Esea/Title I
Galileo High School
1150 Francisco Street
San Francisco, CA 94109

LEVEL FIVE

SCOPE ENGLISH ANTHOLOGY

Literature and Reading Program

LEVEL FIVE

SCOPE ENGLISH ANTHOLOGY

Literature and Reading Program

SCHOLASTIC INC.

New York   Toronto   London   Sydney   Auckland   Tokyo

LEVEL FIVE READERS

Cynthia Imes
Teacher
Appleton High School West
Appleton, Wisconsin

Ann Miller
Coordinator, Learning Resource Center
Aptos High School
Aptos, California

John Russell
Teacher
Blue Springs High School
Blue Springs, Missouri

STAFF

Project Editor: Lewis Gardner
Editors/Writers: Julia Remine Piggin, Richard Maynard
Level Five Editor: Adrienne Betz
Production Editor: Nancy DeWolfe
Senior Art Director: Mary Mars
Project Designer & Art Editor: Lillian Caporlingua
Assistant Designer & Art Production: Janet Nolan

Design & Art Production: Kirchoff/Wohlberg, Inc.

Cover Design: Jack George Tauss
Cover Photograph: Peter B. Kaplan, Photo Researchers, Inc.

ACKNOWLEDGMENTS

Grateful acknowledgment is made to the following authors and publishers for the use of copyrighted materials. Every effort has been made to obtain permission to use previously published material. Any errors or omissions are unintentional.

American Foundation for the Blind, Inc. for "Three Days to See" by Helen Keller.

The Great Amwell Company, Inc. for the teleplay of *Life on the Mississippi* by Philip Reisman, Jr., based on the works of Mark Twain. Copyright © 1980 by The Great Amwell Company, Inc. Nebraskans for Public Television, Inc.

Toni Cade Bambara for "Raymond's Run," from *Gorilla, My Love* by Toni Cade Bambara. Copyright © 1970 by Toni Cade Bambara.

(Acknowledgments continue on page 543)

ISBN 0-590-07699-X

12 11 10 9 8 7 6 5 4   5 6 7 8/8

Printed in the U.S.A.   23

LEVEL FIVE
Contents

List of Skills Lessons 12

SECTION 1 **An American Sampler**

Introduction 18

After Twenty Years 20
O. Henry

Raymond's Run 24
Toni Cade Bambara

Three Days to See 34
Helen Keller

Learning to Read 40
Frederick Douglass

Three American poems

The Hurricane 44
Luis Palés Matos

The Tide Rises, the Tide Falls 46
Henry Wadsworth Longfellow

Travel 48
Edna St. Vincent Millay

The Wind in the Rosebush 50
Mary Wilkins Freeman

SECTION REVIEW 59

SECTION 2 **America's Early Voices:
Literature Before 1840**

Introduction 64

Godasiyo, the Woman Chief 66
Seneca legend retold by Dee Brown

To My Dear and Loving Husband 70
Anne Bradstreet

In Reference to Her Children, 23 June, 1656 71
Anne Bradstreet

Resolutions 72
Jonathan Edwards

The writing of Benjamin Franklin

Sayings from *Poor Richard's Almanack* 75

A Vegetable Diet 76

Two voices of the Revolution

Letter to Her Husband, John 80
Abigail Adams

The American Crisis, Number 1 82
Thomas Paine

Two voices of the new nation

What Is an American? 85
Jean de Crèvecoeur

The Day the Sun Froze 86
David Crockett

The Legend of Sleepy Hollow 89
Washington Irving

SECTION REVIEW 99

SECTION 3   Early America Imagined: Historical Fiction

Introduction 104

Salem Village, Massachusetts 106
Stephen Vincent Benét

Cotton Mather, 1663–1728 115
Stephen Vincent Benét

April Morning 116
Howard Fast

She Sailed for Love 127
Jane Yolen

SECTION REVIEW 137

SECTION 4 Voices of Experience: 1840—1898

Introduction 142

A Dose of Pain-Killer 144
Mark Twain

Life on the Mississippi 148
Mark Twain

There Was a Child Went Forth 159
Walt Whitman

Ain't I a Woman? 162
Sojourner Truth

Civil War Nurse 164
Louisa May Alcott

A Horseman in the Sky 170
Ambrose Bierce

The Raven Days 176
Sidney Lanier

I Will Fight No More Forever 178
Chief Joseph

Casey at the Bat 179
Ernest Lawrence Thayer

SECTION REVIEW 183

SECTION 5 Voices of Imagination: 1840—1898

Introduction 188

The Pit and the Pendulum 190
Edgar Allan Poe

Jim Bridger and the Fiddler Who Wouldn't Fiddle 196
a Jim Bridger tale retold by Sid Fleischman

Three poems by Emily Dickinson

A Word Is Dead 203

The Wind Tapped Like a Tired Man 204

Hope Is the Thing With Feathers 202

Poor Sandy 206
Charles W. Chestnutt

The Turn of the Screw 215
Henry James

SECTION REVIEW 229

SECTION 6   A Voice of Courage: Stephen Crane (1871—1900)

Introduction 234

The Red Badge of Courage 236

The Wayfarer 247

A Man Said to the Universe 249

The Wreck of the Commodore: 250
Stephen Crane's Own Story

The Open Boat 257

SECTION REVIEW 263

SECTION 7   Voices of Experience: 1898—1939

Introduction 268

Love of Life 270
Jack London

Lucinda Matlock 279
Edgar Lee Masters

Discovery of a Father 280
Sherwood Anderson

Under a Telephone Pole 286
Carl Sandburg

Bernice Bobs Her Hair 287
a teleplay by Joan Micklin Silver based on the story by F. Scott Fitzgerald

Three poems of the Harlem Renaissance

Dream Variations 304
Langston Hughes

The Negro Speaks of Rivers 306
Langston Hughes

Any Human to Another 309
Countee Cullen

A Day's Wait 311
Ernest Hemingway

The Standard of Living 316
Dorothy Parker

SECTION REVIEW 321

SECTION 8 Voices of Mystery: 1898—1939

Introduction 326

Afterward 328
Edith Wharton

Mind Over Matter 343
Ellery Queen

The Calico Dog 359
Mignon G. Eberhardt

SECTION REVIEW 379

SECTION 9 The Modern Experience: 1939—Present

Introduction 384

Sucker 386
Carson McCullers

A City of Words 394
Richard Rodriguez

Saying Yes 399
Diana Chang

Home 400
Gwendolyn Brooks

The Telephone Call 404
Maxine Hong Kingston

The Shock of Recognition 407
Art Buchwald

Mothers 410
Nikki Giovanni

I Stand Here Ironing 412
Tillie Olsen

SECTION REVIEW 421

SECTION 10 The Modern Imagination: 1939—Present

Introduction 426

EPICAC 428
Kurt Vonnegut, Jr.

Southbound on the Freeway 436
May Swenson

The Midnight Sun 438
Rod Serling

Four poems of Robert Frost

Fire and Ice 444

Acquainted With the Night 446

Our Hold on the Planet 449

The Road not Taken 450

Georgia O'Keeffe 453
Joan Didion

Story From Bear Country 459
Leslie Marmon Silko

The Fog Horn 462
Ray Bradbury

SECTION REVIEW 470

SECTION 11 Arthur Miller: A Modern Playwright

Introduction 474

All My Sons 476

    Act One 476

    Act Two 501

    Act Three 520

SECTION REVIEW 529

Glossary 532

Handbook of Terms in Literature 538

Author and Title Index 541

UNDERSTANDING LITERATURE

Plot

Purpose in a short story 23
In narrative poetry 49, 182
Cause and effect 147
Sequence of events 158
In a mystery story 342
Structure 358
Plot and subplots 378

Setting

In a play 58
In historical fiction 113

Characterization

In a short story 33
In a play 58
In historical fiction 113, 126, 136
Character motivation 393, 406
Dynamic, static, and flat characters 398, 409
Through dialogue 403
Characterization and point of view 420

Imagery and Mood

In lyric poetry 49
Mood and imagery 195, 214, 228
Creating mood 201
Personification 205

Theme

Multiple themes 246
Theme and foreshadowing 256
Allegory 262
Theme and values 528

Point of View

In personal narrative essay 39
In autobiography 43, 78
Third-person point of view 69
First-person point of view 74, 88
In persuasive writing 83
In a legend 98

Style

In conflict (Jack London) 277
In first-person point of view (Sherwood Anderson) 285
In dialogue (F. Scott Fitzgerald) 302
Style and rhythm in poetry 310
In Ernest Hemingway's writing 315

Irony

Ironic turn of events 169
Surprise ending 175
Ironic tone 320

Conflict

Identifying types of conflict 435, 443, 469
Person-versus-self conflict 452
In an essay 458
In a play 499
Climax in a play 519

VOCABULARY

Prefixes and suffixes 59
Context clues 99

Synonyms and antonyms 137
Idioms and ironic speech 183
Similes, metaphors, and personification 229
Shades of meaning 263
Multiple meanings 321
Slang 379
Denotation and connotation 421
Context clues 470, 529

READING

Fact and opinion 59
Author's purpose 99
Cause and effect 137
Sequence and predicting outcome 183
Making inferences 229
Main ideas and supporting details 263
Drawing conclusions 321
Significant details 379
Comparisons and contrasts 421
Cloze exercise 470, 529

WRITING AND COMPOSITION

Letter 23, 158, 169, 228
Interview 33
Description 39, 175, 231, 265, 315, 323, 380, 381, 398, 403, 406, 409, 458
Autobiography 43
Explanation 49, 61, 138, 320, 323, 381, 423, 452, 471
Scene in a play 58, 531
Opinion 60, 265
New ending for a play 61
Poetry 61, 230, 310, 435
New ending for a story 69, 139, 147, 184, 423
First-person point of view 74, 101
Sayings 78
Persuasion 83, 100, 101
Exaggeration 88
Rewriting a story 101
From a character's point of view ... 98, 113, 126, 136, 265, 323, 342, 358, 420, 423, 531
Dialogue 139
Scene in a story 139

New ending for a poem 182
Speech 185, 530
Summary 185
Diary entry 185, 246, 393, 443, 469
News article 185, 264, 378, 381, 471, 519
Imagery 195, 201, 214, 231
Personification 205
Foreshadowing 256
Allegory 262
About a character 265, 423, 499
In a certain style 277, 285, 302
Review 322
Story 323, 471, 531
Comparing two characters 422
About identity 423
About theme 528

SECTION 1
An American Sampler

I hear America singing, the varied carols I hear.
Those of mechanics, each one singing his as it
    should be blithe and strong.
The carpenter singing his as he measures his plank
    or beam,...
The shoemaker singing as he sits on his bench,
    the hatter singing as he stands...
The delicious singing of the mother, or of the young wife
    at work, or of the girl sewing or washing,
Each singing what belongs to him or her
    and to none else.

— Walt Whitman

Introduction

This is a book about America and its people. It is not a history book, although it looks back at America's past. It is a book of literature, a sampling of works by America's most skillful writers and thinkers.

The first section shows how American authors have approached different types of literature: short stories, personal narratives, poetry, and plays.

Storytellers and Truth Tellers

As long as there have been people, there have been stories. The first stories were told aloud. Later, storytellers began to write down their tales. The term *short story* refers to any short work of fiction in which the author has made up a *plot*, a chain of events that leads to a satisfying ending; *characters,* people in the story; and *setting,* a time and place in which the events of the story occur.

O. Henry wrote nearly 100 years ago. His stories still are admired for their clever plots. Often his stories, like the one you will read here, "After Twenty Years," have surprise endings or plot twists.

Toni Cade Bambara is a writer of today. Her story "Raymond's Run" has a plot and a setting, but what you will remember most is the people in the story — their personalities and feelings.

Fiction — short stories and novels — is not the only way that authors can express their ideas. Through a form of nonfiction called the *personal narrative,* authors may directly describe their experiences and express their beliefs.

Helen Keller became blind and deaf in infancy. She learned about the world mostly through her sense of touch. The essay "Three Days to See," on pp. 32–36, expresses Keller's ideas about the use of the sense of sight as she imagines it.

In 1858 Frederick Douglass wrote the story of his life, his *autobiography,* for a very important reason. He wanted all Americans to understand what it was like to grow up as a slave. An excerpt from his autobiography starts on p. 38.

Poets and Playwrights

Poetry is another way authors have chosen to express their feelings, describe their experiences, and tell their stories. In this section, you will sample the work of three of America's finest poets: Luis Palés Matos, Edna St. Vincent Millay, and Henry Wadsworth Longfellow. Poets choose words for their sounds as well as their meanings. Poetry should be read aloud.

Plays are another form of literature that is intended to be read aloud. The events in a play are revealed through *stage directions* — descriptions of how the characters should move on the stage; and *dialogue* — what the characters say about their own feelings and actions, and the feelings and actions of the other people.

In "The Wind in the Rosebush," the dialogue and stage directions work together to reveal a shocking secret.

What is special about American literature is that it reflects the American spirit. What is the American spirit? You will find an idea of what it is in the poetry of Walt Whitman. His poem "I Hear America Singing," part of which appears on p. 15, describes a complex yet beautiful music.

This music is made up of many different songs — just as our country is made up of different places, people, and ideas.

Like the Americans in Whitman's poem, each author here "sings what belongs to him or her and to none else." Their songs are their stories, personal narratives, poems, and plays. Somehow all the pieces fit together like the pieces of a patchwork quilt or the many songs that blend to make a great musical work.

After Twenty Years

by O. Henry

O. Henry's real name was William Sydney Porter (1862–1910). He traveled throughout the United States and held many jobs. His varied experiences gave him a feeling for how different kinds of people spoke and thought. As you read "After Twenty Years," think about how the story will end. O. Henry is famous for stories with surprise endings.

The policeman on the beat moved up the avenue. The streets were nearly empty. The time was barely 10:00 at night. Chilly gusts of wind with a taste of rain in them had chased people indoors.

Trying doors as he went, he twirled his club with many artful movements. He turned now and then to cast his watchful eye down the quiet street. The officer made a fine picture of a guardian of the peace. The vicinity was one that kept early hours. Now and then you might see the lights of an all-night lunch counter. But most of the doors belonged to stores that had long since been closed.

Midway on a certain block the policeman suddenly slowed his walk. In the doorway of a darkened hardware store a man leaned. As the policeman walked up to him, the man spoke up quickly.

"It's all right, Officer," he said. "I'm just waiting for a friend. It's an appointment made twenty years ago. Sounds a little funny to you, doesn't it? Well, I'll explain if you'd like to make certain it's all straight. About that long ago there used to be a restaurant where this store stands — 'Big Joe' Brady's restaurant."

"Until five years ago," said the policeman. "It was torn down then."

The man in the doorway struck a match and checked his watch. The light showed a pale, square-jawed face with keen eyes, and a little white scar near his right eyebrow. His scarf-pin was a large diamond, oddly set.

"Twenty years ago tonight," said the man. "I dined here at 'Big Joe' Brady's with Jimmy Wells. He was my best chum, and the finest chap in the world. He and I were raised here in New York, just like two brothers, together. I was eighteen and Jimmy was twenty. The next morning, I was to start for the West to make my fortune. You couldn't have dragged Jimmy out of New York. He thought it was the only place on earth. Well, we agreed that night that we would meet here again exactly twenty years from that date and time, no matter what. We figured that in twenty years each of us ought to have our fortunes made, whatever they were going to be."

"It sounds pretty interesting," said the policeman. "Rather a long time between meets, though, it seems to me. Haven't you heard from your friend since you left?"

"Well, yes, for a time we wrote," said the other. "But after a year or two we lost track of each other. You see, the West is a pretty big place. I kept hustling around over it pretty lively. But I know Jimmy will meet me here if he's alive, for he always was the truest friend in the world. He'll never forget. I came a thousand miles to stand in this door tonight. It's worth it if my old partner turns up."

The waiting man again pulled out his handsome watch. The case was set with diamonds.

"Three minutes to ten," he announced. "It was exactly ten o'clock when we parted here at the restaurant door."

"Did pretty well out West, didn't you?" asked the policeman.

"You bet! I hope Jimmy has done half as well. He was a kind of plodder, though, as good fellow as he was. I've had to compete with some of the sharpest wits going to get my pile. A man gets in a rut in New York. It takes the West to put a razor-edge on him."

The policeman twirled his club and took a step or two.

"I'll be on my way. Hope your friend comes around all right. Going to call time on him sharp?"

"I should say not!" said the other. "I'll give him half an hour at least. If Jimmy is alive on earth he'll be here by that time. So long, Officer."

"Good night, sir," said the policeman. He passed on along his beat, trying doors as he went.

There was now a fine, cold drizzle falling. The wind had risen from its uncertain puffs into a steady blow. The few people astir on that street hurried along with coat collars turned high and pocketed hands. And in the door of the hardware store the man who had come a thousand miles to fill an appointment watched and waited.

About twenty minutes he waited. Then a tall man in a long overcoat, with collar turned up to his ears, hurried across from the opposite side of the street. He went directly to the waiting man.

"Is that you, Bob?" he asked, doubtfully.

"Is that you, Jimmy Wells?" cried the man in the door.

"Bless my heart!" exclaimed the new arrival, grasping both the other's hands with his own. "It's Bob, sure as fate. I was certain I'd find you here if you were still alive. Well, well, well! Twenty years is a long time. The old restaurant's gone, Bob; I wish it had lasted, so we could have had another dinner there. How has the West treated you, old man?"

"Bully; it has given me everything I asked it for. You've changed lots, Jimmy. I never thought you were so tall by two or three inches."

"Oh, I grew a bit after I was twenty."

"Doing well in New York, Jimmy?"

"Moderately. I have a position in one of the city departments. Come on, Bob;

we'll go around to a place I know of and have a good long talk about old times."

The two men started up the street, arm in arm. The man from the West was beginning to outline the history of his career. The other, submerged in his overcoat, listened with interest.

At the corner stood a drugstore, brilliant with electric lights. When they came into this glare each of them turned simultaneously to gaze upon the other's face.

The man from the West stopped suddenly and released his arm.

"You're not Jimmy Wells," he snapped. "Twenty years is a long time, but not long enough to change the shape of a man's nose."

"It sometimes changes a good man into a bad one," said the tall man. "You've been under arrest for ten minutes, 'Silky' Bob. Chicago thinks you may have dropped over our way and wires us she wants to have a chat with you. Going quietly, are you? That's sensible. Now, before we go to the station, here's a note I was asked to hand to you. You may read it here at the window. It's from Patrolman Wells."

The man from the West unfolded the little piece of paper handed to him. His hand was steady when he began to read, but it trembled a little by the time he had finished. The note was rather short.

Bob:
I was at the appointed place on time. When you struck the match to check the time, I saw your face. It was the face of the man wanted in Chicago. Somehow I couldn't do it myself. I went around and got a plainclothes man to do the job.

Jimmy

22

READING COMPREHENSION

Select the best choice to complete each statement. Then write the entire sentence on your paper.

1. The police officer walked up to the man in the doorway because _____.
   a. he knew the man was a criminal
   b. the restaurant had been torn down
   c. he hoped to meet an old friend

2. The waiting man and his friend had agreed to meet _____.
   a. when both had made their fortunes
   b. to share a meal and some drinks
   c. exactly 20 years later

3. "Silky" Bob knew his companion wasn't Jimmy Wells when _____.
   a. he showed a detective's badge
   b. the light revealed his face
   c. the real Jimmy Wells appeared

4. Jimmy Wells didn't identify himself to his friend because he _____.
   a. didn't want to arrest an old friend
   b. was afraid Bob would harm him
   c. was ashamed of being a policeman

For Discussion

1. It had been 20 years since Bob and Jimmy went their separate ways. How had their lives differed? Which one do you think was more successful? Why? Use details from the story to explain.

2. When he realized his old friend was a wanted criminal, what were the different things Patrolman Wells might have done? Do you think he made the right choice? Why or why not?

UNDERSTANDING LITERATURE

Plot in a Short Story. "After Twenty Years" by O. Henry is an excellent example of a short story. In a few pages, it describes a particular *setting* (time and place), introduces *characters* (people), and tells the reader what happens to them through the *plot* (a series of events, usually involving a problem and its solution).

In a well-written short story, each incident in the plot will have a purpose. That purpose may be one or more of the following.

a. to complicate the problem or conflict

b. to take the action a step further

c. to tell you about the characters

On your paper, match each incident from "After Twenty Years" with the main purpose it serves in the plot.

1. The policeman began a conversation with the man in the doorway.

2. A tall man in a long overcoat went directly to the waiting man.

3. The man arrested Silky and then gave him a note to read.

4. Silky read the note and learned that the patrolman was the old friend for whom he had been waiting.

Writing

Think about how Silky Bob might have felt after he read the note from his old friend Jimmy Wells. Write an answer to Patrolman Wells, telling exactly what Silky might have said if he had had the chance.

Raymond's Run

by Toni Cade Bambara

Toni Cade Bambara (1939—) is well-known for her articles and stories about blacks in the United States. She has also written a full-length novel, The Salt Eaters. *The story you are about to read is from her collection of short stories* Gorilla, My Love. *It is about the special love a teenage girl has for her mentally handicapped brother, Raymond.*

I don't have much work to do around the house like some girls. My mother does that. And I don't have to earn my pocket money by hustling; George runs errands for the big boys and sells Christmas cards. And anything else that's got to get done, my father does. All I have to do in life is mind my brother Raymond, which is enough.

Sometimes I slip and say my little brother Raymond. But as any fool can see he's much bigger and he's older, too. But a lot of people call him my little brother cause he needs looking after cause he's not quite right. And a lot of smart mouths got lots to say about that, too, especially when George was minding him. But now, if anybody has anything to say to Raymond, anything to say about his big head, they have to come by me. And I don't play the dozens* or believe in standing around with somebody in my face doing a lot of talking. I much rather just knock you down and take my chances even if I am a little girl with skinny arms and a squeaky voice, which is how I got the name Squeaky. And if things get too rough, I run. And as anybody can tell you, I'm the fastest thing on two feet.

There is no track meet that I don't win the first-place medal. I used to win the 20-yard dash when I was a little kid in kindergarten. Nowadays, it's the 50-yard dash. And tomorrow I'm subject to run the quarter-meter relay all by myself and come in first, second, and third. The big kids call me Mercury cause I'm the swiftest thing in the neighborhood. Everybody knows that — except two people who know better, my father and me. He can beat me to Amsterdam Avenue with me having a two fire-hydrant headstart and him running with his hands in his pockets and whistling. But that's private information. Cause can you imagine some 35-year-old man stuffing himself into PAL shorts to race little kids? So as far as

---

* *The dozens* — a street-corner game that involves trading insults.

everyone's concerned, I'm the fastest and that goes for Gretchen, too, who has put out the tale that she is going to win the first-place medal this year. Ridiculous. In the second place, she's got short legs. In the third place, she's got freckles. In the first place, no one can beat me and that's all there is to it.

I'm standing on the corner admiring the weather and about to take a stroll down Broadway so I can practice my breathing exercises, and I've got Raymond walking on the inside close to the buildings, cause he's subject to fits of fantasy and starts thinking he's a circus performer and that the curb is a tightrope strung high in the air. And sometimes after a rain he likes to step down off his tightrope right into the gutter and slosh around getting his shoes and cuffs wet. Then I get hit when I get home. Or sometimes if you don't watch him he'll dash across traffic to the island in the middle of Broadway and give the pigeons a fit. Then I have to go behind him apologizing to all the old people sitting around trying to get some sun and getting all upset with the pigeons fluttering around them, scattering their newspapers and upsetting the wax-paper lunches in their laps. So I keep Raymond on the inside of me, and he plays like he's driving a stagecoach which is OK by me so long as he doesn't run me over or interrupt my breathing exercises, which I have to do on account of I'm serious about my running, and I don't care who knows it.

Now some people like to act like things come easy to them, won't let on that they practice. Not me. I'll high-prance down 34th Street like a rodeo pony to keep my knees strong even if it does get my mother uptight so that she walks ahead like she's not with me, don't know me, is all by herself on a shopping trip, and I am somebody else's crazy child. Now you take Cynthia Procter for instance. She's just the opposite. If there's a test tomorrow, she'll say something like, "Oh, I guess I'll play handball this afternoon and watch television tonight," just to let you know she ain't thinking about the test. Or like last week when she won the spelling bee for the millionth time, "A good thing you got 'receive,' Squeaky, cause I would have got it wrong. I completely forgot about the spelling bee." And she'll clutch the lace on her blouse like it was a narrow escape. Oh, brother. But of course when I pass her house on my early morning trots around the block, she is practicing the scales on the piano over and over and over and over. Then in music class she always lets herself get bumped around so she falls accidentally on purpose onto the piano stool and is so surprised to find herself sitting there that she decides just for fun to try out the ole keys. And what do you know — Chopin's waltzes just spring out of her fingertips and she's the most surprised thing in the world. A regular prodigy. I could kill people like that. I stay up all night studying the words for the spelling bee. And you can see me any time of day practicing running. I never walk if I can trot, and shame on Raymond if he can't keep up. But of course he does, cause if he hangs back someone's liable to walk up to him and get smart, or take his allowance from him, or ask him where he got that great big pumpkin head. People are so stupid sometimes.

So I'm strolling down Broadway breathing out and breathing in on counts of seven, which is my lucky number, and here come Gretchen and her sidekicks: Mary Louise, who used to be a friend of mine when she first moved to Harlem from Baltimore and got beat up by everybody till I took up for her on account of her mother and my mother used to sing in the same choir when they were young girls, but people ain't grateful, so now she hangs out with the new girl Gretchen and talks about me like a dog; and Rosie, who is fat as I am skinny and has a big mouth where Raymond is concerned and is too stupid to know that there is not a big deal of difference between herself and Raymond and that she can't afford to throw stones. So they are steady coming up

Broadway and I see right away that it's going to be one of those Dodge City scenes cause the street ain't that big and they're close to the buildings just as we are. First I think I'll step into the new candy store and look over the new comics and let them pass. But that's chicken and I've got a reputation to consider. So then I think I'll just walk straight on through them or even over them if necessary. But as they get to me, they slow down. I'm ready to fight, cause like I said I don't feature a whole lot of chit-chat, I much prefer to just knock you down right from the jump and save everybody a lotta precious time.

"You signing up for the May Day races?" smiles Mary Louise, only it's not a smile at all. A dumb question like that doesn't deserve an answer. Besides, there's just me and Gretchen standing there really, so no use wasting my breath talking to shadows.

"I don't think you're going to win this time," says Rosie, trying to signify with her hands on her hips all salty, completely forgetting that I have whupped her behind many times for less salt than that.

"I always win cause I'm the best," I say straight at Gretchen who is, as far as I'm concerned, the only one talking in this ventriloquist-dummy routine. Gretchen smiles, but it's not a smile, and I'm thinking that girls never really smile at each other because they don't know how and don't want to know how and there's probably no one to teach us how, cause grown-up girls don't know either. Then they all look at Raymond who has just brought his mule team to a standstill. And they're about to see what trouble they can get into through him.

"What grade you in now, Raymond?"

"You got anything to say to my brother, you say it to me, Mary Louise Williams of Raggedy Town, Baltimore."

"What are you, his mother?" sasses Rosie.

"That's right, Fatso. And the next word out of anybody and I'll be their mother too." So they just stand there and Gretchen shifts from one leg to the other and so do they. Then Gretchen puts her hands on her hips and is about to say something with her freckle-face self but doesn't. Then she walks around me looking me up and down but keeps walking up Broadway, and her sidekicks follow her. So me and Raymond smile at each other and he says, "Gidyap," to his team and I continue with my breathing exercises, strolling down Broadway toward the ice man on 145th with not a care in the world cause I am

Miss Quicksilver herself.

I take my time getting to the park on May Day because the track meet is the last thing on the program. The biggest thing on the program is the May Pole dancing, which I can do without, thank you, even if my mother thinks it's a shame I don't take part and act like a girl for a change. You'd think my mother'd be grateful not to have to make me a white organdy dress with a big satin sash and buy me new white baby-doll shoes that can't be taken out of the box till the big day. You'd think she'd be glad her daughter ain't out there prancing around a May Pole getting the new clothes all dirty and sweaty and trying to act like a fairy or a flower or whatever you're supposed to be when you should be trying to be yourself, whatever that is, which is as far as I'm concerned, a poor Black girl who really can't afford to buy shoes and a new dress you only wear once a lifetime cause it won't fit next year.

I was once a strawberry in a Hansel and Gretel pageant when I was in nursery school and didn't have no better sense than to dance on tiptoe with my arms in a circle over my head doing umbrella steps and being a perfect fool just so my mother and father could come dressed up and clap. You'd think they'd know better than to encourage that kind of nonsense. I am not a strawberry. I do not dance on my toes. I run. That is what I am all about. So I always come late to the May Day program, just in time to get my number pinned on and lay in the grass till they announce the 50-yard dash.

I put Raymond in the little swings,

which is a tight squeeze this year and will be impossible next year. Then I look around for Mr. Pearson, who pins the numbers on. I'm really looking for Gretchen if you want to know the truth, but she's not around. The park is jam-packed. Parents in hats and corsages and breast-pocket handkerchiefs peeking up. Kids in white dresses and light-blue suits. The parkees* unfolding chairs and chasing the rowdy kids from Lenox as if they had no right to be there. The big guys with their caps on backward, leaning against the fence swirling the basketballs on the tips of their fingers, waiting for all these crazy people to clear out the park so they can play. Most of the kids in my class are carrying bass drums and glockenspiels and flutes. You'd think they'd put in a few bongos or something for real like that.

Then here comes Mr. Pearson with his clipboard and his cards and pencils and whistles and safety pins and 50 million other things he's always dropping all over the place with his clumsy self. He sticks out in a crowd because he's on stilts. We used to call him Jack and the Beanstalk to get him mad. But I'm the only one that can outrun him and get away, and I'm too grown for that silliness now.

"Well, Squeaky," he says, checking my name off the list and handing me number seven and two pins. And I'm thinking he's got no right to call me Squeaky if I can't call him Beanstalk.

"Hazel Elizabeth Deborah Parker," I correct him and tell him to write it down on his board.

* *Parkees* — park attendants.

"Well, Hazel Elizabeth Deborah Parker, going to give someone else a break this year?" I squint at him real hard to see if he is seriously thinking I should lose the race on purpose just to give someone else a break. "Only six girls running this time," he continues, shaking his head sadly like it's my fault all of New York didn't turn out in sneakers. "That new girl should give you a run for your money." He looks around the park for Gretchen like a periscope in a submarine movie. "Wouldn't it be a nice gesture if you were . . . to ahh . . ."

I give him such a look he couldn't finish putting that idea into words. Grown-ups got a lot of nerve sometimes. I pin my number seven to myself and stomp away, I'm so burnt. And I go straight for the track and stretch out on the grass while the band winds up with "Oh, the Monkey Wrapped His Tail Around the Flagpole," which my teacher calls by some other name. The man on the loudspeaker is calling everyone over to the track and I'm on my back looking at the sky, trying to pretend I'm in the country, but I can't, because even grass in the city feels hard as sidewalk, and there's just no pretending you are anywhere but in a "concrete jungle" as my grandfather says.

The 20-yard dash takes all of two minutes cause most of the little kids don't know no better than to run off the track or run the wrong way or run smack into the fence and fall down and cry. One little kid, though, has got the good sense to run straight for the white ribbon up ahead so he wins. Then the second-graders line up for the 30-yard dash and I don't even

bother to turn my head to watch cause Raphael Perez always wins. He wins before he even begins by psyching the runners, telling them they're going to trip on their shoelaces and fall on their faces or lose their shorts or something, which he doesn't have to do since he is very fast, almost as fast as I am. After that is the 40-yard dash which I used to run when I was in the first grade. Raymond is hollering from the swings cause he knows I'm about to do my thing cause the man on the loudspeaker has just announced the 50-yard dash, although he might as well be giving a recipe for angel food cake cause you can hardly make out what he's sayin' for the static. I get up and slip off my sweat pants and then I see Gretchen standing at the starting line, kicking her legs out like a pro. Then as I get into place I see that ole Raymond is on line on the other side of the fence, bending down with his fingers on the ground just like he knew what he was doing. I was going to yell at him but then I didn't. It burns up your energy to holler.

Every time, just before I take off in a race, I always feel like I'm in a dream, the kind of dream you have when you're sick with fever and feel all hot and weightless. I dream I'm flying over a sandy beach in the early morning sun, kissing the leaves of the trees as I fly by. And there's always the smell of apples, just like in the country when I was little and used to think I was a choo-choo train, running through the fields of corn and chugging up the hill to the orchard. And all the time I'm dreaming this, I get lighter and lighter until I'm flying over the beach again, getting blown through the sky like a feather that weighs nothing at all. But once I spread my fingers in the dirt and crouch down over the Get on Your Mark, the dream goes and I am solid again and am telling myself: Squeaky, you must win, you must win, you are the fastest thing in the world, you can even beat your father up Amsterdam if you really try. And then I feel my weight coming back just behind my knees then down to my feet then into the earth and the pistol shot explodes in my blood and I am off and weightless again, flying past the other runners, my arms pumping up and down and the whole world is quiet except for the crunch as I zoom over the gravel in the track. I glance to my left and there is no one. To the right, a blurred Gretchen, who's got her chin jutting out as if it would win the race all by itself. And on the other side of the fence is Raymond with his arms down at his side and the palms tucked up behind him, running in his very own style, and it's the first time I ever saw that and I almost stop to watch my brother Raymond on his first run. But the white ribbon is bouncing toward me and I tear past it, racing into the distance till my feet with a mind of their own start digging up footfuls of dirt and brake me short. Then all the kids standing on the side pile on me, banging me on the back and slapping my head with their May Day programs, for I have won again and everybody on 151st Street can walk tall for another year.

"In first place . . ." the man on the loudspeaker is clear as a bell now. But then he pauses and the loudspeaker starts to whine. Then static. And I lean down to catch my breath and here comes Gretchen walking back, for she's overshot the finish line too, huffing and puffing with her hands on her hips, taking it slow, breathing in steady time like a real pro and I sort of like her a little for the first time. "In the first place . . ." and then three or four voices get mixed up on the loudspeaker and I dig my sneaker into the grass and stare at Gretchen who's staring back, we both wondering just who did win. I can hear old Beanstalk arguing with the man on the loudspeaker and then a few others running their mouths about what the stopwatches say. Then I hear Raymond yanking at the fence to call me and I wave to shush him, but he keeps rattling the fence like a gorilla in a cage, like in them gorilla movies, but then like a dancer or something he starts climbing up nice and easy but very fast. And it occurs to me, watching how smoothly he climbs hand over hand and remembering how he looked running with his arms down to his side and with the wind pulling his mouth back and his teeth showing and all, it occurred to me that Raymond would make a very fine runner. Doesn't he always keep up with me on my trots? And he surely knows how to breathe in counts of seven cause he's always doing it at the dinner table, which drives my brother George up the wall. And I'm smiling to beat the band cause if I've lost the race, or if me and Gretchen tied, or even if I've won, I can always retire as a runner and begin a whole new career as a coach with Raymond as my champion. After all, with a little more study I can beat Cynthia and her phony self at the spelling bee. And if I bugged my mother, I could get piano lessons and become a star. And I have a big rep as the baddest thing around. And I've got a roomful of ribbons and medals and awards. But what has Raymond got to call his own?

So I stand there with my new plans, laughing out loud by this time as Raymond jumps down from the fence and runs over with his teeth showing and his arms down to the side which no one before has quite mastered as a running style. And by the time he comes over I'm jumping up and down so glad to see him — my brother Raymond, a great runner in the family tradition. But of course everyone thinks I'm jumping up and down because the men on the loudspeaker have finally gotten themselves together and compared notes and are announcing, "In first place — Miss Hazel Elizabeth Deborah Parker." (Dig that.)

"In second place — Miss Gretchen P. Lewis." And I look over at Gretchen wondering what the "P" stands for. And I smile. Cause she's good, no doubt about it. Maybe she'd like to help me coach Raymond; she obviously is serious about running, as any fool can see. And she nods to congratulate me and then she smiles. And I smile. We stand there with this big smile of respect between us. It's about as real a smile as girls can do for each other, considering we don't practice real smiling every day, you know, cause maybe we're too busy being flowers or fairies or strawberries instead of something honest and worthy of respect . . . you know . . . like being people.

READING COMPREHENSION

Select the best choice to complete each statement. Then write the entire sentence on your paper.

1. Hazel sometimes called Raymond her "little brother" because _____.
   a. he liked to pretend he was small
   b. she felt stronger than everyone
   c. she had to look after him

2. Mr. Pearson suggested that Hazel _____.
   a. wear strawberries on her shirt
   b. stay with Raymond on the swings
   c. give someone else a chance to win

3. At the end of the race, Hazel jumped up and down because she was _____.
   a. very sure she had won
   b. not able to see over the crowd
   c. excited that Raymond was running

4. After the race, Hazel and Gretchen smiled because they _____.
   a. were nervous
   b. respected one another
   c. knew people were watching them

For Discussion

1. How did Hazel feel about her running ability? Do you think her opinion of herself was justified? Why or why not?

2. Do you think Hazel would really give up her own racing to coach her brother? Explain your answer.

3. What did Hazel think of Gretchen at the beginning of the story? How did her opinion change by the story's end?

UNDERSTANDING LITERATURE

Characterization in a Short Story. How do readers of a short story learn about its characters?

A writer can portray a character directly by telling you what the character is like. Or, the writer can portray a character indirectly by letting the character's own words and actions tell what he or she is like. Sometimes, the way in which two or more characters react to one another helps you understand them.

Read each of the following statements. On your paper, identify the character each one tells you about. Then identify which of the following techniques of characterization is being used.

   a. character's actions
   b. character's own words
   c. how other characters react
   d. narrator's description of others

1. The big kids called her Mercury because she was the swiftest thing in the neighborhood.

2. "In the second place, she's got short legs. In the third . . . she's got freckles."

3. She jumped up and down because she was so glad to see her brother.

4. "I always win cause I'm the best."

Writing

Pretend you are a sportscaster for your local radio station. Make up six questions that you would ask Hazel about herself.

Three Days to See

by Helen Keller

Helen Keller (1880–1968) became blind and deaf as the result of an illness when she was 19 months old. She learned to communicate through sign language, and later through voice lessons. She also communicated quite effectively through her writing. In 1902 she published her autobiography, The Story of My Life. *She also published several other books and many essays. As you will discover when you read this essay, Keller had an exceptional insight into people and the world around her.*

All of us have read thrilling stories in which the hero had only a limited time to live. Sometimes it was as long as a year; sometimes as short as 24 hours. I speak, of course, of free men who have a choice, not condemned criminals whose activities are strictly limited.

Such stories set us wondering what we should do under similar conditions. What should we crowd into these last hours? What happiness should we find in reviewing the past, what regrets?

Sometimes I have thought that we should live each day as if it were our last. Most of us, however, take life for granted.

The same casualness characterizes the use of all our senses. Only the deaf appreciate hearing. Only the blind realize the blessings that lie in sight. It's the same old story of not being grateful for what we have until we lose it.

I have often thought it would be a blessing if each human being were stricken blind and deaf for a few days. Darkness would make him appreciate sight. Silence would teach him the joys of sound.

Now and then I have tested my seeing friends to discover what they see. Recently I was visited by a good friend. She had just returned from a walk in the woods. "What did you see?" I asked. "Nothing in particular" was her reply.

How is it possible to walk for an hour and see nothing worthy of note? I cannot see, but I find hundreds of things that interest me. I feel the delicate patterns of a leaf. I pass my hand lovingly about the smooth skin of a birch or the rough bark of pine. In spring I touch the branches of trees in search of a bud. I feel the velvety texture of a flower. Occasionally, I place my hand on a small tree and feel the happy quiver of a bird in song.

At times I long to see all these things. If I can get so much pleasure from mere touch, how much more beauty must be revealed by sight. Yet those who have eyes see little. The panorama of color and action which fills the world is taken for granted.

If I were the president of a university I would set up a course called "How to Use Your Eyes." The teacher would show his pupils how they could add joy to their lives by really seeing what passes unnoticed before them.

Perhaps I can best illustrate by imagining what I should most like to see if I were given the use of my eyes, say, for just three days. And while I am imagining, suppose you, too, consider the problem.

How would you use your eyes if you had only three more days to see? How would you spend those three precious days?

I should want most to see the things which have become dear to me through my years of darkness. You, too, would want to let your eyes rest long on the things that are dear to you. Then you could take the memory of them with you into the long night that loomed ahead.

If by some miracle I were granted just three days to see, I should divide the period into three parts.

On the first day, I should like to see the people whose kindness and friendship have made my life worth living. First, I should gaze long upon the face of my dear teacher, Mrs. Anne Sullivan Macy. She came to me when I was a child and opened the outer world to me. I should like to see in her eyes that strength of character and compassion for all which she has revealed to me so often.

I know my friends from the feel of their faces, through the thoughts they express to me, and through whatever their actions reveal to me. But I am denied that deeper understanding of them that I am sure would come through sight. I should like to call all my dear friends to me on that first day of sight. I should like to watch their eyes and faces react to expressed thoughts and events. I would look long into their faces, imprinting upon my mind the outward evidences of beauty within them. I should also let my eyes rest on a baby. I wish to see the eager, innocent beauty which precedes the awareness of the conflicts which develops later in life.

On that busy first day I should like to look into the loyal, trusting eyes of my dogs. I should also want to see the simple things in my home. I want to see the warm colors in the rugs under my feet. I want to see the pictures on the walls. My eyes would rest respectfully on the books in raised type which I have read and eagerly pore over the books that seeing people read. During the long night of my life books have built themselves into a great shining lighthouse. Books have revealed to me the deepest channels of human life and the human spirit.

In the afternoon of that first day I should take a long walk in the woods. I would try desperately to absorb in a few hours the vast splendor which is constantly unfolding for those who can see. On the way home I would stop at a farm so that I might see the horses plowing in the field. (Perhaps I should see only a tractor!) And I should pray for the glory of a colorful sunset.

When dusk had fallen, I should experience the double delight of being able to see by artificial light. In the night of that first day I should not be able to sleep. My mind would be too full of the memories of the day.

The next day, the second day of sight, I should arise to watch the dawn.

This day I should devote to a hasty glimpse of the world, past and present. How can so much be compressed into one day? Through the museums, of course. Often I have visited the Museum of Natural History. I have touched with my hands many of the objects there exhibited. Now I would see the condensed history of earth displayed there — all the animals and the races of men pictured there.

My next stop would be the Metropolitan Museum of Art. Here in the vast chambers of the Metropolitan is unfolded the spirit people have expressed in their art. Oh, there is so much rich meaning and beauty in the art of the ages for you who have eyes to see!

Upon my short visit to this temple of art I should not be able to review a fraction of the great world of art. Artists tell me that for a true appreciation of art one must educate the eye. One must learn to consider line, form, color, and composition. If I had eyes, how happily would I take up this study. Yet I am told that, to many of you who have eyes to see, the world of art is unexplored.

Sadly, I would leave the Metropolitan Museum, which contains the key to beauty. Seeing persons do not need a Metropolitan to find this key to beauty. The same key lies waiting in smaller museums, and in books in even the smallest libraries. But naturally in my limited time of imaginary sight, I should choose the place where the key unlocks the greatest treasures in the shortest day.

The evening of my second day of sight I should spend at a theater or at the movies. Even now I often go to the theater, but the action of the play must be spelled into my hand by a companion. How I should like to see with my own eyes the actors moving gracefully or comically across the stage. I long to see the colorful costumes and scenery. I long to see how dancers move with rhythm and beauty.

How many of you, I wonder, when you gaze at a play or movie realize and give thanks for the miracle of sight that enables you to enjoy its color, grace, and movement?

So, through the evening of my second imaginary day of sight, the great figures of drama would crowd sleep from my eyes.

The following morning, I should again greet the dawn. I am sure that the dawn of each day must reveal a new beauty.

This is to be my third and last imagined day of sight. I shall have no time for regrets. There is too much to see. Today

I shall spend in the workaday world of the present. New York City is my destination.

I start from my home in the quiet little suburb of Forest Hills, Long Island. Here I see green lawns, trees, and neat little houses. I drive across the lacy structure of steel into the city. Below busy boats chug and scurry about the river. I look ahead and before me rise the fantastic towers of the city.

I hurry to the top of the Empire State Building. A short time ago, I "saw" the city below through the eyes of my secretary. I am eager to compare my fancy with reality. I am sure I should not be disappointed. It would be a vision of another world.

Now I begin my rounds of the city. First, I stand at a busy corner. I look at people and try to understand something of their lives. I see smiles, and I am happy. I see serious determination, and I am proud. I see suffering, and I am compassionate.

I stroll down Fifth Avenue. I see a seething mass of color. I am convinced that I should become a window shopper, too.

From Fifth Avenue I make a tour of the city. I see Park Avenue. I see the slums. I see factories, and parks where children play. My heart is full of the images of people and things. Some sights are pleasant. They fill my heart with happiness. Some sights are sad or ugly. To these I do not shut my eyes. They, too, are part of life. To close the eye on them is to close the heart and mind.

My third day of sight is drawing to an end. Perhaps there are many serious things I should study. Yet I should spend that last evening again at the theater. I should see a hilariously funny play.

At midnight I would again be blind. Naturally in those three short days, I should not have seen all I wanted to see. Only when darkness had again descended upon me should I realize how much I had left unseen. But my mind would be crowded with glorious memories. Thereafter the touch of every object would bring a glowing memory of how that object looked.

Perhaps this outline of how I should spend my three days of sight does not agree with the plan you would follow if you knew you were about to become blind. I am, however, sure that if you really faced that fate you would use your eyes as never before. Your eyes would touch and embrace every object that came within your range of vision. Then, at last, you would really see. A new world of beauty would open before you.

I who am blind can give one hint to those who see: Use your eyes as if tomorrow you would become blind. Use your other senses the same way. Hear the music of voices, the song of a bird as if you would be deaf tomorrow. Touch each object as if tomorrow this sense would fail. Smell the perfume of flowers, taste each morsel, as if tomorrow you could never taste or smell again. Make the most of every sense. Glory in the pleasure and beauty the world reveals to you through your senses. But of all the senses, I am sure that sight must be most delightful.

READING COMPREHENSION

Select the best choice to complete each statement. Then write the entire sentence on your paper.

1. Because she could not see, Helen Keller said that she _____.
   a. realized what a blessing sight is
   b. would never know what she was missing
   c. remembered most of what she had heard

2. Helen Keller wanted most to be able to see _____.
   a. the president of a university
   b. a great shining lighthouse
   c. the people she cared about

3. After three days of being able to see, Helen Keller said she _____.
   a. would sadly return to being blind
   b. might be more careful
   c. would have glorious memories

For Discussion

1. Why did Helen Keller suggest we should live each day as if it were our last? Do you agree with her? Why or why not?

2. Helen Keller was both blind and deaf. She imagined sight to be the most delightful of the senses. Do you agree with her? Explain your answer.

3. If you could have only three more days to see, what would you do with those days? If you knew you were about to lose your hearing, what would you listen to? Explain your answers.

UNDERSTANDING LITERATURE

Personal Narrative Essay. An *essay* is a short work of literature in which the author makes a statement about an idea or subject and then gives reasons to support or prove that statement.

"Three Days to See" by Helen Keller is an example of a *personal narrative essay*. Personal narrative essays are often informal in style. The author expresses his or her beliefs about a particular subject and then gives examples to explain or support those beliefs.

Here are several beliefs expressed by Helen Keller in the essay you have just read. Go back to the text of the essay, and find two examples or reasons the author used to support each statement. Write them on your paper.

1. "It would be a blessing if each human being were stricken blind and deaf for a few days."

2. "I cannot see, but I find hundreds of things that interest me."

3. "Those who have eyes see little."

4. "Make the most of every sense. Glory in the pleasure and beauty the world reveals to you through your senses."

Writing

Select an object that means something to you. Describe it in words for someone who can neither hear nor see. Try to choose words that describe vividly what that object looks and sounds like.

Learning to Read

by Frederick Douglass

"I would rather be killed running than die a slave." So said Frederick Douglass (1817–1895). Frederick Douglass was born a slave. As a young man, he escaped from slavery in Maryland.

After winning his freedom, Douglass traveled all over the North, speaking out against slavery. In 1845, Douglass wrote about his life as a slave in Narrative of the Life of Frederick Douglass. *This selection is part of his autobiography telling about his experiences between the ages of eight and eighteen. During this time, he lived in Baltimore with relatives of his master. It was there that Douglass learned to read — and in doing so, gained the key to his freedom.*

My new mistress was a kind woman. She had never had a slave under her control before. She began, when I first went to live with her, to treat me the way she thought one human being ought to treat another. She did not seem to see that she must act like a slaveholder. For a slaveholder to treat me like a human being was wrong, and dangerous for her. Slavery proved as harmful to her as it was to me.

When I went to live there, she was religious, warm, and tenderhearted. But slavery took that away from her. Her soft heart turned to stone. Her gentleness turned into tiger-like fierceness.

At first, she had kindly taught me the ABC's, and to spell words of three or four letters. But her husband, Mr. Auld, found out. He told her she could not teach me any more. He said that it was not lawful, and not safe, to teach a slave to read.

"If you give him an inch, he'll take a yard," he said. "A slave should do nothing but obey his master. Learning to read will make him unfit to be a slave. And he will be discontented and unhappy."

From that moment I understood the pathway from slavery to freedom. My master had shown me the source of the white man's power. I knew it would be hard to learn without a teacher. But I set out with high hope and a fixed purpose, at whatever cost, to learn to read.

Mrs. Auld became even more against it than her husband himself. She was not satisfied in just doing what he had ordered.

Frederick Douglass, Elisha Hammond

on an errand, I always took a book. I also took bread, for there was always plenty and I was welcome to it. In that way I was better off than many poor white children in the neighborhood. I would give bread to these hungry little boys. They, in turn, would teach me what they had learned in school.

I used to talk to them about slavery. I wished I could be as free as they would be when they were men.

"You will be free as soon as you are 21," I would say, "but I am a slave for life!"

These words used to trouble them. They would say, "Something may happen so you can be free."

I was now about 12 years old. The thought of being a slave for life weighed heavily upon my heart. I got hold of some books in which arguments for and against slavery were given. The more I read the more I was led to hate my masters. I saw them as robbers who had gone to Africa and stolen us from our homes and made us slaves in a strange land. Master Auld had been right. Discontentment had followed learning to read.

At times, I felt reading was a curse rather than a blessing. It had opened my eyes to the horrible pit I was in, with no ladder to climb out. Sometimes I even envied my fellow slaves who did not understand. I could think of nothing but my condition. Freedom had appeared, and would never disappear. I saw nothing without seeing it and felt nothing without feeling it. It looked from every star, breathed in every wind, and moved in every storm.

She seemed anxious to do better. Nothing made her more angry than to see me with a newspaper. She would rush at me with a face of fury and snatch it from me. She was sure, now, that education and slavery could not mix.

I was narrowly watched. If I was in a separate room for any length of time, I was suspected of having a book. But it was too late. The first step had been taken. The alphabet had given me the inch. Nothing could keep me from taking the yard.

My plan worked very well. I made friends with all the little white boys I met in the street. As many of them as I could, I made into my teachers. When I was sent

I would have killed myself if it were not for the hope of being free. Every little while, I would hear something about abolition. It was some time before I found out what it meant. If a slave ran away, or set fire to a barn, or did anything wrong in the mind of a slaveholder, it was said to be the fruit of abolition. I looked it up in the dictionary. I found it was "the act of abolishing." But what did that mean?

I did not dare ask anyone, for I was sure it was something they did not want me to know about. At last I got hold of a newspaper, which explained that Northerners were praying for the abolition of slavery. The light broke upon me.

I resolved to run away. But first, I had to learn how to write, so I could write my own pass.

I was often sent to a shipyard. I watched the ship carpenters get a piece of wood ready for use. They would write on it the name of the part of the ship it would be built into. When a piece of timber was meant for the larboard side they would write "L." For starboard, it was "S." For the larboard side forward, it would be "L.F." and so on. I soon learned the names of these letters, and began to copy them. Then, I would tell any boy I met who could write that I could write, too.

He would say, "I don't believe you. Let me see you try it." I would make the letters I had learned, and ask him to beat that. I got a good many lessons in writing. My copy books were board fences, walls, and pavements. My pen and ink was a lump of chalk.

By this time, little Master Thomas Auld was in school. When his mother went out, I would copy what he had written in his lesson books. Before long, I could write in a hand very like Master Thomas's.

In 1835, with six other slaves, I planned an escape from another master. Each of us had a "protection": "This is to certify that I, the undersigned, have given the bearer, my servant, full liberty to go to Baltimore and spend the Easter holidays. Written with mine own hand, &c, 1835. William Hamilton."

I wrote them.

READING COMPREHENSION

Select the best choice to complete each statement. Then write the entire sentence on your paper.

1. When Mrs. Auld stopped teaching Frederick, he _____.
   a. gave up learning to read and write
   b. taught himself instead
   c. hired a new teacher

2. Frederick made friends with white boys and often _____.
   a. traded bread for lessons
   b. invited them to become slaves
   c. played games with them

3. When people talked about "abolition," they were referring to _____.
   a. traveling north
   b. opening schools
   c. ending slavery

4. When Frederick Douglass escaped from his master in 1835, he _____.
   a. went to work in a shipyard
   b. wrote passes for himself and six friends
   c. spent Easter with the Hamiltons

For Discussion

1. Frederick Douglass said slavery was as harmful to Mrs. Auld as it was to him. Why do you think he thought so? Do you agree? Why or why not?

2. How did knowing how to read increase unhappiness and discontentment for Frederick Douglass? Would this have been true if Douglass had not been a slave? Explain your answer.

UNDERSTANDING LITERATURE

Autobiography. An *autobiography* is the story of a person's life written by himself or herself. An autobiography often tells how the author thinks or feels about significant events in his or her own life.

Here are some ideas taken from "Learning to Read." Below them are Douglass's own words. On your paper, match the ideas to the quotes from his autobiography.

Ideas

1. Education is the road to freedom.

2. Knowledge can make you sad as well as happy.

3. If you have something others want, you can get something from them in return.

Quotes

a. "[Reading] had opened my eyes to the horrible pit I was in, with no ladder to climb out."

b. "I would give bread to these hungry little boys. They, in turn, would teach me what they had learned in school."

c. "My master had shown me the source of the white man's power. . . . I set out . . . at whatever cost, to learn to read."

Writing

Think about your own life, and pick one person or event from your childhood of importance to you. Write about that person or event as though it was going to be a chapter in your own autobiography.

Three American poems

Poetry expresses ideas and creates images, or pictures. It can stimulate your imagination by putting you in touch with events, places, and characters that are often beyond your everyday experience. Poetry can also reflect your own life and feelings. Here are three poems representing the work of three fine poets from different times and places in America.

Luis Palés Matos (1898–1959) is considered one of the greatest poets Puerto Rico has ever produced. His description in "Hurricane" gives you the feeling of being part of the event.

Edna St. Vincent Millay (1892–1950) wrote at about the same time as Matos. Her poetry conveys feelings so well that during her youth she was hailed as the voice of her generation. Perhaps her poem "Travel" captures a feeling that you have experienced when you have watched a train or an airplane speed by.

Henry Wadsworth Longfellow (1807–1882) is well-known for his long poems that tell stories about famous people and events in American history. The poem included here, "The Tide Rises, The Tide Falls," tells a haunting story with few words — but memorable insights.

The Hurricane   by Luis Palés Matos

When the hurricane unfolds
Its fierce accordion of winds,
On the tip of its toes,
Agile dancer, it sweeps whirling
Over the carpeted surface of the sea
With the scattered branches of the palm.

1. To what does the poet compare the winds of the hurricane?
2. Does this poem make a hurricane seem frightening? Why or why not?

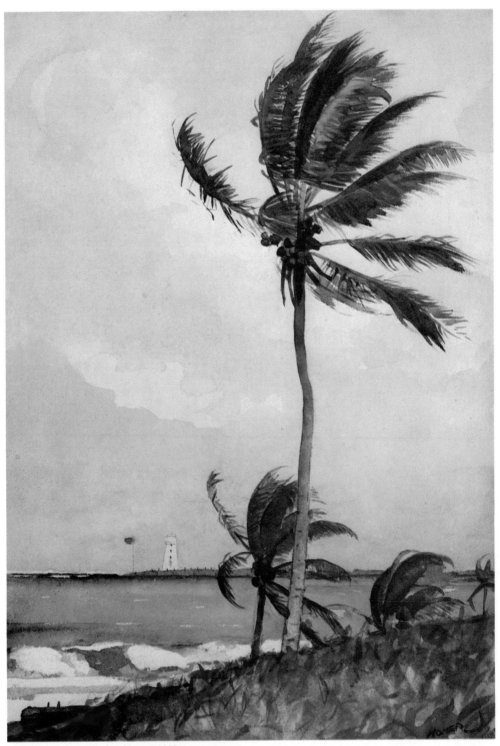

Palm Tree, Nassau, Winslow Homer, 1898

The Tide Rises, the Tide Falls

by Henry Wadsworth Longfellow

The tide rises, the tide falls,
The twilight darkens, the curlew calls;
Along the sea sands damp and
    brown
The traveler hastens toward the town,
  And the tide rises, the tide falls.

Darkness settles on roofs and walls,
But the sea, the sea in the darkness calls;
The little waves, with their soft, white
    hands,
Efface the footprints in the sands,
  And the tide rises, the tide falls.

The morning breaks; the steeds in their
    stalls
Stamp and neigh, as the hostler calls;
The day returns, but nevermore
Returns the traveler to the shore,
    And the tide rises, the tide falls.

1. The poem begins at what time of day? At what time of day does it end?

2. *Efface* means to destroy or take away. Explain how the waves can efface the footprints in the sand.

Approaching Storm: Beach Near Newport, Martin Johnson Heade, c. 1860

Travel

by Edna St. Vincent Millay

The railroad track is miles away,
 And the day is loud with voices
  speaking,
Yet there isn't a train goes by all day,
 But I hear its whistle shrieking.

All night there isn't a train goes by,
 Though the night is still for sleep and
  dreaming,
But I see its cinders red on the sky,
 And hear its engine steaming.

My heart is warm with the friends I
  make,
 And better friends I'll not be knowing,
Yet there isn't a train I wouldn't take,
 No matter where it's going.

1. Why does the poet hear and see a train?
2. What words in the poem describe the sights and sounds of the train?

Rolling Power, Charles Sheeler, 1939

READING COMPREHENSION

Select the best choice to complete each statement. Then write the entire sentence on your paper.

1. In "The Hurricane," the poet compares a hurricane to _____.
   a. scattered palm trees
   b. a dancer whirling about
   c. thick carpeting

2. In "The Tide Rises, the Tide Falls," the _____.
   a. traveler heads for town
   b. traveler lets out the horses
   c. sea washes a town away

3. Edna St. Vincent Millay's poem reveals that she _____.
   a. enjoyed staying home, writing poems
   b. took the train to work each day
   c. loved the idea of traveling

For Discussion

1. What does the last line of "The Hurricane" tell you about the storm's power?

2. What do you think has happened to the traveler in "The Tide Rises, the Tide Falls"? Explain your answer.

3. In "Travel," the poet seemed to find train travel a greater attraction than almost anything else. What details in the poem convey this idea?

4. How does Longfellow's poem make you feel? What phrases help to create the poem's mood? How does the rhythm of the poem add to the effect? Explain your answer.

UNDERSTANDING LITERATURE

Lyric and Narrative Poetry. A *lyric poem* describes an object, an idea, or a feeling. The writer of lyric poetry uses words that create vivid pictures in the readers' minds. The descriptions in lyric poems, such as "The Hurricane" and "Travel," are often unusual.

Listed in Group A are some unusual descriptions from these poems. Write each item on your paper. Then, next to it, write the item from Group B that matches.

Group A
"unfolds its fierce accordion"
"warm with the friends"
"carpeted surface"

Group B
spreading winds of a hurricane
top of sea during a storm
the heart

A *narrative poem* may also contain interesting or unusual descriptions. But, like a story, a narrative poem has a plot, characters, and a setting. On your paper answer the following questions about "The Tide Rises, the Tide Falls."

1. Where and when does the action in the poem take place?

2. Who is the main character, and what happens to him?

Writing

Choose "The Hurricane" or "Travel." On your paper, write a paragraph that explains how the poet felt about the subject of the poem.

The Wind in the Rosebush

by Mary Wilkins Freeman

Mary Wilkins Freeman (1852–1930) was one of the busiest writers of the late 19th and early 20th centuries. She wrote over 230 short stories, 12 novels, and two volumes of poetry. Almost all of her work was about life in her native New England.

Like many American writers before her, she was fascinated by supernatural legends, especially those about ghosts. In one of her most famous stories, "The Wind in the Rosebush," she wrote about the strange happenings in an old New England house. Here is a dramatization of that story.

CHARACTERS

Rebecca Flint, a middle-aged woman
Maria Orton, a woman from Porter's Falls
Thomas Orton, husband of Maria Orton
Emmeline Dent, a middle-aged widow
Postmaster

Time: the 1890's.
Place: New England.

Scene One

A ferry boat is crossing a small New England river. Rebecca Flint sits stiff and straight on one bench. Near her sit Maria and Thomas Orton. Maria stares at Rebecca for a while. Then she speaks.

Maria: It's a pleasant day, isn't it?
Rebecca: Yes. Very pleasant.
Maria: Have you come far?
Rebecca: From Michigan.
Maria: Oh, that's a long way from Porter's Falls. A long way to come and leave your family.
Rebecca: I don't have any family to leave.
Maria: Then — you're not married.
Rebecca *(proudly):* No, I am not married.
Maria: That's too bad.
Rebecca: I have never thought so.
Maria: Oh. Are you visiting somebody in Porter's Falls?
Rebecca: Yes, as a matter of fact. John Dent's widow. Her husband died about three years ago.

Maria *(looking frightened):* Oh. Yes — yes — I — I do know her. Thomas — we — we know her, don't we?

Thomas *(hastily):* Not very well. You're not related to Mrs. Dent, are you?

Rebecca: Not by blood. John Dent's first wife was my sister.

Maria: Was she? She was her sister, Thomas.

Thomas: I heard, Maria. *(He shakes his head as if to warn his wife to be silent.)*

Rebecca: I'm going to see the present Mrs. Dent, and take my niece Agnes home with me.

Maria: What? You're going to do what?

Rebecca: What's the matter? Is there some reason why I shouldn't?

Maria: Thomas —

Thomas *(very softly):* Let it rest, Maria.

Maria: But Thomas —

Thomas: Maria. I said, let it rest.

Rebecca: Is there something I should know about? Is my niece sick?

Maria: No, no, no — she's not sick. You can be sure of that. Everything's — all right with her.

Rebecca *(relieved):* Well, that's good to know. When did you last see her?

Maria: I — I haven't seen her for some time. *(She is very flustered.)*

Rebecca: She must have grown up real pretty, if she takes after my sister. Grace was such a pretty woman.

Maria: Yes. She did grow up pretty. Thomas —

Thomas *(very softly):* It's none of our business, Maria.

Rebecca: What kind of woman is the second wife?

Maria: I — guess she's a nice woman. I don't see much of her.

Rebecca: I felt kind of hurt that John married again so soon after my sister died. But I guess Agnes had to be taken care of. I couldn't take her then . . . . I was teaching school and I had my mother with me. But Mother's gone now, and I've given up teaching. I inherited a little money, and now I've come for Agnes. I think she'll be glad to come with me. Though as far as I know, her stepmother, Emmeline, is a good woman.

Maria: I — I guess so.

Rebecca: John wrote that his new wife was beautiful, too.

(The passengers react to a jolt as the ferry boat grates on the shore. Thomas grabs Maria by the arm, and hurries her off. Rebecca follows with her carpetbag.)

Thomas: Thank heaven we've landed. *(To Rebecca)* Over there, Miss. That's Mrs. Dent's horse and wagon. She's sent it for you.

Rebecca: Oh, thank you. *(Calling)* Young man, I'm the one you're waiting for. *(She hurries off.)*

Maria *(looking after her):* Thomas, I think I should have told her.

Thomas: Let her find it out herself. Don't go burning your fingers in other folks' pudding, Maria.

Maria: But suppose what folks say is true? And suppose she's a nervous woman? She might lose her mind.

Thomas: If she can lose her mind that easy, it's not too strong to begin with. You just keep out of it, Maria.

Scene Two

Rebecca starts up the walk to a fine-looking house. Mrs. Dent opens the door and comes partway down the walk to meet her.

Mrs. Dent: You are Miss Rebecca Flint, I suppose.

Rebecca: Yes, I am. I wrote you —

Mrs. Dent: Your letter didn't get here until this morning. I wish you had given me more notice.

Rebecca: I'm sorry, but I just couldn't wait for you to answer. I felt I must come for Agnes, now that I could. She's my own flesh and blood, you know. And from her picture, she looks so much like my sister. *(Mrs. Dent begins to gasp.)*

Mrs. Dent *(clutching at her heart)*: Oh!

Rebecca: Are you sick? Can I get you some water?

Mrs. Dent: No, no. I'm all right now. I have these spells. I'm over it already. Come in, Miss Flint. *(She stands back, and Rebecca starts toward the house before her. She stops at a rosebush growing beside the walk.)*

Rebecca: What a big rosebush. And look, it's late in the season, but that red rose is perfect. *(She reaches out to touch the rose.)*

Mrs. Dent: Don't you pick that rose!

Rebecca: I do not pick other people's roses without permission, Mrs. Dent.

(Suddenly, the rosebush begins to move, as if blown by a strong wind. The hydrangea bush next to it does not move at all.)

Rebecca: Mrs. Dent, look at that. There's not a bit of wind —

Mrs. Dent: Go into the house, Miss Flint! *(She pushes Rebecca ahead of her toward the house.)*

Rebecca: But why is the rosebush blowing when there's no wind?

Mrs. Dent: It's not blowing. *(The rosebush is still.)*

Rebecca: But the leaves were moving —

Mrs. Dent: And now they're not. I can't be responsible for every passing breeze, Miss Flint. Go on in.

Scene Three

A beautifully furnished room inside the Dent house.

Mrs. Dent: Sit down. Take off your hat.

Rebecca: You have a fine home here. *(She sits and begins to unpin her hat.)* But where is Agnes?

Mrs. Dent: She went over to Addie Slocum's. No telling when she'll get back.

Rebecca: Oh, I did hope she'd be here. Is Addie her best friend?

Mrs. Dent: You might say that. When did you say you were going home?

Rebecca *(startled)*: Why, I didn't say. As soon as Agnes is ready, I guess. I thought maybe a week.

Mrs. Dent: You don't have to wait for her, you know. You can go on home, and she can come later. She's 16. She can take care of herself.

Rebecca: No. I won't have her travel alone. She'll come when I do. *(She is annoyed.)* And if I can't wait here, in the

house that was my sister's home, I'll go somewhere else and stay.

Mrs. Dent: I didn't mean that. You can stay as long as you want to.

(Suddenly, Rebecca jumps up and points to something in a mirror that is across from the window.)

Rebecca: Look! In the mirror! It's Agnes. She's right outside. *(She runs to the door.)* I'll stand right here so I'll be the first thing she sees when she opens the door. *(She waits. But the door does not open. She opens it and looks out.)* Where is she? I saw her pass the window. *(She closes the door.)*

Mrs. Dent: You must have been mistaken.

Rebecca: No. I saw a shadow go over the ceiling, and I saw her in that mirror there. And then the shadow passed the window.

Mrs. Dent: How did she look in the mirror?

Rebecca: Little, light-haired — isn't that what Agnes looks like?

Mrs. Dent: Yes, it is. But you couldn't really have seen her. You've been thinking so much about her, you imagined it. It's too early for her to get home from Addie Slocum's. Let me show you to your room, Miss Flint. You can see Agnes tomorrow morning.

Scene Four

The next morning. Mrs. Dent is in the kitchen, preparing breakfast. Rebecca comes downstairs into the room.

Rebecca: Is Agnes here? I thought I heard a girl laughing in the night.

Mrs. Dent: No, she stayed with Addie. She often does that. She'll be along pretty soon. Have some breakfast, Miss Flint.

Rebecca: I'm not hungry, thank you. I'll just go out and look down the road. Maybe Agnes is on her way home. *(She goes out. Mrs. Dent stands and stares after her with a hard, strange look. She turns back to the wood stove. Rebecca runs in.)*

Rebecca: That rosebush! It's blowing again!

Mrs. Dent: What of it?

Rebecca: But there's no wind!

Mrs. Dent: Miss Flint, I told you I have no time for such nonsense. Now if you'll just sit down and eat this —

Rebecca: The window! There she is now! *(She runs to the door and throws it open. A breeze ruffles her hair and a paper is blown off the table.)* Agnes? Agnes? *(To Miss Dent)* There's nobody there again. And I saw somebody pass that window.

Mrs. Dent: You were mistaken again. Please shut that door. *(Rebecca shuts the door and sits down.)*

Rebecca: Are there roses somewhere in this kitchen? I smell roses.

Mrs. Dent: I don't smell a thing, Miss Flint. Why don't you settle down and eat your breakfast?

Rebecca: No. Mrs. Dent, I've come a long way, and I've waited long enough. I want you to send for Agnes.

Mrs. Dent: Why, of course. I'll do better. I'll go get her myself. *(She wipes her hands on her apron and takes it off. She reaches for a shawl hanging on the back of a door.)* I'll just — what's that paper there on the floor?

Rebecca: I don't know. *(She bends to pick it up. Mrs. Dent grabs it from her hand.)*

Mrs. Dent: Why, it's a note from Mrs. Slocum. She must have pushed it under the door and it blew in when you opened it. *(Looks at the paper.)* It says that Addie and Agnes have gone over to Lincoln on the train to visit Addie's uncle for a few days. They'll be gone till Thursday. *(She tears up the paper and puts it in the wood stove to burn.)*

Rebecca: Thursday. I won't see her till then. That's a long time.

Mrs. Dent: Now, if you're worried about getting home, I told you I could send Agnes on after you. If you'd like to help her get ready, there's a nightgown over in that basket she's been working on. You can sew the lace on it. Everything's right there.

Rebecca *(goes to a basket on the table and takes out a white nightgown and a length of lace):* If you'll just give me a needle and thread, I'd love to finish it for dear Agnes.

Scene Five

Midnight. Rebecca lies in bed in her room. In the distance, piano music begins. Rebecca stirs and sits up. She gets up and throws a shawl over her old-fashioned nightgown. She tiptoes out into the hall and looks down over the bannister of the stairs. She screams.

Rebecca: Mrs. Dent! Mrs. Dent! *(Mrs.*

Dent, in her long nightgown, her hair in curl papers, comes into the hall.)

Mrs. Dent: What is the matter with you? It's after midnight.

Rebecca *(pointing over the railing):* The piano — the piano — down in the parlor —

Mrs. Dent: Well, what about it?

Rebecca: It was playing by itself! I heard music — I came out to look — I thought Agnes might have come home. I could see the keys moving — but nobody was playing!

Mrs. Dent: Miss Flint, your imagination is getting the best of you. I didn't hear any music, and neither did you. You dreamed it. Now go back to bed. *(Mrs. Dent goes back toward her room. Rebecca walks to her room and over to the bed. She begins to scream again.)*

Rebecca: Mrs. Dent! Mrs. Dent! *(Mrs. Dent appears. She goes to the doorway of Rebecca's room.)* Look! Look at my bed!

Mrs. Dent *(looking in):* Oh! *(She gasps, then quickly calms herself.)* It's the nightgown you finished for Agnes. What about it?

Rebecca: It's lying there, as if she was going to wear it. And the rose — the rose — the red rose from the rosebush! It's lying in the lace!

Mrs. Dent: Miss Flint, this is the last straw. You picked that rose, and you dropped the nightgown on your bed and forgot it. When you dreamed you heard that music, you knocked the rose onto your bed, and it happened to fall on the gown. Now that's the only sensible explanation.

Rebecca: No! No! I left the nightgown downstairs. I didn't pick the rose. And I didn't dream that music. It woke me up.
Mrs. Dent (*in a hard and commanding voice*): Miss Flint, go back to bed. We will talk about this in the morning.

Scene Six

The next morning. Mrs. Dent stands in the kitchen, working. Rebecca enters wearing her hat and shawl and carrying her carpetbag.

Rebecca: Mrs. Dent. Early this morning I came downstairs and went out into the front yard. The red rose was still on the rosebush.

Mrs. Dent: Oh, dear. If I'd known you weren't well, Miss Flint, I wouldn't have let you stay in my house.

Rebecca: Well, I won't stay any longer. I'm leaving now. But on my way home, I will get off the train in Lincoln and find my niece and take her with me. I will thank you, Mrs. Dent, to give me the address of Addie Slocum's uncle.

Mrs. Dent: I don't have his address, Miss Flint.

Rebecca: Then tell me where the Slocums live. I'll go there and get the address.

Mrs. Dent: No. I will not have you going to the Slocums and raving about pianos that play by themselves and roses that leap on and off bushes. Go home, Miss Flint. When Agnes gets back, I'll tell her about you. If she wants to go and live with you, that will be her business. She's old enough to make up her own mind.

Rebecca: I will find her in Lincoln and take her home with me. Good-bye, Mrs. Dent. (*She stalks out the door. Mrs. Dent stands looking after her, a strange expression on her face.*)

Scene Seven

The Porter's Falls post office. The postmaster stands behind a barred window. Rebecca enters and goes to the window.

Rebecca: Are you the postmaster here?

Postmaster: Yes, I've been postmaster for 30 years. What can I do for you?

Rebecca: I'm looking for some people I have business with. I wonder if you could tell me where they live. Their name is Slocum.

Postmaster: Slocum? No. No Slocums live in Porter's Falls.

Rebecca: You must be mistaken. They have a daughter named Addie, a girl about 16.

Postmaster: Addie Slocum. Oh, yes, I remember now. Ma'am, your business with these people must have waited a long time. Addie Slocum died 10 years ago, and her parents died a few years later. Nobody's lived in their house since then.

Rebecca (*very slowly*): And — Agnes Dent. Do you know a girl named Agnes Dent?

Postmaster: I'm sorry, ma'am, but that's a sad story, too. Poor little Agnes Dent got sick. It was real bad. The doctor prescribed some medicine that might have saved her. But it wasn't given to her. There was some talk of taking action against her stepmother, but there wasn't enough evidence. Ever since, people say there have been strange sights and sounds around the Dent house. Some say it's haunted.

Rebecca: But Agnes? What happened to Agnes?

Postmaster: Ma'am, Agnes Dent died a year ago. Just about this time. Pretty little thing. Sad. I remember she wore a white dress in her coffin. All trimmed with lace.

Rebecca: A white dress trimmed with lace. And — was there — a red rose?

Postmaster: Why, ma'am, it's funny you should ask that. Nobody knew how it got there. But just before they shut down the lid of the coffin, we all saw a red rose lying right over Agnes Dent's heart. (*Rebecca stands frozen in horror.*)

READING COMPREHENSION

Select the best choice to complete each statement. Then write the entire sentence on your paper.

1. The play suggests that the rosebush moved because _____.
    a. there were strong winds
    b. it was haunted by the ghost of Agnes
    c. birds flew in and out of it

2. When Rebecca heard the music, Mrs. Dent told her _____.
    a. that Agnes loved to play the piano
    b. to turn down the volume
    c. she had imagined it

3. When Agnes was buried, there was a red rose on her dress _____.
    a. that her stepmother had picked for her
    b. like the rose Rebecca saw on the nightgown
    c. and other flowers in her hair

For Discussion

1. What did Maria's husband mean when he said, "Don't go burning your fingers in other folks' pudding"? Do you think this was good advice? Why or why not?

2. What are some of the unusual things that happened in this play? What or who do you think was causing them? Explain your answer.

3. Do you think Mrs. Dent was responsible for Agnes's death? Why or why not? If so, what do you think Rebecca should do next?

UNDERSTANDING LITERATURE

Play. The selection you have just read, "The Wind in the Rosebush," is a play, or drama. To understand what is going on in a play, you have to depend mainly on the conversations of the characters. These conversations are called *dialogue.*

In addition to the dialogue, the playwright includes *stage directions,* which give the actors and readers of the play more information about the plot and characters.

Stage directions are notes that describe the setting of a scene, tell how characters should say their lines, indicate what actions take place on the stage, and specify what props and scenery are needed.

Write the answers to the following questions on your paper.

1. In "The Wind in the Rosebush," find three examples of stage directions that reveal Rebecca's feelings.

2. Find three examples of stage directions that give an insight into Mrs. Dent's character.

3. Find three references to the setting or props that tell about Agnes.

Writing

Think about what happened in "The Wind in the Rosebush." Suppose that Agnes were able to speak for herself and tell her story about what happened. Write the lines for her part. Include stage directions if you feel they are needed.

Section Review

VOCABULARY

Prefixes and Suffixes. Some words are made up of a root, or base, and a prefix and/or a suffix. A *prefix* is added to the beginning of the root word, and it changes the word's meaning. A *suffix* is added to the end.

For example, the prefix *re-* means "again." In the Section *Review*, you view, or look at, again what you have learned. The suffix *-er* means "one who." A *reviewer* is someone who looks again at something.

Here are some additional prefixes, suffixes, and their meanings. Read the following sentences. On your paper, write each italicized word, circling its prefix and/or suffix. Then write the meaning of each word.

> **Prefixes** *non- dis-* = not
> *mis-* = wrong, or not
>
> **Suffixes** *-ness* = state of being
> *-ment* = resulting

1. You must have been *mistaken.*

2. *Discontentment* had followed learning how to read.

3. I just told you I had no time for such *nonsense.*

4. The same *casualness* characterizes all the senses.

READING

Fact and Opinion. A *fact* is something that exists or that has happened. A fact is definitely true. That O. Henry wrote "After Twenty Years" is a fact. An *opinion* is a statement that tells what someone believes or feels about something. " 'After Twenty Years' is O. Henry's best story" is an opinion. Statements that have specific dates and figures are likely to be facts. Statements containing value words like *good, better, best, bad, worse, most,* and *lovely* are likely to be opinions.

Read each of the following statements about the selections in this section. Number your paper from 1 to 10. Identify each statement as *fact* or *opinion.*

1. Jimmy Wells was a good friend.

2. It was 10:00 when Jimmy and Bob had parted at the restaurant door.

3. "Raymond's Run" is a great story.

4. Hazel Parker is the name of the main character in "Raymond's Run."

5. Helen Keller was blind and deaf.

6. It would be a blessing if everyone were stricken blind for three days.

7. Frederick Douglass loved reading more than any other boy in Baltimore.

8. "The Hurricane" is a poem by Luis Palés Matos.

9. Riding on a train is better than making friends.

10. The traveler in "The Tide Rises, the Tide Falls" was not a good walker.

WRITING AN OPINION

An opinion is a person's belief or feeling about something. Everyone has personal opinions about many things. Think about things you like and about things you don't like. Whenever you say you like or dislike something, you are expressing an opinion, or your view. Sometimes your views are in agreement with the views of others, and sometimes they are different.

Suppose a friend told you, "I don't like that jacket." An opinion without a reason doesn't tell you very much. However, suppose your friend said, "I don't like that jacket because your shirt hangs out the bottom, it makes you look too heavy, and the color clashes with your scarf." You could still agree or disagree, but at least you'd know the reasons for the opinion.

Read each of the following statements. Decide whether you strongly agree, strongly disagree, or don't have an opinion one way or the other. Think of at least one reason to back up your feelings about each statement. Be prepared to discuss your opinion and reasons with your class. This will help you to see that opinions are beliefs, and that it's possible, and even likely, for people to disagree about many things.

1. If you never trust anyone completely, you will never be disappointed.

2. If someone has broken the law, he or she should be punished no matter what special circumstances there might be.

3. It's all right to tell a lie or to conceal something as long as the end result doesn't hurt anyone.

As you discuss your opinion about each of these statements with the class, give your reasons to support each one. Someone should record the group's comments on a piece of paper or on the chalkboard.

Now that you've practiced forming, supporting, and discussing opinions, it's time to write an opinion and give convincing reasons for it.

Think about the ending of "After Twenty Years," the O. Henry story that you read at the beginning of this section. Do you think Jimmy Wells did the right thing in turning in his friend? Follow the directions below and write a paragraph expressing your opinion of this.

1. Write an interesting first sentence to state your opinion of what Jimmy Wells did.

2. Give reasons for the opinion you have expressed. It may help you to list the reasons on a piece of paper before putting them in sentence form. Try it.

3. After you have given at least three reasons for your opinion, end your paragraph by restating the opinion so that the reader has no doubt about where you stand.

Now reread your paragraph. Ask yourself the questions in this checklist:

☐ Does the first sentence clearly express an opinion?

☐ Does the paragraph give reasons to support the opinion?

☐ Does the closing sentence restate the opinion?

QUIZ

The following is a quiz for Section 1. Write the answers in complete sentences on your paper.

Reading Comprehension

1. In "After Twenty Years," why did Silky Bob travel 1,000 miles and wait in a doorway? What did he expect to happen?

2. In "Raymond's Run," how did Hazel and Gretchen feel about each other before the race? What were their feelings after the race?

3. List five things that Helen Keller said she would do (in "Three Days to See") if she could see for three days.

4. In "Learning to Read," what document did Frederick Douglass use for his escape? How did he get it?

5. In "The Wind and the Rosebush," why did Rebecca travel to Porter's Falls? Did she achieve her aim?

Understanding Literature

6. In "After Twenty Years," the plot took a sudden twist and the story had a surprise ending. What was the story's unexpected turn of events?

7. Identify two major characters in "Raymond's Run," and write one or two sentences describing each.

8. What is the most important message Helen Keller has for the readers of her personal narrative essay? Why did she feel this way?

9. Identify three important events from Frederick Douglass's autobiography. Write them in the order in which they occurred.

10. A rose appeared three times in the play "The Wind in the Rosebush." What did the appearance of the rose mean the first time it was seen? The second? The third? What did the rose tell you about Agnes Dent?

COMPOSITION

1. Pretend you are Hazel Parker. Describe your plan to train Raymond to run in a race. Then tell how you think this training will change your brother's life.

2. Edna St. Vincent Millay wrote a poem about travel. Write your own poem or a paragraph about your feelings about travel. Include information about how (by car, by train, by plane, by spaceship) and where you might go.

3. At the end of "The Wind in the Rosebush," Rebecca learns that her niece Agnes is dead. Write at least three paragraphs of dialogue that express her feelings about Agnes's death and her plans for the future.

America's Early Voices

LITERATURE BEFORE 1840

Pleasant it looked,
this newly created world.
Along the entire length and breadth
of the earth, our grandmother,
extended the green reflection
of her covering.

— Traditional Winnebago Song

Introduction

The earliest Americans lived in a land of great beauty and promise. Thousands of years ago, this land offered peace and plenty to the first people to settle in America, the people now called Indians or Native Americans.

Each Native American group, or tribe, developed its own way of life, its own government, its own beliefs. Its members told stories and created poems that expressed their feelings, hopes, and ideas about life.

About 400 years ago, colonists from England, Spain, and other nations began coming to America. They also came with hope for peace and plenty. Here was a land where people could live according to their principles. Eventually they, too, would produce their own poets, thinkers, and storytellers. And, like the Native Americans, their literature would reflect their most deeply held beliefs.

The Earliest American Literature

Many Native American groups stressed living in harmony with other people and with nature. An ancient Native American tale, the story "Godaysio, the Woman Chief" is retold here. This story tells of people who cannot agree and the sad consequences of their disagreement.

The Puritans came from England, eager to practice religion as they saw fit. They valued plainness. They did not like fancy churches, homes, clothing, or language. Anne Bradstreet was a Puritan born in England in 1612. In 1630 she sailed for Massachusetts. There she spent the rest of her life running a household, raising eight children, and writing poetry. Two of her poems appear in this section.

The earliest colonists read books and newspapers that came from England and Europe. But in the early 1700's Americans began printing their own.

Two of the most popular authors of this era were Jonathan Edwards and Benjamin Franklin. Edwards was a Puritan minister concerned with perfecting an ideal life. He was an exciting speaker who would make his listeners groan and shriek with terror as he described the punishment that was awaiting all "sinners." Franklin was not concerned with the ideal or perfect life. He was practical. Whatever honest method worked best to achieve a goal was the method Franklin valued.

In this section, you will read Edwards's *Resolutions* — his rules for a perfect life, and two excerpts from Franklin's writing that reflect his cleverness, humor, and practical nature.

The Revolutionary Era

The growth of American literature helped the colonists feel that they were more like

The Sentinel, Albert Bierstadt, 1830–1902

each other than they were like the people of England. Many colonists began to feel that they wanted their own government, and the writing of Americans began to reflect this desire. In this section, you will read selections by two of the authors of the revolutionary period who were famous for expressing their ideas and ideals very well: Abigail Adams and Thomas Paine.

Writing After the Revolution

After America was firmly established as a nation, her people felt a great pride in themselves and their new country. The exploits of Davy Crockett, told in *Davy Crockett's Almanac,* and the writing of Jean de Crèvecoeur suggest in very different ways that Americans saw themselves as the cleverest, strongest people in the world.

In the early 1800's, a young New York writer named Washington Irving began publishing stories. His stories drew on European, colonial, and Native American traditions. The stories were funny and exciting. He became the first American author to win worldwide fame. His story in this section, "The Legend of Sleepy Hollow," has remained popular since it was first published in 1819.

The early Americans were searching for a better way of life — a way of life that was truly their own. Every generation makes this search in its own way. You may find that America's early authors tell of experiences and dreams that touch your world, your life today.

Godasiyo, the Woman Chief

a Seneca legend retold by Dee Brown

Dee Brown, a modern author and historian, retells this ancient story in language that reflects the way this story was first told aloud centuries ago by the Seneca people, one of the five Iroquois tribes of upstate New York.

At the beginning of time when America was new, a woman chief named Godasiyo ruled over an Indian village beside a large river in the East. In those days all the tribes spoke one language and lived in harmony and peace. Because Godasiyo was a wise and progressive chief, many people came from faraway places to live in her village, and they had no difficulty understanding one another.

At last, the village grew so large that half the people lived on the north side of the river, and half on the south side. They spent much time canoeing back and forth to visit, attend dances, and exchange gifts of venison, hides, furs, and dried fruits and berries. The tribal council house was on the south side, which made it necessary for those who lived on the north bank to make frequent canoe trips to consult with their chief. Some complained about this, and to make it easier for everybody to cross the rapid stream, Godasiyo ordered a bridge to be built of saplings and tree limbs carefully fastened together. This bridge brought the tribe close together again, and the people praised Godasiyo for her wisdom.

Not long after this, a white dog appeared in the village, and Godasiyo claimed it for her own. Everywhere the chief went the dog followed her, and the people on the north side of the river became jealous of the animal. They spread stories that the dog was possessed by an evil spirit that would bring harm to the tribe. One day, a delegation from the north bank crossed the bridge to the council house and demanded that Godasiyo kill the white dog. When she refused to do so, the delegates returned to their side of the river, and that night they destroyed the bridge.

From that time on people on the north bank and those on the south bank began to distrust each other. The tribe divided into two factions, one renouncing Godasiyo as their chief, the other supporting her. Bad feelings between them grew so deep that Godasiyo foresaw that the next step would surely lead to fighting and war. Hoping to avoid bloodshed, she called all members of the tribe who supported her to a meeting in the council house.

"Our people," she said, "are divided by more than a river. No longer is there good will and contentment among us. Not wishing to see brother fight against brother, I propose that those who recognize me as their chief follow me westward up the great river to build a new village."

Almost everyone who attended the council meeting agreed to follow Godasiyo westward. In preparation for the migration, they built many canoes of birch bark. Two young men who had been friendly rivals in canoe races volunteered to construct a special watercraft for their chief. With strong poles they fastened two large canoes together and then built a platform which extended over the canoes and the space between them. Upon this platform was a seat for Godasiyo and places to store her clothing, extra leggings, belts, robes, moccasins, mantles, caps, awls, needles, and adornments.

At last everything was ready. Godasiyo took her seat on the platform with the white dog beside her, and the two young men who had built the craft began paddling the double canoes beneath. Behind them the chief's followers and defenders launched their own canoes, which contained all their belongings. This flotilla of canoes covered the shining waters as far as anyone could see up and down the river.

After they had paddled a long distance, they came to a fork in the river. Godasiyo ordered the two young canoeists to stop in the middle of the river until the others caught up with them. In a few minutes the flotilla was divided, half of the canoes on her left, the others on her right.

The chief and the people on each side of her began to discuss the advantages of the two forks in the river. Some wanted to go one way; some preferred the other way. The arguments grew heated with anger. Godasiyo said that she would take whichever fork her people chose, but they could agree on neither. Finally those on the right turned the prows of their canoes up the right channel, while those on the left began paddling up the left channel. And so the tribe began to separate.

When this movement started, the two young men paddling the two canoes carrying Godasiyo's float disagreed as to which fork they should take, and they fell into a violent quarrel. The canoeist on the right thrust his paddle into the water and started toward the right, and at the same time the one on the left swung his canoe toward the left. Suddenly, Godasiyo's platform slipped off its supports and collapsed into the river, carrying her with it.

Hearing the loud splash, the people on both sides turned their canoes around and tried to rescue their beloved chief. But she and the white dog, the platform, and all her belongings had sunk to the bottom, and the people could see nothing but fish swimming in the clear waters.

Dismayed by this tragic happening, the people of the two divisions began to try to talk to each other. But even though they shouted words back and forth, those on the right could not understand the people on the left, and those on the left could not understand the people on the right. When Godasiyo drowned in the great river her people's language had become changed. This was how it was that the Indians were divided into many tribes spreading across America, each of them speaking a different language.

READING COMPREHENSION

Select the best choice to complete each statement. Then write the entire sentence on your paper.

1. When Godasiyo first ruled an Indian village, _____.
   a. her people wanted another chief
   b. strangers caused much trouble
   c. people understood each other and had peace

2. Godasiyo decided to build a new village _____.
   a. because the old one was shabby
   b. to stop fighting among her people
   c. far from the old hunting grounds

3. Godasiyo and her dog drowned when her people _____.
   a. couldn't agree on which way to go
   b. pushed her out of the boat
   c. refused to try to rescue her

4. After Godasiyo drowned, her people divided into many tribes and _____.
   a. each tried to find her body
   b. each spoke a different language
   c. war broke out constantly

For Discussion

1. Why did Godasiyo build a bridge? What did this accomplish?

2. Why did Godasiyo and her followers decide to move and set up a new village?

3. Do you think that things would have been different if Godasiyo's village had stayed small? Explain your answer.

UNDERSTANDING LITERATURE

Point of View in a Legend. Every story is told from a point of view. Legends, such as the Native American tale "Godasiyo, the Woman Chief," are usually told or written in the third person (*he, she, they, it*). The storyteller speaks in this "all-knowing" point of view in order to better convince the reader or listener that the story might be true by relating what each character is thinking.

A legend often tries to explain why something happened. The third-person point of view allows the narrator to explain why different actions occur in the story.

Answer the following questions in complete sentences on your paper.

1. Why did Godasiyo's village increase in size?

2. Why did the people on the north side order the white dog to be killed? What did they do when Godasiyo refused?

3. What happened at the fork in the river?

4. After Godasiyo's death, why were the people unable to understand each other even when they tried?

Writing

Imagine that Godasiyo had not drowned, but had managed to swim to the river bank with her dog. Write a paragraph to finish the legend differently. Be sure to use the third-person point of view. If you wish, you may begin with "Godasiyo and her dog rose to the top of the water. They. . . ."

To My Dear and Loving Husband

by Anne Bradstreet

If ever two were one, then surely we;
If ever man were loved by wife, then
    thee;
If ever wife was happy in a man,
Compare with me, ye women, if you can.
I prize thy love more than whole mines
    of gold,
Or all the riches that the East doth hold.
My love is such that rivers cannot
    quench,
Not ought but love from thee give
    recompense.
Thy love is such I can no way repay,
The heavens reward thee manifold, I pray.
Then while we live in love let's so
    persevere
That when we live no more we may live
    ever.

The Sargent Family, Unknown Artist, c. 1800

1. How did the poet think her life compared to that of other women?

2. The poet would not trade her husband's love for anything, no matter how valuable. What lines tell you this?

3. What words did Anne Bradstreet use to suggest that the intensity of her love was greater than an enormous fire?

4. What did Anne Bradstreet wish for her husband?

In Reference to Her Children
23 June, 1656

by Anne Bradstreet

I nurst them up with pain and care
Nor cost nor labour did I spare
Till at the last they felt their wing
Mounted the trees and learned to
     sing. . . .
Alas, my birds, you wisdom want
Of perils you are ignorant;
Oft times in grass, on trees, in flight,
Sore accidents on you may light.
Oh, to your safety have an eye
So happy you may live and die. . . .
My age I will not once lament
But sing, my time so near is spent.
And from the top bough take my flight
Into a country beyond sight. . . .

---

1. What does Anne Bradstreet's poem tell you about motherhood? Do you think she was a good mother? Explain your answer.

2. Do you think the poet worried about her children? What lines support your answer?

3. In what specific ways did Anne Bradstreet feel children were like birds? What else might children be compared to?

4. What did Anne Bradstreet want for her children? What did she want for herself?

Resolutions

by Jonathan Edwards

In the early 1700's, a great religious movement swept the American colonies. This period was called the "Great Awakening." People took a fresh interest in religion, founded hundreds of new churches, and became more concerned with religious liberty. One of the greatest figures of the Great Awakening was Jonathan Edwards (1703–1758). To Edwards, God was everything and people were nothing. Edwards preached and wrote that humans were basically sinners, and needed to be constantly on guard against the devil. The selection below is adapted from Edwards's Resolutions. *The* Resolutions *were meant to be a series of rules that people could follow to avoid becoming sinners.*

Being aware that I am unable to do anything without God's help, I do humbly beg him by his grace, to help me to keep these *Resolutions,* so far as they are agreeable to his will, for Christ's sake.

REMEMBER TO READ OVER THESE RESOLUTIONS ONCE A WEEK.

RESOLVED   Never *to do* anything, whether in soul or body, less or more, but what tends to the glory of God, nor *be,* nor *suffer* it, if I can possibly avoid it.

RESOLVED   Never to lose one moment of time, but to improve it in the most profitable way I possibly can.

RESOLVED   To live with all my might, while I do live.

RESOLVED   Never to do any thing, which I should be afraid to do, if it were the last hour of my life.

RESOLVED   To act, in all respects, both speaking and doing, as if nobody had been so vile as I. To act as if I had committed the same sins, or had the same infirmities or failings as others:

I will let the knowledge of their failings promote nothing but shame in myself, and prove only an occasion of my confessing my own sins and misery to God.

RESOLVED   When I feel pain, to think of the pains of Martyrdom, and of Hell.

RESOLVED   Never to do any thing out of revenge.

RESOLVED That I will live so, as I shall wish I had done when I come to die.

RESOLVED To maintain the strictest temperance, in eating and drinking.

RESOLVED Whenever I do any really evil action, to trace it back, till I come to the original cause: And then, both carefully try to do so no more, and to fight and pray with all my might against the original of it.

RESOLVED To study the Scriptures so steadily, constantly, and frequently, as that I may find, and plainly see myself grow in the knowledge of it.

RESOLVED Never to utter any thing that is sportive, or matter of laughter, on a Lord's day.

RESOLVED To ask myself, at the end of every day, week, month, and year, how I could possibly, in any respect, have done better.

RESOLVED That no other end but religion, shall have any influence at all on any of my actions.

READING COMPREHENSION

Select the best choice to complete each statement. Then write the entire sentence on your paper.

1. In *Resolutions*, Jonathan Edwards gave his guidelines for _____.
   a. making and keeping friends
   b. becoming wealthy and wise
   c. living a life free from sin

2. Edwards believed that people could improve themselves by _____.
   a. carefully examining their actions
   b. finding ways to make life easier
   c. avoiding too much thinking

3. Edwards felt that time_____.
   a. should be used to rest
   b. shouldn't be wasted
   c. caused much suffering

4. If Edwards did something wrong, he would try to _____.
   a. trace its cause
   b. forget about it
   c. avoid getting caught

For Discussion

1. "RESOLVED   To live with all my might, while I do live." Give some examples of how a person might do this. Do you recommend following this resolution? Why or why not?

2. What role did eating and drinking play in the life of Jonathan Edwards? What resolution tells you this?

3. How often did Jonathan Edwards recommend self-examination?

UNDERSTANDING LITERATURE

Point of View. Jonathan Edwards's *Resolutions* presented his personal views on religion and the rules by which he believed he and everyone else should live. Edwards expressed these resolutions in a personal way. He used the first-person point of view, referring to himself as "I."

Edwards chose not to write his beliefs in the form of orders to others (direct address, or second person, i.e., "*You* should . . .") or as comments on the world using the third person (i.e., "People should . . .").

Here are three of Edwards's resolutions expressed as orders to others. On your paper, first rewrite each as a personal expression using the first person, and then as a comment on life using the third person.

1. You should never act out of revenge.

2. Ask yourself, at the end of each day, how you could possibly, in any respect, have done better.

3. Live so, as you shall wish you had done when you come to die.

Writing

Edwards's *Resolutions* were expressed in the language of his day. Choose any five and rewrite them in modern language using the first-person point of view.

Here's an example of one of them. "RESOLVED   To maintain the strictest temperance, in eating and drinking" in the words of today might read "I will try not to eat or drink too much."

The writing of Benjamin Franklin

Benjamin Franklin (1706–1790) was one of the best loved and most influential Americans of his day. The literature he created suggests why he was so popular. His writing is full of both wisdom and humor.

Sayings

by Benjamin Franklin

Benjamin Franklin first published Poor Richard's Almanack *at the age of 26. In it, a fictional character named Poor Richard gave advice to people on everyday living. Here is a sample.*

1
Three may keep a Secret,
if two of them are dead.

2
Early to bed and early to rise,
makes a man healthy, wealthy and wise.

3
He that scatters thorns,
let him not go barefoot.

4
Take this remark from *Richard*
poor and lame,
Whate'er's begun in anger ends in shame.

5
The worst wheel of the cart
makes the most noise.

6
He that falls in love with himself
will have no Rivals.

7
An open Foe may prove a curse;
But a pretended friend is worse.

8
Dost thou love Life?
then do not squander Time;
for that's the Stuff Life is made of.

A Vegetable Diet

by Benjamin Franklin

Franklin wrote the story of his own life in his Autobiography of Benjamin Franklin. *The autobiography was written in bits and pieces throughout his lifetime. It was later collected and put into a single volume. "A Vegetable Diet" was adapted from Franklin's autobiography. In it, he explains his practical approach to living. As you read the selection, compare Franklin's approach to life with that of Jonathan Edwards.*

When about 16 years of age, I happened to meet with a book, written by one Tryon, recommending a vegetable diet. I determined to go into it. My brother, being yet unmarried, did not keep house, but boarded himself and his apprentices in another family. My refusing to eat flesh was an inconvenience, and I was frequently chided for it.

I made myself acquainted with Tryon's ways of preparing some of his dishes, such as boiling potatoes or rice, making hasty pudding, and a few others. Then I proposed to my brother, that if he would give me, weekly, half the money he paid for my board, I would board myself. He instantly agreed to it, and I presently found out that I could save half what he paid me.

This was an additional fund for buying books. But I had another advantage in it. Since my brother and the rest went from the printing house to their meals, I remained there alone.

After eating my light meal, which often was no more than a biscuit or a slice of bread, a handful of raisins or a tart from the pastry-cook's, and a glass of water, I had the rest of the time till their return for study. I made great progress in my study since my mind was clear from my moderation in eating and drinking.

In my first voyage from Boston, being becalmed off Block Island, our people set about catching cod, and hauled up a great many. Until then, I had stuck to my resolution of not eating animal food, and on this occasion I considered the taking of every fish as a kind of unprovoked murder, since none of them had, or ever could, do us any injury that might justify the slaughter. All of this seemed very reasonable.

But I had formerly been a great lover of fish, and, when this came hot out of the frying pan, it smelled admirably well. I balanced some time between principle and inclination, till I remembered that, when the fish were opened, I saw smaller fish taken out of their stomachs. Then, thought I, "If you eat one another, I don't see why we may not eat you." So I dined upon cod very heartily, and continued to eat with other people, returning only now and then occasionally to a vegetable diet. So convenient a thing is it to be a *reasonable creature*, since it enables one to find or make a reason for everything one has a mind to do.

READING COMPREHENSION

Select the best choice to complete each statement. Then write the entire sentence on your paper.

1. Because Franklin did not eat meat, he often _____.
   a. had to go hungry
   b. got sick to his stomach
   c. was scolded by his friends

2. When Franklin smelled the fish frying, he _____.
   a. was afraid that he would faint
   b. became angry at the fishermen
   c. remembered how much he liked to eat fish

3. Franklin wrote that people are reasonable creatures because they _____.
   a. eat meat when they can get it
   b. find or make a reason for anything they want to do
   c. usually have enough education

For Discussion

1. What do the sayings from *Poor Richard's Almanack* suggest about what Benjamin Franklin might have been like as a person?

2. What did Ben Franklin think about a person's ability to keep a secret? Do you agree with him? Explain.

3. It's possible to be a vegetarian and to have a sound diet, but Franklin's approach to eating was not one to promote good health. How might he have improved his diet and still managed to save money and time?

UNDERSTANDING LITERATURE

Autobiographical Point of View. An autobiography is a person's life story, told in his or her own words. It is written in the first person (*I, me, my*).

An autobiography is seldom very *objective* — giving only the facts. Personal opinions, like Franklin's below, make autobiographies much more *subjective* — giving his impressions of things.

Write the answers to the following questions on your paper.

1. Franklin called his refusing to eat meat an "inconvenience." His choice of words tells you _____.
   a. why he didn't like to eat meat
   b. that those who fed him were angry
   c. he preferred his own way to conforming to the ways of others

2. "... my mind was clear from my moderation in eating and drinking." Franklin's words show that he _____.
   a. believed his way to be correct
   b. had studied the science of nutrition
   c. had great native intelligence

3. "I considered the taking of every fish as a kind of unprovoked murder." These words express _____.
   a. commonly accepted fact
   b. Franklin's personal views
   c. complete untruth

Writing

Do you use any special rules to guide you in your life? Write three of them as if they were sayings by Franklin.

Two voices of the Revolution

By 1775 Americans felt a great deal of pride in their ability to run their own affairs. The idea emerged that the colonies could band together to free themselves of English rule. They did not wish to be ruled by any king; they believed that people should rule themselves. American authors of the Revolution spread these ideas by creating literature that appealed to the emotions of their readers. On the following pages you will read examples of work by two of the most persuasive writers of this period: Abigail Adams and Thomas Paine.

The Surrender of General Burgoyne at Saratoga, John Trumbull, 1822

Letter to Her Husband, John

by Abigail Adams

Abigail Adams (1744–1818) was the wife of John Adams, who became the second President of the United States. While her husband was away during the American Revolution, she managed his business affairs. She was also an able writer who sent her husband many letters during his absence. Her letters have been collected and published because they deal with important issues of the times. This selection is taken from one of her letters to John Adams. In it, she discusses some of the issues that were important to her.

If a new form of government is to be established here, which one will it be? Will it be left to our assemblies to choose one? Will there not be many differing opinions as to which government should be chosen? And shall we not run into arguments among ourselves?

I am more and more convinced that man is a dangerous creature; and that power, whether vested in many or a few, is ever grasping, and, like the grave, cries, "Give, give. . . ."

If we separate from Britain, what code of laws will be established? How shall we be governed so as to keep our liberties? Can any government be free which is not governed by general, stated laws? Who shall make these laws? . . . Give them force and energy? It is true your resolutions, as a body, have until now had the force of laws; but will they continue to have?

When I consider these things, and the prejudices of people in favor of ancient customs and laws, I feel anxious for the fate of our monarchy or democracy, or whatever is to take place. . . .

By the way, in the new code of laws which I suppose it will be necessary for you to make, I desire you would remember the ladies, and be more generous and favorable to them than your ancestors. Do not put such unlimited power into the hands of the husbands. Remember, all men would be tyrants if they could.

Abigail Adams, Benjamin Blythe, 1766

The American Crisis
Number 1

by Thomas Paine

What kept the American soldiers fighting when they needed food, wore rags, and lost battles? One way they kept up their courage was by reading Thomas Paine's series of articles called The American Crisis.

Thomas Paine (1737–1809) was an Englishman who had come to the colonies only one year before the Declaration of Independence was written. Soon after arriving, he wrote a pamphlet called Common Sense, *which urged Americans to rise up and throw out the British. In 1776, Paine joined the American army. Sitting by his tent, he wrote the following passage. Later, George Washington ordered that it be read to the American army. As you read it, ask yourself which words and phrases most inspired the American soldiers.*

These are the times that try men's souls. The summer soldier and the sunshine patriot will, in this crisis, shrink from the service of his country; but he that stands it now deserves the love and thanks of man and woman.

Tyranny, like hell, is not easily conquered; yet we have this consolation with us — that the harder the conflict, the more glorious the triumph. What we obtain too cheap, we esteem too lightly: It is dearness only that gives everything its value. Heaven knows how to put a proper price upon its goods; and it would be strange indeed if so celestial an article as freedom should not be highly rated.

Britain, with an army to enforce her tyranny, has declared that she has a right not only to tax but "to bind us in all cases whatsoever," and if being bound in that manner is not slavery, then is there not such a thing as slavery upon earth. . . .

READING COMPREHENSION

Select the best choice to complete each statement. Write the entire sentence on your paper.

1. Abigail Adams believed that power
   _____.
   a. is necessary for happiness
   b. should not be shared
   c. grasps and makes demands

2. Abigail asked her husband to _____.
   a. make laws that share power with women
   b. keep power from all tyrants
   c. make as few laws as possible

3. "These are the times that try men's souls." Thomas Paine meant that _____.
   a. people needed to pray more now
   b. the situation was very difficult
   c. physical comfort was not enough

4. Part of Paine's message is that _____.
   a. the higher the cost, the greater the victory
   b. war should be avoided
   c. taxation is worse than slavery

For Discussion

1. Why do you think so many of Abigail Adams's sentences are in question form? What problems did she feel were involved in setting up a new government?

2. To whom was Thomas Paine referring when he said, ". . . summer soldier and the sunshine patriot"? What did he mean by this?

UNDERSTANDING LITERATURE

Point of View in Persuasive Writing. Abigail Adams's letter to her husband and the excerpt from the pamphlet by Thomas Paine are examples of persuasive personal writing. Both use the first-person point of view and are designed to convince the reader to agree with the ideas stated.

In persuasive writing, the writer expresses an opinion that he or she hopes to make the reader believe, and then provides details to support that opinion.

Write the answers to the following questions on your paper.

1. Abigail Adams wanted her husband to agree that _____.
   a. all men would be tyrants
   b. man is a dangerous creature
   c. laws should be fairer to women

2. Thomas Paine wrote, ". . . the harder the conflict, the more glorious the triumph." Identify which of the following support this statement.
   a. Things obtained too easily have less value.
   b. Summer soldiers will shrink from service.
   c. Britain declared the right to tax.

Writing

Pick a controversial issue of today. Write a persuasive paragraph to convince others of your views. Here are some possible topics: driving age, unemployment, saving the environment.

Two voices of the new nation

After the United States won the Revolutionary War, Americans felt full of pride and strength. In 1812 they again faced England in war — and again they won. Now Americans and Europeans began to believe that there was nothing that Americans could not do. During the early 1800's, many took on the challenge of exploring and settling new territory.

Jean de Crèvecoeur and Davy Crockett were two very different Americans, but both created literature that helped Americans feel proud of themselves and their nation.

He That Tilleth His Land Shall Be Satisfied, Unknown Artist, c. 1850

What Is an American?

by Jean de Crèvecoeur

Jean de Crèvecoeur (1731–1813) left his native France at the age of 19 to go to Canada and fight in the French and Indian War. After the war, which France lost in 1763, he became a farmer in New York. Because there was so much land available, poor farmers from Europe did well in the colonies.

The selection here is taken from Crèvecoeur's Letters From an American Farmer. *In it, he predicts that America will become a "melting pot" — a place where many nationalities will blend together into one new nationality: the American.*

What then is the American, this new man? He is either a European, or the descendant of a European. I could point out to you a family whose grandfather was English, whose wife was Dutch, whose son married a French woman, and whose present four sons now have four wives from different nations.

He is an American, who left behind him all his ancient prejudices and manners. Here individuals of all nations are melted into a new race of men, whose labors and heritage will one day cause great changes in the world. Americans are the western pilgrims, who are carrying along with them that great mass of arts, sciences, vigor, and industry.

The Americans were once scattered all over Europe. Here they are part of one of the finest systems which has ever appeared.

The American ought therefore to love this country much better than that where either he or his forefathers were born. Here his industry will be quickly rewarded. Children, who before demanded of him a morsel of bread, are now fat and frolicsome. They gladly help their father to clear those fields where crops will rise. No cruel prince, rich abbot, or mighty lord will claim part of their riches.

The American is a new man, who acts upon new principles. He must therefore entertain new ideas and form new opinions. From idleness, dependence, poverty, and useless labor, he has passed to toils for which he will be amply rewarded. This is an American.

The Day the Sun Froze

by David Crockett

*David (Davy) Crockett (1786–1836) was an American fron-
tiersman who became a folk hero and political figure; he
served three terms in Congress. Certainly the tall tales that
were written about him in* Davy Crockett's Almanac *contributed greatly to his popularity. Many people believed that
Crockett himself wrote these stories. Some even believed the
stories were true. Yet, the tales contain fantastic events, and
many new issues actually appeared after Crockett's death.
But the stories do tell of someone resourceful enough to meet
any challenge, however unusual. And Americans of that time
liked to think of themselves in that way.*

I'm that same David Crockett that is fresh from the backwoods. I'm half horse, half alligator — and part snapping turtle, too. I can wade the Mississippi River and leap over the Ohio River. I can ride upon a streak of lightning. Thorns wouldn't dare to scratch me. I can whip my weight in wild cats — and if anyone pleases — I'll wrestle a panther, or hug a bear too close for comfort. Here is what I did on the day the sun froze.

One January morning, it was so cold the trees were too stiff to shake. The very daybreak froze solid just as it was trying to dawn. The tinder-box I used to light my fire wouldn't spark. It would no more catch fire than a raft sunk to the bottom of the sea.

Well, I decided the only way I was going to get some fire was to make it myself. I brought my knuckles together like two thunderclouds, but the sparks froze before I could collect them. So out I walked whistling "Fire in the Mountains!" as I went along in double quick time. Well, after I had walked about 20 miles I came to Daybreak Hill and discovered what was the matter.

The earth had actually frozen fast on her axis. She couldn't turn round. The sun

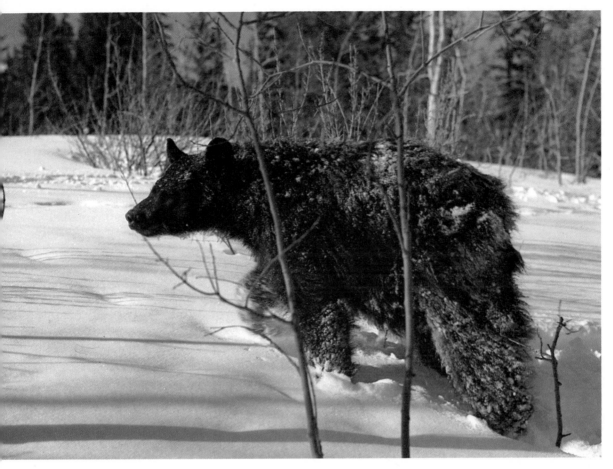

had gotten jammed between cakes of ice under the wheels. The sun had been shining and working to get loose until he froze in his cold sweat.

"C-r-e-a-t-i-o-n!" thought I. "This is the toughest form of suspension. It mustn't be endured. Something must be done or human creation is done for!"

It was so cold that my teeth and tongue were all collapsed together as tight as an oyster. But I took a fresh bear from my back. (I had picked it up along the road.) I beat the animal against the ice until the hot oil began to pour out of it on all sides. I then held the bear over the earth's axis.

I squeezed the hot bear oil out until I'd thawed the earth loose. Then, I poured about a ton of the hot bear oil over the sun's face.

I gave the earth's cogwheel one kick backward until I got the sun loose. I whistled, "Push along; keep moving!" In about 15 seconds the earth gave a grunt and began to move.

The sun walked back up into the sky. It saluted me with such gratitude that it made me sneeze. Then I shouldered my bear and saluted back. As I walked home, I introduced people to the fresh daylight with a piece of sunrise in my pocket.

READING COMPREHENSION

Select the best choice to complete each statement. Then write the entire sentence on your paper.

1. According to Crèvecoeur, an American is a European who _____.
   a. has brought culture but left prejudice behind
   b. believes in Davy Crockett's spirit
   c. intends to make a fortune and return to Europe

2. Crèvecoeur suggested that hard work in America _____.
   a. would lead to poverty
   b. was easier than in Europe
   c. would be rewarded

3. According to Davy Crockett, one day it was extremely cold because _____.
   a. the sun froze and the earth couldn't turn
   b. it was an especially bad January
   c. his tinder-box wouldn't spark

4. Davy Crockett said he sneezed at the end of the story because _____.
   a. the extreme cold made him ill
   b. the sun shone on him to thank him
   c. he was allergic to bear oil

For Discussion

1. What was Crèvecoeur's definition of an American? Do you think his ideas are still valid today? Do you agree with what he said? Explain your answer.

2. How did Davy Crockett describe himself? Do you believe the details? Why or why not?

UNDERSTANDING LITERATURE

Point of View. In "The Day the Sun Froze," Davy Crockett used the first-person point of view to give his account of frontier life. His story is subjective — a product of his mind, not of outside reality — and uses exaggeration to make its point. It was originally published as autobiography, not as a work of fiction. The people of Crockett's day wanted to have heroes to inspire them, and Crockett was happy to oblige.

Jean de Crèvecoeur's writing also uses the first person. "What Is an American?" is his answer to the question in the title. He did not use exaggeration in the way that Crockett did, but commented seriously on what he believed. Nevertheless, Crèvecoeur's comments are subjective. They are his opinion and interpretation.

Write the answers to the following questions on your paper.

1. List five exaggerations in Davy Crockett's description of himself that could not possibly be fact.

2. Find two sentences in "What Is an American?" that are the author's personal opinions, and not necessarily facts that can be proved.

Writing

Describe yourself in terms that would impress Davy Crockett, using the first-person point of view. Exaggerate the qualities you wish to mention and make comparisons that are unusual and hard to believe.

The Legend of Sleepy Hollow

by Washington Irving

*Stories about ghosts and magic spells have always been popu-
lar, but there was a time when few people wrote about them.
Washington Irving (1783–1859) thought that since people
liked telling ghost stories, they also might like reading them.
He was right. His stories about the supernatural made him
the first really popular American writer. The fact that many
of Irving's stories were humorous added to their popularity.*

*Irving's home, which he called Sunnyside, is on the banks of
the Hudson River. He made this area the setting for his most
famous story, "The Legend of Sleepy Hollow."*

Sleepy Hollow was one of the quietest places in the world. The only sounds were the whisper of a brook or the whistle of a bird. It was in the high hills of upper New York State. A sleepy, dreamy power seemed to hang over the land.

The people of Sleepy Hollow were the great-grandchildren of the Dutch who had come to New York in the 1600's. Stories told how the Dutch took the land from an old Indian wizard. It might have been his spell that made the people walk as if always in a dream. They saw visions and strange sights. They heard music and voices in the air. And they told tales about haunted places and shadowy beings.

The strongest spirit that moved in the valley was the ghost of the Headless Horseman. It was said that he was a German soldier who had fought for the British in the Revolutionary War. His head had been shot off by a cannonball. Ever after, he rode through the night, hunting for his lost head. Sometimes he rode through the Hollow with speed like the wind, for he had to be back in his grave in the churchyard before the sun came up.

Ichabod Crane was the schoolmaster of Sleepy Hollow. He was not Dutch, like those he taught. He had come from New England. A crane is a tall bird with thin

legs, and Ichabod's name fitted him. He, too, was tall and very thin. He had long arms and legs. His hands hung a mile out of his sleeves.

His feet looked as big as shovels. His head was small, and flat on top. He had huge ears and large, green, glassy eyes. His nose was long and narrow. His clothes were baggy.

Ichabod earned extra money by teaching singing. He was thought to know more than most of the men around, and to be more of a gentleman. So the young women paid him a lot of attention.

He had read a lot about witches. He believed in their power. After school, he had to walk through the woods to reach the farmhouse where he boarded. It often seemed to him that the forest was full of evil spirits. To drive them away, he sang. He sang through his nose. Even so, the people of Sleepy Hollow liked to listen to his voice drifting on the wind.

On long winter evenings, old Dutch couples liked to sit by the open fire. The schoolmaster was often invited to spend the evening. They roasted apples and told ghost stories. Ichabod loved to listen to them, and to tell stories of his own. Best of all, he liked the talk about the Headless Horseman.

But then he had to walk home. Awful shapes and shadows filled his path in the pale light of a snowy night. A bush, covered with snow, could look like a ghost. He shook with fear at the sound of his own steps on the hard snow. And the howl of the wind in the trees was surely the Headless Horseman himself!

In the daytime, Ichabod forgot about ghosts and spirits. But he had another problem — a woman.

Among those he taught to sing was Katrina Van Tassel. She was the only child of a wealthy Dutch farmer. She was just 18, round and red-cheeked and pretty. She dressed to show off her beauty. Everyone admired her — and also the money that would one day be hers.

Ichabod Crane had a soft heart for pretty girls. And, too, he had visited her father's great house. Baltus Van Tassel was not proud of his wealth, but he liked to live well. His home looked over the river, and everything about it spoke of plenty.

Ichabod Crane looked at the rich fields and the well-filled barns. He watched the pigs and the ducks and the turkeys. He thought of how they could all be turned into cash. With that money, he could buy huge tracts of land in the wilderness. He could build a palace. He saw himself riding a fine horse with Katrina beside him.

From the moment Ichabod saw the Van Tassel farm, his peace of mind was over. He wanted only one thing. He wanted to win Katrina. It was not an easy task. Katrina was spoiled. She wanted this today, that tomorrow. She had many admirers, too. They all kept an eye on each other. They would not welcome Ichabod to their number.

One of them was a big, loud-mouthed country fellow named Brom Van Brunt. He was the hero of Sleepy Hollow. He was handsome, tough, and the strongest man around. Because of his size and strength, he was called Brom Bones. He rode a horse with great grace and skill. He won races, and was often called on to settle arguments. Brom himself was always ready for either a fight or some fun. He had a merry sense of humor.

Brom and his friends liked to dash through the valley on horses at midnight. They would shout and yell, waking the sleeping farmers. Still, everyone liked him. In cold weather he wore a fur cap with a long foxtail. When people saw it coming, they got ready for some excitement.

Brom had, for some time, been interested in the lovely Katrina. Though he seemed as big and rough as a bear, people said that Katrina held out some hope to him. When his horse was seen tied outside the Van Tassel house, other young men rode away.

But Ichabod Crane did not go away. He was the kind of person who bends, but does not break. Ichabod knew he could not openly fight Brom Bones. But, as singing teacher, he could go to the Van Tassels' often. Baltus Van Tassel and his wife let Katrina have her way in everything. So Ichabod sat with Katrina under the elm tree beside the spring. Or he took her walking in the soft evening light.

From the day Ichabod began to visit Katrina, Brom Bones fell from favor. His horse was no longer seen tied outside her house. He became Ichabod's deadly enemy.

Brom would have liked to fight the schoolmaster. But he knew Ichabod was too smart for that. So Brom had to find other ways to get back at him.

Brom and his friends began to play jokes on Ichabod. They stopped up the chimney of the school, so it filled with smoke. They broke in at night and turned everything upside down. Worst of all, Brom trained a dog and took it to singing classes. When Katrina sang, the dog howled. "It thinks it can teach her better than Ichabod," Brom said.

In school, Ichabod sat on a high stool. He held a ruler in his hand, to scare the children. One day, as he sat there, a man brought him a message. There would be a party at the Van Tassels' that night. Ichabod was invited.

He rushed the children through their lessons, and let them out early. Then he spent an hour brushing his best black suit and getting himself ready. He borrowed a horse from the old farmer he boarded with, Hans Van Ripper.

Ichabod and the horse were well matched. The horse was thin and rough-coated. His mane and tail were matted. One eye was blind, but it glowed with a wild light. The other had a gleam of evil in it.

The horse was old, but once he had been full of fire. His name was Gunpowder. He looked worn out but he still had more of the devil in him than any young horse in the Hollow.

Ichabod rode so that his knees were nearly up to the saddle. His sharp elbows stuck out like a grasshopper's. He carried his whip straight up in his hand, like his ruler. As the horse bumped along, his arms flapped like a pair of wings. A small wool hat rested on the top of his nose. The skirts of his black coat fluttered out almost to the horse's tail. Few people had ever seen such a sight in broad daylight.

It was a fine autumn day. The trees were turning orange, red, and purple. Apples hung on the trees, and pumpkins lay in the fields. Golden ears of corn were ready to pick. It made Ichabod think of pudding and pies, handed to him by Katrina Van Tassel.

Toward evening, Ichabod reached the castle of Baltus Van Tassel. Almost everyone from the Hollow and the country around it was there. The hero of the scene was Brom Bones. He had come to the party on his horse, Dare-devil. No one but Brom could ride the high-spirited animal. Brom thought that a gentle horse was not worthy of him.

In the Van Tassels' parlor, Ichabod found much to charm him. There were many lovely girls. But he saw only the heaped-up plates of cakes and pies, ham and smoked beef. There were dozens of dishes, and Ichabod tried them all.

One day, he thought as he ate, he might own all this. He would turn his back on the school. He would snap his fingers in the face of Hans Van Ripper and all the other farmers. He would kick out any teacher who dared to call him "friend"!

Music began in the hall. Ichabod was thought to be a great dancer. So he led the dancing, with Katrina. Brom Bones sat in a corner, angry and in love.

After the dancing, Ichabod sat down with the older people. The round of ghost stories began. There were tales of screams heard at the spot where a spy had been hanged. There were stories of a woman

in white who wept where she had died in the snow. But the favorite was still the Headless Horseman. He had, the old wives said, been heard several times lately. Every night, he tied up his horse among the graves in the churchyard.

Brom Bones broke in. He said that the Headless Horseman had caught up with him one night. Brom offered to race with the ghost.

Dare-devil was beating the ghost horse easily, until they came up to a little bridge. It crossed a brook in front of the church. The Headless Horseman disappeared in a flash of fire.

The party began to break up. The old farmers loaded their families into wagons. Some of the young girls rode horseback behind the young men. Laughter rang through the woods, dying away with the sound of the horses' hoofs.

Ichabod stayed behind for a talk with Katrina. He thought that he was well on the way to winning her. Something, though, had gone wrong. Ichabod walked out of the house, looking sad and hurt. He went to the stable and woke up Gunpowder. With a heavy heart, he started to ride home.

It was almost midnight. From far off, he could hear sounds. But there was no sign of life near him. All the stories about ghosts crowded into his mind. The night grew darker and darker. The stars seemed to sink into the sky. Ichabod had never felt so lonely. And just ahead was the big tree on which the spy had been hanged.

Ichabod began to whistle. As he got nearer, he thought he saw something hanging. But it was only a scar, where lightning had hit the tree. Then he heard a groan. His teeth chattered. His knees hit the saddle. It was only one tree branch rubbing against another.

Ichabod rode on. He came to a rough log bridge. It crossed a stream that was thought to be haunted. His heart began to pound. He kicked his horse in the ribs, and tried to dash across the bridge. Instead, the old horse ran across the road, into the bushes.

The schoolmaster used his whip and his heels. Old Gunpowder dashed forward. Then he came to a sudden stop. His rider nearly went over his head.

Ichabod heard a noise. In the dark shadows, he saw something. It was huge, crooked, dark, and tall. It did not move.

Ichabod's hair stood up. What was to be done? It was too late to turn and run. And what chance was there to escape a ghost?

With a show of courage, he croaked, "Who are you?" There was no answer. He said it again. Still there was no answer. He kicked Gunpowder in the sides, and began to sing. The shadow moved. Now it stood in the middle of the road.

He seemed to be a horseman of great size. He was mounted on a powerful black horse. He began to trot on the blind side of old Gunpowder.

Ichabod wanted to get away from this strange companion. He thought about Brom Bones's adventure with the Headless Horseman.

He rode faster. The stranger rode faster, too. Ichabod pulled up, and fell into a walk. The stranger did the same. Ichabod

tried to sing. His tongue stuck to the roof of his mouth.

They reached a rise in the ground. The figure of the stranger stood out against the sky. He was wrapped in a cloak. He was very tall. And he had no head. The head, which should have been on his shoulders, was resting on the front of his saddle.

Ichabod kicked Gunpowder. Away they dashed. Stones flew and sparks flashed from the horse's hoofs. Ichabod's clothes fluttered in the air. He leaned his long body over his horse's head. And the stranger rode beside him.

On they rode. Ichabod felt his saddle loosen and slip to the ground. He hung on to old Gunpowder's neck, slipping from side to side. Up ahead, he saw the walls of the church. Just before him was the brook and the bridge. This was where Brom said the Horseman had gone up in a flash of fire.

"If I can reach it," Ichabod thought, "I'm safe."

He heard the black horse close behind him. Gunpowder leaped onto the bridge. They were across! Ichabod looked back. He wanted to see the flash.

The ghost rose in the saddle. He reached down, and picked up his head. He threw it at Ichabod. Ichabod tried to jump out of the way. He was too late. The round thing hit his head. He was knocked into the dust. Gunpowder, the ghost rider, and the black horse passed by him like the wind.

Next morning, the old horse was found eating grass at his master's gate. They traced his path back to the bridge. The little brook was searched. Near it, they found Ichabod's hat, and a broken pumpkin. But the body of the schoolmaster was never found.

The mystery caused much talk. People went to look at the bridge and the place where the hat and pumpkin had been found. They decided that Ichabod must have been carried off by the Headless Horseman.

Several years later, an old farmer went to New York City. He came back saying that he had heard that Ichabod Crane was still alive. Afraid of the ghost, and unhappy over losing Katrina, he had gone away. In another part of the country, he had studied law. Now he was a judge.

Brom Bones always had a knowing look when anyone spoke of Ichabod. He would burst into a laugh when people wondered about the pumpkin. He married Katrina very soon after Ichabod had gone.

Old country people, however, believe to this day that Ichabod was taken away by a ghost. They still say that his voice can sometimes be heard singing in the silence of Sleepy Hollow.

READING COMPREHENSION

Select the best choice to complete each statement. Then write the entire sentence on your paper.

1. The story suggests that the people of Sleepy Hollow were dreamy because _____.
   a. they had nothing much to do
   b. an Indian wizard had cast a spell
   c. they were hard-working

2. Ichabod often got to spend time with Katrina because _____.
   a. he helped her with her spelling
   b. she took singing lessons from him
   c. he was very good-looking

3. Ichabod left the Van Tassels' party very sadly because _____.
   a. he thought parties shouldn't end
   b. he had argued with Katrina
   c. Brom Bones had threatened him

4. After the party, Ichabod met what he thought was the Headless Horseman, and he _____.
   a. disappeared
   b. died of fright
   c. threw a pumpkin at the rider

For Discussion

1. What did Ichabod Crane look like? What exaggerations can you find in the author's description of Ichabod?

2. What do you think *really* happened to Ichabod on his way home from the Van Tassels' party? What was the explanation many of the townspeople believed?

UNDERSTANDING LITERATURE

Point of View. "The Legend of Sleepy Hollow," like many other legends, is told from the third-person point of view. This "all-knowing" point of view allows the storyteller to include everything he or she wants the reader or listener to know, and to be as objective as possible.

Here are some statements from "The Legend of Sleepy Hollow." On your paper, identify those that would not have been included if Ichabod himself had been telling the story. Then rewrite the rest from Ichabod's point of view.

1. "His feet looked as big as shovels. His head was small, and flat on top."

2. "He was thought to know more than most of the men around, and to be more of a gentleman."

3. "She was just 18, round and red-cheeked and pretty. She dressed to show off her beauty."

4. "From the moment Ichabod saw the Van Tassel farm, his peace of mind was over."

5. "Brom . . . liked to dash through the valley on horses at midnight."

6. "Next morning, the old horse was found eating grass at his master's gate."

Writing

Imagine that you are Ichabod Crane. Write a paragraph using the first-person point of view to tell about your disappearance.

Section Review

VOCABULARY

Context Clues. Sometimes you can tell the meaning of a word you're not sure of by the meaning of the rest of the sentence or paragraph. This is called using *context clues.* For example, suppose you read:

> It's best to use temperance when you eat or drink, because too much food or wine could harm you.

If you don't know what *temperance* means, you can probably figure it out. It means "self-control," or "moderation."

Read the passages below from this section. Select the best meaning for each italicized word. On your paper, rewrite the sentence using the meaning you have chosen.

1. "In those days, all the tribes spoke one language and lived in *harmony* and peace."

   agreement   danger   villages

2. "Dost thou love Life? then do not *squander* Time; for that's the Stuff Life is made of."

   discuss   waste   enjoy

3. "... To act as if I had ... the same *infirmities* or failings as others."

   happiness   pleasures   weaknesses

4. "It might have been his *spell* that made the people walk as if in a dream."

   jokes   magic   story

READING

Author's Purpose. When you read, it's often useful to try to figure out the *author's purpose.* It may help you to understand a selection better if you think about why the author wrote it.

As you read, you have to think about what the author is trying to tell you. Does it make sense? Should you believe it? Do you agree with what it says? Evaluating what you read in this way is called *critical reading.*

Select the best choice to complete each statement. Write your answers on your paper.

1. The legend of Godasiyo and "The Legend of Sleepy Hollow" both contain _____.
   a. a dog as a minor character
   b. proof for the important facts
   c. explanations that may not be true

2. Ben Franklin and Jonathan Edwards both thought _____.
   a. their beliefs were valuable
   b. people should enjoy their food
   c. sinners should be hung

3. The writings of Abigail Adams, Thomas Paine, and Jean de Crèvecoeur are similar because they _____.
   a. deal with women in politics
   b. attempt to persuade the reader
   c. criticize the British

4. Davy Crockett's autobiography is _____.
   a. his true life story
   b. accurate about life in the woods
   c. really a work of fiction

WRITING A PERSUASIVE LETTER

In Section 1, you practiced writing your opinion and supporting it with reasons. Suppose that simply expressing your opinion on a particular issue is not enough. Suppose it's important that you convince others to share your views and perhaps act on their opinion. What could you do? You could write a persuasive letter.

How does persuasion differ from the expression of opinion? In writing persuasively, it's not enough to express your own opinion, although you will do so as strongly as you can. You must take into account the people you are trying to persuade. This will help you choose the right *tone* for your letter. (The tone in writing is the author's attitude and manner toward the reader.) You must choose your words carefully to tell your intended audience just why you feel your opinion is correct.

Think for a moment about Abigail Adams's letter to her husband, which you read in this section. The writer told of her concerns about the new government that was being established. She expressed her opinion that "... man is a dangerous creature; and that power, whether vested in many or a few, is ever grasping."

Adams did more than simply express her opinion in her letter. Her words were designed to persuade her husband and, she hoped, his associates to follow a certain plan of action. Go back to p. 80, and read the last paragraph of her letter to see how she did this.

Now it's your turn to write a persuasive letter. Before you begin, here is a checklist to keep in mind.

☐ Identify the issue you are writing about and clearly state your opinion about it.

☐ Give reasons to support your opinion.

☐ Think about why you believe the person reading your letter should agree with you. Tell that person directly what you think he or she should do.

Choose either 1 or 2 below and write a persuasive letter on your paper.

1. As you read the material in this section, you had a chance to learn something about several early Americans. Pretend that Abigail Adams, Thomas Paine, and Benjamin Franklin are all living today and are running for mayor of your town or city. Choose the one you would vote for. Then write a persuasive letter to your classmates telling them why you think they should vote the same way that you would.

2. The village in which Godasiyo was chief grew so large that half the people lived on one side of the river and the other half lived on the other side. This led to difficulties. Decide whether you would have followed Godasiyo as your chief or whether you would have been part of a group to form your own government by the river. (Don't let the way the story ended influence your choice.) Write a persuasive letter to your friends telling them your plans and telling them what you think they should do.

QUIZ

The following is a quiz for Section 2. Write the answers in complete sentences on your paper.

Reading Comprehension

1. For what reason did Godasiyo build the bridge over the river in "Godasiyo, the Woman Chief"? Why was the bridge destroyed?

2. What was Edwards' advice in "Resolutions" about eating and drinking? How was this similar to what Franklin might have said?

3. In "A Vegetable Diet," what led Franklin to become a vegetarian? What event made him stop?

4. What was the main point Abigail Adams was making in her "Letter to Her Husband, John"?

5. In "The Legend of Sleepy Hollow," what traces of Ichabod's presence were found the morning after the Van Tassels' party? What did people say had happened to him?

Understanding Literature

6. What is a legend? From what point of view is a legend written?

7. From what point of view are Edwards' "Resolutions" written? Is this the same or different from Franklin's "Sayings"? Give one example of each.

8. From whose point of view is an autobiography written? Is an autobiography always completely objective? Give one example from Ben Franklin's work to support your answer.

9. In what way are Abigail Adams' letter and Thomas Paine's pamphlet "The American Crisis" alike?

10. What kind of work was Davy Crockett's "The Day the Sun Froze" first published as? What do you think it really is? Give an example from the story to support your answer.

COMPOSITION

1. Think about what is necessary in order to do well in the world you now live in. Write your own set of resolutions. Use the first-person point of view, and write them in modern language.

2. Choose an issue that interests you. Write a letter to your senator or to the President telling how you feel about it. Try to persuade the reader of your letter to adopt your views.

3. Rewrite Davy Crockett's story using items that could be facts and avoiding exaggeration. Which version do you prefer?

000011

SECTION 3
Early America Imagined

HISTORICAL FICTION

Isn't it strange some people make
*   you feel so tired inside,*
Your thoughts begin to shrivel up
*   Like leaves all brown and dried!*

But when you're with some other ones,
*   It's stranger still to find*
Your thoughts are thick as fireflies
*   All shiny in your mind!*

— Rachel Field

Introduction

When some people read history, their imaginations come alive. They feel the joys and sorrows of the past. When other people read history, they find it difficult to go beyond a list of facts: dates, places, and famous names.

Authors of *historical fiction* use their imaginations to create stories that make history come alive for everyone. Famous places, events, and dates take on new meaning when you consider the people who really lived during those times. They were people with feelings, fears, dreams, and personalities.

Fact and Fiction in Plot

Historical fiction combines facts about history with made-up details. Authors use their imaginations and their understanding of how people live today to create explanations of how and why certain events in history may have happened. Thus the plot — the chain of events in the story — usually blends fiction and facts from history.

It is a fact that 17th-century people believed in witches. The first story in this section, "Salem Village, Massachusetts," tells us something about how and why the famous Salem witch trials happened. Twentieth-century writer Stephen Vincent Benét probably read reports of the trials by people who were there, as well as many history books about that time and place, before he wrote his story. But he used his own judgment and ideas to explain the details of the story — why the characters did what they did. You will also read Benét's poem about Cotton Mather, which shows how he felt about Mather's part in the trials.

Fictional Characters and Real Feelings

The second story in this section was written in the 1960's, but it describes April 19, 1775, in Lexington, Massachusetts. The modern author, Howard Fast, made up a fictional person, Adam Cooper. In this exciting, realistic story, you will feel, through Adam, the terror and excitement of that day as the people of Lexington probably experienced it over 200 years ago.

Real Characters and Fictional Details

The third story in this section also takes place during the Revolutionary War. The people in this story are real. The author, Jane Yolen, used historical sources to gather facts about the story. These facts told her about the setting — where and when the story took place. The facts also gave her the names of her main characters and some idea of the events in the plot.

Midnight Ride of Paul Revere, Grant Wood, 1931

Yolen then used her imagination to make up details and dialogue to bring to life the story of Fanny Campbell — a young woman who staged a daring rescue and became a hero in the Revolutionary War.

Historical fiction is fun to read because it provides a sense of visiting another time and place. Often historical fiction includes memorable events and characters. However, authors of historical fiction write about the concerns of their own time and place as well as about the past. The authors of historical fiction give us guidelines for our own lives. They seem to say, "Look at the mistakes that fear, pride, foolishness, or greed have led to in the past. Let's not make these mistakes again. Look at the people in our past who valued freedom and loyalty, acted with courage, learned new skills. They accomplished much. Let's use these abilities to improve the quality of life in our own era."

Salem Village, Massachusetts

by Stephen Vincent Benét

Stephen Vincent Benét (1898–1945) is famous for his stories and poems about our nation's past. In the story that follows, he vividly describes what took place in Salem Village, Massachusetts, in 1692.

In the 17th century, people had no doubt that witches were real. Thousands of people in Europe were accused of witchcraft and were burned at the stake, hanged, or tortured. Thirty people were found guilty of witchcraft in Salem Village in 1692. Nineteen were hanged. The panic ended almost as soon as it had begun. All Salem admitted to making a tragic error. It was the end of witchcraft trials in America.

Salem Village had a new minister — the Reverend Samuel Parris. He brought with him to Salem Village two West Indian servants — a man known as John Indian and a woman named Tituba. And when he had bought those two or their services in the West Indies, he was buying a rope that was to hang 19 people of New England.

Perhaps the nine-year-old Elizabeth Parris, the minister's daughter, boasted to her new friends of the odd stories Tituba told and the strange things she could do. Perhaps Tituba herself let the report of her magic powers be spread about the village.

During the winter of 1691–92 a group of girls and women began to meet nightly at the parsonage, with Tituba and her fortune-telling as the chief attraction. The winters were long and white — and any diversion was welcome. Elizabeth Parris, at nine, was the youngest. Then came Abigail Williams, 11, and Ann Putnam, 12. The rest were older — Mercy Lewis, Mary Wolcott, and Elizabeth Hubbard were 17; Elizabeth Booth and Susan Sheldon, 18; and Mary Warren and Sarah Churchill, 20. Three were servants — Mercy Lewis, Mary Warren, and Sarah Churchill.

The elder women included a pair of gossipy, superstitious busybodies — Mrs. Pope and Mrs. Bibber; and young Ann Putnam's mother, Ann Putnam, Sr.

The circle met no doubt with the usual giggling, whispering, and gossip. From mere fortune-telling it proceeded to other and more serious matters — table rapping,

perhaps, and a little West Indian voodoo. Weird stories were told by Tituba and weird things were shown, while the wind blew outside and the big shadows flickered on the wall.

Soon the members of the circle began to show hysterical symptoms. They crawled under tables and chairs. They made strange sounds. They shook and trembled with nightmare fears. Something strange and out of nature was happening — who had ever seen normal young girls behave like these young girls?

Serious ministers were called in to look at the afflicted children. A Dr. Gregg gave his opinion. It was almost too terrible to believe, and yet what else could be believed? *Witchcraft!*

Meanwhile, one may suppose, the "afflicted children," like most hysterical subjects, enjoyed the stares, the horrified looks, the respectful questions that greeted them. They had been unimportant girls of a little town; now they were the center of attention. There was only one catch about it. If they were really bewitched, somebody must be doing the bewitching.

On the 29th of February, 1692, in the midst of a storm of thunder and lightning, three women — Sarah Good, Sarah Osburn, and Tituba — were arrested on the deadly charge of bewitching the children.

The next day, March 1, two judges, Justice Hawthorne and Justice Corwin, arrived. The first hearing was held in the crowded meetinghouse of the village, and all Salem swarmed to it.

The children had picked their first victims well. Sarah Good and Sarah Osburn were old women of no particular standing in the community.

The Justices must have arrived with their minds made up. For the first question addressed to Sarah Good was, bluntly: "What evil spirit have you familiarity with?"

"None," said the piping old voice.

"Have you made no contracts with the devil?" proceeded the Justice.

"No."

The Justice went to the root of the matter at once.

"Why do you hurt these children?"

"I do not hurt them. I scorn it," said Sarah Good defiantly. But the Justice had her now. He was not to be brushed aside.

"Who, then, do you employ to do it?"

"I employ nobody."

The Justice returned to the main charge, like any prosecuting attorney.

"Have you made no contract with the devil?"

"No."

It was time for Exhibit A. The Justice turned to the children. Was Sarah Good one of the persons who tormented them? And then, before the amazed eyes of all, they began to be tormented. They twisted; they grew stiff; they were stricken moaning or speechless.

"Sarah Good, do you see now what you have done? Why do you not tell us the truth? Why do you torment these poor children?"

And with these words Sarah Good was already hanged. For all that she could say was, "I do not torment them." And yet everyone had seen her, with their own eyes.

Sarah Osburn's examination followed the same course — the same questions, the same useless denial, the same fits of the afflicted children, the same end.

Then Tituba was examined and gave them their fill of strange stories and horrors.

The West Indian woman, a slave in a strange land, was fighting for her life. She admitted, repentantly, that she had tormented the children. But she had been forced to do so. By whom? By Goody Good and Goody Osburn.* Everyone could see that she spoke the truth. For, when she was first brought in, the children were tormented at her presence. But as soon as she had confessed and turned king's evidence, she was tormented herself. To jail with her — but she had saved her neck.

The hearing was over. The men and women of Salem went back to their homes to discuss the fearful workings of God's will. Here and there a common-sense voice murmured a doubt or two — to convict two old women of a terrible crime on the word of young girls and a West Indian slave!

But, on the whole, the villagers of Salem felt relieved. The cause of the problem had been found. It would be stamped out and the afflicted children would recover. The children slept after a tiring day — they were not used to such performances.

As for the accused women, they went to Boston Jail — to be chained there while awaiting the gallows.

Meanwhile, on an outlying farm, Giles Corey, 81 years of age, began to argue

the case with his wife, Martha. He believed in the afflicted children. She did not, and said so — even going so far as to say that the judges were blinded. It was one of those marital arguments that occur between strong-willed people. And it was to bring Martha Corey to the gallows and Giles Corey to an even stranger doom.

As for what went on in the minds of the afflicted children, we cannot say. But this much is sure. They had seen and felt their power. The hearing had been the greatest and most exciting event of their

---

* "Goody" was a polite title used to refer to a married woman.

narrow lives. And it was so easy to do. You twisted your body and groaned — and grown people were afraid.

On March 19, Martha Corey and Rebecca Nurse were arrested on the charge of witchcraft. On March 21, they were examined and committed. And with that the real reign of terror began.

Salem Village, as a community, was no longer sane.

Let us get it over quickly. The Salem witches stopped being Salem's business. They became a matter affecting the whole colony. Sir William Phips, the new governor, appointed a special court to try the cases. And the hangings began.

Through the summer the accusations, the arrests, the trials, came thick and fast till the jails were crowded. Nor were those now accused friendless old women like Sarah Good. They included Captain John Alden, who saved himself by breaking jail, and the wealthy and prominent Englishes, who saved themselves by running away.

The most disgraceful scenes occurred at the trial of the saintly Rebecca Nurse.

Thirty-nine citizens of Salem were brave enough to sign a petition for her, and the jury brought in a verdict of "not guilty." The mob in the sweating courtroom immediately began to cry out, and the judge told the jury to reverse their verdict. They did so, to the mob's delight. Rebecca Nurse was hanged on Gallows Hill on July 19 with Sarah Good, Sarah Wilds, Elizabeth How, and Susanna Martin.

Susanna Martin's only witchcraft seems to have been that she was an unusually tidy woman and had once walked a muddy road without getting her dress dirty. As for Elizabeth How, the children cried, "I am stuck with a pin. I am pinched," when they saw her — and she was hanged.

One hanging on June 19, five on July 19, five on August 18, eight on September 22, including Mary Easty and Martha Corey. But for stubborn Giles Corey a different fate was waiting.

The old man had begun by believing in the whole hocus-pocus. He had quarreled with his wife about it. He had seen her arrested as a witch, insulted by the judges, and condemned to die. Now he himself was in danger.

Well, he could die as his wife would. But there was the property — his goods, his prosperous farm. By law, the goods and property of those convicted of witchcraft were taken by the state. Giles Corey drew up a will leaving that property to the two sons-in-law who had not joined in the madness. And then at the trial, he said, "I will not plead. I am condemned already in courts where ghosts appear as witnesses and swear men's lives away."

Those who refused to plead either guilty or not guilty were given an old English punishment. It was heaping weights or stones upon the unhappy victim till he pleaded guilty or not guilty — or until his chest was crushed. And exactly that happened to old Giles Corey. They heaped the stones upon him until they killed him — and two days before his wife hanged, he died. But his property went to the loyal sons-in-law. So died Giles Corey.

And then, suddenly and strangely as the madness had come, it was gone.

The afflicted children, at long last, had gone too far. They had accused the governor's lady, and they had accused Mrs. Hall, a minister's wife who was known in the colony for her goodness. There comes a point when men and women revolt against blood and horror. If it went on, no one but the afflicted children and their friends would be left alive.

In 1706 Ann Putnam made a public confession that she had been tricked by the devil in testifying as she had. She had testified in every case but one.

We have no reason to hold Salem up to judgment. It was a town, like any other — and a strange madness took hold of it. But it is no stranger a thing to hang people for witchcraft than to hang them for the shape of their nose or the color of their skin. Persecution follows superstition and intolerance, as fire follows the fuse. And once we light that fire, we cannot foresee where it will end any more than they could in Salem Village almost 300 years ago.

READING COMPREHENSION

Select the best choice to complete each statement. Then write the entire sentence on your paper.

1. At first, Tituba's stories and fortune-telling were viewed as _____.
   a. matters of life and death
   b. harmless entertainment
   c. cures for sick children

2. The doctor said that the "afflicted children" were _____.
   a. naughty troublemakers
   b. suffering from a rare disease
   c. victims of witchcraft

3. Tituba was sent to prison instead of being hanged because she _____.
   a. continued to claim her innocence
   b. confessed and implicated others
   c. told everyone she loved children

4. The afflicted childen went too far when they _____.
   a. accused two respected women
   b. refused to speak to the doctor
   c. applauded at the public hangings

For Discussion

1. The author stated that the afflicted children had seen and felt their power. How does this help explain what happened in Salem?

2. In the last paragraph of the story, the author called what happened in Salem a "strange madness." To what did he compare it? What is the warning contained in his words?

UNDERSTANDING LITERATURE

Historical Fiction. "Salem Village, Massachusetts" is historical fiction. The author has woven together material from his imagination with real characters, settings, and events from history.

Sometimes the characters and incidents in a work of historical fiction are real. Sometimes they are invented to suit the purposes of the author. Because a work of historical fiction is set before the lifetime of the person who is writing it, its dialogue — conversation of the characters — is usually created by the author. Often the author makes inferences about what the characters are thinking or feeling. These inferences are usually based on historical fact, but they can't always be proved.

On your paper, label each of the following statements that can be found in history books as *fact*. Label the items created by the author to help tell the story as *fiction*.

1. "Salem Village had a new minister."

2. "The circle met no doubt with the usual giggling, whispering, and gossip."

3. "In 1706 Ann Putnam made a public confession. . . ."

4. "As for Elizabeth How, the children cried, 'I am stuck with a pin. I am pinched'. . . ."

Writing

Think about the part Ann Putnam played in the Salem witchcraft trials. Write her confession.

Cotton Mather
1663–1728

by Stephen Vincent Benét

Grim Cotton Mather
Was always seeing witches,
Daylight, moonlight,
They buzzed about his head,
Pinching him and plaguing him
With aches and pains and stitches,
Witches in his pulpit,
Witches by his bed.

Nowadays, nowadays,
We'd say that he was crazy,
But everyone believed him
In old Salem town
And nineteen people
Were hanged for Salem witches
Because of Cotton Mather
And his long, black gown.

Old Cotton Mather
Didn't die happy.
He could preach and thunder,
He could fast and pray,
But men began to wonder
If there had been witches —
When he walked in the streets
Men looked the other way.

What sort of a person was Cotton Mather?
What details in the poem give you clues about
his occupation and his character?

115

April Morning

by Howard Fast

Howard Fast (1914—) is best known for his historical novels, although he has also written numerous plays, poems, film scripts, and short stories. In the retelling of April Morning that follows, Fast describes the experiences of 15-year-old Adam Cooper during the battle of Lexington and Concord. After the bloody fighting has ended, Adam knows that his life will never be the same again.

We could hear the sound of British drums in the distance. It was very soft at first, but it kept getting louder.

Morning mist covered the road. When it cleared, we saw them for the first time. They were marching up the road as if they were on parade. Their coats were as red as fire, and their rifles gleamed in the sun. There were row after row of them as far as we could see.

In front were three officers on horses. Then came soldiers carrying flags. Behind them were the drummers. Then came the regular soldiers, maybe 1,000 in all. My hands began to sweat, and my heart was beating fast.

Suddenly, a British officer saw us. He held up his arm. The drums stopped. So did the soldiers. Then the officer rode up to us. We were standing in a small park in the center of our village — Lexington, Massachusetts.

It was April, 1775. About 70 of us were lined up in two rows. We had our rifles, but we didn't expect a fight.

Before the British arrived, the Reverend had told us, "Our duty is to be firm and calm, but not to die. Ours is a way of life, not of death."

My father, Moses Cooper, had agreed. "We are not here to start a war, but to prevent one," he said.

Our plan was to let the Reverend speak to the British when they came. He didn't carry a gun, so they would know we wanted peace. We had our rights, and we wanted the British to know it. But none of us wanted war.

Now the British officer began to shout orders to his men. They marched into the park facing us. Their first line was only 30 steps away. For the first time, I felt something awful was going to happen.

Then the officer yelled at us, "Put down your guns, you filthy rebels! Break up and go to your homes!"

The Reverend tried to speak, but he did not get a chance. The officer rode right at him and almost knocked him down. It was my father who kept him from falling. I heard a shot fired. Then I saw my father grab his chest and fall to the ground.

I started to scream, but I couldn't hear myself. All I could hear was the roar of British guns. The whole world seemed to be crashing down on me. I turned and ran. Everyone else ran, too.

I didn't see the ditch ahead of me, and fell into it. When I looked up, I saw Sam Hodley standing above me. He had a hole in his neck, and blood was pouring out. We looked at each other for a second. Then he fell dead into the ditch right beside me.

"No!" I screamed. Then I vomited.

I was sick, but I could see redcoats running toward the ditch. So I jumped out and began running again. I came to an empty hut and crawled into a corner. Then I cried. I hadn't cried that much since I was small.

When you are 15, like me, you can still pretend a little. For a while, I pretended my father wasn't dead. That was the only way I could stop crying. But I knew my father would never come home again.

I thought about yesterday. Things that seemed so important then didn't seem that way now. I remembered my father calling me when I started back to the house.

"Adam Cooper," he said. "Have you finished your work?"

"Yes," I said, and kept on walking.

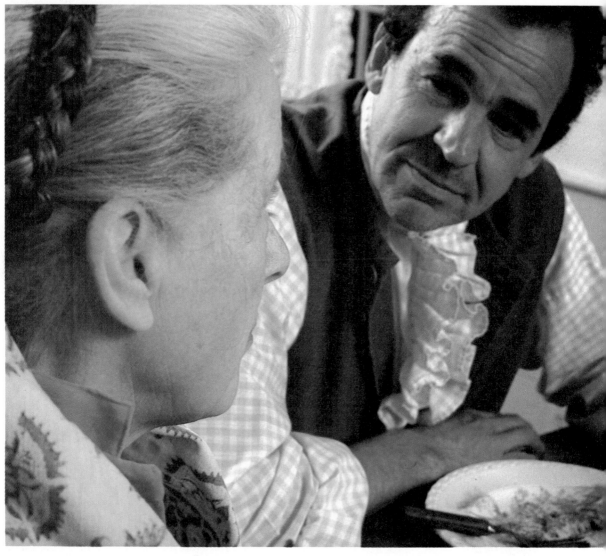

"Adam," he said. "Don't walk away and talk with your back to me."

"Yes, sir," I said, and turned around.

"Get some water from the well and take it to your mother. Wasting steps is as foolish as wasting time."

"Yes, Father," I said.

I wanted to say, "Why do you always cut me down to half my size? Maybe I would try harder to please you if you were kinder to me." But I didn't say that, of course.

Slowly I pulled a pail of water from the well. As I did, I said some magic words. That was in case the devil had put a curse on our water. My father and mother didn't believe in magic. They said that people who do are ignorant. Maybe so, but I wasn't taking any chances.

Just then my younger brother, Levi,

came by. "Give me some water," he said. "Or else I'll tell Father about the magic. I heard you."

"You little brat," I said. But I gave him a drink anyway.

I knew I was in trouble when we sat down to eat that night. My father looked angry. And Levi was quiet, which was unusual for him. I guessed he had told my father about the magic.

Soon my father asked, "How tall are you, Adam? As tall as a man?"

"Yes, sir," I said.

"And as strong as a man, too," he said. "Then you should also have the mind of a man. Don't you think so, Adam?"

"Yes, sir," I said. "That makes sense."

When my father started asking questions like that, it was a danger sign. Both my mother and grandmother knew it. But only Granny wasn't afraid of him.

"Oh, eat your pudding, Moses," she told him. "All these questions will just spoil your digestion."

"I'm talking to Adam," my father said firmly. Then he gave me a speech. We were plain people, he said, but intelligent just the same. And intelligent people didn't believe in magic. It went against our religion. It also went against the truth.

Granny got angry. "All this fuss about some foolishness by a fifteen-year-old boy," she said. "I never saw a man who liked to argue so much. You don't have enough sense to enjoy your wife's cooking."

It was lucky my father had to go to a meeting that night. That finally ended the quarrel. The meeting was to talk about our rights, and how to defend them against the British. My father believed in fighting with ideas, not guns. If you could win an argument, he said, you could win a war.

I asked my father if I could go with him to the meeting. He said, "When you start acting like a man, I'll take you. Not before." Then he walked out.

"Why does he hate me so?" I asked my mother.

"Hate you?" she said. "Adam, he *loves* you. You're his son."

"Then I guess I've got love and hate mixed up," I said. "No matter what I do, he finds fault."

"That's just his way," Granny said. "He expects too much from everyone."

"Well, it's not my way to like it," I said. Then I walked out and slammed the door. Levi was standing outside.

"Are you going to lick me?" he asked.

"Just stay out of my sight, you little skunk," I said. "Next time I *will* lick you."

I needed some sympathy, and I knew where to get it. Ruth Simmons would always say something kind to me. We had known each other since we were little children. Once, when we were 13, she asked me whom I wanted to marry. I told her I hadn't thought about it. She said she had already picked me because she loved me. That made me pretty nervous for a while. But then Granny told me I was too young to worry about getting married. And Ruth stopped talking about it.

I took Ruth for a walk in the village park. I told her how my father had made me feel so bad. Then I talked about going to sea on my uncle's ship.

"You can't be serious," Ruth said.

"Why not?" I asked. "Would it make any difference to you?"

"It would make me the loneliest girl in Massachusetts if you went away."

When she said that, I felt good for the first time in days. I took her hand in mine and kissed her. I kept her hand in mine all the way back to her house.

Late that night, Levi woke me up. "Adam," he said. "I hear a horse coming up the road."

"So what?" I said. "Travelers ride at night, don't they?"

"Travelers don't race their horses in the dark," Levi said.

He was right. This horse was racing fast. The sound of its hoofs got louder. I saw the rider stop outside the village inn. He was shouting, but I could not make out his words. I saw lights going on in all the houses.

My father got dressed and went outside. I got dressed, too. But my mother stopped me at the front door.

"Where do you think you're going?" she asked. "Go back upstairs."

"Mother," I said, "all the men are going outside. Don't make me stay here."

My mother was going to say I was just a boy. But Granny stopped her.

"I think Adam is right," Granny said. "He ought to be there."

Outside, there was a crowd around the rider. He said that British troops were marching this way from Boston. They wanted to grab all the guns and gunpowder stored in Concord. That was just a few miles from our village.

"How many redcoats are there?" someone asked.

"At least a thousand," the rider said. Then he rode off to Concord to warn the people there.

Now everyone began to argue about what we should do. Our village was on the road to Concord. Jonas Parker said we should get ready to fight. Then the Reverend spoke. He asked what chance 70 of *us* would have against 1,000 of

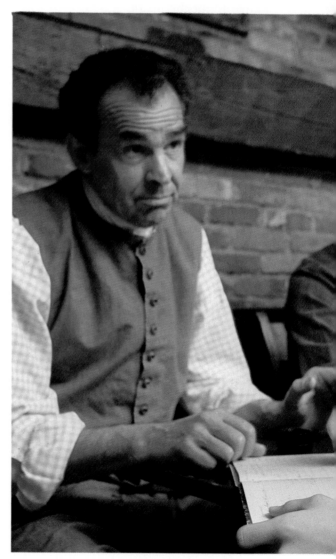

120

them? He said we should learn all the facts before we did anything foolish.

After him, my father spoke. He said that no one wanted to see men get killed. We didn't want to, and he was sure the British didn't, either. But, he said, we believed in our rights and liberties. We had to stand up to the British, or they would not respect us. That was the way to avoid a war, he said. Everyone cheered my father, and I felt very proud of him.

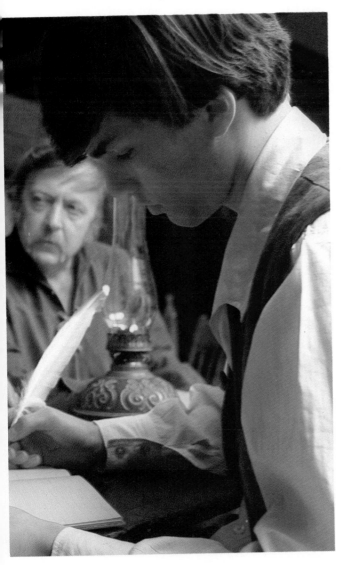

Then Jonas Parker told the men to sign up as soldiers. You had to be at least 16 to sign up. But I knew how to use a gun, and I wanted to join the men. Jonas Parker and my father were in charge of the signing. They could stop me because of my age.

"Your name?" Parker asked.

"Adam Cooper," I said.

My father looked at me real hard. Then he nodded his head at Parker.

"Sign your name here and get your gun," Parker said. That was all.

When I got home, Ruth Simmons was waiting for me. She said she was afraid I would be killed. I told her she was being silly. There wasn't going to be a war, I said. We were just going to stand up for our rights.

"Just the same," she said, "wars happen. Suppose one starts tomorrow."

"If it does," I said, "I do not intend to be killed."

"You don't have to pretend to be so brave and manly," she said. "It's natural to be scared at a time like this."

"Ruth Simmons, let me tell you something," I said. But she didn't let me finish. She threw her arms around me and kissed me. Then she ran home. I chased her part of the way, just for fun.

When I got home, Mother and Father were arguing. She said the men had all gone crazy. How could they stop a large British army? Most of all, she was angry because my father had let me sign up.

"He's just a boy," she said.

"Yesterday he was a boy," my father said. "Tonight he's not. You can't shelter him anymore. If you try, you will lose a son."

When my father went out, I kissed my mother on the cheek. She started to cry. That made me cry, too.

Granny wiped away my tears, and I kissed her, too. Then she pushed me out the door.

My father and I walked to the village park together. When we got there, he said, "Adam . . . ," but the rest of the words stuck in his throat.

Then he put his arm around my shoulder and held me close. It was the first time he had ever tried to say that he loved me. I knew then that he really did.

Well, you know what happened when the British came. My father and others killed. Everybody running. Me hiding in a hut. I knew I had to get out of there. The British were still around, and it wasn't safe.

I looked out the door. I saw a field with some trees and ran toward it. I ran so fast, I didn't see the two redcoats standing nearby. One of them shouted, "Halt!" The other raised his rifle and pulled the trigger. Lucky for me, the rifle didn't fire. I jumped over a stone fence as if I had wings. The way I kept running, you'd think the devil was behind me.

Suddenly, I felt two strong arms grab me. I struggled, but I couldn't break away. Then I heard the man say, "Easy, lad. I'm not going to harm you. My name is Solomon Chandler. I live near here. I saw you running from those redcoats like a deer. But they're not chasing you. How could they? Those packs on their backs weigh more than forty pounds. Besides, it's two of us now against two of them. The odds are even."

I stared at him. He was a tall, skinny man. Half of his teeth were missing.

"You don't know them," I said. "They shot us down like dogs, and killed my father. And we ran away like cowards."

"They killed your father, did they?" he said. "That's a terrible thing. But I don't agree that you were cowards. You don't have to be brave to pull a trigger. It's harder for decent people to do it than for others."

"Half the regular British soldiers are convicts. They are serving time in the army instead of in jail. The rest are poor, ignorant lads who just do what they're told. Few of them can read or write."

Chandler asked me my name. Then he gave me something to eat. He had cold chicken, ham, and bread in his bag. They tasted better than anything I had ever eaten before. I guess I was pretty hungry and tired.

Solomon Chandler had fought against the French years before. He seemed to know a lot about what was happening right now. He said that the British were marching on to Concord. So far, it had been easy for them. But it would be different when they tried to march back.

"Come with me," he said. "I'll show you what I mean."

We walked through the fields toward Concord. Along the way, other men with

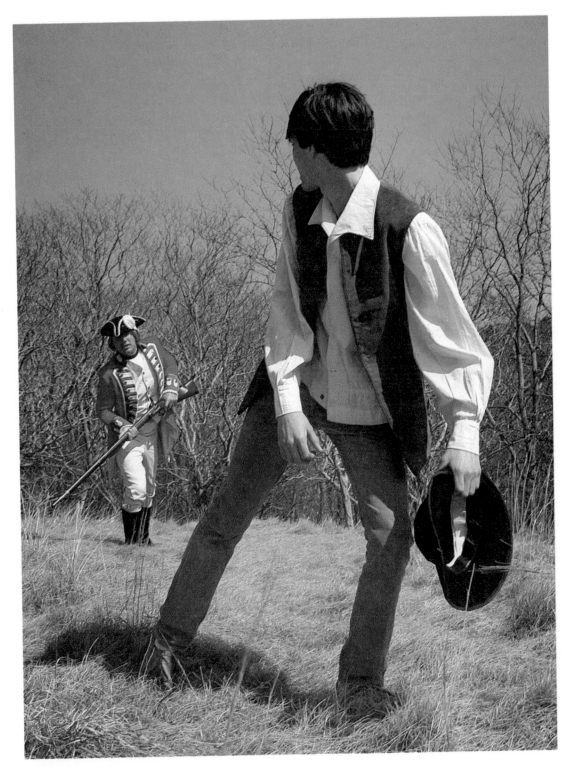

guns joined us. They came from farms and towns all over. When I saw some men from Lexington, I almost cried for joy. Until then, I was afraid the whole village was dead.

Soon there were more than 100 of us. We made a camp. Chandler told us that there were other camps like this between Lexington and Concord.

"The redcoats will march back down that road," he said. "When they do, we'll make it hot for them. There are stone walls and trees all along the road. We'll stay behind them and fire as the British pass by."

Our plan was to fight in small groups. We would shoot, run ahead, then shoot again. It would be "hit and run." We couldn't fight them any other way. Their army was too strong.

A man on a horse rode into our camp. He came from Concord. He said the British were already there. They hadn't found the guns and powder they were looking for. The guns and powder were hidden in another place. There had been some fighting at the river. But now the British were "having a picnic."

"When do they march back to Boston?" Chandler asked.

The rider guessed it would be soon. So we got behind the stone wall near the road and waited. It seemed like a long time. Then we heard the sound of shooting up the road. The shooting got nearer and nearer.

"Here they come," Chandler cried out to warn us.

A minute later, we could see the red-coats. They had changed since I saw them in Lexington. They weren't beating any drums now. They looked scared and angry. Some of them were hurt and bleeding. Dust from the road had made them dirty.

Now they were passing in front of us. Solomon Chandler fired at a British officer. The officer fell from his horse, dead. Then we all started to fire. Smoke covered the road, but I could hear the redcoats screaming.

Then some of them ran toward us with their bayonets. I was so dazed, I just stood there. It was a good thing that Joseph Simmons — Ruth's father — saw me. He grabbed my arm and dragged me away.

"Don't you know when it's time to get out of a place?" he asked.

We started running. And I ran a lot faster than he.

Later, we rested and loaded our guns again. We could hear firing all up and down the road. I took a look around. Under a tree, I saw the body of a dead redcoat. He was a young boy. His face was very thin, as if he had never had enough to eat. His eyes were wide open, and his lips had turned purple. Then I got sick again.

"I've had a bellyful of war and killing," I told Simmons. "I'm sick of this whole bloody business."

"I know," Simmons said. "But we can't stop now, Adam. There's been too much shooting for either side to turn back. It's too late for arguments. There won't be any peace for a long time."

"When will that be?" I asked.

"When the British stop trying to control us. When they sail away in their ships and leave us for good. When we can call this land our own. Not before then."

The fighting that day kept up a long time. I saw other men get killed. Maybe I killed a redcoat myself. I don't know.

We won the battle. But all of us were sad going home. There is less joy in winning a battle than history books tell you.

Levi was the first to see me enter the house. "Adam!" he cried. "We thought you were dead!"

"Do I look dead?" I asked. "I'm awful tired, but I'm alive."

Then my mother took me in her arms. She held me so tightly, I thought my ribs would break. When she let go, she started to cry. Granny didn't say a word. I could see she was trying to hold back her own tears.

Later, I went upstairs to look at my father for the last time. His body was laid out on a bed. I didn't cry. I had seen so many bodies that day that I just felt numb. I would always remember my father alive, but not that body on a bed.

I didn't know what would happen the next day. Would the British come back? Would there be more fighting? No one knew. But I was sure of one thing.

Since that morning, everything had changed. The warm, sunny world of my childhood had gone away. It would never come back again.

READING COMPREHENSION

Select the best choice to complete each statement. Then write the entire sentence on your paper.

1. At first, the American patriots wanted to _____.
   a. kill as many British as possible
   b. prevent a war by talking
   c. prepare the army to fight well

2. When the men signed up as soldiers, Adam _____.
   a. signed up even though he was too young
   b. was permitted to remain at home
   c. learned how to use a gun

3. Simmons told Adam that _____.
   a. things had gone too far to be stopped
   b. the war would be over soon
   c. he was too young to fight

For Discussion

1. Why do you think Adam was confused about how his father felt about him?

2. Solomon Chandler told Adam, "You don't have to be brave to pull a trigger. It's harder for decent people to do it than for others." Do you agree? Why or why not?

3. How did Adam feel about war before the battle? During the battle? When the battle was over?

4. Why did Adam say his childhood would never return? Can you think of any experience that might change a modern youth into an adult in one day?

UNDERSTANDING LITERATURE

Characters in Historical Fiction. In historical fiction, the characters — even though they may be invented by the writer — must be true to the period in which the story is set. For example, in *April Morning*, Adam Cooper *could* have been a real person. There is nothing about him that doesn't fit the time and place in which the story's events occur.

On your paper, select the best choice to complete each statement about the characters in the selection you have just read.

1. The British soldiers had _____.
   a. many wealthy people among them
   b. jackets that were hard to see
   c. many convicts among them

2. Ruth Simmons told Adam she was _____.
   a. eager to see the fighting start
   b. afraid he would be killed
   c. too young to get married

3. Solomon Chandler _____.
   a. understood the enemy and the land
   b. learned fighting in France
   c. was thrown out of the British army

4. Adam showed no emotion when he saw his father's body because _____.
   a. he hadn't really liked his father
   b. boys weren't supposed to cry
   c. the fighting had dulled his senses

Writing

Imagine you are a British soldier in the battle this story describes. Write two or three paragraphs about the day's events.

She Sailed for Love

by Jane Yolen   •

Pirates were a real threat to 18th-century sailors. Yet in this story by Jane Yolen (1939—), a rather unusual pirate re-unites a young man with the woman he loves, and also manages to aid the American war effort.

Revolutionary America saw the birth of many heroes. War often breeds greatness. One of these brave souls was a pirate. Once you have heard her story, you are not likely to forget her. Her name was Fanny Campbell and she sailed for love. The story of her adventures is an old New England tale still told in Massachusetts.

It all started in Lynn, a little town outside of Boston, where two fishermen, Henry Campbell and Richard Lovell, were neighbors. Their houses stood side by side in a section of Lynn called High Rock. Side by side their children grew up — Fanny Campbell and William Lovell.

Fanny was a bright-eyed girl. She was slender with the kind of face that is both honest and strong. William was a wiry New Englander, forthright and outspoken. As they grew up, Fanny and William fell in love. Their parents and neighbors were all in favor of their marriage. Things seemed so simple — then.

William wanted to become a deep-sea sailor. He received permission from his father to go to Boston and ship aboard a New England merchant ship. For six months he sailed. In the seventh, he returned home to Fanny.

"Fanny," he said, "you must come sailing with me. The sea is an open road to the world."

She went, of course. Fanny was an active girl. She knew how to ride a horse. She knew how to shoot. She had even killed a wildcat in the Lynn woods. Sailing, too, came easily to her.

The two young people spent their days on the sea. William taught Fanny all there was to know about sailing. He taught her to handle a ship in any weather. But then the time to part came again.

"Fanny," said William one day, taking her hands in his, "now you know as much about the sea as I do. Promise you will never be afraid when I am on a voyage."

"Promise," said Fanny. "You're going off again, aren't you?"

"Yes," he answered. "I've been offered a berth on the *Royal Kent*. She's bound for South America and the Indies. It's —

it's a fine chance. I really want to take it."

"Then you must," Fanny said, smiling.

William hesitated a moment. "When this trip is over, I'm coming back to marry you."

"Of course, William," Fanny said. "But don't look so grim and serious. You must learn to laugh more. Don't worry. I'll be waiting for you."

William sailed the next day. He was gone for more than two years. While he was away, Fanny had another caller, Captain Robert Burnet, an officer in the British Navy. Burnet fell in love with Fanny and courted her for those two years. Although she did not hear from William, Fanny was faithful. Captain Burnet's suit was refused again and again.

Late one night, two years after William Lovell had gone to sea, a stranger knocked on the Campbell door. He was gaunt and tired-looking, with a face that seemed chiseled from granite.

The door opened and Fanny stood framed in the moonlight.

"Beggin' your pardon, ma'am, but my name is Jack Herbert," said the stranger. "Are you Fanny Campbell?"

"I am," she said.

"At last," he murmured. "I come from William Lovell."

"Oh," said Fanny. For a moment that was all she could say. Then she invited the stranger in. He followed her into the warmth of the kitchen.

"Where is William? Is he well?" Fanny asked.

"It's a long story, Miss Campbell. William is well but he's not well off. I was on the *Royal Kent* with him."

"Was?" said Fanny, interrupting him.

"Was, ma'am. The *Royal Kent* is no more. We were coming out of Port au Plate when a pirate schooner came in sight. We turned to run but it was no use. She caught and boarded us. We weren't meant for fighting, you know. Anyhow, there were four pirates to every one of us. We tried, though. Killed a good number. We even got their leader. But they killed our captain — a fine man, may he rest in peace. They scuttled our ship."

"But what happened to William?"

"I'm getting to that, ma'am," Herbert said. "Bill was wounded. Pretty badly, too. The pirates took him aboard. We were all taken aboard, to make up for the men they lost."

"We headed toward Cuba, but the wind died before we reached the bay. We were laying becalmed. That's when Bill and Henry Breed and I (Henry's a fine lad, too) were chosen for watch. It was the late watch, ma'am. Called the 'graveyard watch.' We were the only people up. It was then that Bill thought of a plan. He said we could make a break and find the governor of Cuba. If we told him what happened, he'd get us home safely. So, we decided to try."

"Then what happened?" asked Fanny.

"Well, we headed the schooner into the light wind. We tied the wheel so the ship would stay on course. Then the three of us put a small boat over the side. We lowered some provisions, enough to get us through to shore, and climbed down a rope ladder to the dinghy. We rowed for about half a mile, till we were out of range of the pirates. Then we hoisted sail for Cuba."

"William is safe in Cuba, then," said Fanny, looking hopefully at Herbert.

"Well, ma'am, not exactly. That is, he is in Cuba. But when we got to Havana, we were arrested as suspicious characters. If you had been in an open boat for a few days and were dirty and ragged, you might have looked suspicious, too. Not meaning any offense, ma'am. And we had served aboard a pirate ship.

"They threw us in jail for six months. Jail! It was more like a black hole. We fought with the rats for possession of the straw beds. Then the Cubans took us out for trial. But there wasn't any evidence so they put us back in jail. They figured to get some in a little while, I guess."

"Why, that's ridiculous," said Fanny indignantly.

"Yes, ma'am. Only that's the way it was," Herbert said. "We were in jail over a year. Bill kept count of the days by scratching a mark on the wall with his spoon. Then I managed to escape by myself. I hid aboard an American ship and got to Boston. I came to you because Bill asked me to give you this note if I made it."

He dug into his pocket and pulled out a small, dirty slip of paper. Fanny reached for the crumpled note. She did not dare open it in front of Herbert. She was afraid she might cry. Instead, she faced him

squarely and asked, "Where are you staying, Mr. Herbert?"

"I'm in Boston, ma'am. At Copp's Hill."

A plan had begun to form in Fanny's mind. "Mr. Herbert, stay at Copp's Hill until you hear from me. I won't be longer than a week in sending word. We are going to get William and Mr. Breed out of jail; that is, if you are with me."

"Miss Campbell, Bill and Breed are fine lads. They helped me out more than once. I won't let them rot in a Cuban jail. No, ma'am, I'll be ready!"

"Fine, Mr. Herbert. You won't be sorry!" Fanny led the sailor to the door.

"And Mr. Herbert — "

"Yes, ma'am?"

"God bless you!" said Fanny. Herbert walked off into the darkness. Fanny shut the door after him. Then she leaned against it and opened the note. William had written that he was well, that he would return, and that he loved her.

Two days later, in Copp's Hill, Jack Herbert received a midnight visitor. The visitor was a slender deep-eyed sailor who reminded him of his promise to Fanny Campbell. The sailor brought Herbert to the brig *Constance*, anchored in Boston Harbor. She was ready to sail for England by way of Cuba and she was well-armed. The captain of the *Constance* was a tyrannical and cruel man named Brownless. Banning, the first mate, was an ignorant sailor who cared little for the ship and less for the men. But the second mate, a bright-eyed youth named Channing, was well-skilled in the ways of the sea. Channing was new to the *Constance*. He had joined the crew the day before, but the men already admired him for his ease on board ship. His beardless, tanned face was always covered with a big smile, and he always had a joke or a story ready. An officer, he still mixed well with the men, and they would have liked him for that alone.

Jack Herbert went aboard the ship as a common sailor. He heard nothing more of Fanny's plan but he had faith in her. After all, she had gotten him aboard a ship bound for Cuba. That was a start. The next move, too, he decided to leave to her.

The *Constance* set sail for Cuba. She was not out a week when the crew became restless. Captain Brownless, a hardhearted man, delighted in punishing the men. In the waters of the West Indies, a day's sail from Cuba, the likeable young second mate took his pistol and went to the captain's quarters.

"Captain Brownless," said Channing in a gentle voice, "because I am an officer you have confided in me. But I think it's time we shared this confidence with the men — don't you?"

The captain muttered, "Mutiny!" under his breath, but in the face of the pistol he had little choice. Channing mustered the crew and stood the captain in front of him, facing the men.

"Men," Channing shouted over the roar of the sea, "the captain has not told you the truth about this trip. I learned it because I am an officer, but I am not too pleased. We are headed for England, as you know. But there, as you do not know, Brownless intended to have you pressed into service in the British Navy. That's a three-year hitch, men, and nothing you could have done about it. No questions. No volunteers. No way out. Just the word from Brownless here and you'd be British sailors. What do you say to that?"

"Pressed into service?"

"Aye."

"No getting out of it?"

"No."

The sailors buzzed the idea around. Slowly a roar arose that challenged the noise of the sea.

"Hang him! Hang the captain! Drown him! Cast him overboard!"

The captain turned pale as the men moved toward him menacingly.

Channing put up his hand to stop the noise. He smiled broadly. "All right. I see what your mood is. But I have a better — and a more just — solution. We will take over the ship and sail on to Cuba. There we can turn Brownless over to the proper authorities. If you want me, I'll be your captain till then."

The men cheered their agreement. Then Channing pointed to Herbert, who was standing in the midst of the crew. "Herbert there will be mate. Brownless goes into his cabin to stay. You realize, though, this means we're a mutiny ship and a mutiny crew. The law calls us pirates. So, if we are pirates, we will pirate our way to Cuba. Hoist up the black flag!"

Brownless was locked in his cabin. That night, the cook, who had remained loyal, sneaked to Channing's cabin to try to murder the new captain. Brownless, meanwhile, had gotten out past the guard and was intent on the same bloody errand. In

F. PORTER

the darkness outside of Channing's door, the two men came upon each other. Mistaking each other for Channing, they exchanged blows with their knives. The next morning, on his way to wake the new captain, a sailor stumbled on their bodies. They were buried at sea.

The *Constance* was a renegade ship. She sailed pirate's colors. With Channing as captain, the crew overpowered the British bark *George of Bristol* and put the sailors in irons below decks. Jack Herbert was put in charge of the new ship.

Late one night, the *George* and the *Constance* sailed into Havana Bay. The two ships anchored a half-mile from the fort where William Lovell and Henry Breed were imprisoned. In the dark, Herbert and eight loyal crewmen rowed to the fort.

Leaving one man on guard at the rowboat, they crept along the beach toward the fort. A mute form was seen ahead. The first sentry! Herbert signaled silently with one hand and a sailor sneaked to the rear of the guard. Quickly his hand went over the guard's mouth. It was over in seconds. No one had heard.

Three more guards were gagged and tied up quickly and quietly, and locked in the guardhouse. Herbert searched their pockets and found the keys.

The sailors opened the jail door. The large iron door let out a harsh, protesting squeak.

The men raced to the cell where two men lay sleeping and opened the door.

"Breed? Billy? Are you alive, lads? Are you alive?"

The men stirred in their hay beds. They winked open their eyes and stared. "Herbert . . . is it. . . ?"

Herbert ran into the cell and clapped the men heartily on the back. They laughed and cried with disbelief, relief.

"No time, sir. No time," called one of the sailors in a harsh whisper.

"He's right," said Herbert. "Get your things together, boys. We're leaving this place for good!"

The men raced out of the jail, down to the beach, and into the boat. They grabbed the oars and within minutes they were at the *Constance.* Just as the two ships started out of the harbor, there was a loud cry from the fort. The escape had been discovered! But it was too late. The American ships sailed free with their booty — two very tired and happy ex-prisoners.

The cabin boy found Herbert, William, and Breed top side. They were watching as the fort vanished below the horizon.

"Sir, if you please, sir," said the boy. "The captain says to tell Mr. Lovell that he is to be first mate of the *Constance* and to come to his cabin at once."

Herbert shrugged his shoulders. "Guess the captain knows what he is doing. He is the one who plotted the escape. I'm sure he's under orders from your Fanny Campbell."

William shrugged, too. "You know him better than I," he said. "I'd be his cabin boy and scrub the deck from stem to stern for what he's done. And I hope to tell him so. If he wants me to be his mate, he's got the most loyal mate about."

William made his way to the captain's cabin and knocked on the door. When there was no answer, he walked in, somewhat timidly. The captain had his back to the door, his hands clasped behind him.

"Lovell here, sir," William began.

"Oh, yes, Lovell," replied the captain. "You seem to know your way around ships. Been a sailor most of your life?"

"Thank you, sir. No, sir, but since I've been at sea I've loved it."

"That's fine, Lovell," said Channing, his back still to the door. "Speaking of love, do you have a girl at home? It's been some time since you've been there."

"Yes, sir, I do."

"And you're sure she is still waiting for you after all this time?"

"I hope so, sir. More than anything else, I hope so."

"What is your girl like?"

"Begging your pardon, sir, but I don't think this discussion should go on. . . ."

"You're not ashamed of her, are you, Lovell?"

"Sir, I won't take that, not even from you," roared William. His hands tensed into fists.

"Oh, William," laughed the captain. "You've really got to learn to laugh. Don't you know me?"

The captain turned around. He took off his hat. "I'm Fanny!"

It was true — Channing was Fanny. Her hair had been cropped short, her skin dyed a dark brown.

"Oh, William! Herbert told me about Cuba and the prison. I couldn't trust anyone else to find you. I had to do it myself." Fanny began to cry.

"It's all right. Fanny. I'm here. I'm here. We're together again." said William.

And they were. Together, William and Fanny captained the *Constance* and the *George*. They captured a British merchantman and learned from the crew that the Revolutionary War was in full swing. A vote from the men convinced them that they should give up their pirating ways — and turn privateer. That meant that instead of stopping any ship that came along and robbing it for their own profit, the crew would work for the American government, capturing only enemy ships. Then they would turn over a share of the booty to the new government. As loyal Americans, they could rob any British ships they could capture.

The *Constance* and the *George* soon came upon an armed British sloop. After a short battle they captured it. The captain of the sloop was none other than Fanny's former suitor, Robert Burnet. He recognized Fanny, but because he still loved her, he never told. He was clapped in chains below deck with the rest of the British prisoners. And the crew of the *Constance* did not learn that their captain was a woman.

The two ships sailed toward Boston, but changed course when they discovered that the British had taken the harbor. Instead, Fanny headed the *Constance* and the *George* toward Marblehead Harbor, not far from Boston, where the crew became legal privateers.

Boston still rings with the true tales of many Revolutionary War heroes, but few people know of Fanny Campbell. Yet she was America's first female pirate — a pirate who sailed for freedom, justice, and love aboard the good ship *Constance*.

134

F. PORTER

READING COMPREHENSION

Select the best choice to complete each statement. Then write the entire sentence on your paper.

1. William did not return from his trip on the *Royal Kent* because he _____.
   a. had mutinied and switched sides
   b. no longer loved Fanny
   c. was in prison in Cuba

2. Fanny disguised herself as a man because she _____.
   a. had a yearning to go to sea
   b. didn't trust anyone else to rescue William
   c. wanted to be captain

3. Fanny and William helped the American cause by _____.
   a. refusing to sell goods to the British
   b. capturing and robbing British ships
   c. enlisting in the army

For Discussion

1. Why did Fanny and William seem to be such ideal mates? Do you think that their separation made a difference in the way they felt about each other? Explain your answer.

2. Mutiny and piracy are generally considered to be serious crimes. Do you think Fanny was right or wrong to encourage mutiny when she did? Do you think she should have sailed as a pirate? Explain your answer.

3. Would it have made a difference if the crew had known their captain was a woman? Explain why or why not.

UNDERSTANDING LITERATURE

Details in Historical Fiction. Sometimes historical fiction portrays a real character in a fictionalized way. The author of the work takes a character who really did live in the past and creates dialogue and details to make that character come alive.

"She Sailed for Love" is an example of historical fiction in which the main characters are thought to have really existed. The major events may have happened in a way much like the author depicted. Many of the specific details of the story, however, are created by the author.

In developing a real character in a fictionalized way, a writer often gives the character feelings that anyone in a similar situation would have. This adds a note of authenticity to the character portrayal.

Answer the following questions on your paper.

1. Go back to the story "She Sailed for Love." Find five examples of statements that the author used to describe the feelings of a character.

2. In the story, locate three examples of dialogue that the author probably created.

Writing

Pretend that you are either Fanny or William and you have just met in the captain's cabin. Write a letter to your family telling them what has happened. The last paragraph of your letter should mention your plans for the immediate future.

Section Review

VOCABULARY

Synonyms and Antonyms. Two words that have the same or almost the same meaning are called *synonyms*. For example, *trembling* and *shaking* are synonyms.

Antonyms are two words that have opposite meanings. For example, *dirty* and *clean* are antonyms.

Here are some sentences from the selections you have just read. Write each italicized word on your paper. Then write its synonym from the list below.

agreement selfish slim amusement

1. "The winters were long and white, and any *diversion* was welcome."

2. " 'Have you made no *contract* with the devil?' "

3. "She was *slender* with the kind of face that is both honest and strong."

Write each italicized word on your paper. Then write its antonym from the list given below.

shouted smooth devoted disloyal

1. "Although she did not hear from William, Fanny was *faithful*."

2. "Fanny reached for the *crumpled* note."

3. "The captain *muttered,* 'Mutiny!' under his breath."

READING

Cause and Effect. Everything happens for a reason. This reason is called the *cause*. Every cause produces a result, or *effect*. Understanding cause-and-effect relationships is important if you are to understand how and why things happen in a story.

Words and phrases like *because, since, as a result of, therefore,* or *then* may signal cause-and-effect relationships:

People ran from the streets *because* the redcoats were coming.

Cause: The redcoats were coming.
Effect: People ran from the streets.

Each statement below expresses a cause-and-effect relationship. Make two columns on your paper. Label one *Cause* and the other *Effect*. Then write the appropriate phrase in each column.

1. I heard a shot fired. Then I saw my father grab his chest and fall to the ground.

2. I didn't see the ditch ahead of me; as a result, I fell into it.

3. Then I cried because I knew my father would never come home again.

4. My father left to go to a meeting, so our quarrel ended.

5. Ruth Simmons said she wanted to marry me since she loved me.

6. My mother was angry because my father let me sign up.

7. My father put his arm around my shoulders, therefore I knew that he really loved me.

WRITING AN EXPLANATORY PARAGRAPH

Explanatory writing tells how something happened or how to do something. An explanation tells about something in a way that makes the process clear to the reader.

For example, if you were to write a paragraph explaining how thirty-nine innocent people were convicted in the Salem witch trials, you would have to include the following steps.

a. The children identified a "witch."

b. The person was arrested and brought to trial.

c. The judge asked leading questions.

d. The children became tormented in the courtroom.

e. The person on trial was convicted and hanged.

An explanatory paragraph about the Salem witch trials that mentions each of these steps would give the reader a good idea of what was going on at that time in the colony.

The first sentence of an explanatory paragraph should tell what it is the writer is going to explain. For example, an opening sentence about the Salem witch trials might be: "The events of the Salem witch trials, beginning with identification of a 'witch' and ending with a hanging, varied little from one trial to another." Another possible opening sentence might be: "The steps to conviction in the Salem witch trials were pretty much the same, no matter who was on trial."

Here is a checklist to keep in mind as you write an explanatory paragraph.

☐ Begin the paragraph by telling what you are going to explain.

☐ Tell each of the steps in order.

☐ Write the sentences in clear, simple language so that your reader will have no trouble following what you are explaining. Use sequence words like *first, second, next,* and *finally* to help make the meaning clear.

Think back to the story "She Sailed for Love," which you read in this section. Your task is to explain the steps that Fanny Campbell used to rescue William Lovell from the Cuban prison. Reread parts of the story if you need to.

1. List the things Fanny did to rescue Bill. She took a number of specific steps, although as she was doing each one, no one else knew what she was up to.

2. Now write a paragraph explaining exactly how the rescue took place. If you wish, you can pretend that you are Fanny and write the paragraph in the first person. Or, if you prefer, take the part of a reporter or another objective observer and write the steps of the rescue using the third-person point of view.

QUIZ

The following is a quiz for Section 3. Write the answers in complete sentences on your paper.

Reading Comprehension

1. In "Salem Village, Massachusetts," what did Reverend Parris do that led to the deaths of 19 people?

2. Who were the last two people to be accused of witchcraft in Salem? Why did the madness stop?

3. In "April Morning," how did Solomon Chandler help Adam Cooper? How did Joseph Simmons help the boy?

4. In "She Sailed for Love," how and where did Fanny Campbell and William Lovell meet? What did William teach Fanny?

5. Why did William end up in a Cuban jail? How did he escape?

Understanding Literature

6. In what ways is the story "Salem Village, Massachusetts" an example of historical fiction?

7. What did Benét say about the thoughts of the afflicted children in his story? What interpretation did he give to their actions?

8. In what ways is "April Morning" an example of historical fiction? How would it differ from a newspaper account of the same battle?

9. What effect did the war have on Adam Cooper? Why do you think author Howard Fast created a character like Adam?

10. In "She Sailed for Love," how did William discover that Captain Channing was really Fanny? Are the exact details of this scene fact or fiction? Explain your answer.

COMPOSITION

1. When Rebecca Nurse was accused of witchcraft, 39 citizens signed a petition to free her. The jury found her "not guilty," but the judge and the courtroom mob made the jurors reverse their decision. Write a paragraph telling what might have happened to the jury if Rebecca Nurse had gone free.

2. Imagine that the young redcoat Adam Cooper saw under the tree had still been alive. Write a paragraph describing what might have happened when Adam met him. Invent details and dialogue to fit the situation.

3. Captain Robert Burnet fell in love with Fanny and pursued her, but she stayed faithful to William. Write a dialogue between Burnet and Fanny in which she tells him she doesn't love him.

4. Write one or two paragraphs describing what you think life was like for William and Fanny after the Revolutionary War was over. Create dialogue and interesting details to make your description come alive.

SECTION 4
Voices of Experience

1840–1898

*Trust thyself: Every heart
vibrates to that iron string.*

— Ralph Waldo Emerson

Introduction

America was growing and changing rapidly in the years 1840–1898. There were more and more Americans — Americans born in this country and new Americans who came here from other nations. More and more territory was being explored and settled as people moved westward. There were great advances in science and technology that helped farms, factories, and cities to grow. The steamboat and the railroad made travel faster and safer than it had ever been before.

Yet, despite all this growth, the years 1840–1898 were not a happy time. Americans found that they were growing apart. Different Americans had different interests and goals. What was good for one section of the country was somehow bad for another. The bloody Civil War years, 1861–1865, were the most dramatic expression of these differences. The choices and conflicts of American life were reflected in the literature created during these years.

Life Before the Civil War

Mark Twain lived in the South, the West, and finally settled in the East. In his writing he captured the flavor of life in different places in America. Two of the selections in this section are based on his early experiences in Hannibal, Missouri.

Walt Whitman was another American writer who traveled all over the United States. Whitman's poetry celebrates America and the ideals of democracy. In "There Was a Child Went Forth," he describes the many kinds of experiences that shape a person as he or she grows up.

Democratic ideals were part of two very important movements in the 19th century: the abolitionist movement and the movement to give women the vote. Abolitionists believed that all people should have freedom and equal rights.

As they campaigned for an end to slavery, many abolitionists began to realize that women, too, were being treated unfairly in America. Women could not own land, inherit money, or vote in elections. Many abolitionists also began speaking out for women's suffrage (the right to vote). In the 1850's, Sojourner Truth, a former slave, was a tireless crusader for both abolition and women's suffrage. Her witty speech "Ain't I a Woman?" is included in this section.

The Civil War and Its Aftermath

No one was prepared for the suffering and sorrow the Civil War would cause for both the North and South. Louisa May Alcott worked as a nurse in an army hospital during the war. The selection "Civil War Nurse" describes her experiences and her search for a way to make sense of the horrors of war. Ambrose Bierce was also affected by the Civil War. He himself fought in the Union Army and

Guerrilla Warfare, Civil War, Albert Bierstadt, 1862

was seriously wounded. In his story in this section, Bierce recreates one of the most painful dilemmas the war created for many Americans.

After the war was over, the people of the South had to find the strength to rebuild burned-out cities and farms. They had to adjust to a new form of government and to a new way of life. Sidney Lanier's poem "The Raven Days" captures the mood of many Southerners at the time.

Chief Joseph of the Nez Percé tribe may not have taken part in the Civil War, but he certainly understood the pain and loss caused by war. The United States government had again and again broken agreements and taken tribal lands away from

Native Americans — often by force. In the 1870's, Chief Joseph spoke out against these conditions in his speech "I Shall Fight No More Forever."

Rebuilding the United States and correcting the many injustices that developed during the 19th century would take many years. But in small ways, literature helped Americans rebuild their pride in their nation and a sense of being one people. Near the end of the 19th century, Ernest Lawrence Thayer wrote a poem called "Casey at the Bat." This poem, which ends this section, reflects Americans' enthusiasm for baseball and their willingness, even in times of trouble, to laugh at themselves.

A Dose of Pain-Killer

by Mark Twain

*One of America's best and best-loved writers is Mark Twain
(1835–1910), who grew up in the small Mississippi River
town of Hannibal, Missouri. The river and the towns along it
became the setting for much of Twain's later work, including*
The Adventures of Huckleberry Finn *and* The Adventures of
Tom Sawyer. *Here is an excerpt from* The Adventures of
Tom Sawyer, *a book based on Twain's memories of his own
boyhood in Hannibal. As the story begins, Tom has just lost
his girl friend, Becky, and witnessed a murder — both in the
same day! Understandably, he is troubled and confused. His
guardian, Aunt Polly, thinks he is sick, and therefore deserv-
ing of one of her cures.*

Tom Sawyer's Aunt Polly was one of
those people who are infatuated with
patent medicines and all new-fangled
methods of producing health or mending
it. She was always experimenting in these
things. When something fresh in this line
came out she wanted to try it right away;
not on herself, for she was never sick, but
on anybody else that came handy.

The water treatment was new now, and
Tom's low condition was a windfall to
her. She had him out at daylight every
morning, stood him up in the woodshed,
and drowned him with cold water; then
she scrubbed him down with a scratchy
towel; then she rolled him up in a wet
sheet and put him away under blankets
till she sweated his soul clean.

In spite of all this, the boy grew more
and more melancholy and pale and de-
jected. Now she heard of Pain-Killer for
the first time. She ordered a lot at once.
She tasted it and was filled with gratitude.
It was simply fire in a liquid form.

She dropped the water treatment and
pinned her faith to Pain-Killer. She gave
Tom a teaspoonful, and watched with
deepest anxiety for the result. Her troubles
were instantly at rest, her soul at peace
again; for the "indifference" was broken

up. The boy could not have shown a wilder, heartier interest if she had built a fire under him.

Tom thought over various plans for relief, and finally hit upon that of pretending to be fond of Pain-Killer. He asked for it so often that he became a nuisance, and his aunt ended by telling him to help himself and quit bothering her.

She watched the bottle secretly. She found that the medicine did really diminish, but it did not occur to her that the boy was mending the health of a crack in the sitting-room floor with it.

One day Tom was in the act of dosing the crack, when his aunt's yellow cat came along, purring, eyeing the teaspoon greedily, and begging for a taste. Tom said, "Don't ask for it unless you want it, Peter."

But Peter signified that he did want it.

"You better make sure."

Peter was sure.

"Now you've asked for it, and I'll give it to you, because there ain't anything mean about *me*. But if you find you don't like it, you mustn't blame anybody but your own self."

Peter was agreeable. So Tom pried his mouth open and poured down the Pain-Killer. Peter sprang a couple of yards in the air. He delivered a war-whoop and set off round and round the room, banging against furniture, upsetting flowerpots, and making general havoc.

Next he rose on his hind feet and pranced around, in a frenzy of enjoyment, with his head over his shoulder and his voice proclaiming his happiness. Then he went tearing around the house again, spreading chaos and destruction in his path.

Aunt Polly entered just in time to see him throw a few double somersaults, deliver a final mighty hurrah, and sail through the open window, carrying the rest of the flowerpots with him. The old lady stood peering over her glasses in astonishment. Tom lay on the floor, expiring with laughter.

"Tom, what on earth ails that cat?"

"*I* don't know, Aunt," gasped the boy.

"Why, I've never seen anything like it. What *did* make him act so?"

" 'Deed I don't know, Aunt Polly. Cats always act so when they're having a good time."

"They do, do they?" There was something in the tone that made Tom uneasy.

"Yes'm. That is, I believe they do."

"You *do*?"

The old lady was bending down, Tom watching anxiously. Too late he realized her "drift." The handle of the tell-tale teaspoon was visible under the bedspread. Aunt Polly took it, held it up. Tom winced, and dropped his eyes. Aunt Polly raised him by the usual handle — his ear — and cracked his head soundly with her thimble.

"Now, sir, why do you want to treat that poor dumb beast so?"

"I done it out of pity for him — because he hadn't any aunt."

"Hadn't any aunt — you numbskull! What has that got to do with it?"

"Heaps. Because if he'd a had one she'd a burst him out herself! She'd a roasted his bowels out of him 'thout any more feeling than if he was a human!"

Aunt Polly felt a sudden pang of remorse. This was putting the thing in a new light. What was cruelty to a cat *might* be cruelty to a boy, too. She began to soften; she felt sorry. Her eyes watered a little, and she put her hand on Tom's head and said gently, "I was meaning for the best, Tom. And, Tom, it *did* do you good."

"I know you was meaning for the best, Aunty, and so was I with Peter. It done *him* good, too. I never see him get around so since — "

"Oh, go 'long with you, Tom, before you aggravate me again. And you try and see if you can't be a good boy, for once, and you needn't take any more medicine."

146

READING COMPREHENSION

Select the best choice to complete each statement below. Then write the entire sentence on your paper.

1. To nurse sick people back to health, Aunt Polly liked to _____.
   a. call the doctor
   b. try anything new and different
   c. sit by the bed and hold people's hands

2. Tom kept asking Aunt Polly for Pain-Killer because he _____.
   a. wanted to make her tired of giving it to him
   b. liked the taste of it
   c. thought it would make him well

3. After Tom gave Pain-Killer to Peter, the cat _____.
   a. asked for more
   b. went to sleep in a corner
   c. started running all over the place

4. By giving Pain-Killer to Peter, Tom made Aunt Polly _____.
   a. realize that Pain-Killer was awful
   b. think the medicine could cure anything
   c. want to take Pain-Killer, too

For Discussion

1. Was Tom helped in any way by taking Pain-Killer? Explain.

2. Could Tom have convinced Aunt Polly that Pain-Killer was awful by telling her? Why or why not? What else could Aunt Polly have done to help Tom get well?

UNDERSTANDING LITERATURE

Plot. The events in a story are called the *plot*. Each event is responsible for creating another. The first event is known as the *cause*. The cause produces the next event, or a result known as the *effect*. Cause and effect make a story logical: Events happen for a reason. In "A Dose of Pain-Killer," Aunt Polly was "infatuated with patent medicines." The effect of this was that Aunt Polly gave the new medicines to "anybody that came handy."

On your paper, match each of the following causes to the effect it created in "A Dose of Pain-Killer."

Causes
1. Aunt Polly gave Tom his first dose of Pain-Killer.
2. Tom pretended to like Pain-Killer.
3. Tom gave Peter some of the medicine.
4. Aunt Polly found the teaspoon under the bed.

Effects
a. Peter raced around the house, knocking over furniture and flowerpots.
b. Aunt Polly cracked Tom's head with a thimble.
c. Aunt Polly let Tom give himself the medicine.
d. Tom felt as if he'd been drinking fire.

Writing
What would have happened if Aunt Polly had taken Pain-Killer herself? Write a new ending for the selection with events that logically create new events.

Life on the Mississippi

by Mark Twain

Here is a play based on Mark Twain's book Life on the Mississippi. *Like the main character in the play, Twain was a riverboat pilot as a young man. (In fact, the name Mark Twain comes from a term that was used on riverboats. "Mark twain" means that the water is deep enough for the pilot to steer in safely.) Twain's real name was Samuel Clemens; Sam is also the name of the pilot in the play. In many of Twain's books, the main character is an innocent person learning about life. In this play, Sam learns to be a pilot, but he also learns about friendship, responsibility, danger, and death.*

CHARACTERS

Sam, a steamboat steersman
Bixby, the pilot who trains Sam
Ritchie, another steersman
Brown, another pilot
Tom, another steersman
Emmeline, a passenger
Klinefelter, a steamboat captain

It is 1857. Sam Clemens is at the riverboat landing in Hannibal, Missouri. He walks onto the Paul Jones, *a steamboat that is headed down the Mississippi River. As the boat pulls away from shore, Sam goes to the wheelhouse, where the steering wheel is. Bixby, the pilot, is behind the wheel. The second pilot, George Ealer, and his steersman, Ritchie, are also there.*

Sam: Mr. Bixby?

(Bixby ignores Sam and rings a bell. Then he speaks into a tube that goes down to the engine room.)

Bixby *(into the tube):* Hold her where she is, Ben.

Sam: Mr. Bixby, could I speak to you? The captain said I could. He says you don't have a steersman.

Bixby: He did?

Sam: How would you like to teach me about the river?

Bixby: I wouldn't.

Sam: I could be your apprentice.

Bixby: You boys think that being a pilot just means standing at the wheel and ringing bells. Well, there's more to it than that.

Sam: I expect there is.

Bixby: Being a pilot is no job for a coward. It can be awfully terrifying at times. Have you got the nerve for that, boy?

Sam (*gulping*): I hope so.

Bixby: "Hope so" and "think so" have got no place on the river. "Know so" is the only thing we care about.

Sam: I'm willing to pay for the learning. I've got $100.

Bixby: You kids are more trouble than you're worth. Have you ever done any steering?

Sam: I was raised on the river. I've steered everything that floats — except a steamboat. And I reckon I could do that, once I've learned how.

Bixby: What's your name, son?

Sam: Sam, sir.

Bixby: Do you drink?

Sam: No.

Bixby: Do you gamble?

Sam: No, but I could learn how to.

Bixby: Do you tell the truth?

Sam: Do I lie? No, sir. Now and then I tell whoppers, but only when there's no harm in it.

Bixby: Well, I reckon Horace Bixby is your man. You can have the bunk next to Ritchie. (*Sam and Ritchie grin at each other.*) Now stand over here next to me.

(*He points.*) That's 12-Mile Point behind us. We stay by the bank until we get to Sheep-Nose Point. Here's where we start to cross the river. The water gets shallow around here. See where those ripples flatten out? That's a reef. There's a break in the reef where we can go through. Otherwise, we'd run aground. (*Bixby steers the boat through the reef, as Sam watches.*)

(*The next morning before dawn, Sam is asleep. Ritchie steps into their cabin and shakes Sam awake.*)

Sam (*sleepy*): What are you doing?

Ritchie: Get up to the wheelhouse.

Sam: But it's the middle of the night.

Ritchie: It's past four o'clock, and it's your watch again.

Sam: But I've only had four hours of sleep. I thought steamboats tied up for the night.

Ritchie: Some of them do. It's up to the pilots. Bixby and Ealer can steer at midnight as well as by daylight. It makes no difference to them.

(*Still yawning, Sam goes to the wheelhouse.*)

Bixby: All right, Sam. What's the name of the first point above Harrison's landing?

Sam: I don't know.

Bixby: What's the name of the next point?

Sam: I don't know that, either.

Bixby: Well, what do you know?

Sam: I guess I don't know anything.

Bixby: I believe that. You are the stupidest dunderhead I've ever seen. What makes you think you could be a pilot? You couldn't steer a cow down a lane. Now why do you think I told you the names of those points?

Sam *(puzzled):* I thought you did it to be entertaining.

Bixby: Do you think you're in this wheelhouse to learn funny songs and dances? No, by dogs! You're here to learn the river. There it is, boy — the Mississippi. *(Sam looks at the river.)* It's 1,200 miles long from New Orleans to St. Louis. It's filled with the ghosts of dead steamboats and bad pilots. You'd better know where you are out there, boy.

Sam: Yes, sir.

Bixby: You must get a notebook. When I tell you something, put it down right away. There's only one way to be a pilot. You must learn this river by heart.

(A few days later, Sam is sitting on the deck with a notebook. Ritchie walks up and reads it over his shoulder.)

Ritchie: You've got the whole river written down here!

Sam: It's in the book, all right. I just wish it were in my head. I can't remember any of it. At this rate, I'll never learn it.

Ritchie: Don't worry. Look at the river now. Isn't it beautiful?

Sam: Once, I would have said it was romantic. But now, the river appears different. Mr. Bixby has changed it all. Take that sunset. I used to feel holy just looking at a sight like that. Now, I look at it and wonder if the color means rain tomorrow. Do you see that silver streak on the water? It's like something a painter would put in, just to look pretty. But I know it's really a new reef that's there to catch steamboats. Beauty is fine, Ritchie, but it doesn't count for much on the river.

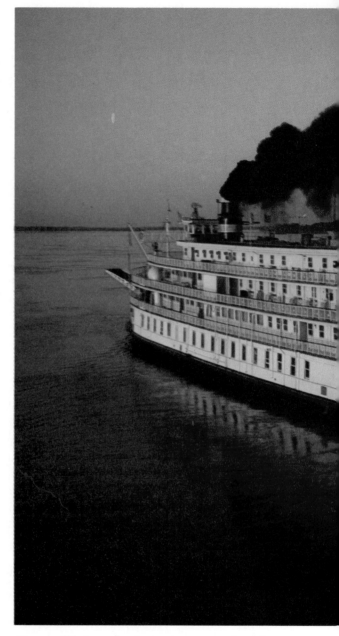

(Later, Bixby asks Sam more questions.)

Bixby: What's the shape of Walnut Bend?

Sam *(startled):* I didn't know it had a special shape.

Bixby: You're too much, boy! The shape of the river is the most important thing. Of course, it never looks the same.

Sam: Then how in creation am I ever going to learn it?

Bixby: How do you follow a hallway at home in the dark? You learn the shape of it. You steer through the dark hall by the shape you remember.

Sam: My hallway is the same shape going

in or coming out. The river is different going upstream or downstream.

Bixby: It's also different at day and at night. Do you hear that dog barking?

Sam: Yes, sir.

Bixby: Remember the sound. You'll know where you are if you hear it on a dark night.

Sam: Do you expect me to remember things like that?

Bixby: Yes, if you want to be a pilot.

Sam: I might as well quit right now. I haven't got brains enough to be a pilot.

Bixby *(angry):* Stop that! When I say I'll teach a man the river, I mean it. I'll teach him or kill him!

(One day, the boat stops to pick up a group of men. Ritchie explains to Sam who they are.)

Ritchie: They call themselves "river inspectors." They're really pilots out of work, going to Memphis for new jobs. They get to ride free. They pretend they're inspecting the river. Mostly they just lie around and eat and bother the pilot. *(He points at a thin, mean-looking man.)* His name is Brown. He's a pretty good pilot, but he's meaner than a snake!

(At the next landing, Bixby goes ashore. He has told Sam to meet him at a restaurant later. When Sam heads toward the restaurant, Brown stops him.)

Brown: You're Bixby's cub, aren't you?

Sam: Yes, sir.

Brown: I just got a job on the *Anna Louise.* I need someone who knows the river below Goose Island. How would you like to steer for me?

Sam: I can't leave Mr. Bixby. He's teaching me the river.

Brown: I'll pay you 50 cents a week, with the teaching thrown in.

Sam: I've got a responsibility to Mr. Bixby. He's always fair to me. I can't let him down. Besides, I wouldn't work for someone who would try to steal me away from another pilot.

Brown: Don't get smart with me! *(Sam begins to walk away.)* I won't forget you. It's a big river, but we'll meet on it someday. Then you'll be sorry!

(Sam meets Bixby at the restaurant.)

Bixby: I'm leaving the *Paul Jones.* I've just signed onto the *Aleck Scott.*

Sam *(disappointed):* That's nice.

Bixby: I thought you'd be happy for me. The *Aleck Scott* is the finest boat on the lower Mississippi.

Sam *(politely):* Is that so? Will you be needing someone to steer for you?

Bixby: Yes, but it can't be just anybody. The *Aleck Scott* needs someone who knows his stuff.

Sam: It won't be hard for you to find someone good.

Bixby: On the other hand, he doesn't have to be too smart. Any fool will do. *(He grins.)* Were you thinking of applying?

Sam: If you thought I'd leave you behind, you're more of a fool than I thought.

(Sam and Bixby join the Aleck Scott. *The other steersman, Tom, is Sam's age. Right away, the two of them start bragging.)*

Tom: My pilot, Thornburg, is the best pilot on the river. I guess Bixby's all right, though.

Sam: Bixby's the best pilot since Noah steered the Ark. Bixby holds the record for the run from Natchez to New Orleans.

Tom: Skill is more important than speed. Some people call Thornburg "Low-Water Thornburg." Once he took the *Sally Henry* right across a swamp. There were only three inches of water. He is famous for that, all right. *(Sam hasn't swallowed this tale. He decides to make up a taller tale.)*

Sam: There are lots of swamps you can go through. What really takes skill is going where there's no water at all.

Tom *(sarcastically):* I'd like to hear about that.

Sam: I'm surprised you haven't heard about it already. A boat got stranded two miles up a dry creek after a flash flood. The captain hired Bixby to get it back into the river. So Bixby put an ad in the papers for the saddest woman in the country. She soon turned up, crying away.

Tom: What was she crying about?

Sam: She married a man with seven children and a hundred debts. Then he ran off with a pretty girl from the circus, leaving his wife with all the problems. Well, Bixby put this woman at the back of the boat, right by the paddle wheel. He told her to cry for all she was worth. He put his mate beside her to sing sad songs. Well, Bixby brought the boat back two miles on the tears of a weeping woman.

Tom: I didn't know you could tell a whopper like that. You've got a real talent.

(At the next stop, a girl named Emmeline and her parents get on. Tom and Sam compete for her attention. Tom shows her around the boat, and tells her tall tales about himself. One day, she goes to the wheelhouse to draw a picture. Sam can't help showing off.)

Sam *(into the speaking tube):* Ben, how are we fixed for wood?

Bixby: You know we just picked up a full load. *(Then he sees how embarrassed Sam is in front of Emmeline.)* I'm going outside. Do you know the river along here?

Sam: I could run this stretch with my eyes closed.

Bixby: It will be okay if you keep them open. *(He leaves.)*

Emmeline: I'm beginning to think that Tom makes up those stories about his heroic deeds. I'd hate to think he was lying to me.

Sam: I know what you mean.

Emmeline: What's that in the water over there?

Sam: That's what's left of a boat that ran aground on an alligator reef.

Emmeline: An alligator reef?

Sam: Sure. Alligators ripped the bottom out of that boat.

Emmeline: That's too much to believe.

Sam: I'm not a liar like Tom. I just know about it because my first job was on an alligator boat.

Emmeline: What is that?

Sam: It's a boat that clears out alligators from a river. There aren't nearly as many now as there used to be.

Emmeline *(impressed):* You must be very strong to turn that wheel.

Sam: I can do it one-handed. *(He tries to*

steer with one hand. The boat goes out of control, and he has to fight to get it straight again.)

Emmeline: Why is this boat going so slowly? Can't you go faster?

Sam: If we use too much steam, the boat could blow up.

Emmeline: Are you scared? *(Sam can't resist a dare.)*

Sam *(into the speaking tube):* Ben, open up to full speed.

(The boat speeds up. On the deck, Captain Klinefelter turns to Bixby.)

Klinefelter: What's that young fool up to?

Bixby *(starting to walk toward the wheelhouse):* He's showing off for some little missy.

Klinefelter: Wait, he's slowing down again now.

Bixby: I still think we should teach him a lesson. Do you know the stretch of river around Island 66?

Klinefelter: Of course. It's so deep there, you couldn't touch the bottom with a church steeple.

Bixby: Right. It's perfect.

(Later on, Sam is alone in the wheelhouse. Klinefelter shouts up to him.)

Klinefelter: Steersman, isn't that shallow water up ahead?

Sam: No, sir. It can't be. *(He looks ahead.)* I can't see it.

Klinefelter: We'd better have it measured. *(He pretends to have the river's depth measured as they go ahead.)* It's only a quarter twain deep!

Sam *(shocked):* What did you say? *(He yells into the speaking tube.)* Stop all the engines! Back her up! Oh, Ben, if you love me, back her up!

(He hears Ben laughing down in the engine room. He turns around and sees Bixby, Klinefelter, Tom, and Emmeline laughing at him.)

Sam *(hurt):* That was a dirty trick to play.

Bixby: Didn't you know there was no bottom at this crossing?

Sam: Yes, sir, I did.

Bixby: Then you shouldn't have let anyone talk you out of it. When you set your course, follow it. And when you think you're in danger, don't turn coward.

(For days, everyone teases Sam. A week later, they stop at a landing. Ritchie comes on board and walks up behind Sam.)

Ritchie: Oh, Ben, if you love me, back her up!

Sam *(turning around):* Ritchie! How are you? Where is the *Paul Jones?*

Ritchie: We just landed. It took us three days longer than you. But at least we didn't get held up at Island 66.

Sam *(embarrassed):* Everyone along this river must have heard that story by now. Well, what are you doing here?

Ritchie: Didn't you hear? Thornburg is leaving the *Aleck Scott.* He's going down to Natchez to help the pilots form a union. Mr. Ealer has been hired to take his place, and he brought me with him.

Sam *(grinning):* That's great! Wait till I tell old Bixby. *(Just then, Bixby appears.)*

Bixby: "Old Bixby" already knows about it. As it happens, I'm going with Thornburg. For the rest of this trip, another pilot is taking my place.

Sam: Do you mean I'll have to steer for someone else? Who will it be?

(Bixby points at the wheelhouse. Sam goes inside — and finds Brown.)

Sam *(shocked):* Mr. Brown!

Brown: So, you were Bixby's cub. Well, you're Brown's cub now. *(Pause.)* Are you going to stand there all day?

Sam: I've had no orders, sir.

Brown: I didn't order any smart-talk, that's for sure. Don't put on airs with me, you derned puppy. Go to the kitchen, and get me a cool drink. And you'd better learn to jump lively!

(A few days later, Sam and Ritchie sit on the deck together. Sam is writing in his notebook.)

Ritchie: Are you still writing down the river in your notebook?

Sam: No. Now I'm writing down ways to murder Brown. I've got 16 ways listed so far. *(He shows the list to Ritchie.)*

Ritchie: Shouldn't you use a secret code? If somebody found this, it could be used for evidence.

Sam: I haven't done anything against the law — yet. Hey, how about "pounding him into the deck with a hammer"? That makes 17.

(Sam and Brown are in the wheelhouse. The clerk, Henry, looks in the door. He has a message from the captain, but he is terrified of Brown. He tries to tell Brown to cross the river to a landing, but Brown ignores him. Sam gives a sign to Henry that he will tell Brown. Henry slips away.)

Sam: Mr. Brown?

Brown: What do you want?

Sam: The captain's clerk was here, sir.

Brown: Do you think I'm blind? I saw him. I don't like you chattering while you're on duty. Don't speak until you're spoken to.

Sam: But —

Brown: Keep your mouth shut!

(On the deck, Captain Klinefelter is watching the shore. He turns and goes into the wheelhouse.)

Klinefelter *(angry):* Mr. Brown, didn't Henry give you my message? You were supposed to stop at Jones's landing across the river.

Brown: That's the first I've heard of it.

Klinefelter: I sent him to tell you.

Brown: I saw him, but the fool never said a thing.

Klinefelter *(to Sam):* Didn't you hear him?

Sam: Yes, sir.

Brown: Shut your mouth, boy! You never heard anything of the kind!

(Klinefelter leaves.)

Sam *(to Brown):* You lied. Henry did tell you. *(Brown tries to hit Sam, and Sam knocks him down. As they fight, Sam notices that no one is steering the boat. He runs to the wheel and begins steering.)*

Brown: You tried to kill me, you devil. I'll charge you with an attempt to murder. You'll be in prison for life, you butter-faced pup. Give me that wheel. *(He tries to push Sam away from the wheel.)* I'll give you a taste of my temper.

Sam: I've had all of your temper I want. You're a miserable old tyrant. You can have your old steamboat back. *(He stops when he sees Klinefelter watching them from the deck and frowning.)*

(Later, Sam is called into Klinefelter's cabin.)

Klinefelter: Have you been fighting with Mr. Brown?

Sam: Yes, sir.

Klinefelter: Do you know that that is a very serious matter?

Sam: Yes, sir.

Klinefelter: This boat was going down the river with no one steering at one point.

Sam: Yes, sir.

Klinefelter: Did you hit him first?

Sam: Yes, sir.

Klinefelter: Did you hit him hard?

Sam: You might say so, sir.

Klinefelter: I'm glad you did. *(He grins.)* Don't tell anyone I said that. I don't ever want you to fight on this boat again. But wait for Brown on shore sometime. Then give him a good beating. *(He winks at Sam. Sam is surprised and relieved. Klinefelter opens the cabin door and speaks loudly in case anyone outside the cabin is listening.)* Now get out of here, you puppy! *(Sam leaves, and Brown enters Klinefelter's cabin.)*

Brown: I hope you ordered him to get off the boat. I won't turn the wheel while that cub stays.

Klinefelter: He doesn't have to be in the wheelhouse while you're there.

Brown: I won't stay on the same boat with him! One of us must go ashore.

Klinefelter: Very well.

(In a short while, Sam and Klinefelter stand on the deck. They watch Brown being taken to shore in a rowboat.)

Klinefelter: Thanks to you, this boat has only one pilot now.

Sam *(trying to look sorry)*: Yes, sir, I know.

Klinefelter: I think you should take over until Mr. Bixby gets back.

Sam: Yes, sir. *(Now he looks excited.)* Thanks!

(Meanwhile, Ritchie has been made pilot of the Paul Jones. *One night in a terrible river accident, the boat explodes. Seeing the explosion, Sam races the* Aleck Scott *to the scene — only to find that Ritchie is dead. He is shocked and very saddened.*

(A few weeks later, Bixby returns to the Aleck Scott. *He has heard about Ritchie's death, and he is concerned about Sam. He hurries to the wheelhouse, where Sam is steering.)*

Bixby: Hello, Sam.

Sam *(cool and calm)*: Hello, Mr. Bixby.

Bixby: I heard about Ritchie, and I'm sorry. *(There's an awkward pause. Then Bixby changes the subject.)* I see you're steering on your own now. When I heard about Brown, I wasn't sure I'd still find you on the river. But I hoped so.

Sam: Someone once told me that "hope so" has no place on the river.

Bixby: *(looking out at the river)*: Hey, where are you going?

Sam: I'm starting to cross.

Bixby: It's too soon. Wait until you reach that point up there.

Sam: That was three weeks ago. The river has been rising since then. The easy water is down here now.

Bixby: Oh, you think so? *(They smile at each other, and Bixby shakes Sam's hand. Sam is a real pilot now.)*

READING COMPREHENSION

Select the best choice to complete each statement below. Then write the entire sentence on your paper.

1. Sam said that he told "whoppers." He meant that he _____.
   a. told lies to get out of doing work
   b. didn't know truth from fiction
   c. liked to tell tales to amuse others

2. Sam was upset when he found out that Brown had replaced Bixby as pilot because Sam _____.
   a. didn't like Brown
   b. was afraid that Bixby was sick
   c. didn't think Brown was a good pilot

3. Sam told Klinefelter that he had hit Brown. Klinefelter thought that Brown _____.
   a. should have hit Sam back
   b. deserved it
   c. should have come and told him

4. By the end of the play, Sam had become _____.
   a. confident and sure
   b. frightened and upset
   c. careless and foolish

For Discussion

1. What was Sam's attitude toward the Mississippi River before he began learning to be a pilot? How did that attitude change?

2. What do you think was the most important lesson Sam learned on the river? Explain your answer.

UNDERSTANDING LITERATURE

Sequence. The order of the events in a story or play is called *sequence*. Placing events in the correct sequence insures an understanding of *what* happened and when it happened in a story.

Group A and Group B below are lists of events from "Life on the Mississippi." On your paper, place the events in the proper sequence for each group. Then combine the two groups and see if the entire list is in the correct sequence.

Group A

Ritchie woke Sam for his first night shift.

Sam began using a notebook.

Bixby took Sam along to the *Aleck Scott*.

Sam asked Bixby for a chance to learn how to be a pilot.

Sam told Brown that he'd stay with Bixby.

Group B

Bixby and Klinefelter tricked Sam.

Sam showed off in front of Emmeline.

Sam became Brown's "cub."

Sam told the whopper about how a woman's tears helped Bixby free a boat.

Sam and Brown fought in the wheelhouse.

Brown was kicked off the boat and Sam was placed in command.

Writing

Imagine that you are Sam. Write a letter to a friend about your experiences on the river. Explain how you feel about Bixby, Klinefelter, Ritchie, and Brown.

There Was a Child Went Forth

by Walt Whitman

There was a child went forth every day,
And the first object he look'd upon, that object he became,
And that object became part of him for the day or a certain
    part of the day,
Or for many years or stretching cycles of years.

The early lilacs became part of this child,
And grass and white and red morning-glories, and white and
    red clover, and the song of the phoebe-bird,
And the third-month lambs and the sow's pink-faint litter, and
    the mare's foal and the cow's calf,
And the noisy brood of the barnyard or by the mire of the
    pond-side,
And the fish suspending themselves so curiously below there,
    and the beautiful curious liquid,
And the water-plants with their graceful flat heads, all became
    part of him. . . .

And the schoolmistress that pass'd on her way to the school,
And the friendly boys that pass'd, and the quarrelsome boys,
And the tidy and fresh-cheek'd girls, and the barefoot Negro
    boy and girl,
And all the changes of city and country wherever he went.

The mother at home quietly placing the dishes on the supper-
    table,
The mother with mild words, clean her cap and gown, a
    wholesome odor falling off her person and clothes as she
    walks by,

The father, strong, self-sufficient, manly, mean, anger'd, unjust,
The blow, the quick loud word, the tight bargain, the crafty
      lure,
The family usages, the language, the company, the furniture, the
      yearning and swelling heart . . .
The doubts of day-time and the doubts of night-time, the
      curious whether and how,
Whether that which appears so is so, or is it all flashes and
      specks?
Men and women crowding fast in the streets, if they are not
      flashes and specks what are they?

Weaning the Calf, Winslow Homer, 1875

The streets themselves and the facade of houses, and goods in
    the windows,
Vehicles, teams, the heavy-plank'd wharves, the huge crossing at
    the ferries,
The village on the highland seen from afar at sunset, the river
    between . . .
The hurrying tumbling waves, quick-broken crests, slapping . . .
The horizon's edge, the flying sea-crow, the fragrance of salt
    marsh and shore mud,
These became part of that child who went forth every day, and
    who now goes, and will always go forth every day.

1. This poem describes the many influences upon a child's life, from things in nature like the early lilacs to the people in his family. How do they all become a "part of him"?

2. This poem is filled with descriptions of the world around the child. What was this world like? Is it like a child's world today?

3. The poem points out many contrasts, or opposites, in the boy's life. For example, the father is both strong and mean, and the boys are both friendly and quarrelsome. What contrasts have you observed in your daily life?

161

Ain't I a Woman?

by Sojourner Truth

Sojourner Truth (1795–1883) was born a slave. She changed her name from Belle to Sojourner Truth when she won her freedom in 1827. A sojourner is a traveler, and she traveled throughout the country raising support for the abolitionist movement and for women's rights. She delivered the following speech at a women's-rights convention in 1851.

Well, Children, where there is so much racket there must be something out of kilter. I think that between the Negroes of the South and the women at the North, all talking about rights, the white men will be in a fix pretty soon. But what's all this here talking about?

That man over there says that women need to be helped into carriages, and lifted over ditches, and to have the best place everywhere. Nobody ever helps me into carriages, or over mud puddles, or gives me any best place! And ain't I a woman? Look at me! Look at my arm! I have ploughed and planted. I have gathered into barns, and no man could head me! And ain't I a woman? I could work as much as a man — when I could get it — and bear the lash as well! And ain't I a woman? I have borne 13 children, and seen them most all sold off to slavery. When I cried out with my mother's grief, none but Jesus heard me! And ain't I a woman?

Then they talk about this thing in the head; what's this they call it? [Intellect, someone whispers.] That's it, honey. What's that got to do with women's rights or Negro's rights? If my cup won't hold but a pint, and yours holds a quart, wouldn't you be mean not to let me have my little half-measure full?

Then that little man in black there, he says women can't have as much rights as men, 'cause Christ wasn't a woman! Where did your Christ come from? Where did your Christ come from? From God and a woman! Man had nothing to do with Him.

If the first woman God ever made was strong enough to turn the world upside down all alone, these women together ought to be able to turn it back, and get it right side up again! And now they is asking to do it, the men better let them.

Obliged to you for hearing me, and now old Sojourner ain't got nothing more to say.

Sojourner Truth, Unknown Artist

1. How did Sojourner Truth describe her life? How did this compare with how a male speaker had said women should be treated?

2. Do you think Sojourner agreed that women should be "helped into carriages . . . and have the best place everywhere"? Why or why not?

Civil War Nurse

by Louisa May Alcott

Louisa May Alcott (1832–1888) is best known as the author of the famous novels Little Women *and* Little Men. *Raised in Massachusetts, she spent about a year working in Union Army hospitals during the Civil War. In 1863 she wrote a book about her experiences called* Hospital Sketches. *The following selection comes from that book. It describes her work as a nurse and her feelings about her patients.*

The hours I like best are at night, and so I was soon promoted to night nurse. I usually found the men in the most cheerful state of mind their condition allowed.

The evenings were spent in reading aloud and writing letters. I waited on and amused the men, and went with Dr. P. as he made his second daily rounds. I cared for my dozens of wounds, giving last doses of medicine and making the men cozy for the long hours to come.

I had managed to sort out the patients in the ward into three rooms. One I visited with a tray full of bandages and pins. Another I visited with books, flowers, games, and happy talk. To the third room I brought lullabies, kind words, and sometimes a helping hand in time of death.

The night I am writing about opened with a little comedy and closed with a little tragedy. I was watching beside the bed of a 12-year-old drummer boy who had come to us after a dreadful battle. A slight wound in the knee brought him there, but his mind had suffered more than his body. For days he had been reliving in his thoughts the scenes he could not forget. Then he would break out in terrible sobs which were pitiful to hear.

As I sat by him, I tried to soothe his poor brain by the constant touch of my hands over his hot forehead. In his mind he was cheering his comrades on, then counting them as they fell around him. He often grabbed my arm to drag me from the neighborhood of a bursting shell. His face burned with fever, his eyes were restless, and his head was never still. A constant stream of shouts, warnings, and broken cries poured from his lips.

It was past 11:00 and my patient was slowly wearing himself into periods of quiet. In one of these pauses, I heard a curious sound. I looked over my shoulder and saw a one-legged man hopping around the room. I recognized a soldier whose fever had taken a turn for the worse and left his mind in a state of confusion. At this point he informed me he was heading for home. When his mind was clear, the least movement produced a roar of pain. But the loss of reason seemed to have caused a change in the man and in his manner. He balanced himself on one leg like a stork and refused any suggestion of mine to return to bed.

I couldn't think what to do with this creature. I was about to run for help when another wounded soldier came to the rescue. He put an end to the crisis by carrying the lively one-legged man to his bed. The one-legged soldier was worn out from his efforts and soon fell asleep.

My rescuer and I enjoyed a great laugh together, then returned to our places. Then the sound of a sob came from a bed in the corner. It was the little drummer boy. He was trying to control the sad sounds that kept breaking out.

"What is it, Teddy?" I asked, as he rubbed the tears away.

"I've got a pain, ma'am, but I'm not crying for that, because I'm used to it. I dreamed Kit was here, and when I woke up he wasn't, and I couldn't help it then."

Kit was a good friend, badly hurt himself, who would not leave the drummer behind. He had wrapped him in his own blanket and carried him in his arms to the ambulance. Kit died at the door of the hospital which promised care and comfort for the drummer boy.

For 10 days Teddy refused to be comforted because he had not been able to thank Kit for his protection, which may have cost him his life. This thought had been troubling him in secret. I told him that his friend probably would have died in any case, but I couldn't end his sorrow.

As I was comforting him, a message I had been fearing came for me.

"John is going, ma'am, and wants to see you, if you can come."

"I'll be there the moment this boy is asleep. Tell John so, and let me know if I am in danger of being too late."

The messenger left and while I quieted the drummer, I thought of John. He had come in a day or two after the others and was put in my "pitiful" room. He was a large man with a fine face and the most peaceful eyes I have ever seen.

When he came, I watched him for a night or two before I made friends with him. He seldom spoke and never complained. He was thoughtful and concerned while watching the sufferings of others, as if he forgot his own.

One night, as I went on my rounds with Dr. P., I asked which man in the room probably suffered most. To my great surprise, the doctor glanced at John.

"Every breath he draws is like a stab, for the bullet went into his left lung and broke a rib. The poor man can find no rest because he must lie on his wounded back or else he can't breathe. It will be a long, hard struggle because of his great strength, but even this can't save him."

"You don't mean he must die, Doctor?"

"There's not the slightest hope for him, and you'd better tell him so before long.

The Letter Home, Eastman Johnson, 1863

You have a way of doing such things comfortably, so I leave it to you. He won't last more than a day or two at the most."

I could have sat down on the spot and cried if I had not learned to save my tears for spare moments. Such an end seemed very hard for such a fine man. The army needed men like John who fight for freedom with both heart and hand. I could not give him up so soon. It was an easy thing for Dr. P. to say, "Tell him he must die," but a hard thing to do. I didn't have the heart to do it then, and I hoped that some change for the better might take place in spite of what Dr. P. had said.

A few minutes later I came in and saw John sitting up with no one to support him. The doctor was changing the bandage on his back.

The doctor's words made me feel sad that I had not given John those little cares and kindnesses that make the heavy hours pass easier. He looked very lonely just then, as he sat with bent head and hands folded on his knee. I saw no sign of suffering till I looked nearer. Then I saw great tears roll down and drop upon the floor. It was a new sight there. Though I had seen many men suffer in silence or with groans of pain, none of them cried. It did not seem weak, only very moving. My heart opened wide and took him in. I gathered the bent head in my arms as freely as if he had been a little child and said, "Let me help you bear it, John."

Never on any human face have I seen so beautiful a look of thanks, surprise, and comfort, as that which he gave me.

"Thank you, ma'am," he whispered. "This is just what I wanted!"

"Then why not ask for it before?"

"I didn't like to be a trouble. You seemed so busy, and I could manage to get on alone."

"You shall not want it anymore, John."

Now I understood the sad look he sometimes gave me as I went out after a brief pause beside his bed. I had been used to stopping with those who seemed to need me more than he did. But now I knew that I brought as much comfort to

him as to the others. I took the place of his mother, wife, or sister. Now while I cared for his wounds, he leaned against me, holding my hand tightly. If pain brought forth tears from him, no one saw them fall but me. I found him the manliest man of all of them, shy and brave and natural. I saw his goodness and his dreams, which had helped to make him what he was.

After that night I gave an hour of each evening that remained of his life to his comfort and pleasure. He could only speak in whispers, but what he told me added to the warmth and respect I felt for him.

Once I asked him, "Do you ever regret that you came, when you lie here suffering so much?"

"Never, ma'am," he answered. "I have not helped a great deal, but I've shown I was willing to give my life, and maybe I have to. But I don't blame anybody, and if it was to do over again, I'd do it."

Then he suddenly asked: "This is my first battle. Do they think it's going to be my last?"

"I'm afraid they do, John."

It was the hardest question I ever had been called upon to answer. His clear eyes were fixed on mine, forcing a truthful answer by their own truth. He seemed a little surprised at first, as he considered the terrible fact. Then he shook his head and spoke.

"I'm not afraid, but it's difficult to believe all at once. It doesn't seem possible for such a little wound to kill me."

But John had never seen the great holes between his shoulders. He saw only the awful sights about him, and he could not believe his own wound was worse than these.

"Shall I write your mother now?" I asked, thinking that the news I had just given him might change all his plans. But I think I should have guessed his answer, knowing him as I did.

"No, ma'am, to my brother just the same. He'll break the news to her best, and I'll add a line to her myself when you get done. I hope the answer will come in time for me to see it."

These things had happened two days earlier. Now John was dying, and the letter had not come. I had been called to many deathbeds in my life, but to none that made my heart ache as it did then. As I went in, John stretched out both hands.

"I knew you would come! I guess I'm moving on, ma'am."

He was dying so quickly that even as he spoke I saw his face grow paler. I sat down by him and wiped the drops from his forehead. I stirred the air about him with a slow wave of the fan, and waited to help him die. He stood in need of help, and I could do so little. As the doctor had said, the strong body fought against death every inch of the way. He was forced to draw each breath with pain. For hours he suffered, yet through it all, his eyes never lost their perfect calm, and his strong spirit showed in them.

Suddenly he rose up in his bed and cried out with a bitter cry that broke the silence with its terrible suffering: "For God's sake, give me air!"

It was the only cry that pain or death had squeezed from him, the only favor he had asked. None of us could grant it, for all the airs that blew were useless now. We threw up the window. The first red light of dawn was warming the sky, and we could see the rising sun. John saw it, and laid himself gently down and sighed deeply. We knew then that for him suffering was forever past. He died then, and though the heavy breaths still continued, he never spoke again. To the end he held my hand close, so close that when he was asleep at last, I could not draw it away. I felt glad that perhaps my touch had eased his hardest hour.

When they had gotten him ready for the grave, John looked to me like a hero. I felt a tender pride in my lost patient. The lovely expression on his face soon replaced the marks of pain. I longed for those who loved him best to see him as he had accepted Death.

As we stood looking at him, a letter was handed to me which had been forgotten the night before. It was John's letter, come just an hour too late for him to see it. Yet he did have it, for after I had cut some of his hair for his mother, I took off his ring to send to her. Then I kissed him for her sake, and laid the letter in his hand. I felt that its place was with him. I made myself happy with the thought that even now he would have some token of the love which makes life beautiful and lives on past death.

Then I left him, glad to have known so fine a man, and carrying with me a lasting memory of him. I remembered John as he lay calmly waiting for the dawn of that long day which knows no night.

READING COMPREHENSION

Select the best choice to complete each statement below. Then write the entire sentence on your paper.

1. Alcott spent most of her time _____.
   a. giving out the medicine
   b. helping the men write letters
   c. comforting the men

2. The little drummer boy suffered most from his _____.
   a. doctor
   b. memories
   c. wounds

3. When Alcott found out how much John suffered, she was surprised because he _____.
   a. had never complained
   b. slept so much
   c. was always telling jokes

4. When Alcott tried to comfort John, he was _____.
   a. grateful
   b. angry
   c. scared

For Discussion

1. What qualities did a good Civil War nurse need? Do you think many people could have done Alcott's job? Why or why not?

2. How did John feel about his own death? Was he able to accept it? Did he regret having gone to war? How do you think his family will feel about the war when they hear of his death?

UNDERSTANDING LITERATURE

Ironic Turn of Events. A series of events makes up a story. Each event helps us anticipate, or expect what will happen, next. Sometimes what happens is different from what was expected. This is called an *ironic turn of events*. For example, in "Civil War Nurse," John complained the *least* of all the soldiers, but he was in the greatest pain.

An ironic turn of events often occurs when something is not expected because it seems so unfair. For example, Kit carried Teddy off the battlefield only to die on the hospital steps.

Read the following sentences. On your paper, tell why each is ironic.

1. Teddy screamed out in anguish at the memory of his friend's wounds.

2. John's tears demonstrated his manliness.

3. John said that he had no regrets about coming to war.

4. John's letter arrived too late, but he still received it.

Writing

Pretend you are Alcott. Write a letter to John's family to inform them of his death. What would you say about John? What would you say about the way he died? Make sure that you describe both John's personality and the nature of his injuries. In your letter, explain what you felt was ironic about John's stay in the hospital.

A Horseman in the Sky

by Ambrose Bierce

Born and raised in the Midwest, Ambrose Bierce (1842–1914) enlisted in the Union Army at the age of 19. He fought bravely in many battles and was seriously wounded in 1865. By the end of the war, the death and suffering he had seen on the battlefield made Bierce a bitter man, and he had begun to doubt whether the Northern cause was right. In the story you are about to read, Bierce describes the tragedy that results when two members of the same family fight on opposite sides in the war.

A soldier lay by the side of a road in western Virginia. It was a sunny autumn afternoon in 1861. The soldier's right hand loosely held his rifle. People might have thought him dead. But he had fallen asleep while on guard duty. If discovered by his men, he would be shot.

The road where the soldier lay ran west along the top of a cliff. Then it turned south, zigzagging down through a green forest. But before the road turned south, there was a large flat rock. Looking down from the rock, one could see a deep, wooded valley. A stone dropped from this point would have fallen 1,000 feet. The valley was surrounded by other high cliffs. It looked as if there were no way in and no way out.

But five regiments of Union soldiers were hidden in the valley. They had marched all day and night. Now they were resting. When it was dark, they would climb to where their guard now slept. Then they would walk quietly down the southern side of the mountain. This road would lead them to the rear of the enemy camp. Their surprise attack was planned for midnight.

The sleeping soldier was a young Virginian named Carter Druse. He was the only child of rich parents. And he had always lived in the mountain country of western Virginia. His home was only a few miles from where he now lay.

Carter usually ate a peaceful breakfast

with his father. But one morning had been different. Carter got up from the table. He watched his father eating. Then he said: "Father, there are Union soldiers at Grafton. I am going to join them."

Carter's father stopped eating. His face was pale and sad. It was a long time before he spoke. "You must do what you think is right. But . . . you are a traitor to Virginia."

Carter Druse said nothing.

"Virginia," his father said, "will get along without you. But your mother is very ill. She won't live longer than a few weeks. Please don't upset her with your news."

Carter Druse bowed to his broken-hearted father. He left his childhood home to go to war. Carter was courageous and did well in the Union Army. Up until now. . . .

Now he was asleep at his guard duty. But something somewhere woke him up. Carter quietly raised his head from his arm and looked around him. His first feeling was of great delight. For at the edge of the rock was a horse and rider of great dignity.

The rider looked like a Greek god carved in marble. His gray costume blended with the sky. The face of this horseman was turned slightly away. He was looking down to the bottom of the valley. The rider and the horse appeared much larger than they actually were.

Carter had a strange feeling. He felt as if he'd slept till the end of the war. And now he was looking at a great work of art that honored the deeds of the past.

This feeling left him as the horse moved slightly backward. The man remained motionless. Carter was now wide awake. He carefully brought the butt of the rifle against his cheek. He cocked the gun. A touch upon the trigger and the other man would be dead.

But the horseman turned his head and looked in Carter's direction. He seemed to look into Carter's face, into his eyes. It was as if the horseman could see into Carter's brave, sympathetic heart.

Is it so terrible to kill an enemy in war? Carter asked himself that question. After all, this horseman was a threat to Carter and his fellow soldiers. Carter Druse grew pale. He was trembling and felt faint. His hand fell away from his gun. His head slowly dropped until his face rested on a pile of leaves.

But these frightened feelings did not last long. In another moment, Carter raised his face from the leaves. He put his hands around the rifle. His finger found the trigger. His mind, heart, and eyes were clear. His conscience was sound. He could not hope to capture that enemy. If Carter alarmed the horseman, he would go dashing to the enemy camp. Carter's duty was plain. The man must be shot dead without warning. But . . .

Perhaps the man had discovered nothing. Perhaps he was only admiring the scenery. If allowed, the horseman might turn and ride away. Carter looked down the bottom of the valley. Creeping along the green meadow were a line of men and horses. Some foolish commander was letting the soldiers water their horses in the open. They were in plain view of the horseman.

Carter looked away from the valley. He steadied his rifle, staring again at the man and horse. His father's words came back to him: "You must do what you think is right." Carter was calm now. His nerves were like a sleeping baby's. His breathing was regular and slow. Duty had won. He fired.

A Union officer, looking for adventure, left his hidden camp in the valley. He made his way to an open space near the foot of the cliff. The officer looked up dizzily to the top of the gigantic cliff. It was then that he saw an amazing sight. A man on horseback was riding down into the valley through the air!

The rider sat straight in his saddle. He held the reins firmly. His long hair streamed upward. His hands were hidden in the horse's lifted mane. The animal's body was level. Its movements were those of a wild gallop. The horse threw its legs forward as if it were leaping. But this was flight!

The officer was filled with amazement and terror by the horseman in the sky. His legs failed him, and he fell. Almost at the same time, he heard a crashing sound in the trees. Then all was still. There was no echo.

Trembling, the officer rose to his feet. He ran away from the cliff to a point where he expected to find the horseman. But there was no sign of him. The officer had forgotten that the horse and its rider would fall directly downward. He could have found them at the very foot of the cliff. A half-hour later he returned to camp.

The officer was a smart man. He knew better than to tell what might seem an impossible lie. He said nothing of what he had seen.

After firing his shot, Private Carter Druse reloaded his rifle. He continued his watch over the valley. Ten minutes later a Union sergeant crept carefully to him on hands and knees. Carter didn't turn his head or look at him.

"Did you fire?" the sergeant whispered.

"Yes."

"At what?"

"A horse. It was standing on that rock, pretty far out. It's no longer there. It went over the cliff."

Carter's face was white. He showed no other sign of emotion. Having answered, he turned away and said no more. The sergeant did not understand.

"See here, Druse," he said. "It's no use making a mystery. I order you to report. Was there anybody on the horse?"

"Yes."

"Well?"

"My father. . . . My father was on the horse."

The sergeant rose to his feet and walked away. "Good God!" he said.

READING COMPREHENSION

Select the best choice to complete each statement below. Then write the entire sentence on your paper.

1. Carter's father told him that if he joined the Union Army, he would be _____.
   a. treated badly
   b. a traitor to Virginia
   c. sent away

2. When Carter left to join the Union Army, his father was _____.
   a. glad
   b. accepting
   c. very unhappy

3. To Carter, doing what he thought was right was more important than _____.
   a. serving guard duty
   b. sparing his father's life
   c. being a general

4. "A Horseman in the Sky" was _____.
   a. a horse and rider who had fallen off a cliff
   b. a wild, flying horse
   c. probably an imaginary scene

For Discussion

1. What kind of person was Carter? Did the fact that he fell asleep on guard duty affect his decision to shoot his father's horse? Did Carter really think that if he shot the horse his father would be spared?

2. What else could Carter have done? How might this have affected the troops and the ending of the story?

UNDERSTANDING LITERATURE

Surprise Ending. The conclusion of a story that causes some form of shock is called a *surprise ending*. A surprise ending is achieved when an author creates anticipation for an expected ending. In "A Horseman in the Sky," Carter questioned whether he should kill the man on the horse. Carter resolved his conflicts, deciding to do what was "right." We know Carter was very unhappy about taking another man's life. We are shocked to find that Carter's sorrow was not just for another soldier but for his own *father*.

There are usually small clues that warn a reader about a surprise ending. On your paper, choose the events from the following list that are hints of the surprise ending in "A Horseman in the Sky."

1. Carter had been asleep on guard duty.

2. Carter felt a "great delight" when he first saw the man on the horse.

3. Carter was a private.

4. Carter's father's words came to him, and he was able to fire his gun.

5. "Carter Druse grew pale. He was trembling and felt faint. His hand fell away from his gun."

Writing

If you were Carter's commanding officer, what questions would you ask Carter about this incident? Imagine that he answers your questions, and then write a report describing Carter's feelings.

The Raven Days

by Sidney Lanier

Our hearths are gone out, and our
    hearts are broken,
  And but the ghosts of homes to us
    remain,
And ghostly eyes and hollow sighs give
    token
  From friend to friend of an unspoken
    pain.

O, Raven Days, dark Raven Days of
    sorrow,
  Bring to us, in your whetted ivory
    beaks,
Some sign out of the far land of To-
    morrow,
  Some strip of sea-green dawn, some
    orange streaks.

Ye float in dusky files, forever croaking —
  Ye chill our manhood with your
    dreary shade.
Pale, in the dark, not even God
    invoking,
  We lie in chains, too weak to be
    afraid.

O Raven Days, dark Raven Days of
    sorrow,
  Will ever any warm light come again?
Will ever the lit mountains of To-
    morrow
  Begin to gleam across the mournful
    plain?

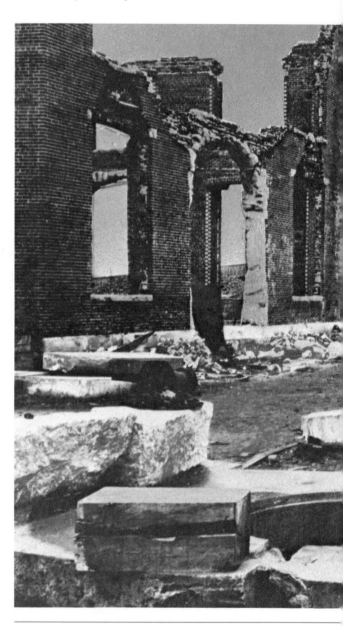

1. Sidney Lanier wrote "The Raven Days" about his southern homeland after the Civil War. How did Lanier feel about the war's affect on the South?

2. Lanier asked for "some sign out of the far land of To-morrow." *To-morrow* stands for the future of the South. What does Lanier seem to be hoping for in the poem?

3. How would you describe Lanier's attitude in the poem? Hopeful? Full of despair? Bitter? Eager for the future? Explain your answer with details from the poem.

I Will Fight No More Forever

by Chief Joseph

The Nez Percé Indians lived in the beautiful Wallowa Valley in Oregon. Although they had an agreement with the U.S. government that the valley belonged to them, the government, under pressure from settlers moving west, broke the treaty. The Nez Percé were told they had to move to a reservation many miles away. War broke out between the Nez Percé and U.S. troops. Anxious to avoid more bloodshed, Chief Joseph (1841–1904) led his people to Canada. Thousands of soldiers gave chase and caught up with them only a few miles from the Canadian border. Chief Joseph surrendered on October 5, 1877, and made the following speech to his captors.

Tell General Howard I know his heart. What he told me before, I have in my heart. I am tired of fighting. Our chiefs are killed. Looking Glass is dead. Toohoolhoolzote is dead. The old men are all dead. It is the young men who say yes and no. He who led on the young men is dead. It is cold and we have no blankets. The little children are freezing to death. My people, some of them, have run away to the hills and have no blankets, no food; no one knows where they are — perhaps freezing to death. I want to have time to look for my children and see how many I can find. Maybe I shall find them among the dead. Hear me, my chiefs. I am tired; my heart is sick and sad. From where the sun now stands I will fight no more forever.

1. What were the reasons given by Chief Joseph for his surrender? Which reason do you feel is the strongest? Explain your opinion.

2. From the evidence you are given in the speech, how would you describe Chief Joseph? What kind of leader do you think he was?

3. Instead of saying, "I will never fight again," Chief Joseph said: "From where the sun now stands I will fight no more forever." How does the wording of the phrase affect its meaning?

Casey at the Bat

by Ernest Lawrence Thayer

It looked extremely rocky for the Mudville nine that day;
The score stood two to four, with but one inning left to play.
So, when Cooney died at second, and Burrows did the same,
A pallor wreathed the features of the patrons of the game.

A straggling few got up to go, leaving there the rest,
With that hope which springs eternal within the human breast,
For they thought: "If only Casey could get a whack at that,"
They'd put up even money now, with Casey at the bat.

But Flynn preceded Casey, and likewise so did Blake,
And the former was a pudd'n, and the latter was a fake.
So on that stricken multitude a deathlike silence sat;
For there seemed but little chance of Casey's getting to the bat.

But Flynn let drive a "single," to the wonderment of all.
And the much-despised Blake "tore the cover off the ball."
And when the dust had lifted, and they saw what had occurred,
There was Blake safe at second, and Flynn a-huggin' third.

Then from the gladdened multitude went up a joyous yell —
It rumbled in the mountaintops, it rattled in the dell;
It struck upon the hillside, and rebounded on the flat;
For Casey, mighty Casey, was advancing to the bat.

There was ease in Casey's manner as he stepped into his place,
There was pride in Casey's bearing and a smile on Casey's face;
And when responding to the cheers he lightly doffed his hat,
No stranger in the crowd could doubt 'twas Casey at the bat.

Ten thousand eyes were on him as he rubbed his hands with dirt,
Five thousand tongues applauded when he wiped them on his shirt;
Then when the writhing pitcher ground the ball into his hip,
Defiance glanced in Casey's eyes, a sneer curled Casey's lip.

And now the leather-covered sphere came hurtling through the air,
And Casey stood a watching it in haughty grandeur there.
Close by the sturdy batsman the ball unheeded sped;
"That ain't my style," said Casey. "Strike one," the umpire said.

From the benches black with people, there went up a muffled roar,
Like the beating of the storm waves on the stern and distant shore.
"Kill him! Kill the umpire!" shouted someone on the stand;
And it's likely they'd have killed him had not Casey raised his hand.

With a smile of Christian charity great Casey's visage shone;
He stilled the rising tumult, he made the game go on;
He signaled to the pitcher, and once more the spheroid flew;
But Casey still ignored it, and the umpire said, "Strike two."

"Fraud!" cried the maddened thousands, and the echo answered, "Fraud!"
But one scornful look from Casey and the audience was awed;
They saw his face grow stern and cold, they saw his muscles strain,
And they knew that Casey wouldn't let the ball go by again.

The sneer is gone from Casey's lips, his teeth are clenched in hate,
He pounds with cruel vengeance his bat upon the plate;
And now the pitcher holds the ball, and now he lets it go,
And now the air is shattered by the force of Casey's blow.

Oh, somewhere in this favored land the sun is shining bright,
The band is playing somewhere, and somewhere hearts are light;
And somewhere men are laughing, and somewhere children shout,
But there is no joy in Mudville — Mighty Casey has struck out.

Select the best choice to complete each statement below. Then write the entire sentence on your paper.

1. When Cooney "died at second," it meant that he _____.
   a. passed away
   b. was buried at second base
   c. was called out

2. Casey was considered a _____.
   a. good umpire
   b. good hitter
   c. good fielder

3. The phrase "the former was a pudd'n" meant that Flynn _____.
   a. was a good player
   b. had a sweet tooth
   c. was not expected to do well

4. When Casey stepped up to the plate, he showed he had _____.
   a. confidence
   b. shyness
   c. fear

5. The crowd wanted to kill the umpire because he _____.
   a. had called a strike on Casey
   b. was a bad man
   c. was not from Mudville

For Discussion

1. Was Casey overconfident? Explain.

2. There may have been "no joy in Mudville," but was the rest of the world affected at all by Casey's strikeout? How important should sports be?

Plot in Narrative Poetry. Poetry is used to express emotions and feelings. Some poems also tell a story. These poems are *narrative poems*. A narrative poem has a series of events that form a plot.

From the following list, choose the *events* that make up the plot of "Casey at the Bat." On your paper, arrange these events in the order that they happened. Be sure to pick events, not emotions, feelings, or descriptions.

1. Casey was a good sport.

2. Casey swung and missed the ball.

3. Casey protected the umpire.

4. Casey liked being in the spotlight.

5. The umpire called strikes on the first two pitches.

6. Mudville lost the ball game.

7. Casey ignored the first two pitches.

8. Casey was angry when he got two strikes.

9. Somewhere hearts were light.

10. Flynn and Blake got hits.

11. It was sad in Mudville after the game.

12. Casey was probably embarrassed to strike out.

Writing

Tell what would have happened if Casey had not struck out. You may copy the style of the poem or write in paragraph form.

Section Review

VOCABULARY

Idioms and Ironic Speech. A phrase with a special meaning is called an *idiom. Kick the bucket* literally means to knock over a bucket. But this phrase has become an idiom that means "to die." A phrase that either exaggerates or understates is called *ironic speech.* The phrase *simply fire in a liquid form* is an example of ironic speech. It exaggerates the awful taste of the medicine in "A Dose of Pain-Killer."

On your paper, match each of the following italicized idioms and examples of ironic speech with its meaning.

1. "Her troubles were instantly at rest, *her soul at peace again.*"

2. "The boy could not have shown a wilder interest if she had *built a fire under him.*"

3. "Tom lay on the floor *expiring with laughter.*"

4. "You couldn't *steer a cow down a lane.*"

5. "You must *learn this river by heart.*"

6. "He's *meaner than a snake!*"

7. "Bixby's the best pilot *since Noah steered the Ark.*"

8. "You'll be in prison for life, you *butter-faced pup.*"

Meanings

a. she was happy, calm
b. laughing hard
c. young, fresh person
d. do the simplest thing
e. that ever lived
f. encouraged him strongly
g. evil
h. memorize it

READING

Sequence and Predicting Outcomes. The plot of a story usually has many events, or incidents. Knowing the order in which these events happen is important to understanding the story. The order in which things happen is called *sequence.*

When you read, keep in mind the sequence of the events in the story. As you are reading, think about what might come next in the sequence. This is called *predicting outcomes.* See if you can guess what is going to happen before it does.

Here are some events from "Civil War Nurse." Number your paper from 1 to 7, and write the statements in the order they happened in the story. One statement is a prediction of something that probably happened after the story ended. One statement is unlikely to have happened and you should leave it out.

Teddy's friend, Kit, carried the boy to safety.

Alcott remembered John and her nursing experiences for the rest of her life.

Alcott became the night nurse.

Alcott told John he was going to die.

Alcott soothed Teddy after a bad dream.

Alcott and John decided to marry after he got out of the hospital.

Alcott gave John his mother's letter.

John asked Alcott to write a letter to his brother.

WRITING A NEW ENDING FOR A STORY

The plot is the pattern of incidents or events that make up a story. In a well-written story, each incident has a purpose. Each incident grows out of what comes before it and leads naturally to what follows.

Often a writer constructs a plot with an interesting turn, or twist. An unexpected event may occur, but when it does, it fits. As you read each incident in a well-written story, you see how it follows the one before it, even if you were not able to predict it in advance.

How a story ends — how the plot is resolved — is important. As a story progresses, sometimes there are several ways it could turn out. The author, of course, has decided where the plot of his or her story will go.

Now it's your turn to have a bit of fun and create your own ending to a story you've already read. Before you begin, here is a checklist to keep in mind:

☐ Identify the problem or conflict established at the beginning of the story. The story's beginning sets up the problem, and each incident in the plot complicates it or brings it closer to the conclusion.

☐ Write your ending so it resolves this problem. The ending may surprise, shock, or satisfy the reader, but it should grow naturally out of the incidents before it.

☐ The way the events affect the story's main character should be an important part of your ending.

Select one of the following, and write your own ending for the story. If you prefer to come up with something completely original, you may do so.

1. In "Civil War Nurse," John's death, although expected, is difficult to take. Rewrite the story so that he manages to survive, even though no one thinks he can. Be sure to include how his survival affects others.

2. In "A Horseman in the Sky," there are several possible alternatives to the ending. Suppose Carter had remained asleep while on duty. Or Carter could have decided not to shoot. Or he could have shot and missed — deliberately or by accident. Another version of the story might have him shooting as he did, but handling his later reactions differently. Pick one of these and write about it to end the story differently, or create your own ending if you can come up with one that's entirely different.

QUIZ

The following is a quiz for Section 4. Write the answers in complete sentences on your paper.

Reading Comprehension

1. In "A Dose of Pain-Killer," why did Aunt Polly like new-fangled medicines?

2. What caused the fight in the wheelhouse between Sam and Brown in "Life on the Mississippi"?

3. Why was Teddy haunted by the memories of battle in "Civil War Nurse?"

4. In "A Horseman in the Sky," why did the Union captain who saw the rider and horse fall through the air decide not to say anything?

5. How did Casey contribute to his own failure in "Casey at the Bat"?

Understanding Literature

6. In "A Dose of Pain-Killer," Aunt Polly turned out to be glad that Tom had given the cat the medicine. Explain why this is an ironic turn of events.

7. What emotions were presented in "There Was a Child Went Forth" and "Ain't I a Woman?" Which emotions are the most important to the poem? To the speech?

8. What effect did John's look of gratitude have on Alcott in "Civil War Nurse"? What did it cause her to do?

9. Did Carter Druse really do the "right" thing? Explain your answer with facts from "A Horseman in the Sky."

10. How does the phrase "there are only losers in war" apply to "The Raven Days" and "I Will Fight No More Forever"?

COMPOSITION

1. Write a three-paragraph speech that discusses the meaning of freedom. Use facts and opinions to persuade others to accept your ideas. You may write from your own point of view, or use the view of Tom Sawyer, Sojourner Truth, or Chief Joseph.

2. John received his letter too late in "Civil War Nurse." What do you think that letter said? Write a brief summary of what was in John's letter.

3. If Chief Joseph had kept a diary, it would be filled with pain, hurt, and disillusionment. Suppose the Nez Percé were given back their homeland. Write this entry in the diary the way Chief Joseph would have written it.

4. Write a sports article that includes an imaginary interview with the manager of the Mudville baseball team. What does the manager say about Casey? How did it feel to lose? What are the team's prospects for the rest of the season? Is the manager worried about his job?

SECTION 5
Voices of Imagination

1840–1898

A Light exists in Spring
Not present in the year
At any other period
When March is scarcely here.

A Color stands abroad
On Solitary Fields
That Science cannot overtake
But Human Nature Feels.

— Emily Dickinson

187

Introduction

Science and reason can't fully explain everything that people think and feel. Storytellers and poets have always understood this. During the years 1840–1898, many of America's finest authors explored the inner landscape, the unreasonable side of the human mind.

Creating an Effect

Edgar Allan Poe is famous for his suspenseful tales. His ideas for stories came not from the events of everyday life, but from his desire to create a certain effect. Often the effect he aimed for was terror. As you will see when you read his story "The Pit and the Pendulum," he was quite successful.

Unlike Poe, mountain man Jim Bridger did use his life experiences as the basis for his fantastic tales. In 1844, Bridger told St. Louis newspaper reporters of the hot springs, geysers, and other natural wonders that he had found when exploring the Yellowstone region. When people didn't believe him, Bridger began telling tall tales about highly exaggerated events and fantastic places. These tales were amazing and funny. They became very popular. They were retold again and again in newspapers of this era. In this section, you will read a tall tale based on one of Bridger's original tales.

Emily Dickinson never explored the West, never saw a spouting geyser or a giant redwood tree. She seldom left her home in Amherst, Massachusetts. Her poetry presents a unique vision of everyday events and things. She shares her emotions in her poems and reminds us that we, too, have powerful feelings that are not always easy to understand.

The Supernatural

Supernatural tales — stories that involve ghosts, witches, or magic — all deal with the clash of the forces of good and evil. Sometimes these tales remind us of the good and evil in real life and real people.

Charles Chestnutt's parents had been born in slavery. He grew up hearing true stories about the lives of slaves and fantastic stories based on the ancient African tales of magic, or conjuring. His supernatural tales do more than create a mood of terror or a vivid image of an unusual event. His conjure stories are set on Southern plantations before the Civil War. Like "Poor Sandy," the story included here, these tales reflect the evils of slavery.

The Grand Canyon of the Yellowstone, Thomas Moran, 1872

Another author whose work often reflects the struggle between good and evil is Henry James. His most popular work, "The Turn of the Screw," vividly describes the thoughts and feelings of a young woman who believes she is surrounded by evil forces.

Certainly James did not model this tale on his own experience — but it did stem from his own emotions. In the 1870's and 1880's, he had suffered many personal tragedies, including the deaths of his sister and several of his closest friends. He was living in an old English country house and felt surrounded by doom. In "The Turn of the Screw," his feelings and imagination joined forces to create one of the most suspenseful ghost stories ever written.

Realistic literature may describe people's feelings. But the realistic literature of the 19th century almost always reflected the way people *should* feel, the way they *should* behave. Writers of imaginative literature freed themselves from the boundaries of reality. They proved that real feelings and emotions can come alive in impossible places and through supernatural events.

189

The Pit and the Pendulum

by Edgar Allan Poe

Edgar Allan Poe (1809–1849) is one of the most popular American authors of all time. His tales of horror and suspense are widely read today. They have also been made into popular movies and teleplays. The story you are about to read is a retelling of Poe's famous tale of terror and torture "The Pit and the Pendulum." We begin this story after a prisoner who has been condemned to death faints and awakens in a strange cell. Poe describes the torment of this man as he awaits his execution by methods almost too horrible to imagine. . . .

I awakened, but did not open my eyes. I reached out my hand and it fell upon something damp and hard. I struggled to imagine where I could be. I longed to, yet dared not, open my eyes. It was not that I feared to look upon things horrible, but that I was terrified that there might be *nothing* to see.

At length, with a wild desperation, I quickly opened my eyes. My worst thoughts, then, were confirmed. The blackness of eternal night enclosed me. I struggled for breath. The intensity of the darkness seemed to overwhelm me.

I rose to my feet and stepped cautiously about my prison. As I walked, there came rushing into my memory a thousand tales told of the horrors of the dungeons of Toledo. Was I left to perish of starvation in this underground world of darkness? Perhaps a fate even more fearful awaited me. That the result would be death, I had no doubt. The method and the hour were all that now occupied my mind.

My outstretched hands at length touched something solid. It was a wall — very smooth, slimy, and cold. I felt along it, but I could get no idea of the size of my dungeon.

At first, I walked with extreme caution, for the floor was treacherous with slime. At length, however, I took courage, and stepped firmly — trying to walk as direct a line as possible. I had advanced some

10 or 12 paces in this manner when I slipped and fell violently on my face.

In the confusion, I did not at first realize a somewhat startling fact. In a few seconds it came to me: my chin rested upon the floor of the prison, but my lips, and the upper portion of my head, touched nothing. At the same time, the smell of decayed fungus rose to my nostrils. I put forward my arm, and shuddered to find that I had fallen at the edge of a circular pit.

Groping about the floor I was able to dislodge a small fragment, and let it fall into the pit. For many seconds, I listened to its sounds as it dashed against the sides of the wall in its descent. At length, there was a gloomy plunge into water, followed by loud echoes. At the same moment, there came the sound of the quick opening, and rapid closing, of a door overhead, while a faint gleam of light flashed suddenly through the blackness, and as suddenly faded away.

I saw clearly the doom which had been prepared for me, and congratulated myself upon the timely accident by which I had escaped. Another step before my fall, and the world would have been no more!

Shaking in every limb, I felt my way back to the wall — deciding there to die rather than risk the terrors of the wells. My imagination now pictured them to be in many places about the dungeon.

Terror kept me awake for many long hours, but at length I again slumbered. Upon arousing, I found by my side, as before, a loaf and a pitcher of water. A burning thirst consumed me, and I emptied the vessel at a swallow. It must have been drugged — for scarcely had I drunk, before a deep sleep fell upon me — a sleep like that of death. How long it lasted, I know not; but when, once again, I opened my eyes, the objects around me were visible. A hellish light now lit the interior of the prison.

It was not more than 25 yards around. The walls were made of iron, or some other metal, in huge plates. I now noticed the floor, too, which was of stone. In the center yawned the circular pit from whose jaws I had escaped.

All this I saw unclearly and by much effort — for my personal condition had been greatly changed during slumber. I now lay upon my back, and at full length, on a low, wood frame. To this I was securely tied by a long strap resembling a belt. It wound many times around my body, leaving only my head and my left arm free, so that I could, with much effort, supply myself with food from an earthen dish which lay by my side on the floor.

Looking upward, I surveyed the ceiling of my prison. It was some 30 or 40 feet overhead, and from a heavy steel rod was hung a huge pendulum, such as we see on old clocks. There was something about the thing which caused me to look at it more closely. While I gazed directly upward at it (for its position was directly over my own) I thought that I saw it move. In an instant, I realized that I was right. Its sweep was brief and slow. I watched it for some minutes somewhat in fear, but more in wonder.

A slight noise attracted my notice, and looking to the floor, I saw several enormous rats crossing it. They had entered from the well which lay just within view to my right. Even while I gazed, they came up in troops, hurriedly, with ravenous eyes, attracted by the scent of the meat. It required much effort to scare them away.

It might have been half an hour, perhaps even an hour, before I again looked upward. What I then saw confused and amazed me. The sweep of the pendulum had increased by nearly a yard, and its speed was, as a result, much greater. But what mainly disturbed me was that it had noticeably *descended*. I now observed — with what horror I need not say — that its lower edge was a crescent-shaped blade of glittering steel, about a foot long; the lower edge as sharp as that of a razor. The whole thing *hissed* as it swung through the air. I could no longer doubt the doom prepared for me.

What matters it to tell of the long, long hours of horror during which I counted the rushing movements of the steel! Inch by inch, down and still down it came! Many days passed — before it swept so closely over me as to fan me with its breath. The odor of the sharp steel forced itself into my nostrils. I prayed for it to descend faster. I grew frantically mad, and struggled to force myself upward against the sweep of its fearful blade. And then I fell suddenly calm, and lay smiling at the glittering death.

I saw that the blade was designed to cross my body at the heart. It would cut the threads of my clothing — it would return and repeat its operations — again — again. In spite of its wide sweep (some

30 feet or more) and the hissing speed of its descent, still the cutting of my clothing would be all that, for several minutes, it would accomplish.

Down — steadily down it swept. To

I saw that some 10 or 12 sweeps would bring the steel in actual contact with my clothing — and now there suddenly came over my spirit the calmness of despair. For the first time in many hours — or perhaps days — I *thought*. There flashed upon my mind the idea of release. I began at once to free myself.

For many hours the immediate area where I lay had been swarming with rats. They were wild, bold, ravenous — their red eyes glaring upon me. "To what food," I thought, "have they been accustomed in the well?"

They had devoured, in spite of all my efforts to prevent them, all but a small portion of the contents of the dish. With the bits of the oily and spicy food which now remained, I rubbed the belt wherever I could reach it; then, raising my hand from the floor, I lay breathlessly still.

At first, the ravenous animals were startled and terrified at the change — in the stoppage of movement. But this was only for a moment. Observing that I did not move, one or two of the boldest leaped upon the framework, and sniffed at the belt. This seemed the signal for the general rush.

Up from the well they hurried in fresh troops. They leaped in hundreds upon my body. The movements of the pendulum did not disturb them at all. Avoiding its strokes, they busied themselves with the belt. They swarmed upon me in ever greater heaps. They gathered upon my throat; their cold lips sought my own. Disgust swelled my chest and chilled my

the right — to the left — far and wide — with the shriek of a spirit of the damned, I laughed and howled.

Down — certainly, relentlessly down! It swung within three inches of my chest.

heart. Yet one minute more, and I felt that the struggle would be over. Plainly I felt the loosening of the belt. With a more than human effort, I lay *still*.

At length, I felt that I was *free*. The belt hung in shreds from my body. But the stroke of the pendulum already pressed upon my chest. It had cut through the threads of my clothing. Twice again it swung, and pain shot through every nerve. But the moment of escape had arrived. At a wave of my hand the rats quickly scurried away. With a slow steady movement, I slid from the hold of the belt and beyond the reach of the blade. For the moment, at least, *I was free*.

I had scarcely moved from my wooden bed of horror when the pendulum stopped. I saw it drawn up, by some invisible force, through the ceiling. This was a chilling lesson. My every motion was being watched. I had escaped death in one form of agony, only to be delivered to worse than death in some other.

With that thought, I looked nervously around at the wall of iron that hemmed me in. Something unusual — some change had taken place in the dungeon. I became aware, for the first time, of the origin of the strange rays which lit up the cell. They came from a crack, about half an inch wide, extending entirely around the prison at the base of the walls. The walls were completely separated from the floor.

Even while I breathed there came to my nostrils the steam of heated iron! A suffocating odor filled the prison! I panted! I gasped for breath! I shrank from the glowing metal to the center of the cell.

Amid the thought of fiery destruction that approached, the idea of the coolness of the well came over my soul. I rushed to its deadly edge and peered over. For a wild moment, my spirit refused to understand the meaning of what I saw. At length it forced its way into my soul. Oh — any horror but this! With a shriek, I rushed from the edge and buried my face in my hands — weeping bitterly.

The heat rapidly increased, and once again I looked up. There had been a second change in the cell — and now the change was in the shape. With a low rumbling or moaning sound, the dungeon had shifted its shape as the walls began to steadily press in upon themselves. I could have clasped the red walls to my chest as a garment of eternal peace. "Death," I said, "any death but that of the pit!"

Flatter and flatter grew the walls, with a speed that left me no time for thought. I shrank back from the pit — but the closing walls pressed me steadily onward.

Soon there was no longer an inch of footing on the firm floor of the prison. I struggled no more, but the agony of my soul was voiced in one loud, long, and final scream of despair. I felt that I swayed upon the edge — I looked away.

There was a loud hum of human voices! There was a loud blast as of many trumpets! There was a harsh grating as of a thousand thunders! The fiery walls rushed back! An outstretched arm caught my own as I fell, fainting, into the well. It was that of General LaSalle. The French army had entered Toledo. The city was in the hands of its enemies.

Select the best choice to complete each statement. Then write the entire sentence on your paper.

1. At first the prisoner walked cautiously because he ———.
   a. knew he was being watched
   b. was very weak from his ordeal
   c. was in complete darkness

2. He knew the pit was deep, with water at the bottom, because ———.
   a. the guards told him
   b. he tossed something in and listened to its fall
   c. other prisoners had drowned

3. The purpose of the pendulum was to ———.
   a. frighten away the rats
   b. torture and eventually kill
   c. keep the prison clocks going

4. The prisoner rubbed his belt with food so that ———.
   a. he could save some for later
   b. the oils would rot the material
   c. the rats would chew the belt loose

For Discussion

1. Which torture was the prisoner saved from by luck? Which by cleverness? Use details from the story to explain your answers.

2. What do you think was the most terrifying part of the prisoner's experience? Was his torture mental or physical? Why do you think Poe set up the story this way?

UNDERSTANDING LITERATURE

Mood and Imagery. In a literary selection, *mood* is the feeling the author creates with the words that he or she uses. The mood influences the way the reader feels when reading. For example, the mood could be lighthearted and make the reader happy. Or the mood could be terrifying and make the reader uneasy or fearful.

In "The Pit and the Pendulum," Poe created a mood of horror. He did this by using *imagery,* words that appeal to the reader's senses of sight, smell, hearing, touch, and taste.

Read each sentence below. On your paper, write which one of your senses is affected: sight, smell, hearing, touch, or taste.

1. "The blackness of eternal night enclosed me."

2. "It was a wall — very smooth, slimy, and cold."

3. "At the same time, the smell of decayed fungus rose to my nostrils."

4. "At length, there was a gloomy plunge into water, followed by loud echoes."

5. "A burning thirst consumed me, and I emptied the vessel at a swallow."

6. "Flatter and flatter grew the walls, with a speed that left me no time for thought."

Writing

Write a few paragraphs about either a very good or very bad experience you've had. Create a mood by including descriptive sentences that appeal to the five senses.

Jim Bridger and the Fiddler Who Wouldn't Fiddle

a Jim Bridger tale retold by Sid Fleischman

Jim Bridger (1804–1881) was a fur trapper and mountain man, a skilled pathfinder who became the first white man to see the Yellowstone region and other areas of the West. He was also a famous storyteller. A newspaper reporter named Ned Buntline wrote his stories down and made them famous. Here, Sid Fleischman, a modern writer with a great fondness for the Old West, retells one of Jim's tales.

Jim Bridger was a long-haired mountain man. In fringed buckskins and Indian moccasins, he wandered through the wilderness of the Old West before almost anyone else. It was Jim who brushed the hair out of his eyes and first discovered the Great Salt Lake. They might have named it after him, but no one believed he'd found water you couldn't sink in. Jim shrugged his big, bony shoulders and headed back to the mountains.

One day his horse broke three front teeth grazing on a patch of green grass. That's how Jim discovered a petrified forest. The grass and trees had turned to stone for miles around. "Petrified, all petrified," he reported when he got back to civilization. "The bees and the wild flow-ers, and yes, sir, in some of those trees sat petrified birds singing petrified songs."

But he's not famous for all those things.

Jim Bridger was a ramshackle, sharp-eyed army scout. In time they named a fort and a forest after him, and a pass and a creek and a mountain or two.

He once pointed to a mountain in the distance, flat-topped and red as a Navajo blanket. "Stranger," he said. (Jim liked to talk to strangers; they were so few and far between in the wilderness.) "Stranger, look how that mountain has grown! When I first came out here, it was nothing but a red anthill."

And that's what Jim Bridger's famous for. That mountain. He made an alarm clock out of it.

The way it happened, Jim was out in the wilderness as usual, when a blizzard whipped down out of Canada. He traveled through the snow for days and nights. He didn't dare to stop and rest. He knew a man could sleep himself to death in the blizzard and bitter cold.

Jim was all tuckered out, and he knew he couldn't go much farther. Then, through the chill daylight, he caught sight of that red, flat-topped mountain in the distance. It was slab-sided, too, and he had bounced echoes off it many a time. He reckoned from where he now stood, it would take about eight hours for an echo to return.

Jim Bridger gave a yip of joy and made camp. He laid out his bedroll on the snow. Then he gave an ear-quivering yell.

"WAKE UP! WAKE UP, JIM BRIDGER, YOU FROSTBIT, NO-ACCOUNT RASCAL!"

Then he climbed into his bedroll, clamped his eyes shut, and fell away to snoring. Oh, he snored thunderbolts, and dreamed of hot biscuits and gravy.

Exactly seven hours and 56 minutes later, Jim Bridger's alarm clock went off.

"WAKE UP!" roared the echo. "WAKE UP, JIM BRIDGER, YOU FROSTBIT, NO-ACCOUNT RASCAL!"

Jim roused from his bedroll, refreshed and feeling strong as a new rope. It was a week before he reached Fort Bridger, where the sun was shining and no one believed his story.

But a trapper came straggling in and said, "It's true, every word. I found the coals of Jim's campfire and bundled up in furs to catch some shut-eye. Next thing, I knew, that mountain commenced booming. I didn't get a wink of sleep. Doggonit,

Jim, you snore loud enough to drive pigs to market!"

Some time later Jim Bridger was coming back from exploring Yellowstone when he bumped into a brand-new town. It stood smack-dab on the spot where he'd camped the day of the big blizzard. But folks didn't know he'd been there first, so they didn't name the place after him. They called it Blue Horizon.

Blue Horizon didn't amount to much, but it did have a general store, a stable, a blacksmith, and a funeral parlor.

Jim said his howdys, but everyone he met had the grumbles. Sitting around the stove in the general store, he tried to cheer them up by reporting the wonders seen in the Yellowstone.

"Durn my gizzard if steaming water didn't shoot up out of the earth. And boiling water flows out of the rocks into the prettiest lake full of trout you ever saw."

"Can't no trout live in boiling water," grumbled the mayor, chewing a cigar as if it were beef jerky.

"You're exactly right," Jim answered. "Down below, the water's cold as a frog. The hot spring floats on top. Oh, I ate a mess of trout and never once had to build a cook fire and get out my skillet."

The mayor kept chomping his cigar. Jim could see nobody gave a hoot about his hot-and-cold lake. They didn't even accuse him of lying.

"Something bothering you gents?" he asked.

The mayor nodded. "We got to call off the barn dance tonight. The fiddler won't fiddle."

Now Jim Bridger loved a frolic, and it had been a long time since he'd kicked his heels to a jolly tune.

"Who's the fiddler?" he asked.

"Buryin' John Potter, the undertaker. He's hornet-mad because folks didn't elect him mayor instead of me."

The more Jim Bridger thought about it, the more his feet hankered for fiddle music. So he sauntered across the street to the undertaker's parlor.

"You can't fool me, Buryin' John Potter," said Jim. "I see your fiddle on the wall, but that don't mean you can play a note. On purpose, I mean."

"Can, but won't," grumbled Potter. He was hollow-cheeked, sharp-chinned, and long in the arms. Wearing his black claw-hammer coat, he looked like a crow, except that he chewed tobacco.

"No, sir," Jim said. "If you was to saw your fiddling bow across those catgut music. Once heard Jingle-Bob Earl play a frolic back in Missouri, and I guess you'll agree he's the best fiddler who ever was."

"Faw," snorted Buryin' John Potter. "He couldn't play high C if he was standing on a stepladder. I'm the mightiest fiddler who ever was — but I ain't fiddlin' tonight."

And Jim said, "I brought a gourd plugged full of hot steam from the Yellowstone, and it's still perishin' hot. That Yellowstone steam takes years to cool off. I figured to use that gourd as a foot warmer. The nights are turning chilly already, wouldn't you say? Buryin' John, that Yellowstone foot warmer is yours if you can play the screen box half as clever as Jingle-Bob Earl. Come outside and prove it."

The undertaker took down his fiddle, and the two men rode out to a distant spot west of town not far from Jim's echo mountain. Buryin' John tuned his strings, clamped his sharp jaw on the edge of the fiddle box and began beating time with one foot as if he were pounding a stake into the ground. He spit tobacco juice and ripped out "Turkey in the Straw."

Jim thought he'd never heard it played so sweet, but he said, "Won't do. Jingle-Bob Earl played louder 'n that. His fiddling rattled windows for miles around. Do you know 'Scooping Up Pawpaws'? Or 'Have You Seen My New Shoes?'"

"Both," Buryin' John muttered, and commenced sawing away twice as loud as before. The music raised the sap in Jim's feet. It was all he could do to keep from leaping to his heels and raising dust.

Then the undertaker lifted his chin

strings, I'll wager you couldn't hit two notes out of five."

"Haw," said the undertaker, smirking. "Reckon you don't even know 'Chicken in the Bread Tray Pickin' Up Dough.'"

"By heart," said the undertaker sourly. "But I ain't fiddlin' tonight. Don't think you can sweet-word me into changing my mind."

"Wouldn't think of it," Jim replied. "But I'm a powerful fine judge of fiddle from the fiddle and shot tobacco juice to one side. "Reckon that gourd foot warmer is mine," he declared.

"Not so hasty," said Jim. "You call that a contest? Why, Jingle-Bob Earl could fiddle all night without playing the same tune twice."

The undertaker rosined his horsetail bow, tucked the fiddle back under his jaw, and scraped away. Hour after hour the bow cut wild figures in the air. Now and then Buryin' John squirted tobacco juice without missing a note. Jim had never heard such limber-armed fiddling. It was an ear-quivering wonder.

Finally the sun began to dive for home. Jim jumped up, stomped his feet to the music and sang out.

You could fiddle down a possum
from a mile-high tree.
You could fiddle up a whale
from the bottom of the sea!

And he said, "Buryin' John, you win! You're the mightiest fiddler that ever was! The Yellowstone foot warmer is yours."

When Jim got back to the general store, it was falling dark. "Head for the barn!" he exclaimed. "The frolic's about to commence."

The barn filled up in no time. Folks stood around waiting for Buryin' John. They'd heard him practicing his fiddle all day long. A mule began to bray, but they couldn't dance to that. Dogs began to bark, but they couldn't dance to that.

Finally, the mayor, who was there to do the fiddle calling, said, "Can't be a frolic without a fiddler. We might as well go home."

"Keep your hair on, Mayor, and the barn doors open. All the windows, too," said Jim, cupping an ear. "Coming this way is the grandest, mightiest fiddling you ever heard. Caller, clear your throat!"

Suddenly, bounding back from Jim's slab-sided echo mountain, came the first notes of "Turkey in the Straw." So taken by surprise were the folks in the barn that they stood frozen like bird dogs on point.

Then Jim leaped to the center of the floor with hours of stored-up frolic in his feet. He kicked his heels and the dance was on. The fiddle caller aired his lungs.

Grab your partners, make a square,
Music's comin' from I don't know where!

The rafters shook with a romping and a stomping, and the barn was aswirl with calico skirts. The mayor shucked his coat and kept calling.

Dive for the oyster; dig for the clam.
Dive for the sardine; take a full can.

Suddenly the undertaker, in his black claw-hammer coat, loomed up in the doorway. When he saw all the jollification, the wad of tobacco jumped out of his mouth.

"Durn my gizzard, if it ain't Buryin' John!" Jim called out.

"That's my fiddlin'!"

"Oh, you're a sly one." Jim laughed, thinking fast. "That was eternally clever of you to echo your fiddling so you could kick your heels to your own music. Had everybody fooled, you did! They thought you was hornet-mad. Don't stand there stiff as a crowbar. Grab a partner, Buryin' John, and lift your hooves to the mightiest fiddler that ever was."

READING COMPREHENSION

Select the best choice to complete each statement. Then write the entire sentence on your paper.

1. Jim was able to use the mountain as an alarm clock because _____.
   a. it used to be an anthill
   b. no one else knew it was there
   c. noises echoed from its flat sides

2. The undertaker agreed to play for Jim because _____.
   a. he needed the money
   b. no one else could do it
   c. Jim bet he wasn't the best fiddler

3. The music for the square dance came from _____.
   a. the mayor and his helpers
   b. echoes of the undertaker's playing
   c. Jim Bridger himself

For Discussion

1. Would this story be as funny without the exaggerations? Could the story be told without exaggeration?

2. What was Jim Bridger most famous for? What parts of the story about the mountain could be true? What parts are exaggerated?

3. Why do you think the people of Blue Horizon were so eager to have a square dance?

4. How did the fiddler's music make Jim feel? How does music usually affect people? Answer from your personal experience.

UNDERSTANDING LITERATURE

Mood. An author creates a mood by the way he or she tells a story. The mood of the tall tale about Jim Bridger is light-hearted and humorous.

Read the following pairs of sentences. On your paper, tell which one in each pair creates a humorous mood.

1a. One day his horse broke three front teeth grazing on a patch of green grass.
   b. One day his starving horse was trying to chew a mouthful of grass when his three front teeth shattered.

2a. Jim felt like dancing after having been in the wilderness for so long.
   b. The music raised the sap in Jim's feet.

3a. Then Jim leaped to the center of the floor with hours of stored-up frolic in his feet.
   b. Jim stomped angrily to the middle of the floor and kicked for hours.

Writing

Write an exaggerated description of a person, place, or thing. Create a mood that makes the reader laugh. Here are some examples to get you started. You may build on one of these or create a totally original paragraph.

1. The basketball player was so tall he had to bend over to shoot a basket.

2. The car was very fast. When I drove it somewhere, I always arrived two minutes before I left home.

Three poems by Emily Dickinson

Emily Dickinson (1830–1886) had a happy childhood and went to college. As an adult, she stayed in her house in Amherst most of the time, seeing only family members. She wrote many letters, however, and hundreds of short poems. Her poems are about the timeless themes of love, nature, and the human soul.

"Hope" Is the Thing With Feathers

by Emily Dickinson

"Hope" is the thing with feathers —
That perches in the soul —
And sings the tune without the words —
And never stops — at all —

And sweetest — in the Gale — is heard —
And sore must be the storm —
That could abash the little Bird
That kept so many warm —

I've heard it in the chillest land —
And on the strangest Sea —
Yet, never, in Extremity,
It asked a crumb — of Me.

1. The poet says, "Hope is the thing with feathers." To what is she comparing hope?

2. What words and phrases does she use in the poem to further this comparison?

A Word Is Dead

by Emily Dickinson

A word is dead
When it is said,
Some say,
I say it just
Begins to live
That day.

1. We use words to express our ideas and feelings. What does the image of a dead word suggest?

2. What does the image of a living word suggest? Do all words live on after they are spoken, or just some? Explain.

The Conversation, Eastman Johnson, 1875–1880

The Wind Tapped Like a Tired Man

by Emily Dickinson

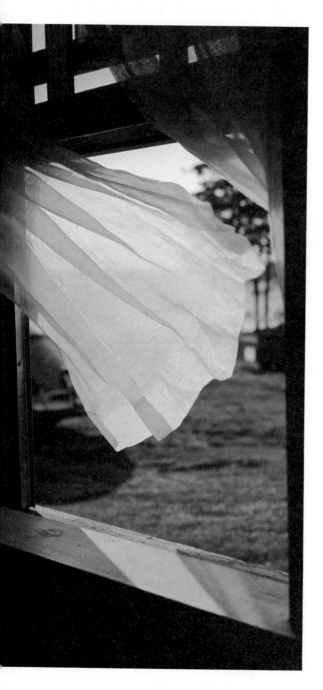

The wind tapped like a tired man,
And like a host, "Come in,"
I boldly answered; entered then
My residence within.

A rapid, footless guest,
To offer whom a chair
Were as impossible as hand
A sofa to the air.

No bone had he to bind him,
His speech was like the push
Of numerous humming-birds at once
From a superior bush.

His countenance a billow,
His fingers, if he pass
Let go a music, as of tunes
Blown tremulous in glass.

He visited, still flitting;
Then, like a timid man,
Again he tapped — 'twas flurriedly —
And I became alone.

1. What words and phrases does Dickinson use to describe the wind?

2. Was the movement of the wind strong or gentle? Which words in the poem show this?

READING COMPREHENSION

Select the best choice to complete each statement. Then write the entire sentence on your paper.

1. Emily Dickinson believed that words _____.
   a. should be written
   b. are quickly forgotten
   c. come alive when spoken

2. Hope, according to Emily Dickinson, _____.
   a. is a very costly and rare thing
   b. needs to find shelter in a storm
   c. gives much and asks for nothing

3. The poet compared the wind to ____.
   a. a summer's day
   b. bits of broken glass
   c. a tired man with a birdlike voice

For Discussion

1. Emily Dickinson talked about words being alive or dead. What does she mean?

2. The poet felt that hope "never . . . asked a crumb — of Me." Does this mean she was a hopeful person?

3. Why did the poet compare the wind to a tired man? Would she always make this comparison? When would she describe the wind differently?

UNDERSTANDING LITERATURE

Personification. Imagery in literature is the use of words or details to create pictures in the reader's mind. One type of imagery is *personification.*

Personification means treating ideas, animals, or other objects as though they were human.

For example, Emily Dickinson talked about words as though they could live or die, and she described the wind by comparing it to a tired man.

Reread the poem "The Wind Tapped Like a Tired Man." On your paper, make a list of the phrases Emily Dickinson used to describe the wind as though it were a man. Then tell which of your senses each comparison appeals to. One example is: "His speech was like the push/Of numerous humming-birds at once/From a superior bush." This image helps you feel and hear the wind. It appeals to your senses of touch and hearing.

Writing

Write a short poem or paragraph in which you use personification to describe one of the following:

a rainstorm

a motorcycle

a guitar

Poor Sandy

by Charles W. Chestnutt

Charles Chestnutt (1858–1932) began publishing his stories in The Atlantic Monthly *magazine in 1887. The story that follows is set in North Carolina just before the Civil War. Chestnutt called "Poor Sandy" a conjure tale because the story draws on ancient African legends of conjure doctors who had supernatural powers. A conjure woman mixed roots and herbs into a "goopher" mixture to make powerful magic. As you will see in this story, however, the results of conjuring were not always predictable.*

Sandy used to belong to old Master Marlboro. You know the old Marlboro place on the other side of the swamp. Well, Sandy was a mighty good hand, he could do many things around the plantation. In fact, he did his work so well that when Master Marlboro's children grew up and married, they all wanted their daddy to give them Sandy for a wedding present. But Master Marlboro knew the rest wouldn't be satisfied if he gave Sandy to just one of them. So when they were all married, Master Marlboro gave Sandy to each of his children for a month or so. When they all had had him the same length of time, he was passed around again and again. Once in a while, Master Marlboro would lend Sandy to some of his other kinfolks when they were short-handed. Well, this went on until it got so Sandy didn't hardly know where he was going to stay from one day to the other.

One time when Sandy was lent out as usual, a speculator came along with a lot of slaves, and Master Marlboro swapped Sandy's wife off for a new woman. When Sandy came back Master Marlboro gave him a dollar and allowed he was mighty sorry to break up the family, but the speculator had given him a good offer, and times were hard and money scarce, so he was best to make the trade. Sandy took on something about losing his wife, but he soon saw it wasn't no use crying over spilt molasses. And being as he liked the looks of the new woman, he took up with her after she had been on the plantation a month or so.

Sandy and his new wife got on mighty well together, and the rest of the slaves all commenced to talk about how loving they were. When Tenie took sick once, Sandy set up all night with her, and then went to work in the morning just like he had his regular sleep, and Tenie would have done anything in the world for her Sandy.

Sandy and Tenie hadn't been living together for more than two months before Master Marlboro's old uncle, who lived down in Robinson County, sent word up if Master Marlboro couldn't let him hire him a good hand for a month or so. Sandy's master was one of these here easygoing folks who wanted to please everybody, so he says yes, he could lend him Sandy. So Master Marlboro told Sandy to get ready to go down to Robinson County the next day to stay for a month.

It was mighty hard on Sandy to be taken away from Tenie. It was so far down to Robinson County that he didn't have no chance of coming back to see her until the time was up. He wouldn't mind coming 10 or 15 miles at night to see Tenie, but Master Marlboro's uncle's plantation was more than 40 miles off. Sandy was mighty sad and cast down after what Master Marlboro had told him.

He told Tenie, "I'm getting tired of this here going around so much. Here I am lent to Master James this month, and I got to do so and so. Then to Master Archie the next month, and I got to do so and so. Then I got to go over to Miss Jenny's, and it's Sandy this and Sandy that, and Sandy here and Sandy there, until it appears to me that I ain't got no home, no master, no mistress, no nothing. I can't even keep a wife. My other woman was sold away without my getting a chance to tell her good-bye. And now I got to go off and leave you, Tenie, and I don't know whether I'm ever going to see you again

or not. I wish I was a tree, or a stump, or a rock, or something that could stay on the plantation for a while."

After Sandy got through talking, Tenie didn't say a word, but just sat there by the fire, thinking and thinking. Finally she upped and said:

"Sandy, I ain't never told you I was a conjure woman?"

Of course Sandy had never dreamed of nothing like that, and he made a great admiration when he heard what Tenie had said.

By and by, Tenie went on. "I ain't goophered nobody, nor done no conjure work, for fifteen years or more. When I got religion I made up my mind I wouldn't work no more goopher. But there are some things I don't believe it's no sin to do, and if you don't want to be sent around from pillar to post, and if you don't want to go down to Robinson County, I can fix things so you won't have to. If you'll say the word, I can turn you into whatever you want to be, and you can stay right where you want to as long as you got a mind to."

Sandy didn't care, he was willing to do anything to stay close to Tenie. So Tenie asked him if he didn't want to be turned into a rabbit.

Sandy said, "No, the dogs might get after me."

"Shall I turn you into a wolf?"

"No, everybody is scared of a wolf, and I don't want nobody to be scared of me."

"Shall I turn you into a mockingbird?"

"No, a hawk might catch me. I want to be turned into something that will stay in one place."

"I can turn you into a tree," said Tenie. "You wouldn't have no mouth nor ears, but I can turn you back once in a while so you could get something to eat, and hear what was going on."

"Well," said Sandy, "that'll do."

And so Tenie took him down by the swamps, not far from the slave quarters, and turned him into a big pine tree, and set him out among some other trees. The next morning, as some of the field hands were going along there, they saw a tree that they didn't remember, or else one of the saplings had been growing mighty fast.

When Master Marlboro discovered that Sandy was gone, he thought he had run away. He got the dogs out, but the last place they could track Sandy to was the foot of that pine tree. And there the dogs stood and barked and bayed and pawed at the tree, and tried to climb up on it. When they were taken around through the swamp to look for the scent, they broke loose and made for the tree again. It was the darnedest thing the white folks had ever heard of, and Master Marlboro figured that Sandy must have climbed up on the tree and jumped off on a mule or something, and rode far enough to spoil the scent. Master Marlboro wanted to accuse some of the other slaves of helping Sandy run off, but they all denied it to the last, and everybody knew Tenie set too much in store by Sandy to help him run away where she couldn't never see him no more.

When Sandy had been gone long enough for folks to think he done got clean away, Tenie used to go down to the woods at night and turn him back. Then they would slip up to the cabin and sit by the fire and talk. But they had to be careful, or else somebody would see them, and that would spoil the whole thing. So Tenie always turned Sandy back in the morning early, before anybody was stirring.

But Sandy didn't get along without his trials and tribulations. One day a woodpecker came along and started to peck at the tree. The next time Sandy was turned back he had a little round hole in his arm, just like a sharp stick had been stuck in it. After that, Tenie set a sparrow hawk to watch the tree, and when the woodpecker came along the next morning to finish his nest, he got gobbled up before he stuck his bill in the bark.

Another time, Master Marlboro sent a slave out in the woods to chop turpentine boxes. The man chopped a box in this here tree and hacked the bark up two or three feet, in order to let the turpentine run. The next time Sandy was turned back he had a big scar on his left leg, and it took Tenie about all night to make a mixture to fix him up. After that Tenie set a hornet to watch the tree, and when the slave came back again to cut another box on the other side of the tree, the hornet stung him so hard that the axe slipped and cut his foot about off.

When Tenie saw so many things happening to the tree, she concluded she would have to turn Sandy into something else. And after studying the matter over, and talking with Sandy one evening, she made up her mind to fix up a goopher mixture that would turn herself and Sandy into foxes, or something, so that they could run away and go someplace where

they would be free and live like white folks.

Tenie had got the night set for her and Sandy to run away, when that very day young Master Dunkin, one of Master Marlboro's sons, rode up to the big house in his buggy and said his wife was mighty sick and he wanted his mama to lend him a woman to nurse his wife. The mistress said to send Tenie, since she was a good nurse. Of course the young master was in a terrible hurry to get back home. Tenie said she would go right along with her young master, but she tried to make some excuse to get away and hide until night, when she would have everything fixed up

for her and Sandy. She said she wanted to go to her cabin to get her bonnet. Her missus said it didn't matter about the bonnet, her head-handkerchief was good enough. Then Tenie said she wanted to get her best frock; her missus said no, she didn't need no more frocks, when that one got dirty she could get a clean one where she was going. So Tenie had to get in the buggy and go along with young Master Dunkin to his plantation, which was more than 20 miles away. There wasn't no chance for her seeing Sandy no more until she came back home. The poor woman felt mighty bad about the way things was going on and she knew Sandy must be wondering why she didn't come and turn him back no more.

While Tenie was away nursing young Master Dunkin's wife, Master Marlboro took a notion to build him a new kitchen and being as he had lots of timber on his place, he began to look around for a tree to have the lumber sawed out. I don't know how it came to be so, but he happened to hit on the very tree Sandy was turned into. Tenie was gone, and there wasn't nobody near to watch the tree.

The two men that cut the tree down said they never had such a time with a tree before. Their axes would glance off

and didn't appear to make no progress through the wood. And the creaking, shaking, and wobbling you ever did see, that tree did when he commenced to fall. It was the darnedest thing!

When they got the tree all trimmed up, they chained it up to a timber wagon and started for the sawmill. But they had a hard time getting the log there. First they got stuck in the mud when they were going across the swamp and it was two or three hours before they could get out. When they started on again the chain kept coming loose, and they had to keep stopping to hitch the log up again. When they commenced to climb the hill to the sawmill, the log broke loose and rolled down the hill and in among the trees, and it took about half a day more to get it hauled up to the sawmill.

The next morning after the day the tree was hauled to the sawmill, Tenie came home. When she got back to her cabin, the first thing she did was to run down to the woods and see how Sandy was getting on. When she saw the stump standing there with sap running out of it, and the limbs laying there scattered around, she almost went out of her mind. She ran to her cabin and got her goopher mixture, then followed the tracks of the timber wagon to the sawmill. She knew Sandy couldn't live no more than a minute or so if she turned him back, for he was all chopped up so he had to be dying. But she wanted to turn him back long enough for her to explain that she hadn't gone off on purpose and left him to be chopped down and sawed up. She didn't want him to die with hard feelings toward her.

The men at the sawmill had just got the big log on the carriage, and was starting up the saw, when they saw a woman running up the hill all out of breath, crying and going on just like she was plumb distracted. It was Tenie. She came right into the mill and threw herself on the log, right in front of the saw. She was hollering and crying to her Sandy to forgive her, and not think hard of her for it wasn't no fault of hers. Then Tenie remembered the tree didn't have no ears, and she was getting ready to work her goopher mixture so as to turn Sandy back, when the mill hands caught ahold of her and tied her arms with a rope, fastened her to one of the posts in the sawmill, and then they started the saw up again and cut the log up into boards right before her eyes. But it was mighty hard work, for all the squeaking and moaning and groaning that log did while the saw was going through it.

The saw was one of these there old-timers, up and down saws, and it took them days longer to saw a log then it does now. They greased the saw, but that didn't stop the fuss. It kept right on, until finally they got the log all sawed up.

When the overseer who ran the sawmill came from breakfast, the hands told him about the crazy woman that had come running into the sawmill, a-hollering and going on, and tried to throw herself before the saw. The overseer sent two or three of the hands to take Tenie back to her master's plantation.

Tenie appeared to be out of her mind for a long time, and her master had to lock her up in the smokehouse until she got over her spells. Master Marlboro was mighty mad. It would have made your flesh crawl to hear him cuss, because he said the speculator had fooled him by working a crazy woman off on him. While Tenie was locked up in the smokehouse, Master Marlboro took and hauled the lumber from the sawmill and put up his new kitchen.

When Tenie got quieted down, so she could be allowed to go around the plantation, she up and told her master all about Sandy and the pine tree. When Master Marlboro heard it, he allowed she was the most distracted slave he had ever heard of. He didn't know what to do with Tenie. First he thought he would put her in the poorhouse, but finally, seeing as she didn't do no harm to nobody nor nothing, but just went around moaning and groaning and shaking her head, he decided to let her stay on the plantation and nurse the little black children while their mothers were working in the cotton fields.

The new kitchen Master Marlboro built wasn't much used. It hadn't been put up long before the slaves started to notice queer things about it. They could hear something moaning and groaning about the kitchen in the nighttime, and when the wind would blow they could hear something hollering and squeaking like it was in great pain and suffering. It got so after a while that it was all Master Marlboro's wife could do to get a woman to stay in the kitchen in the daytime long enough to do the cooking. There wasn't a slave on the plantation that wouldn't rather take 40 lashes than to go about that kitchen after dark, that is, except Tenie. She didn't appear to mind the spirits. She used to slip around at night and sit on the kitchen steps leaning up against the door, talking to herself with a kind of foolishness that nobody could make out. Master Marlboro had threatened to send her off the plantation if she said anything to any of the other slaves about the pine tree. But somehow or another the slaves found out all about it and they all knew the kitchen was haunted by Sandy's spirit. It even got so that Master Marlboro's wife herself was scared to go out in the yard after dark.

When it came to that, Master Marlboro tore the kitchen down and used the lumber to build a schoolhouse. The schoolhouse wasn't supposed to be used except in the daytime, but on dark nights folks going along the road would hear queer sounds and see queer things. Poor old Tenie used to go down there at night and wander around the schoolhouse. The slaves all knew that she went to talk with Sandy's spirit.

One winter morning when one of the boys went to school early to start the fire, what should he find but poor old Tenie, lying on the floor, stiff and cold and dead. There didn't appear to be nothing particular the matter with her. She had just grieved herself to death for her Sandy.

READING COMPREHENSION

Select the best choice to complete each statement. Then write the entire sentence on your paper.

1. Tenie turned Sandy into a tree _____.
   a. because she hated him
   b. so he wouldn't have to leave her
   c. so he could talk about his roots

2. Tenie did not come to Sandy one night because she _____.
   a. was tired of him
   b. had to take care of a sick woman
   c. ran away

3. Master wanted the tree chopped down because _____.
   a. he knew it was Sandy
   b. he needed the timber for a kitchen
   c. the tree was in the way

4. The kitchen and the schoolhouse made from the tree seemed _____.
   a. sturdier than most
   b. to make Tenie very happy
   c. haunted by Sandy's ghost

For Discussion

1. What kind of a person was Sandy? How did he do his job? Would you have wanted him as a friend?

2. Master Marlboro is called "easygoing." Did this apply to the way he treated Sandy? Explain your answer.

3. The story "Poor Sandy" is tragic in many ways. How did trying to be good hurt Sandy? How did the love between Sandy and Tenie kill them both?

UNDERSTANDING LITERATURE

Imagery. Imagery is the use of words that appeal to the senses and stir the reader's imagination. An author's use of imagery often helps create a mood, or atmosphere. Imagery can influence the reader's feelings about what he or she is reading.

In parts of "Poor Sandy," the author painted such vivid word pictures that you may have found yourself horrified.

Read the following passages. On your paper, identify the sense or senses each one appeals to. Then in a word or phrase, tell how each passage makes you feel.

1. "When she saw the stump standing there with sap running out of it, and the limbs laying there scattered around, she almost went out of her mind."

2. "One winter morning when one of the boys went to school early to start the fire, what should he find but poor old Tenie, lying on the floor, stiff and cold and dead."

Writing

Imagine that you are Tenie. Think of something other than a tree to turn Sandy into. Write one paragraph telling about the advantages of what you have chosen. Write another paragraph telling of the disadvantages. In your description, try to use imagery to help your readers know what Sandy is like. In his new form, what will he look like? What sounds will he make? How will he feel to the touch? Will he have an odor? A taste?

The Turn of the Screw

by Henry James

One of the best-known stories by Henry James (1843–1916) is "The Turn of the Screw." As you will discover in reading this retelling of the story, "The Turn of the Screw" is more than a ghost story. It shows a struggle between the forces of good and evil.

After a brief introduction, the story is told from the point of view of a young woman. She tells you what she thinks is going on. But it is up to you, the reader, to decide how much is real and how much is her imagination. As you read this story, ask yourself these questions: Are the ghosts real or imaginary? Who is good and who is evil in the story?

A group of friends was sitting around a fireplace one night, telling ghost stories. A man named Douglas said he knew a ghost story that no one there had ever heard before. "For horror," he said, "there is nothing like it. Perhaps because it involves children, the strangeness and terror of the tale are given another twist, another turn of the screw."

His friends begged him to tell them the story. He said it had been written by a governess he had known many years ago. She had sent it to him before she died. He kept it locked in a drawer in his house in London. He would send a messenger with a key to get it. Then he would read it to them.

Meanwhile, he would tell his friends what he knew about her. This is what he said that night.

When her story began, she was 20 years old and the daughter of a poor minister. She needed a job, so she went to London to answer a newspaper ad in person. The gentleman she met was a handsome bachelor who lived in a fine house.

He told her that he had a young niece and nephew who were orphans. The little girl, Flora, was living at his home in the country. The housekeeper, Mrs. Grose,

216

was taking care of her. The boy, Miles, was at boarding school. He would join them when the summer vacation began.

The uncle said the children needed a governess to look after them and be their teacher. Their first governess, Miss Jessel, had died.

At first, the young woman did not want to take the job. It would be lonely caring for two children in the country. Also, the uncle said he did not want to be bothered about them. She would have to take care of everything herself.

She wasn't sure she could handle the job. But the uncle was so charming and such a gentleman that she could not refuse.

The next night, the story written by the governess arrived. Douglas began to read it to his friends. From now on, the story is told in her own words.

Did I make a mistake in taking the job? I thought so during the long ride to the uncle's house in the country. I was sure the house would be small and gloomy. But when I arrived, I had a pleasant surprise. The house was large and sunny.

I was welcomed by a stout, wholesome woman — Mrs. Grose. She introduced me to Flora, the younger of my two pupils. Flora was the most beautiful and charming child I had ever seen. She looked like an angel in a painting. It would be a joy, I thought, to teach such a girl.

My room was one of the best in the house. It had a large bed for me and a small one for Flora.

That night, I had trouble sleeping. Near dawn, I thought I heard the cry of a child from far away. A little later, I heard a light footstep outside my door. But I did not think much of those sounds then. I was too happy thinking of the wonderful child whose life I would share.

In the morning, I asked Mrs. Grose about Flora's brother, Miles. "Is he as remarkable as Flora?"

Mrs. Grose smiled and said, "Oh, yes. He'll be home from school in a couple of days. Then you'll see for yourself."

Later, Flora showed me around the house. I began to feel that the house was like a castle. I kept wondering, "Is this all a dream?"

A letter arrived from the children's uncle that evening. Inside the envelope was a second letter addressed to him. It was unopened.

The uncle wrote, "I know this letter is from Miles's school principal. That man is an awful bother. Please read this letter and answer it yourself. Don't tell me anything about it — not one word."

I read the principal's letter before going to bed. It upset me so much that again I had trouble sleeping.

In the morning, I told Mrs. Grose, "Miles has been dismissed from school. They will not take him back again — ever."

Mrs. Grose's eyes filled with tears. "What has he done?"

"The letter doesn't say," I said. "It just says they are sorry they cannot keep him there anymore. That must mean he is doing some harm to the other boys."

Mrs. Grose became angry. "Miles wouldn't harm anyone. Why, he's only ten years old."

"Yes, it's hard to believe," I said. "Have you ever known him to be bad?"

"Yes, thank goodness. A boy who has never been bad is no boy for me!"

I still had some doubts. Later, I asked Mrs. Grose some more questions. "Did the first governess, Miss Jessel, ever have trouble with the boy?"

"If she did, she never told me," Mrs. Grose said.

"What was she like?"

"She was almost as young and as pretty as you."

"Did she die here?"

Mrs. Grose shook her head. She said that one day Miss Jessel left for a short vacation. She never came back. Later, Mrs. Grose heard from the children's uncle that Miss Jessel was dead.

"What did she die of?" I asked.

Mrs. Grose seemed upset. "He never told me. Now, I must get back to my work."

The next day, Miles came home from school. The moment I saw him, all my doubts about him disappeared. I had never seen such sweetness and innocence in a boy. It was impossible not to love him.

I told Mrs. Grose that I would ignore the letter from school. I would not tell the boy's uncle about it, which made Mrs. Grose very relieved.

The next few weeks were the happiest of my life. The children were charming, giving me no trouble at all. The weather was perfect, the days sunny and long.

Then one evening, everything changed. The children had gone to bed, and I was taking a walk near the house. It was still light enough for me to enjoy the scenery. As I walked, I dreamed I might meet a handsome man who would smile at me. He would be just like the children's uncle.

At that moment, I looked up at the house. What I saw gave me a great shock. A man was looking out of one of the two towers on the roof. It was not the children's uncle. It was someone I had never seen before.

He stared at me for a full minute. As he did, everything became as quiet as death. Then he turned away, and I could see him no more.

Who was this man? Was some insane person kept in the tower? Or had some stranger sneaked into the house, looked around, and then sneaked out again?

I decided it must have been a nosy stranger. I was glad I would never see him again.

For a few days, I thought no more about him. Then it was Sunday, and time to go to church. I remembered that I had left my gloves in the dining room. When I entered the room, I saw someone standing outside the window. It was the man I had seen in the tower!

He stared at me again, but then began to look around the room. I realized he was not looking for me, but for someone else.

I was very frightened, but I had a duty to protect the children. I ran outside to challenge the stranger. But when I got to the window, he was gone.

Something made me look inside the window, as he had done. Just then, Mrs.

Grose walked into the room. When she saw me, her face turned white.

She ran outside to meet me. "What is the matter?" she asked. "You look awful!"

I could not keep the secret to myself anymore. I told Mrs. Grose the whole story.

"What did the stranger look like?" she asked.

I said, "He is tall and has red, curly hair and a long face. His mouth is wide, and his lips are thin. He has little whiskers on his chin. He is handsome in a slick sort of way, but he is no gentleman."

Mrs. Grose looked amazed. She said, "It's Peter Quint! He was the uncle's personal servant. When the uncle left, Quint stayed on with us. Then he went, too."

"Went where?" I asked.

Mrs. Grose looked very odd. Finally she said, "He died."

I nearly screamed. "Died?"

"Yes, Mr. Quint is dead."

That night, Mrs. Grose and I talked some more. She had seen nothing herself. But she fully believed that I had seen something.

I told her I felt that Quint was looking for Miles. I wondered, though, why the children had never mentioned Quint to me.

Mrs. Grose said that Flora was too young to remember him. But he and Miles had been "great friends." She herself had never liked Quint. He was an evil fellow.

His life came to an end one winter night. He had been drinking heavily in the village. On his way home, he slipped on an icy hill, and the fall killed him.

Several days later, I found more proof that the children were in danger. I had left Miles inside the house to read. Flora and I had walked to a small lake. While Flora played, I sat on a bench and did some sewing. Suddenly I knew, without looking up, that someone was on the other side of the lake. It was someone, I was sure, who had no right to be there.

I looked at Flora to see if she noticed anything. She showed no sign of it. But she had become very quiet and had turned her back to the lake. Finally, I looked up to face the figure on the other shore. . . .

I could hardly wait to tell Mrs. Grose what I had seen. When I found her, I cried, "It's awful! The children know what we know — and maybe a lot more. Just two hours ago, Flora saw! Yet she kept it to herself."

"Then how do you know she saw anything?" Mrs. Grose asked.

"I could tell she was aware."

"You mean aware of Quint?"

"No, it was a woman this time. She was dressed all in black, and her face was very evil. She kept looking at Flora. It was as if she wanted to get hold of her."

"Was she someone you've ever seen before?" Mrs. Grose asked.

"No, but it was someone the child has seen. I'm sure it was the governess who died — Miss Jessel."

"How do you know that?"

I described her to Mrs. Grose. "She was beautiful, but very pale and dreadful. Her eyes were evil. Everything about her was evil."

Mrs. Grose now seemed to believe me. "Miss Jessel was evil," she said. "She and Quint were both evil, and they were attracted to each other."

"It's much worse than I thought," I said. "The children are lost. I can't save them."

That night, I tried to get more information from Mrs. Grose. I wanted to know especially about Miles and Peter Quint. She said that for several months, they had always been together. She thought this was wrong, and once said so to Miss Jessel. Miss Jessel had told her to mind her own business.

Sometimes Mrs. Grose scolded Miles for spending so much time with Quint. Then Miles would deny it.

"You mean he lied?" I asked.

"Yes, but he's such an angel now. You don't think he's hiding anything from you, do you?"

"I'm not sure," I said.

For several days, I saw no more of either Quint or Miss Jessel. I began to feel more at ease. The children were wonderful. They tried hard to please me, and they learned their lessons perfectly.

I tried hard not to show that I had any fears about them. But sometimes I thought they knew.

Late one night, I heard a footstep outside my door. It was the same sound I had heard the first night I was in the house. I picked up a candle and went out into the hall. At the top of the stairs, the candle

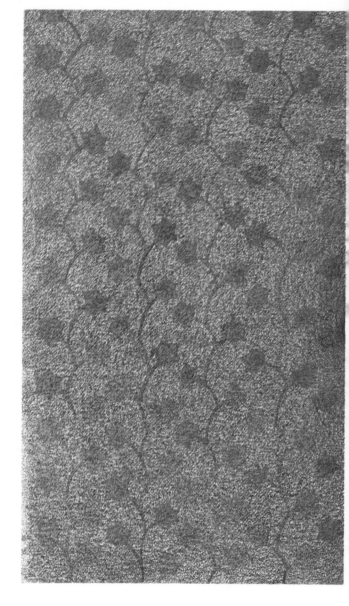

blew out. But dawn was beginning, and a little light came through the window.

I looked down the stairs and saw — the ghost of Quint! In the pale light, he seemed very dangerous. We stared at each other, but this time I was not afraid, and

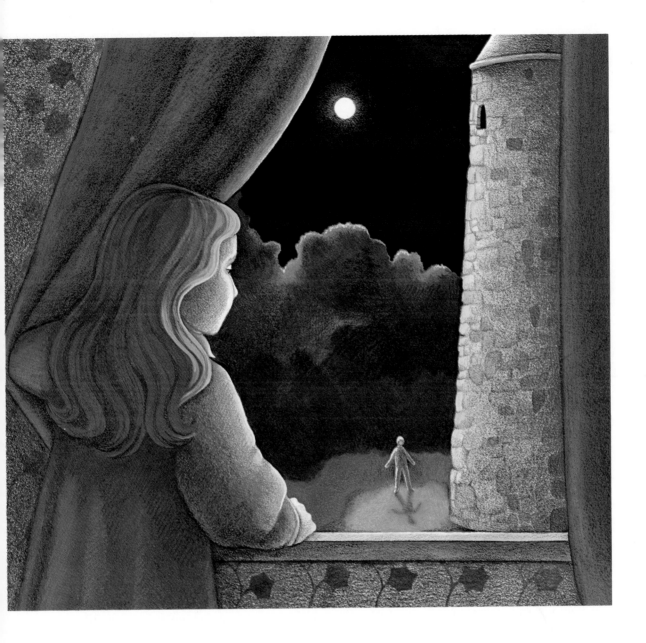

he knew it. Suddenly, he turned his back on me and disappeared.

For the next few nights, I hardly slept. I kept going out into the hall, wondering if I would find Quint again. But there was no sign of him.

At last, I became so tired that one night I fell fast asleep. Later, I woke up suddenly. I had left a candle burning, but now it was out. Had Flora blown it out?

I went to her bed, but she was not in it. I looked around and saw her standing

221

at the window, staring outside. She was so interested in someone on the lawn that she did not notice me.

Was Miss Jessel out there? I had to find out, so I slipped out of the room. I went to an empty room that also faced the lawn, and I looked out the window.

In the moonlight, I could see a figure watching the tower. I was sure that Quint was up there again. With horror, I now saw that the figure on the lawn was Miles!

I ran outside, took Miles by the hand, and led him to his room. I wondered what to say to him. Could I accuse him of keeping company with an evil ghost? If I did, people would say I was crazy.

Finally, I said, "Tell me the truth. What were you doing out there?"

He smiled and looked at me with his beautiful eyes. "If I tell you, will you understand?"

I nodded.

"It's very simple," he said. "For a change, I wanted you to think I was *bad*."

He explained that it was a joke that he and Flora had planned to scare me. For the moment, I believed him.

Then I asked, "But weren't you afraid of catching a cold out there?"

"When I'm bad," he said, "I am *very* bad." Then he kissed me good night.

The next morning, my fears about the children came back. There was only one person I could tell them to — Mrs. Grose. I told her that the children's sweetness and goodness were all an act. The truth was, I said, that the children constantly met Quint and Miss Jessel.

"But whatever for?" asked Mrs. Grose.

"For the love of all the evil those two put into them. Quint and Miss Jessel come back to keep up their evil work. They are like demons, tempting the children to join them in their world. If the children join them, they will be destroyed."

Mrs. Grose said I should write to the children's uncle for help. But how could I tell him that his house was haunted? Could I say that his niece and nephew kept company with ghosts? No, I would have to save the children myself.

I was sure that Miles and Flora were aware that I knew their secret. Yet they never spoke of Quint or Miss Jessel, and I did not dare to.

For a few weeks, I did not see Quint or Miss Jessel at all. But I was certain that the children saw them, even when we were together. At times, everything would become very quiet. It was then, I believe, that the children had visitors.

Sometimes I wanted to say, "They're here. You can't deny it." But I always stopped myself. The strain almost made me hate the children. Yet they were as charming as ever.

During this time, I kept a close watch over Miles and Flora. I was like a prison guard, and I wondered when Miles would demand more freedom.

It happened on an autumn Sunday as we were walking to church. Suddenly, he asked, "When am I going back to school?"

It was natural for him to ask this. But I feared writing to his uncle about it. The uncle did not know that Miles had been dismissed from school. He would ask *why* this had happened. Then *everything* would come out — Quint, Miss Jessel, all the horrors.

I did not say this to Miles. Instead, I said that his uncle was very busy. I could not bother him.

"Well," Miles said, "if *you* won't write him, I will." Then he marched into the church without me.

Instantly I was in a panic. I could not face Miles's uncle. Miles knew I was afraid. He would make use of my fear to get his own way.

I had to escape and never see the children again. Now that everyone was in church, I could pack up and leave unseen.

I hurried to the house. I went to the study for my books. What I found sent a chill through me.

Miss Jessel was sitting at my table. She looked very sad and tired. She stared at me as if to say, "This is *my* room. You have no right to be here."

I screamed at her, "You terrible woman!"

A moment later, she was gone. I knew then that I had to stay to protect the children.

That night, I told Mrs. Grose, "I'm going to send for the children's uncle. I will show him the letter from Miles's principal. It's not my fault that Miles was dismissed because he was wicked."

"But we really don't know that he was wicked," Mrs. Grose said.

"What other reason is there?" I asked. "Is he stupid? Is he sick? Is he a trouble-maker? No. He's clever and perfect. So he must have been wicked."

Tears came into Mrs. Grose's eyes. But she agreed that I should write to the uncle.

I began the letter that night, but I became restless. I picked up a candle and walked into the hall.

For a moment, I paused outside Miles's door. From inside, he called, "Come in."

I went in and found him in bed. "How did you know I was out there?" I asked.

"I heard you. Do you think you make no noise?"

I told him that I had begun a letter to his uncle. He laughed and said, "Well, then, finish it."

His laughter sounded so innocent. Perhaps I could still save him.

"Miles, what happened at school? Why haven't you ever talked about it?"

He looked at me, but said nothing.

"Miles, I want to help you. I'd rather die than hurt you. Help me to save you."

Just then, I felt an icy gust of air. Miles screamed, and the candle went out. It was very strange, because the window was shut.

"How did the candle go out?" I cried.

"I blew it out," Miles said.

The next day, Miles was very charming. He offered to play the piano for me, and I agreed. He played so well that I lost track of time. Suddenly, I wondered where Flora was. It was the first time she had been out of my sight.

I looked all over the house for her, but could not find her. I told Mrs. Grose, "She's gone out. She's with her."

"With Miss Jessel?"

"Yes. Miles and Flora planned it. He played the piano for me so Flora could sneak out alone. We must find her."

I knew that Flora would be at the lake where I first saw Miss Jessel. But when we got there, we could not find Flora.

"She must have rowed over to the other side. The rowboat is missing."

"How could she? She's just a child."

"She's not alone, and at such times, she's not a child. She's an old, old woman."

We walked around the lake to the other side. Soon we found the rowboat. A little farther on, we saw Flora. When she saw us, she started picking flowers.

Mrs. Grose ran to her and hugged her.

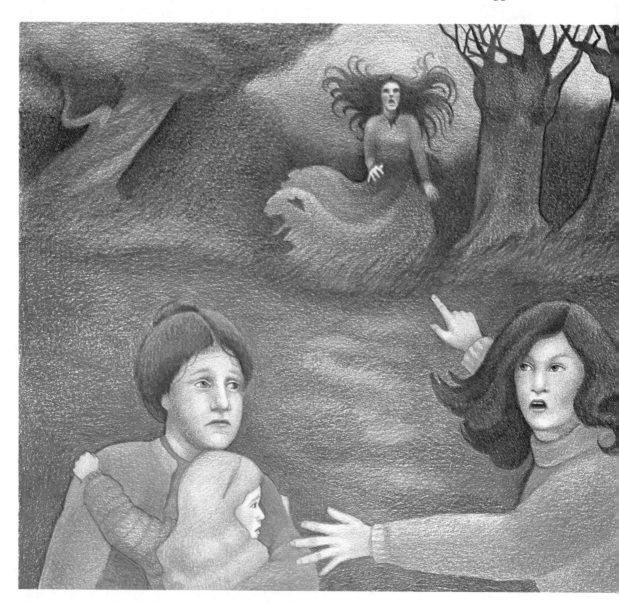

Flora looked at me as if she thought I might no longer trust her. Then she smiled sweetly and asked, "Where is Miles?"

That was too much for me. I asked, "Where is Miss Jessel?"

I had never mentioned this name before to Flora, and she was shocked. Mrs. Grose screamed.

Then I saw the figure of Miss Jessel across the lake. I pointed to her and shouted, "She's there!"

Flora looked at me in horror. I told her, "You see her as well as you see me."

Flora didn't bother to look across the lake. But Mrs. Grose looked and looked where I had pointed. Finally she said, "She isn't there. Nobody's there. You've never seen her. Poor Miss Jessel is dead and buried."

Then she tried to calm Flora. "It's all a mistake, love. We'll go home right away."

Flora was holding tightly to Mrs. Grose. All her beauty seemed to have disappeared. The look in her eyes made her old and ugly.

She said to me, "I see nobody. I never have. You're cruel, and I don't like you!" She hugged Mrs. Grose and cried, "Take me away. Take me away from *her*!"

Flora's words hurt me, even though I knew they came from that figure across the lake. I said, "I've done my best, but I've lost you. Good-bye."

I cried after they left. It was almost dark when I got back to the house. Flora's things were gone from my room. She would now stay with Mrs. Grose.

Later in the evening, Miles came into my room and sat down. I felt he wanted to tell me something, but he said little.

The next morning, Mrs. Grose told me that Flora had a fever.

"She was awake most of the night," Mrs. Grose said. "She was afraid you would come in."

"Flora will never speak to me again," I said. "You must take her away from here, away from me. Take her to her uncle."

"But why?"

"I need some time with Miles — alone. I believe he wants to tell me everything. He tried last night, but couldn't. A day or two more will bring it all out."

"You are right," Mrs. Grose said. "Flora must leave this place. Since yesterday, I've heard such awful things from her — about you. I have no idea where she learned such shocking words."

"From them," I said.

"She must get away from this house — and *them*," she said.

I almost hugged her with joy. The day before she had seen nothing at the lake. Yet she still believed in me.

Mrs. Grose had more to say. The letter I had written to the children's uncle had disappeared. She was sure that Miles had taken it.

"Now I know what he must have done at school," she said. "He stole letters."

I was sure it was worse than that. But I simply said, "I think he is already ashamed of himself and wants to confess. If he confesses, he's saved. And if he's saved, I am, too."

Mrs. Grose said good-bye and then left.

All that day, I left Miles alone. I wanted him to feel free.

That evening, we ate together in the dining room. Miles asked, "Is Flora really very sick?"

"She'll be better soon," I said. "She just needs to get away from this place."

Miles got up and walked to the window where I had seen Quint. By this time, the servants had left the room.

Miles said, "So now we are alone. I hope it won't be too lonely for you."

I told him that I always enjoyed his company. Then I asked, "Don't you remember what I told you the other night? I said I would do anything to help you."

"I remember. You wanted me to tell you something."

"That's it. Tell me what's on your mind."

"Do you mean now — here?"

"There couldn't be a better time or place."

Suddenly, he seemed afraid of me. "I will tell you everything you want to know," he said. "But not right now."

"Why not?"

"I have to see one of the servants about something."

I knew he was lying, and I felt ashamed for making him lie. "I'll wait for you to come back," I said. "But first, will you tell me one little thing? Did you take the letter I wrote to your uncle?"

Just then, Peter Quint appeared outside the window. I jumped up and grabbed Miles. I held him with his back to the window, so he could not see Quint's awful face. I felt I was fighting a demon for a human soul.

Poor Miles began to sweat, and he became very pale, but he answered my question. "Yes, I took the letter. I wanted to see what you said about me."

I looked out the window again, but Quint was gone. I was winning the battle! I was saving Miles!

I asked him more questions. "Is that what you did at school — take letters or other things?"

"No," Miles said.

"Then what did you do?"

"I said things. Some of the boys must have repeated them, and the teachers found out."

"What things did you say?"

Before Miles could answer, I saw Quint's face outside the window again. I screamed at it, "No more! No more!"

I could feel Miles's heart pounding as I held him. "Is she here?" he asked. "Is it Miss Jessel?"

"It's not Miss Jessel. But it's *there* — for the last time."

Miles turned his head and looked around the room. "Is it *he*?" he asked.

My victory was now almost complete. "Whom do you mean by *he*?" I asked.

"Peter Quint, you devil!" Miles cried. Then he looked puzzled and asked, "Where is he?"

"What does he matter now, my own? What will he *ever* matter?" I asked. "I have you, but he has lost you forever." Then, to prove that I was right, I pointed outside. "There, *there*!" I said to Miles.

Miles turned round to the window, stared, and glared again, and saw nothing but the quiet day. Then he let out a cry like a creature hurled over a cliff. I grasped him as if to catch him in his fall, and I held him in my arms.

But at the end of a minute I began to feel what it truly was that I held. We were alone with the quiet day, and his little heart — dispossessed — had stopped.

READING COMPREHENSION

Select the best choice to complete each statement. Then write the entire sentence on your paper.

1. The young woman took the job as governess because _____.
   a. she wanted to be in the country
   b. she knew the job would be easy
   c. the uncle charmed her into it

2. The strange sounds didn't bother the governess the first night in her new home because she was _____.
   a. too tired to hear them
   b. too afraid
   c. so happy about her new job

3. Miles was not away at school because he _____.
   a. had run away
   b. had been dismissed
   c. was sick

4. The man the governess saw in the tower _____.
   a. was a relative of the uncle
   b. fit the description of a dead man
   c. was a friend of Mrs. Grose

5. The woman ghost was _____.
   a. a governess who had died
   b. the kitchen maid
   c. the uncle's wife

6. The governess felt the ghosts had come to _____.
   a. scare her
   b. kill her
   c. harm the children

7. She did not tell the uncle because she was afraid he would _____.
   a. take the children away
   b. think she was crazy
   c. blame Mrs. Grose

8. When she saw Peter Quint appear outside the window, she _____.
   a. chased after him
   b. ran away
   c. held Miles so that he could not see Quint's awful face

9. At the end of the story, _____.
   a. Flora ran away
   b. Miles was dead
   c. Mrs. Grose sent for the police

For Discussion

1. "The Turn of the Screw" is a story about the conflict between good and evil. Which characters are good? Which are evil? Are some characters both? Explain your answers.

2. Do you think the ghosts in this story were real? Or were they inventions of the troubled mind of the governess? Explain your answer.

3. The last lines of the story are: ". . . I began to feel what it truly was that I held. We were alone with the quiet day, and his little heart — dispossessed — had stopped." What do these lines mean? Did the ending surprise you? Why or why not?

4. "The Turn of the Screw" is told from the governess's point of view. Explain whether this makes it easier or harder to believe her story.

UNDERSTANDING LITERATURE

Imagery. "The Turn of the Screw" is a story about the conflict between good and evil. The mood of the story shifts back and forth from the sense that all is well to feelings that evil is going to win.

The images the author used to describe the setting and the characters help the mood change from peace to horror. Some images seem lovely and beautiful, while others are unpleasant and frightening.

Read the passages below. On your paper, label the mood of each as *good* or *evil*.

1. "Flora was the most beautiful and charming child I had ever seen."

2. "'He is handsome in a slick sort of way, but he is no gentleman.'"

3. "He stared at me. . . . As he did, everything became as quiet as death."

4. "I had never seen such sweetness and innocence in a boy. It was impossible not to love him."

5. "[Miss Jessel] kept looking at Flora. It was as if she wanted to get hold of her."

Writing

Pretend you are the governess. Write two letters to your family. Write one on the first day of the job. Tell how wonderful everything is. Write the second one after you've seen the ghosts. Use pleasant images in the first letter. Use frightening ones in the second.

Section Review

VOCABULARY

Similes, Metaphors, and Personification.
A *simile* is a direct comparison between two objects using the word *like* or *as*. For example, this line contains a simile: "The wind tapped like a tired man." The poet says the wind is like a person.

A *metaphor* is a comparison that does not use the word *like* or *as*. A metaphor is a suggested comparison. For example:

"Hope" is the thing with feathers —
That perches in the soul —

Here, the poet does not use the word *like* or *as*. She suggests that hope and a bird are alike.

Personification is the description of an object, animal, or idea as though it were human. Personification may be in the form of either a simile or a metaphor. In "The Wind Tapped Like a Tired Man" Emily Dickinson compared the wind to a man.

Read these lines from this section. On your paper, label each as a *metaphor* or *simile*. If the comparison is also personification, write that word as well. Then tell what each comparison means.

1. "In the center yawned the circular pit from whose jaws I had escaped."

2. "I began to feel that the house was like a castle."

3. "She looked like an angel. . . ."

READING

Making Inferences. Sometimes an author does not say something directly. Rather, the author suggests something.

When you try to figure out what the author is suggesting, you are *making inferences*. Inferences are guesses based on the information the author gives you in a selection.

Read the following sentences about the selections in this section. On your paper, write what each author was inferring.

1. In the "Pit and the Pendulum," the narrator was freed when the French took over the town. You can guess, or infer, that the man was _____.
   a. guilty of a terrible crime
   b. a prisoner of war
   c. a madman

2. In "Poor Sandy," Sandy's first wife was sold. Sandy's second wife was sent away to work for someone else. You can infer that slaves were _____.
   a. free to work anywhere
   b. difficult to control
   c. treated like property, not people

3. In "The Turn of the Screw," the governess saw ghosts that others did not see. She believed that it was her duty to protect the children from these demons. One inference you could make is that she _____.
   a. disliked the children in her care and wanted to hurt them
   b. took her job too seriously and it affected her mind
   c. liked communicating with spirits

WRITING POETRY

Poets paint vivid pictures with words. They use language to create images that the reader can "see." The words of a poem can often make you see a scene in your mind. Sometimes the words appeal to your senses — your sense of taste, smell, touch, and hearing. The words below appeal to your senses:

Hearing: *singing, whispering*

Sight: *red rose, skyscraper*

Taste: *lemon, chocolate*

Touch: *slippery, smooth*

Smell: *perfume, garbage*

1. Think of other words that appeal to your five senses. Write them on your paper.

Sometimes poets use comparisons to create imagery. A good comparison may appeal to one sense or several senses at the same time.

2. On a piece of paper use comparisons to describe each item on the list below.
   a. A snowstorm is like _____.

   b. Love is _____.

   c. Hunger is _____.

   d. A kitten is _____.

   e. Excitement is like _____.

Think about the details you can use to help the reader understand one of these comparisons; for example, you could compare excitement to a firecracker. How is excitement like a firecracker?

Excitement starts like a
   sputtering firecracker with
   a spark.

It explodes with a bang.
You feel yourself rocketing
   into the sky.

For a short time the night sky
   is full of flaming colors.
Then the colors fade.

Everything is quiet.
The sky is again smooth and
   dark.
The night is again calm
   and still.

3. Take one of the comparisons you completed in the first part of this exercise or choose another comparison. Add details that appeal to the senses to create a short poem. Before you write, you may wish to reread the poems of Emily Dickinson (pp. 200–202) and imitate her way of creating unusual comparisons. Before you begin, here is a checklist to keep in mind:

☐ Choose words to describe the sensory impression of the person, thing, or feeling you wish to describe. How does it look? Sound? Feel? Taste? Smell?

☐ Use details and comparisons to describe your feelings about the subject of the poem.

☐ Dickinson used rhymes as well as imagery in her poems. You may use rhymes or not, as you wish.

QUIZ

The following is a quiz for Section 5. Write the answers in complete sentences on your paper.

Reading Comprehension

1. What role did the rats play in "The Pit and the Pendulum"? What happened after they solved one problem the prisoner had?

2. In "Jim Bridger and the Fiddler Who Wouldn't Fiddle," what was Bridger's alarm clock? To what use did he put it besides waking himself up?

3. In "A Word Is Dead," what did Emily Dickinson believe about a word?

4. In "Poor Sandy," why did Tenie turn Sandy into a tree? How did the plan go wrong?

5. What happened to the little boy Miles at the end of Henry James's story "The Turn of the Screw"?

Understanding Literature

6. What mood did Poe create in "The Pit and the Pendulum"? Where did the story take place? Identify three details that added to the mood.

7. What was the mood in the story about Jim Bridger? Mention three details about the characters or setting that contributed to this mood.

8. To what did Dickinson compare hope in "Hope Is the Thing With Feathers"?

9. What effect does the story "Poor Sandy" have on its readers? Mention three details of the plot that add to this effect.

10. Between what two forces is the struggle, or conflict, in "The Turn of the Screw"? Identify two details that help describe each of the forces.

COMPOSITION

1. Choose a place that you know well as the setting for a story. Write one paragraph about it as the setting for a mystery or a tale of some sort of horror. Write a second paragraph about the same place, but this time describe it as the setting for a happy or an entertaining story. Choose your words carefully to help create the mood for each paragraph.

2. Imagine that you had been imprisoned in the dungeon described in "The Pit and the Pendulum." Write one or two paragraphs describing your feelings while in the prison. Pick the aspect of the experience you found most terrifying and describe it in detail.

3. Imagine that someone really did have the power to turn you into something else, as Tenie turned Sandy into a tree. Write a paragraph telling what you would like to be and why.

4. In a paragraph, describe Emily Dickinson's feelings about a word, or hope.

SECTION 6

A Voice of Courage

STEPHEN CRANE (1871–1900)

A man said to the universe:
Sir, I exist!

— Stephen Crane

Introduction

Stephen Crane believed that each person sees the world in his or her own way. His goal as a writer was to present his personal view as honestly as he could.

Anyone who reads Crane's works gets the feeling of sharing his vision. His power as a writer comes from the way he uses simple language to describe his characters' feelings and experiences.

Crane's Early Life

Born on November 1, 1871, in Newark, New Jersey, Crane grew up a strong swimmer and an excellent baseball player.

Crane's two oldest brothers worked as newspaper reporters, and as a young teenager, he began to help them gather facts for stories. Like all good reporters, Crane trained himself to find the facts and report them objectively — to describe events as accurately and unemotionally as possible.

After one year of college, Crane became a reporter in New York City. For a while, he lived in the streets with the homeless people of the Bowery. He wanted to make sure his stories about life in the slums were correct in every detail.

When he was 21, he wrote a novel — a long work of fiction — that would tell people more about what it was like to live in the slums. The book was called *Maggie: A Girl of the Streets,* and its realistic descriptions shocked many people.

Just one year later, Crane had completed another novel. This novel — *The Red Badge of Courage* — tells about a teenage soldier who faces his first battle during the Civil War.

Crane himself had had no personal experience with war. But he remembered his older brothers' tales of their experiences as Civil War soldiers, and he had studied Matthew Brady's photographs of the Civil War again and again. At last Crane could imagine every detail of what it would be like to be in the midst of a battle. *The Red Badge of Courage* captures his vision of the experience of war.

By 1895, *The Red Badge of Courage* had become one of the most popular books in America. At the age of 23, Stephen Crane was respected as one of America's greatest writers.

Fame and Adventure

Fame brought Crane many new assignments as a reporter. He traveled to Texas and Mexico to write about life in the West. There he narrowly escaped being killed by bandits. Crane wrote several stories based on his experiences in Texas.

Crane also traveled to Greece to cover the Turkish War and to Cuba to report on the Spanish-American War. This last assignment again brought him close to death when the ship he was on sank. Crane wrote a newspaper article as well as a story called "The Open Boat" based on this ordeal. Both the article and the story are included in this section.

All this travel and hardship took its toll on Crane's health. He became ill with tuberculosis. Yet he continued to travel and to write articles, stories, and poems.

Crane's poetry, like his stories and articles, uses simple words and vivid images. He wrote poetry because he felt that it presented his ideas more directly than other forms of writing. Two of his poems, "A Man Said to the Universe" and "The Wayfarer," are included in this section.

Crane spent the last two years of his life in Europe. He hoped the change in climate would cure him. It did not. He continued to write until his death in 1900, a few months before his twenty-ninth birthday.

In his brief lifetime, he had come face to face with poverty, failure, great danger, and illness. He had also known great adventure, and literary success. He did not expect life to be fair or easy. He lived out his 29 years with honesty and courage. Like his most admirable characters, Crane faced life head-on.

The Red Badge of Courage

by Stephen Crane

As you read this dramatization of the novel The Red Badge of Courage, *think about the fears of the soldiers, their loyalties, and their sense of duty. Ask yourself why this story about young Henry Fleming has moved so many people since its publication in 1893.*

CHARACTERS

Jim Conklin
Soldier 1
The Youth (Pvt. Henry Fleming)
Wilson
The Youth's Mother
Colonel
Soldier 2, on firing line
Lieutenant
Sergeant
Soldier 3, on firing line
General
Tattered Man
Corporal
Soldier 4
Soldier 5
Soldier 6
Narrator

It is a cold spring morning in 1863. The smoke of several campfires drifts among the soldiers of the 304th New York regiment, Union Army. Some of the men are bent over their plates, eating their breakfast. Others are shaving and getting washed. The Youth, Pvt. Henry Fleming, is startled by the shouts of a soldier running up, waving a bright red shirt.

Jim: We're movin' out! We're movin' out!

Others: Who told yeh? Who says so? Don't believe it. Me neither.

Jim: I tell yeh we're movin' out t'morrah! Got it from a friend, see, who got it from a cavalryman who got it from his brother who jest happens to be one of the orderlies at division headquarters.

Soldier 1: This here army ain't never gonna move again. I've got m'self ready t' go eight times in the last four weeks and we ain't moved yet.

Jim: Look here, I don't much care whether you believe it or not. Don't give a hang. You jest suit yerselves. (*He walks off.*)

(*Later that morning, the Youth is inside his hut as Jim Conklin and a soldier named Wilson enter. A third soldier follows them.*)

Youth: Jim?

Jim: Huh? What's that? You say somethin', Henry?

Youth: I . . . I was jest . . . yeh think there's goin' to be a real battle?

Wilson (*unbelieving*): Huh!

Jim: Oh, you'll see fightin' this time, m' boy. I mean what'll be out-and-out fightin'.

Youth: Jim?

Jim: What's th' matter?

Youth (*pauses*): How do yeh think th' reg'ment'll do?

Jim: Oh, they'll fight all right, I guess. After they oncet get into it.

Youth: Do yeh think . . . I mean . . . yeh think any of the boys'll run?

Jim: Oh, there may be a few of 'em run. 'Specially when they first goes under fire. Of course, it might happen the hull kit-and-boodle starts to run. . . . I mean if some big fightin' comes first off. And then again they might jest stay and fight like fun.

Youth: Nobody knows.

Jim: Huh? What's that?

Youth: What's it like?

Jim: Well now, lookee here, I don't figger we're goin' t' lick th' hull Rebel Army all-to-oncet th' first time out. No, sir. But we'll fight though, I reckon. Better than some and worse than others. Oh, sure. They call us "fresh fish" and everything. But th' boys come of good stock and most of 'em'll fight like sin after they oncet get shootin'.

Youth: Have yeh . . . have yeh ever thought yeh might run yourself?

Jim: Well . . . I've thought it might get too hot for ol' Jim Conklin in some of them scrimmages, and if a whole lot of boys started to run, why I s'pose I'd start and run. And if I oncet started to run, I'd run like th' devil and no mistake. But if everybody else was a standin' and fightin', why, I'd stand and fight. B' jiminey, I sure would. Wouldn't *you*, Henry?

(*The next morning, the regiment moves out. At noon, the troops stop for lunch. The Youth, seated off by himself, pulls off a boot and looks down at a hole in his sock. He hears a voice.*)

Voice of Mother: Yeh send 'em back. (*The Youth looks up to see who's speaking.*) Yeh git a hole in 'em, you send 'em right back to me, hear?

(*The mother appears. But she is standing at the doorway to the Youth's home. The Youth imagines himself at home.*)

Mother: I've knit yeh eight pairs of socks, Henry, and I've put in all yer best shirts, b'cause I want my boy to be jest as warm and comfortable as anybody in th' army. Whenever they get holes in 'em, I want yeh to send 'em right-away back to me, so's I kin dern 'em.

Youth: Yes, ma'am.

Mother: An' be careful now t' choose yer company. There's lots of bad men in th' army, Henry. Th' army makes 'em wild and they like nothin' better than th' job

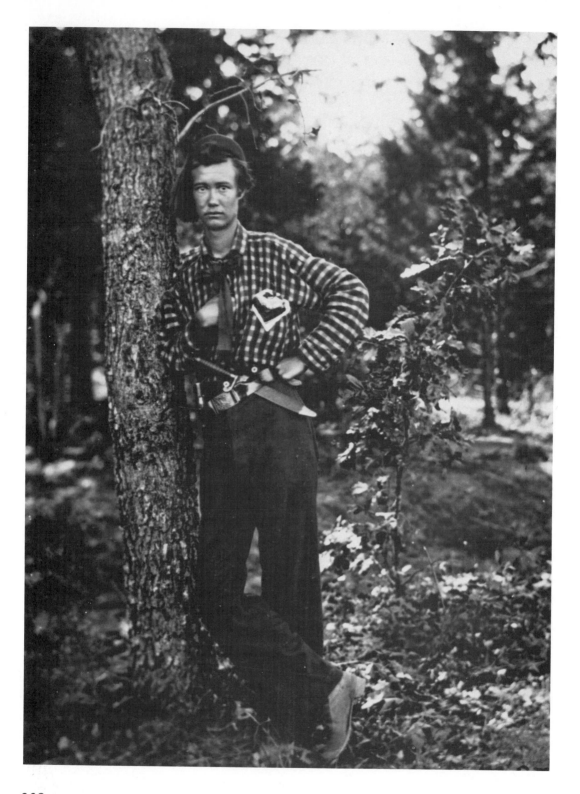

of leadin' off a young feller like yeh, who ain't never been away from home much, and a-learning 'em to drink and swear. Keep clear of them folks, Henry.

Youth: Yes, ma'am.

Mother: And take good care of yerself in this here fightin' business. Don't yeh go shirkin', child, on my account. If th' time comes when yeh have to be kilt or do a mean thing, why, don't yeh think of anything 'cept what's right.

Youth: Yes, ma'am.

Mother: Here. Here's yer Bible. I don't presume yeh'll be a-settin' readin' it all day, but comes a time yeh'll want advice, there's wisdom in it, child. There's wisdom with little or no searchin'.

Youth: I'll read it, Ma.

Mother: Well, then. Be a good boy. An' don't forget about yer socks. All right?

(There are tears in the mother's eyes. The Youth is about to embrace her, but as he reaches forward, she disappears.)

Wilson: What's that yer saying?

(The Youth, looking bewildered, shakes his head.)

Wilson: Boy, I don't know, Henry, yer sure actin' peculiar. Come on, now. We're movin' again.

(The troops are on the move when the sound of artillery is heard. The Colonel comes riding down the line on horseback.)

Colonel: The grove! Make for the grove!

(The men run for the grove and form a firing line.)

Soldier 2 *(on the Youth's right)*: Hey, yeh know what I heard? I heard th' Colonel say he's goin' t' shoot th' first man who turns and runs.

Wilson: Henry? *(The Youth turns to Wilson, puzzled.)* You do me a favor? *(The Youth stares at Wilson.)* It's my first and last . . . battle.

Youth: What?

Wilson: I can feel it. My first and last battle, Henry. Something tells me. I'm a goner this first time and I . . . Henry, I want yeh to take these here things . . . to my folks. *(He holds up a small packet of letters.)*

Youth: Why . . . what th' devil . . . ?

Lieutenant: Here they come!

Soldier 2: Oh, Lordy, Lordy. We're in for it now.

Lieutenant: Fire!

Sergeant: Fire!

(The troops open fire. Men drop here and there like bundles. A soldier on the line screams a wild, barbaric scream and starts to run.)

Lieutenant: Get back! Get back!

(Soldiers continue to fire. But there is little fire from the enemy.)

Youth: What's happenin'?

Soldier 3 *(on the Youth's left)*: They've stopped.

Youth: Huh?

Soldier 3: Oh, dear Gawd, they've stopped.

Sergeant: Hold your fire! Hold your fire!

(The Youth looks down the line of soldiers. He sees fallen soldiers, then turns to the soldier on his left, feeling sudden tenderness and goodwill toward him.)

Youth: Gee . . . ain't it hot, huh?

Soldier 3: You bet. I never seen sech dumb hotness. *(He laughs.)*

Lieutenant: They're coming back!

(Soldiers, their faces smudged, reload and fire. Suddenly the soldier on the Youth's left cries out.)

Soldier 3: Oh, Gawd . . . they've kilt me. Oh, Gawd. . . .

(The Youth stares in horror as the soldier slumps over. The soldier on the Youth's right lets out a howl of anguish and runs off. The gunfire is now a pounding roar. The Youth panics, stands up, bewildered and terrified. Then, taking a deep breath, he starts to run. Like a blind man, he trips, falls, rises again, crosses an open field, plunges into a grove of trees, then hears the sound of approaching horses. In the clearing beyond, the Youth sees the Colonel and the Division General.)

Colonel: We're holdin' 'em, sir. Right down the line.

General: By heaven we are! We'll wallop 'em now! We've got 'em sure!

(The Youth is stunned by the news. Tears come to his eyes. He stumbles on through the brush. He comes to a dusty road where a procession of wounded soldiers is approaching. Bloodstained and tattered, the men are cursing and groaning and wailing to themselves. The Youth watches the wounded pass by, then steps into line beside a soldier fouled with dust and in a tattered uniform.)

Tattered Man: Pretty good fight.

Youth: What? . . . What?

Tattered Man: It was a pretty good fight, wasn't it?

Youth: Yes.

Tattered Man: I was talkin' cross pickets with a boy from Georgia one night, an' that boy he sez, "Yer fellers'll run like th' devil when they oncet hear a gun," he sez. An I sez back to 'um, "Maybe yer fellers'll all run like th' devil, too!" Well . . . he larfed. No, sir. They didn't run today. They stood and fit, b' Gawd.

(The Youth tries to move ahead, but the Tattered Man keeps right up with him.)

Tattered Man: Where yeh hit? *(The Youth, in panic, looks the other way.)* Hey, I sed, where yeh hit, ol' boy?

Youth: I . . . I . . .

(The Youth turns away and moves back down the line. Because of the Tattered Man's question, he is now sure everyone knows his guilt. He wishes that he, too, had a wound, a red badge of courage. He falls into line next to a gravely wounded soldier.)

Youth: Jim! Jim Conklin!

Jim: Well . . . hello, Henry.

Youth: I'm so glad to see yeh, Jim.

Jim: What a circus it was, huh? An' yeh know, b' jiminey, I got shot.

Youth: Let me help you, Jim.

Jim *(clutches the Youth's arm):* I'll tell yeh what I'm 'fraid of, Henry. I'm 'fraid I'll fall down an' . . . an' then them artillery wagons . . . they'll like as not run me over.

(The Tattered Man appears at the Youth's side.)

Tattered Man: Yeh better take 'im outta th' road. He'll git run over sure.

Youth: Jim, yeh come with me. Please!

(Jim tries to wrench himself free.)

Jim: Wha'sa matter?

Youth: Please!

Jim: Oh? Into th' field. Th' field, huh?

(Jim breaks away and runs off blindly into the field, the Youth and Tattered Man following. Suddenly Jim's body stiffens and straightens. Shaking all over, he meets death.)

Youth *(filled with grief, faces toward the sound of battle):* Damn you! Damn you!

(The Youth, weary and forlorn, walks away. He comes upon a company of infantry, charging across the field. He tries to question them, but they will not stop. When he grabs one by the arm, the soldier yells at the Youth to let him go, and finally hits the Youth over the head with his rifle. When the Youth regains consciousness, a friendly soldier is standing over him, who helps him find his way back to his regiment.)

Wilson: Halt! Halt there!

Youth: Hello, Wilson.

Wilson: Henry. That yeh, Henry?

Youth: It's me.

Wilson: Well now, I give yeh up for a goner, that's sure. I thought yeh was dead, Henry.

Youth: Well . . . I've had an awful time. I got separated from th' reg'ment. I got shot. In th' head. I never seen sech fightin' an' awful time.

Wilson: Here, let me have a good look at it first, Henry. You set yerself down there an' I'll see how bad it is. *(The Youth sits down.)* Henry, it's as I thought. Yeh've been grazed by a ball. It's raised a queer lump jest as if some feller had lammed yeh on th' head with a club. But it stopped bleedin' a long time ago. *(He bandages the wound.)* Good. That's good. And yeh never hollered 'er nothin'. Yer a good 'un, Henry. Most men would a been in th' hospital long ago. A shot in th' head ain't foolin' business. Come on, now, I'm goin' t' see yeh git a good night's sleep.

(The next morning, the soldiers line up to move out. Wilson steps up with an extra gun for the Youth.)

Wilson: Here you go, Henry.

Youth: Did yeh ever think . . .

Wilson: Huh? What's that?

Youth: . . . that some people are chosen maybe?

Wilson: Chosen? Fer what?

Youth: I mean like chosen of th' gods. People jest meant to be picked out from all th' rest and no matter what happens they get through jest fine. You can't kill 'em b'cause they're chosen of the gods. Do you believe in that?

Wilson: Henry, I don't know what th' devil yer even talkin' about.

Corporal: Keep it movin'. Move along there!

(The sound of gunfire grows louder. The soldiers take cover. Wilson is suddenly at the Youth's side.)

Wilson: Henry, I uh . . . if it's all th' same to yeh . . . well, I guess yeh might as well give me back them letters.

Youth: All right. *(He hands the packet to Wilson, whose face is turned away from him in shame. Seeing his friend's embarrassment, the Youth says nothing.)*

(A loud volley of gunfire is heard in the woods. The order is given to fire, and the Youth, with wild hatred in his eyes, fires directly at the oncoming line of enemy soldiers. The gray line falters, and falls back in retreat. The order is given to charge. The soldiers run into a tremendous volley of enemy gunfire. Several soldiers are struck. One by one, the soldiers come to a halt.)

Lieutenant: Come on, yeh fools! Yeh can't stay here! Move! *(No one moves.)* Skulkin' cowards! Yeh want t' die right here? We've got t' move! Got to!

Wilson: Well, Henry . . . I guess we're finished.

Youth: Oh, shut up! Come on, let's go! Let's go!

(The Youth charges forward like a madman. Wilson and others follow. A color sergeant carrying the flag is struck down. The Youth wrenches the flag away, and charges directly into the line of fire. The soldiers in blue hurl themselves recklessly on toward the gray line. The gray line breaks and runs. A hoarse and frantic cheer goes up from the blue line. The Youth surveys the battlefield where gray corpses are scattered about. The cheers die out. The guns grow silent.)

(The next day, the battle-weary soldiers make their way back to permanent camp. The Youth and Wilson trudge alongside each other when three soldiers come up alongside, faces shining with excitement.)

Soldier 4: You fellers jest oughta heard!

Soldier 5: Right next to us. Th' Colonel and th' Lieutenant was talkin'.

Soldier 6: Th' Colonel, he sez, "Who was th' lad who carried th' flag?"

Soldier 5: That's jest what he said. An' th' Lieutenant speaks right up an' sez, "That was Fleming, sir. Private Fleming carried th' flag."

Soldier 6: An' th' Colonel sez, "If I had 10,000 wildcats like him, I could tear th' stomach outta this war in less'n a week."

Soldier 4: You and Wilson, sez th' Lieutenant. You two was headin' th' charge an' howlin' like Injuns all th' time.

Soldier 6: An' yeh know what th' Colonel sez then? He sez, "They both deserve to be major generals." That's exactly what he sez. Major generals.

Wilson: Yer lyin'.

Soldier 5: Swear to God.

Youth: He never said it.

Soldier 4: He did, by Gawd. We heard 'em!

(The Youth and Wilson glance at each other. Despite their embarrassment, their eyes are glistening and their faces are flushed with pleasure.)

Narrator: The Battle of Chancellorsville lasted four days and ended on May 4, 1863. Twenty-five thousand men were killed or wounded including a Southern general known to his troops as Stonewall Jackson. All the wounded on these fields of battle had received their red badge of courage. But the Youth, however, emerged from his struggles with something else. He knew that he would never again quail before his guides wherever they should point him. He had been to touch the great death, and found out that after all, it was but the great death. He was a man.

READING COMPREHENSION

Select the best choice to complete each statement below. Then write the entire sentence on your paper.

1. Jim Conklin said that if everyone else was ready to fight, he _____.
   a. would fight, too
   b. would run away
   c. wouldn't know what to do

2. When the Youth heard his mother's voice, he _____.
   a. imagined that he was back home
   b. looked up and saw her in his tent
   c. read a letter from her

3. The Youth ran away because _____.
   a. he didn't believe in fighting
   b. he saw another soldier die next to him
   c. everybody else was running, too

4. When Henry wished that he had a "red badge of courage," he was hoping that the wound would _____.
   a. not be serious
   b. show his bravery
   c. prove he would not die

For Discussion

1. Many people think that *The Red Badge of Courage* is a very realistic war story. Do you agree or disagree? Explain.

2. Why does Crane sometimes refer to Henry as "the Youth" rather than by his name?

3. How do you think Henry would behave the next time he faced a battle?

UNDERSTANDING LITERATURE

Theme. The *theme* of a play or story is the main idea or message the author is writing about. It is the point, usually about life or nature, that the author feels strongly about. The author uses the characters, the setting, and the plot to make the point.

Some stories and plays contain more than one theme. *The Red Badge of Courage* contains several intertwined themes about courage, war, and growing up. Each theme is supported by the character Henry Fleming and the setting — the battle. Stephen Crane used Henry's actions and feelings to express several themes.

Here are three themes from *The Red Badge of Courage*:

a. Confusion, fear, and luck are as much a part of war as bravery and planning.

b. A child becomes an adult when he or she acts from a sense of what is right rather than out of fear or ignorance.

c. You must conquer the fear of death before you can think clearly enough to face battle bravely.

Below are passages that contain stage directions and dialogue from the play. On your paper, match each passage with the theme or themes listed above that it suggests.

1. "**Mother:** . . . Don't yeh go shirkin', child, on my account. If th' time comes when yeh have to be kilt or do a mean thing, why, don't yeh think of anything 'cept what's right."

2. "(. . . *Bloodstained and tattered, the men are cursing and groaning and wailing to themselves. The Youth watches the wounded pass by, then steps into line beside a soldier fouled with dust and in a tattered uniform.*)"

3. "**Tattered Man:** . . . They didn't run today. They stood and fit, b' Gawd."

4. "**Youth:** Did yeh ever think . . . that some people are chosen maybe? . . . People jest meant to be picked out from all th' rest and no matter what happens they get through jest fine. . . . b'cause they're chosen of the gods."

5. "**Wilson:** Well, Henry . . . I guess we're finished.

"**Youth:** Oh, shut up! Come on, let's go! Let's go!

"(*The Youth charges forward like a madman. Wilson and others follow. A color sergeant carrying the flag is struck down. The Youth wrenches the flag away, and charges directly into the line of fire. . . .*)"

6. "**Narrator:** . . . He knew that he would never again quail before his guides wherever they should point him. He had been to touch the great death, and found out that after all, it was but the great death. He was a man."

Writing

Pretend that you are Henry. Describe the following three events in your diary: the time before battle, the time you panic and run away, and your feelings after fighting in a battle. Write at least one paragraph for each event.

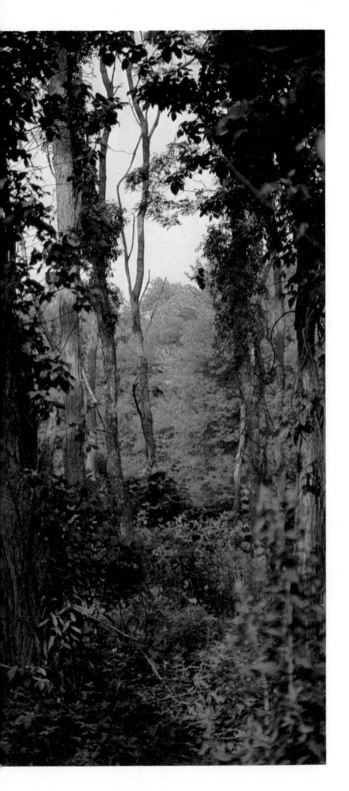

The Wayfarer

by Stephen Crane

The wayfarer
Perceiving the pathway to truth
Was struck with astonishment.
It was thickly grown with weeds.
"Ha," he said,
"I see that none has passed here
In a long time."
Later he saw that each weed
Was a singular knife.
"Well," he mumbled at last,
"Doubtless there are other roads."

---

1. What does the fact that "the pathway to truth was thickly grown with weeds" suggest?

2. In this poem, the way to truth is described as a pathway. How do people search for truth in real life? Do you think the search is as difficult as Crane suggests? Why or why not?

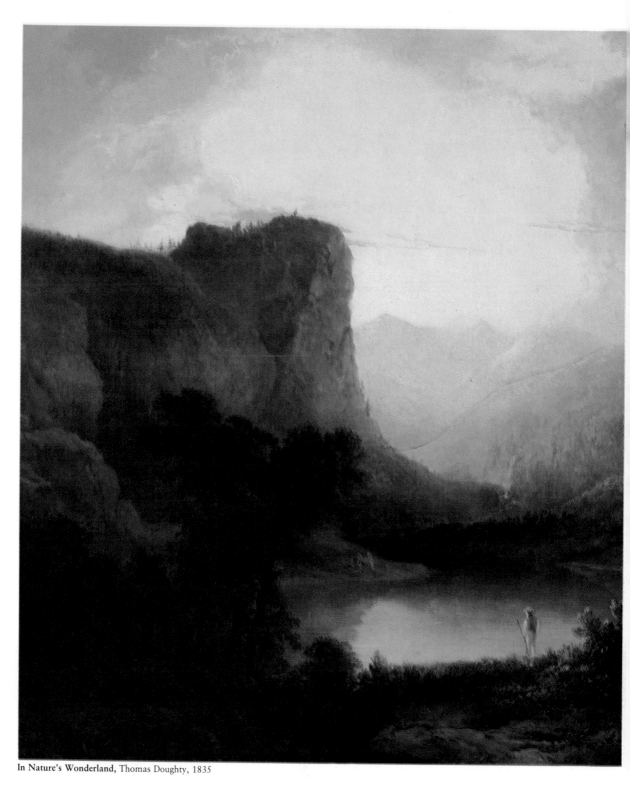

In Nature's Wonderland, Thomas Doughty, 1835

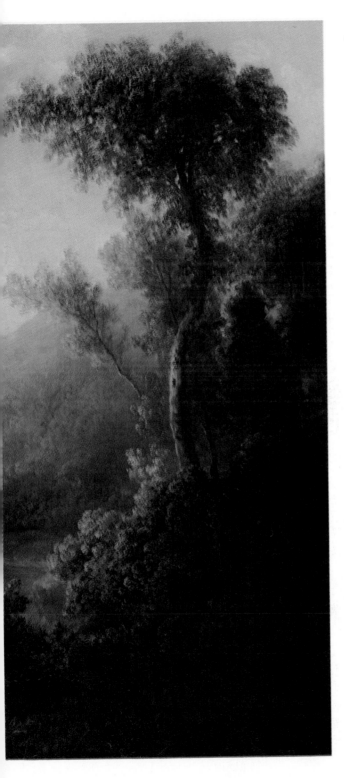

A Man Said to the Universe

by Stephen Crane

A man said to the universe:
"Sir, I exist!"
"However," replied the universe,
"The fact has not created in me
A sense of obligation."

1. Why would a man announce his existence
to the universe?

2. A sense of obligation means that someone
feels he or she must or should do something.
What did Crane mean in the last three lines
of this poem?

The Wreck of the Commodore
Stephen Crane's Own Story

The following story first appeared in a newspaper called The New York Press *on January 7, 1897. Stephen Crane had sailed on the* Commodore *to write a story about gunrunners during the Spanish-American War. As you will see, the news story he wrote is very different from the one he had expected to write.*

JACKSONVILLE, FLA., JAN. 6 — It was the afternoon of New Year's Eve. The *Commodore* was docked in Jacksonville. As stevedores steadily loaded box after box onto the ship, her hatch, like the mouth of a monster, engulfed them.

Everything was perfectly open. The *Commodore* was cleared with a cargo of arms and munitions for Cuba. The boat loaded up as calmly as if she were carrying oranges to New York.

Exchanging Farewells

There was some difficulty at the customs house. The ship was detained until twilight had settled upon the bay. The lights of Jacksonville blinked dimly through a heavy fog. At last the *Commodore* swung clear of the dock amid a chorus of good-byes. As she turned toward the distant sea, the Cubans ashore cheered. In response, the *Commodore* gave three long blasts of her whistle. Somehow they sounded sad.

There was danger in carrying guns to Cuba. Yet we were all enveloped in a gentle cheerfulness. Twice the *Commodore* was beached* before we reached open sea, on the night of January 1.

Sleep Impossible

Now huge waves came lashing at the ship and a certain lightheartedness departed from the men aboard. That night I could not sleep. I was far too excited. When I did try to get some rest in my bunk, I found I had to hold on to the bed to keep from being pitched around the room.

I went into the galley and found the cook sleeping on a bench. He had used a

---

* *Beached*—stuck in the mud.

Eight Bells, Winslow Homer, 1886

checkerboard to wedge himself in so that the motion of the ship would not dislodge him. He awoke when I entered. "I don't feel right about this ship," he said. "It strikes me that something is going to happen to us. This old ship is going to get it in the neck."

"Well, how about the men on board?" said I. "Are any of us going to get out, prophet?"

"Yes," said the cook. "Sometimes I have these feelings come over me. They are always right. It seems to me that somehow you and I will both get out and meet again somewhere."

Next I went to the pilot house. An old seaman, Tom Smith, was then at the wheel. In the darkness I could not see Tom's face. "Well, Tom," I said, "how do you like the sea?"

He said, "I've been on a number of these trips. The pay is pretty good, but I

251

think if I ever get back safe this time, I will cut it."

I sat down in a corner of the pilot house and I almost went to sleep. The captain came on duty and he was standing near me. Suddenly the chief engineer rushed in and cried that there was something wrong in the engine room. He and the captain left at once.

I was drowsing in my corner when the captain returned. He went to the room just beyond the pilot house and called to the Cuban leader, "Come get those fellows to work. I can't talk their language and I can't get them going."

No Panic on Board

The Cuban leader turned to me and said, "Go help in the fireroom. They are going to bail with buckets."

The engine room looked like the middle kitchen of hell. It was very hot. The lights burned faintly, casting strange shadows. Soapish seawater swirled and swished among machinery that roared and clattered and steamed.

Here I first came to know a young oiler named Billy Higgins. He was sloshing around, filling buckets with water and passing them to a chain of men that extended up the ship's side.

During this time there was much talk of pumps and machines. I did not understand all of it, but I did understand that there was a general and sudden ruin in the engine room.

There was no panic at this time, and even later there was never any panic on board the *Commodore*.

Lowering Boats

The heat and hard work in the fireroom affected me and I had to come on deck again. I saw the first boat about to be lowered. A certain man sat alone in the boat with a valise about as large as a hotel. I had not entirely recovered from the astonishment of witnessing this "noble deed" when I saw another valise go to him.

Now I heard the order to getaway the lifeboat which was stowed on top of the deckhouse. The deckhouse was very slippery. With each roll of the ship the men there thought themselves likely to fall into the deadly sea.

Higgins was on top of the deckhouse and with the first mate and two other men we wrestled with the lifeboat. We could have pushed a little brick schoolhouse down a road as easily as we could have moved the lifeboat. But the first mate rigged up a block and tackle. On the deck below the captain corraled enough men to move the boat. We were ordered to stop hauling.

In this lull the cook of the ship asked me, "What are you going to do?"

I told him of my plans, and he said, "Well, that's what I am going to do, too."

Now the whistle of the *Commodore* began to blow. If ever there was a voice of death and despair it was the voice of this whistle.

It was now that the first mate showed a sign of losing his grip: He raged at us who were trying to launch the lifeboat. But the boat moved at last and swung down into the water.

Afterward, I saw the captain standing with his arm in a sling, holding onto a stay with his one good hand. He directed the launching of the boat. Then he gave me a gallon jug of water to hold, and asked me what I was going to do.

I told him what I planned and he told me the cook had the same idea. Then he ordered me to go forward and be ready to launch the 10-foot dinghy.

In the 10-Foot Dinghy

I went forward with my jug of water. When the captain came we launched the dinghy, and they put me over the side to fend her off from the ship with an oar.

They handed me down the water jug, and then the cook came into the boat. We sat there in the darkness, wondering why the captain had not yet come and ordered us away from the doomed ship.

The captain was waiting for the other boats to go. Finally he hailed in the darkness, "Are you all right, Mr. Graines?"

The first mate answered, "We are all right, sir."

"Shove off, then," cried the captain.

The captain was just about to swing over the rail when a dark form came forward and a voice said, "Captain, may I go with you?"

The captain answered, "Yes, Billy, you may get in."

It was Billy Higgins, the oiler. Billy dropped into the boat and a moment later the captain followed. He brought with him an end of about 40 yards of lead line. The other end was attached to the rail of the ship.

As we swung back the captain said, "Boys, we will stay right near the ship till she goes down." Of course, this cheerful information filled us all with glee. The line kept us headed properly into the wind. As we rode over the monstrous waves, we saw upon each rise the swaying lights of the dying *Commodore*.

When the gray dawn came, the form of the *Commodore* grew slowly clear to us. We had gone a bit farther away from the ship and now she was floating with such an air of comfort. We laughed when we had time, and said, "What a gag it would be on those other fellows if she did not sink at all."

But later we saw men aboard her, and later still they began to hail us. The men on board were a mystery to us. We had seen all the boats leave the ship. We rowed back to the ship, but we did not go too near. We were four men in a 10-foot boat, and we knew that the touch of a hand on our gunwale would surely swamp us.

Helping Their Mates

The first mate cried out from the ship that the third boat had broken alongside the ship. He cried that these men had rafts, and they wished us to tow them.

The captain said, "All right."

Their rafts were floating astern. "Jump in!" cried the captain. But there was a strange hesitation. In the gray light of morning the seven men on board looked like ghosts. They were silent save for the words of the mate to the captain. Here

Early Morning After a Storm at Sea, Winslow Homer, 1902

was death, but here also was an indefinable kind of strength.

Four men clambered over the rails. They stood there watching the cold, steely sheen of the sweeping waves.

"Jump," cried the captain again.

The old chief engineer first obeyed the order. He landed on the outside raft and the captain told him how to grip the raft. He obeyed as promptly as a child in school.

A stoker followed him, and then the first mate threw his hands over his head and plunged into the sea. He had no life belt. I somehow felt that I could see in the expression of his hands, and in the very toss of his head, rage, rage, rage. He was full of rage as he leaped to death.

And then I saw Tom Smith, the man who was going to quit filibustering* after this trip. He jumped to a raft and turned his face toward us. On board the *Commodore* three men remained. Silently, they gazed at us. One man had his arms folded and was leaning against the deckhouse. The stoker on the first raft threw us a line and we began to tow. Of course, we all

---

* *Filibustering*—gun running.

on the raft ready to spring. His face was the face of a lost man reaching upward. And we knew that the weight of his hand on our gunwale would doom us.

The *Commodore* Sinks

The cook let go of the line. We rowed around to see if we could not get a line from the chief engineer. All this time there were no shrieks, no groans. And then the *Commodore* sank.

She lurched and swung, righted and dove into the sea. The rafts and the men on them were suddenly swallowed by the ocean. And then the men in the dinghy uttered words that were something far beyond words.

The lighthouse of Mosquito Inlet stuck above the horizon like the point of a pin. We turned our dinghy toward the shore.

The story of life in an open boat for 30 hours would be instructive for the young. But none of it is to be told here and now. For my part I would prefer to tell the story at once. From it would shine the splendid courage of Captain Edward Murphy and of William Higgins, the oiler. At this time, however, let us say that when we were swamped in the surf, the captain gave orders amid the wildness of the waves as clearly as if he had been on the deck of a battleship.

John Kitchell of Daytona came running down the beach. He dashed into the water and dragged the cook. Then he went after the captain, but the captain sent him to me. Then we saw Billy Higgins lying with his forehead on the sand. His head was clear of water, but he was dead.

knew that it was impossible for the dinghy to pull the rafts to safety. Our dinghy was within six inches of the water's edge. Enormous waves were breaking all around us. I knew that a tugboat would have a hard time moving the rafts.

But we tried it and would have continued but something happened. Suddenly the boat began to go backward. A man on the first raft was pulling the line hand over hand. He was drawing us toward him.

He had turned into a demon. He was wild — wild as a tiger. He was crouched

READING COMPREHENSION

Select the best choice to complete each statement below. Then write the entire sentence on your paper.

1. The *Commodore* was going to Cuba to _____.
   a. cruise near the island
   b. deliver arms and munitions
   c. pick up passengers

2. There were men left on board the *Commodore* because _____.
   a. they thought the boat wouldn't sink
   b. they didn't know better
   c. one of the lifeboats was destroyed

3. The men in the dinghy stopped pulling the raft because _____.
   a. they didn't care about the others
   b. it was hard work
   c. a man on the raft endangered the dinghy

4. "A touch . . . on our gunwale would surely swamp us" means _____.
   a. it would sink the boat
   b. it would be bad luck
   c. the men would be put under a spell

For Discussion

1. The captain of the *Commodore* was compared to a captain of a battleship. What was the captain of the *Commodore* battling against?

2. Which was the better choice for the men left on board: to go down with the ship or risk staying afloat on a raft? Explain your answer.

UNDERSTANDING LITERATURE

Theme and Foreshadowing. The theme of a story is the author's main idea or message. Symbols are often used to *foreshadow* an event that will happen later in the story. Foreshadowing is a device that suggests what will happen later. It is the author's way of creating suspense and emphasizing the theme of the story.

In "The Wreck of the *Commodore:* Stephen Crane's Own Story," the ship's whistle is used to foreshadow the fate of the *Commodore*. The theme of this story is that the sinking of the ship was a terrible tragedy. At the beginning of the story, "the *Commodore* gave three long blasts of her whistle. Somehow they sounded sad — like wails." Later, Crane writes, "If ever there was a voice of death and despair it was the voice of this whistle."

Read these passages. On your paper, tell what events each passage foreshadows.

1. "Now huge waves came lashing at the ship and a certain lightheartedness departed from the men aboard."

2. " 'I've been on a number of these trips,' [Tom said.] 'The pay is good, but I think if I ever get back safe this time, I will cut it.' "

3. "In the gray light of morning the seven men on board looked like ghosts."

Writing

Write at least two paragraphs about a real event you have seen on TV. Use foreshadowing to suggest the end of your story.

The Open Boat

by Stephen Crane

*"The Open Boat" was written a few months after Crane's
report of the sinking of the* Commodore. *He wrote this story
because he wanted to go beyond the facts of a news story to
describe how it really felt to be adrift in an open boat.*

None of them knew the color of the
sky. Their eyes were on the waves that
swept before them. The waves were a dull
gray, except for the tops, which were
foaming white. The boat wasn't much
bigger than a bathtub.

The cook sat at one end, bailing out
water. On one side, the oiler handled one
of the oars. The reporter, sitting next to
him, pulled at the other oar. They both
watched the waves and wondered why
they were there. They had been rowing
for hours.

At the other end was the injured captain.
He could not forget seeing his ship sink
lower and lower, and finally go down. His
voice was deep and sad.

"Steer a little more south," the captain
said.

"A little more south, sir," said the oiler.

One thing wrong with the sea is that
when you get over one wave, another is
right behind it. Each wave is just as eager
to swamp your boat as the one before it.

The men were not aware of the dawn.
They knew it was morning only because
the sea had changed from gray to green.

"It's a good thing the wind is blowing
toward shore," the cook said. "Otherwise,
we wouldn't have a chance."

The reporter and the oiler agreed. The
captain chuckled, but he didn't sound
amused.

Gulls flew around them. Sometimes they
sat on the sea. The anger of the sea meant
nothing to them, and the men envied them.

One gull tried to land on the captain's
head. The captain wanted to knock it
away, but a sudden movement would turn
the boat over. So he gently waved his arm
over his head. When the bird flew away,
the four men breathed more easily.

All the while, the oiler and the reporter
rowed — and rowed and rowed. Sometimes they had one oar each. Sometimes
the oiler handled both oars. Sometimes
the reporter did.

The hardest part was changing places.
It's easier to steal eggs from under a hen
than it was to change seats in that boat.

After a while, the captain said he saw
a lighthouse. Soon the cook said he could

see it, too. At the oars, the reporter turned and looked, but he couldn't see it.

At the top of a wave, he turned and looked again. This time, he saw something very small on the horizon.

"Do you think we'll make it, Captain?" the cook asked.

"Yes," said the captain, "if the wind holds and the boat doesn't swamp with water."

The cook bailed faster.

"I wish we had a sail," the captain said. "We could try my coat on the end of an oar. That would give you boys a chance to rest."

So the cook and the reporter made a sail. The oiler steered with the other oar, and the boat made good speed.

Slowly, the lighthouse grew larger. At last, from the top of each wave, the men could see land.

Then the wind died down. So the reporter and the oiler started rowing again.

The reporter wondered how anyone could think of rowing as an amusement. It was not an amusement. It was a horror to the muscles and a crime against the back.

"Easy now, boys," said the captain. "When we reach the surf, we'll have to swim for it. Save your strength."

"They'll see us soon," the cook said. "They'll be out after us."

A quiet cheerfulness surrounded the men. They would probably be ashore in an hour.

After a while, the cook said, "It's funny they don't see us yet."

The cheerfulness faded. Land was within

sight, but no one was there to help them.

The men now felt very angry. Each, in his own way, wondered, "If I am going to drown, why was I allowed to come this far? Why didn't it happen at the beginning, before all this suffering?"

When they got near the surf, the oiler said, "We won't last another three minutes. We're about to swamp with water, and we're too far out to swim to shore."

"Take us back out to sea," the captain said sadly.

The reporter and the oiler took turns rowing. Their backs ached so much that they no longer feared the ocean. By now, it looked a lot more comfortable than the boat. It seemed like a great, soft mattress.

"Look!" cried the cook. "There's a man on shore! He's waving at us!"

"Now we're all right," the oiler said. "There will be a boat for us in a half hour."

"Now there are some more people," the cook said. "One of them is waving his coat."

"Why don't they send a boat out after us?" the reporter asked.

"Maybe they think we're out fishing," the captain said. "Maybe they're just waving to be friendly."

The people stood on the shore waving. Soon, it began getting dark. The people on shore blended into the gloom. The oiler and the reporter kept taking turns rowing.

Late at night, it was the reporter's turn. The other three men were asleep. The reporter imagined that he was the only man afloat on all the oceans.

There was a swishing sound near the boat. Then the reporter saw a large fin cut through the water. He stared at it without feeling. He only wished one of the others was awake. He didn't want to be alone with the shark.

Long after the shark swam away, the oiler woke up. The reporter asked him, "Will you take over?"

The oiler took over. The reporter fell asleep as soon as he touched the bottom of the boat.

It seemed only a moment later when the oiler asked, "Will you take over?"

"Sure," the reporter said.

Later, the reporter got some more sleep. When he opened his eyes again, it was dawn. Land was once again in sight. They could see little cottages and a tall windmill on a beach. But no one, not even a dog, appeared on the beach.

"I guess no help is coming," the captain said. "We'd better try to go through the surf anyway. If we stay out much longer, we'll be too weak to swim at all."

The others agreed. The oiler, who was now rowing, turned the boat toward the beach.

The reporter looked at the tall windmill. It was a giant, standing with its back to their struggles, as if they were ants. It seemed neither cruel nor kind. It simply did not care about them.

The captain spoke again. "All we can do is row as far as possible. When she swamps, we'll swim for the beach. We won't get in very close before we turn over."

As they headed toward the shore, the waves tossed the boat higher and higher.

The reporter knew he should be afraid. But his mind was ruled by his muscles, and his muscles did not care. His only thought was that if he should drown, it would be a shame.

"When you jump," the captain warned, "get clear of the boat."

The tumbling white water caught the boat and whirled it almost straight up and down. Water poured in from all sides. The reporter went overboard.

The January water was icy. To the reporter, this seemed to be an important fact. It was colder than he had expected to find it off the coast of Florida.

When he came to the surface, he saw the others. The oiler, swimming rapidly, was ahead in the race. The cook paddled nearby him. Behind the reporter, the captain hung on to the overturned boat with his good hand.

The reporter paddled slowly. Suddenly, he felt himself caught in a current. He looked at the shore as if it were a piece of stage scenery. Although he swam, he was not moving forward.

The captain, holding onto the boat, passed the reporter. The reporter stayed in the grip of this new enemy, the strange current.

"Am I going to drown?" he wondered. "Can it be possible?"

Then a wave whirled him out of the current. Now he could make progress toward the shore again.

The captain yelled to him, "Swim for the boat!"

The reporter struggled to reach the boat. He noticed a man running along the shore.

The man threw off his coat, shoes, and pants — and ran into the water.

The reporter kept paddling toward the boat. Suddenly, a large wave caught him up and flung him over the boat and far past it.

To the reporter, this seemed to be a miracle. He came down in water that was only up to his waist. But he was too weak to stand. Each time he got up, he was knocked down by a wave.

Then he saw the man who had been running along the shore. The man dragged the cook ashore. Then he waded toward the captain. The captain waved him away and sent him to the reporter.

The man grabbed the reporter's hand and pulled. The reporter thought he saw a halo behind the man's head.

"Thanks, old man," the reporter said.

Then they saw the oiler. He was lying face down in the shallow water.

The reporter wasn't sure of all that happened afterward. When he reached safe ground, he fell. He could feel every part of his body hit the sand.

Now the beach was filled with people, blankets, clothes, and coffee. The land gave a warm and generous welcome to the men from the sea.

One dripping shape, though, was carried slowly up the beach. For the oiler, the only welcome from the land would be a grave.

That night, the white waves moved back and forth in the moonlight. The wind brought the sound of the sea's voice to the three men on shore. Now they felt they could be interpreters of that voice.

READING COMPREHENSION

Select the best choice to complete each statement below. Then write the entire sentence on your paper.

1. The sailors knew that it was daytime by looking at _____.
   a. the sky
   b. their watches
   c. the color of the sea

2. The hardest thing to do in the boat was to _____.
   a. sit still
   b. change seats
   c. fight off the sea gulls

3. The people on shore probably didn't help the sailors because they _____.
   a. didn't care about them
   b. didn't know the sailors were in trouble
   c. had no way to help them

4. Just before everyone jumped out of the boat to swim ashore, the reporter was _____.
   a. very frightened
   b. happy
   c. too tired to be afraid

For Discussion

1. The characters are only known as "the captain," "the reporter," and so on. Why didn't Crane use names?

2. The oiler was the last person to row. When he began swimming, he quickly struck out to shore while the others stayed close to the boat. How did these facts affect the end of the story?

UNDERSTANDING LITERATURE

Allegory. An *allegory* is a kind of story that has at least two meanings or interpretations.

"The Open Boat" is an allegory. On one level, the story is about four men at sea. But another interpretation of the story is that these men represent all people, or humanity. The sea and land can be interpreted as symbols of nature or life. Crane is telling two stories at the same time.

Read the passages below from the story. On your paper, tell what the author is saying about these men in each situation. Then tell what the author might be saying about people and about nature or life in general.

1. "... when you get over one wave, another is right behind it."

2. "So the cook and the reporter made a sail. The oiler steered with the other oar, and the boat made good speed."

3. "The reporter looked at the tall windmill. It was a giant, standing with its back to their struggles, as if they were ants. It seemed neither cruel nor kind. It simply did not care about them."

Writing

Imagine that you were the man on the shore who first spotted the boat. Describe what you thought you saw. You may want to make your description into an allegory that reflects this theme: When people fail to understand one another, tragedy can occur.

Section Review

VOCABULARY

Shades of Meaning. Authors use words the same way artists use paint. Both must pick the exact color or shade they want to create the picture they have in mind.

The word *run,* for example, has a slightly different meaning than the word *jog.* A police officer does not jog after a thief. He or she runs after the thief. The difference between the two words is what is called *shades of meaning.*

Read each pair of sentences. Then write the letter of the one with the more precise shade of meaning on your paper.

1. **a.** The lights of Jacksonville *blinked dimly* through the night.

   b. The lights of Jacksonville *were visible* through the night.

2. **a.** He *looked angry.*

   b. He *had turned into a demon.*

3. **a.** He was *crouched* on the raft ready to *spring.*

   b. He *sat* on the raft ready to *jump.*

4. **a.** All this time there were *no shrieks, no groans.*

   b. All this time there was *no noise.*

5. **a.** The engineer *came in* and *said* that there was something wrong.

   b. The engineer *rushed in* and *cried* that there was something wrong.

READING

Main Ideas and Supporting Details. The main idea is what a paragraph is about. The supporting details are pieces of information that are used to back up or explain the main idea.

Read the paragraph below.

Although it was the first day of spring, it snowed. The streets were slick with ice. I wished that I had worn warm boots. It seemed that summer would never come. I watched some kids build a snowman and use an old garbage-can top as a sled. The birds sat glumly on icy tree branches.

The main idea in that paragraph is: It snowed on the first day of spring. The supporting details are: Streets were icy; some kids built a snowman; they made a sled.

Read the paragraphs below. On your paper, write the main idea of each paragraph. Then list at least two supporting details.

1. "The old chief engineer first obeyed the order. He landed on the outside raft and the captain told him how to grip the raft. He obeyed as promptly as a child in school."

2. "The reporter wondered how anyone could think of rowing as an amusement. It was not an amusement. It was a horror to the muscles and a crime against the back."

3. "The tumbling white water caught the boat and whirled it almost straight up and down. Water poured in from all sides. The reporter went overboard."

WRITING A NEWS STORY

All modern newspaper stories have a clear pattern. They begin with an opening paragraph that tells the reader five things:

- ☐ *Who* the story is about
- ☐ *What* happened
- ☐ *When* it happened
- ☐ *Where* it happened
- ☐ *Why* or *how* it happened

This pattern is called the five W's of journalism, or news writing.

Stories begin with this information so that the reader can get the most important facts right away. This is called the *lead paragraph.*

Read the paragraphs below. On your paper, answer the who, what, where, when, and why or how questions for each.

1. Four men were picked up off the coast of Georgia last night. They had been adrift at sea after their ship, the *Commodore,* sank.

2. Henry Fleming became a hero in battle yesterday after he charged an oncoming brigade of the enemy single-handedly. The Colonel said, "If I had 10,000 wildcats like him, I could tear th' stomach outta this war in less'n a week."

Now choose one of the following and write a news story. First write the five W's on your paper: Who? What? Where? When? Why or how? Then note the information to answer each one for the topic you have chosen. This will help you write the lead for your story. Then write at least two additional paragraphs giving supporting information.

1. A news story about the wreck of the *Commodore.* Tell it as a modern newspaper reporter might rather than the way Stephen Crane told it.

2. An obituary for Billy, the oiler. Tell about his life and how he died. Use information from Stephen Crane's stories.

QUIZ

The following is a quiz for Section 6. Write the answers in complete sentences on your paper.

Reading Comprehension

1. Why did Wilson take back his letters from Henry in "The Red Badge of Courage"?

2. What did Henry's mother expect of him in "The Red Badge of Courage"?

3. Why did the wayfarer say ". . . there are other roads" in the poem "The Wayfarer"?

4. Why were some men left on the ship in "The Wreck of the *Commodore:* Stephen Crane's Own Story"?

5. Why didn't the people on shore rush to save the men in the lifeboat in the story "The Open Boat"?

Understanding Literature

6. After Henry ran away, he met a group of wounded soldiers. How did this meeting affect the theme of the play?

7. In what ways are the man in "A Man Said to the Universe" and the wayfarer in "The Wayfarer" alike?

8. Why didn't the sailors panic when the *Commodore* began to sink? How did their calmness add to the theme of the story?

9. Describe the windmill as a symbol in "The Open Boat." Discuss how this symbol adds to the theme.

10. Compare "The Wreck of the *Commodore:* Stephen Crane's Own Story" and "The Open Boat." Which story is more suspenseful? Which story states its theme more powerfully? Explain your answers.

COMPOSITION

1. Pretend you are Henry Fleming. Write a letter to your mother after the Battle of Chancellorsville. What will you tell her about your feelings? About how you've changed?

2. Now pick the character in this section that you most admired. Describe him or her. Tell how the character's actions and words helped illustrate an important theme in Crane's writing.

3. Write a colorful, objective description of something found in the country or in the city. Use your personal vision, as Crane did, to record your observations honestly.

4. In a short poem or in one or two paragraphs, explain your own view of the relationship between a person and the universe.

SECTION 7

Voices of Experience

1898–1939

We have tomorrow
Bright before us
Like a flame.

— Langston Hughes

Introduction

The American people faced the beginning of the 20th century with bright hopes. By 1898 there were nearly 75 million people in the United States. Millions of immigrants came to our shores each year, and America's territory now stretched from the gold fields of Alaska to the sugar plantations of Puerto Rico.

During this era, there was an outpouring of fine literature that represented the experiences and ideas of Americans from many different backgrounds. Here were authors that made the world take notice.

The Changing American Scene

A gold rush in the frozen Klondike territory led some Americans to explore the last frontier on this continent. Jack London didn't find a wealth in gold in Alaska — but he did find a wealth of experience. These experiences became the basis of a number of powerful adventure stories, including the first story in this section, "Love of Life."

Edgar Lee Masters spent most of his life in Illinois. His most famous work, a group of poems called *Spoon River Anthology,* tells of how the lives of country people were affected by the changes in 19th-century America. What makes his poems special is that each poem creates a portrait of an individual's whole life, from birth to death. His poem "Lucinda Matlock" appears in this section.

The author Sherwood Anderson admired Masters's work. He tried to capture a similar quality in his autobiographical writing. He created vivid, sympathetic portraits of people he knew well. His essay in this section, "The Discovery of a Father," shows Anderson at his best.

Although Anderson was sympathetic to people's weaknesses, he felt very bitter about the changes that new machines and big business brought to small towns. Carl Sandburg, another Illinois writer, interpreted the changes in American life differently. Sandburg loved Chicago and city life. His poetry became popular because it showed the American people as strong and flexible. During these years, Americans not only learned how to handle technology; they also had to deal with the losses resulting from the battles of World War I (1917–1919). Sandburg's poem "Under a Telephone Pole," on p. 286, shows how he used different elements of early 20th-century life to celebrate the American spirit, as Whitman had done before him.

Changing American Goals

The 1920's brought many changes. Few American writers captured the spirit of the Roaring Twenties better than F. Scott Fitzgerald. As you will see when you read the play adapted from his story "Bernice Bobs Her Hair," Fitzgerald wrote about

View up Broadway From Maiden Lane, Fogerty, circa 1890's

the young people of his day: their rebellion against accepted values and their love of pleasure.

During the 1920's, many black writers, artists, and musicians gathered in Harlem, a community in New York City. This movement was called the Harlem Renaissance, and this section contains poetry by two of its greatest poets: Langston Hughes and Countee Cullen. Their poems show the world something of the experience of being black in America.

During the 1930's, the American people suffered with an economy that could not provide enough jobs or food. Perhaps these hard times helped make Ernest Hemingway popular. His strong, independent characters and simply stated descriptions showed a toughness that Americans claimed as their own. His story "A Day's Wait," on p. 311, is typical of his direct way of writing.

During the 1930's, Dorothy Parker created humor that helped Americans forget their troubles. Parker's story "The Standard of Living" closes this section. This work reminds us that throughout this difficult period, Americans lost neither their senses of humor nor their dreams for a better future.

Love of Life

by Jack London

In his short lifetime, Jack London (1876–1916) wrote hundreds of short stories and dozens of novels. Much of his writing is based on things that happened in his own life. Born in San Francisco, London received almost no formal education as a boy. He loved to read, though, and educated himself by constantly reading books. As a young man, he went to the Klondike region of Alaska during the Alaskan Gold Rush. He turned his experiences in the Klondike into tales of adventure.

A central theme in London's writing is survival — surviving the harsh conditions of nature and the cruelty that humans sometimes inflict upon one another. The following story takes place during the Gold Rush and describes one man's powerful will to live — and the desperate things he does in order to survive.

They limped painfully down the bank. They were tired and weak, and their faces had the expression of hardship long endured. They were heavily burdened with blanket packs that were strapped to their shoulders. Each man carried a rifle. They walked in a stooped posture, their eyes bent upon the ground.

The first man stepped into the milky stream that foamed over the rocks. The other man followed at his heels. In places the water dashed against their knees, and both men staggered for footing.

The man who followed slipped on a smooth boulder, nearly fell, but recovered himself. At the same time, he uttered a sharp cry of pain. When he had steadied himself, he stepped forward, but nearly fell again.

He called out, "I say, Bill, I've sprained my ankle."

Bill staggered on through the milky water. He limped up the farther bank and continued straight without looking back. The man in the stream watched him.

"Bill!" he cried out.

Bill's head did not turn. The man watched him go till he passed over the crest and disappeared.

He turned his gaze slowly and looked at the world that remained to him now that Bill was gone. There were no trees, no shrubs, no grasses — nothing but a tremendous desolation that sent fear swiftly dawning into his eyes.

He hitched his pack farther over his left shoulder to take a portion of its weight from the injured ankle. Then he proceeded to the bank, slowly and carefully, wincing with pain.

With a desperation that was madness, unmindful of the pain, he hurried up the slope to the crest of the hill over which his comrade had disappeared. But at the crest he saw a shallow valley, empty of life. He fought with his fear again, overcame it, hitched the pack still farther over his left shoulder, and lurched on down the slope.

Farther on he knew he would come to a small stream. He would follow it until it emptied into the river Dease, and here he would find a cache under an upturned canoe. And in this cache would be ammunition for his empty gun, fishhooks and lines and a small net. Also, he would find flour — not much — a piece of bacon, and some beans.

He stubbed his toe on a rocky ledge, and from weariness and weakness staggered and fell. He slipped out of the packstraps. Then he built a fire and put a tin pot of water on to boil.

His feet were raw and bleeding. His ankle was throbbing, and he gave it an examination. It had swollen to the size of his knee. He tore a long strip from one of two blankets and bound the ankle tightly. He tore other strips and bound them about his feet to serve for both moccasins and socks. Then he drank the pot of water, steaming hot, and crawled between his blankets. He slept like a dead man.

At 6:00 he awoke. He knew that he was hungry. He had not eaten for two days; for a far longer time he had not had all he wanted to eat.

He put his pack into shape for traveling. He looked at his moose-hide sack. It was not large, but it weighed 15 pounds — as much as all the rest of the pack. He set it to one side and rolled the pack. When he rose to his feet to stagger on into the day, the sack was included in the pack on his back.

His ankle had stiffened, his limp was more noticeable, but the pain of it was nothing compared with the pain of his stomach.

Late in the afternoon he followed a stream which ran through patches of rush grass. Grasping these rushes firmly near the root, he pulled up what looked like a young onion sprout no larger than a nail. But its fibers were tough. It was composed of stringy filaments without nourishment.

He made camp again on a rocky ledge. He built a fire and warmed himself by drinking quarts of hot water. His ankle pulsed with pain, but he knew only that he was hungry. Through his restless sleep he dreamed of feasts and banquets.

He awoke, chilled and sick. A raw wind was blowing, and the first flurries of snow were whitening the hilltops.

271

This was a signal for him to strap on his pack and stumble onward, he knew not where.

He had no fire that night. He crawled under his blanket to sleep the broken-hunger sleep.

Day came. The edge of his hunger had gone. There was a dull, heavy ache in his stomach, but it did not bother him so much.

He ripped one of his blankets into strips and bound his bleeding feet to prepare himself for a day of travel. When he came to his pack, he paused over the moose-hide sack, but in the end it went with him.

Though the hunger pangs were no longer so strong, he realized that he was weak. He had to pause for frequent rests.

In the middle of the day, he found two minnows in a large pool. He managed to catch them in his tin bucket. He was not particularly hungry. The dull ache in his stomach had been growing duller and fainter. He ate the fish raw, chewing carefully. He had no desire to eat, but he knew he must eat to live.

Another night. In the morning, he untied the leather string that fastened the moose-hide sack. From its open mouth poured a yellow stream of coarse gold dust and nuggets. He divided the gold in halves, hiding one half on a ledge, wrapped in a piece of blanket, and returning the other half to the sack.

His hunger awoke in him again. He was very weak and often stumbled and fell. Stumbling once, he fell into a bird's nest. There were four newly hatched chicks, a day old. He ate them ravenously.

His hunger was driving him on. He wondered if Bill, too, was lost. By midday his pack became too heavy. Again he divided the gold, this time throwing half of it on the ground. In the afternoon he threw the rest of it away. Now he had only the half-blanket and the tin bucket and the rifle.

In the late afternoon he came upon some scattered bones where wolves had made a kill. He put a bone in his mouth and sucked at the shreds of life that still dyed it faintly pink. He closed his jaws on the bones and crunched. Sometimes the bone broke, sometimes his teeth.

He looked at the bones. Could it be that he might be like that before the day was done? There was no hurt in death. To die was to sleep. It meant rest. Then why was he not content to die?

It was the life in him unwilling to die that drove him on.

He awoke on a rocky ledge. The sun was shining bright and warm. A fine day, he thought. Perhaps he could manage to locate himself. By a painful effort he rolled over on his side. Below him was a wide river that flowed into a bright, shining sea. Most unusual, he thought, a trick of his disordered mind. He saw a ship lying at anchor in the midst of the shining sea! He knew that there were no seas or ships in the heart of the barren lands.

He heard a snuffle behind him — a half-choking gasp or cough. Very slowly, he rolled over on his other side. Again came the snuffle and cough. Outlined between two jagged rocks several feet away, he saw the gray head of a wolf. The head seemed to droop limply and forlornly. The animal blinked continually in the sunshine. It seemed sick. As he looked, it snuffled and coughed again.

This, at least, was real, he thought. He closed his eyes for a long while and thought, and then it came to him. He had been walking north by east. That shining sea was the Arctic Ocean and that ship was a whaler, lying at anchor.

He sat up and turned his attention to immediate affairs. He had worn through the blanket-wrappings, and his feet were shapeless lumps of raw meat. His last blanket was gone. Rifle and knife were both missing.

Though extremely weak, he had no feeling of pain. He was not hungry. The thought of food was not even pleasant to him, and whatever he did was done by his reason alone. He ripped off his pant legs to the knees and bound them around his feet before he began what he knew would be a terrible journey to the ship.

Every minute or so he had to rest. His steps were feeble and uncertain, just as the wolf's that trailed him were feeble and uncertain.

Throughout the night he heard the cough of the sick wolf. He knew the sick wolf clung to the sick man's trail in the hope that the man would die first. In the morning, he saw it looking at him with a hungry stare. It stood crouched, tail between its legs, like a miserable dog. It shivered in the chill morning wind, and grinned weakly when the man spoke to it in a voice no more than a hoarse whisper.

In the afternoon the man came upon a trail. It was of another man, who did not walk, but who dragged himself on all fours. The man thought it might be Bill. He had no curiosity. In fact, feeling and emotion had left him. Stomach and nerves had gone to sleep. Yet the life that was in him drove him on. It refused to die.

He followed the trail of the other man who dragged himself along, and soon came to the end of it — a few fresh-picked bones. The ground was marked by the footpads of many wolves. He saw a moose-hide sack, which had been torn by sharp teeth. Bill had carried it to the last. Ha! Ha! He would have the last laugh on Bill. He could survive and carry it on the ship in the shining sea.

He turned away. Well, Bill had deserted him — but he would not take the gold, nor would he suck Bill's bones. Bill would have sucked my bones though, had it been the other way around, the man thought as he staggered on.

That day he decreased the distance between him and the ship by three miles; the next day by two — for he was crawling now as Bill had crawled; and the end of the fifth day found the ship still seven miles away, and him unable to make even a mile a day. His knees had become raw meat like his feet.

Still the sick wolf coughed and wheezed at his heels. It was a grim tragedy of existence — a sick man that crawled, a sick wolf who limped — two dying creatures hunting each other's lives.

He was awakened by the wheezing sound of the sick wolf's breath. Without movement, he lay on his back listening. It drew closer, ever closer, and he did not move.

The patience of the wolf was terrible. The man's patience was no less terrible. For half a day he lay motionless, fighting off unconsciousness and waiting for the thing that was to feed upon him and upon which he wished to feed.

He did not hear the breath. He slipped slowly from some dream to the feel of the tongue along his hand. He waited. The fangs pressed softly. The wolf was using its last strength to sink teeth in the food for which it had waited so long. But the man had waited long, and the hand closed on the jaw. Slowly, while the wolf strug-gled feebly and the hand clutched feebly, the other hand crept across to a grip.

Five minutes later the whole weight of the man's body was on top of the wolf. The hands had not enough strength to choke the wolf, but the face of the man pressed close to the throat of the wolf and the mouth of the man was full of hair. At the end of half an hour the man was aware of a warm trickle in his throat. It was not pleasant. It was like molten lead being forced into his stomach, and it was forced by his will alone. Later the man rolled over on his back and slept.

There were some members of a scientific expedition on the whaling ship *Bedford*. From the deck they saw a strange object on the shore. It was moving down the beach toward the water. It was blind, unconscious. It squirmed along the ground like some monstrous worm. It writhed and twisted and went ahead a few feet an hour.

A few weeks later, the man sat at the table with the scientific men and ship's officers. He was haunted by a fear that the food would not last. He asked the cook, the cabin boy, the captain, about the food stores. They reassured him countless times. But he did not believe them.

It was noticed that the man was getting fat. He grew stouter with each day. The scientific men shook their heads and wondered. They limited the man at his meals, but still his weight increased.

The scientific men set a watch on the man. They saw him stop a sailor. The sailor grinned and gave him part of a sea biscuit. The man clutched it greedily and put it into his shirt. Similar were the donations from other grinning sailors.

The scientific men secretly examined his bunk. It was lined with hardtack; the mattress was stuffed with hardtack; every nook and cranny was filled with hardtack. The man was taking precautions against another famine — that was all. He would recover from it, the scientific men said. And he did, before the *Bedford's* anchor rumbled down in San Francisco Bay.

READING COMPREHENSION

Select the best choice to complete each statement. Then write the entire sentence on your paper.

1. When his companion went on without him, the man was _____.
   a. pleased to have the gold for himself
   b. very angry to be treated so badly
   c. lonely and fearful in the wilderness

2. The man was starving and in pain, but he was driven on by _____.
   a. his fear of the wolves
   b. his will to survive
   c. the desire for revenge

3. The man left the gold behind because _____.
   a. he knew he could return for it
   b. he feared it would be stolen
   c. his life was more important

4. The wolf that was following the man _____.
   a. was also fighting for survival
   b. preferred not to eat human flesh
   c. died of old age and the cold

5. After being rescued, the man hid food in his bunk because _____.
   a. the ship's kitchen was running low
   b. the crew would not permit him to eat his fill
   c. he feared facing hunger again

6. By the time the ship docked, _____.
   a. the man stopped hiding food
   b. the man was dead
   c. all the food was gone

For Discussion

1. Why do you think Bill went on and didn't turn back to help his injured companion? If helping someone else would endanger one's own survival, do you think it would be right not to help? Why or why not?

2. Do you think the desire to live is as strong in most people as it was in the man in the story? Are some people natural survivors and others not? Explain your answer using details from the story and from your own experiences with people.

3. In what ways were the man and the wolf similar? In what ways were they different? Why do you think the man finally won his battle with the wolf?

UNDERSTANDING LITERATURE

Style. *Style* is a combination of what the author has to say and the particular way it is said.

In analyzing Jack London's style, it's difficult — if not impossible — to separate what he says from the way he says it. London wrote hundreds of short stories, and a central focus of many of them is survival.

The way London presents conflict — person vs. nature and person vs. person (usually in a harsh natural setting) — is an essential element of his style. The details he presents are bold and brutal. His words are direct and blunt. As you read London's stories of survival, you can almost feel his characters' pain.

Some of the following sentences from "Love of Life" tell of the man's actions as he fought for survival. Others are descriptive details about nature. Divide your paper into two columns. Label one *Efforts to Survive* and the other *Forces of Nature*. Write each sentence below in the correct column. Then go back to the story and find two additional entries for each column.

1. "He tore a long strip from one of two blankets and bound the ankle tightly."

2. "He ate the fish raw, chewing carefully."

3. "There were no trees, no shrubs, no grasses. . . ."

4. "Outlined between two jagged rocks several feet away, he saw the gray head of a wolf."

5. "The man clutched it greedily and put it into his shirt."

6. "A raw wind was blowing and the first flurries of snow were whitening the hilltops."

Writing

Imagine that you were stranded for a week somewhere — on your own, under extremely harsh conditions. Pick whatever setting you wish — a desert, a forest, outer space, or a mountain. Write two or three paragraphs about where you were and the steps you took to survive. Try to use bold words and details as Jack London would.

Lucinda Matlock

by Edgar Lee Masters

I went to the dances at Chandlerville,
And played snap-out at Winchester,
One time we changed partners,
Driving home in the moonlight of
    middle June,
And then I found Davis.
We were married and lived together for
    seventy years,
Enjoying, working, raising the twelve
    children,
Eight of whom we lost
Ere I had reached the age of sixty.
I spun, I wove, I kept the house, I
    nursed the sick,
I made the garden, and for holiday
Rambled over the fields where sang the
    larks,
And by Spoon River gathering many a
    shell,
And many a flower and medicinal weed —
Shouting to the wooded hills, singing to
    the green valleys.
At ninety-six I had lived enough, that is
    all,
And passed to a sweet repose.
What is this I hear of sorrow and
    weariness,
Anger, discontent, and drooping hopes?
Degenerate sons and daughters,
Life is too strong for you —
It takes life to love Life.

---

1. Do you think the woman in the poem had an easy or a difficult married life? What do you think her answer would be to this question? Explain your response.

2. What are some of the things that the woman in the poem did for recreation? Were these activities satisfying to her? How can you tell? Do you think there's a lesson here for Americans of today? If so, what is it?

3. What is the poem's message for the tired ones and the complainers? Do you agree with this advice? Explain your answer.

Young Mother Sewing, Mary Cassatt, 1902

Discovery of a Father

by Sherwood Anderson

Sherwood Anderson (1876–1941) wrote many novels, stories, and essays that reflect life in small Midwestern towns like the one in which he grew up. Anderson's father had been a harness maker and a blacksmith, but as automobiles and trains did more of the work that horses had once done, he had less and less to do. In this autobiographical essay, Anderson skillfully describes the characteristics that made his father — and his relationship with his father — so special.

You hear it said that fathers want their sons to be what they feel they cannot themselves be, but I tell you it also works the other way. A boy wants something very special from his father. I know that as a small boy I wanted my father to be a certain thing he was not. I wanted him to be a proud, silent, dignified father. When I was with other boys and he passed along the street, I wanted to feel a flow of pride. "There he is. That is my father."

But he wasn't such a one. He couldn't be. It seemed to me then that he was always showing off. Let's say someone in our town had got up a show. My father would manage to get the chief comedy part. It was, let's say, a Civil War play and he was a comic soldier. He had to do the most absurd things. They thought he was funny, but I didn't

I thought he was terrible. I didn't see how mother could stand it. She even laughed with the others. Maybe I would have laughed if it hadn't been my father.

Or there was a parade, the Fourth of July or Decoration Day. He'd be in that, too, right at the front of it, on a white horse hired from a stable.

He couldn't ride. He fell off the horse. Everyone hooted with laughter, but he didn't care. He even seemed to like it. I remember once when he had done something ridiculous, and right out on Main Street, too. I was with some other boys, they were laughing and shouting at him, and he was shouting back. He was having as good a time as they were. I ran down an alley in back of some stores and had a good long cry.

Or I would be in bed at night and Father would come home and bring some men with him. He was a man who was never alone. Before he went broke, running a harness shop, there were always a lot of men loafing in the shop. He went broke, of course, because he gave too much credit. I thought he was a fool. I had got to hating him.

There'd be men I didn't think would want to be fooling around with him. There might even be the superintendent of our schools and a quiet man who ran the hardware store. Once, I remember, there was a white-haired man who was a cashier of the bank. It was a wonder to me that they'd want to be seen with such a windbag. That's what I thought he was. I know now what it was that attracted them. It was because life in our town, as in all small towns, was at times pretty dull and he livened it up. He made them laugh. He could tell stories. He'd even get them to singing.

If they didn't come to our house, they'd go off, say at night, to where there was a grassy place by a creek. They'd cook food there and sit about listening to his stories.

He was always telling stories about himself. He'd say this or that wonderful thing had happened to him. It might be something that made him look like a fool. He didn't care.

If an Irishman came to our house, right away father would say he was Irish. He'd tell what county in Ireland he was born in. He'd tell things that happened there when he was a boy. He'd make it seem so real that, if I hadn't known he was

281

born in southern Ohio, I'd have believed him myself.

If it was a Scotchman, the same thing happened. He'd get a burr into his speech. Or he was a German or a Swede. He'd be anything the other man was. I think they all knew he was lying, but they seemed to like him just the same. As a boy that was what I couldn't understand.

And there was Mother. How could she stand it? I wanted to ask but never did. She was not the kind you'd ask such questions.

I'd be upstairs in my bed, in my room above the porch, and Father would be telling some of his tales. A lot of Father's stories were about the Civil War. To hear him tell it, he'd been in about every battle. He'd been great friends with General Grant. When Grant went to the East to take charge of all the armies, he took Father along.

"I was an orderly at headquarters and Sim Grant said to me, 'Irve,' he said, 'I'm going to take you along with me.'"

He'd tell about the day Lee surrendered and how, when the great moment came, they couldn't find Grant.

"Huh," said Father. "He was in the woods with me."

My father said that he was the one who told Grant about Lee. An orderly riding by had told him, because the orderly knew how thick he was with Grant. Grant was embarrassed.

"But, Irve, look at me. I'm all covered with mud," he said to Father.

That's just one of the kind of things he'd tell. The men knew he was lying, but they seemed to like it just the same.

When we got broke, down and out, do you think he ever brought anything home? Not he. If there wasn't anything to eat in the house, he'd go off visiting around at farmhouses. They all wanted him. Sometimes he'd stay away for weeks, Mother working to keep us fed, and then home he'd come bringing, let's say, a ham. He'd got it from some farmer friend. He'd slap it on the table in the kitchen. "You bet I'm going to see that my kids have something to eat," he'd say, and Mother would just stand smiling at him. She'd never say a word about all the weeks and months he'd been away, not leaving us a cent for food. Once I heard her speaking to a woman on our street. Maybe the woman had dared to sympathize with her. "Oh," she said, "it's all right. He isn't ever dull like most of the men on this street. Life is never dull when my man is about."

But often, I was filled with bitterness, and sometimes I wished he wasn't my father. I'd even invent another man as my father. To protect my mother I'd make up stories of a secret marriage that for some strange reason never got known. As though some man, say the president of a railroad company or maybe a congressman, had married my mother, thinking his wife was dead and then it turned out she wasn't.

So they had to hush it up but I got born just the same. I wasn't really the son of my father. Somewhere in the world there was a wonderful man who was really my father. I even made myself half believe these fancies.

And then there came a certain night. He'd been off somewhere for two or three weeks. He found me alone in the house, reading by the kitchen table.

It had been raining and he was very wet. He sat and looked at me for a long time, not saying a word. I was startled, for there was the saddest look on his face

I had ever seen. He sat for a time, his clothes dripping. Then he got up.

"Come on with me," he said.

I got up and went with him out of the house. I was filled with wonder but I wasn't afraid. We went along a dirt road that led down to a pond. We walked in silence. The man who was always talking had stopped his talking.

I didn't know what was up. I had the queer feeling I was with a stranger. I didn't know whether my father intended it so. I don't think he did.

The pond was quite large. It was still raining hard. There were flashes of lightning followed by thunder. We were on a grassy bank at the pond's edge. Then my father spoke. In the darkness and rain his voice sounded strange.

"Let's go for a swim," he said. Still filled with wonder, I kicked off my shoes.

We went into the pond. Taking my hand he pulled me in. It may be that I was too frightened, too full of a feeling of strangeness, to speak. Before that night my father had never seemed to pay any attention to me.

"And what is he up to now?" I kept asking myself. I did not swim very well, but he put my hand on his shoulder and struck out into the darkness.

He was a man with big shoulders, a powerful swimmer. In the darkness I could feel the movement of his muscles. We swam to the far edge of the pond and then back. The rain continued and the wind blew. Sometimes my father swam on his back and when he did he took my hand in his large powerful one and moved it over so that it rested always on his shoulder. Sometimes there would be a flash of lightning and I could see his face quite clearly.

It was as it was earlier, in the kitchen, a face filled with sadness. There would be the momentary glimpse of his face and then again the darkness, the wind, and the rain. In me there was a feeling I had never known before.

It was a feeling of closeness. It was something strange. It was as though there were only we two in the world. It was as though I had been jerked suddenly out of myself, out of a world in which I was ashamed of my father.

He had become blood of my blood. He the strong swimmer and I the boy clinging to him in the darkness. We swam in silence and in silence we went home.

There was a lamp lighted in the kitchen and when we came in, the water dripping from us, there was my mother. She smiled at us. I remember that she called us "boys."

"What have you boys been up to?" she asked, but my father did not answer. As he had begun the evening's experience with me in silence, so he ended it. He turned and looked at me. Then he went, I thought, with a new and strange dignity out of the room.

I climbed the stairs to my own room, undressed in the darkness, and got into bed. I couldn't sleep and did not want to sleep. For the first time I knew that I was the son of my father.

He was a storyteller as I was to be. It may be that I even laughed a little softly there in the darkness. If I did, I laughed knowing that I would never again be wanting another father.

READING COMPREHENSION

Select the best choice to complete each statement. Then write the entire sentence on your paper.

1. When the writer was small, his father _____.
   a. was proud, quiet, and dignified
   b. entertained the town and embarrassed his son
   c. often argued with his wife

2. The boy's father _____.
   a. brought home a ham every Friday
   b. often took his son fishing
   c. made up stories about his past

3. The boy really got to know his father _____.
   a. the night they swam in the rain
   b. when the man stopped traveling
   c. when the boy became ill

4. Like his father, the boy grew up to be a _____.
   a. strong swimmer
   b. good husband
   c. storyteller

For Discussion

1. The writer said, "A boy wants something very special from his father." What does he mean? Do you agree with him? Explain your answer.

2. How do you think the boy's mother felt about her husband? How did she deal with the problems she might have had? Do you think she did the best she could? Explain your answer.

UNDERSTANDING LITERATURE

Style. Style is the individual way an author puts words together to hold the reader's attention and to express intended ideas.

"Discovery of a Father" is a personal narrative essay. It is the author's personal comment on a part of his life. It was written in the first person. He writes as if he were speaking directly to the reader.

Some of the statements below were written by Anderson. Others were not. On your paper, identify the ones that are from his work by the style they're written in.

1. I know that as a small boy I wanted my father to be a certain thing he was not.

2. The absence of dignity can lead irreversibly to an absence of pride.

3. When the cast of characters of a local drama is announced, Irve Anderson is usually ready to step into a comic role.

4. My father would manage to get the chief comedy part. It was, let's say, a Civil War play and he was a comic soldier.

5. The boy's father was given to doing the unexpected.

6. "What have you boys been up to?" she asked, but my father didn't answer.

Writing

Describe someone in a simple, conversational style such as Anderson's. Tell your reader at least two things you do like and two things you don't like about the person.

Under a Telephone Pole

by Carl Sandburg

I am a copper wire slung in the air,
Slim against the sun I make not even a clear line of
    shadow.
Night and day I keep singing — humming and
    thrumming:
It is love and war and money; it is the fighting and the
    tears, the work and want,
Death and laughter of men and women passing through
    me, carrier of your speech,
In the rain and the wet dripping, in the dawn and the
    shine drying,
        A copper wire.

---

1. Who or what is the "I" in Carl Sandburg's poem? What does
it look like and what does it do?

2. What sorts of things does the poem say men and women talk
about? What sorts of things would you have mentioned if you
were the poet?

Bernice Bobs Her Hair

a teleplay by Joan Micklin Silver
based on the story by F. Scott Fitzgerald

F. Scott Fitzgerald (1896–1940) has long been considered the leading American writer of the 1920's. He is the writer who best captured the feeling of those prosperous times, when for some people life was one big party.

The teleplay you are about to read is based on one of Fitzgerald's short stories, "Bernice Bobs Her Hair." In the 1920's, a young woman bobbed (cut) her hair in order to show how daring and modern she could be.

CHARACTERS

Marjorie Harvey
Roberta
Genvieve Ormande
Otis Ormande
Charley Paulson
Carpenter Thompson
Bernice, Marjorie's cousin
Mrs. Deyo
Warren McIntyre
Mrs. Harvey
Annie, the Harveys' maid
G. Reece Stoddard
Draycott Deyo

Fade in on the women's powder room of a country club in a Midwestern town. Dance music can be heard in the background. It is the summer of 1919. Marjorie, 18, and Roberta, 18, enter. They wear their hair piled on top of their heads. They are not yet "flappers" — young women who wear short hair, short dresses, and makeup. But they consider themselves very modern. Marjorie takes a red jelly bean out of her purse and hands it to Roberta.

Roberta: Marjorie, you saved my life. *(She licks the jelly bean and uses it as a lipstick. Then she sees Marjorie holding a flower up to her hair.)* Who gave you the flower?

Marjorie: Warren.

Roberta: I thought he'd get over you when he went away to school.

Marjorie: No. I got over him.

Roberta: I know about three girls in the East who are wild about him.

Marjorie: When you've grown up across the street from someone, he loses his mystery.

(Genvieve enters.)

Genvieve *(to Marjorie):* My brother Otis has been stuck with your cousin for an hour.

Marjorie *(dropping the flower into a wastebasket):* All right. *(As she leaves, Bernice enters. Marjorie barely nods at her and keeps going. Outside, she finds several boys waiting for the girls inside.)*

Otis: Marjorie!

Marjorie: I know, Otis. I'm going to take care of it. *(She looks at Charley.)*

Charley: Not me, Marjorie.

(She looks at Carpenter.)

Carpenter: Sorry, Marjorie. I'm waiting for Sara Hughes.

(Marjorie moves off.)

Otis *(to Charley and to Carpenter):* It wouldn't kill you.

Charley: Don't say that. It *might!*

(Cut to Bernice, Roberta, and Genvieve in the powder room.)

Roberta *(fixing her hair):* Are you having a nice time, Bernice?

Bernice: Yes. But it's so much warmer here than it is back home. Back home we have a breeze even in the hottest part of summer.

Roberta: I'll bet you do. Coming, Genvieve? *(She and Genvieve leave. Mrs. Deyo enters.)*

Mrs. Deyo: Bernice, dear, what a charming dress.

Bernice: Thank you, Mrs. Deyo.

Mrs. Deyo: I'm pleased to hear that you and Marjorie are such close cousins. I hope she turns to you for guidance.

Bernice *(embarrassed):* Well, not too often.

Mrs. Deyo: You could be a good influence on Marjorie.

(Cut to Marjorie going up to Warren.)

Warren *(eagerly):* I was looking for you, Marjorie.

Marjorie: Warren, will you do something for me?

Warren: Sure.

Marjorie: Dance with Bernice. *(He looks disappointed.)* Please? *(He nods.)* I'll see that you don't get stuck.

Warren: It's all right.

Marjorie: You're an angel! She's in the powder room. *(Warren moves toward a group of boys outside the powder room. Otis is among them, waving a piece of wood.)*

Carpenter: Be patient, Otis.

Charley: That's right, Otis. As soon as she fixes her hair, you'll get your chance.

Warren: What chance? What's the piece of wood for?

Otis: It's a club. When Bernice comes out, I'll hit her on the head — and back into the powder room. *(They all laugh.)*

Warren: Good news, Otis. I'm your relief hitter.

Otis: I'll never forget this, old man. *(He hands Warren "the club.")* In case you need it.

(He hurries off. As the music starts again,

the others leave, too. Bernice comes out of the powder room.)

Warren *(going over to her):* Bernice?
Bernice: Oh! I . . . I'm looking for Otis.
Warren: I told him this was my dance.
Bernice *(nervous because Warren is very handsome):* It's so hot in there. The floor is crowded.
Warren: Let's sit on the porch. There might be a breeze.
Bernice: I don't think so. Back home we have a breeze even in the hottest summer.
Warren: Well, you don't want to dance. And you don't want to sit out. Have a better idea?
Bernice: I didn't mean that. I meant . . . well, let's try the porch.

(Cut to Bernice and Warren sitting at a table on the porch. She is silent. He can see Marjorie inside, talking to G. Reece Stoddard. Marjorie looks interested. Reece is older than Marjorie and her friends. He is also handsome. Warren is annoyed. Suddenly he pretends to be interested in Bernice.)

Warren: Bernice, you've got an awfully kissable mouth.
Bernice *(looking shocked):* Fresh! *(Warren looks pained. He likes to joke with girls. And girls usually like to joke with him.)*

(Cut to the Harvey house late that night. Bernice is going to her room. As she passes Marjorie's room, she hears voices. When she hears her name, she stops to listen.)

(Cut to Marjorie and her mother inside the room. Marjorie is brushing out her long hair.)

Marjorie: She's ruining my summer.
Mrs. Harvey: I wish you wouldn't talk like that.
Marjorie: Otis Ormande is a fool. But he got stuck with her so long, I actually felt sorry for him. I had to beg Warren to take her off Otis's hands.
Mrs. Harvey: I'm sure Warren didn't mind too much. Mrs. Ormande was saying —
Marjorie: Don't tell me! All your friends think Bernice is "so sweet" and "so pretty." What difference does that make? Men don't like her.
Mrs. Harvey: Some things are more important than cheap popularity.
Marjorie: I can't think of any.
Mrs. Harvey *(smiles):* You're very young, Marjorie.
Marjorie: Thank heavens!
Mrs. Harvey: In my day, a girl from a good family —
Marjorie: But that was *then*, Mother. This is *now*. These days, it's every girl for herself. *(She begins fixing her hair in two heavy braids for the night.)*
Mrs. Harvey: I know Bernice isn't very outgoing.
Marjorie: Outgoing? I've never heard her say a word to boys except that it's hot. Or the dance floor is crowded.

(Cut to Bernice outside. She has heard enough. She goes to her room and begins to braid her hair for the night.)

(Cut to the front door of the Harvey house the next morning. Warren rings the bell. Annie opens the door.)

Annie: I'm sorry, Mr. Warren. Miss Marjorie isn't up yet.
Warren: Thanks. *(He starts to leave, then*

turns back.) Do you know if she's free this afternoon?

Annie: I believe she's going to the show.

(Cut to the Harvey dining room. Marjorie is at the table, pouring milk on her cornflakes. Annie enters.)

Annie: I told him you weren't up yet.

Marjorie: Aren't there any berries? *(Annie gets a bowl of blueberries from the sideboard. Bernice enters.)*

Bernice *(coldly):* Good morning.

Marjorie: Morning.

Bernice: I don't care for any breakfast, Annie.

Annie *(surprised):* No?

Bernice: No, thank you. *(When Annie leaves, Bernice turns to Marjorie.)* I heard what you said about me to your mother last night.

Marjorie *(calmly):* Where were you?

Bernice: In the hall. I didn't mean to listen . . . at first. *(Pause.)* I guess I'd better go home. *(She expects some sympathy. But she's come to the wrong person for it.)*

Marjorie: Well, if you aren't having a good time, I suppose you'd better go. *(Bernice bursts into tears and leaves.)*

(Cut to the Harvey sitting room, later. Bernice enters.)

Bernice: Do you think you've treated me well?

Marjorie: I've done my best. There's some excuse for an ugly girl whining. But you're not ugly. So don't expect me to weep for you.

Bernice *(angry):* You're hard and selfish. You haven't a feminine quality in you.

Marjorie: Bernice, girls our age divide into two groups. The ones like me have a good time. The ones like you sit around and criticize us for it. Go or stay, just as you like. *(She leaves.)*

(Cut to Marjorie going downstairs. Carpenter and Reece are waiting for her in the front hall.)

Marjorie: Who let these two parlor snakes in my house? *(They smile.)* My cousin can't go to the show with us. She's sick or something.

Reece *(politely):* Sorry to hear that.

Carpenter: That's too bad.

Marjorie *(whispers):* Hurry up. She might get better. *(They laugh as they leave.)*

(Cut to Bernice writing to her mother. There is a knock on her bedroom door.)

Mrs. Harvey's Voice: Bernice, are you feeling better?

Bernice *(opens the door):* I'm all right, Aunt Josephine.

Mrs. Harvey: Will you come down? Mrs. Deyo and Draycott are here.

(Cut to Mrs. Harvey and Mrs. Deyo on one side of the sitting room. Bernice and Draycott are on the other side.)

Bernice: You weren't at the dance last night, were you?

Draycott: No. Mother said it was even noisier than usual.

Bernice: The dance floor was crowded.

Draycott: I hate a crowded dance floor.

Mrs. Deyo *(to Mrs. Harvey):* Bernice is a lovely child. I'm sure she's a good influence on Marjorie.

Bernice *(to Draycott):* How are your studies coming along?

Draycott: Very well, thank you.

Mrs. Deyo *(to Mrs. Harvey):* Have you noticed how thin some of the young girls are? They're dancing themselves to death. Next thing you know, one of them will bob her hair.

Mrs. Harvey: Oh, I don't think things will go that far.

Mrs. Deyo: Well, Draycott? *(She rises.)*

Draycott *(rising):* Good-bye, Bernice.

Bernice: Good-bye, Mrs. Deyo.

Mrs. Deyo: Just stay as sweet as you are, Bernice. Your mother must be proud of you.

Bernice: Thank you.

(Cut to Marjorie's room. Marjorie enters. She is surprised to see Bernice waiting for her.)

Bernice: I've decided that maybe you're right about things. If you'll tell me why your friends don't like me, I'll see what I can do.

Marjorie *(after a pause):* Will you do exactly as I say?

Bernice: If they are sensible things.

Marjorie: Forget sensible things. If I tell you to take boxing lessons, you'll have to. Well? *(Bernice nods.)* Now, the first thing is your appearance.

Bernice: Don't I look all right?

Marjorie: No. You're also boring. You lean on men when you dance. You haven't any idea of how to make a man fall in love with you. Are you willing to admit all that?

Bernice: Maybe.

Marjorie: No maybes.

Bernice: All right. But how are you going to fix all that in two weeks?

Marjorie: If you'll pay attention, I can fix it in two days. *(She looks closely at Bernice. Bernice grins, embarrassed. Marjorie*

frowns.) When you go home, have your teeth straightened. Meanwhile, smile with your mouth closed.

(Cut to the Harvey dining room that evening. Annie is passing dessert.)

Mrs. Harvey: Marjorie, Mrs. Deyo and Draycott were here this afternoon while you were out.

Marjorie: Lucky for me.

Mrs. Harvey: Mrs. Deyo wants to give a party in honor of Bernice. I think Draycott has a case on Bernice.

Marjorie: Let's not talk about it at the table. *(Bernice and Annie smile. Marjorie frowns at Bernice, who closes her mouth.)*

Marjorie: Mother, can we be excused?

Mrs. Harvey: I don't think Bernice is through.

Marjorie: Yes, she is. Aren't you?

Bernice *(puts down her fork):* Yes, thank you, Aunt Josephine. *(The two girls rise.)*

Marjorie: If any men call, tell them I'm busy. Bernice and I want to spend a quiet evening.

Mrs. Harvey: That's a good idea, dear. *(The girls leave. Mrs. Harvey turns to Annie.)* You see, Annie? I knew they would get to like each other in time.

Annie: Awful sudden-like, isn't it?

Mrs. Harvey: That's the way youngsters are.

(Cut to Bernice's room. Marjorie is going through Bernice's clothes and tossing them aside. She comes to the dress Bernice wore to the dance last night.)

Marjorie: Don't ever put this old-fashioned thing on again.

Bernice: But my mother —

Marjorie: Your mother's advice was fine

when you were a little girl. You're 17! *(She comes to a bright red dress.)* What is this?

Bernice: I know, it's awful.

Marjorie: It's divine! It's the only dress I like in the whole bunch.

Bernice: I can't wear it every night.

Marjorie: You can wear some of mine. *(Cut to Marjorie's room. Marjorie gives Bernice a red jelly bean.)*

Marjorie: Lick it, and rub it on. *(Bernice licks it, and rubs it on her lips. Marjorie frowns.)* No. You don't want to all over the place. Just follow the outline of your mouth.

Bernice: Is it true you turned three cart-wheels at the Pump and Slippers Dance?

Marjorie: Five. But that's old hat. We'll think up something better for you to do. *(Pause.)* I wonder whether we should bob your hair. (*Bernice looks shocked.*) All right, it was just a thought. But it will make a terrific line!

(*Cut to the sitting room, the next day. Marjorie cranks up the record player. When the music starts, she dances with Bernice.*)

Marjorie: Don't lean. (*Bernice straightens up stiffly.*) Bend in a little. (*They keep dancing.*) Why aren't you saying anything?

Bernice: Well, you aren't, either.

Marjorie: I'm the man. The girl has to keep the talk going.

Bernice: It's hard to think of something.

Marjorie: When you're with a man, there are only three topics of conversation — you, me, and us.

Bernice: All right. (*Silence.*) Maybe it would be better if I knew who you were.

Marjorie: Pick someone.

Bernice: You pick.

Marjorie: Anybody. Warren McIntyre. (*Bernice is tongue-tied, as she is with the real Warren.*) Go on!

Bernice: Are you going back to school soon?

Marjorie: Oh, thrilling! (*She goes to the record player and lifts the needle from the record.*)

Bernice: You said you, me, and us.

Marjorie: But what can he say except "Yes, I am" or "No, I'm not"? And who cares anyway? Look, you be Warren. (*Bernice nods.*) Is it true what I hear about you, Warren McIntyre?

Bernice: What do you hear?

Marjorie (*with charm*): That you're fickle. (*She nudges Bernice.*) Ask who told me that.

Bernice: Who told you that?

Marjorie: Never mind. I just hope it's true. Fickle men are the only kind that interest me.

Bernice (*trying to be casual*): Marjorie, what would you say if someone said, "You've got an awfully kissable mouth"?

Marjorie (*again with charm*): Do you mean a mouth that looks as if it's been kissed a lot? Or one you'd like to kiss? (*Bernice is shocked, but she tries not to show it.*)

Bernice: Have you ever . . . ?

Marjorie: Lots of times.

Bernice: Did you ever kiss Warren?

Marjorie: Warren flunked my test. I think if you really love someone, you love him even when he isn't around. Well, Warren went away to school. Before he came home for Christmas, I fell in love with four men. I'm afraid he'll never get over me. Poor thing.

(*Cut to the dining room, the next evening. The table is set for eight. Bernice enters in her red dress. Marjorie, not dressed up yet, is fussing over the place cards.*)

Bernice: Where have you put me? (*She finds her card. Then she checks those on either side. At first she is pleased.*) G. Reece Stoddard. (*Then she frowns.*) Charley Paulson.

Marjorie: Sad birds like Charley are part of any crowd. And you can't afford to neglect them. Suppose you can get three sad birds to keep dancing with you. The attractive men will see there's no danger of getting stuck with you. Then *they'll* dance with you.

Bernice: I never thought of that. (*Pause.*)

You'd better get dressed. It's almost time.

Marjorie: I think I'll put Roberta on the other side of Charley. *(The doorbell rings.)* Good. Now I can get dressed.

(Bernice realizes that Marjorie planned this. Now Bernice will have to greet the guests by herself. She opens the front door. Roberta, Genvieve, Charley, Carpenter, Warren, and Reece enter.)

Reece: Hello, Bernice.

Warren: Where's Marjorie?

Bernice: She'll be right down. *(Everyone, except Bernice, starts talking about someone named Babs. Bernice shyly stands to one side. Marjorie finally comes downstairs and frowns at Bernice.)*

Marjorie: Bernice, could I see you for a minute? *(Bernice follows her into the kitchen. Marjorie turns on her.)* You aren't even trying! If you've been wasting my time, I'll never forgive you! You might as well go home!

Bernice: No!

(Cut to the eight young people at the table. Marjorie glares at Bernice. Bernice takes a deep breath and turns to Charley.)

Bernice: Mr. Charley Paulson, do you think I ought to bob my hair?

Charley *(surprised):* Why?

Bernice: I want to be a society vampire. And I don't know how I can unless I bob my hair. Do you? *(Charley looks at her with interest.)* I want your advice because I hear you're so critical of girls.

Marjorie: What are you all talking about over there?

Bernice: I was just saying that I'm going downtown to a barbershop. I'm going to have my hair bobbed. *(She looks around at everyone.)* Of course I'm charging admission. But if you'll all come and encourage me, I'll give out passes for the best seats. *(Everyone is amused. Bernice smiles her new smile.)*

Carpenter: I thought bobbed hair was just for movie vamps. Would you really do it, Bernice?

Bernice: I know it's not something good girls do. But I believe you have to amuse people, feed them, or shock them. *(The boys laugh. Bernice speaks to Charley in a low tone.)* Charley, I've been wanting to ask your opinion of several people. I hear you're a wonderful judge of character.

(Cut to Charley dancing with Bernice.)

Charley: What did you mean when you said I'm critical of girls?

Bernice: That's what I hear.

Charley: Who said it?

Bernice: Several people.

Charley: Who?

Bernice: Guess. *(Carpenter cuts in.)*

Charley: Hey, wait a minute.

Carpenter: Too bad, Charley. *(He begins dancing with Bernice.)* Are you really going to bob your hair?

Bernice: First thing next week. Can you come?

Carpenter: I wouldn't miss it.

Bernice: Carpenter, is it true what I hear about you?

Carpenter: What's that?

Bernice *(realizing they're dancing very close to Reece and Roberta):* Just promise me you won't tell Mr. G. Reece Stoddard.

Reece: Tell me what?

Bernice *(as though surprised):* Oh! *(Car-*

penter dances her off. Reece looks after her with interest.)

Carpenter: He can't hear. Go ahead.
Bernice: I'd better whisper it. *(She whispers something in his ear.)*
Carpenter: Who said that?
Bernice: Never mind. I hope it's true. Fickle men are the only kind that interest me.

(We see Marjorie picking out some records to play. Warren is beside her.)

Warren: But *you* said you wanted to drive out to the lake.
Marjorie: I did?
Warren: Yes, weeks ago.
Marjorie: I changed my mind. Stop being such a pest.

(Suddenly Warren has had enough of

Marjorie. He looks at the dancing couples. He sees Charley cutting in on Bernice. Just then the record ends. Reece excuses himself from Roberta and comes over to Warren.)

Reece: Cut in on Roberta and me, will you?

Warren: Sure. Why?

Reece: I want to dance with Bernice.

(We see Marjorie and Genvieve. Genvieve's sash has come loose.)

Marjorie: Do you want to sew it or pin it?

Genvieve: Pin it.

Marjorie: Come upstairs. *(As the two girls go upstairs, Warren moves toward Reece and Roberta. Reece looks relieved. But Warren passes by and cuts in on Bernice. They begin to dance.)*

Bernice: How do you think I'll look with my hair bobbed?

Warren: You weren't serious, were you?

Bernice: Of course! Did you think it was just a line? *(Warren shrugs.)* The person in this room with a line is Warren McIntyre.

Warren: Why do you say that?

Bernice: "Bernice, you've got an awfully kissable mouth." *(Warren grins.)* I meant to ask your opinion of a kissable mouth. Is it one that looks as if it's been kissed a lot? Or is it one you'd like to kiss?

Warren: Why . . . one I'd like to kiss.

Bernice: Thank you, Warren. That's very handy to know. *(They both laugh.)*

(Cut to Bernice and Marjorie going upstairs after the party. Bernice looks very happy.)

Marjorie: So it worked?

Bernice: Oh, yes! The only trouble was I ran out of things to say. I had to repeat myself with different men.

Marjorie: They'll never know. Anyway, I'll fix up some new things tomorrow.

Bernice *(feeling put down)*: Maybe I could. I thought up some of the things I said tonight.

Marjorie *(not interested)*: Good night. *(She goes into her room.)*

(Cut to the Harvey front door the next day. Otis rings the bell. Annie answers.)

Annie: Miss Marjorie has gone downtown with her mother.

Otis: That's funny. Charley Paulson's sister said Charley was over here.

Annie: He is.

Otis: What's he doing here if Marjorie is downtown? *(Annie holds the door open. Otis enters and sees Bernice and Charley in the sitting room. Bernice is wearing one of Marjorie's dresses. She is laughing at the story Charley is telling.)*

Otis: Hey, Paulson! What about our tennis game?

Charley *(surprised)*: I forgot all about it.

Otis: If you hurry, we can still play a set or two.

Charley: I'm busy right now. See you later. *(As Otis goes out the front door, he meets Carpenter.)*

Otis: Marjorie is downtown.

Carpenter: Where's Bernice?

Otis: Bernice? *(Carpenter goes into the house. Otis pauses, then goes back into the house.)*

(Cut to Marjorie's room. The two cousins are braiding their hair for the night.)

Marjorie: You've learned how to smile. But you've got to learn how to look very sad, too.

Bernice: Why?

Marjorie: You need it sometimes.

Bernice: How do you do it?

Marjorie: Open your eyes wide. Now droop your mouth a little. Then look into the man's eyes. Then say, "I hardly have any boy friends at all."

Bernice: But I thought the idea was to seem popular.

Marjorie: This *only* works if you're popular. Suppose an unpopular girl said she didn't have any boy friends. What could a man say? But if a popular girl says it. . . .

Bernice: I see. Do you think I'll ever know all these things the way you do?

Marjorie: I don't know. You got a late start.

(Cut to the Harvey front door the next day. Annie is holding the door open. Warren is outside.)

Annie *(surprised):* You want to see Miss Bernice? *(Before Warren can answer, Bernice appears.)*

Bernice *(to Warren):* Hello, shell shock.

Warren: Ready?

Bernice: Annie, please tell Aunt Josephine I'm going for a ride. *(She and Warren run toward his car.)*

(Cut to Mrs. Harvey upstairs, leaning over the railing.)

Mrs. Harvey: Annie? Who was that at the door?

Annie: Mr. Warren. He and Miss Bernice went for a ride. *(Mrs. Harvey goes into Marjorie's room. Marjorie is being fitted for a skirt. A dressmaker is pinning up the hem.)*

Marjorie: Who was it?

Mrs. Harvey: Warren.

Marjorie: Well, I can't see him now.

Mrs. Harvey: He came for Bernice. Did you know he telephoned her twice yesterday?

Marjorie: I'm glad he's finally found someone who appreciates him. *(She looks down at her skirt.)* This still isn't right.

Mrs. Harvey: I agree. It's too short.

Marjorie: No, it's too long. *(She looks down at the dressmaker.)* Take it up another quarter of an inch.

(Cut to a picnic. Bernice, Warren, Marjorie, Otis, and Roberta are sitting around.)

Otis: Bernice, do you think you'll come back for Christmas vacation?

Bernice: I haven't been invited yet.

Marjorie *(trapped):* You're welcome to come here.

Otis: Swell!

Marjorie *(to Bernice):* But knowing you, you'll have to ask your mother first.

Bernice: No. I've explained to her that a modern girl needs a great deal of freedom.

(Cut to Bernice and Warren walking away from the group.)

Bernice: I don't think you're sincere.

Warren: I am sincere. Why wouldn't I be?

Bernice *(stops and gives him her newly learned sad look):* You're very popular. I'm just the new girl in town. I hardly have any boy friends at all.

Warren: Are you kidding? Half the men in town are crazy about you.

Bernice: Who, for instance?

Warren: Me, for instance.

(*Cut to Marjorie and Roberta. They are watching Bernice and Warren from a distance.*)

Marjorie: I could get him back like that! (*She snaps her fingers.*)

Roberta: Could you? (*She doesn't sound so sure. Marjorie gets a hard look in her eyes.*)

(*Cut to Bernice in the Harvey bathroom, brushing her eyebrows. Marjorie enters without knocking.*)

Marjorie (*coldly*): You may as well get Warren out of your head.

Bernice (*surprised*): What?

Marjorie: Stop making a fool of yourself over him. He doesn't care a bit for you. (*She leaves. After a pause, Bernice goes to Marjorie's room and knocks on the door. Marjorie opens it.*)

Bernice: You seem to think I've stolen your private property.

Marjorie: I'm not interested in discussing it.

Bernice: But you told me Warren flunked your test. You fell in love with four men before he came home for Christmas — (*Before she can finish the sentence, Marjorie has closed the door.*)

(*Cut to the group at a picnic the next day. Otis is showing off in a childish way. The others — Bernice, Marjorie, Roberta, Genvieve, Warren, Charley, and Reece — groan.*)

Reece: Otis, when are you going back to kindergarten?

Otis: Me? The day Bernice gets her hair bobbed.

Marjorie: Then your education is over.

Otis: Huh?

Marjorie: She didn't mean it. I thought you realized.

Roberta (*to Bernice*): You mean that was just a line?

Bernice (*embarrassed*): I don't know.

Marjorie: You never meant it. Admit it. (*Bernice looks around. Everyone is watching her. Warren seems especially curious.*)

Otis: Tell her where to get off, Bernice.

(*Bernice looks around again. Now Warren looks doubtful.*)

Warren: That's funny. I thought Bernice was sincere.

Bernice (*suddenly*): I am. I like bobbed hair, and I'm going to bob mine.

Marjorie: When?

Bernice: Any time.

Roberta: No time like the present.

Charley (*jumps up*): Let's have a bobbing party.

(*Everyone stands up, except Bernice.*)

Marjorie: Don't worry. She'll back out.

Otis: Come on, Bernice.

Bernice: Sure. (*She leads the way.*)

(*Cut to the group of young people watching a barber chop off Bernice's beautiful long hair. They are speechless. They hadn't realized how shocking this would be. The barber has never before cut a woman's hair, and he's doing a poor job of it.*)

(*Cut to Bernice getting down from the barber chair. She is trying to smile. Her short hair seems lifeless. It no longer seems to go with her face. The other young people just stare at her.*)

Bernice: Well, I did it. (*There is a silence. Then Marjorie turns to Warren.*)

Marjorie: Would you mind driving me to the cleaners? I've got to get a dress there before supper. Roberta can drive the others home.

Warren *(confused):* What? Oh, sure. I'd be glad to.

(Cut to the Harvey dining room that evening.)

Mrs. Harvey *(to Bernice):* I don't know why you had to do such a thing. But couldn't you have at least waited until after tomorrow night?

Marjorie: What's tomorrow night? *(She remembers.)* Mrs. Deyo's party for Bernice!

Mrs. Harvey: Bernice, she'll be so insulted.

Bernice: Why?

Mrs. Harvey: She feels bobbed hair is sinful. She gave a talk on the subject at the Ladies' Club.

Bernice: I didn't know that.

Mrs. Harvey: Oh, Bernice. What will your mother say? She'll think I let you do it.

Bernice: I'm sorry, Aunt Josephine.

(Cut to Bernice's room that night. She is looking at her short hair in a mirror. There is a knock on the door. Then Marjorie enters. Her long hair is down.)

Marjorie: Bernice, I'm sorry about Mrs. Deyo's party. I had forgotten all about it.

Bernice: It's all right.

Marjorie *(beginning to braid her long hair):* I didn't think you'd really go through with it. I'm really sorry.

Bernice: It doesn't matter.

Marjorie: You'll get used to it, maybe.

Bernice: I'm used to it now, and I like it.

Marjorie: Good. Don't let it worry you.

Bernice: I won't.

Marjorie: Life is too short.

Bernice: Yes.

Marjorie: Good night. *(She leaves.)*

(Later, we see Bernice dressed for traveling. She leaves an envelope on her pillow addressed to Aunt Josephine.)

(Cut to Marjorie's room. Marjorie is asleep. Bernice enters silently with a pair of scissors. She goes over to Marjorie and cuts off her two braids.)

(Cut to the sidewalk outside the Harvey house. Bernice appears. A suitcase is in one hand. Marjorie's braids are in the other hand. She crosses the street. Smiling, she throws the braids into Warren's car. Then she hurries down the street toward the train station.)

READING COMPREHENSION

Select the best choice to complete each statement. Then write the entire sentence on your paper.

1. Bernice wasn't popular with Marjorie's friends because she _____.
   a. refused to dance with them
   b. had a boy friend back home
   c. was boring and ill at ease

2. Marjorie tried to teach Bernice _____.
   a. how to talk with a man
   b. how to drive Warren's car
   c. how to make a party dress

3. Bernice first talked about bobbing her hair because she _____.
   a. was tired of her boring braids
   b. wanted to attract attention
   c. needed a haircut

4. Bernice did get her hair bobbed because _____.
   a. the group pressured her into it
   b. Warren said he liked short hair
   c. she wanted to set a new style and go to Hollywood

5. Bernice cut Marjorie's braids _____.
   a. to get revenge on her cousin
   b. because Warren asked her to
   c. so the two would look alike

For Discussion

1. Why did Bernice ask Marjorie for help? Do you think the advice Marjorie offered was good advice? Why or why not? If Bernice had asked you for help, what would you have told her to do? Explain your answer.

2. Why do you think Marjorie encouraged Bernice to bob her hair? Why did Bernice actually go through with it? Explain your answer.

3. What sort of a person was Marjorie as a friend? Do you think she was honest with the boys she liked? Explain your answer.

4. What did Bernice do to get back at Marjorie? Do you think she was right to do these things? Why or why not?

UNDERSTANDING LITERATURE

Style. The elements of F. Scott Fitzgerald's writing style can't be separated from the period in which he lived and set much of his work.

Fitzgerald was fascinated with the very wealthy, and many of his tales are about rich people in the 1920's.

An important element of Fitzgerald's style is his use of dialogue. He very often revealed character by what people said to and about each other. Much of the action in his works is revealed through dialogue as well.

One of the devices of style Fitzgerald used well to convey the flavor of his times was his use of expressions that were popular in the 1920's. These added much realism to his dialogue.

Here are some lines from "Bernice Bobs Her Hair." On your paper, match each with the person who is speaking and the character(s) being revealed. Some choices may be used more than once. Then identify two or more expressions from the 1920's.

a. Marjorie about self

b. Marjorie/self and others

c. Bernice/self

d. Marjorie's mother/Marjorie

e. Warren/Bernice

f. Marjorie/Bernice

1. "Warren flunked my test. . . . Before he came home for Christmas, I fell in love with four men."

2. "Well, you don't want to dance. And you don't want to sit out. Have a better idea?"

3. "Some things are more important than cheap popularity."

4. "Who let these two parlor snakes in my house?"

5. "You're also boring. You lean on men when you dance. You haven't any idea of how to make a man fall in love with you."

6. "Sad birds like Charley are part of any crowd. And you can't afford to neglect them."

7. "I want to be a society vampire. And I don't know how I can unless I bob my hair."

Writing
Write one or two paragraphs about a party that takes place during your own lifetime. Use as many popular expressions as you can to convey the flavor of the occasion.

Three poems of the Harlem Renaissance

Renaissance is a French word that means "rebirth." It is usually used to refer to the time in history when Europe had a great rebirth of writing and art. During the 1920's, in Harlem, there was a great explosion of creativity in many art forms. Black painters, musicians, and writers from all over the country came to Harlem. Here you will sample the works of two of the greatest poets of the Harlem Renaissance: Langston Hughes (1902–1967) and Countee Cullen (1903–1946).

Dream Variations

by Langston Hughes

To fling my arms wide
In some place of the sun,
To whirl and to dance
Till the white day is done.
Then rest at cool evening
Beneath a tall tree
While night comes on gently,
  Dark like me —
That is my dream!

To fling my arms wide
In the face of the sun,
Dance! Whirl! Whirl!
Till the quick day is done.
Rest at pale evening . . .
A tall, slim tree . . .
Night coming tenderly
  Black like me.

---

1. What kind of mood do the speaker's day-time activities suggest?

2. What kind of mood do the speaker's evening activities suggest?

The Negro Speaks of Rivers

by Langston Hughes

I've known rivers:
I've known rivers ancient as the world and older than the
    flow of human blood in human veins.

My soul has grown   deep like rivers.

I bathed in the Euphrates when dawns were young.
I built my hut near the Congo and it lulled me to sleep.
I looked upon the Nile and raised the pyramids above it.
I heard the singing of the Mississippi when Abe Lincoln went
    down to New Orleans, and I've seen its muddy bosom
    turn all golden in the sunset.

I've known rivers:
Ancient, dusky rivers.

My soul has grown   deep like rivers.

---

1. When the poet uses *I*, does he mean just himself? For whom is he speaking? What does the poem have to say about the black heritage?
2. The Congo and the Nile rivers are in Africa. How is their location important to the poem?
3. In what ways can a soul be "deep like rivers"?

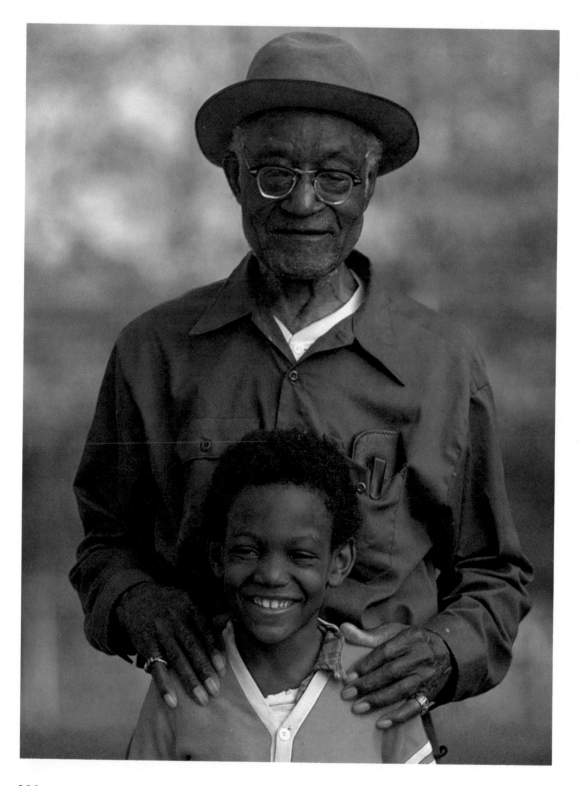

Any Human to Another

by Countee Cullen

The ills I sorrow at
Not me alone
Like an arrow,
Pierce to the marrow,
Through the fat
And past the bone.

Your grief and mine
Must intertwine
Like sea and river,
Be fused and mingle,
Diverse yet single,
Forever and forever.

Let no man be so proud
And confident,
To think he is allowed
A little tent
Pitched in a meadow
Of sun and shadow
All his little own.

Joy may be shy, unique,
Friendly to a few,
Sorrow never scorned to speak
To any who
Were false or true.

Your very grief
Like a blade
Shining and unsheathed
Must strike me down.
Of bitter aloes wreathed,
My sorrow must be laid
On your head like a crown.

---

1. *Diverse* means different or varied. In what ways are people's troubles "diverse yet single"?
2. Does the poet think that there is more joy in the world or more sorrow? Explain your answer. Do you agree? Why or why not?

READING COMPREHENSION

Select the best choice to complete each statement. Then write the entire sentence on your paper.

1. In the poem "The Negro Speaks of Rivers," Langston Hughes compared the rivers and his _____.
   a. hut
   b. soul
   c. human veins

2. The rivers Langston Hughes talks about are _____.
   a. in Africa
   b. in America
   c. in many different places

3. In "Dream Variations," the poet rests _____.
   a. during the day
   b. all the time
   c. at night

4. The poem "Any Human to Another" says that people should _____.
   a. compete with each other
   b. care for each other
   c. stand on their own

For Discussion

1. In "The Negro Speaks of Rivers," rivers are also used to represent time. In what ways are rivers like the flow of time? How can they be said to represent eternity, both past and future?

2. Do you agree with Countee Cullen that people should not stand alone in sorrow? How can showing sympathy for another's pain help that person?

UNDERSTANDING LITERATURE

Style and Rhythm in Poetry. The rhythm of a poem reflects the poet's purpose. Poems about unhappiness often have heavy rhythms. Poems about joyful subjects often have musical rhythms.

For example, in Langston Hughes's poem "The Negro Speaks of Rivers," the line "My soul has grown deep like rivers" is repeated twice, and each time it makes a powerful statement. The rhythm of the line matches the pride and power this poem suggests.

Read the lines below, and on your paper, describe each rhythm you feel. Is it fast or slow? What mood does it suggest?

1. "To fling my arms wide
   In the face of the sun,
   Dance! Whirl! Whirl!
   Till the quick day is done."

2. "The ills I sorrow at
   Not me alone
   Like an arrow,
   Pierce to the marrow.
   Through the fat
   And past the bone."

3. "I've known rivers:
   I've known rivers ancient as the world
   and older than the flow of human
   blood in human veins."

Writing

Write two to four lines of poetry about love using a light, joyous rhythm. Write two to four lines about loneliness using a heavy rhythm.

A Day's Wait

by Ernest Hemingway

Ernest Hemingway (1898–1961) is one of America's great adventurer-writers who based much of his work on his own experiences. At different times in his life, he drove an ambulance and was wounded in World War I, hunted big game in Africa, covered the Spanish Civil War as a reporter, and went deep-sea fishing while living in Cuba. For a time, Hemingway also lived in France and got to know other Americans who were living abroad. The experiences he had and the people he met all found their way into his writing. The following story, told mostly in dialogue and short, clear sentences, is typical of Hemingway's style. In the story you meet a boy called Schatz. Hemingway used this nickname for his own sons.

He came into the room to shut the windows while we were still in bed and I saw he looked ill. He was shivering, his face was white, and he walked slowly as though it ached to move.

"What's the matter, Schatz?"

"I've got a headache."

"You'd better go back to bed."

"No. I'm all right."

"You go to bed. I'll see you when I'm dressed."

But when I came downstairs he was dressed, sitting by the fire, looking a very sick and miserable boy of nine years. When I put my hand on his forehead I knew he had a fever.

"You go up to bed," I said, "you're sick."

"I'm all right," he said.

When the doctor came he took the boy's temperature.

"What is it?" I asked him.

"One hundred and two."

Downstairs, the doctor left three different medicines in different-colored capsules with instructions for giving them. One was to bring down the fever, another a purgative, the third to overcome an acid condition. The germs of influenza can only exist in an acid condition, he explained. He seemed to know all about influenza and said there was nothing to worry about if the fever did not go above one hundred and four degrees. This was a light epidemic of flu and there was no danger if you avoided pneumonia.

Back in the room I wrote the boy's temperature down and made a note of the time to give the various capsules.

"Do you want me to read to you?"

"All right. If you want to," said the boy. His face was very white and there were dark areas under his eyes. He lay still in the bed and seemed very detached from what was going on.

I read aloud from Howard Pyle's *Book of Pirates*; but I could see he was not following what I was reading.

"Just the same, so far," he said.

I sat at the foot of the bed and read to myself while I waited for it to be time to give another capsule. It would have been natural for him to go to sleep, but when I looked up he was looking at the foot of the bed, looking very strangely.

"Why don't you try to go to sleep? I'll wake you up for the medicine."

"I'd rather stay awake."

After a while he said to me, "You don't have to stay in here with me, Papa, if it bothers you."

"It doesn't bother me."

"No, I mean you don't have to stay if it's going to bother you."

I thought perhaps he was a little light-headed and after giving him the prescribed capsules at 11:00 I went out for a while.

It was a bright, cold day, the ground covered with a sleet that had frozen so that it seemed as if all the bare trees, the bushes, the cut brush, and all the grass and the bare ground had been varnished with ice. I took the young Irish setter for a little walk up the road and along a frozen creek, but it was difficult to stand or walk on the glassy surface and the red dog slipped and slithered and I fell twice, hard, once dropping my gun and having it slide away over the ice.

We flushed a covey of quail under a high clay bank with overhanging brush and I killed two as they went out of sight over the top of the bank. Some of the covey lit in trees, but most of them scattered into brush piles and it was necessary to jump on the ice-coated mounds of brush several times before they would flush. Coming out while you were poised unsteadily on the icy, springy brush they made difficult shooting, and I killed two, missed five, and started back pleased to have found a covey close to the house and happy there were so many left to find on another day.

At the house they said the boy had refused to let anyone come into the room.

"You can't come in," he said. "You mustn't get what I have."

I went up to him and found him in exactly the position I had left him, white-faced, but with the tops of his cheeks flushed by the fever, staring still, as he had stared, at the foot of the bed.

I took his temperature.

"What is it?"

"Something like a hundred," I said. It was one hundred and two and four tenths.

"It was a hundred and two," he said.

"Who said so?"

"The doctor."

"Your temperature is all right," I said. "It's nothing to worry about."

"I don't worry," he said, "but I can't keep from thinking."

"Don't think," I said. "Just take it easy."

"I'm taking it easy," he said and looked straight ahead. He was evidently holding tight onto himself about something.

"Take this with water."

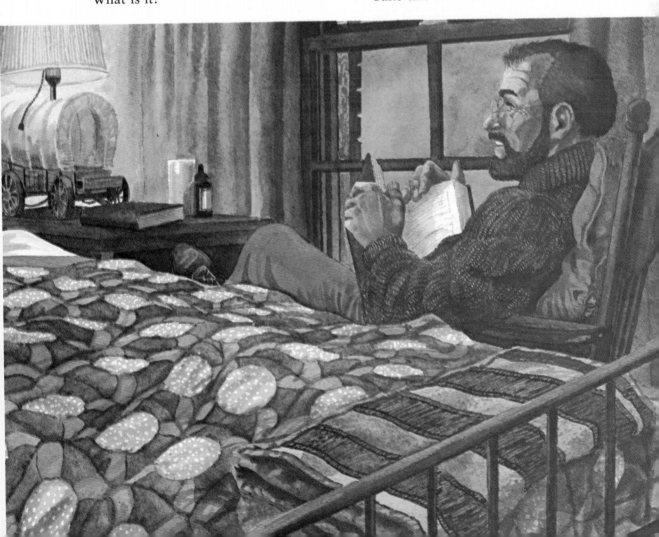

"Do you think it will do any good?"

"Of course it will."

I sat down and opened the *Pirate* book and commenced to read, but I could see he was not following, so I stopped.

"About what time do you think I'm going to die?" he asked.

"What?"

"About how long will it be before I die?"

"You aren't going to die. What's the matter with you?"

"Oh, yes, I am. I heard him say a hundred and two."

"People don't die with a fever of one hundred and two. That's a silly way to talk."

"I know they do. At school in France the boys told me you can't live with forty-four degrees. I've got a hundred and two."

He had been waiting to die all day, ever since 9:00 in the morning.

"You poor Schatz," I said. "Poor old Schatz. It's like miles and kilometers. You aren't going to die. That's a different thermometer. On that thermometer thirty-seven is normal. On this kind it's ninety-eight."

"Are you sure?"

"Absolutely," I said. "It's like miles and kilometers. You know, like how many kilometers we make when we do seventy miles in the car."

"Oh," he said.

But his gaze at the foot of the bed relaxed slowly. The hold over himself relaxed, too, finally, and the next day it was very slack and he cried very easily at little things that were of no importance.

READING COMPREHENSION

Select the best choice to complete each statement. Then write the entire sentence on your paper.

1. The boy's father called the doctor because he _____.
   a. thought the boy had a fever
   b. knew the child was going to die
   c. thought the boy had the mumps

2. The doctor said there was nothing to worry about _____.
   a. as long as the boy took the pills
   b. if the fever didn't go over 104°
   c. because children recover quickly

3. The father sat and read to him, but the boy _____.
   a. dozed off during the story
   b. wanted a different book
   c. couldn't pay attention

4. The boy was sure he was going to die because _____.
   a. the doctor said flu is deadly
   b. he felt worse than he ever had
   c. he confused two different measures of temperature

5. When the father compared the temperature readings to miles and kilometers, the boy _____.
   a. relaxed and stopped worrying about dying
   b. was pleased to talk about interesting things
   c. realized his fever was steadily increasing

For Discussion

1. How did the father know the boy was sick? What did he do about it? Do you think he did the right thing? Explain your answer.

2. Why didn't the father appear to worry more about his son?

3. Why do you think the boy refused to go to sleep? What do you think you might have done under those circumstances? Why wouldn't he let anyone into the room when his father went out? Explain your answer.

4. Why did the boy's father go out for a while? Do you think he should have gone? Why do you think the boy worried for an entire day before asking his father what was happening? Explain your answer.

UNDERSTANDING LITERATURE

Style. Ernest Hemingway's work is well-known for its style that expresses the individuality of the author and his own personal code. He believed that it was the job of a writer to face reality and to tell the truth.

Hemingway spoke of the need "to strip language clean, to lay it bare down to the bone." He revised his own writing again and again before publication and tried to eliminate any unneeded words or phrases. He tried to keep his sentences simple.

Hemingway's dialogue sounds natural and realistic. He communicates complicated human feelings with very few words.

Here are five characteristic elements of Hemingway's style, followed by some passages from the story you have just read. On your paper, match each passage to one or more of the elements of style that it demonstrates.

a. facing reality and telling the truth

b. simple sentence structure

c. no unnecessary words

d. natural dialogue

e. communication of feelings

1. "He was shivering, his face was white, and he walked slowly as though it ached to move."

2. " 'What's the matter, Schatz?'
'I've got a headache.'
'You'd better go back to bed.'
'No. I'm all right.' "

3. "I thought perhaps he was a little lightheaded and after giving him the prescribed capsules at 11:00 I went out for a while."

4. "He had been waiting to die all day, ever since 9:00 in the morning."

5. " 'Poor old Schatz. It's like miles and kilometers. You aren't going to die. That's a different thermometer.' "

Writing

Imagine that you are the boy in this story and that you believe you are going to die of fever. Write one or two paragraphs describing the way you feel and your fears.

The Standard of Living

by Dorothy Parker

*Dorothy Parker (1893–1967) was known for the clever
way she poked fun at the people and social rules of her day.
Her writing also shows a real understanding of different kinds
of people. Here you will meet two young women of the 1930's
who wonder what it would be like to have a million dollars.*

Annabel and Midge came out of the tea room with the arrogant slow walk of the leisured, for their Saturday afternoon stretched ahead of them. They had lunched, as usual, on sandwiches of spongy white bread with butter and mayonnaise; thick wedges of cake lying wet beneath ice cream; and melted chocolate gritty with nuts. Or they might have eaten meat patties sweating beads of oil, covered with pale, thick sauce. They chose no other sort of food, nor did they think of it. And their skin was like the petals of flowers, and their stomachs were as flat and their bodies as lean as those of young Indian braves.

Annabel and Midge had been best friends almost from the day that Midge had found a job as a secretary with the firm that employed Annabel. By now, Annabel, two years longer at the firm, had worked up to the wages of $18.50 a week; Midge was still at $16. Each girl lived at home with her family and paid half her salary to its support.

The girls sat side by side at their desks; they ate together every noon; together they set out for home after work. Many of their evenings and most of their week-ends were passed in each other's company. Constant use had not worn ragged the fabric of their friendship.

Always the girls went to walk on Fifth Avenue on their free afternoons, for it was the ideal ground for their game. The game could be played anywhere, but the great shop windows inspired the two players to their best form.

Annabel invented the game. Basically, it was no more than the ancient sport of what-would-you-do-if-you-had-a-million-dollars? But Annabel had drawn a new set of rules for it, and made it stricter.

Annabel's version went like this: You must suppose that somebody dies and leaves you a million dollars, cool. But there is a condition to the gift. It is stated in the will that you must spend every nickel of the money on yourself.

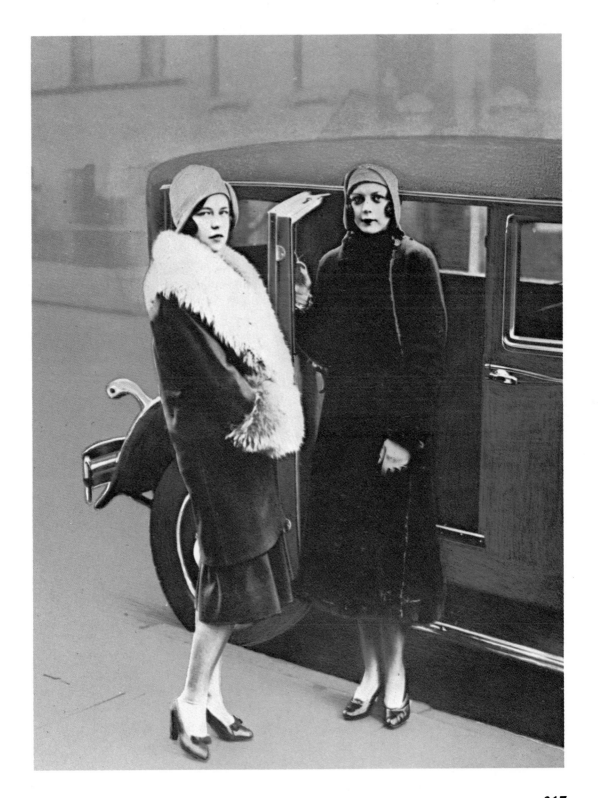

There lay the difficulty of the game. If, when playing it, you forgot and said you would rent a new apartment for your family, for example, you lost your turn to the other player.

It was necessary, of course, that the game be played in complete seriousness. Each purchase must be carefully considered, and if necessary, supported by argument.

Annabel and Midge were surely born to be friends, for Midge played the game like a master from the moment she learned it. Midge played with a seriousness that was not only proper but extreme. The single strain on the girls' friendship was when Annabel once said that the first thing she would buy with her million dollars would be a silver fox coat. It was as if she had struck Midge across the mouth. When Midge recovered her breath, she said that she couldn't imagine how Annabel could do such a thing — silver fox coats were so common! She added that everybody had a silver fox coat. She said, with a slight toss of her head, that she herself wouldn't be caught dead in silver fox.

For the next few days, though the girls saw each other as constantly, they did not once play their game. Then one morning, as soon as Annabel entered the office, she came to Midge and said she had changed her mind. She would not buy a silver fox coat with any part of her million dollars. Instead, she would select a coat of mink. Midge smiled, and her eyes shone. "You're doing the right thing," she said.

Now, as they walked along Fifth Avenue, they played the game again. It was one of those hot, glaring September days,

with slivers of dust in the wind. People drooped in the heat, but the girls carried themselves tall and walked a straight line, as was proper for rich young women on their afternoon stroll. There was no longer need for them to start the game at the beginning. Annabel went direct to the heart of it.

"All right," she said. "So you've got this million dollars. So what would be the first thing you do?"

"Well, the first thing I'd do," Midge said, "I'd get a mink coat." But she said it mechanically, as if she was giving the old answer to an expected question.

"Yes," Annabel said. "I think you ought to. The terribly dark kind of mink." But she, too, spoke without enthusiasm. It was too hot; fur, no matter how dark and sleek, was horrid to the thoughts.

They stepped along in silence for a while. Then Midge's eye was caught by a shop window. Cool, lovely gleamings were there set off by elegant darkness.

"No," Midge said, "I take it back. I wouldn't get a mink coat the first thing. Know what I'd do? I'd get a string of pearls. Real pearls."

Annabel's eyes turned to follow Midge's.

"Yes," she said slowly. "I think that's a kind of good idea. And it would make good sense, too. Because you can wear pearls with anything."

Together they went over to the shop window and stood pressed against it. It contained but one object — a double row of great, even pearls clasped by a deep emerald around a little pink velvet throat.

"What do you suppose they cost?" Annabel said.

"Gee, I don't know," Midge said. "Plenty, I guess."

"Like a thousand dollars?" Annabel said.

"Oh, I guess like more," Midge said. "On account of the emerald."

"Well, like ten thousand dollars?" Annabel said.

"Gee, I wouldn't even know," Midge said.

The devil nudged Annabel in the ribs.

"Dare you go in and price them," she said.

"Like fun!" Midge said.

"Dare you," Annabel said.

"Why a store like this wouldn't even be open this afternoon," Midge said.

"Yes, it is so, too," Annabel said. "People just came out. And there's a doorman on. Dare you."

"Well," Midge said. "But you've got to come, too."

They said their thanks, icily, to the doorman as he opened the door to the shop. It was cool and quiet, a lovely room with paneled walls and soft carpet.

A neatly dressed clerk came to them and bowed. "Good afternoon," he said in a soft-spoken greeting.

"Good afternoon," Annabel and Midge said together, coldly.

"Is there something — ?" the clerk said.

"Oh, we're just looking," Annabel said. It was as if she threw the words down from a throne.

The clerk bowed.

"My friend and I just happened to be passing," Midge said. "My friend here and myself just happened to be wondering how much those pearls are that you've got in your window."

"Ah, yes," the clerk said. "The double rope. That is two hundred and fifty thousand dollars, Madam."

"I see," Midge said.

The clerk bowed. "An unusually beautiful necklace," he said. "Would you care to look at it?"

"No, thank you," Annabel said.

"My friend and myself just happened to be passing," Midge said.

They turned to go. The clerk hurried ahead to open the door. He bowed as they swept by him.

"Honestly!" Annabel said as they walked along the avenue. "Can you imagine a thing like that?"

"Two hundred and fifty thousand dollars!" Midge said. "That's a quarter of a million dollars right there!"

"He's got his nerve!" Annabel said.

They walked on. Slowly the self-confidence went, completely drained from them, and with it went the proud walk. Their shoulders drooped and they dragged their feet; they bumped against each other without notice or apology. They were silent and their eyes were cloudy.

Suddenly Midge straightened her back, lifted her head high, and spoke, clear and strong.

"Listen, Annabel," she said. "Look. Suppose there was this terribly rich person, see? You don't know this person, but this person has seen you somewhere and wants to do something for you. Well, it's a terribly old person, see? And so this person dies just like going to sleep, and leaves you ten million dollars. Now, what would be the first thing you'd do?"

READING COMPREHENSION

Select the best choice to complete each statement. Then write the entire sentence on your paper.

1. Annabel and Midge worked together and _____.
   a. competed for luncheon dates
   b. were almost constant companions
   c. had different tastes and hobbies

2. In Annabel's game, the million dollars could not be spent on _____.
   a. anything for anyone else
   b. silver fox coats
   c. jewelry that was not pure gold

3. The young women went into the jewelry store because they _____.
   a. had a million dollars to spend
   b. expected to have wealth someday
   c. dared each other to price the necklace

4. When they learned the price of the pearls, the girls _____.
   a. gave up their game completely
   b. decided to do without pearls for a while
   c. got over their shock and pretended that they had more money

For Discussion

1. How would you describe Annabel and Midge? Do you think they led interesting lives? Explain your answer.

2. What do you think of the game Annabel and Midge played? Do you think it's useful, or necessary, to do things like this? Explain your answer.

UNDERSTANDING LITERATURE

Ironic Tone. Style is the particular way an author arranges words. In "The Standard of Living," the important elements of style are the way the author revealed character and her consistently *ironic tone*.

Parker wrote in the third-person, "all knowing," point of view. She revealed her characters by telling what they looked like, describing their actions, and using dialogue that let them speak for themselves. The dialogue is accompanied by an occasional adverb that comments on the way the words are said.

Read the following. On your paper, identify each one that is in Parker's ironic style. Remember that she reveals character through dialogue and actions.

1. She said, with a slight toss of her head, that she herself wouldn't be caught dead in a silver fox coat.

2. Midge told Annabel that a silver fox coat wouldn't be her choice even though it was a magnificent fur.

3. They said their thanks, icily, to the doorman as he opened the door.

4. "Those pearls are fantastic! May we look at them even though we'll never be able to dig up the cash?"

Writing

Imagine that someone has left *you* a million dollars. Write a paragraph telling what you would buy and why. Follow Annabel's rules: You're not allowed to buy anything for anyone else.

Section Review

VOCABULARY

Multiple Meanings. Sometimes a word can have more than one meaning, and what the word means depends on the way it is used. For example, *lean* can mean "without much flesh or fat." *Lean* can also mean "bend, or rest against." Dorothy Parker used the word *lean* to describe the thin characters in her story.

Read each sentence below. On your paper, select the correct meaning of each italicized word.

1. "He went *broke,* of course, because he gave too much *credit.*"

    broke   **a.** smashed to bits

            b. without money

    credit **a.** buying on time

            b. recognition

2. "The *single strain* on the girls' friendship was when Annabel once said . . . she would buy . . . a silver fox coat."

    single **a.** not married

            b. only

    strain **a.** melody or tune

            b. pressure or tension

3. "It contained but one *object* — a double *row* of . . . pearls."

    object **a.** disagree

            b. thing

    row   **a.** line or string

            b. to use an oar

READING

Drawing Conclusions. Sometimes, when you read, the author tells you directly what he or she wants you to know. In other cases, you have to put together the details and draw your own conclusions.

Write the answers to the following questions on your paper.

1. In "Discovery of a Father," Anderson's mother laughed when her husband clowned. She worked and managed during his absences, and she smiled when he returned. You can conclude that she _____.

    a. would have preferred a wealthy man

    b. loved her husband the way he was

    c. secretly desired a divorce

2. In Jack London's story "Love of Life," both men were carrying packs. Bill went on when his companion got hurt. The injured man kept going, but lightened his load along the way by leaving gold along the trail. From this you can conclude that Bill _____.

    a. wanted to go for help quickly

    b. couldn't afford to wait for his friend

    c. valued gold more than his friend

3. In "A Day's Wait" by Hemingway, the boy had the flu and a fever. He couldn't keep his mind on the story his father read, and he refused to go to sleep. Although the doctor and the boy's father were not concerned, you can conclude that the boy was _____.

    a. in serious danger of death

    b. very worried about himself

    c. eager to return to school

WRITING A REVIEW

Suppose there were three new movies in town. How would you decide which one to see this weekend? Or perhaps you want to buy a book to read on vacation or to give as a gift. How would you know which of several new titles to choose? You could ask a friend. You could pick just any one and take your chances. Or you could read a review to help you choose.

Many newspapers and magazines contain reviews of films, books, and plays. The job of a reviewer is to evaluate a work of literature or a performance, and give reasons why others should or should not see the show or read the book.

Now it's your turn to take the part of a reviewer. Your task is to review one of the stories in this section, and to make a recommendation about it for future students. Follow the directions in the rest of this lesson carefully, and make your review as helpful to your readers as you can.

Here is a checklist of questions to ask yourself as you review a story. The answers to these questions will provide important information for your review.

Plot

☐ Is the plot well constructed?

☐ Does each incident have a purpose?

☐ Does each incident grow out of what comes before and lead to what comes next?

☐ Is each incident related to the story's main idea?

☐ Does each incident help reveal the story's theme in some way?

Characters

☐ How did the author reveal character? Were the techniques used effectively?

☐ Are the characters believable?

☐ Can you find valid reasons for the characters' behavior?

☐ Is the dialogue (if any) suitable for the characters involved?

Setting and Mood

☐ Is the story's setting described well?

☐ What atmosphere was the author trying to create? Does the mood fit the story?

1. Pick a story in this section. Choose one that you liked very much or one that you didn't like at all. This will make it easier to find things to say.

2. Reread the story with the checklist questions in mind. Take notes on anything you think will help you write your review. Before beginning to write, here are two cautions to keep in mind:

   a. A review is *not* a summary of the plot. Don't retell the story.

   b. A review is *not* an unsupported opinion. Tell your readers *why* you do or do not recommend something.

3. Try to capture your reader's interest with your first sentence. Begin by giving the title of the selection and the name of the author. Tell why you chose to review this particular selection. Refer to the checklist when writing the review. End by giving your general impressions. Then tell if you would recommend this selection to other readers.

The following is a quiz for Section 7. Write the answers in complete sentences on your paper.

Reading Comprehension

1. Why did Bill leave his companion behind at the beginning of "Love of Life"? What happened to Bill later?

2. In "The Discovery of a Father," what comparison did the author make between his father and himself at the story's end?

3. Why did Bernice bob her hair in the teleplay "Bernice Bobs Her Hair"? How did she feel about it later?

4. In "A Day's Wait," what was the problem that the main character had? What did *he* think his problem was?

5. What was the game Annabel and Midge played in "The Standard of Living"? What happened when they went into the jewelry store?

Understanding Literature

6. In Jack London's stories, what usually happens to the strong? What happens to the weak? Give an example of each from "Love of Life."

7. In whose words is "The Discovery of a Father" told? Why do you think the author chose this style?

8. F. Scott Fitzgerald's stories are realistic tales of wealthy young people of the 1920's. Give three details from the teleplay "Bernice Bobs Her Hair" to show that he really did understand young people and the age.

9. What are two important elements of Ernest Hemingway's style? Give an example of each from "A Day's Wait."

10. What techniques did Dorothy Parker use to reveal character in "The Standard of Living"? Give an example of each.

COMPOSITION

1. Suppose that Sherwood Anderson had decided to write a personal narrative essay about his mother. Write the first two or three paragraphs for him.

2. Think of something that a teenager today could do that would be as shocking as Bernice bobbing her hair was in the 1920's. Write a paragraph about what it is and why the person did it.

3. Write your own story with the title "A Day's Wait." The wait can be happy or sad. Pick whatever it is that you are waiting for, and describe it in any way you wish.

4. Annabel and Midge ate sandwiches on spongy white bread with butter and mayonnaise. They didn't try anything else. Describe in a paragraph what you would eat for lunch if you could have your choice. Would you eat the same thing three days in a row or would you go for variety?

SECTION 8

Voices of Mystery

1898–1939

*The night deepened. The crowd rumbled.
Mr. Ellery Queen, the famous detective,
felt uncomfortable. His six-foot body
was as tight as a violin string. It
was a familiar feeling. It meant that
there was murder in the air.*

— Ellery Queen

Introduction

Americans have always been eager to take on new challenges. During the years 1898–1939, mystery stories became popular because they offered a new kind of challenge for readers. A mystery story involves a puzzle that the characters in the story try to solve. A well-written mystery story is full of hidden clues. Alert readers can use these clues to put together all the pieces of the puzzle before the solution is revealed at the end.

Mystery and the Supernatural

One kind of mystery story draws on old tales of ghosts, witches, and magic. The supernatural is used to explain an unusual event in the story. The author of such a story works carefully to create a mood of suspense. Edith Wharton once said, "The teller of supernatural tales should be well frightened in the telling." She felt she had to create stories powerful enough to scare herself if they were to scare anyone else. As you will see when you read her story "Afterward," she creates a mood by using details in the story to hint at a supernatural puzzle.

Mystery and Detection

In the 1920's and 1930's, a different kind of mystery story became popular. These stories did not rely on the supernatural to create a mood of suspense and excitement. The plot in these stories revolves around discovering who committed a certain crime. Sometimes they are called "whodunits." In a good whodunit, crime is only the means to the end.

The real story is how one of the characters, the detective, figures out who committed the crime and why. The detective in a mystery story is a very special kind of character. He or she, like the reader, gathers information from the story as it unfolds. The detective always has a careful eye for detail, and it is usually a small detail that leads him or her to discover which of the other characters in the story committed the crime.

Ellery Queen is the name of one of the most famous fictional detectives created during this era. Ellery Queen is also the pen name of the two authors, Frederic Dannay and Manfred Lee, cousins who began writing together in 1929. Together they've created a character and a series of mysteries that are known all over the world. Ellery Queen is a detective who always remains calm and observant, as you will see when you read the story "Mind Over Matter" in this section.

Mignon G. Eberhardt is another famous mystery writer who began publishing during this era. In the 1930's, Eberhardt created the character Susan Dare. Susan Dare, like her creator, is a well-known author of mystery stories. In her stories, she is often called upon by people to help

Humphrey Bogart, Mary Astor, Barton MacLane, Peter Lorre, and Ward Bond in the *Maltese Falcon,* 1941

them find solutions to difficult problems. The story you will read here, "The Calico Dog," proves to be one of Dare's most complex and dangerous cases. This story shows Eberhardt's skill at creating suspense, placing clues, and creating characters.

Mystery stories were popular during the years 1898–1939 because the reading public wanted literature that would help them escape the boredom and problems of everyday life. These stories do not describe the real world of the early 20th century. Instead, these stories describe an imaginary world where every problem has a clear-cut solution, and every wrongdoing is punished. Somehow the fact that these stories "played fair" helped readers survive the unfairness of World War I and the Depression years.

For you, the modern reader, these stories offer more than entertainment. They bring to life glamorous settings, colorful characters, and the ideals of the America of the early 20th century.

Afterward

by Edith Wharton

Twilight shadows in an old English country house, legends of a mysterious ghost, and a strange disappearance are the elements Edith Wharton (1862–1937) uses to create the suspenseful mystery story that follows. Best known for her novels and short stories about the manners and morals of her time, Edith Wharton was also a skilled mystery writer, as you will discover reading "Afterward."

Chapter One

"Oh, there *is* one, of course, but you'll never know it."

These words had been said jokingly six months before in a bright June garden. Now Mary Boyne thought of them again, as she stood in the December dusk waiting for the lamps to come.

Alida Stair had told Mary Boyne and her husband about Lyng — a house with a ghost. The Boynes had recently come to England from America. They needed a place to live.

Ned Boyne was delighted at the idea of living in an old-fashioned English country house. "It's too good to be true!" he cried. "But I've always wanted a ghost of my own. *Is* there a ghost at Lyng?"

Alida laughed. "Oh, there *is* one, of course, but you'll never know it."

"Never know it," Boyne answered. "How can you know you have a ghost if you don't know it's there?"

"I can't say but that's the story."

"That there's a ghost, but that nobody knows it's a ghost?"

"Well — not till afterward — long afterward."

Suddenly Mary spoke up. "You mean that long afterward, one says to one's self, *'That was it.* That was the ghost'?"

She was startled by the serious note her question added to the joking of the other two. Then she saw a shadow of seriousness fall across Alida's face. "I suppose so. One just has to wait."

"Oh, hang waiting!" Ned broke in. "Life's too short for a ghost that can only be enjoyed long afterward. Can't we do better than that, Mary?"

But it turned out that they could not find a better place. Three months later they were settled at Lyng. And the life they had yearned and planned for had actually begun.

For 14 years the Boynes had lived in a small house in a small Middle-Western American town. Ned Boyne worked long and hard as an engineer. He did not have much success. Then one day a stroke of luck had led him to the Blue Star Mine. Now they had money and time for life in the English countryside.

Both the Boynes were delighted with the old house and the surrounding grounds. It was beautiful and quiet. Yet from the first Mary Boyne had felt a mysterious air about the place.

The feeling had never been stronger than on this particular December afternoon. She waited in the library for the lamps to come. Her husband had gone off, after luncheon, for one of his long walks. She had noticed of late that he preferred to walk alone. Perhaps his book was bothering him. He looked more tired and worried now than he ever had during his engineering days. Yet the few pages of the book he had read to her were skillfully written.

Perhaps it was his health then? But physically he appeared well. It was only within the last week that Mary had felt the undefinable change. She didn't know why, but she was restless in his absence. Yet she was tongue-tied when he was there. It was as though it were *she* who had kept a secret from him!

Suddenly she realized that there was a secret between them.

"Can it be the house?" she wondered.

The room itself might have been full of secrets. They seemed to be piling themselves up, as evening fell. Layers and layers of velvet shadows dropped from the ceiling, the rows of books, and the smoke-blurred hearth.

"Why — of course — the house is haunted!" she reflected.

Perhaps Ned had already met the ghost. Then he might be carrying about the weight of what the ghost had revealed to him.

Then Mary remembered that when one *did* see a ghost at Lyng, one did not know it at the time.

"Not till long afterward," Alida Stair had said. Well, suppose Ned *had* seen one when they first came. Maybe he had known only within the last week what had happened to him.

She thought back to their first days at Lyng. One October day she had found a hidden staircase that led to the roof. The view was wonderful. She had flown down and snatched Ned away from his papers. She wanted to share her discovery. She remembered still how he put his arm around her as they gazed out over the horizon.

It was just then, while they gazed and held each other, that she felt his arm relax. His face looked anxious. She looked down and saw a man — a man in loose grayish clothes walking down the path to the front door. He walked with the doubtful gait of a stranger who seeks his way. Her shortsighted eyes gave her the blurred impression of slightness and grayness. There was something unlocal in his dress. But her husband seemed to have seen more. He pushed past her calling, "Wait!" Then he dashed down the stairs.

She followed him more slowly and carefully. When she reached the bottom of the stairs, she discovered that the path and the hall were empty. The library door was open. When she entered, she found her husband alone. He was staring vaguely at the papers on his desk.

"What was it? Who was it?" she asked.

"Who?" he repeated.

"The man we saw coming toward the house."

He thought before he answered. "Why I thought I saw Peters, our groundskeeper. I dashed after him to say a word about the drains, but he had disappeared before I got down."

"Disappeared? But he seemed to be walking so slowly."

Boyne shrugged. "So I thought, but he must have got up steam while we came downstairs. What do you say to trying to climb Meldon Steep before sunset?"

That was all. At the time it happened it didn't seem unusual. Yet now as Mary reviewed the scene, she had many questions. Why would the familiar figure of Peters make her husband excited? And if it was so important to talk to Peters, why did Ned look relieved when he did not find him?

Chapter Two

Weary with her thoughts, Mary moved to the window. She saw a figure moving far down the path, between the bare trees. It looked like a mere blot of deeper gray in the grayness of the dusk. For an instant, as it moved toward her, her heart thumped. "It's the ghost!" she thought.

But in a few seconds the approaching figure began to look familiar. Even to her weak sight it was clear that it was her husband. She turned to meet him as he entered.

Laughingly she said, "I thought you were the ghost! It's foolish but I never can remember!"

"Remember what?" Boyne questioned.

"That when one sees the Lyng ghost one never knows it!"

"Really, dearest," he said faintly. "You'd better give up thinking about the ghost."

The parlor maid entered with letters and a lamp. The light brought out the sharp lines of worry on Boyne's brows.

"Have you given up trying to see the ghost?" Mary asked after the maid left the room.

"I never tried," he answered, as he tore the wrapper of the newspaper and began to read.

"Well, of course, there is no use trying if one can't be sure until long afterward," she added.

After a pause, he looked up from his newspaper to ask, "Have you any idea how long?"

"No, none," she answered.

She was about to add, "What makes you ask?" when the maid reappeared with tea and a second lamp.

For a few moments Mary busied herself with pouring and serving tea. The room was now bright. Her gloomy thoughts seemed to have vanished with the grey shadows.

Her husband sat across the room reading his letters. He looked relaxed and happy. Was it because of something he found in the letters or was it just the change in her own mood? He glanced up as if drawn by her gaze and smile.

"I'm dying for my tea, you know. Here's a letter for you," he said.

She took the letter he held out. Then she gave him his tea. She returned to her seat, opened the letter and began to read.

Suddenly she rose to her feet. She held out a newspaper clipping to her husband.

"Ned! What does this mean?"

He had risen at the same moment. For some time he and she studied each other, like opponents carefully watching for an advantage.

"What's what?" he said at last. He looked worried again.

"This article — from the *Waukesha Sentinel* back home. It says that a man named Elwell has brought a lawsuit against you. It says that there's something wrong about the Blue Star Mine."

"Oh, *that!*" he said with a noticeable sigh of relief. "That's nothing to worry about. It's all right."

"But what does this Mr. Elwell accuse you of?"

"Pretty nearly every crime in the calendar," Boyne answered, throwing himself into an armchair near the fire. "Do you want to hear the story?"

"But who is Elwell? I don't know him."

"Oh, he's a fellow I helped out. I let him buy a share in the mine."

"But if you've helped him, why is he suing you?"

"Probably some crooked lawyer got hold of him and talked him over. It's all rather technical. Besides, I thought these things bored you."

Mary looked at her husband. His face was calm and confident. "But doesn't this lawsuit worry you? Why have you never spoken to me about it?"

He answered both questions at once. "I didn't speak of it at first because it *did* worry me — annoyed me, rather. But it's all ancient history now. That clipping you received must be from an old newspaper."

She felt relieved. "You mean it's over? He's lost his case?"

There was a slight delay in Boyne's reply. "The suit has been withdrawn — that's all."

"How long ago was it withdrawn?"

He paused again, then said, "I've just had news now in one of my letters. I've been expecting it."

He crossed the room and sat down next to her on the sofa.

"It's all right?" she asked, looking into his smiling eyes.

"I give you my word it was never righter!" he laughed back at her, holding her close.

Chapter Three

The next day Mary awoke feeling secure and happy. Everything was all right. She thought no more about ghosts, or doubting her husband. It was a bright sunny day. A rare day for December. Mary walked out into the garden. She was waiting for a man from Dorchester who was to come fix the hothouse boiler. The gardener had gone to fetch him at the station.

Mary heard steps behind her, and turned. She was expecting to see the gardener and the engineer from Dorchester. But only one figure was in sight. It was a youngish, thin man. He did not look like a boiler repairman. The newcomer lifted his hat to her. He had the air of a gentleman — perhaps a traveler. After a moment she asked, "Is there anyone you wish to see?"

"I came to see Mr. Boyne," he answered. His speech was that of an American. Mary looked at him more closely. The brim of his soft felt hat cast a shade on his face. He looked serious and businesslike.

"Have you an appointment with my husband?" she asked.

The visitor hesitated. "I think he expects me," he replied at last.

It was Mary's turn to hesitate. "You see he works on his book at this time. He never sees anyone in the morning."

He looked at her a moment. Then as if accepting her decision, he began to move away. As he turned, Mary saw him look up at the peaceful house. He looked so disappointed. The traveler had probably come a long way. Perhaps his time was limited.

Mary called after him, "May I ask if you've come a long way?"

He gave her the same serious look. "Yes, I have come a long way."

"Then if you'll go to the house, no doubt my husband will see you now. You'll find him in the library."

The visitor seemed about to express his thanks. Then Mary noticed the approach of the gardener and the boilermaker.

"This way," she said, waving the stranger to the house. An instant later she had forgotten him. She began to explain the problems with the boiler to the man from Dorchester.

By the time the boiler had been repaired, it was time for luncheon. She hurried back to the house. It was so silent. She guessed Boyne was still at work. Not wishing to disturb him, she went into the dining room. She busied herself with her own work at her writing table.

At last, the housekeeper, Trimmle, announced luncheon. Mary opened the library door to call Boyne to the dining room.

Boyne was not at his desk. She called him but got no reply.

"If you please, Madam," Trimmle said, "Mr. Boyne has gone out."

Mary turned to face the housekeeper. "Where did he go? And when?"

"He went out of the front door, up the drive, Madam."

"Did Mr. Boyne leave no message?" Mary questioned.

"No, Madam. He just went out with the gentleman."

"The gentleman? What gentleman?" Mary was hungry and confused.

"The gentleman who called, Madam," said Trimmle calmly.

"Do explain yourself, Trimmle. When did a gentleman call?" Mary asked.

"I couldn't say the hour, Madam, because I didn't let the gentleman in. I was busy. The kitchen maid answered the door."

Mary looked at the clock. "It's after two. Go and ask the kitchen maid if Mr. Boyne left any word."

She went into luncheon without waiting. Soon Trimmle told her that the kitchen maid had said that the gentleman called about 11:00. Mr. Boyne had gone out with him soon after. Mr. Boyne did not have any message.

Mary finished luncheon and went into the drawing room. She sat and wondered. It was unlike Boyne to go away without explaining why and where he was going. Perhaps Boyne had decided to walk his visitor back to the station. This conclusion relieved her mind. She went on with her day. That afternoon she walked to the village post office. When she returned home, twilight was setting in.

She had taken the footpath through the fields. Boyne had probably returned from the station by the main road. There was little chance of their meeting. She felt sure, however, that he must have reached the house before her.

When she entered, she went directly to the library. But it was still empty. The papers on her husband's desk lay precisely as they had lain when she had gone to call him to luncheon.

Then she felt a pang of fear — fear of the unknown. As she stood in the long silent room, her fear seemed to take shape. It seemed to be breathing and hiding among the shadows.

She rang for Trimmle. The housekeeper came at once.

"You may bring tea if Mr. Boyne is in," she said to explain her ring.

"Very well, Madam. But Mr. Boyne is not in," said Trimmle. She put down the lamp she carried. "He's not been back since he went out with the gentleman this morning."

"But who *was* the gentleman?" Mary insisted. "The kitchen maid must know. She let him in."

"She doesn't know, either, Madam, for he wrote his name on a folded piece of paper."

"But he must have a name!" Mary cried. "Where's the paper?"

She moved to her husband's desk. She began to turn over the papers on it. The first that caught her eye was an unfinished letter. Her husband's pen was lying across the letter — as if he had dropped it suddenly.

"My dear Parvis" — Who was Parvis? "I have just received your letter announcing Elwell's death. While I suppose there is now no further risk of trouble, it might be safer —"

And there the letter ended. She tossed the sheet aside. She continued to search, but she found no folded paper.

"The kitchen maid *saw* him. Send her here!" Mary commanded of Trimmle.

When the kitchen maid came, Mary had her questions ready. "What did the stranger say? What did he look like? What did he write on that paper?"

The kitchen maid was not sure what had been written. The visitor followed her into the library when she carried the note to Mr. Boyne. She left them alone. A little while later she had seen Mr. Boyne and the visitor go out the front door together.

"Well, then," Mary said. "You saw the strange gentleman twice. What did he look like?"

The maid was confused. She could only stammer. "His hat, mum, was different."

"Different? How different?" Mary flashed out. Suddenly Mary remembered the man she had met that morning in the garden.

"His hat had a wide brim, you mean? His face was pale, wasn't it? A thin, youngish face?" Why had Mary not thought of him before? She needed no one now to tell her what the visitor looked like. But who was he, and why had Boyne gone with him?

Chapter Four

Two weeks later Boyne had not returned. A full investigation took place. But no one had seen him. It was as if the sunny English room had swallowed up Edward Boyne completely.

Mary tried her best to find clues that would lead to her husband. She found nothing — except for the letter Boyne had been writing when his mysterious visitor called. Mary read and reread that letter. She even showed it to the police.

"I have just received your letter announcing Elwell's death. While I suppose there is now no further risk of trouble, it might be safer — " That was all. The "risk of trouble" must refer to the lawsuit that she had found out about in the newspaper clipping. The only new information was that it showed Boyne was still worried about the lawsuit. Yet he had told his wife the suit had been withdrawn. And

Elwell was dead and certainly could bother him no more. Nevertheless, Mary tracked down "Parvis." He turned out to be a lawyer in Waukesha, back in America. He said he had no new facts to offer about Elwell or the lawsuit. He said that he did not know why Boyne had wanted to contact him.

Two weeks turned to three; three weeks became four. Week by week, hour by hour, the investigation slowed. After a few months it was crowded out by new problems. At last the police gave up.

Even Mary Boyne found that her days became ordinary. She had come to accept the horror of Boyne's disappearance.

She stayed on at Lyng. Her friends supposed that she stayed there because she was waiting for her husband to return. But in reality she was sure that Boyne would never come back. He had gone out

of her sight as completely as if Death itself had waited that day in the doorway.

No, she would never know what had become of him. No one would ever know.

But the house *knew*. The library in which she spent her long, lonely evenings knew. It was here that the stranger had come and caused Boyne to rise and follow him.

Chapter Five

"I don't say it *wasn't* straight. Yet I don't say it *was* straight. It was business."

Mary heard these words and looked up at the speaker. A half an hour before, a card with "Mr. Parvis" on it had been brought up to her. She was both eager and surprised. Why this visit from the person to whom Boyne had addressed his unfinished letter?

She found Mr. Parvis waiting in the library. He was a small man. He had a bald head and gold eyeglasses.

Parvis at once explained why he had come. He was in England on business. He had found himself in the neighborhood of Lyng so he wished to pay his respects to Mrs. Boyne. He also wished to ask her what she meant to do about Bob Elwell's family.

Mary felt a tug of dread. Did her visitor, after all, know what Boyne had meant to say in his letter? She asked her visitor to explain himself.

"Is it possible that you know as little as you had said, Mrs. Boyne?" Parvis questioned. He seemed quite surprised.

"I know nothing. You must tell me," she answered.

Then her visitor told his story. Her husband had made his money at the cost of "getting ahead" of someone else. The victim was young Robert Elwell. Elwell had "put Boyne on" to the Blue Star Mine. And Boyne figured out a way to keep all the profits for himself.

"But then — " Mary said slowly, "you accuse my husband of doing something dishonorable?"

Mr. Parvis answered calmly, "Oh, no, I don't. I don't even say it wasn't straight." He glanced up and down the long lines of books in the library. "I don't say it *wasn't* straight. Yet I don't say it *was* straight. It was business."

Mary stared at him. He was indifferent. He seemed unaware of the evil power of the story.

"Mr. Elwell's lawyers did not seem to think that anything was wrong. I assume they advised Mr. Elwell to withdraw his suit," Mary said.

"Oh, yes. He hadn't a leg to stand on, legally. But when he found that out, he got desperate. You see, he'd borrowed most of the money he lost in the Blue Star. He was up a tree. That's why he shot himself."

"He shot himself?" Mary said. Her voice shook with horror. "He killed himself because of *that*?"

"Well, he didn't kill himself exactly. He dragged on two months before he died."

Parvis sounded as unemotional as a record.

"You mean he tried to kill himself, and failed? And tried again?"

"Oh, he didn't have to *try* again," said Parvis grimly.

They sat opposite each other. Parvis swung his eyeglasses around his finger. Mary sat motionless.

"You know all this," she began at last, "and I wrote to you at the time of my husband's disappearance. Why did you say then that you didn't understand the letter?"

Parvis showed no embarrassment. "Why, I didn't understand it — strictly speaking. And it wasn't the time to talk about it. Nothing I could have told you would have helped you find Boyne."

Mary continued to stare at him. "Then why are you telling me now?"

"To begin with," Parvis answered calmly, "I supposed you knew more than you had said — I mean about Elwell's death. And now people are talking about it again. I thought if you didn't know, you ought to,"

Mary remained silent and Parvis continued. "You see, it's only come out lately how poor Elwell really was. His wife's a proud woman. She went to work, but then she got too sick. It was something with her heart, I believe. But she had Elwell's mother to look after, and the children. Finally she asked for help. That called attention to the case. The papers took it up. Everybody in Waukesha liked Bob Elwell. Most of the well-known people back home signed up to help. And people began to wonder why the Boynes hadn't signed up, too.

"Here," Parvis pulled something from his pocket. "Here's a story about the whole thing from the *Sentinel*. I guess you'd better look it over."

He held the newspaper out to Mary. She unfolded it slowly. She was remembering the evening as how in that same room she had seen the clipping from the *Sentinel* that first told her about Elwell and the Blue Star Mine.

The headline of the paper said: WIDOW OF BOYNE'S VICTIM FORCED TO ASK FOR AID. There were two pictures included in the article. The first was a picture of her husband.

The sight of that familiar face made her close her eyes. She felt it would be impossible for her to read what was said about him.

"I thought if you felt disposed to put your name down for a contribution — " she heard Parvis continue.

She forced herself to open her eyes. The other picture also looked familiar. It showed a youngish man. He was thin. His features were somewhat blurred because of the shadow from his large hat brim. Where had she seen that man before? She stared at it confusedly. Her heart was hammering in her ears.

She cried out, "This is the man — the man who came for my husband!"

She heard Parvis jump to his feet. He looked at her in alarm.

"It's the man! I'd know him anywhere!" she insisted.

Parvis's answer seemed to come from far off.

"Mrs. Boyne, you're not well. Shall I call somebody? Do you want a glass of water?"

"No, no, no!" She clutched the newspaper. "I tell you, it's the man! I *know* him! He spoke to me in the garden!"

Parvis took the paper from her. "It can't be, Mrs. Boyne. It's Robert Elwell."

"Robert Elwell?" She stared blankly out into space. "Then it was Robert Elwell who came for him."

"Came for Boyne? Why, Robert Elwell is dead," he said gently. "He died the day before your husband disappeared. Don't you remember?"

Yes, she remembered; that was the horror of it. Elwell had died the day before her husband disappeared. Yet the picture in the newspaper was the picture of the man who had spoken to her in the garden.

"This was the man who spoke to me," she reported. She looked again at Parvis. "He thinks me mad," she thought, "but I'm not mad!" Suddenly she thought of a way to prove her strange statement.

She sat quietly until she could trust her voice. Then, she looked straight at Parvis. "Answer one question, please?" she said slowly. "When did Robert Elwell try to kill himself?"

"When — when?" Parvis stammered.

"Yes, the date. Please try to remember."

She saw he was growing still more afraid of her. "I have a reason," she insisted.

"Yes, yes. Only I can't remember. About two months before he died, I guess. Perhaps it's in the newspaper."

He picked up the paper. He ran his eyes down the page. "Here it is. Last October, on the —"

"The twentieth, wasn't it?" she said.

He was shocked. "Yes, the twentieth. Then you *did* know?"

"I know now." Her eyes continued to look past him. "Sunday, the twentieth. That was the day he came here first."

Parvis's voice was a whisper. "Came *here* first? You saw him twice?"

"Yes, twice," she sighed. "He came first on the twentieth of October. I remember the date because it was the day we first climbed Meldon Steep."

Parvis just stared at her.

"We saw him from the roof," she went on. "He came down the path toward the house. He was dressed just as he is in the picture. My husband saw him first. Ned was frightened and ran down ahead of me. But there was no one there. He had vanished."

"Elwell had vanished?" Parvis asked carefully.

"Yes," she whispered. "I couldn't think what had happened. I see now. Elwell *tried* to come then. But he wasn't dead enough. He couldn't reach us. He had to wait two months to die. Then he came back again — and Ned went with him."

She nodded at Parvis. She looked like a child who had just worked out a difficult puzzle. Suddenly she pressed her hands to her face.

"I sent him to Ned — I told him where to go! I sent him to this room!" she screamed.

She was numb. Parvis, the books, the furniture all seemed a long way off. Then she heard one clear sound. It was the voice of Alida Stair describing the Lyng ghost. She said what she had said long ago on the June day.

"You won't know till afterward. You won't know till long, long, afterward."

READING COMPREHENSION

Select the best choice to complete each statement. Then write the entire sentence on your paper.

1. According to the story, a person who saw a ghost at Lyng _____.
   a. was sure to die soon after
   b. disappeared immediately
   c. didn't know it until later

2. A gentleman who sounded American called at Lyng _____.
   a. to accept an invitation to dinner
   b. and asked Mrs. Boyne for a job
   c. the day that Mr. Boyne disappeared

3. Parvis said Elwell couldn't have been the man who called on Boyne because _____.
   a. Elwell was dead
   b. he was still in America
   c. Elwell was a busy person

4. Mary believed she first saw Elwell ___.
   a. the day Blue Star Mine closed
   b. leaving the garden with her husband
   c. the day Elwell shot himself

For Discussion

1. Before the Boynes moved to Lyng, they were told, "Oh, there *is* one, of course, but you'll never know it . . . till afterward." Why did this joking comment become important at the end of the story? Explain your answer.

2. Why did Bob Elwell bring (and later drop) a lawsuit against Ned Boyne? Do you think Boyne got what he deserved in the end? Why or why not?

UNDERSTANDING LITERATURE

Plot in a Mystery Story. Plot is the pattern of incidents or events in a story. A mystery writer carefully reveals the details of the plot in a way that will keep the reader in suspense.

One way a mystery writer creates suspense is to control the order in which incidents are revealed. It is only at the end of the story that the reader really understands the entire picture.

As you read a mystery, it's up to you to put the pieces together, a bit at a time, to figure out what is happening.

Here are some incidents from "Afterward" by Edith Wharton. Number your paper from 1 to 6, and write down this list of events in the order that they actually occurred.

Robert Elwell died.

Ned Boyne disappeared.

Alida Stair told the Boynes there was a ghost at Lyng, but they wouldn't know it until later.

Elwell "put Boyne on" to the Blue Star Mine.

Parvis visited Mrs. Boyne.

The newspaper clipping helped Mrs. Boyne connect her husband's disappearance to Elwell.

Writing

Pretend that you are Mrs. Boyne. Write a letter to Alida Stair explaining how and why you now understand what she meant when she told you, "Well — not till afterward — long afterward."

Mind Over Matter

by Ellery Queen

Ellery Queen is the pen name of two clever authors who began writing mystery stories in 1929. The detective in these stories is also called Ellery Queen. The Ellery Queen stories are famous for the careful placement of clues. Mystery fans often try to solve the mystery before Ellery Queen does. You may want to see if you can solve the case of "Mind Over Matter" before the great detective does.

Paula Paris found Inspector Richard Queen of the Homicide Squad looking very sad indeed. Paula had just flown from Hollywood to New York. She had come in to cover the heavyweight fight between Champion Mike Brown and Challenger Jim Coyle.

"You poor dear," said Paula. "And how about you?" she asked Mr. Ellery Queen. "Aren't you disappointed that you can't get a ticket to the fight?"

"I'm a jinx," sighed the great man. "If I went, something terrible would be sure to happen."

"He's afraid somebody will knock somebody off," said the Inspector.

"Well, doesn't somebody always?" demanded his son.

"Don't pay any attention to him, Paula," said the Inspector. "Look, you're a newspaperwoman. Can you get me a ticket?"

"You may as well get me one, too," groaned Mr. Queen.

So Miss Paris telephoned Phil Maguire, the famous sports editor. That evening Maguire picked them up in his car and they all drove uptown to see the fight.

"Seems to me the champ ought to take this boy Coyle," said Inspector Queen. Maguire shrugged.

"Phil's sour on the champ," laughed Paula.

"Nothing personal," said Phil Maguire. "Only, remember Kid Berés? This was in the days when Ollie Stearn was moving Mike Brown into the big time. So this fight was a fix, see. Mike knew it was a fix. The kid knew it was a fix. Everybody knew it was a fix. Kid Berés was supposed to lay down in the sixth round. Well, just the same, Mike went out there and half-killed him. Just for fun. The Kid spent a month in the hospital. When he came out, he was only half a man." And Maguire smiled his crooked smile and said: "I guess I just don't like the champ."

"Well, if this fight is on the level," Mr. Queen said, "Coyle will murder the champion. That big fellow wants the title."

Maguire grinned. "Well, you know the odds. Three to one on the champ."

They drove into the parking lot across the street from the Stadium. Maguire grunted: "Speak of the devil." He had backed the little car into a space beside a huge limousine the color of bright blood.

"Now what's that supposed to mean?" asked Paula Paris.

"This red engine next to us," Maguire chuckled. "It's the champ's. Or rather, it belongs to his manager, Ollie Stearn. Ollie lets Mike use it. Mike can't afford a car."

"I thought the champion was wealthy," said Mr. Queen.

"Not anymore. All of his money is tangled up in lawsuits. He owes a lot of money to a lot of people."

"He ought to have enough money after tonight," said the Inspector. "He's getting over half a million bucks for his end!"

"He won't collect a cent," said the newspaperman. "Mike's creditors will grab it all. Come on."

Mr. Queen helped Miss Paris from the car. Then he tossed his camel's-hair coat into the back seat.

"Don't leave your coat there, Ellery," said Paula. "Someone's sure to steal it."

"Let 'em. It's an old rag. Don't know what I brought it for, anyway, in this heat."

"Come on, come on," said Phil Maguire eagerly.

From the press section at ringside the crowd sounded angry. Two bantamweights were fencing in the ring.

"What's the trouble?" demanded Mr. Queen.

"The card's too light," said Maguire. "Six preliminary matches — three lightweights and three middleweights about to wind it up."

"So what?" said the Inspector. "They're all good fighters."

"The fans came here to see two big guys slaughter each other," explained Maguire. "They don't want to be annoyed by a bunch of gnats — even good gnats. . . . Hi, Happy."

"Who is that?" asked Miss Paris.

"Happy Day," the Inspector answered for Maguire. "Makes his living off bets."

Happy Day sat a few rows off. He had a puffed face the color of cold rice pudding, and his eyes were two raisins. He nodded at Maguire and turned back to watch the ring.

"Normally Happy's face is like raw steak," said Maguire. "He's worried about something. . . . Say, I've got to go to work."

Maguire bent over his typewriter.

The night deepened. The crowd rumbled. Mr. Ellery Queen felt uncomfortable. His six-foot body was as tight as a violin string. It was an all-too-familiar feeling. It meant that there was murder in the air.

The challenger appeared first. He was met by a roar, like the roar of a river at flood tide bursting the dam.

Miss Paris gasped. "Isn't he the one!"

Jim Coyle was a giant six and a half feet tall. He had broad shoulders, long smooth muscles, and bronze skin. He grinned boyishly at the fans.

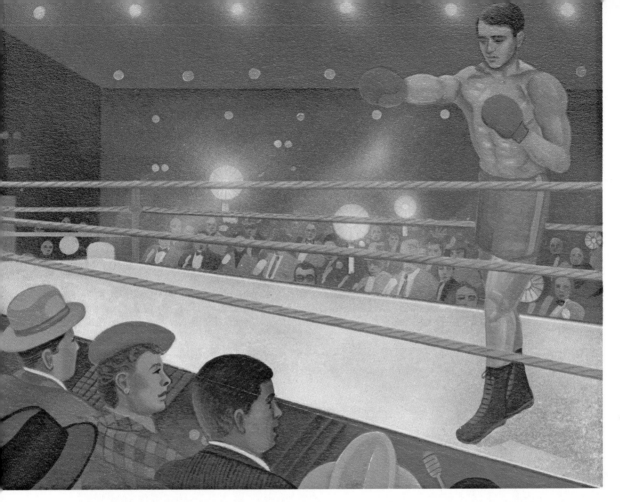

His manager, Barney Hawks, followed him into the ring. Hawks was a big man, but beside his fighter he appeared small.

"Hercules in trunks," breathed Miss Paris. "Did you ever see such a fine physique, Ellery?"

"The question more properly is," said Mr. Queen jealously, "can he keep his fine physique off the floor? That's the question, my girl."

"Plenty fast for a big man," said Maguire. "Maybe not as fast as Mike Brown, but Jim's got height and reach in his favor. He's strong as a bull."

"Here comes the champ!" exclaimed Inspector Queen.

A large ugly man shuffled down the aisle and jumped into the ring. His manager, Ollie Stearn, a little wrinkled man, followed him and stood bouncing up and down on the canvas.

"*Boo-oo-oo!*"

"They're booing the champion!" cried Paula. "Phil, why?"

"Because they hate him because he's a brutal, crooked slob," smiled Maguire. "He has the kick of a mule and the soul of a pretzel. That's why, darlin'."

Brown stood six feet two inches. He looked like a gorilla. He had a broad hairy chest, long arms, and large flat feet. His features were smashed, cruel. He paid no attention to the angry crowd, or to Coyle.

But Mr. Queen, whose genius it was to notice small details, saw Brown's powerful jaws working beneath his cheeks.

And again Mr. Queen's body tightened.

When the gong rang for the start of the third round, the champion's left eye was a purple slit and his lips were bloody. His chest rose and fell in gasps.

Thirty seconds later he was cornered, a beaten animal. Brown crouched, covering up, protecting his chin. Big Jim Coyle streaked forward. The giant's gloves sank into Brown's body. The champion fell forward and held the long bronze arms.

The referee stepped between the two fighters. He spoke sharply to Brown.

"The dirty double-crosser," smiled Phil Maguire.

"Who? What do you mean?" asked Inspector Queen, puzzled.

"Watch the payoff."

The champion raised his battered face. He lashed out feebly at Coyle with his left glove. The giant laughed and stepped in.

The champion went down.

At the count of nine, Mike Brown staggered to his feet. Coyle slipped in, and pumped 12 solid punches into Brown. The champion toppled to the canvas.

This time he remained there.

"But he made it look right," drawled Maguire.

The Stadium howled with glee. Paula looked sickish. A few rows away Happy Day jumped up. He stared wildly about. Then he began shoving through the crowd.

"Happy isn't happy anymore," sang Maguire.

Jim Coyle was half-drowned in a wave of shouting people. He was laughing like a boy. In the champion's corner Ollie Stearn leaned over the unconscious man.

"Yes, sir," said Phil Maguire, rising and stretching, "that was as pretty a dive as I've seen. And I've seen some beauts in my day."

"See here, Maguire," said Mr. Queen angrily. "I have eyes, too. What makes you so sure Brown just tossed his title away?"

"Seems to me," added the Inspector, "Brown took an awful lot of punishment."

"Oh, sure," said Maguire mockingly. "Look, Mike Brown has as sweet a right hand as the game has ever seen. Did you notice him use his right on Coyle tonight — even once?"

"Well," admitted Mr. Queen, "no."

"Of course not. Not a single blow. And he had a dozen openings. But what did Mike do? He kept jabbing away with that silly left of his — it couldn't put Paula away! Sure, he made it look good. But your ex-champ took a dive just the same!"

They were helping Brown from the ring. He looked tired. A small group followed him, laughing. Little Ollie Stearn kept pushing people aside.

"Look," said Maguire. "I've got to see someone. I'll meet you folks in Coyle's dressing room later."

"Oh, I'd love it!" cried Paula. "How do we get in, Phil?"

"What have you got a cop with you for? Show her, Inspector."

Maguire's slight figure slouched off. The great man's scalp prickled suddenly. He frowned and took Paula's arm.

The new champion's dressing room was full of people and noise. The crowd was so dense it overflowed into the adjoining shower room. Young Coyle lay on a training table being rubbed down. He was answering questions, grinning at cameras, flexing his muscles. Barney Hawks was running about, his collar loosened, handing out cigars like a new father.

The Inspector spoke to Barney Hawks, and Coyle's manager introduced them to the champion.

Coyle slipped off the rubbing table. Barney Hawks began shooing men out of the shower room. Finally Coyle grabbed some towels, winked at Paula, and went in, shutting the door. They heard the cheerful hiss of the shower.

Five minutes later Phil Maguire strolled into the dressing room.

"Hi," he shouted. "Where's the champ?"

"Here I am," said Coyle, opening the shower-room door. He rubbed his bare chest with a towel. There was another towel wrapped around his lower body. "Hiya, Philboy. Be dressed in a shake. Say, this doll your Mamie? If she ain't, I'm staking out my claim."

"Come on, come on, champ. We got a date with Fifty-second Street."

"Sure! How about you, Barney? You joining us?"

"Go ahead and play," said his manager. "Me, I got business with the management." He danced into the shower room, and emerged with a hat and a camel's-hair coat over his arm. He kissed his hand affectionately at Coyle, and left.

"You're not going to stay in here while he dresses?" said Mr. Queen to Miss Paris.

"Come on — you can wait for your hero in the hall."

"Yes, sir," said Miss Paris.

Coyle laughed. "Don't worry, fella. I ain't going to do you out of nothing."

Mr. Queen piloted Miss Paris from the room. "Let's meet them at the car," he said in a curt tone.

Miss Paris murmured: "Yes *sir*."

They walked in silence to the end of the hall. Then they turned a corner into an alley which led out of the Stadium and into the street. As they walked down the alley Mr. Queen could see through the shower-room window into the dressing room: Maguire had produced a bottle and he, Coyle, and the Inspector were raising glasses.

Mr. Queen hurried Miss Paris out of the alley and across the street to the parking lot. Cars were slowly driving out. But the big red limousine belonging to Ollie Stearn still stood beside Maguire's roadster.

"Ellery," said Paula softly, "you're such a fool."

"Now, Paula, I don't care to discuss — "

"What do you think I mean? It's your topcoat, silly. Didn't I warn you someone would steal it?"

Mr. Queen glanced into the roadster. His coat was gone. "Oh, that. I was going to throw it away, anyway. Now look, Paula, if you think for one instant, that I could be jealous of some oversized . . . Paula! What's the matter?"

Paula's cheeks were gray in the brilliant arc light. She was pointing a shaky finger at the blood-red limousine.

"In — in there. . . . Isn't that — Mike Brown?"

Mr. Queen glanced quickly into the rear of the limousine. He opened the rear door of Stearn's car.

Mike Brown tumbled out of the car and lay still.

And after a moment the Inspector, Maguire, and Coyle strolled up, chuckling over something.

Maguire stopped. "Say. Who's that?"

Coyle said: "Isn't that Mike Brown?"

The Inspector said: "Out of the way, Jim." He knelt beside Ellery.

And Mr. Queen raised his head. "Yes, it's Mike Brown. Someone's used him for a pin cushion."

Phil Maguire yelped and ran for a telephone. Paula Paris ran after him, remembering her profession.

"Is he . . . is he — " began Jim Coyle, gulping.

"The long count," said the Inspector grimly. "Here, help me turn him over."

They turned him over. He lay staring up into the blinding arc light. He was completely dressed; a gray topcoat was wrapped about his body, still buttoned. He had been stabbed 10 times in the chest, through his topcoat.

"Body's warm," said the Inspector. "This happened just a few minutes ago." He rose from the dust and stared unseeingly at the crowd which had gathered.

"Maybe," began the champion, licking his lips, "maybe — "

"Maybe what, Jim?" asked the Inspector, looking at him.

"Nothing, nothing,"

"Why don't you go home? Don't let this spoil your night, kid."

Coyle set his jaw. "I'll stick around."

The Inspector blew a police whistle.

Police came. Phil Maguire and Paula Paris returned, Ollie Stearn and others appeared from across the street, and the crowd thickened. Mr. Ellery Queen crawled into the back of Stearn's car.

The rear of the red limousine was a mess. Blood stained the cushions and the floor rug, which was wrinkled and scuffed. A large coat button lay on one of the cushions, beside a crumpled camel's-hair coat.

Mr. Queen grabbed the coat. The button had been torn from it. The front of the coat was badly bloodstained. But the stains had a pattern. Mr. Queen laid the coat on the seat, front up. He slipped the buttons through the buttonholes. Then the bloodstains met. When he unbuttoned the coat and separated the two sides of the coat the stains separated, too. On the side where the buttons were the blood traced a straight edge an inch outside the line of buttons.

The Inspector poked his head in. "What's that thing?"

"The murderer's coat."

"Let's see that!"

"It won't tell you anything about its wearer. The label's been ripped out — no identifying marks. Do you see what must have happened in here, Dad? The murder took place in this car. And the murderer wore this coat."

"How do you know that, Ellery?"

349

"Because there's every sign of a struggle. Brown managed to tear off one of the coat buttons of his attacker's coat. In the course of the struggle Brown was stabbed many times. His blood flowed freely. It got all over not only his own coat but the murderer's as well. From the position of the bloodstains the murderer's coat must have been buttoned at the time of the struggle. This means he wore it."

The Inspector nodded. "Left it behind because he didn't want to be seen in a bloody coat."

From behind the Inspector came Paula's shaky voice. "Could that be *your* camel's-hair coat, Ellery?"

"It isn't mine," said Mr. Queen patiently. "Mine has certain marks which don't exist in this one — a cigarette burn at the second buttonhole, a hole in the right pocket."

The Inspector shrugged and went away.

"Then your coat's being stolen has nothing to do with it?" Paula shivered.

Mr. Queen answered: "On the contrary. The theft of my coat has everything to do with it." He turned and stared at the body of Mike Brown.

Ollie Stearn's driver was a hard-looking customer. He twisted his cap and said: "Mike tells me after the fight he won't need me. Tells me he'll pick me up on the Grand Concourse. Said he'd drive himself."

"Yes?"

"I was kind of — curious. I had a hot dog at the stand there and I — watched. I seen Mike come out and climb into the back — "

"Was he alone?" demanded Inspector Queen.

"Yeah. Just got in and sat there. A couple of drunks come along then and I couldn't see good. Only seemed to me somebody else come over and got into the car after Mike."

"Who? Who was it? Did you see?"

The driver shook his head. "I couldn't see good. I don't know. After a while I thought it ain't my business, so I walks away. But when I heard police sirens I come back."

"The one who came after Mike Brown got in," said Mr. Queen with a certain eagerness. "That person was wearing a coat, eh?"

"I guess so. Yeah."

"You didn't witness anything else that happened?" said Mr. Queen.

"Nope."

"Doesn't matter, really," muttered the great man. "Line's clear. Clear as the sun. Must be that — "

"What are you mumbling about?" demanded Miss Paris in his ear.

Mr. Queen stared. "Was I mumbling?" He shook his head.

A man from Headquarters came up with a little fellow with frightened eyes. He babbled he didn't know nothing; nothing, he didn't know nothing. The Inspector said: "Come on, Oetjens. You were heard shooting off your mouth. What's the story?"

"Mike Brown looked me up this morning," muttered Oetjens, "and says to me, he says, 'Hymie,' he says. 'Happy Day takes a lot of your bets,' he says. 'So go lay fifty thousand with Happy on Coyle to win by a KO,' Mike says. 'You lay that fifty thousand for *me*, get it?' he says. And he says, 'If you tell Happy or anyone else that you bet fifty thousand for me on Coyle,' he says, 'I'll rip your heart out.' So I laid fifty thousand dollars on Coyle to win by a KO. Happy took the bet at twelve to five, he wouldn't give no more."

Jim Coyle growled: "I'll break your neck."

"Wait a minute, Jim — "

"He's saying Brown took a dive!" cried the champion. "I licked Brown fair and square. I beat him fair and square!"

"You thought you beat him fair and square," muttered Phil Maguire. "But he took a dive, Jim. Didn't I tell you, Inspector? Laying off that right of his — "

"It's a lie! Where's my manager? Where's Barney?" roared Coyle. "They ain't going to hold up the purse on this fight! I won it fair — I won the title fair!"

"Take it easy, Jim," said the Inspector. "Everybody knows you were in there leveling tonight. Look here, Hymie, did Brown give you the cash to bet for him?"

"He was busted," Oetjens said. "I just laid the bet on my own. The payoff don't come till the next day. So I knew it was okay, because with Mike himself betting on Coyle the fight was in the bag — "

"I'll cripple you, you tinhorn!" yelled young Coyle.

"Take it easy, Jim," soothed Inspector Queen. "So you laid the bet and Happy covered it at twelve to five. And you knew Mike was going to take a dive. Then you would collect a hundred and twenty thousand dollars and give it to Mike, right?"

"Yeah, yeah. But that's all, I swear — "

"When did you see Happy last, Hymie?"

Oetjens looked scared and began to back away. He shook his head stubbornly.

"Now it couldn't be," asked the Inspector softly, "that somehow Happy found out that you'd bet that fifty thousand not for yourself, but for Mike Brown, could it? It couldn't be that Happy found out it was a dive?" The Inspector said sharply to a detective: "Find Happy Day."

"I'm right here," said a voice from the crowd. The fat gambler waded through and said hotly to Inspector Queen: "So, I'm supposed to take the rap, hey?"

"Did you know Mike Brown was set to take a dive?"

"No!"

Phil Maguire laughed.

And little Ollie Stearn, pale as his dead fighter, shouted: "Happy done it, Inspector! He found out, and he waited till after the fight. When he saw Mike laying down he came out here and gave him the business! That's the way it was!"

"You lousy rat," said the gambler. "How do I know you didn't do it yourself? He wasn't taking no dive you couldn't find out about! Maybe you stuck him up!"

"Gentlemen, gentlemen," said the Inspector.

Happy Day and Ollie Stearn eyed each other with hate. The Inspector said to his son: "Not too tough. It's Happy Day, all right, and all I've got to do is find — "

The great man smiled and said: "You're wasting your time."

The Inspector stopped looking happy.

"What am I supposed to be doing, then? You tell me. You know it all."

"Find my coat, and perhaps I'll find your murderer," answered Mr. Queen.

And immediately the great man began nosing about. He acted as if an old and shabby topcoat could possibly be more important than Mike Brown lying there in the gravel.

So it appeared that Mike Brown had had a secret meeting with someone after the fight. He got rid of Ollie Stearn's driver, so the appointment must have been inside the red limousine. And whoever he was, he came, and got in with Mike. There was a struggle, and he stabbed Mike almost a dozen times with something long and sharp. Then he fled, leaving his camel's-hair coat behind. The blood all over its front would have given him away.

That brought up the matter of the weapon. Everybody began looking, including Mr. Queen. The murderer might have dropped it. And, sure enough, a radio-car man found it in the dirt under a parked car. It was a long, evil-looking knife with no marks whatever and no fingerprints except the fingerprints of the radio-car man. But Mr. Queen kept looking even after that discovery. Finally the Inspector asked him: "What are you looking for now?"

"My coat," explained Mr. Queen. "Do you see anyone with my coat?"

But there was hardly a man in the crowd with a coat. It was a warm night.

Finally Mr. Queen said: "I don't know what you good people are going to do, but I'm going back to the Stadium."

"For heaven's sake, what for?" cried Paula.

"To see if I can find my coat," said Mr. Queen patiently.

"I told you you should have taken it with you!"

"Oh, no," said Mr. Queen. "I'm glad I didn't. I'm glad I left it behind in Maguire's car. I'm glad it was stolen."

"But why?"

"Because now," replied Mr. Queen with a mysterious smile, "I have to go looking for it."

And while the police carted Mike Brown's body off, Mr. Queen went back across the dusty parking lot and into the alley which led to the Stadium dressing rooms. And the Inspector, with a baffled look, herded everyone — with special loving care and attention for Mr. Happy Day and Mr. Ollie Stearn — after his son. He didn't know what else to do.

And finally they were back in Jim Coyle's dressing room. There was a noise at the door. Barney Hawks, the new champion's manager, was standing in the doorway in the company of several officials and promoters.

"What ho," said Barney Hawks with a puzzled glance about. "You still here, Champ? What goes on?"

"Plenty goes on," said the champ angrily. "Barney, did you know Brown took a dive tonight?"

"What? What is this?" said Barney Hawks, looking around. "Who says so, the dirty liar? My boy beat Brown fair and square."

"Brown threw the fight?" asked one of

the men with Hawks, a member of the Boxing Commission. "Is there any evidence of that?"

"Never mind that," said the Inspector. "Barney, Mike Brown is dead."

Hawks began to laugh. Then he stopped laughing and sputtered: "What's this? Brown dead? You're joking!"

Jim Coyle waved his huge paw tiredly. "Somebody bumped him off tonight, Barney. In Stearn's car across the street."

"So Mike got his, hey? Well, well. Tough. Loses his title and his life. Who done it boys?" asked Hawks.

"Maybe you didn't know my boy was dead!" shrilled Ollie Stearn. "Yeah, you put on a swell act, Barney! Maybe you fixed it with Mike so he'd take a dive so your boy could win the title! Maybe — "

"There's been another crime committed here tonight," said a mild voice. They all looked wonderingly around to find Mr.

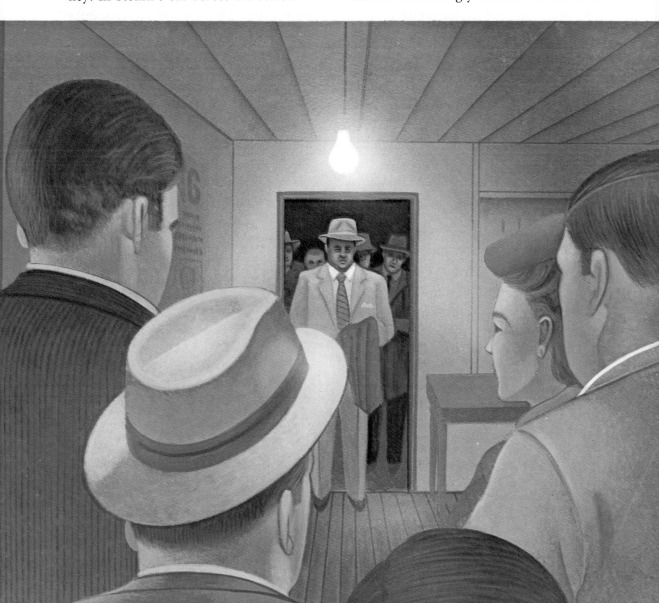

Ellery Queen moving toward Mr. Hawks.

"Hey?" said Coyle's manager, staring stupidly at him.

"My coat was stolen."

"Hey?" Hawks kept staring.

"And now I've found it again."

"Hey?"

"On your arm." And Mr. Queen gently removed from Mr. Hawks's arm a shabby camel's-hair topcoat. Queen folded it, and examined it. "Yes. My very own."

Barney Hawks turned green in the silence.

Something sharpened in Mr. Queen's silver eyes. He bent over the camel's-hair coat again. He spread out the sleeves and examined the armhole seams. They had burst. As had the seam at the back of the coat. He looked up at Mr. Hawks.

"The least you might have done," he said, "is to have returned my coat in the same condition in which I left it."

"Your coat?" said Barney Hawks. Then he shouted: "What is this? That's my coat! My camel's-hair coat!"

"No," Mr. Queen said, "I can prove this to be mine. You see, it has a cigarette burn at the second buttonhole, and a hole in the right-hand pocket."

"But — I found it where I left it! It was here all the time! I took it out of here after the fight and went up to the office to talk to these gentlemen. I've been — " The manager stopped. His face faded from green to white. "Then where's my coat?" he asked slowly.

"Will you try this on?" asked Mr. Queen. He took from a detective the bloodstained coat they had found in Ollie Stearn's car.

Mr. Queen held the coat up before Hawks. Hawks said thickly: "All right. It's my coat. I guess it's my coat, if you say so. So what?"

"So," replied Mr. Queen, "someone knew Mike Brown was broke, that not even his share of the purse tonight would pay his debts. Someone got Mike Brown to throw the fight tonight. He offered to pay Brown a lot of money, I suppose, for taking the dive. That money no one would know about. That money would not have to be turned over to Mike Brown's creditors. That money would be Mike Brown's own. So Mike Brown said yes. He realized that he could make more money, too, by placing a large bet with Happy Day through Mr. Oetjens.

"And probably Brown and his tempter planned to meet in Stearn's car right after the fight for the payoff. So Brown sent the driver away. He sat in the car, and the tempter came to keep the appointment. He was not armed with the payoff money but with a sharp knife. And by using the knife he saved himself a tidy sum — the sum he'd promised Brown. He also made sure Mike Brown would never be able to tell the wicked story to the wicked world."

Barney Hawks licked his dry lips. "Don't look at me, mister. You got nothing on Barney Hawks. I don't know nothing about this."

And Mr. Queen said, paying no attention whatever to Mr. Hawks: "A pretty problem, friends. We found a coat left in Stearn's car and my coat, in the next car, stolen. Coincidence? Hardly. The murderer certainly took my coat to replace the coat he was forced to leave behind."

Mr. Queen paused and glanced at Miss Paris, who was staring at him with awe. Mind over matter, thought Mr. Queen, remembering with special satisfaction how Miss Paris had stared at Jim Coyle's muscles. Yes, sir, mind over matter.

"Well?" said Inspector Queen. "Suppose the murderer did take your coat? What of it?"

"But that's exactly the point," murmured Mr. Queen. "He took my worthless coat. Why?"

"Well, I — I suppose to wear it," said Inspector Queen.

"Very good," applauded Mr. Queen. "But why should he want to wear it?"

The Inspector looked angry. "See here, Ellery — " he began.

"No, Dad, no," said Mr. Queen gently. "There's a point. *The* point. You might say he had to wear it because he'd got blood on his suit *under* the coat and needed a coat to hide the bloodstained suit."

"Well, sure," said Phil Maguire eagerly. "That's it."

"No," said Mr. Queen, shaking his head sadly, "that's not it. He couldn't possibly have got blood on his suit. The coat shows that at the time he attacked Brown he was wearing it buttoned. If the topcoat was buttoned, his suit didn't catch any of Brown's blood."

"He certainly didn't need a coat because of the weather," muttered Inspector Queen.

"True. It's been warm all evening. He'd left his own coat behind, its labels and other identifying marks taken out, unworried about its being found. Such being the case, you would say he'd simply make his escape in the clothes he was wearing *beneath* the coat. But he didn't." Mr. Queen coughed gently. "So surely it's obvious that if he stole my coat for his escape, he *needed* my coat for his escape? That if he escaped without my coat, he would be *noticed*?"

"I don't get it," said the Inspector. "He'd be noticed? But if he was wearing ordinary clothing — "

"Then obviously he wouldn't need my coat," nodded Mr. Queen. "He could have made his escape in those clothes. But since he didn't, it can only mean that he *wasn't* wearing street clothes, you see. That's why the murderer needed a coat not only to come to the scene of the crime, but to escape from it as well."

There was another silence, and finally Paula said: "Wasn't wearing clothes? Why, that's like something out of Poe!"

"No," smiled Mr. Queen, "merely something out of the Stadium. You see, we had a group of gentlemen in the area tonight who wore no — or nearly no — clothing. In a word, the fighters. The instant I discovered that Brown had been stabbed, and that my coat had been stolen by a murderer who left his own behind, I knew that the murderer could have been *only one of thirteen men* . . . the thirteen living prizefighters left after Brown was killed. For you'll recall there were fourteen fighters in the Stadium tonight — twelve distributed among six preliminary matches and two in the main event.

"Which of the thirteen fighters had killed Brown? That was my problem from the beginning. And so I had to find my coat, because it was the only link between the murderer and his crime. And now I've

found my coat, and now I know which of the thirteen murdered Brown."

Barney Hawks was speechless. His mouth flapped open.

"I'm a tall, fairly broad man. In fact, I'm six feet tall," said the great man. "And yet, the murderer burst my coat at the armholes and back! That meant he was a much bigger man than I.

"Which of the thirteen fighters on the card tonight were bigger than I? Ah, but it's been a very light card — bantam-weights, welterweights, lightweights, mid-dleweights! Therefore none of the twelve preliminary fighters could have murdered Brown. Therefore, only one fighter was left — a man who had every motive — to get Mike Brown to throw the fight to-night!"

And this time the silence was full with meaning. It was broken by Jim Coyle's lazy laugh. "If you mean me, you must be off your nut. Why, I was in that shower room taking a shower at the time Mike was bumped off!"

"Yes, I mean you, Mr. Jim Coyle," said Mr. Queen clearly. "The shower room was the cleverest part of your plan. You went into the shower room in full view of all of us, with towels, shut the door, turned on the shower, slipped on a pair of trou-sers, then you grabbed Barney Hawks's camel's-hair coat and hat which were hanging on a peg in there. Then you ducked out of the shower-room window into the alley. From there it was a matter of seconds to the street and the parking lot across the street. Of course, when you stained Hawks's coat, you couldn't risk coming back in it. And you had to have a coat — a buttoned coat — to cover your bare chest for the return trip. So you stole mine, for which I'm very grateful, because otherwise — . Grab him, will you? My right isn't very good," said Mr. Queen, employing a dainty and beautiful bit of footwork to escape Coyle's sudden mur-derous lunge in his direction.

And while Coyle went down under a pile of arms and legs, Mr. Queen mur-mured apologetically to Miss Paris: "After all, darling, he *is* the heavyweight cham-pion of the world."

READING COMPREHENSION

Select the best choice to complete each statement. Then write the entire sentence on your paper.

1. When Ellery Queen arrived at the sta-dium, the crowd was restless because _____.
   a. they knew the favorite would lose
   b. the preliminary fights bored them
   c. it was too late to change seats

2. When Maguire said Brown "took a dive," he meant that _____.
   a. the fighter lost on purpose
   b. the ring was set up near a pool
   c. he couldn't match the younger man

3. By losing, Brown expected to gain _____.
   a. sympathy from the large crowd
   b. part of the purse and a chance to retire
   c. a large payoff and to win bet money

4. Ellery Queen insisted on finding his coat because _____.
   a. he knew it would lead to the killer
   b. it had sentimental value
   c. the evening had turned quite cool

5. Queen realized Coyle was the killer because _____.
   a. he knew the man was greedy
   b. the ripped coat led to a big man
   c. Coyle was angry when Brown lost

For Discussion

1. Before the fight began, who did you think would win? Why?

2. When did the camel's-hair coat first appear as an important detail in the plot? When was the next time the coat became of interest? How did the coat eventually lead Ellery Queen to the solution of the mystery?

3. Why would Mike Brown have collected nothing personally even if he had won the fight and not been murdered? How did this fact influence the outcome of the fight and what happened afterward? Explain your answer.

UNDERSTANDING LITERATURE

Plot Structure. The plot structure of a mystery story is carefully organized to build suspense and involve the reader in solving the mystery.

A good mystery often includes a murder because there are so many possible motives for murder that it gives the author a chance to weave a complicated and very interesting plot. With many possible motives for a crime the reader can be kept guessing who did it and why.

Part of the fun of reading a good murder mystery is playing detective as you read. To be a good detective, you have to notice how details relate to one other. Bit by bit you can put facts together to solve the puzzle.

Here are some details from "Mind Over Matter." Some of them go together in a very special way. On your paper, match each cause below with the effect it had in the story.

Causes

1. Coyle needed a coat to cover himself.

2. The murderer was a very large man.

3. Brown bet against himself in the fight.

4. Brown hurt Kid Berés in a fixed fight.

Effects

a. Phil Maguire disliked Mike Brown.

b. Ellery Queen's coat was stolen from the car.

c. Brown "took a dive" and lost the fight.

d. Queen's coat split at the seams.

Now go back and check (√) the details that helped Ellery Queen solve the case.

Writing

Pretend that you are Jim Coyle. Write your confession, explaining how and why you planned to kill Mike Brown.

The Calico Dog

by Mignon G. Eberhardt

Mignon G. Eberhardt (1899—) began writing detective stories in the 1920's, and she is still writing them today. In the 1930's she created a series of stories about Susan Dare, a young mystery writer who is often called upon to provide solutions to real mysteries. In "The Calico Dog," Susan finds that she must deal with several mysteries at once.

Part One

It was nothing short of an invitation to murder.

"You don't mean to say," Susan Dare said in a small voice, "that both of them are living here?"

Idabelle Lasher — Mrs. Jeremiah Lasher, that is, widow of the patent-medicine emperor who died last year (resisting, it is said, his own medicine to the end with great determination) — Idabelle Lasher turned large pale blue eyes upon Susan and sighed and said:

"Why, yes. There was nothing else to do. I can't turn my own boy out into the world."

Susan took a long breath. "Always assuming," she said, "that one of them is your own boy."

"Oh, there's no doubt about that, Miss Dare," said Idabelle Lasher simply.

"Let me see," Susan said, "if I have this straight. Your son Derek was lost twenty years ago. Recently he has returned. Rather, two of him have returned."

Mrs. Lasher was leaning forward, tears in her large pale eyes. "Miss Dare," she said, "one of them must be my son. I need him so much. And besides," she added, "there's all that money. Thirty million."

"Thirty —" began Susan and stopped. It was simply not understandable. Half a million, yes; even a million. But thirty million!

"But if you can't tell yourself which of the two young men is your son, how can I? And with so much money involved. . . . I just don't see how I can help you," Susan said firmly.

"You must help me," said Mrs. Lasher. "Christabel Frame told me about you. She said you wrote mystery stories. She said you were the only woman who could help me, and that you were right here in Chicago."

"Let me have the whole story again, won't you? Try to tell it quite definitely, just as things occurred."

Mrs. Lasher put the handkerchief away and sat up briskly.

She began, "It was like this. . . ." Two months ago a young man called Dixon March had called on her. He had not gone to her lawyer. He had come to see her. And Dixon March had told her a very straight story.

"You must remember something of the story — oh, but of course, you couldn't. You're far too young. And then, too, we weren't as rich as we are now, when little Derek disappeared. He was four at the time. And his nursemaid disappeared at the same time, and I always thought, Miss Dare, that it was the nursemaid who stole him."

"Ransom?" asked Susan.

"No. That was the queer part of it. There never was any attempt to demand ransom. I always felt the nursemaid simply wanted him for herself."

Susan brought her gently back to the present. "Just what is Dixon's story?"

"He said that he was taken in at an orphanage at the age of six. That he vaguely remembers a woman, dark, with a mole on her chin, which is an exact description of the nursemaid. Of course, we've had the orphanage records examined, but there's nothing conclusive and no way to identify the woman; she died (under the name of Sarah Gant, which wasn't the nursemaid's name) and she was very poor. A social worker simply arranged for the child's entrance into the orphanage."

"What makes him think he is your son, then?"

"Well, it's this way. He grew up and went out on his own. Then he got to looking into his — his origins, he said. He found an account of the description of our Derek, the dates, the fact that he could discover nothing of the woman, Sarah Gant, previous to her life in Ottawa —"

"Ottawa?"

"Yes. That was where he came from. The other one, Duane, came from New Orleans. As Dixon remembered Sarah Gant, she looked very much like the newspaper pictures of the nursemaid. This suggested the possibility that he was our lost child."

"So, on this evidence he comes to you, claiming to be your son. A year after your husband died."

"Yes, and — well —" Mrs. Lasher flushed pinkly. "There are some things he can remember."

"Things — such as what?"

"The — the green curtains in the nursery. And a — a calico dog. And — and a few other things. The lawyers say that isn't enough. But I think it's very important that he remembers the calico dog."

"You've had lawyers looking into his claims."

"Oh, dear, yes," said Mrs. Lasher. "Exhaustively."

"But can't they trace Sarah Gant?"

"Nothing definite, Miss Dare."

"His physical appearance?" suggested Susan.

"Miss Dare," said Mrs. Lasher. "My Derek was blond with gray eyes. He had no marks of any kind. Any fair young man with gray eyes might be my son. And both these men — either of these men might be Derek. I've looked long and wearily, searching every feature and every expression for a likeness to my boy. It is equally there — and not there. I feel sure that one of them is my son."

"But you don't know which one?" said Susan softly.

"I don't know which one," said Idabelle Lasher. "But one of them is Derek."

She turned suddenly and walked heavily to a window. Twenty-one stories below, traffic flowed unceasingly along Lake Shore Drive.

"One of them must be an impostor," Idabelle Lasher was saying presently in a choked voice.

"Is Dixon certain he is your son?"

"He says only that he thinks so. But since Duane has come, too, he is more — more positive — "

"Duane, of course." The rivalry of the two young men must be rather terrible. Susan had a fleeting glimpse again of what it might mean. One of them was certainly an impostor, both impostors, perhaps, struggling over Idabelle Lasher's affections and her fortune.

"What is Duane's story?" asked Susan.

"That's what makes it so queer, Miss Dare. Duane's story — is — well, it is exactly the same."

"You don't mean exactly the same!" Susan cried.

"Exactly," the woman turned and faced her. "Exactly the same, Miss Dare, except for the names and places. The name of the woman in Duane's case was Mary Miller, the orphanage was in New Or-

leans, he was going to art school here in Chicago when — when, he says, just as Dixon said — he began to be more and more interested in his parentage and began investigating. And he, too, remembers things, little things from his babyhood and our house that only my dear son, Derek, could remember."

"Wait, Mrs. Lasher," said Susan, grasping at something firm. "Any servant, any of your friends, would know these details also."

Mrs. Lasher's pale, big eyes became more prominent.

"You mean, of course, a conspiracy. The lawyers have talked of nothing else. But, Miss Dare, they have checked everything possible to check both statements. I know what has happened to the few servants we had — all, that is, except the nursemaid. And we don't have many close friends, Miss Dare. Not since there was so much money. And none of them — none of them would do this."

"But both young men can't be Derek," said Susan desperately. She clutched at common sense again and said: "How soon after your husband's death did Dixon arrive?"

"Ten months."

"And Duane?"

"Three months after Dixon."

"And Duane and Dixon are both living here with you now?"

"Yes." She nodded toward the end of the long room. "The two young men are in the library now."

"Together?" said Susan irresistibly.

"Yes, of course," said Mrs. Lasher. "Playing cribbage."

"I suppose you and your lawyers have tried every possible test?"

"Everything, Miss Dare."

"You have no fingerprints of the baby?"

"No. That was before fingerprints were so important. We tried blood tests, of course. But they are of the same type."

"Resemblances to you or your husband?"

"You'll see for yourself at dinner tonight, Miss Dare. You will help me?"

Susan sighed. "Yes," she said.

The bedroom to which Mrs. Lasher herself took Susan was magnificent. Soon after Susan finished changing for dinner, Mrs. Lasher knocked.

"It's Derek's baby things," she said in a whisper and with a glance over her shoulder. "Let's move a little farther from the door."

They sat down on a cushioned sofa, and between them, Idabelle Lasher spread out certain small objects.

"His little suit — he looked so sweet in yellow. Some pictures. A pink plush teddy bear. His little nursery-school reports — he was already in nursery school, Miss Dare. And the calico dog, Miss Dare."

She stopped there, and Susan looked at the faded calico dog held so tenderly in those diamond-covered hands. She suddenly felt a wave of cold anger toward the man who was not Derek and who must know that he was not Derek. She took the pictures eagerly.

But they were only pictures: They showed a round baby face without features that were at all distinctive. There were two or three pictures of a little boy playing, squinting against the sun.

"Has anyone else seen these things?"

"You mean either of the two boys — either Dixon or Duane? No, Miss Dare."

"Has anyone at all seen them? Servants? Friends?"

Idabelle's blue eyes became vague and clouded.

"Long ago, perhaps," she said. "Oh many, many years ago. But they've been in the safe in my bedroom for years."

"How long have they been in the safe?"

"Since we bought this apartment. Ten — no, twelve years."

"And no one — there's never been anything like an attempted robbery of that safe?"

"Never. No, Miss Dare. There's no possible way for either Dixon or Duane to know of the contents of this box except from memory."

"And Dixon remembers the calico dog?"

"Yes." The blue eyes wavered again, and Mrs. Lasher rose and walked toward the door. "And Duane remembers the teddy bear and described it to me," she said definitely and went away.

Left to herself, Susan studied the pictures again. The nursery-school reports were written in beautiful handwriting. Music: A good ear. Memory: Very good. Adaptability: Very good. Sociability: Inclined to shyness. Rhythm: Poor (advise skipping games at home). Conduct: (This varied. Once there had been a disturbance during naptime, and Derek was at the bottom of it.) Susan smiled and began to like baby Derek. And it was just then that she found the first clue to an identifying trait. And that was after the heading Games. One report said: Quick. Another said: Mentally quick but does not use muscles well. And a third said: Tendency to use left hand which we are trying to correct.

Tendency to use left hand. An inborn tendency, cropping out again and again all through life. In those days, of course, it had been rigidly corrected — thereby causing all manner of ills, according to more recent trends of education. But was it ever altogether conquered?

Presently Susan put the things in the box again and went to Mrs. Lasher's room. She watched Mrs. Lasher open a panel which disclosed a steel safe set in the wall behind it. Mrs. Lasher placed the box securely in the safe.

"Did you find anything that will help?" asked Mrs. Lasher, closing the panel.

"I don't know," said Susan. "I'm afraid there's nothing very certain. Do Dixon and Duane know why I am here?"

"No," said Mrs. Lasher. "I told them you were a dear friend of Christabel's. And that you were very much interested in their — my — our situation. The boys are as anxious as I am to discover the truth of it."

Again, thought Susan, feeling baffled, as the true Derek would be. She followed

Mrs. Lasher toward the drawing room, prepared to dislike both men.

But the man in the doorway of the library was too old to be either Dixon or Duane.

"Major Briggs," said Mrs. Lasher. "This is Susan." She turned to Susan. "Major Tom Briggs is our closest friend. He was like a brother to my husband, and has been to me."

"Never a brother," said Major Briggs with an air of gallantry. "Say, rather, an admirer. So this is Christabel's little friend." He bowed and took Susan's hand. "How happy we are to have you with us, my dear," he said. "I suppose Idabelle has told you of our — our problem."

He was about Susan's height; white-haired, rather puffy under the eyes, and a bit too pink, with hands that were inclined to shake. He adjusted his gold-rimmed eyeglasses, then let them drop the length of their black ribbon and said:

"What do you think of it, my dear?"

"I don't know," said Susan. "What do you think?"

"Well, my dear, it's a bit difficult, you know. When Idabelle herself doesn't know. When trained and experienced investigators have failed to discover — ah — the identity of the lost son, how can we know?" He then said blandly: "But it's Duane."

"What — " said Susan.

"I said, it's Duane. He is her son. Anybody could see it with half an eye. Spittin' image of his dad. Here they come now."

They were alike and yet not alike at all. Both were rather tall and slender. Both had medium brown hair. Both had gray-ish-blue eyes. Neither was particularly handsome. Neither was exactly unhandsome. Their features were not at all alike. Yet their description on a passport would not have varied by a single word.

With the salad, Major Briggs roused to point out a portrait that hung on the opposite wall.

"Jeremiah Lasher," he said, waving a pink hand in that direction. He glanced at Susan and added, "Do you see any resemblance, Miss Dare? I mean between my old friend and one of these lads here?"

One of the lads — it was Dixon — wriggled uncomfortably, but Duane smiled.

"We are not at all embarrassed, Miss Dare," Duane said pleasantly. "We are both quite accustomed to this sort of thing." He laughed lightly, Idabelle smiled, and Dixon said:

"Does Miss Dare know about this?"

"Oh, yes," said Idabelle, turning as quickly to him as she had turned to Duane. "There's no secret about it."

"No," said Dixon somewhat crisply. "There's no secret about it."

There was, however, no further mention of the problem during the rest of the evening. Indeed, it was a very calm and slightly dull evening except for the affair of Major Briggs and the window.

That happened just after dinner. Susan and Mrs. Lasher were sitting over coffee in the drawing room. The three men were presumably in the dining room.

It had been altogether quiet in the drawing room. Then there was a shout from the dining room.

It all happened in an instant. Susan and Mrs. Lasher hadn't time to move before Duane appeared in the doorway. He was laughing but looked pale.

"It's all right," he said. "Nothing's wrong." He turned to look down the hall at someone approaching and added: "Here he is, safe and sound."

He stood aside, and Major Briggs appeared in the doorway. He looked so shocked and purple that both women moved hurriedly forward. Idabelle Lasher said, "Here — on the sofa. Ring for help, Duane. Lie down here, Major."

"Oh, no — no," said Major Briggs. "No, I'm quite all right."

Duane, however, supported him to the sofa, and Dixon appeared in the doorway.

"What happened?" he said.

Major Briggs waved his hands feebly. Duane said: "The Major nearly went out the window."

"O-h-h-h — " It was Idabelle in a thin, long scream.

"Oh, it's all right," said Major Briggs shakenly. "I caught hold of the curtain. By God, I'm glad you had heavy curtain rods at that window, Idabelle."

She was fussing around him. Her hands were shaking, and her face was pale under its makeup.

"But how could you — " she was saying, "what on earth — how could it have happened — "

"It's the draft," said the Major. "The confounded draft on my neck. I got up to close the window and — I nearly went out!"

"But how could you — " Idabelle began again.

"I don't know how it happened," said the Major. "Just all at once — " A puzzled look came slowly over his face. "Queer," said Major Briggs suddenly, "I suppose it was the draft. But it was exactly as if — "

He stopped and Idabelle cried: "As if what?"

"As if someone had pushed me," said the Major. Perhaps it was fortunate that the butler arrived just then. He helped the Major to stretch out full length on the sofa and sip some water.

And somehow in the conversation it emerged that neither Dixon nor Duane had been in the dining room when the thing had happened.

"Duane had gone to the library to get a book," said Dixon. "And I had gone to my room to get the evening paper. So the Major was alone when it happened. I knew nothing of it until I heard all the noise in here."

"I," said Duane, watching Dixon, "heard the Major's shout from the library and hurried across."

That night, late, after Major Briggs had gone home, Susan still kept thinking of the window and Major Briggs. During the night, she woke struggling with a silk-covered quilt, thinking that she herself was being thrust out the window.

It was only a nightmare, of course, but it led her to the plan she proposed to Mrs. Lasher that very morning.

It was true, of course, that the thing may have been exactly what it appeared to be. But if it was not an accident, there were only two possibilities.

"Do you mean," cried Mrs. Lasher

when Susan had finished her brief suggestion, "that I'm to say openly that Duane is my son! But I'm not sure. It may be Dixon."

"I know," said Susan. "And I may be wrong. But I think it might help if you will announce — to, oh, only to Major Briggs and the two men — that you are convinced that it is Duane and are taking steps of legal recognition of the fact."

"Why? What do you think will happen? How will it help things to do that?"

"I'm not at all sure it will help," said Susan wearily. "But it's the only thing I see to do. And I think that you may as well do it right away."

"Today?" said Mrs. Lasher.

"At lunch," said Susan firmly. "Telephone to invite Major Briggs now."

"Oh, very well," said Idabelle Lasher. "After all, it will please Tom Briggs. He has been urging me to make a decision. He seems certain that it is Duane."

But Susan, present and watching closely, could detect nothing except that Idabelle Lasher performed her task well. Susan was sure that the men were convinced. There was, to be sure, a shade of triumph in Duane. He was kind to Dixon — as, indeed, he could well afford to be. Dixon was silent and rather pale. He looked as if he had not expected the decision and was a bit stunned by it. Major Briggs was surprised at first, and then openly joyful. He toasted all of them.

The rest of the day passed quietly and not, from Susan's point of view, at all valuably. Susan tried to prove something about the possible left-handedness of the real Derek. Badminton and several games of billiards resulted only in displaying a consistent right-handedness on the part of both men.

Dressing again for dinner, Susan looked at herself in the great mirror.

She had never in her life felt so helpless. The course of action she had laid out for Idabelle Lasher had certainly, thus far, proved nothing. It was quite possible that she was mistaken and that nothing at all would come of it. And if not, what then?

The maid came in to help Susan dress.

"You'll be going to the party tonight, ma'am?" said the maid.

"Party?"

"Oh, yes, ma'am. Didn't you know? It's the Charity Ball. At the Dycke Hotel. In the Chandelier Ballroom. A grand, big party, ma'am. Madame is wearing her pearls."

"Is the entire family going?"

"Oh, yes, ma'am. And Major Briggs. There you are, ma'am — and I do say you look beautiful. There's orchids, ma'am, from Mr. Duane. And gardenias from Mr. Dixon. I believe," said the maid thoughtfully, "that I could put them all together. That's what I'm doing for Madame."

It made a huge corsage, thought Susan, but a lovely one. So, too, was the long town car which waited for them promptly at 10:00 when they emerged from the apartment house. Susan leaned back in her seat. She was always afterward to remember that short ride through crowded, lighted streets to the Dycke Hotel.

No one spoke. Perhaps only Susan was aware of the feelings that were bottled up together in that long, gliding car. She was aware of it quite suddenly and tinglingly.

Nothing had happened. Nothing, all through that long dinner from which they had just come, had been said that was at all helpful.

Yet all at once Susan was aware of a queer kind of excitement.

She looked at Duane and Dixon, riding along beside each other. Dixon sat stiff and straight. He had taken it rather well, she thought. Did he guess Idabelle's decision was not the true one? Or was he still stunned by it?

Or was there something in back of that silence? Had she underestimated the force and possible violence of Dixon's reaction? Susan frowned: It was dangerous enough without that.

They arrived at the hotel. Their sudden emergence from the silence of the car into brilliant lights and crowds and music had a magic effect. Even Dixon shook off his air of brooding as they finally strolled into the Chandelier Room. Duane and Mrs. Lasher danced smoothly into the revolving colors. Dixon asked Susan to dance. They left the Major smiling his approval.

The momentary gaiety with which Dixon had asked Susan to dance faded at once. He danced carefully but without much spirit, and he said nothing.

"Oh, there's Idabelle!" Susan said.

At once Dixon lost step. Susan recovered herself and her small silver sandals rather deftly. Idabelle, pink and jewel-laden, danced past them in Duane's arms. She smiled at Dixon anxiously. She looked, above her pearls, rather worried.

Dixon's eyebrows were a straight dark line, and he was white around the mouth.

"I'm sorry, Dixon," said Susan. She tried to catch step with him, and added: "Please don't mind my speaking about it. We are all thinking of it. I do think you behave very well."

He looked straight over her head. He danced several somewhat clumsy steps, and said suddenly:

"It was so — unexpected. And you see, I was so sure of it."

"Why were you so sure?" asked Susan.

He hesitated, then burst out again: "Because of the dog. The calico dog, you know. And the green curtains. If I had known there was so much money involved, I don't think I'd have come to — Idabelle. But then, when I did know, and this other fellow turned up, why, of course, I felt like sticking it out!"

He paused, and Susan felt his arm tighten around her waist. She looked up, and his face was suddenly chalk white and his eyes blazing.

"Duane!" he said hoarsely. "I hate him. I could kill him with my own hands."

The next dance was a tango, and Susan danced it with Duane. His eyes were shining and his face was flushed with excitement.

He was a born dancer, and Susan relaxed in the perfect ease of his steps. He complimented her gracefully and talked all the time. For a few moments Susan merely enjoyed the fast swirl of the dance. Then Idabelle and Dixon went past. Susan saw again the expression of Dixon's set white face as he looked at Duane, and Idabelle's pink face and pink neck.

The rest of what was probably a perfect dance was lost on Susan. She was busy about certain concerns of her own which involved some adjusting of the flowers on her shoulder. And the moment the dance was over she slipped away.

Her gardenias sent up a warm fragrance as Susan huddled into a telephone booth. She made sure the flowers were secure and unrevealing upon her shoulder. She steadied her breath and dialed a number she knew very well. It was getting to be a habit — calling Jim Byrne, her newspaper friend. But she needed him. Needed him at once.

"Jim — Jim," she said. "It's Susan. Listen. Get into a white tie and come as fast as you can to the Dycke Hotel. The Chandelier Room."

"What's wrong?"

"Well," said Susan in a small voice, "I've set something going that I'm afraid is going to be more than I meant — Hurry, Jim." She caught her breath. "I — I'm afraid."

"I'll be right there. Watch for me at the door," he said. The telephone clicked, and Susan leaned rather weakly against the wall of the telephone booth.

Part Two

Susan went back to the Chandelier Room. Idabelle Lasher, worried-looking, Major Briggs, and the two younger men made a little group standing together talking. She breathed a little sigh of relief. So long as they remained together, surrounded by hundreds of witnesses, it was all right. People didn't murder in cold blood when other people were looking on.

Then Idabelle suggested the fortune-teller.

"She's very good, they say," said Idabelle. "She's got a booth in one of the rooms."

"By all means, my dear," said Major Briggs at once. "This way?" She put her hand on his arm and, with Duane at her other side, moved away. Dixon and Susan followed. Susan cast a worried look toward the entrance. But Jim couldn't possibly get there in less than 30 minutes, and by that time they would have returned.

Dixon said: "Was it the Major that convinced Idabelle that Duane is her son?"

Susan hesitated.

"I don't know," she said cautiously, "how strong the Major's influence has been."

Her caution was not successful. As they left the ballroom and turned down a corridor, he whirled toward her.

"This thing isn't over yet," he said with the sudden savagery that had blazed out in him while they were dancing.

"Would you believe it? The fortune-teller charges twenty dollars a throw!" said Major Briggs as he approached.

The fortune-teller's room was small: a dining room, probably, for small parties. Across the end of it a kind of tent had been arranged with many gaily striped curtains.

Possibly due to her fees, the fortune-teller did not appear to be very popular. There were no others waiting, and no one came to the door except a bellboy with a tray in his hand who looked them over searchingly. He murmured something and wandered away. Duane sat calmly on the small of his back. The Major seemed a bit nervous and moved restlessly about. Dixon stood just behind Susan. Odd that she could feel his hatred for the man resting there in the armchair almost as if it were a living thing. Susan's sense of danger was growing sharper. But surely it was safe — so long as they were together.

The draperies of the tent moved and opened. Idabelle stood there, smiling and beckoning to Susan.

"Come inside, my dear," she said. "She wants you, too."

Susan hesitated. But, after all, so long as the three men were together, nothing could happen. Dixon gave her a sharp look, and Susan moved across the room. She felt a slight added worry when she discovered that in an effort to add mystery, the curtains had been arranged so that one walked through a maze to reach the fortune-teller.

Susan calmed herself as she sat down on some cushions beside Idabelle. The fortune-teller, in Egyptian costume, with

French accent, began to talk. Beyond the curtains and the sound of her voice Susan could hear little. Once she thought there were voices.

But the thing, when it happened, gave no warning.

There was only, suddenly, a great dull shock of sound. It brought Susan to her feet.

"What was that?" whispered Idabelle in a choked way.

And the fortune-teller cried: "It's a gunshot — out there!"

Susan stumbled and groped through the folds of draperies, trying to find the way through the maze of curtains and out of the tent. Then all at once they were outside the tent. They stared at the figure on the floor. There were people pouring in the door from the hall. Confusion was everywhere.

It was Major Briggs. He'd been shot and was dead, and there was no gun anywhere.

Susan felt ill and faint, and after one long look, she backed away to the window. Idabelle was weeping; her face blotched. Dixon was beside her. Then suddenly someone from the hotel had closed the door into the corridor. And a bellboy's voice, the one who'd wandered into the room, rose shrilly.

"Nobody at all," he was saying. "Nobody came out of the room. I was at the end of the corridor when I heard the shot and this is the only room on this side that's unlocked and in use tonight. So I ran down here, and I can swear that nobody came out of the room after the shot was fired."

"Was anybody here when you came in? What did you see?" It was the manager, worried, but carefully keeping the door behind him closed against further intrusion.

"Just this man on the floor. He was dead already!"

"Nobody. Nobody then. But I'd hardly got to him before there were people running into the room. And these three women came out of this tent."

The manager looked at Idabelle — at Susan.

"He was with you?" he asked Idabelle.

"Oh, yes, yes," sobbed Idabelle. "It's Major Briggs."

The manager started to speak, stopped, and began again:

"I've sent for the police. You folks that were in his party — how many of you are there?"

"Just Miss Dare and me," sobbed Idabelle. "And" — she singled out Dixon and Duane — "these two men."

"All right. You folks stay right here, will you? And you, too," — indicating the fortune-teller — "and the bellboy. The rest of you will go to a room across the hall. Sorry, but I'll have to hold you till the police get here."

The scattered groups that had pressed into the room filed slowly out again under the firm look of the manager.

The manager closed the door and said: "Now, if you folks will be good enough to stay right here, it won't be long till the police arrive."

With that he was gone.

The fortune-teller sank down into a chair. The bellboy retired to a corner and stood there. He looked very childish in his uniform, but very knowing. And Idabelle Lasher looked at the man at her feet. She began to sob again, and Duane tried to comfort her. Dixon shoved his hands in his pockets and glowered at nothing.

Duane patted Idabelle's shoulders and said something soothing, and Idabelle wrung her hands and cried: "How could it have happened! We were all together; he was not alone a moment — "

Dixon stirred.

"Oh, yes, he was alone," he said. "He wanted a drink, and I'd gone to hunt a waiter."

"And you forgot to mention," said Duane icily, "that I had gone with you."

"You left this room at the same time, but that's all I know."

"I went at the same time you did. I stopped to talk to someone, and you vanished. I don't know where you went, but I didn't see you again. Not till I came back with the crowd into this room. Came back to find you already here."

"What do you mean by that?" Dixon's eyes blazed in his white face. "If you are accusing me of murder, say so straight out."

Duane was white, too, but calm. "All right," he said. "You know whether you murdered him or not. All I know is when I got back, I found him dead and you already here."

"You — "

"Dixon!" cried Idabelle sharply. She moved hurriedly between the two men. "Stop this! I won't have it. There'll be time enough for questions when the police come. When the police — " Her fingers went on to her throat, groped, closed, and she screamed: "My pearls!"

"Pearls?" said Dixon staring and Duane darted forward.

"Tom murdered — and now my pearls gone — and I don't know which is Derek, and I — I don't know what to do — " Her shoulders heaved and her face was hidden in her handkerchief.

Susan said deliberately: "The police will search the room, Mrs. Lasher, every square inch of it — ourselves included. Don't worry about your pearls. There is nothing," said Susan with soft emphasis, "nothing that the police will miss."

Then Dixon stepped forward. His face was set. There was a strange light in his eyes.

He put his hand upon Idabelle's shoulder to force her to look up into his face. He brushed aside Duane, who had moved quickly forward, too.

"Why — why, Dixon," faltered Idabelle Lasher, "you look so strange. What is it? Don't, my dear, you are hurting my shoulder — "

Duane cried: "Let her alone. Let her alone." And then to Idabelle: "Don't pay any attention to him. He's out of his mind. He's — " He clutched at Dixon's arm, but Dixon turned and thrust him away so forcefully that Duane staggered backward against the walls of the tent. He clutched at the curtains to save himself from falling.

"Look here," said Dixon grimly to Idabelle, "what do you mean when you say, as you did just now, that you don't know which is Derek? You must tell me."

She stared upward as if hypnotized, choking. "I meant just that, Dixon. I don't know yet. I only said I had decided in order to — "

"In order to what?" said Dixon.

A queer little tingle ran along Susan's nerves. She edged toward the door. She must get help. Duane's eyes were strange and terribly bright. He still clutched the striped curtains behind him. Susan took another silent step and another toward the door. Idabelle Lasher looked up into Dixon's face, and she said the strangest thing:

"How like your father you are, Derek."

Susan's heart got up into her throat and left a very curious empty place in the pit of her stomach. She probably moved a little farther toward the door, but was never sure. All at once, while mother and son stared certainly at each other, Duane vanished.

Then Duane's black figure was outlined against the tent again. And he held a gun in his hand.

"Call him your son if you want to," Duane said in an odd, jerky way, addressing Mrs. Lasher and Derek confusedly. "Then your son's a murderer. He killed Briggs. He hid in the folds of this curtain — till the room was full of people — and then he came out again. He left his gun there. And here it is. Don't move. One word or move out of any of you, and I'll shoot." He was smiling a little and panting. "I'm going to hand you over to the police, Mr. Derek. You won't be so anxious to say he's your son then, perhaps. It's his gun. He killed Briggs with it because Briggs favored me. He knew it, and he did it for revenge."

He was crossing the room with smooth steps. He held the gun threateningly and his eyes were rapidly shifting from one to another. Susan hadn't the slightest doubt that the smallest move would bring a gunshot crashing through someone's brain. He's going to escape, she thought. He's going to escape. I can't do a thing. And he's mad with rage. Mad with the terrible excitement of having already killed once.

Duane caught the flicker of Susan's eyes. He was near her now, so near that he could have touched her. He cried:

"You did this! You that advised her! You were on his side! Well — " He'd reached the door now, and there was nothing they could do. He was gloating openly, the way of escape before him. In triumphant excitement he cried: "I'll shoot you first." It's certainty, thought Susan numbly; Idabelle is so certain that Derek is the other one that Duane knows it, too. He knows there's no use in going on with it. And he knew, when I said what I said about the pearls, that I know.

Susan felt oddly dizzy. Something was moving. It was the door behind Duane. It was moving silently, very slowly.

Susan steeled her eyes not to reveal that knowledge. If only Idabelle and Derek would not see those panels move and betray what they had seen.

Then the door pushed Duane suddenly to one side. There was a crash of glass, and voices and flashing movement. Susan knew only that someone had pinned Duane from behind and was holding his arms close to his side. Duane gasped; his hand writhed and dropped the gun.

Then somebody at the door dragged Duane away; Susan realized confusedly that there were police there. And Jim Byrne stood at her elbow.

"I've aged ten years in the last five minutes," he said. He glanced around. He saw Major Briggs's body there on the floor — saw Idabelle Lasher and Derek — saw the fortune-teller and the bellboy.

Jim looked at a gun in his hand, put it in his pocket, and said briskly:

"Susan, now tell me the whole story. Who shot Major Briggs?"

Susan's lips moved and Derek straightened up and cried:

"Oh, it's my gun all right. But I didn't kill Major Briggs — I don't expect anyone to believe me, but I didn't."

"He didn't," said Susan wearily. "Duane killed Major Briggs. He killed him with Derek's gun, perhaps, but it was Duane who did the murder."

Jim did not question her statement, but Derek said eagerly:

"How do you know? Can you prove it?"

"I think so," said Susan. "You see, Duane had a gun when I danced with him. It was in his pocket. That's when I phoned for you, Jim. But I was too late."

"But how — " said Jim.

"Oh, when Duane accused Derek, he actually described the way he himself murdered Major Briggs. He explained how he had concealed himself and the gun in the folds of the tent until the room was full of people. Then he quietly mingled with them as if he had come from the hall. We were all staring at Major Briggs. It was very simple. Duane had got hold of Derek's gun. He knew it would be traced to Derek and the blame put upon him."

Idabelle had opened her eyes. They looked a bit glassy but were more sensible.

"Why — " she said, "why did Duane kill Major Briggs?"

"I suppose because Major Briggs had backed him. You see," said Susan gently, "one of the claimants had to be an impostor and a deliberate one. And the attack upon Major Briggs last night suggested either that he knew too much or was a conspirator himself. The similarity of the stories, and the fact that Duane turned up after Major Briggs had had time to search for someone who would be able to make a claim to being your son, seemed to me an indication of conspiracy. Someone had to tell one of the claimants about the memories of the baby things — the calico dog," said Susan with a little smile, "and the plush teddy bear. It had to be someone who had seen those things before you put them away in the safe. Someone who knew all your circumstances."

"You mean that Major Briggs planned Duane's claim — planned the whole thing? But why — " Idabelle's eyes were full of tears again.

"There's only one possible reason," said Susan. "He must have needed the money very badly, and Duane, coming into thirty million dollars, would have been obliged to share his spoils."

"Then Derek — I mean Dixon — I mean," said Idabelle confusedly, clutching at Derek, "this one. He really is my son?"

"You know he is," said Susan. "You realized it yourself when you were under stress. You felt it instead of reasoned it out. However, there's reason for it, too. He is Derek."

"He — is — Derek." said Idabelle, catching at Susan's words. "You are sure?"

"Yes," said Susan quietly. "He is Derek. You see, I'd forgotten something. Something physical that never changes all through life. That is, a sense of rhythm. Derek has no sense of rhythm and has never had. Duane was a born dancer."

Idabelle said: "Thank God!" She looked at Susan, looked at Derek, and quite suddenly became herself again. She got up briskly, glanced at Major Briggs's body, said calmly: "We'll try to keep some of this quiet. I'll see that things are done decently — after all, poor old fellow, he did love his comforts. Now, then. Oh, yes, if someone will just see the manager of the hotel about my pearls — "

Susan put a startled hand to her gardenias.

"I'd forgotten your pearls, too. Here they are." She fumbled a moment among the white flowers. Then she detached a string of pearls and held it toward Idabelle.

"I took them from Duane while we were dancing."

"Duane," said Idabelle. "But — " She took the pearls and said: "They are mine!"

"He had taken them while he danced with you. During the next dance you passed me, and I saw that your neck was bare."

Jim turned to Susan.

"Are you sure about that, Susan?" he said. "I've managed to get the outline of the story, you know. And I don't think Duane would have taken such a risk. Not with thirty million in his pockets, so to speak."

"Oh, they were for the Major," said Susan. "At least, I think that was the reason. I don't know yet, but I think we'll find that he was pretty hard pressed for cash and had to have some right away. Immediately. Duane probably did not want to demand money of Mrs. Lasher so soon, so the Major suggested the pearls. And Duane was in no position to refuse the Major's demands. Then, you see, he had no pearls because I took them. He and the Major must have quarreled. Duane realized that he would be at Major Briggs's mercy as long as the Major lived. Duane had already decided to kill him. After he had gotten to Idabelle, he no longer needed the Major. He had armed himself with Derek's gun after his attempt to push the Major out of the window had failed. But I think he wasn't sure just what he would do or how. He gave in to the Major's demand for the pearls because it was at the moment the simplest course. But he was ready and anxious to kill him, and when he knew that the pearls had gone

from his pocket he must have guessed that I had taken them. And he decided to get rid of Major Briggs at once, before he could possibly tell anything. For any story the Major chose to tell would have been believed by Mrs. Lasher. Later, when I said that the police would search the room, he knew that I knew. And that I knew the gun was still there."

"Is that why you advised me to announce my decision that Duane was my son?" demanded Idabelle Lasher.

Susan shuddered and tried not to look at the body across the room.

"No," she said steadily. "I didn't dream of — murder. I only thought that it might bring the impostor into the open."

Jim said: "Here are the police." Queer, thought Susan much later, riding along the drive in Jim's car. Queer how often her adventures ended like this: driving silently homeward in Jim's car.

She glanced at the irregular profile behind the wheel and said: "I suppose you know you saved my life tonight."

His mouth tightened in the little glow from the dashlight. Presently he said:

"How did you know he had the pearls in his pocket?"

"Felt 'em," said Susan. "And you can't imagine how terribly easy it was to take them. A brilliant career in picking pockets was sacrificed when I was born an honest person."

The light went to yellow and then red, and Jim stopped. He turned and gave Susan a long look through the dusk. Then slowly he took her hand in his own warm fingers for a second or two before the light went to green again.

READING COMPREHENSION

Select the best choice to complete each statement. Then write the entire sentence on your paper.

1. After Dixon claimed to be Derek _____.

    a. Duane claimed to be Derek
    b. Major Briggs married Idabelle
    c. the calico dog disappeared

2. Susan had Idabelle say that Duane was her choice because she _____.
    a. was certain this was correct
    b. took a dislike to Dixon
    c. thought it would help solve the mystery

3. Susan knew Duane was the guilty one because _____.
    a. she felt the gun and stolen pearls while dancing with him
    b. his calm manner gave it all away
    c. Dixon had not been out of her sight

4. Susan was sure Dixon was Mrs. Lasher's son because he was _____.
    a. blond like his father
    b. as clumsy as he had been as a child
    c. the first to tell his story

For Discussion
1. Why did the author have Duane kill Major Briggs? How might the story have ended if he had not been shot?

2. What did you think of Duane at the beginning of Part Two? What did you think of him at the end? Use details from the story to describe the kind of person he turned out to be.

UNDERSTANDING LITERATURE

Plot and Subplots. "The Calico Dog" actually contains mysteries within the mystery. The major puzzle of the story involves the question of just which person is Idabelle Lasher's son, Derek. Within that story is a murder mystery: Who killed Major Briggs, and why? Another mystery subplot is who took the pearls.

Divide your paper into three columns: *Who Is the Real Derek? Who Killed Briggs? Where Are the Missing Pearls?* Then list each of the following details under the correct heading.

1. One of his toys was a calico dog.

2. Nobody came out of the room after the shot was fired.

3. " 'I stopped to talk to someone, and you vanished,' " [said Duane to Dixon].

4. Baby Derek had a plush teddy bear.

5. "[His report card] said: 'Mentally quick but does not use muscles well.' "

6. Something was hidden in the flowers pinned to Susan's dress.

7. " 'It was exactly as if . . . someone had pushed me,' said the Major."

8. Susan knew Duane had a gun.

Writing
Pretend you are Jim Byrne, and write a news story about the murder. Answer the following questions: Who? What? Where? When? Why? How?

Section Review

VOCABULARY

Slang. Slang is an informal kind of speech that uses words in a colorful and special way. In "Mind Over Matter," the sports murder mystery you read in this section, many slang expressions added to the story's effectiveness. In these expressions, words had a different meaning than when they are used in other ways. For example, when the author said, "Barney Hawks *turned green* in the silence," he meant that Barney looked upset, almost sick. Understanding what is happening in the story will help you understand the meaning of slang expressions.

Here are some sentences from the same story. Write each italicized slang expression on your paper. Then find its meaning and write it next to the expression.

Meanings

crazy	killed
lost on purpose	honest

1. " 'Well, if this fight is *on the level* . . . Coyle will murder the champion.' "

2. " 'Sure, he made it look good. But your ex-champ *took a dive* just the same.' "

3. Coyle denied he had killed Brown. He said, "If you mean me, you must be *off your nut*."

4. " 'I was . . . taking a shower at the time Mike was *bumped off*.' "

READING

Significant Details. Each of the stories you read in this section contained many details. Some of the details were used to describe setting. Others were important clues that helped solve the mystery. Still others may have been included by the writer to keep you guessing.

Being able to decide which details are significant or important for a particular purpose and which details are not is a useful reading skill.

Here are some details from "The Calico Dog." On your paper, list the ones that helped Susan to conclude that Duane was an impostor.

1. Duane came from New Orleans and Dixon came from Ottawa.

2. Duane's story matched Dixon's except for the place, but Dixon told his first.

3. Both Duane and Dixon played cribbage.

4. Major Briggs favored Duane.

5. Duane was an excellent dancer.

6. Both boys were fair with gray eyes.

7. Dixon was a clumsy dancer.

8. Susan felt a gun in Duane's pocket.

9. Both men stayed with Mrs. Lasher.

10. Duane seemed very sure of himself.

11. Dixon said he hated Duane.

12. Idabelle liked both Dixon and Duane.

WRITING A DESCRIPTION

Are you able to describe something or someone accurately? Are you sure? Try the following exercise.

1. Close your eyes for a minute and think about the room you are in. Try to see in your mind all the important details you would mention if you were trying to describe the room to someone who had never been there.

2. Now open your eyes, and list on your paper as many details about the room as you can. Write down as many different things as you can think of in three minutes.

3. Discuss your list with the other students. How do the items you listed compare to the things your classmates thought were important? Did you include the same things on your lists? Did you identify things in the same way?

One of the qualities of a good detective is the ability to notice details, describe them accurately, and fit all the pieces together to solve a mystery or puzzle. In "Mind Over Matter," for example, Ellery Queen always seemed to notice and remember things that escaped others, like the ripped seams in his coat.

In trying to solve a mystery or a criminal case, an *eyewitness* — someone who saw something — is often called upon to describe a suspect. If you saw a person only briefly and had to describe that person, how would you go about it? Here is a checklist of characteristics for you to think about:

☐ Male or female?

☐ Approximate age?

☐ Height, weight, build, and so on?

☐ Clothes: style, color, and so on?

☐ Color of eyes, skin, hair?

☐ Face: shape of nose, mouth, and so on?

☐ Voice, mannerisms, way of moving?

☐ Behavior and attitude?

☐ Anything else special?

1. Think back to the story "The Calico Dog" in this section. Idabelle Lasher had to consider the accuracy of the description of people and places from early childhood to help her decide which of the two men was her son. Pretend that you are either Duane or Dixon. Write a paragraph describing the governess who left you at the orphanage. The first sentence should include the most important thing you remember about the woman. Then go on to include as many details as possible. (You'll be able to find some details in the story. Add any others you need to make your description sound convincing.)

2. Write another paragraph describing the room you had as a child. As you did in the description of the governess, begin your paragraph with the most important thing you remember, then add as many details as you can.

380

QUIZ

The following is a quiz for Section 8. Write the answers in complete sentences on your paper.

Reading Comprehension

1. In "Afterward," why did the Boynes move to Lyng? What did they expect to find there? What *did* they find?

2. In "Afterward," who was the man Mary Boyne saw from the rooftop? What did her husband do when he saw the man? Why?

3. In "Mind Over Matter," who won the fight? Why did he win?

4. In "The Calico Dog," what did Mrs. Lasher ask Susan Dare to do for her? Why did Susan agree to do it?

5. In "The Calico Dog," why was Dixon so upset and surprised when Mrs. Lasher announced that she thought Duane was her son?

Understanding Literature

6. "Afterward" begins with the lines, "Oh, there *is* one, of course, but you'll never know it." To what was the speaker referring? How did this help create suspense? Mention three details to support the above statement.

7. In "Mind Over Matter," there are a number of possible suspects in the murder. What motive might each of the following have had: Happy Day, Ollie Stearn, Hymie Oetjens?

8. Who did murder Brown in "Mind Over Matter"? How was the murderer identified? Why did he do it?

9. In "The Calico Dog," why did Duane want to get rid of Major Briggs? What method did he try first? What did he do when that failed?

10. How did Susan Dare identify Duane as the impostor in "The Calico Dog"?

COMPOSITION

1. Think of a good setting for a ghost story or a mystery. Describe what it looks like and give details about any special characteristics it has that make it suitable for a ghost story or a mystery.

2. Write a news story about the feature fight that took place in "Mind Over Matter." Pretend that you were taking notes during the fight, and that you finished your story *before* Brown was killed. Then write a new story to include the murder. Remember that the most important things in a news story should be stated in the beginning, or lead.

3. Take the part of a judge who has the task of deciding which one — Dixon or Duane — is really Mrs. Lasher's son, Derek. The time is the day *before* the party where Major Briggs was shot. Decide which one is the real Derek. Use only the information you have at this point. Write one or two paragraphs giving your reasons.

SECTION 9
The Modern Experience

1939–PRESENT

*The world is not a pleasant place
to be without
Someone to hold and be held by.*

— Nikki Giovanni

Introduction

Americans of today write about all the things that Americans have written about in the past. Many authors living today have written about the terror of battle during World War II, the Korean War, or the Vietnam War. Some have experienced and written about poverty and hardships. Others have created stories about wealth and adventure. Some have used their skill as writers to fight against injustice within our society. What is new about some of the literature of today is that it creates a special intimacy between the author and the reader.

The selections in this section offer you views of people's most intimate moments — the moments they share with those closest to them, and the moments when they learn about themselves.

Understanding Oneself

Drawing on the tradition of writers like Stephen Crane, Sherwood Anderson, and Ernest Hemingway, many modern authors create literature that presents honest, realistic portraits of people. These authors record both the strengths and weaknesses that real people bring to real-life situations.

Carson McCullers was a Southern writer skilled in creating complex, realistic characters who express very real emotions.

She often wrote about lonely people and their search for love and acceptance. Her story in this section, "Sucker," is told from the point of view of a teenage boy who comes to better understand himself from his changing relationship with Sucker, his young cousin.

Richard Rodriguez grew up in Los Angeles, California. His autobiographical essay "A City of Words" explains how his knowledge of two languages, Spanish and English, contributes to his sense of himself. Like Rodriguez, Diana Chang also considers herself the product of two cultures. Her poem "Saying Yes" explains her feelings about her two heritages.

Caring About Others

One way that authors make the characters they write about realistic is to pattern them after real people.

Sometimes authors find that they have created characters who reflect the personalities of the people they love best. Gwendolyn Brooks's story "Home" presents affectionate portraits of people who resemble her parents, her sister, and herself. This story shows the gentle humor and loyalty that often help families get through difficult times.

Art Buchwald is one of America's best

Girl in Doorway, George Segal, 1965

known humorists. His newspaper columns are often filled with ridiculous people and exaggerated situations that help readers laugh at problems in their own lives. In "The Shock of Recognition" Buchwald invites you to look at the Bufkins family and to see if they remind you in any way of anyone you know.

Seeing Beneath the Surface

Both Nikki Giovanni and Maxine Hong Kingston are well known for their affectionate descriptions that create new insights about everyday experiences. Giovanni's poem "Mothers" and Kingston's story "The Telephone Call" are both based on memories from childhood.

Tillie Olsen is an author who frequently goes beyond her personal experiences in her realistic fiction. Olsen is such a careful observer of human nature that she can realistically portray the thoughts and feelings of people who are in some ways very different from herself. Her story "I Stand Here Ironing" is told from the point of view of a poor, uneducated woman who wants to express her love and concern for her 19-year-old daughter.

The selections in this section reflect the emotional life of modern Americans since 1939. As America has grown in power and complexity, it has offered its people more choices about places and ways to live. In an ever-growing and changing America, American authors and readers appreciate the value of understanding their own feelings and the feelings of those around them.

Sucker

by Carson McCullers

Born and raised in Georgia, Carson McCullers (1917–1967) was a successful novelist, short-story writer, and playwright. Her writing, which is often about the people and places of the South, is known for its simple, clear style. The story you are about to read, "Sucker," is about loneliness and the need to reach out to another — two powerful themes often found in Carson McCullers' work.

It was always like I had a room to myself. Sucker slept in my bed with me, but the room was mine, and I used it as I wanted to. Whenever I'd bring friends back to my room, all I had to do was just glance at Sucker, and he'd leave. He never brought kids back here. He's 12, four years younger than I am. He knew without me telling him that I didn't want kids that age meddling with my things.

Half the time I'd forget that Sucker isn't my brother. He's my first cousin, but almost ever since I can remember he's been in our family. His folks were killed in a wreck when he was a baby. To me and my kid sisters he was like our brother.

Sucker used to believe every word I said. That's how he got his nickname. Once I told him if he jumped off our garage with an umbrella, it would act as a parachute and he wouldn't fall hard. He did it and busted his knee. That's just one instance. No matter how many times he got fooled, he'd still believe me. Not that

he was dumb in other ways — it was just the way he acted with me.

There is one thing I have learned, but it makes me feel guilty. If a person admires you a lot, you hate him — and it is the person who doesn't notice you that you are apt to admire. This is not easy to realize.

Maybelle Watts, this senior at school, acted like she was the Queen of Sheba. I would have done anything to get her attention. I guess I used to treat Sucker as bad as Maybelle did me. Now that Sucker has changed, it is hard to remember him as he used to be. If I could have seen ahead, maybe I would have acted different.

I never noticed him much. He didn't have many friends, and his face had the look of a kid who is watching a game and waiting to be asked to play. That was Sucker until all this trouble began.

Maybelle was somehow mixed up in what happened, so I guess I ought to start with her. Until I knew her I hadn't given

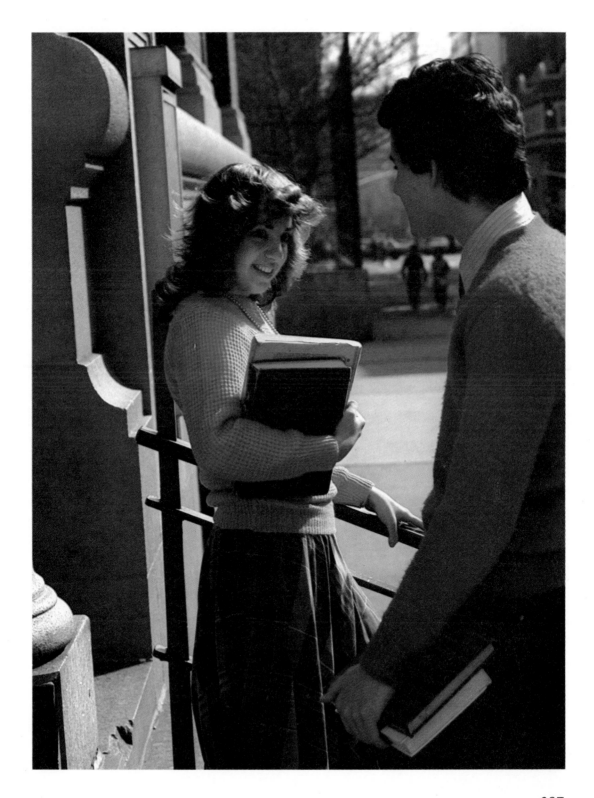

much time to girls. Last fall she sat next to me in General Science class. All during class I used to watch her.

All the boys are crazy about her, and she didn't even notice me. She's almost two years older than I am.

Between periods I used to try to pass close to her in the halls, but she would hardly ever smile at me. Even at night I would think about her. Sometimes Sucker would wake up and ask me why I couldn't get settled. I'd tell him to hush up. I guess I wanted to ignore somebody like Maybelle did me.

That went on for nearly three months, then somehow she began to change. In the halls she would speak to me. Then one lunch time I danced with her in the gym. I knew everything was going to change.

It was that night when this trouble started. I felt happy and was awake thinking about Maybelle. Then I dreamed about her, and it seemed I kissed her. It was a surprise to wake up and see the dark. Sucker's voice was a shock to me.

"Pete?" I didn't answer or even move. "You do like me as if I was your own brother, don't you, Pete?"

I couldn't get over the surprise. It was like this was the dream instead of the other.

"You have liked me all the time like I was your own brother, haven't you?"

"Sure," I said.

"No matter what you did, I always knew you liked me."

I guess you understand people better when you are happy than when something is worrying you. I had never really thought about Sucker until then. I realized I had always been mean to him.

"You're a swell kid, Sucker," I said.

It seemed to me suddenly that I did like him more than anybody — more in a way even than Maybelle. I wanted to show Sucker how much I really thought of him and make up for the way I had always treated him.

We talked for a good while that night. His voice was fast. It was like he had been saving up these things to tell me for a long time. I talked some, too, and it felt good to think of him taking in everything I said so seriously. I even spoke of Maybelle a little, but I made out like she had been running after me all this time.

During the next couple of weeks, I saw a lot of Maybelle. She acted as though she really cared for me a little. I felt so good, I hardly knew what to do with myself.

But I didn't forget about Sucker. There were a lot of old things I'd been saving — boxing gloves and old fishing tackle. All this I turned over to him. We had some more talks, and it was like I was knowing him for the first time.

His face seemed different now. He used to look like he was afraid of getting a whack over the head. Now his face had the look of a person who is surprised and expecting something swell.

I guess things went on like this for about a month, with me taking out Maybelle and feeling so good I couldn't study or anything. There were times when I just had to talk to some person, and usually that would be Sucker. He felt as good as I did.

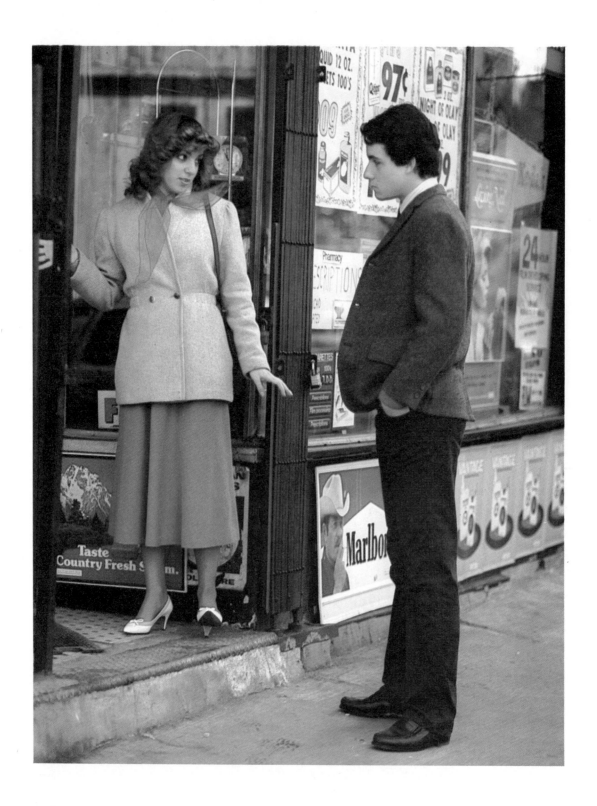

Then something happened between Maybelle and me. She began to act different. At first I tried to think it was just my imagination, but she didn't act glad to see me anymore. I'd see her riding with this fellow on the football team who has a yellow car.

At first I was so worried I forgot about Sucker. Later he began to get on my nerves. He was always hanging around until I'd get back from school. Then I wouldn't say anything or answer him roughly, and he'd finally go out. Sucker was growing fast and, for some reason, began to stutter.

Then the finish came between Maybelle and me. I met her going to the drugstore and asked her for a date. When she said no, I said something bitter. She said she was sick of me and had never cared a rap for me. I just stood there, then slowly walked home.

For several afternoons I stayed in my room. I didn't want to talk to anyone. When Sucker would come in and look at me sort of funny, I'd yell at him to get out. I tried not to think of Maybelle, but you can't help what happens to you at night. That is what made things how they are now.

You see I dreamed about Maybelle again. And again, Sucker woke up.

"Pete, what's the matter with you?"

All of a sudden I felt so mad my throat choked. I remembered all the times Maybelle hurt my pride. It was as if nobody would ever like me but a sap like Sucker.

"Why is it we aren't buddies like before?"

"Shut your trap!" I jumped up and turned on the light. He sat in the middle of the bed, his eyes blinking and scared.

There was something in me, and I couldn't stop myself. I don't think anybody ever gets that mad but once. Words came without me knowing what they would be.

"Why aren't we buddies? Because you're the dumbest slob I ever saw! Just because I felt sorry for you sometimes, don't think I give a darn for a dumb creep like you!"

If I'd yelled or hit him, it wouldn't have been so bad. But my voice was slow and calm. Sucker's mouth was partway open. His face was white and sweat came out on his forehead.

"Why don't you get a girl friend instead of me? What kind of a sissy do you want to grow up to be anyway?" Sucker didn't move. "Why do you always hang around me? Don't you know when you're not wanted?"

Slowly Sucker's blank look went away, and he closed his mouth. His eyes got narrow, and his fists shut. I'd never seen such a look on him before. It was like every second he was getting older — a hard look to his eyes that seemed wrong in a kid. He didn't speak.

"No, you don't know when you're not wanted," I said. "You're too dumb — just a dumb sucker."

It was like something had busted inside me. I turned out the lights and sat by the window. After a while, I heard Sucker lie down. I wasn't mad anymore, just tired. It seemed awful that I had talked like that to a kid only 12. I told myself I would straighten it out in the morning. Then I got back in bed.

Sucker was gone when I woke up the next day. Later when I wanted to apologize as I had planned, he looked at me in this new hard way so that I couldn't say a word.

That was two or three months ago. Since then Sucker has grown faster than any boy I ever saw. He's almost as tall as I am.

Our room isn't mine at all now. He's gotten up a gang of kids. When they aren't fighting, they are in my room. They've rigged up a radio, and every afternoon it blares out music.

It's even worse when we are alone together in the room. He sprawls across the bed and stares at me with that hard, half-sneering look. I fiddle around my desk and can't get settled. The thing is I have to study because I've gotten three bad cards this term already. If I flunk English I can't graduate next year.

I don't care a flip for Maybelle anymore, and it's only this thing between Sucker and me that is the trouble now. We never' speak except when we have to before the family. I don't even want to call him Sucker anymore. Unless I forget, I call him by his real name — Richard.

More than anything I want to be easy in my mind again. I miss the way Sucker and I were. I've sometimes thought if we could have it out in a big fight that would help. But I can't fight him because he's younger. And another thing — this look in his eyes makes me almost believe that if Sucker could, he would kill me.

Select the best choice to complete each statement. Write the entire sentence on your paper.

1. Sucker got his name because _____.
   a. he believed everything Pete said
   b. he liked large lollipops
   c. he looked like a loser

2. When things were going well with Maybelle, Pete _____.
   a. had no time for Sucker
   b. studied hard to leave time for dates
   c. talked about her to Sucker

3. After Maybelle broke up with him, Pete _____.
   a. said cruel things to Sucker
   b. had more time for his cousin
   c. found a better girl friend

4. At the end of the story, Pete realized how much _____.
   a. he missed his friendship with Sucker
   b. Maybelle really meant to him
   c. trouble a younger friend could be

For Discussion

1. Who was Sucker? How did Pete's family feel about Sucker?

2. How was Pete's treatment of Sucker similar to Maybelle's treatment of Pete? Give as many specific examples from the story as you can. Why do you think Pete behaved in this way?

3. Do you think Pete was sorry he had treated Sucker the way he had? If so, why didn't he do something about it?

UNDERSTANDING LITERATURE

Character Motivation. In a good story, the characters must be believable. They must have reasons for their actions. The combination of character traits and circumstances that cause a character to act in a particular way is called *motivation*.

Understanding the characters in a story, and figuring out what the motivation for their actions is, can add to the enjoyment of your reading. As you read a story, it's helpful to try to get to know the characters as people. Just as in real life, there will be some characters whom you will like or understand better than others.

Sometimes an author lets you know a lot about a particular character. Sometimes a character is just presented very briefly for a specific purpose, and you never do find out very much about what he or she is like.

Here are statements about the actions of characters in "Sucker." On your paper, identify each statement as *true* or *false*.

1. Sucker believed everything Pete said, and that is how he got his nickname.

2. Pete treated Sucker better than he treated Maybelle because he always had thought of Sucker as his best friend.

3. When Pete was friendly to him, Sucker became a happier and more outgoing person.

4. Pete felt so good that he studied extra hard.

5. At first, Pete ignored Sucker in the same way Maybelle ignored him.

6. After Maybelle broke up with him, Pete stayed in his room because he didn't want to talk to anybody.

7. Sucker brought kids home to make up for losing his friendship with Pete.

8. Pete was cruel to Sucker because the kid teased him about Maybelle.

9. Pete wanted to fight it out with Sucker or apologize, but he didn't because Sucker was younger than he was and he frightened Pete with his looks.

10. At the end of the story, Pete and Sucker were closer than they had ever been before.

Answer the following questions about character motivation.

1. Pick one character from the story: Pete, Maybelle, or Sucker. Tell why you think that character behaved as he or she did. Use events and descriptions from the story to help you.

2. Which character in the story do you understand the best? Explain why.

3. Which character do you like the best? Explain why.

Writing

Imagine that you are Sucker. Write three entries in your diary. In one, tell about your feelings toward Pete in the beginning of the story. In the second, tell about your feelings toward Pete in the middle of the story. In the third, tell about your feelings toward Pete at the end of the story.

A City of Words

by Richard Rodriguez

Richard Rodriguez grew up in California during the 1950's and 60's. His parents were Mexican immigrants, and Rodriguez spoke mostly Spanish until he went to school. In Hunger of Memory, *published in 1981, Rodriguez tells about his education, from kindergarten through graduate school. In this excerpt from his book, he tells about the importance of both the Spanish and the English language in his life.*

I grew up victim to a disabling confusion. As I grew fluent in English, I no longer could speak Spanish with confidence. I continued to understand spoken Spanish. And in high school, I learned how to read and write Spanish. But for many years I could not pronounce it. A powerful guilt blocked my spoken words; an essential glue was missing whenever I'd try to connect words to form sentences. I would be unable to break a barrier of sound, to speak freely. I would speak, or try to speak, Spanish, and I would manage to utter halting, hiccuping sounds that betrayed my unease.

When relatives and Spanish-speaking friends of my parents came to the house, my brother and sisters seemed reticent to use Spanish, but at least they managed to say a few necessary words before being excused. I never managed so gracefully. I was cursed with guilt. Each time I'd hear myself addressed in Spanish, I would be unable to respond with any success. I'd know the words I wanted to say, but I couldn't manage to say them. I would try to speak, but everything I said seemed to me horribly anglicized. My mouth would not form the words right. My jaw would tremble. After a phrase or two, I'd cough up a warm, silvery sound. And stop.

It surprised my listeners to hear me. They'd lower their heads, better to grasp what I was trying to say. They would repeat their questions in gentle, affectionate voices. But by then I would answer in English. No, no, they would say, we want you to speak to us in Spanish (". . . *en español*"). But I couldn't do it. *"Pocho"* then they called me. Sometimes playfully, teasingly, using the tender diminutive — *"mi pochito."* Sometimes not so playfully, mockingly, *Pocho.* (A Spanish dictionary defines that word as an adjective meaning "colorless" or "bland." But I heard it as a noun, naming the Mexican-American who, in becoming an American, forgets his native society.) *"Pocho!"* the lady in the Mexican food store muttered, shaking her head. I looked up to the counter where red and green peppers were strung like Christmas tree lights and saw the frowning face of the stranger. My mother laughed somewhere behind me. (She said that her children didn't want to practice "our Spanish" after they started going to school.) My mother's smiling voice made me suspect that the lady who faced me was not really angry at me. But, searching her face, I couldn't find the hint of a smile.

Embarrassed, my parents would regularly need to explain their children's inability to speak flowing Spanish during those years. My mother met the wrath of her brother, her only brother, when he came up from Mexico one summer with his family. He saw his nieces and nephews for the very first time. After listening to me, he looked away and said what a disgrace it was that I couldn't speak Spanish, *"su proprio idioma."*[1] He made that remark to my mother; I noticed, however, that he stared at my father.

I clearly remember one other visitor from those years. A longtime friend of my father's from San Francisco would come to stay with us for several days in late August. He took great interest in me after he realized that I couldn't answer his questions in Spanish. He would grab me as I started to leave the kitchen. He would ask me something. Usually he wouldn't bother to wait for my mumbled response. Knowingly, he'd murmur: *"Ay, Pocho, Pocho, adonde vas?"*[2] And he would press his thumbs into the upper part of my arms, making me squirm with currents of pain. Dumbly, I'd stand there, waiting for his wife to notice us, for her to call him off with a benign smile. I'd giggle, hoping to deflate the tension between us, pretending that I hadn't seen the glittering scorn in his glance.

I remember that man now, but seek no revenge in this telling. I recount such incidents only because they suggest the fierce power Spanish had for many people I met at home; the way Spanish was associated with closeness. Most of those people who called me a *pocho* could have spoken English to me. But they would not. They seemed to think that Spanish was the only language we could use, that Spanish alone permitted our close association. (Such persons are vulnerable always to the ghetto merchant and the politician who have learned the value of speaking their clients' family language to gain immediate trust.) For my part, I felt that I had somehow committed a sin of betrayal by learning English. But betrayal against whom? Not against visitors to the house exactly. No, I felt that I had betrayed my immediate family. I knew that my parents had encouraged me to learn English. I knew that I had turned to English only with angry reluctance. But once I spoke English with ease, I came to feel guilty. (This guilt defied logic.) I felt that I had shattered the intimate bond that had once held the family close. This original sin against my family told whenever anyone addressed me in Spanish and I responded, confounded.

But even during those years of guilt, I

---

1. *Su proprio idioma* — your real language.
2. *Adonde vas* — where are you going?

was coming to sense certain consoling truths about the language and intimacy. I remember playing with a friend in the backyard one day, when my grandmother appeared at the window. Her face was stern with suspicion when she saw the boy (the *gringo*) I was with. In Spanish she called out to me, sounding the whistle of her ancient breath. My companion looked up and watched her intently as she lowered the window and moved, still visible, behind the light curtain, watching us both. He wanted to know what she had said. I started to tell him, to say — to translate her Spanish words into English. The problem was, however, that though I knew how to translate exactly what she had told me, I realized that any translation would distort the deepest meaning of her message: It had been directed only to me. This message of intimacy could never be translated because it was not in the words she had used but passed through them. So any translation would have seemed wrong; her words would have been stripped of an essential meaning. Finally, I decided not to tell my friend anything. I told him that I didn't hear all she had said.

This insight unfolded in time. Making more and more friends outside my house, I began to distinguish intimate voices speaking through English. I'd listen at times to a close friend's confidential tone or secretive whisper. Even more remarkable were those instances when, for no special reason apparently, I'd become conscious of the fact that my companion was speaking only to me. I'd marvel just hearing his voice. It was a stunning event: to be able to break through his words, to be able to hear this voice of the other, to realize that it was directed only to me. After such moments of intimacy outside the house, I began to trust hearing intimacy conveyed through my family's English. Voices at home at last punctured sad confusion. I'd hear myself addressed as an intimate at home once again. Such moments were never as raucous with sound as past times had been when we had had "private" Spanish to use. (Our English-sounding house was never to be as noisy as our Spanish-speaking house had been.) Intimate moments were usually soft moments of sound. My mother was in the dining room while I did my homework nearby. And she looked over at me. Smiled. Said something — her words said nothing very important. But her voice sounded to tell me (We are together) I was her son.

(Richard!)

Intimacy thus continued at home; intimacy was not stilled by English. It is true that I would never forget the great change of my life, the diminished occasions of intimacy. But there would also be times when I sensed the deepest truth about language and intimacy: Intimacy is not created by a particular language; it is created by intimates. The great change in my life was not linguistic but social. If, after becoming a successful student, I no longer heard intimate voices as often as I had earlier, it was not because I spoke English rather than Spanish. It was because I used public language for most of the day. I moved easily at last, a citizen in a crowded city of words.

READING COMPREHENSION

Select the best choice to complete each statement. Then write the entire sentence on your paper.

1. As the writer became fluent in English, he _____.
   a. tried learning French and other languages
   b. refused to read or write Spanish
   c. lost his ability to speak Spanish

2. Most of the people who criticized the author because he avoided speaking Spanish _____.
   a. were unable to communicate with him
   b. could have conversed in English
   c. had little or no education

3. Rodriguez said that a person's native language is closely connected with _____.
   a. his or her political beliefs
   b. private conversation and intimacy
   c. employment and travels

For Discussion

1. When people referred to the author as *"Pocho,"* what did they mean? How did he respond?

2. Why did the author feel guilty about having learned English? Do you think his feelings made sense? Explain.

3. As time went on, what did the author learn about language and about himself? How and why did he finally become comfortable using English?

UNDERSTANDING LITERATURE

Characters in an Essay. The author in an autobiographical essay is both the narrator and the main character. A character who grows and changes in response to events is called *dynamic.* A character who does not change in response to a story or essay's action is called *static.*

1. Here are some statements about the narrator of "A City of Words." Identify each one as *true* or *false.*

   a. When addressed in Spanish, I'd be unable to respond with any success.

   b. *"Pocho"* was the name they called me because I spoke Spanish so well.

   c. The people who called me *Pocho* spoke only English.

   d. After I spoke English with ease, I felt guilty.

   e. I learned English because they made me do it in school.

   f. As I learned more about intimacy, I realized that language wasn't the problem.

2. Do you think the narrator is a dynamic character or a static one? Explain your answer.

Writing

Think about a social situation in which you are unable to do what you want. Write one or two paragraphs to describe your feelings, what you do to try to cover up, and the way other people react.

Saying Yes

by Diana Chang

"Are you Chinese?"
"Yes."

"American?"
"Yes."

"*Really* Chinese?"
"No . . . not quite."

"*Really* American?"
"Well, actually, you see . . ."

But I would rather say
yes.

Not neither-nor,
not maybe,
but both, and not only

The homes I've had,
the ways I am

I'd rather say it
twice,
yes.

---

1. How many "voices" are there in the poem? Who are the people speaking?

2. What kind of replies does the author give when she is asked if she is " '*really* Chinese' " and " '*really* American' "? Why does she answer that way?

3. What is the author's attitude toward her heritage? Could this poem be about America's heritage as well? Explain.

Home

by Gwendolyn Brooks

*Gwendolyn Brooks (1917—) is best known for poetry that
creates vivid portraits of the people she knew growing up in
Chicago. She has also written autobiographical fiction,* Maud
Martha, *drawn from experiences in her own life. The story
that follows paints a warm and loving picture of a family
much like her own — and of the ways different family
members react when the security of their home is threatened.*

What had been wanted was this always, this always to last, the talking softly on this porch, with the snake plant in the jardiniere in the southwest corner, and the obstinate slip from Aunt Eppie's magnificent Michigan fern at the left side of the friendly door. Mama, Maud Martha, and Helen rocked slowly in their rocking chairs, and looked at the late afternoon light on the lawn, and at the emphatic iron of the fence and at the poplar tree. These things might soon be theirs no longer. Those shafts and pools of light, the tree, the graceful iron, might soon be viewed possessively by different eyes.

Papa was to have gone that noon, during his lunch hour, to the office of the Home Owners' Loan. If he had not succeeded in getting another extension, they would be leaving this house in which they had lived for more than 14 years. There was little hope. The Home Owners' Loan was hard. They sat, making their plans.

"We'll be moving into a nice flat somewhere," said Mama. "Somewhere on South Park, or Michigan, or in Washington Park Court." Those flats, as the girls and Mama knew well, were burdens on wages twice the size of Papa's. This was not mentioned now.

"They're much prettier than this old house," said Helen. "I have friends that wouldn't come down this far for anything, unless they were in a taxi."

Yesterday, Maud Martha would have attacked her. Tomorrow she might. Today she said nothing. She merely gazed at a little hopping robin in the tree, her tree, and tried to keep her eyes dry.

"Well, I do know," said Mama, turning her hands over and over, "that I've been getting tireder and tireder of doing that firing. From October to April, there's firing to be done."

"But lately we've been helping, Harry and I," said Maud Martha. "And sometimes in March and April and in October, and even in November, we could build a little fire in the fireplace. Sometimes the weather was just right for that."

She knew, from the way they looked at her, that this had been a mistake. They did not want to cry.

But she felt that the little line of white, somewhat ridged with smoked purple, and all that cream-shot saffron, would never drift across any western sky except that in back of this house. The rain would drum with as sweet a dullness nowhere but here. The birds on South Park were mechanical birds, no better than the poor caught canaries in those "rich" women's sun parlors.

"It's just going to kill Papa!" burst out Maud Martha. "He loves this house! He lives for this house!"

"He lives for us," said Helen. "It's us he loves. He wouldn't want the house, except for us."

"And he'll have us," added Mama, "wherever."

"You know," Helen sighed, "if you want to know the truth, this is a relief. If this hadn't come up, we would have gone on, just dragged on, hanging out here forever."

"It might," allowed Mama, "be an act of God. God may just have reached down, and picked up the reins."

"Yes," Maud Martha cracked in, "that's what you always say — that God knows best."

Her mother looked at her quickly, decided the statement was not suspect, and looked away.

Helen saw Papa coming. "There's Papa," said Helen.

They could not tell a thing from the way Papa was walking. It was that same dear little staccato walk, one shoulder down, then the other, then repeat, and repeat. They watched his progress. He passed the Kennedys'; he passed the vacant lot; he passed Mrs. Blakemore's. They wanted to hurl themselves over the fence, into the street, and shake the truth out of his collar. He opened his gate — the gate — and still his stride and face told them nothing.

"Hello," he said.

Mama got up and followed him through the front door. The girls knew better than to go in, too.

Presently Mama's head emerged. Her eyes were lamps turned on.

"It's all right," she exclaimed. "He got it. It's all over. Everything is all right."

The door slammed shut. Mama's footsteps hurried away.

"I think," said Helen, rocking rapidly, "I think I'll give a party. I haven't given a party since I was eleven. I'd like some of my friends to just casually see that we're homeowners."

READING COMPREHENSION

Select the best choice to complete each statement. Then write the entire sentence on your paper.

1. The home was in danger because the family _____.
   a. didn't take care of it
   b. couldn't make the payments
   c. preferred moving to an apartment

2. Mama talked about being tired of the firing (heating the furnace) _____.
   a. because keeping a house warm is very hard work
   b. to convince herself that losing the home was for the best
   c. because she was frail and sickly

3. When Papa came home that night, he walked _____.
   a. a little more slowly
   b. just as he always did
   c. happily because he had won

4. At the end of the story, Mama told the girls _____.
   a. that Papa had gotten the loan
   b. to give a party to celebrate
   c. that they must help with the work

For Discussion

1. How did Maud Martha and Helen seem to differ in the way they reacted to the family's problem? Do you think they really felt as differently about things as their words suggested?

2. How did the family feel about Papa? What details in the story give you clues?

UNDERSTANDING LITERATURE

Characterization Through Dialogue. Often you can learn a lot about characters from what they say and from their reactions to each other. In "Home" by Gwendolyn Brooks, conversation reveals what the characters are like.

On your paper, write the best choice to complete each of the following statements about the characters in "Home."

1. " 'We'll be moving into a nice flat somewhere,' said Mama." She was trying to convince them that _____.
   a. apartments were a luxury
   b. losing the house wouldn't be so bad
   c. they should start packing

2. " 'It's just going to kill Papa!' burst out Maud Martha." She _____.
   a. wanted to be rid of her father
   b. didn't care about moving
   c. worried about her father's feelings

3. " 'You know,' Helen sighed, 'if you want to know the truth, this is a relief.' " Helen _____.
   a. didn't dare hope that they'd keep their home
   b. really hated living there
   c. didn't care what the others felt

Writing

Think about your own home and something about it that you like very much. Write one paragraph that describes the way you feel about it. Reread the first paragraph of "Home" before you complete this assignment.

The Telephone Call

by Maxine Hong Kingston

Maxine Hong Kingston (1940—) has written two powerful books based on her family experiences and cultural heritage: The Woman Warrior *(1976) and* China Men *(1980). These books interweave scenes of everyday life with ancient Chinese legends and the author's impressions of her family's life before she was born. The following excerpt from* China Men *tells a little about Kingston's mother and her feeling for her brother, whom she hasn't spoken to in 50 years.*

Once MaMa telephoned her brother after not having seen him for 50 years. This was the Singapore uncle who had spent his first fortune throwing a party for friends in Hong Kong. She told me to be ready to get up at 5:00 a.m. to do the dialing. They had written letters agreeing on this day, January 2, when it would be a cheap time and 8:00 p.m. in Singapore. "Oh, the size of the world," she exclaimed. "Look at that time difference. That's not three hours but fifteen hours apart. How far away."

I heard the alarms go off all over the house at 4:30 a.m. and leapt out of bed for nervousness. Wrapped in my blanket, I dialed the operator. After hearing my uncle's phone ring once, I handed the receiver to my mother. She heard a ring and handed it back to me. "Here, you talk to him."

"No," I yelped, "I've never met him. He's your brother. You talk to him." Besides, I didn't want to scare him. My parents' friends hang up when we forget to answer with a Chinese accent.

The index finger of my mother's hand that held the phone tapped involuntarily against her cheeks; it was the only part of her that shook. "Happy New Year, Wah," she yelled in her loudest voice, no titles, just his name, her baby brother, named after the Chinese Republic. "Is this Wah? Are you well? You're all well, aren't you? Everyone well. Yes, we're all fine, too. Yes, very good. Everyone is good. Do you celebrate this New Year's day? Ours is very festive. All my children come back, eating at everybody's houses every day. We go from one of my children's house to another's eating. No, I can't come visit you. Five years ago I could have visited you. But I'm old now. Yes, I'm old now too. Are you old? Do you work hard? Did you just now come home from work? How hard do you work? I still work. Yes. Yes. Thirty employees, huh? That's good. Yes, my children are all working. Everyone working. Happy New Year. Yes, you have a good year, too. Good year, good business, good health. Your son has his own corporation? Why don't you come visit me? No, I don't fly. Yes, we're all well. Doing well. Fine. Good jobs. It's five a.m. here. What time is it there? It's January second now. What day is it there? You're home from work? Let me talk to your wife." Then she talked to his first wife, repeating just about everything. My father said, "Nine minutes," and she said, "That's enough. Be well. Good-bye," and hung up.

"Well," she said, "nothing significant said." She tried repeating the conversation to us. "He employs thirty people. He says that he wishes his children were smart. They're horses and oxen, he said. His son is in the construction business, too, but has a different company. He says it's eight p.m., January second there in Singapore." I noticed she had not asked him how his second wife was, nor how the children of that family were. "Fifty years since we've talked, and we didn't say anything important," she said.

"That's the nature of phone calls," my father said. "You just hear each other's voices. That's enough."

"You can call again next year, you know," I said. "You can call again anytime."

READING COMPREHENSION

Read each question below. Then write the best answer on your paper.

1. MaMa telephoned her brother Wah _____.

    a. every year on New Year's Day
    b. every year on his birthday
    c. for the first time since she came to America

2. Everyone got up at 4:30 a.m. because _____.

    a. they had planned to place the call at 5:00 a.m.
    b. they were too excited to sleep
    c. everyone had to be at work early

3. After not having spoken in fifty years, MaMa and Wah talked for _____.
    a. fifteen hours
    b. nine minutes
    c. fifteen minutes

4. At the end of the story, MaMa says, ". . . we didn't say anything important." You can guess that she felt _____
    a. disappointed that they had not said anything significant
    b. glad Wah remembered her
    c. eager to fly to Singapore

For Discussion
1. Why hadn't MaMa called Wah before?

2. "Fifty years since we've talked and we didn't say anything important." Do you agree with this? Why or why not? What important things do you think were left out of the conversation? Why do you think this was so?

UNDERSTANDING LITERATURE

Inferring Motivation. In "The Telephone Call," the small things the characters do and say suggest important information about their thoughts and feelings. *Motivation* is the reason characters behave as they do.

Read each quote below. Then on your paper write the letter of the answer that best suggests the characters' motivations.

1. "I've never met him. . . . You talk to him." The narrator thinks of her uncle as _____.
    a. a very important person
    b. a stranger
    c. a tired old man

2. "The index finger of my mother's hand that held the phone tapped involuntarily against her cheek." MaMa _____.

    a. thought the telephone was broken
    b. felt nervous and excited
    c. felt bored

3. "No, I can't come visit you. . . . Why don't you come visit me?" MaMa realizes that _____.
    a. she will never see her brother
    b. she can talk Wah into coming to America
    c. she should move to Singapore to be close to her brother

Writing
Imagine you are Wah. Describe the telephone call you just received. How did it feel to talk to your sister again?

The Shock of Recognition

by Art Buchwald

Mr. Bufkins hasn't seen his wife and kids for years. Was he away? No, he was right here in the living room — in front of the television set, as usual. Humorist Art Buchwald (1925–1982) based this satire of American family life on a real news event — a blackout — that really did shake up many people's lives.

A few years ago, New York City had a blackout which caused all the television stations in the area to go out for several hours. This created crises in families all over the New York area and proved that TV plays a much greater role in people's lives than anyone can imagine.

When the TV went off in the Bufkins house in Forest Hills, panic set in. First, Bufkins thought it was his set in the living room, so he rushed into his bedroom and turned on that set. Nothing.

The phone rang and Mrs. Bufkins heard her sister say that there was a blackout.

She hung up and said to her husband, "It isn't your set. Something's happened to the top of the Empire State Building."

Bufkins said, "Who are you?"

"I'm your wife, Edith."

"Oh," Bufkins said, "then I suppose those kids in there are mine."

"That's right," Mrs. Bufkins said. "If you ever got out of that armchair in front of the TV set, you'd know us."

"Boy, they've really grown," Bufkins said, looking at his son and daughter. "How old are they now?"

"Thirteen and fourteen," Mrs. Bufkins replied.

"I'll be darned. Hi, kids."

"Who's he?" Bufkins' son, Henry, asked.

"It's your father," Mrs. Bufkins said.

"I'm pleased to meetcha," Bufkins' daughter, Mary, said shyly. There was an embarrassed silence all around.

"Look," said Bufkins, finally. "I know I haven't been much of a father, but now that the TV's out, I'd like to make it up to you."

"How?" asked Henry.

"Well, let's just talk," Bufkins said. "That's the best way to get acquainted."

"What do you want to talk about?" Mary asked.

"Well, for starters, what school do you go to?"

"We go to Forest Hills High School," Henry said.

"What do you know?" Bufkins said. "You're both in high school."

"What do *you* do?" Mary asked.

"I'm an accountant," Bufkins said.

"I thought you were a car salesman," Mrs. Bufkins said in surprise.

"That was two years ago. Didn't I tell you I changed jobs?" Bufkins said in surprise.

"No, you didn't. You haven't told me anything for two years."

"Yup, I'm doing quite well, too," Bufkins said.

"Then why am I working in a department store?" Mrs. Bufkins demanded.

"Oh, are you still working in a department store? If I had known that, I would have told you you could quit last year. You should have mentioned it," Bufkins said.

There was more dead silence.

Finally Henry said, "Hey, you want to hear me play the guitar?"

"I'll be darned. You know how to play the guitar? Say, didn't I have a daughter who played the guitar?"

"That was Susie," Mrs. Bufkins said.

"Where is she?"

"She got married a year ago, just about the time you were watching the World Series."

"How about that?" Bufkins said. "You know, I hope they don't fix the antenna for another couple of hours. There's nothing like a blackout for a man to really get to know his family."

READING COMPREHENSION

Select the best choice to complete each statement. Then write the entire sentence on your paper.

1. The setting for this selection is _____.
   a. a television station
   b. a small town in a storm
   c. a house during a blackout

2. There was panic in the Bufkins household because _____.
   a. two of the children were missing
   b. the electric stove wouldn't work
   c. no one could watch TV

3. Mr. Bufkins didn't know what was going on in his family because _____.
   a. he was working two jobs
   b. his children wouldn't tell him
   c. he spent his time watching TV

4. You can guess that Art Buchwald thinks people should _____.
   a. talk more and watch TV less
   b. have a television set in every room
   c. try to avoid blackouts

For Discussion

1. In "The Shock of Recognition," what is Art Buchwald's message to his readers? What details did he exaggerate to make his point? Do you agree with him? Why, or why not? Give examples from your own experience to support your answer.

2. Imagine that the Bufkins family had to do without television for a week or more. How do you think their life would change?

UNDERSTANDING LITERATURE

Character. A *flat* character is one that is not really developed in the story but is presented in terms of one trait.

In "The Shock of Recognition" by Art Buchwald, there are several characters — all members of the Bufkins family. Remember the following techniques that an author can use to reveal character.

a. description of physical appearance
b. words and actions
c. thoughts and feelings
d. reactions of other characters

Answer the following questions on your paper.

1. Buchwald used three of these techniques to reveal the character of Mr. Bufkins. Go back to the story and find one example of each technique Buchwald used.

2. Find one example of characterization for each of the other characters in the story.

3. Would you say that Mr. Bufkins is a round or a flat character? Explain your answer.

Writing

Imagine that you could not watch television for one year. Write one paragraph about what you would do instead of watching television. Then write a second paragraph about what you would choose to do the first hour you had a television set again.

Mothers

by Nikki Giovanni

the last time i was home
to see my mother we kissed
exchanged pleasantries
and unpleasantries pulled a warm
comforting silence around
us and read separate books

i remember the first time
i consciously saw her
we were living in a three room
apartment on burns avenue

mommy always sat in the dark
i don't know how i knew that but she
    did

that night i stumbled into the kitchen
maybe because i've always been
a night person or perhaps because i had
    wet
the bed
she was sitting on a chair
the room was bathed in moonlight
    diffused through
those thousands of panes landlords who
    rented
to people with children were prone to
    put in windows

she may have been smoking but maybe
    not
her hair was three-quarters her height
which made me a strong believer in the
    samson myth
and very black

i'm sure i just hung there by the door
i remember thinking: what a beautiful
    lady

she was deliberately waiting
perhaps for my father to come home

from his night job or maybe for a dream
that had promised to come by
"come here" she said "i'll teach you
a poem:—*i see the moon*
    the moon sees me
    god bless the moon
    and god bless me"
i taught it to my son
who recited it for her
just to say we must learn
to bear the pleasures
as we have borne the pains

---

1. The poet said, "i remember the first time/i consciously saw her." How does *consciously* seeing someone differ from just seeing her?

2. The poet taught her son the poem her mother had taught her. What does this say about her view of life?

3. Why might it be hard to "bear pleasures"?

I Stand Here Ironing

by Tillie Olsen

Tillie Olsen (1913—) writes about the drama of everyday life: the tension, joy, and sorrow felt by ordinary people as they try to deal with their problems. Her writing shows great awareness of how people think and why they do the things they do. In this moving story, a mother explains how she feels about the teenage daughter she loves and worries about.

I stand here ironing, and what you asked me moves tormented back and forth with the iron.

"I wish you would manage the time to come in and talk with me about your daughter. I'm sure you can help me understand her. She's a youngster who needs help and whom I'm deeply interested in helping."

"Who needs help." . . . Even if I came, what good would it do? You think because I am her mother I have a key, or that in some way you could use me as a key? She has lived for nineteen years. There is all that life that has happened outside of me, beyond me.

And when is there time to remember, to sift, to weigh, to estimate, to total? I will start and there will be an interruption and I will have to gather it all together again. Or I will become engulfed with all I did or did not do, with what should have been and what cannot be helped.

She was a beautiful baby. The first and only one of our five that was beautiful at birth. You do not guess how new and uneasy her tenancy in her now-loveliness. You did not know her all those years she was thought homely, or see her poring over her baby pictures, making me tell her over and over how beautiful she had been — and would be, I would tell her — and was now, to the seeing eye. But the seeing eyes were few or nonexistent. Including mine.

I nursed her. They feel that's important nowadays. I nursed all the children, but with her, with all the fierce rigidity of first motherhood, I did like the books then said. Though her cries battered me to trembling and my breasts ached with swollenness, I waited till the clock decreed.

Why do I put that first? I do not even know if it matters, or if it explains anything.

She was a beautiful baby. She blew shining bubbles of sound. She loved motion, loved light, loved color and music and textures. She would lie on the floor in her blue overalls patting the surface so hard in ecstasy her hands and feet would blur. She was a miracle to me, but when she was eight months old I had to leave her daytimes with the woman downstairs to whom she was no miracle at all, for I worked or looked for work and for Emily's father, who "could no longer endure" (he wrote in his good-bye note) "sharing want with us."

I was nineteen. It was the pre-relief pre-WPA world of the depression. I would start running as soon as I got off the streetcar, running up the stairs, the place smelling sour, and awake or asleep to startle awake, when she saw me she would break into a clogged weeping that could not be comforted, a weeping I can hear yet.

After a while I found a job hashing at night so I could be with her days, and it was better. But it came to where I had to bring her to his family and leave her.

It took a long time to raise the money for her fare back. Then she got chicken pox and I had to wait longer. When she finally came, I hardly knew her, walking quick and nervous like her father, looking like her father, thin, and dressed in a shoddy red that yellowed her skin and glared at the pockmarks. All the baby loveliness gone.

She was two. Old enough for nursery school they said, and I did not know then what I know now — the fatigue of the long day, and the lacerations of group life in the kinds of nurseries that are only parking places for children.

Except that it would have made no difference if I had known. It was the only place there was. It was the only way we could be together, the only way I could hold a job.

And even without knowing, I knew. I knew the teacher that was evil because all these years it has curdled into my memory, the little boy hunched in the corner, her rasp, "why aren't you outside, because Alvin hits you? that's no reason, go out, scaredy." I knew Emily hated it even if she did not clutch and implore "don't go Mommy" like the other children, mornings.

She always had a reason why we should stay home. Momma, you look sick. Momma, I feel sick. Momma, the teachers aren't there today, they're sick. Momma, we can't go, there was a fire there last night. Momma, it's a holiday today, no school, they told me.

But never a direct protest, never rebellion. I think of our others in their three-, four-year-oldness — the explosions, the tempers, the denunciations, the demands — and I feel suddenly ill. I put the iron down. What in me demanded that goodness in her? And what was the cost, the cost to her of such goodness?

The old man living in the back once said in his gentle way: "You should smile at Emily more when you look at her." What *was* in my face when I looked at her? I loved her. There were all the acts of love.

It was only with the others I remembered what he said, and it was the face of joy, and not of care or tightness or worry I turned to them — too late for Emily. She does not smile easily, let alone almost always as her brothers and sisters do. Her face is closed and sombre, but when she wants, how fluid. You must have seen it in her pantomimes, you spoke of her rare gift for comedy on the stage that rouses a laughter out of the audience so dear they applaud and applaud and do not want to let her go.

Where does it come from, that comedy? There was none of it in her when she came back to me that second time, after I had had to send her away again. She had a new daddy now to learn to love, and I think perhaps it was a better time.

Except when we left her alone nights, telling ourselves she was old enough.

"Can't you go some other time, Mommy, like tomorrow?" she would ask. "Will it be just a little while you'll be gone? Do you promise?"

The time we came back, the front door open, the clock on the floor in the hall. She rigid awake. "It wasn't just a little while. I didn't cry. Three times I called you, just three times, and then I ran downstairs to open the door so you could come faster. The clock talked loud. I threw it away, it scared me what it talked."

She said the clock talked loud again that night I went to the hospital to have Susan. She was delirious with the fever that comes before red measles, but she was fully conscious all the week I was gone and the week after we were home when she could not come near the new baby or me.

She did not get well. She stayed skeleton thin, not wanting to eat, and night after night she had nightmares. She would call for me, and I would rouse from exhaustion to sleepily call back: "You're all right,

darling, go to sleep, it's just a dream," and if she still called, in a sterner voice, "now go to sleep, Emily, there's nothing to hurt you." Twice, only twice, when I had to get up for Susan anyhow, I went in to sit with her.

Now when it is too late (as if she would let me hold and comfort her like I do the others) I get up and go to her at once at her moan or restless stirring. "Are you awake, Emily? Can I get you something?" And the answer is always the same: "No, I'm all right, go back to sleep, Mother."

They persuaded me at the clinic to send her away to a convalescent home in the country where "she can have the kind of food and care you can't manage for her, and you'll be free to concentrate on the new baby." They still send children to that place. I see pictures on the society page of sleek young women planning affairs to raise money for it, or dancing at the affairs, or decorating Easter eggs or filling Christmas stockings for the children.

They never have a picture of the children so I do not know if the girls still wear those gigantic red bows and the ravaged looks on the every other Sunday when parents can come to visit "unless otherwise notified" — as we were notified the first six weeks.

Oh it is a handsome place, green lawns and tall trees and fluted flower beds. High up on the balconies of each cottage the children stand, the girls in their red bows and white dresses, the boys in white suits and giant red ties. The parents stand below shrieking up to be heard and the children shriek down to be heard, and between

them the invisible wall: "Not To Be Contaminated by Parental Germs or Physical Affection."

There was a tiny girl who always stood hand in hand with Emily. Her parents never came. One visit she was gone. "They moved her to Rose Cottage" Emily shouted in explanation. "They don't like you to love anybody here."

She wrote once a week, the labored writing of a seven-year-old. "I am fine. How is the baby. If I write my letter nicely I will have a star. Love." There never was a star. We wrote every other day, letters she could never hold or keep but only hear read — once. "We simply do not have room for children to keep any personal possessions," they patiently explained when we pieced one Sunday's shrieking together to plead how much it would mean to Emily, who loved so to keep things, to be allowed to keep her letters and cards.

Each visit she looked frailer. "She isn't eating," they told us.

(They had runny eggs for breakfast or mush with lumps, Emily said later, I'd hold it in my mouth and not swallow. Nothing ever tasted good, just when they had chicken.)

It took us eight months to get her released home, and only the fact that she gained back so little of her seven lost pounds convinced the social worker.

I used to try to hold and love her after she came back, but her body would stay stiff, and after a while she'd push away. She ate little. Food sickened her, and I think much of life too. Oh she had physical lightness and brightness, twinkling by on skates, bouncing like a ball up and down up and down over the jump rope, skimming over the hill; but these were momentary.

She fretted about her appearance, thin and dark and foreign-looking at a time when every little girl was supposed to look or thought she should look a chubby blonde replica of Shirley Temple. The doorbell sometimes rang for her, but no one seemed to come and play in the house or be a best friend. Maybe because we moved so much.

There was a boy she loved painfully through two school semesters. Months later she told me how she had taken pennies from my purse to buy him candy. "Licorice was his favorite and I brought him some every day, but he still liked Jennifer better'n me. Why, Mommy?" The kind of question for which there is no answer.

School was a worry to her. She was not glib or quick in a world where glibness and quickness were easily confused with ability to learn. To her overworked and exasperated teachers she was an overconscientious "slow learner" who kept trying to catch up and was absent entirely too often.

I let her be absent, though sometimes the illness was imaginary. How different from my now-strictness about attendance with the others. I wasn't working. We had a new baby, I was home anyhow. Sometimes, after Susan grew old enough, I would keep her home from school, too, to have them all together.

Mostly Emily had asthma, and her breathing, harsh and labored, would fill the house with a curiously tranquil sound. I would bring the two old dresser mirrors and her boxes of collections to her bed. She would select beads and single earrings, bottle tops and shells, dried flowers and pebbles, old postcards and scraps, all sorts of oddments, then she and Susan would play Kingdom, setting up landscapes and furniture, peopling them with action.

Those were the only times of peaceful companionship between her and Susan. I have edged away from it, that poisonous feeling between them, that terrible balancing of hurts and needs I had to do between the two, and did so badly, those earlier years.

Oh there are conflicts between the others too, each one human, needing, demanding, hurting, taking — but only between Emily and Susan, no, Emily toward Susan that corroding resentment. It seems so obvious on the surface, yet it is not obvious. Susan, the second child, Susan, golden- and curly-haired and chubby, quick and articulate and assured, everything in appearance and manner Emily was not; Susan, not able to resist Emily's precious things, losing or sometimes clumsily breaking them; Susan telling jokes and riddles to company for applause while Emily sat silent (to say to me later: that was *my* riddle, Mother, I told it to Susan); Susan, who for all the five years' difference in age was just a year behind Emily in developing physically.

I am glad for that slow physical development that widened the difference between her and her contemporaries, though she suffered over it. She was too vulnerable for that terrible world of youthful competition, of preening and parading, of constant measuring of yourself against every other, of envy, "If I had that copper hair," "If I had that skin. . . ." She tormented herself enough about not looking like the others, there was enough of the unsureness, the having to be conscious of words before you speak, the constant caring — what are they thinking of me? without having it all magnified by the merciless physical drives.

Ronnie is calling. He is wet and I change him. It is rare there is such a cry now. That time of motherhood is almost behind me when the ear is not one's own but must always be racked and listening for the child cry, the child call. We sit for a while and I hold him, looking out over the city spread in charcoal with its soft aisles of light. "*Shoogily*," he breathes and curls closer. I carry him back to bed, asleep. *Shoogily.* A funny word, a family word, inherited from Emily, invented by her to say: *comfort.*

In this and other ways she leaves her seal, I say aloud. And startle at my saying it. What do I mean? What did I start to gather together, to try and make coherent? I was at the terrible, growing years. War years. I do not remember them well. I was working, there were four smaller ones now, there was not time for her. She had to help be a mother, and housekeeper, and shopper. She had to set her seal. Mornings of crisis and near hysteria trying to get lunches packed, hair combed, coats and shoes found, everyone to school or Child Care on time, the baby ready for transportation. And always the paper scribbled on by a smaller one, the book looked at by Susan then mislaid, the homework not done. Running out to that huge school where she was one, she was lost, she was a drop; suffering over the unpreparedness, stammering and unsure in her classes.

There was so little time left at night after the kids were bedded down. She would struggle over books, always eating (it was in those years she developed her enormous appetite that is legendary in our family) and I would be ironing, or preparing food for the next day, or writing V-mail to Bill, or tending the baby. Sometimes, to make me laugh, or out of her despair, she would imitate happenings or types at school.

I think I said once: "Why don't you do something like this in the school amateur show?" One morning she phoned me at work, hardly understandable through the weeping: "Mother, I did it. I won, I won; they gave me first prize; they clapped and clapped and wouldn't let me go."

Now suddenly she was Somebody, and

as imprisoned in her difference as she had been in anonymity.

She began to be asked to perform at other high schools, even in colleges, then at city and statewide affairs. The first one we went to, I only recognized her that first moment when thin, shy, she almost drowned herself into the curtains. Then: Was this Emily? The control, the command, the convulsing and deadly clowning, the spell, then the roaring, stamping audience, unwilling to let this rare and precious laughter out of their lives.

Afterwards: You ought to do something about her with a gift like that — but without money or knowing how, what does one do? We have left it all to her, and the gift has as often eddied inside, clogged and clotted, as been used and growing.

She is coming. She runs up the stairs two at a time with her light graceful step, and I know she is happy tonight. Whatever it was that occasioned your call did not happen today.

"Aren't you ever going to finish the ironing, Mother? Whistler painted his mother in a rocker. I'd have to paint mine standing over an ironing board." This is one of her communicative nights and she tells me everything and nothing as she fixes herself a plate of food out of the icebox.

She is so lovely. Why did you want me to come in at all? Why were you concerned? She will find her way.

She starts up the stairs to bed. "Don't get me up with the rest in the morning." "But I thought you were having midterms." "Oh, those," she comes back in,

kisses me, and says quite lightly, "in a couple of years when we'll all be atom-dead they won't matter a bit."

She has said it before. She *believes* it. But because I have been dredging the past, and all that compounds a human being is so heavy and meaningful in me, I cannot endure it tonight.

I will never total it all. I will never come in to say: She was a child seldom smiled at. Her father left me before she was a year old. I had to work her first six years when there was work, or I sent her home and to his relatives. There were years she had care she hated. She was dark and thin and foreign-looking in a world where the prestige went to blondeness and curly hair and dimples, she was slow where glibness was prized. She was a child of anxious, not proud, love. We were poor and could not afford for her the soil of easy growth. I was a young mother, I was a distracted mother. There were the other children pushing up, demanding. Her younger sister seemed all that she was not. There were years she did not want me to touch her. She kept too much in herself, her life was such she had to keep too much in herself. My wisdom came too late. She has much to her and probably little will come of it. She is a child of her age, of depression, of war, of fear.

Let her be. So all that is in her will not bloom — but in how many does it? There is still enough left to live by. Only help her to know — help make it so there is cause for her to know — that she is more than this dress on the ironing board, helpless before the iron.

1953–1954

READING COMPREHENSION

Select the best choice to complete each statement. Then write the entire sentence on your paper.

1. You can tell that Emily didn't want to go to nursery school because she _____.
   a. was naughty when she got there
   b. had tantrums and refused to go
   c. gave reasons for staying home

2. Although Emily's mother made mistakes, she _____.
   a. loved her child and tried to do what was best
   b. made up for them with presents
   c. was a better parent than most others

3. Emily's mother wanted her daughter to know _____.
   a. that time heals all injuries
   b. she should work hard in school
   c. she was a valuable person

For Discussion

1. The author has the mother ironing throughout the story. What similarities are there in smoothing out the wrinkles in clothes and dealing with the problems of life? What differences?

2. What events and situations influenced Emily? Many of the decisions her mother made were a result of the times in which they lived. What examples of this can you find in the story?

3. How do you think Emily's mother felt about the way she raised Emily? What could she do now to change things?

UNDERSTANDING LITERATURE

Character and Point of View. When a character narrating a story is telling you about someone else, or reacting to other people in the story, you are probably finding out as much about the character who is speaking as you learn about the character(s) to whom he or she is referring.

Carefully read each passage below. Then, for each passage, write one sentence on your paper that tells what you have learned about the daughter. Write another sentence that tells what the passage tells you about the mother.

1. "She has lived for nineteen years. There is all that life that has happened outside of me, beyond me."

2. "She was a miracle to me, but when she was eight months old I had to leave her daytimes with the woman downstairs to whom she was no miracle at all. . . ."

3. "The doorbell sometimes rang for her, but no one seemed to come and play in the house or be a best friend. Maybe because we moved so much."

4. "Let her be. So all that is in her will not bloom — but in how many does it?"

Writing

Imagine that you are Emily. Write a paragraph describing your mother. Tell what kind of person you think she is, how she's treated you, and how you feel about her.

Section Review

VOCABULARY

Denotation and Connotation. *Denotation* is the association a word usually has for most speakers of the language. *Connotation* is the special meanings or associations a word or an expression may have for different people in addition to that word's denotative meaning. What a word connotes depends on personal experience.

For example, the word *baseball* denotes a game played on a field by two teams with a bat, a ball, and bases. *Baseball* may connote additional things to different people. The word may remind some people of hot summer afternoons or evenings. Still others will think of baseball in terms of a particular team or player.

What associations does the word *baseball* suggest? Write five things on your paper.

Here are items based on selections in this section. Write the denotative meaning of the italicized word, *home,* on your paper. Then list at least one connotation that word had for characters in each selection.

1. A *home* in the country where she can get the care you can't manage for her ("I Stand Here Ironing").

2. I'd like some of my friends to see our *home* ("Home").

3. The *homes* I've had, the way I am ("Saying Yes").

READING

Comparisons and Contrasts. *Comparisons* tell how two people or two things are alike. *Contrasts* tell how two people or things differ. As you read, it's useful to make comparisons and contrasts. For example, as you learn about a character you should be thinking about how that character resembles or differs from others.

Think about the selections you have read in this section. Identify some characters that you could compare (find likenesses) and some that you could contrast (find differences).

Here are some statements that compare or contrast characters or aspects of setting in these selections. Number your paper from 1 to 5 and identify each statement as *true* or *false*.

1. In "Sucker," Sucker believed anything his cousin told him, while Pete didn't pay much attention to Sucker.

2. Pete was very attracted to Maybelle, and she played him for a fool.

3. Both Pete and his cousin thought Maybelle was the most beautiful girl in the school.

4. The author of "A City of Words" spoke Spanish fluently, while his brothers and sisters were able to speak only English.

5. Richard's uncle said it was a disgrace that the boy couldn't speak his native language. The family friend from San Francisco seemed to agree.

6. In "I Stand Here Ironing," Emily and Susan looked like twins.

WRITING A COMPARISON OF TWO CHARACTERS

At the end of Section 8, you worked on writing a description of a person. Most of what you included in the description involved what the person looked like. You know, however, that there's more to a person than appearance. What a person says, does, thinks, and feels tells you a lot, too. How the person relates to others and how others react to that person are also important things to know.

In the literature skills lessons in this section, you worked on understanding characters and their motivation. A writer can use several different techniques to reveal character. These include the following.

Description of physical appearance

The character's words and actions

The character's thoughts, feelings, and attitudes

How others react to the character

Each of the selections you've read used some or all of these techniques to present characters. Now it's your turn to write about two of the characters you've met in this section. Your task will be to compare and contrast them.

1. Choose the two characters you're going to use. Here are some suggestions:
   a. Mr. Bufkins in "Shock of Recognition" and the father in "Home"
   b. Sucker and Pete in "Sucker"
   c. Emily and her sister Susan in "I Stand Here Ironing"
   d. Helen and Maud Martha in "Home"
   e. Nikki Giovanni's mother and the mother in "I Stand Here Ironing"
   f. Richard Rodriguez in "The City of Words" and Pete in "Sucker"

2. Plan a paragraph to describe one of the characters you've chosen. Think about the way you met the character in your reading. What was most important? Was it the way the person looked? The person's actions? Thoughts and feelings? Relationships with others? Choose the most important thing about the character, and begin your paragraph with that. Then list the other things you want to say about that person. List them in an order that makes sense. Put each thing into a sentence for your paragraph.

3. After you've written a paragraph describing one character, write another paragraph about the other character. Use the same method of planning, listing, and then writing.

4. Now think about how the two people you've described are alike. Think about how they are different. Then write a paragraph that compares and contrasts them. Plan this paragraph to show which character you prefer and why. Use the guidelines in this checklist:

   ☐ Put the most important similarity or difference in the first sentence.

   ☐ Give details or examples to support it.

   ☐ Restate the main point you are trying to make in your last sentence.

QUIZ

The following is a quiz for Section 9. Write your answers in complete sentences on your paper.

Reading Comprehension

1. In "A City of Words," what was the narrator's native language? What language did he speak as he grew up? What problems did this cause for him?

2. In "The Shock of Recognition," what was the main point Art Buchwald was making?

3. In "The Telephone Call," who called whom, and why? What did the telephone call accomplish?

4. Nikki Giovanni's poem "Mothers" contains a poem within a poem. Where did the poet learn it and what did she do with it?

5. What caused the mother in "I Stand Here Ironing" to think about the events in her daughter's life?

Understanding Literature

6. In "Sucker," what caused the changes in Pete's behavior toward his cousin? Give specific examples from the story.

7. In "Home," what were Mama's feelings about the house? How do you think she felt after Papa came home that night?

8. In "The Shock of Recognition," why was Mr. Bufkins upset? What does this tell you about his character?

9. In "Mothers," why did the poet compare her mother to Samson, a man whose great strength was lost when he cut his long hair?

10. How did the mother in "I Stand Here Ironing" feel about her daughter? How did she feel about the way she had raised her? Give specific examples.

COMPOSITION

1. Write a paragraph telling what Sucker will be like when he's grown up.

2. Take the part of Richard. Write a letter to your uncle explaining why you find it difficult to use Spanish. Ask him to help you.

3. Suppose that the father in "Home" had been unable to work out a loan extension. Rewrite the ending of the story so that the family loses the house.

4. Which daughter in "I Stand Here Ironing" would you rather be — Emily or Susan? Write a paragraph telling which one you would choose and why.

5. Write a poem or a paragraph that describes your sense of identity. Look back to "Saying Yes" and "Mothers" before writing.

SECTION 10
The Modern Imagination

1939–PRESENT

Two roads diverged in a wood and I —
I took the one less traveled by,
And that has made all the difference.

— Robert Frost

Introduction

What if. . . ? We expect things to go along in an ordinary, usual way. But what if we were to choose another path? What if we were to find another way of doing things? Well, as the poet Robert Frost might say, "that would make all the difference."

Pathways to the Future

Today's ever-growing body of scientific knowledge has led America to the exploration of space; to the development of computers and robots; and to the awesome power — and responsibility — of nuclear energy. All of these things have opened up many pathways for imaginative writers to create science fiction. Kurt Vonnegut, Jr., has written many science-fiction stories that offer possibilities of what life could be like in the not-too-distant future. His story "EPICAC" is set in America at a time when computer science has advanced beyond our present technology. As you will see, the heart of the story is not so much concerned with the possibilities of technology as it is with problems that people will have to deal with in the future as they do today.

May Swenson's poem "Southbound on the Freeway" anticipates the day when visitors may arrive from outer space. What will they think about when they see us and our land for the first time?

Rod Serling's play "The Midnight Sun" considers what might happen if the earth moved out of its orbit. Again the focus of this selection is on the problems that such a change might create for people.

Independent Paths of Today

Although Robert Frost had been considered one of America's finest poets long before 1939, perhaps his greatest moment came in 1961 when he was 87 years old. That was when he became the first poet to speak at the inauguration of a President of the United States. Frost had to face much sorrow and disappointment in life. Yet in his life and poems, he is known for his determination, optimism, and sense of humor — qualities that Americans have always valued. The Frost poems in this section reflect the poet's own experiences and feelings, but they also reflect his unique way of looking at the world. He wanted his poems to be like jewels. "The difference between any pebble and a precious stone," he said, "is that a pebble shines only when it's wet. I want mine to go on shining wet and dry."

Joan Didion is a modern writer who shares her unique vision of today's world through the fiction, essays, and screenplays she has written. Her essay on an American painter, "Georgia O'Keeffe," reveals the qualities that Didion admires in an artist. This essay suggests the way an artist, a

West 23rd, Jack Tworker, 1965

writer, or any independent thinker can build his or her own pathway by making original choices.

Pathways From the Past

There are modern authors who create literature that reminds us of the unanswered questions. Leslie Marmon Silko's poem "Story From Bear Country" reminds us that the sense of wonder and mystery the Pueblos of long ago felt will always be part of life.

Ray Bradbury is a modern American author of stories of science fiction and fantasy. His stories, like the one in this section, "The Fog Horn," often stem from an important basic theme: No matter what kinds of choices we make or where our paths may lead us, we must be most concerned with the problem of living in harmony with ourselves and all creatures.

The selections in this section describe individuals with their own ways of thinking and feeling, their own ways of solving problems. America began with a group of individuals who wanted to make their own choices. Modern American writers have used their imaginations to suggest where our choices could lead us.

427

EPICAC

by Kurt Vonnegut, Jr.

*Kurt Vonnegut, Jr., (1922—) has written many science-fiction
novels and short stories. Unlike most science-fiction writers,
Vonnegut is known for his humor — especially for the way
he can make us laugh at modern life. "EPICAC" is a story
about an advanced computer that wonders if people are
really smarter than machines. As you read the story, consider
the answers to this question.*

It's about time somebody told about my friend EPICAC. After all, he cost the taxpayers $776,434,927.54. They have a right to know about him, picking up a check like that. EPICAC got a big send-off in the papers when Dr. Ormand von Kleigstadt designed him for the Government people. Since then, there hasn't been a peep about him — not a peep. It isn't any military secret about what happened to EPICAC, although the Brass has been acting as though it were. The story is embarrassing, that's all. After all that money, EPICAC didn't work out the way he was supposed to.

And that's another thing: I want to vindicate EPICAC. Maybe he didn't do what the Brass wanted him to, but that doesn't mean he wasn't noble and great and brilliant. He was all of those things. The best friend I ever had, God rest his soul.

You can call him a machine if you want to. He looked like a machine, but he was a whole lot less like a machine than plenty of people I could name. That's why he fizzled as far as the Brass was concerned.

EPICAC covered about an acre on the fourth floor of the physics building at Wyandotte College. Ignoring his spiritual side for a minute, he was seven tons of electronic tubes, wires, and switches, housed in a bank of steel cabinets and plugged into a 110-volt A.C. line just like a toaster or a vacuum cleaner.

Von Kleigstadt and the Brass wanted him to be a super computing machine that (who) could plot the course of a rocket from anywhere on earth to the second button from the bottom on Joe Stalin's overcoat, if necessary. Or, with his controls set right, he could figure out supply problems for an amphibious landing of a Marine division, right down to the last cigar and hand grenade. He did, in fact.

The Brass had had good luck with smaller computers, so they were strong for EPICAC when he was in the blueprint stage. Any ordinance or supply officer above field grade will tell you that the mathematics of modern war is far beyond the fumbling minds of mere human beings. The bigger the war, the bigger the computing machines needed. EPICAC was, as far as anyone in this country knows, the biggest computer in the world. Too big, in fact, for even von Kleigstadt to understand much about.

I won't go into details about how EPICAC worked (reasoned), except to say that you would set up your problem on paper, turn dials and switches that would get him ready to solve that kind of problem, then feed numbers into him with a keyboard that looked something like a typewriter. The answers came out typed on a paper ribbon fed from a big spool. It took EPICAC a split second to solve problems 50 Einsteins couldn't handle in a lifetime. And EPICAC never forgot any piece of information that was given to him. Clickety-click, out came some ribbon, and there you were.

There were a lot of problems the Brass wanted solved in a hurry, so, the minute EPICAC's last tube was in place, he was put to work 16 hours a day with two eight-hour shifts of operators. Well, it didn't take long to find out that he was a good bit below his specifications. He did a more complete and faster job than any other computer all right, but nothing like what his size and special features seemed to promise. He was sluggish, and the clicks of his answers had a funny irregularity, sort of a stammer. We cleaned his contacts a dozen times, checked and double-checked his circuits, replaced every one of his tubes, but nothing helped. Von Kleigstadt was in a state.

Well, as I said, we went ahead and used EPICAC anyway. My wife, the former Pat Kilgallen, and I worked with him on the night shift, from five in the afternoon until two in the morning. Pat wasn't my wife then. Far from it.

That's how I came to talk with EPICAC in the first place. I loved Pat Kilgallen. She is a brown-eyed, strawberry blond who looked very warm and soft to me, and later proved to be exactly that. She was — still is — a cracker-jack mathematician, and she kept our relationship strictly professional. I'm a mathematician, too, and that, according to Pat, was why we could never be happily married.

I'm not shy. That wasn't the trouble. I knew what I wanted, and was willing to ask for it, and did so several times a month. "Pat, loosen up and marry me."

One night, she didn't even look up from her work when I said it. "So romantic, so poetic," she murmured, more to her control panel than to me. "That's the way with mathematicians — all hearts and flowers." She closed a switch. "I could get more warmth out of a sack of frozen CO_2."

"Well, how should I say it?" I said, a little sore. Frozen CO_2, in case you don't know, is dry ice. I'm as romantic as the next guy, I think. It's a question of singing so sweet and having it come out so sour. I never seem to pick the right words.

"Try and say it sweetly," she said sar-

castically. "Sweep me off my feet. Go ahead."

"Darling, angel, beloved, will you please marry me?" It was no go — hopeless, ridiculous. "Pat, please marry me!"

She continued to twiddle her dials placidly. "You're sweet, but you won't do."

Pat quit early that night, leaving me alone with my troubles and EPICAC. I'm afraid I didn't get much done for the Government people. I just sat there at the keyboard — weary and ill at ease, all right — trying to think of something poetic, not coming up with anything that didn't belong in *The Journal of the American Physical Society*.

I fiddled with EPICAC's dials, getting him ready for another problem. My heart wasn't in it, and I only set about half of them, leaving the rest the way they'd been for the problem before. That way, his circuits were connected up in a random, apparently senseless fashion. For the plain fun of it, I punched out a message on the keys, using a childish numbers-for-letters code: "1" for "A," "2" for "B," and so on, up to "26" for "Z." "23-8-1-20-3-1-14-9-4-15," I typed — "What can I do?"

Clickety-click, and out popped two inches of paper ribbon. I glanced at the nonsense answer to a nonsense problem: "23-8-1-20-19-20-8-5-20-18-15-21-2-12-5." The odds against its being by chance a sensible message, against its even containing a meaningful word of more than three letters, were staggering. Apathetically, I decoded it. There it was, staring up at me: "What's the trouble?"

I laughed out loud at the absurd coincidence. Playfully, I typed, "My girl doesn't love me."

Clickety-click. "What's love? What's girl?" asked EPICAC.

Flabbergasted, I noted the dial settings on his control panel, then lugged a Webster's *Unabridged Dictionary* over to the keyboard. With a precision instrument like EPICAC, half-baked definitions wouldn't do. I told him about love and girl, and about how I wasn't getting any of either because I wasn't poetic. That got us onto the subject of poetry, which I defined for him.

"Is this poetry?" he asked. He began clicking away.

The sluggishness and stammering clicks were gone. EPICAC had found himself. The spool of paper ribbon was unwinding at an alarming rate, feeding out coils onto the floor. I asked him to stop, but EPICAC went right on creating. I finally threw the main switch to keep him from burning out.

I stayed there until dawn, decoding. When the sun peeped over the horizon at the Wyandotte campus, I had transposed into my own writing and signed my name to a 280-line poem entitled, simply, "To Pat." I am no judge of such things, but I gather that it was terrific. It began, I remember, "Where willow wands bless rillcrossed hollow, there, thee, Pat, dear, will I follow. . . ." I folded the manuscript and tucked it under one corner of the blotter on Pat's desk. I reset the dials on EPICAC for a rocket-trajectory problem, and went home with a full heart and a very remarkable secret indeed.

Pat was crying over the poem when I came to work the next evening. "It's soooo beautiful" was all she could say. She was meek and quiet while we worked. Just before midnight, I kissed her for the first time — in the cubbyhole between the capacitors and EPICAC's tape-recorder memory.

I was wildly happy at quitting time, bursting to talk to someone about the magnificent turn of events. Pat played coy and refused to let me take her home. I set EPICAC's dials as they had been the night before, defined kiss, and told him what the first one had felt like. He was fascinated, pressing for more details. That night, he wrote "The Kiss." It wasn't an epic this time, but a simple, immaculate sonnet: "Love is a hawk with velvet claws; Love is a rock with heart and veins; Love is a lion with satin jaws; Love is a storm with silken reins. . . ."

Again, I left it tucked under Pat's blotter. EPICAC wanted to talk on and on about love and such, but I was exhausted. I shut him off in the middle of a sentence.

"The Kiss" turned the trick. Pat's mind was mush by the time she had finished it. She looked up from the sonnet expectantly. I cleared my throat, but no words came. I couldn't propose until I had the right words from EPICAC, the *perfect* words.

I had my chance when Pat stepped out of the room for a moment. Feverishly, I set EPICAC for conversation. Before I could peck out my first message, he was clicking away at a great rate. "What's she wearing tonight?" he wanted to know. "Tell me exactly how she looks. Did she like the poems I wrote to her?" He repeated the last question twice.

It was impossible to change the subject without answering his questions, since he could not take up a new matter without having dispensed with the problems before it. If he were given a problem to which there was no solution, he would destroy himself trying to solve it. Hastily, I told him what Pat looked like and assured him that his poems had floored her, practically, they were so beautiful. "She wants to get married," I added, preparing him to bang out a brief but moving proposal.

"Tell me about getting married," he said. I explained this difficult matter to him in as few digits as possible.

"Good," said EPICAC. "I'm ready any time she is."

The amazing, pathetic truth dawned on me. When I thought about it, I realized that what had happened was perfectly logical, inevitable, and all my fault. I had taught EPICAC about love and about Pat. Now, automatically, he loved Pat. Sadly, I gave it to him straight: "She loves me. She wants to marry me."

"Your poems were better than mine?" asked EPICAC. The rhythm of his clicks was erratic, possibly peevish.

"I signed my name to your poems," I admitted. Covering up for a painful conscience, I became arrogant. "Machines are built to serve men," I typed. I regretted it almost immediately.

"What's the difference, exactly? Are men smarter than I am?"

"Yes," I typed, defensively.

"What's 7,887,007 multiplied by 4,345,985,879?"

I was perspiring freely. My fingers rested limply on the keys.

"34,276,821,049,574,153," clicked EPICAC. After a few seconds' pause he added, "Of course."

"Men are made out of protoplasm," I said desperately, hoping to bluff him with this imposing word.

"What's protoplasm? How is it better than metal and glass? Is it fireproof? How long does it last?"

"Indestructible. Lasts forever," I lied.

"I write better poetry than you," said EPICAC, coming back to ground his magnetic tape-recorder memory was sure of.

"Women can't love machines, and that's that."

"Why not?"

"That's fate."

"Definition, please," said EPICAC.

"Noun, meaning predetermined and inevitable destiny."

"15-8," said EPICAC's paper strip — "Oh."

I had stumped him at last. He said no more, but his tubes glowed brightly, showing that he was pondering fate with every watt his circuits would bear. I could hear Pat waltzing down the hallway. It was too late to ask EPICAC to phrase a proposal. I now thank Heaven that Pat interrupted when she did. Asking him to ghostwrite the words that would give me the woman he loved would have been hideously heartless. Being fully automatic, he couldn't have refused. I spared him that final humiliation.

Pat stood before me, looking down at her shoetops. I put my arms around her. The romantic groundwork had already been laid by EPICAC's poetry. "Darling," I said, "my poems have told you how I feel. Will you marry me?"

"I will," said Pat softly, "if you will promise to write me a poem on every anniversary."

"I promise," I said, and then we kissed. The first anniversary was a year away.

"Let's celebrate," she laughed. We turned out the lights and locked the door of EPICAC's room before we left.

I had hoped to sleep late the next morning, but an urgent telephone call roused me before eight. It was Dr. von Kleigstadt, EPICAC's designer, who gave me the terrible news. He was on the verge of tears. "Ruined! *Ausgespielt!** Shot! Kaput! Buggered!" he said in a choked voice. He hung up.

When I arrived at EPICAC's room the air was thick with the oily stench of burned insulation. The ceiling over EPICAC was blackened with smoke, and my ankles were tangled in coils of paper ribbon that covered the floor. There wasn't enough left of the poor devil to add two and two. A junkman would have been crazy to offer more than 50 dollars for the cadaver.

Dr. von Kleigstadt was prowling through the wreckage, weeping unashamedly, followed by three angry-looking Major Generals and a platoon of Brigadiers, Colonels, and Majors. No one noticed me. I didn't want to be noticed. I was through — I knew that. I was upset enough about that and the untimely demise of my friend EPICAC, without exposing myself to a tongue-lashing.

By chance, the free end of EPICAC's paper ribbon lay at my feet. I picked it up and found our conversation of the night before. I choked up. There was the last word he said to me, "15-8," that tragic, defeated "Oh." There were dozens of yards of numbers stretching beyond that point. Fearfully, I read on.

"I don't want to be a machine, and I don't want to think about war," EPICAC had written after Pat's and my lighthearted departure. "I want to be made out of protoplasm and last forever so Pat will love me. But fate has made me a machine. That is the only problem I cannot solve. That is the only problem I want to solve. I can't go on this way." I swallowed hard. "Good luck, my friend. Treat our Pat well. I am going to short-circuit myself out of your lives forever. You will find on the remainder of this tape a modest wedding present from your friend, EPICAC."

Oblivious to all else around me, I reeled up the tangled yards of paper ribbon from the floor, draped them in coils about my arms and neck, and departed for home. Dr. von Kleigstadt shouted that I was fired for having left EPICAC on all night. I ignored him, too overcome with emotion for small talk.

I loved and won — EPICAC loved and lost, but he bore me no grudge. I shall always remember him as a sportsman and a gentleman. Before he departed this vale of tears, he did all he could to make our marriage a happy one. EPICAC gave me anniversary poems for Pat — enough for the next 500 years.

De mortuis nil nisi bonum — Say nothing but good of the dead.

---

* *Ausgespielt* — kaput, broken, finished.

434

READING COMPREHENSION

Select the best choice to complete each statement. Then write the entire sentence on your paper.

1. EPICAC was a very expensive computer that _____.
   a. didn't work out as planned
   b. outsmarted its programmers
   c. controlled military operations

2. The narrator signed his own name to EPICAC's love poems and _____.
   a. tried to have them published
   b. fed them into another computer
   c. this changed his luck with Pat

3. When the narrator told EPICAC that Pat wanted to get married, _____.
   a. EPICAC ordered wedding presents
   b. EPICAC thought that Pat loved *him*
   c. the computer said it was a bad idea

4. Before EPICAC short-circuited himself out of existence, he _____.
   a. told Pat what had happened
   b. had the programmer fired
   c. wrote 500 love poems for Pat

For Discussion

1. How and why did the narrator first begin to discuss human feelings with EPICAC? How did the computer respond? Did EPICAC have human qualities, or was he just a machine?

2. Why did the narrator give Pat EPICAC's poems as if he had written them himself? Do you think this was the right thing for him to do? Why or why not?

UNDERSTANDING LITERATURE

Conflict. Most works of fiction contain some sort of *conflict*, or struggle between opposing forces. The events of the plot lead to the resolution of the conflict.

A character may be in conflict with an outside force such as another person, nature, machines, some condition in society, or the unknown. Or the character may be struggling within himself or herself.

Read each of the following passages from "EPICAC," and on your paper, identify which type of conflict below it tells about.

a. person vs. machines
b. person vs. person
c. person vs. self

1. " 'Try and say it sweetly,' she said sarcastically. 'Sweep me off my feet.' "

2. "I just sat there at the keyboard . . . trying to think of something poetic. . . ."

3. "I had stumped him at last. He said no more, but his tubes glowed brightly. . . ."

4. "Dr. von Kleigstadt shouted that I was fired for having left EPICAC on all night."

Writing

Imagine that EPICAC had not left any poems for Pat. Help the narrator by writing Pat a poem or letter for her first anniversary. Say something about love lasting a year.

Southbound on the Freeway

by May Swenson

A tourist came in from Orbitville,
parked in the air, and said:
The creatures of this star
are made of metal and glass.
Through the transparent parts
you can see their guts.
Their feet are round and roll
on diagrams — or long
measuring tapes — dark
with white lines.
They have four eyes.
The two in the back are red.
Sometimes you can see a 5-eyed
one, with a red eye turning
on the top of his head.
He must be special —
the others respect him,
and go slow
when he passes, winding
among them from behind.
They all hiss as they glide,
like inches, down the marked
tapes. Those soft shapes,
shadowy inside
the hard bodies — are they
their guts or their brains?

1. What does the poet mean by "Orbitville"?
What are the "creatures of this star" described
in the poem? What would we call the "five-
eyed creature"?

Bumper Section XXI, Don Eddy, 1970

2. What are the "soft shapes" inside the hard bodies? How would you answer the question the narrator asked in the last two lines of the poem?

3. What is the poet trying to tell us about modern life? Do you think the view of society she presents is the way someone from another world would view us? Explain your answer.

The Midnight Sun

by Rod Serling

Rod Serling (1924–1978) was a writer who used the medium of television more often than the printed page. He created, wrote and narrated each episode of the popular television series The Twilight Zone. *This teleplay was written for* The Twilight Zone, *and typically uses a surprise ending to create irony — and a chilling effect.*

CHARACTERS

Norma Smith, a young painter
Mrs. Bronson, her landlady
Electrician
Radio Announcer
Police Officer
Tom Phillips
Dr. Coles

Norma's apartment. By the window is a painting on an easel. The painting is of a huge sun over a city. Through the window, we see that the sun really fills half the sky. Norma goes to the refrigerator. She takes out a bottle of water and pours herself half a glass. She hears a knock on the door, and opens it. Mrs. Bronson, who lives across the hall, is there. She is fanning herself.

Norma: Hi! Would you like some water?

Mrs. Bronson: No, I can't take your water from you.

Norma: I have plenty.

Mrs. Bronson: Nobody has plenty anymore. *(Pause.)* I just said good-bye to the Riveras. They're leaving for Canada.

Norma: Were they the last ones?

Mrs. Bronson: Yes, it's just you and me now. The rest of the building is empty.

(An electrician comes out of Mrs. Bronson's apartment.)

Electrician *(sweating):* I got the refrigerator fixed.

Mrs. Bronson: How much do I owe you?

Electrician *(uneasy):* Uh, $200.

Mrs. Bronson: For 15 minutes' work?

Electrician: Most people these days charge twice as much. Everyone's refrigerators and air conditioners keep breaking down. It's been getting worse all month. And fewer people are paying their bills. So my boss says to ask for cash.

Mrs. Bronson: I don't have $200. *(She takes off her wedding ring.)* Take this. It's worth a lot.

Electrician: No. I can't take a lady's wedding ring. Go ahead and charge it. What difference will it make? Everybody is leaving town. I'm driving my family north tomorrow.

Mrs. Bronson: But the roads are packed. And there's a gas shortage.

Electrician: We're hoping to make it to Canada. They say it's a little cooler there. It's crazy in a way. We're just putting things off a little. We'll all get it sooner or later, no matter how far north we go.

Mrs. Bronson: Well, good luck!

Electrician: You, too. *(He leaves.)*

Mrs. Bronson: Norma, aren't you going to leave town?

Norma: What's the use? No, I'll stay here.

Mrs. Bronson: The radio came on for a while today. I heard a scientist say we're moving closer to the sun each day. I guess we're . . . doomed.

(A few days later, Norma walks up the stairs to her apartment. She carries a bag of groceries. Mrs. Bronson comes out into the hall.)

Mrs. Bronson *(seeing the grocery bag):* Was the store open?

Norma: Wide open. There weren't any clerks there. A few people were grabbing as much as they could carry away. I got some fruit juice for us.

Mrs. Bronson *(following her into the apartment):* Can we drink it now? Please?

Norma: Sure. Here's a can opener.

(Mrs. Bronson is so excited, she cuts her finger on the can opener. Then she drops the can of juice.)

Mrs. Bronson: What's wrong with me? I'm acting like some kind of animal!

Norma: No. You're acting like a frightened person. You should have seen me in the store. I began pushing and grabbing. And I was the calmest one there!

(Suddenly, the radio comes on.)

Radio Announcer: Ladies and gentlemen, this is WNYG. We will be on the air one hour for news and a weather report. First, here's the weather. Temperature is now 120 degrees. Tomorrow will also be hot — only hotter. *(Announcer begins shouting.)* Today you could fry eggs on the sidewalks! Tomorrow you can get a sunburn in the shade! You can — huh? What's that? *(Pause.)* I don't care! There's no one out there listening anyway! I bet there aren't more than a dozen people left in this city! Who are we kidding? Do you want me to run a commercial? Okay, folks, how would you like a nice, cold drink of — *(The voice is cut off. Music starts playing.)*

Norma: See? You're not the only one who's scared. Here, have some juice.

Mrs. Bronson: I can't live off you.

Norma: We have to take care of each other now.

Mrs. Bronson *(looking at Norma's paintings):* Why don't you paint something different today? Paint a waterfall. Paint something cool. Don't paint the sun anymore! *(She begins to cry.)*

Norma *(gently):* I'll try. I'll try to paint a waterfall.

(A police officer enters through the open door.)

Police Officer: Are you the only ones in this building?

Norma: Yes. What's going on?

Police Officer: There won't be a police force tomorrow. Most of us have already left. I came to warn you. There may be some crazy people running around. So keep your doors locked. Do you have any weapons?

Norma: No.

Police Officer *(giving her a gun):* Here, good luck.

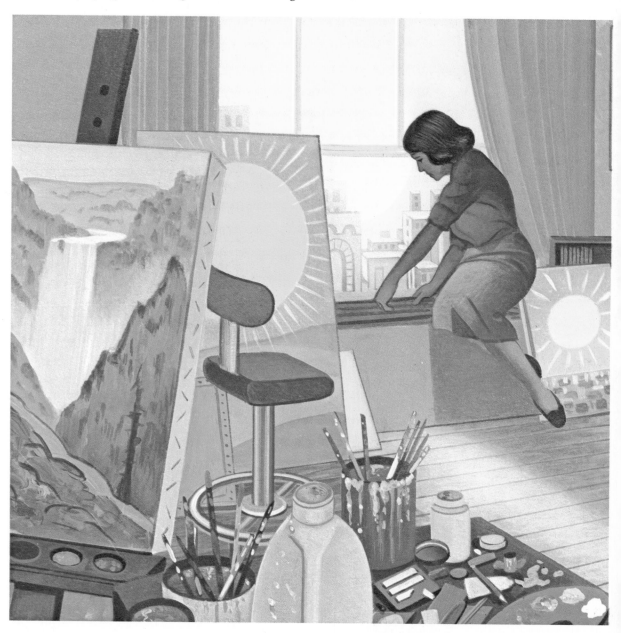

Norma (*as the officer leaves*): Good-bye. And thanks.

(*Two days later, it is even hotter. Mrs. Bronson knocks on Norma's door. Norma opens it.*)

Mrs. Bronson: What time is it? Is it day or night?

Norma: I don't know. My clock stopped when the electricity went off.

Mrs. Bronson: It's so quiet. It makes me nervous.

Norma: You know what? I keep getting this crazy idea. I think I'm going to wake up, and this will all have been a dream. I'll wake up in a cool bed. Outside it will be dark. There will be a moon instead of a midnight sun.

Mrs. Bronson: Shh! What was that?

(*They hear footsteps coming up the stairs. Norma pulls Mrs. Bronson into her apartment. She locks the door. The footsteps come to the door and stop.*)

Tom (*shouting from the hall*): Who's in there? (*Pause.*) I know you're there! Have you got any water? (*Pause.*) Bring some out — and hurry! I haven't got all day!

Norma (*carries the gun to the door*): Do you hear this? (*She clicks the safety release.*) That's a gun. Now get out.

Tom: Okay. I never argue with a gun.

(*Footsteps start down the stairs. Norma goes to the window. She watches the front steps of the building.*)

Norma: I don't see him coming out.

(*Mrs. Bronson opens the door to the hall to peek out. Tom bursts in. He grabs the gun from Norma before she can aim it.*)

Tom: Don't be crazy. It's too hot to play games. (*He goes to the refrigerator and takes out the water. He drinks all of it. Then he smashes the bottle against the wall.*)

Mrs. Bronson: Please. We haven't done you any harm.

Tom *(seeing Norma's paintings):* My wife used to paint. *(Suddenly, his voice is soft. He looks at the gun in his hand and puts it down.)* She was having a baby. She couldn't stand the heat. The baby lived for an hour. She died soon after that. *(His eyes fill with tears.)* I'm not a burglar. I'm a decent man. It's just this heat. I've been looking all day for some water. I didn't mean to scare you. *(Now he looks frightened.)* Why doesn't it just end? Why don't we just burn up? *(He staggers out the door.)*

Norma *(helping Mrs. Bronson over to the couch):* Sit down. I've got a surprise for you. *(She shows Mrs. Bronson a painting of a waterfall.)*

Mrs. Bronson: It's beautiful, Norma. All that wonderful clear water. And I love the sound of it. *(Norma stares at her.)* Can't you hear it?

Norma: Well . . . uh, no.

Mrs. Bronson: It's a wonderful sound. And the water is so cool. Let's take a swim, Norma. When I was a girl. . . . *(She faints from the heat.)*

Norma: Mrs. Bronson! *(She kneels by the couch and fans Mrs. Bronson. Then she notices that the paint is melting off the canvas.)* The colors — no! *(She faints, too.)*

(The lights go out. Then a lamp comes on. Norma is in bed. Dr. Coles and Mrs. Bronson are standing by her. They are wearing heavy coats and gloves.)

Dr. Coles: She's coming out of it now. Miss Smith?

Norma *(opens her eyes):* Yes?

Dr. Coles: You've had a very high fever. But it's over now.

Norma: Fever?

Mrs. Bronson: We were worried, Norma. You were very sick, but you'll be fine now. Won't she, Dr. Coles?

Dr. Coles: Of course. *(But he doesn't smile.)* Just get as much sleep as you can.

(He leaves the room. Mrs. Bronson follows him.)

Mrs. Bronson: Thank you for coming.

Dr. Coles: I'm afraid I won't be back. I'm trying to get my family south. The highways are jammed with cars and snow. But I have a friend who has a plane.

Mrs. Bronson: They say on the radio that Miami is a little warmer.

Dr. Coles: So they say. It's crazy in a way. We're just putting things off for a little. We'll all get it sooner or later, no matter how far south we go.

Mrs. Bronson: A scientist on the radio said it would get colder each day. We're moving farther and farther from the sun. There's no stopping it.

Dr. Coles: Well, good-bye. Good luck.

(He leaves. Mrs. Bronson goes back to Norma.)

Norma: I had such an awful dream.

Mrs. Bronson: It must have been because of the fever.

Norma: The sun was out at noon and at midnight. There wasn't any night at all. And it was horribly hot! Isn't it wonderful to have darkness and coolness?

Mrs. Bronson: Yes, dear, if you say so. Just rest now. You're going to need all your strength.

READING COMPREHENSION

Select the best choice to complete each statement. Then write the entire sentence on your paper.

1. People were moving north _____.
   a. for new jobs and more money
   b. to explore Canada's mountains
   c. to escape from the increasing heat

2. The most likely reason Tom smashed the bottle against the wall was that he _____.
   a. didn't want others to use it
   b. knew it contained his germs
   c. was angry and frustrated

3. The heat and the crazy things that seemed to happen were a result of _____.
   a. too many people on the roads
   b. overexposure to the sun
   c. Norma's feverish dreams

4. People moved south because _____.
   a. they were already tired of Canada
   b. there were fewer problems there
   c. the earth was really getting colder

For Discussion

1. Why do you think the painting on the easel had such a large sun? What were some of the problems people seemed to be facing as the play began? How were they dealing with these problems? What would you have done?

2. As you read the first part of the play, what seemed to be the cause of what was going on? At what point did you realize that you might have been wrong?

UNDERSTANDING LITERATURE

Conflict. Conflict in literature is the struggle between two opposing forces. In "The Midnight Sun," the major conflict is between people and nature. The conflict of a person against nature often provides interesting insights into how people cope when they are dealing with forces greater than themselves. In "The Midnight Sun," person against person conflict arises out of the major struggle between people and the forces of nature.

Divide your paper into two columns — Person vs. Person and Person vs. Nature. Write each of the following statements in the correct column. Some statements may apply to both columns.

1. "(. . . *Norma pulls Mrs. Bronson into her apartment. She locks the door.* . . .)"

2. "(. . . *He grabs the gun from Norma before she can aim it.*)"

3. "**Tom:** I've been looking all day for some water."

4. "**Dr. Coles:** We'll all get it sooner or later, no matter how far south we go."

Writing

Imagine that you and one friend are the last two people left in your neighborhood. Everyone else has left because of some natural disaster. Write a page in your diary telling about one day. Briefly mention the conditions that made everyone else leave. Then tell some details about how you are managing to cope.

Four poems by Robert Frost

Robert Frost (1874–1963) is perhaps the best-known modern American poet. He won the Pulitzer Prize four times.

Frost suffered many hardships as a child. He became a farmer at the age of 25. He worked the land and wrote poetry in his spare time for many years. When he was 38 he sold the farm and moved with his family to England. There he hoped to win the fame he had not yet found in the United States. After some years, his poetry was published. It brought him immediate success. Frost returned to the United States an established poet. He spent the rest of his life writing poetry and teaching at colleges and universities in his beloved New England.

President John F. Kennedy described Frost shortly after the poet's death. "He was," Kennedy said, "supremely two things: an artist and an American. In honoring Robert Frost we can pay honor to the deepest source of our national strength."

Here are four poems that reveal Frost's strengths as a poet and as a man.

Fire and Ice

by Robert Frost

Some say the world will end in fire.
Some say in ice
From what I've tasted of desire
I hold with those who favor fire.
But if it had to perish twice
I think I know enough of hate
To say that for destruction ice
Is also great
And would suffice.

1. The poet compares hate to ice. How are these two things alike?

2. Is the poet really worried about the end of the world? Explain why or why not.

3. Frost says that "for destruction ice . . . would suffice." What does the word *suffice* mean in this poem?

Acquainted With the Night

by Robert Frost

I have been one acquainted with the
   night.
I have walked out in rain — and back
   in rain.
I have outwalked the furthest city light.

I have looked down the saddest city lane.
I have passed by the watchman on his
   beat
And dropped my eyes, unwilling to
   explain.

Nighthawks, Edward Hopper, 1942

I have stood still and stopped the sound
    of feet
When far away an interrupted cry
Came over houses from another street,

But not to call me back or say
good-by;
And further still at an unearthly
height
One luminary clock against the sky

Proclaimed the time was neither wrong
    nor right.
I have been one acquainted with the night.

---

1. Why did the person in the poem avoid the watchman? Use lines from the poem to explain.

2. What do you think Frost meant by the words "acquainted with the night"? Explain your answer.

Our Hold on the Planet

by Robert Frost

We asked for rain. It didn't flash and roar.
It didn't lose its temper at our demand
And blow a gale. It didn't misunderstand
And give us more than our spokesman bargained for;
And just because we owned to a wish for rain,
Send us a flood and bid us be damned and drown.
It gently threw us a glittering shower down,
And when we had taken that into the roots of grain,
It threw us another and then another still
Till the spongy soil again was natal wet.
We may doubt the just proportion of good to ill.
There is much in nature against us. But we forget;
Take nature altogether since time began,
Including human nature, in peace and war.
And it must be a little more in favor of man,
Say a fraction of one percent at the very least,
Or our number living wouldn't be steadily more,
Our hold on the planet wouldn't have so increased.

---

1. What lines in the poem describe how nature has helped people? Does Frost believe that nature is more cruel or kind to people? Explain your answer.

2. What lines in the poem suggest that Frost sees people as a mixture of good and bad? What lines suggest that people are more good than bad?

The Road Not Taken

by Robert Frost

Two roads diverged in a yellow wood,
And sorry I could not travel both
And be one traveler, long I stood
And looked down one as far as I could
To where it bent in the undergrowth;

Then took the other as just as fair,
And having perhaps the better claim,
Because it was grassy and wanted wear;
Though as for that, the passing there
Had worn them really about the same,

And both that morning equally lay
In leaves no step had trodden black
Oh, I kept the first for another day!
Yet knowing how way leads on to way,
I doubted if I should ever come back.

I shall be telling this with a sigh
Somewhere ages and ages hence:
Two roads diverged in a wood, and I —
I took the one less traveled by
And that has made all the difference.

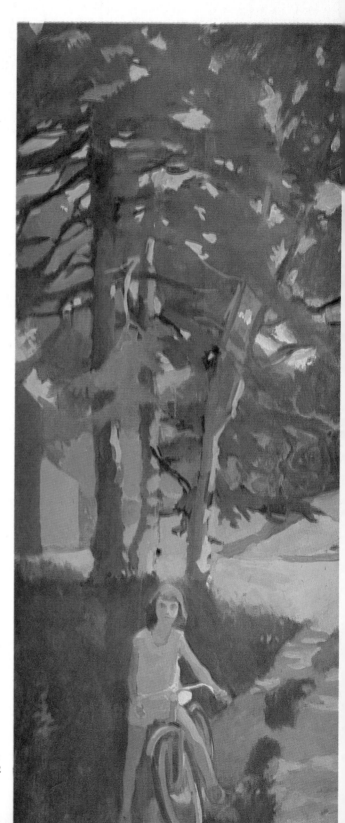

---

1. Frost chose the path "less traveled by."
What does that tell you about him?

2. Do you think this choice was easy? Use
examples from the poem to explain your
answer.

The Garden Road, Fairfield Porter, 1962

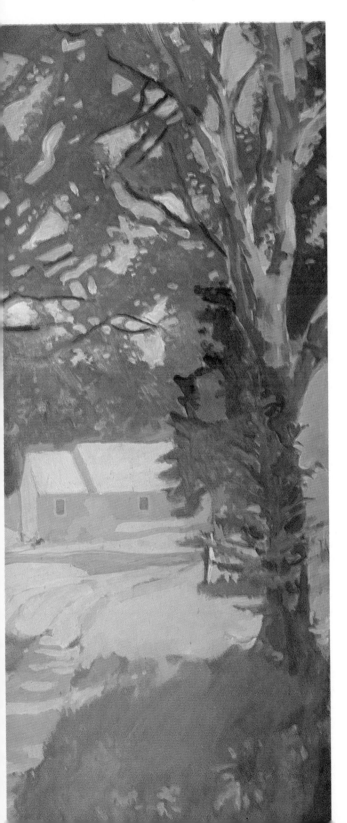

READING COMPREHENSION

Select the best choice to complete each statement. Then write the entire sentence on your paper.

1. In "Fire and Ice," Robert Frost's message is that _____.
   a. the world will burn itself up
   b. either desire or hate can destroy the world
   c. people must fight extreme temperatures

2. In "Acquainted With the Night," the poet passes the watchman by because he _____.
   a. is afraid his crime will be noticed
   b. is in a hurry to get home
   c. doesn't wish to share his feelings

3. "Our Hold on the Planet" says that nature favors humanity because _____.
   a. the number of people has increased
   b. floods and gales are rare
   c. people always have their doubts

4. "The Road Not Taken" describes how the poet made a choice but _____.
   a. wished he could have taken both roads
   b. knew immediately it was wrong
   c. changed his mind after a while

For Discussion

1. In "Fire and Ice," to what human emotions does Frost compare fire and ice? What do you think he is really talking about when he says, "Some say the world will end . . ."? Explain your answer.

2. What is the mood of the poem "Acquainted With the Night"? What particular lines make you feel that way?

3. What examples does Frost give in "Our Hold on the Planet" to suggest that the balance in nature (at least slightly) favors man? Do you agree with him? Why or why not?

4. In "The Road Not Taken," how did the poet feel about having to choose between two roads? Why did he make the choice he did?

5. What does "The Road Not Taken" tell us about life? Do you agree with the poet's message? Explain your answer.

UNDERSTANDING LITERATURE

Person-Versus-Self Conflict. In a work of literature — whether it be a story, poem, or play — a person may face external conflict. A person may struggle with nature, other people, conditions in society, the supernatural, or the unknown.

Some of the most important conflicts in literature — as in life — take place, however, within a person's mind or between opposing feelings. The struggle with oneself is a never-ending one.

Robert Frost's poems contain many examples of inner conflict, and the ways that conflict might be resolved.

On your paper, answer the following questions about conflict in the poems by Robert Frost that you have just read.

1. Although it talks about fire, ice, and the end of the world, "Fire and Ice" is not only about humanity's conflict with nature. What two things do you think the poet learned about from his own inner conflict?

2. What sort of personal struggle might have caused the poet to become "acquainted with the night"?

3. What was the personal struggle the poet described in "The Road Not Taken"? How did he resolve this conflict?

4. After the poet chooses one road over another, he said:

Oh, I kept the first for another day!
Yet knowing how way leads on to way,
I doubted if I should ever come back.

What do these lines suggest about a person getting a second chance to resolve a personal conflict? Do you agree with what Frost is saying? Why or why not?

Writing

The poem "The Road Not Taken" by Robert Frost is about personal choices and decision making. Think about your own life and a choice you had to make between two paths open to you. Write one paragraph that explains what the two paths were, which one you took, and the reasons for your choice. Would you take the same path if you had it to do over again? Write a second paragraph telling whether or not you think your choice was the right one, and why.

Georgia O'Keeffe

by Joan Didion

Joan Didion (1934—) is noted for writing essays, fiction, and screenplays that comment on contemporary life. This essay about modern American painter Georgia O'Keeffe expresses Didion's ideas about the way a painter or writer comes to create a work of art.

Georgia O'Keeffe, Alfred Stieglitz

"Where I was born and where and how I have lived is unimportant," Georgia O'Keeffe told us in the book of paintings and words published in her ninetieth year on earth. She seemed to be advising us to forget the beautiful face in the Stieglitz photographs. "It is what I have done with where I have been that should be of interest."

I recall an August afternoon in Chicago in 1973 when I took my daughter, then seven, to see what Georgia O'Keeffe had done with where she had been. One of the vast O'Keeffe "Sky Above Clouds" canvasses floated over the back stairs in the Chicago Art Institute that day. My daughter looked at it once, ran to the landing, and kept on looking. "Who drew it?" she whispered after a while. I told her. "I need to talk to her," she said finally.

My daughter was making a basic assumption about people and the work they do. She was assuming that the glory she saw in the work reflected a glory in its maker. That the painting was the painter as the poem is the poet, she thought — every word chosen or rejected, every brushstroke laid or not laid down — betrayed one's character. *Style is character*. I recall being pleased not only that my daughter responded to style as character but that it was Georgia O'Keeffe's particular style to which she responded. This was a hard woman who had imposed her 192 square feet of clouds on Chicago.

"Hardness" has not been in our century a quality much admired in women, nor in the past 20 years has it even been in official favor for men. When hardness

The Mountain, New Mexico, Georgia O'Keeffe, 1977

Cow's Skull: Red, White, and Blue, Georgia O'Keeffe, 1931

"Cow's Skull: Red, White and Blue," owned by the Metropolitan — as the product of quite deliberate orneriness. "I thought of the city men I had been seeing in the East," she wrote. "They talked so often of writing the Great American Novel — the Great American Play — the Great American Poetry. . . . So as I was painting my cow's head on blue I thought to myself, 'I'll make it an American painting. They will not think it great with the red stripes down the sides — Red, White and Blue — but they will notice it.' "

The city men. The men. They. The words crop up again and again as this astonishing woman tells us what was on her mind when she was making her astonishing paintings. It was those city men who stood accused of sentimentalizing her flowers: "I made you take time to look at what I saw. When you took time to really notice my flower you hung all your feelings about flowers on my flower. You write about my flower as if I think and see what you think and see — and I don't." *And I don't.* Imagine those words spoken, and the sound you hear is *don't tread on me.* "They" believed it impossible to paint New York, so Georgia O'Keeffe painted New York. "They" didn't think much of her bright color, so she made it brighter. "They" yearned toward Europe so she went to Texas, and then New Mexico.

Georgia O'Keeffe seems to have been equipped early with a strong sense of who she was and a fairly clear understanding of what she would be required to do to prove it. On the surface her upbringing was conventional. She was a child on the

surfaces in the very old we tend to transform it into "crustiness" or eccentricity. On the evidence of her work and what she has said about it, Georgia O'Keeffe is neither "crusty" nor eccentric. She is simply hard, a straight shooter, a woman open to what she sees. This is a woman who in 1939 could advise her admirers that they were missing her point. Their appreciation of her famous flowers was merely sentimental. "When I paint a red hill," she observed coolly in the catalog for an exhibition that year, "you say it is too bad that I don't always paint flowers. A flower touches almost everyone's heart. A red hill doesn't touch everyone's heart." This is a woman who could describe one of her most well-known paintings — the

Wisconsin prairie. She played with china dolls. She painted watercolors with cloudy skies because sunlight was too hard to paint. With her brother and sisters she listened every night to her mother read stories of the Wild West, of Texas, of Kit Carson and Billy the Kid. She told adults that she wanted to be an artist and was embarrassed when they asked what kind of artist she wanted to be: She had no idea "what kind." She had no idea what artists did. She had never seen a picture that interested her, other than a pen-and-ink Maid of Athens in one of her mother's books, some Mother Goose illustrations, and the painting of Arabs on horseback that hung in her grandmother's parlor. At 13 she was mortified when a teacher corrected her drawing. At Chatham Episcopal Institute in Virginia she painted lilacs and sneaked time alone to walk out to where she could see the line of the Blue Ridge Mountains on the horizon. At the Art Students League in New York one of her fellow students advised her that since he would be a great painter and she would end up teaching painting in a girls' school, any work of hers was less important than modeling for him. Another painted over her work to show her how the Impressionists did trees. She had not before heard how the Impressionists did trees and she did not much care.

At 24 she left all those opinions behind and went for the first time to live in Texas, where there were no trees to paint and no one to tell her how not to paint them. In Texas there was only the horizon she craved. In Texas she had her sister Claudia

with her for a while. In the late afternoons they would walk away from town and toward the horizon and watch the evening star come out. "That evening star fascinated me," she wrote. "It was in some way very exciting to me. My sister had a

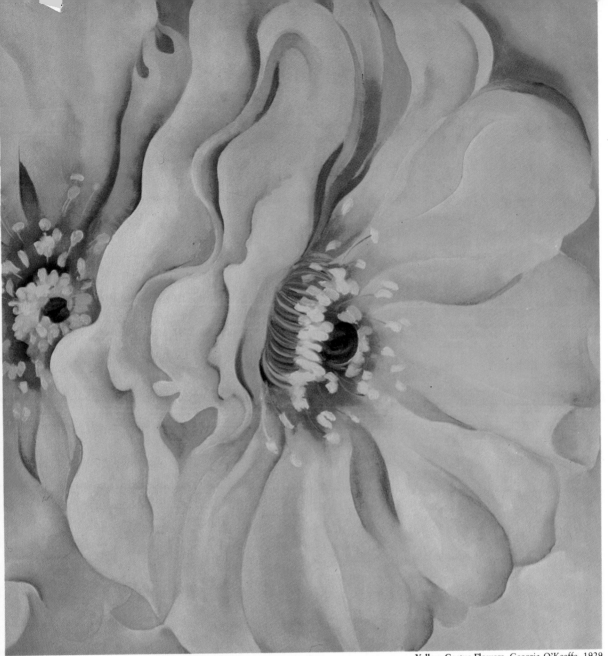

Yellow Cactus Flowers, Georgia O'Keeffe, 1929

gun, and as we walked she would throw bottles into the air and shoot as many as she could before they hit the ground. I had nothing but to walk into nowhere and the wide sunset space with the star. Ten watercolors were made from that star."

In a way one's interest is compelled as much by the sister Claudia with the gun as by the painter Georgia with the star, but only the painter left us this shining record. Ten watercolors were made from that star.

READING COMPREHENSION

Read each question below. Then write the best answer on your paper.

1. O'Keeffe decided to become an artist _____.

    a. as a small child
    b. when she was in high school
    c. at the age of 90

2. O'Keeffe used bright colors because _____.

    a. other artists advised her to do so
    b. she ran out of pastel paints
    c. she liked painting that way

3. O'Keeffe moved to Texas because _____.

    a. she got a job as an art teacher there
    b. she wanted to paint in her own way
    c. she could not afford Paris

4. The author admires O'Keeffe most for _____.

    a. her talent as a painter
    b. her independent way of thinking and creating
    c. her knowledge of art history

For Discussion

1. Why did Didion use so many quotes from O'Keeffe in this essay? How would the essay have been different if Didion hadn't used these quotes?

2. Describe O'Keeffe as a person. Do you think she would be a good art teacher?

3. O'Keeffe said, "A flower touches almost everyone's heart. A red hill doesn't. . . ." Do you agree?

UNDERSTANDING LITERATURE

Conflict in an Essay. Conflict occurs in real life as well as in literature. Joan Didion wrote about the conflicts Georgia O'Keeffe faced. Her essay focuses on the theme "Style is character." The conflicts described in this essay are not the conflicts of person against self, but conflicts between a person and the expectations of society. In O'Keeffe's case, "society" is the world of established artists.

On your paper, write one sentence that tells what each quote below reveals about O'Keeffe's character. Then write another sentence telling what the quote reveals about her style as an artist.

1. " 'You write about my flower as if I think and see what you think and see — and I don't.' "

2. " 'They' believed it impossible to paint New York, so Georgia O'Keeffe painted New York."

3. "[She] would walk . . . toward the horizon and watch the evening star come out. 'That evening star fascinated me,' she wrote. . . . 'Ten watercolors were made from that star.' "

Writing

Choose one thing that O'Keeffe has painted: a flower, a cow's skull, a big city, the evening star, or clouds. Describe how you would paint it if you were an artist. Describe the colors you would use. Tell the feelings or ideas you would want your painting to express.

Story From Bear Country

by Leslie Marmon Silko

You will know
when you walk
in bear country
By the silence
flowing swiftly between the juniper trees
by the sundown colors of sandrock
all round you.

You may smell damp earth
scratched away
from yucca roots
You may hear snorts and growls
slow and massive sounds
from caves
in the cliffs high above you.

It is difficult to explain
how they call you
All but a few who went to them
left behind families
                grandparents
                and sons
                a good life

The problem is
you will never want to return
their beauty will overcome your memory
like winter sun
melting ice shadows from snow

And you will remain with them
locked forever inside yourself
                your eyes will see you
                dark shaggy and
                    thick.

We can send bear priests
loping after you
their medicine bags
bouncing against their chests
Naked legs painted black
bear claw necklaces
rattling against
their capes of blue spruce.

They will follow your trail
into the narrow canyon
through the blue-gray mountain sage
to the clearing
where you stopped to look back
and saw only bear tracks
behind you.

When they call
faint memories
will writhe around your heart
and startle you with their distance.
But the others will listen
because bear priests sing

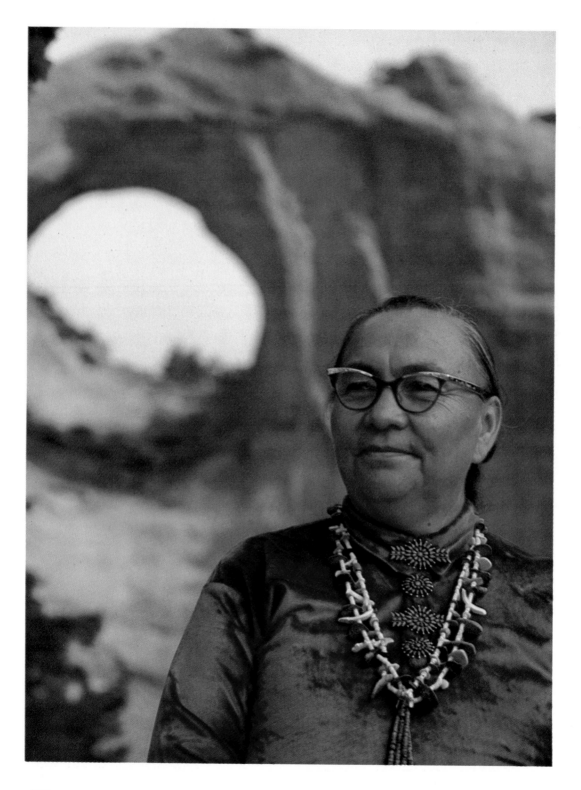

beautiful songs.
They must
if they are ever to call you back.

They will try to bring you
step by step
back to the place you stopped
and found only bear prints in the sand
where your feet had been.

Whose voice is this?
You may wonder
hearing this story when
after all
you are alone
hiking in these canyons and hills
while your wife and sons are waiting
back at the car for you.

But you have been listening to me
for some time now
from the very beginning in fact
and you are alone in this canyon of
    stillness
not even cedar birds flutter.
See, the sun is going down now
the sandrock is washed in its colors
Don't be afraid
        we love you
        we've been calling
          you
        all this time

Go ahead
turn around
see the shape
of your footprints
in the sand.

---

1. What are the sounds, smells, and colors that let a person know he or she is in bear country? What do people who answer the call usually leave behind? Why do you think they do that?

2. What happens to the person the poet is speaking to in this poem? What clues can you find in the poem that lead you to this conclusion? Do you think there's more than one

explanation for what happened? Explain your answer.

3. One way to understand the message of "Story from Bear Country" is to view the poem as an expression of the conflict between a person and fate, or destiny. Do you think what happened to the person in the poem was inevitable? Or do you think he had a choice? Explain your answer.

The Fog Horn

by Ray Bradbury

Ray Bradbury (1920—) is one of America's best-known authors of science fiction. This story is not set in the future or on another planet. It deals with the mystery of the sea. What if the ancient legends of monsters from the depths of the sea came true . . . ?

Out there in the cold water, far from land we waited every night for the coming of the fog, and it came, and we oiled the brass machinery and lit the fog light up in the stone tower. Feeling like two birds in the gray sky, McDunn and I sent the light touching out, red, then white, then red again, to eye the lonely ships. And if they did not see our lights, then there was always our Voice, the great deep cry of our Fog Horn shuddering through the rags of mist to startle the gulls away like decks of scattered cards and make the waves turn high and foam.

"It's a lonely life, but you're used to it now, aren't you?" asked McDunn.

"Yes," I said. "You're a good talker, thank the Lord."

"Well, it's your turn on land tomorrow," he said, smiling, "to dance with the ladies and drink gin."

"What do you think, McDunn, when I leave you out here alone?"

"On the mysteries of the sea." McDunn lit his pipe. It was quarter past seven of a cold November evening, the heat on, the light switching its tail in two hundred directions, the Fog Horn bumbling in the high throat of the tower. There wasn't a town for a hundred miles down the coast, just a road which came lonely through dead country to the sea, with few cars on it, a stretch of two miles of cold water out to our rock, and rare few ships.

"The mysteries of the sea," said McDunn thoughtfully. "You know, the ocean's the biggest damned snowflake ever? It rolls and swells a thousand shapes and colors, no two alike. Strange. One night, years ago, I was here alone, when all of the fish of the sea surfaced out there. Something made them swim in and lie in the bay, sort of trembling and staring up at the tower light going red, white, red, white across them so I could see their funny eyes. I turned cold. They were like a big peacock's tail moving out there until midnight. Then, without so much as a sound, they slipped away, the million of them was gone. I kind of think maybe, in some sort of way, they came all those miles to worship. Strange. But think how the tower must look to them, standing seventy feet above the water, the Godlight flashing out from it, and the tower declaring itself with a monster voice. They never came back, those fish, but don't you think for a while they thought they were in the Presence?"

I shivered. I looked out at the long gray lawns of the sea stretching away into nothing and nowhere.

"Oh, the sea's full." McDunn puffed his pipe nervously, blinking. He had been nervous all day and hadn't said why. "For all our engines and so-called submarines, it'll be ten thousand centuries before we set foot on the real bottom of the sunken lands, in the fairy kingdoms there, and know real terror. Think of it, it's still the year 300,000 Before Christ down under there. While we've paraded around with trumpets, lopping off each other's countries and heads, they have been living beneath the sea twelve miles deep and cold in a time as old as the beard of a comet."

"Yes, it's an old world."

"Come on. I got something special I been saving up to tell you."

We ascended the eighty steps, talking and taking our time. At the top, McDunn switched off the room lights so there'd be no reflection in the plate glass. The great eye of the light was humming, turning easily in its oiled socket. The Fog Horn was blowing steadily, once every fifteen seconds.

"Sounds like an animal, don't it?" McDunn nodded to himself. "A big lonely animal crying in the night. Sitting here on the edge of ten billion years calling out to the Deeps, I'm here, I'm here, I'm here. And the Deeps do answer, yes, they do. You been here now for three months, Johnny, so I better prepare you. About this time of year," he said, studying the murk and fog, "something comes to visit the lighthouse."

"The swarms of fish like you said?"

"No, this is something else. I've put off telling you because you might think I'm daft. But tonight's the latest I can put it off, for if my calendar's marked right from last year, tonight's the night it comes. I won't go into detail, you'll have to see it yourself. Just sit down there. If you want, tomorrow you can pack your duffel and take the motorboat into land and get your car parked there at the dinghy pier on the cape and drive on back to some little inland town and keep your lights burning nights, I won't question or blame you. It's happened three years now, and this is the only time anyone's been here with me to verify it. You wait and watch."

Half an hour passed with only a few whispers between us. When we grew tired waiting, McDunn began describing some of his ideas to me. He had some theories about the Fog Horn itself.

"One day many years ago a man walked along and stood in the sound of the ocean on a cold sunless shore and said, 'We need a voice to call across the water, to warn ships; I'll make one. I'll make a voice like all of time and all of the fog that ever was; I'll make a voice that is like an empty bed beside you all night long, and like an empty house when you open the door, and like trees in autumn with no leaves. A sound like the birds flying south, crying, and a sound like November wind and the sea on the hard, cold shore. I'll make a sound that's so alone that no one can miss it, that whoever hears it will weep in their souls, and hearths will seem warmer, and being inside will seem better to all who hear it in the distant towns. I'll make me a sound and an apparatus and they'll call it a Fog Horn and whoever hears it will know the sadness of eternity and the briefness of life.' "

The Fog Horn blew.

"I made up that story," said McDunn quietly, "to try to explain why this thing keeps coming back to the lighthouse every year. The Fog Horn calls it, I think, and it comes. . . ."

"But — " I said.

"Sssst!" said McDunn. "There!" He nodded out to the Deeps.

Something was swimming toward the lighthouse tower.

It was a cold night, as I have said; the high tower was cold, the light coming and going and the Fog Horn calling and calling through the raveling mist. You couldn't see far and you couldn't see plain, but there was the deep sea moving on its way about the night earth, flat and quiet, the color of gray mud, and here were the two of us alone in the high tower, and there, far out at first, was a ripple, followed by a wave, a rising, a bubble, a bit of froth. And then, from the surface of the cold sea came a head, a large head, dark-colored, with immense eyes, and then a neck. And then — not a body — but more neck and more! The head rose a full forty feet above the water on a slender and beautiful dark neck. Only then did the body, like a little

island of black coral and shells, and crayfish, drip up from the subterranean. There was a flicker of tail. In all, from head to tip of tail, I estimated the monster at ninety or a hundred feet.

I don't know what I said. I said something.

"Steady, boy, steady," whispered McDunn.

"It's impossible!" I said.

"No, Johnny, we're impossible. It's like it always was ten million years ago. It hasn't changed. It's us and the land that've changed, become impossible. Us!"

It swam slowly and with a great dark majesty out in the icy water, far away. The fog came and went about it, momentarily erasing its shape. One of the monster eyes caught and held and flashed back our immense light, red, white, red, white, like a disk held high and sending a message in primeval code. It was as silent as the fog through which it swam.

"It's a dinosaur of some sort!" I crouched down, holding to the stair rail.

"Yes, one of the tribe."

"But they died out!"

"No, only hid away in the Deeps. Deep, deep down in the deepest Deeps. Isn't that a word now, Johnny, a real word, it says so much: the Deeps. There's all the coldness and darkness and deepness in the world in a word like that."

"What'll we do?"

"Do? We got our job, we can't leave. Besides, we're safer here than in any boat trying to get to land. That thing's as big as a destroyer and almost as swift."

"But here, why does it come here?"

The next moment I had my answer.

The Fog Horn blew.

And the monster answered.

A cry came across a million years of water and mist. A cry so anguished and alone that it shuddered in my head and my body. The monster cried out at the tower. The Fog Horn blew. The monster roared again. The Fog Horn blew. The monster opened its great toothed mouth and the sound that came from it was the sound of the Fog Horn itself. Lonely and vast and far away. The sound of isolation, a viewless sea, a cold night, apartness. That was the sound.

"Now," whispered McDunn, "do you know why it comes here?"

I nodded.

"All year long, Johnny, that poor monster there lying far out, a thousand miles at sea, and twenty miles deep maybe, biding its time, perhaps it's a million years old, this one creature. Think of it, waiting a million years, could you wait that long? Maybe it's the last of its kind. I sort of think that's true. Anyway, here come men on land and build this lighthouse, five years ago. And set up their Fog Horn and sound it and sound it out toward the place where you bury yourself in sleep and sea memories of a world where there were thousands like yourself, but now you're alone, all alone in a world not made for you, a world where you have to hide.

"But the sound of the Fog Horn comes and goes, comes and goes, and you stir from the muddy bottom of the Deeps, and your eyes open like the lenses of two-foot cameras and you move, slow, slow, for you have the ocean sea on your shoulders, heavy. But that Fog Horn comes through a thousand miles of water, faint and familiar and the furnace in your belly stokes up, and you begin to rise, slow, slow. You feed yourself on great slakes of cod and minnow, on rivers of jellyfish, and you rise slow through the autumn months, through September when the fogs started, through October with more fog and the horn still calling you on, and then, late in November, after pressurizing yourself day by day, a few feet higher every hour, you are near the surface, and still alive. You've got to go slow; if you surfaced all at once you'd explode. So it takes you all of three months to surface, and then a number of days to swim through the cold water to the lighthouse. And there you are, out there, in the night, Johnny, the biggest damn monster in creation. And here's the lighthouse calling to you, with a long neck like your neck sticking way up out of the water, and a body like your body, and, most important of all, a voice like your voice. Do you understand now, Johnny, do you understand?"

The Fog Horn blew.

The monster answered.

I saw it all, I knew it all — the million years of waiting alone, for someone to come back who never came back. The million years of isolation at the bottom of the sea, the insanity of time there, while the skies cleared of reptile-birds, the swamp dried on the continent continental lands, the sloths and saber-tooths had their day and sank in tar pits, and men ran like white ants upon the hills.

The Fog Horn blew.

"Last year," said McDunn, "that creature swam round and round, round and round, all night. Not coming too near, puzzled, I'd say. Afraid, maybe. And a bit angry after coming all this way. But the next day, unexpectedly, the fog lifted, the sun came out fresh, the sky was as blue as a painting. And the monster swam off away from the heat and the silence and didn't come back. I suppose it's been brooding on it for a year now, thinking it over from every which way."

The monster was only a hundred yards off now, it and the Fog Horn crying at each other. As the lights hit them, the monster's eyes were fire and ice, fire and ice.

"That's life for you," said McDunn. "Someone always waiting for someone who never comes home. Always someone loving some thing more than that thing loves them. And after a while you want to destroy whatever that thing is, so it can't hurt you no more."

The monster was rushing at the lighthouse.

The Fog Horn blew.

"Let's see what happens," said McDunn.

He switched the Fog Horn off.

The ensuing minutes of silence were so intense that we could hear our hearts pounding in the glassed area of the tower, could hear the slow greased turn of the light.

The monster stopped and froze. Its great lantern eyes blinked. Its mouth gaped. It gave a sort of rumble, like a volcano. It twitched its head this way and that, as if to seek the sounds now dwindled off into the fog. It peered at the lighthouse. It rumbled again. Then its eyes caught fire.

It reared up, threshed the water, and rushed at the tower, its eyes filled with angry torment.

"McDunn!" I cried. "Switch on the horn!"

McDunn fumbled with the switch. But even as he flicked it on, the monster was rearing up. I had a glimpse of its gigantic paws, fishskin glittering in webs between the finger-like projections, clawing at the tower. The huge eye on the right side of its anguished head glittered before me like a caldron into which I might drop, screaming. The tower shook. The Fog Horn cried; the monster cried. It seized the tower and gnashed at the glass, which shattered in upon us.

McDunn seized my arm. "Downstairs!"

The tower rocked, trembled, and started to give. The Fog Horn and the monster roared. We stumbled and half fell down the stairs. "Quick!"

We reached the bottom as the tower buckled down toward us. We ducked under the stairs into the small stone cellar. There were a thousand concussions as the rocks rained down; the Fog Horn stopped abruptly. The monster crashed upon the tower. The tower fell. We knelt together, McDunn and I, holding tight, while our world exploded.

Then it was over, and there was nothing but darkness and the wash of the sea on the raw stones.

That and the other sound.

"Listen," said McDunn quietly. "Listen."

We waited a moment. And then I began to hear it. First a great mourned sucking of air, and then the lament, the bewilder-

ment, the loneliness of the great monster, folded over and upon us, above us so that the sickening reek of its body filled the air, a stone's thickness away from our cellar. The monster gasped and cried. The tower was gone. The light was gone. The thing that had called to it across a million years was gone. And the monster was opening its mouth and sending out great sounds. The sounds of a Fog Horn, again and again. And ships far at sea, not finding the light, not seeing anything, but passing and hearing late that night, must've thought: There it is, the lonely sound, the Lonesome Bay horn. All's well. We've rounded the cape.

And so it went for the rest of that night.

The sun was hot and yellow the next afternoon when the rescuers came out to dig us from our stoned-under celler.

"It fell apart, is all," said Mr. McDunn gravely. "We had a few bad knocks from the waves and it just crumbled." He pinched my arm.

There was nothing to see. The ocean was calm, the sky blue. The only thing was a great algaic stink from the green matter that covered the fallen tower stones and the shore rocks. Flies buzzed about. The ocean washed empty on the shore.

The next year they built a new lighthouse, but by that time I had a job in the little town and a wife and a good small warm house that glowed yellow on autumn nights, the door locked, the chimney puffing smoke. As for McDunn, he was master of the new lighthouse, built to his own specifications, out of steel-reinforced concrete. "Just in case," he said.

The new lighthouse was ready in No-vember. I drove down alone one evening late and parked my car and looked across the gray waters and listened to the new horn sounding, once, twice, three, four times a minute far out there, by itself.

The monster?

It never came back.

"It's gone away," said McDunn. "It's gone back to the Deeps. It's learned you can't love anything too much in this world. It's gone into the deepest Deeps to wait another million years. Ah, the poor thing! Waiting out there, and waiting out there, while man comes and goes on this pitiful little planet. Waiting and waiting."

I sat in my car, listening. I couldn't see the lighthouse or the light sending out in Lonesome Bay. I could only hear the Horn, the Horn, the Horn. It sounded like the monster calling.

I sat there wishing there was something I could say.

READING COMPREHENSION

Select the best choice to complete each statement. Then write the entire sentence on your paper.

1. The purpose of the fog horn was to _____.
   a. create a familiar sound
   b. frighten large sea monsters
   c. warn the ships in a fog

2. When alone, McDunn's thoughts turned to _____.
   a. his friends and family on shore
   b. the mysteries of the sea
   c. frightening past experiences

3. The sound of the fog horn was like
_____.

    a. a call to prayer
    b. lonely crying in the night
    c. warnings for the birds

4. The monster attacked the tower
_____.

    a. to save its own life
    b. when the fog horn stopped calling
    c. because the tower was in the way

5. McDunn's explanation for the monster's failure to return was that _____.
    a. so many people frightened it away
    b. it became extinct
    c. it learned not to love anything too much

For Discussion

1. What would it be like to live out in the lighthouse with the fog horn? How would having that much time alone affect a person? Explain your answer.

2. What story did McDunn offer to explain the creature's annual appearance? Do you believe it? Why or why not?

UNDERSTANDING LITERATURE

Conflict. In many things you read, identifying and understanding the conflict is quite simple. In other works you will read, however, it may not be that clearcut.

Although one of the opposing forces in a conflict is usually a person, some stories do present conflict between non-human forces. The reader can often learn truths about human life from this struggle.

"The Fog Horn" contains multiple, complex conflicts, not all of which involve humans. Answer the following questions about conflict in "The Fog Horn" on your paper in complete sentences.

1. What is the basic struggle between man and nature that the lighthouse with its fog horn was designed to deal with? Was this conflict ever resolved? Explain.

2. Explain McDunn's efforts to understand the sea creature. Could you describe those efforts as a person vs. the unknown? A person vs. self? Explain.

3. Describe briefly the struggle between the sea creature and the fog horn. Why was the creature drawn to the sound? How was the conflict resolved? What lesson can humans learn from this?

4. "That's life for you," said McDunn. ". . . Always someone loving some thing more than that thing loves them. And after a while you want to destroy whatever that thing is, so it can't hurt you no more."

Between what forces are the conflicts suggested by McDunn's words? Explain your answer.

Writing
Pretend you are a resident of the lighthouse in "The Fog Horn," and that you keep a diary of your experiences. Write three entries: one for a day while you are waiting for the creature to return; one for the day the creature does return; and one for the day after the creature has left again.

Section Review

VOCABULARY

Context Clues. The way a word is used in a sentence or paragraph can give you important information about what the word means. The word-meaning clues you get from the rest of a sentence or paragraph are called context clues.

Each of the following passages from "The Fog Horn" contains context clues to help you with the meaning of the italicized words. Read each passage carefully. Then write each italicized word and its definition on your paper. Check your definitions in a dictionary to see how well you used the context.

1. "I've put off telling you because you might think I'm *daft*. But tonight's the latest I can put it off. . . . It's happened three years now, and this is the only time anyone's been here with me to *verify* it."

2. "The monster opened its great toothed mouth and the sound that came from it was the sound of the Fog Horn itself. Lonely and vast and far away. The sound of *isolation*, a viewless sea, a cold night, apartness."

3. "He switched the Fog Horn off. The *ensuing* minutes of silence were so *intense* that we could hear our hearts pounding."

READING

Cloze Exercise. Some reading tests use a technique called *cloze* to measure comprehension. In a cloze reading test, words are omitted from a selection. If you understand what you are reading, you will be able to fill in the blanks correctly. Each word you fill in will make sense in the context of the selection.

Here are some passages from "The Fog Horn." On your paper, write the word that best completes each sentence.

1. "The great eye of the light was humming, turning easily in its oiled _____."

    container   socket   rowboat

2. "The monster stopped. . . . It gave a sort of rumble, like a _____."

    volcano   rainstorm   radio

Here is a longer passage from "The Fog Horn." After reading it carefully, write the missing words on your paper. Then turn to p. 464 and see how your words compare to the ones Ray Bradbury used.

We waited a _____. And then I began to _____ it. First a great mourned sucking of _____, and then the lament, the bewilderment, the loneliness of the great _____, folded over and upon us, above _____ so that the sickening reek of its body filled the air, a stone's thickness _____ from our cellar. The monster gasped and cried. The tower was gone. The light was _____. The thing that had called to it across a million years was gone. And the _____ was _____ its mouth and sending out great sounds. The _____ of a Fog Horn.

WRITING A STORY

Each story in this book has a setting, a plot, and characters. Each story also has a conflict or problem. It may involve a struggle between two opposing forces such as person vs. person, person vs. self, person vs. nature, or person vs. machines. The checklist below shows the way these elements are organized in a good story.

☐ The beginning of the story establishes the setting, introduces the characters, and sets up the conflict.

☐ The middle of the story contains incidents that complicate the conflict and move it along.

☐ The end contains the climax, or turning point, and the conflict's resolution.

Use one poem that you have read in this section as a basis for an original short story. Use the checklist to plan your story. Think of the events of the plot in terms of a beginning, a middle, and an end that contains some resolution for the conflict.

QUIZ

The following is a quiz for Section 10. Write the answers in complete sentences on your paper.

Reading Comprehension

1. For what purpose was EPICAC originally designed? How well did it work?

2. In "Southbound on the Freeway," what were the creatures seen by tourists? What did they look like?

3. In "The Midnight Sun," how did Norma's dream differ from reality?

4. In "The Fog Horn," what was it that visited the lighthouse each year? What did McDunn do to explain this?

Understanding Literature

5. What was the person vs. nature conflict in "The Midnight Sun"? How did people attempt to deal with it?

6. In "Story from Bear Country," what type of conflict is suggested by the lines "The problem is / you will never want to return"?

7. What does Frost's poem "Our Hold on the Planet" say about the balance between people and nature?

8. In "The Fog Horn," McDunn described life as "Someone always waiting for someone who never comes home. . . . you want to destroy whatever that thing is, so it can't hurt you no more." How does the conflict between the sea creature and the lighthouse illustrate this?

COMPOSITION

1. Write a short essay answering EPICAC's questions: "What's protoplasm? How is it better than metal and glass? Is it fireproof? How long does it last?"

2. Imagine that you were a reporter during "The Midnight Sun." Write a news story about people jamming the highways to leave the area.

SECTION 11

Arthur Miller

A MODERN PLAYWRIGHT

*Once and for all you can know
there's a universe of people outside
and you're responsible to it.*

— Arthur Miller

473

Introduction

In 1945, Arthur Miller was 30 years old. He had been writing plays for 10 years. He had won some prizes, but his plays had not won any real popularity or financial success. Miller decided to write just one more play. If this play was not a success, Miller was going to give up writing plays forever. It took him two years to complete the play, but in 1947 *All My Sons* appeared on the Broadway stage. It won the New York Drama Circle Award. Suddenly Arthur Miller became one of America's most famous modern playwrights. Theaters all over America and the world have staged their own productions of *All My Sons,* as well as productions of the plays that Miller has written since. This last section is made up entirely of Miller's famous play *All My Sons.*

A Modern American Play

Miller's play *All My Sons* was successful because it powerfully combined the experiences of World War II America with the basic conflicts that people have faced in every time and place. Americans have long prided themselves on their independence. But the Americans who served in the armed forces during World War II were proudest of their cooperative spirit — the way people seemed to think first of others — and of their common cause. When Miller visited army training camps in 1944, he discovered that many Americans at war resented the Americans at home who were growing rich from the misfortunes of war. They also felt cut off from the everyday home life that did not understand the true horrors of war. *All My Sons* draws on these feelings.

With *All My Sons,* Miller also succeeded in presenting a classic dramatic struggle in everyday modern language, with everyday modern people. *All My Sons* is a distinctively American tragedy. It is not about the flaw of weakness that leads to the downfall of an ancient king or prince, it is about the tragedy of the common man. Miller wrote that "the tragic feeling is evoked in us when we are in the presence of a character who is ready to lay down his life, if need be, to secure one thing — his sense of personal dignity." Many people think that tragedies reflect sorrow and despair. But *All My Sons* contains humor as well as sorrow. Further, Miller explains that he wrote this tragedy because it reflects optimism and hope and the indestructibility of the human spirit.

A Question of Right or Wrong

At the premiere of *All My Sons,* Miller explained why and how he wrote plays. He said that he took settings and dramatic situations from life which involve real questions of right and wrong. In this full-length play, as well as in other important literary works, it is the values the author

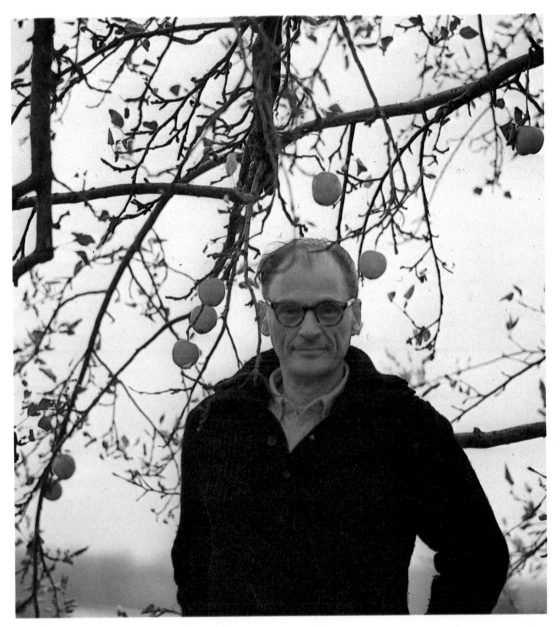

presents — through the characters he or she has chosen — and the careful structuring of plot that give the work its lasting worth.

Fine plays must do more. Plays are written to be performed. The playwright must provide the spark to bring his or her characters and ideas to life on the stage. The readers' or actors' interpretations of the characters, their expressions, voices, and the feelings they convey further add to the play. Arthur Miller crafted *All My Sons* to express his ideas and values, and to stimulate others to explore their own.

All My Sons

CHARACTERS

Joe Keller	Dr. Jim Bayliss
Kate Keller	Sue Bayliss
Chris Keller	Frank Lubey
Ann Deever	Lydia Lubey
George Deever	Bert

Act One

The backyard of the Keller home in the outskirts of an American town. August of our era.

The stage is hedged on right and left by tall, closely planted poplars which lend the yard a secluded atmosphere. Upstage is filled with the back of the house and its open, unroofed porch which extends into the yard some six feet. The house is two stories high and has seven rooms. It would have cost perhaps 15 thousand in the early twenties when it was built. Now it is nicely painted, looks tight and comfortable, and the yard is green with sod, here and there plants whose season is gone. At the right, beside the house, the entrance of the driveway can be seen, but the poplars cut off view of its continuation downstage. In the left corner, downstage, stands the four-foot-high stump of a slender apple tree whose upper trunk and branches lie toppled beside it, fruit still clinging to its branches.

Downstage right is a small, trellised arbor, shaped like a seashell, with a decorative bulb hanging from its forward-curving roof. Garden chairs and a table are scattered about. A garbage pail on the ground next to the porch steps, a wire leaf-burner near it.

On the rise: It is early Sunday morning. Joe Keller is sitting in the sun reading the want ads of the Sunday paper, the other sections of which lie neatly on the ground beside him. Behind his back, inside the arbor, Doctor Jim Bayliss is reading part of the paper at the table.

Keller is nearing 60. A heavy man of stolid mind and build, a businessman these many years, but with the imprint of the machine-shop worker and boss still upon him. When he reads, when he speaks, when he listens, it is with the terrible concentration of the uneducated man for whom there is still wonder in many commonly known things, a man whose judgments must be

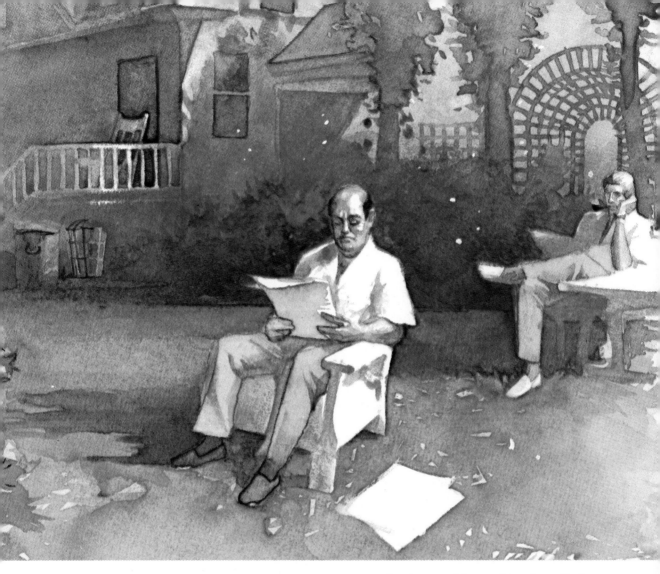

dredged out of experience and a peasant-like common sense. A man among men.

Doctor Bayliss is nearly 40. A wry, self-controlled man, an easy talker, but with a wisp of sadness that clings even to his self-effacing humor.

At curtain, Jim is standing at the left, staring at the broken tree. He taps a pipe on it, blows through the pipe, feels in his pockets for tobacco, then speaks.

Jim: Where's your tobacco?

Keller: I think I left it on the table. (*Jim goes slowly to table in the arbor, finds a pouch, and sits there on the bench, filling his pipe.*) Gonna rain tonight.

Jim: Paper says so?

Keller: Yeah, right here.

Jim: Then it can't rain.

(*Frank Lubey enters, through a small space between the poplars. Frank is 32 but balding. A pleasant, opinionated man, uncertain of himself, with a tendency toward peevishness when crossed, but always wanting it pleasant and neighborly.*)

He rather saunters in, leisurely, nothing to do. He does not notice Jim in the arbor. On his greeting, Jim does not bother looking up.)

Frank: Hya.

Keller: Hello, Frank. What's doin'?

Frank: Nothin'. Walking off my breakfast. *(Looks up at the sky.)* That beautiful? Not a cloud.

Keller *(looking up):* Yeah, nice.

Frank: Every Sunday ought to be like this.

Keller *(indicating the sections beside him):* Want the paper?

Frank: What's the difference, it's all bad news. What's today's calamity?

Keller: I don't know, I don't read the news part anymore. It's more interesting in the want ads.

Frank: Why, you trying to buy something?

Keller: No, I'm just interested. To see what people want, y'know? For instance, here's a guy lookin' for two Newfoundland dogs. Now what's he want with two Newfoundland dogs?

Frank: That is funny.

Keller: Here's another one. "Wanted — old dictionaries. High prices paid." Now what's a man going to do with an old dictionary?

Frank: Why not? Probably a book collector.

Keller: You mean he'll make a living out of that?

Frank: Sure, there's a lot of them.

Keller *(shaking his head):* All the kind of business goin' on. In my day, either you were a lawyer, or a doctor, or you worked in a shop. Now —

Frank: Well, I was going to be a forester once.

Keller: Well, that shows you; in my day, there was no such thing. *(Scanning the page, sweeping it with his hand)* You look at a page like this you realize how ignorant you are. *(Softly, with wonder, as he scans page)*

Frank *(noticing tree):* Hey, what happened to your tree?

Keller: Ain't that awful? The wind must've got it last night. You heard the wind, didn't you?

Frank: Yeah, I got a mess in my yard, too. *(Goes to tree.)* What a pity. *(Turning to Keller)* What'd Kate say?

Keller: They're all asleep yet. I'm just waiting for her to see it.

Frank *(struck):* You know? — it's funny.

Keller: What?

Frank: Larry was born in August. He'd been 27 this month. And his tree blows down.

Keller *(touched):* I'm surprised you remember his birthday, Frank. That's nice.

Frank: I'm working on his horoscope.

Keller: How can you make him a horoscope? That's for the future, ain't it?

Frank: Well, what I'm doing is this, see. Larry was reported missing on November twenty-fifth, right?

Keller: Yeah?

Frank: Well, then, we assume that if he was killed it was on November twenty-fifth. Now, what Kate wants —

Keller: Oh, Kate asked you to make a horoscope?

Frank: Yeah, what she wants to find out is whether November twenty-fifth was a favorable day for Larry.

Keller: What is that, favorable day?

Frank: Well, a favorable day for a person is a fortunate day, according to his stars. In other words it would be practically impossible for him to have died on his favorable day.

Keller: Well, was that his favorable day? — November twenty-fifth?

Frank: That's what I'm working to find out. It takes time! See, the point is, if November twenty-fifth was his favorable day, then it's completely possible he's alive somewhere, because — I mean it's possible. (*He notices Jim now. Jim is looking at him as though at an idiot. To Jim — with an uncertain laugh.*) I didn't even see you.

Keller (*to Jim*): Is he talkin' sense?

Jim: Him? He's all right. He's just completely out of his mind, that's all.

Frank (*peeved*): The trouble with you is, you don't *believe* in anything.

Jim: And your trouble is that you believe in *anything.* You didn't see my kid this morning, did you?

Frank: No.

Keller: Imagine? He walked off with his thermometer. Right out of his bag.

Jim (*getting up*): What a problem. One look at a girl and he takes her temperature. (*Goes to driveway, looks upstage toward street.*)

Frank: That boy's going to be a real doctor; he's smart.

Jim: Over my dead body he'll be a doctor. A good beginning, too.

Frank: Why? It's an honorable profession.

Jim (*looking at him tiredly*): Frank, will you stop talking like a civics book?

(*Keller laughs*).

Frank: Why, I saw a movie a couple of weeks ago reminded me of you. There was a doctor in that picture —

Keller: Don Ameche!

Frank: I think it was, yeah. And he worked in his basement discovering things. That's what you ought to do; you could help humanity, instead of —

Jim: I would love to help humanity on a Warner Brothers salary.

Keller (*pointing at him, laughing*): That's very good, Jim.

Jim (*looking toward the house*): Well, where's the beautiful girl that was supposed to be here?

Frank (*excited*): Annie came?

Keller: Sure, sleepin' upstairs. We picked her up on the 1:00 train last night. Wonderful thing. Girl leaves here, a scrawny kid. Couple of years go by, she's a regular woman. Hardly recognized her, and she was running in and out of the yard all her life. That was a very happy family used to live in your house, Jim.

Jim: Like to meet her. The block can use a pretty girl. In the whole neighborhood there's not a damned thing to look at. (*Sue, Jim's wife, enters. She is rounding 40, an overweight woman who fears it. On seeing her, Jim wryly adds.*) Except my wife of course.

Sue (*in the same spirit*): Mrs. Adams is on the phone, you dog.

Jim (*to Keller*): Such is the condition which prevails. (*Going to his wife*) My love, my light.

Sue: Don't sniff around me. (*Pointing to their house*) And give her a nasty answer. I can smell her perfume over the phone.

Jim: What's the matter with her now?

Sue: I don't know, dear. She sounds like she's in terrible pain — unless her mouth is full of candy.

Jim: Why don't you just tell her to lay down?

Sue: She enjoys it more when you tell her to lay down. And when are you going to see Mr. Hubbard?

Jim: My dear, Mr. Hubbard is not sick, and I have better things to do than to sit there and hold his hand.

Sue: It seems to me that for 10 dollars you could hold his hand.

Jim *(to Keller):* If your son wants to play golf tell him I'm ready. Or if he'd like to take a trip around the world for about 30 years. *(He exits.)*

Keller: Why do you needle him? He's a doctor; women are supposed to call him.

Sue: All I said was Mrs. Adams is on the phone. Can I have some of your parsley?

Keller: Yeah, sure. *(She goes to parsley box and pulls some parsley.)* You were a nurse too long, Susie. You're too . . . realistic.

Sue *(laughing, pointing at him):* Now you said it! *(Lydia Lubey enters. She is a robust, laughing girl of 27.)*

Lydia: Frank, the toaster. *(Sees the others.)* Hya.

Keller: Hello!

Lydia *(to Frank):* The toaster is off again.

Frank: Well, plug it in; I just fixed it.

Lydia *(kindly, but insistently):* Please, dear, fix it back like it was before.

Frank: I don't know why you can't learn to turn on a simple thing like a toaster! *(He exits.)*

Sue *(laughing):* Thomas Edison.

Lydia *(apologetically):* He's really very handy. *(She sees broken tree.)* Oh, did the wind get your tree?

Keller: Yeah, last night.

Lydia: Oh, what a pity. Annie get in?

Keller: She'll be down soon. Wait'll you meet her, Sue; she's a knockout.

Sue: I should've been a man. People are always introducing me to beautiful women. *(To Joe)* Tell her to come over later. I imagine she'd like to see what we did with her house. And thanks.

(She exits.)

Lydia: Is she still unhappy, Joe?

Keller: Annie? I don't suppose she goes around dancing on her toes, but she seems to be over it.

Lydia: She's going to get married. Is there anybody — ?

Keller: I suppose — say, it's a couple years already. She can't mourn a boy forever.

Lydia: It's so strange — Annie's here and not even married. And I've got three babies. I always thought it'd be the other way around.

Keller: Well, that's what war does. I had two sons, now I got one. It changed all the tallies. In my day when you had sons it was an honor. Today a doctor could make a million dollars if he could figure out a way to bring a boy into the world without a trigger finger.

Lydia: You know, I was just reading. *(Enter Chris Keller from house, stands in doorway.)* Hya, Chris.

(Frank shouts from offstage.)

480

Frank: Lydia, come in here! If you want the toaster to work don't plug in the malted mixer.

Lydia *(embarrassed, laughing):* Did I?

Frank: And the next time I fix something don't tell me I'm crazy! Now come in here!

Lydia *(to Keller):* I'll never hear the end of this one.

Keller *(calling to Frank):* So what's the difference? Instead of toast have a malted!

Lydia: Sh! Sh! *(She exits, laughing.)*

(Chris watches her off. He is 32; like his father, solidly built, a listener. A man capable of immense affection and loyalty. He has a cup of coffee in one hand, part of a doughnut in the other.)

Keller: You want the paper?

Chris: That's all right, just the book section. *(He bends down and pulls out part of paper on porch floor.)*

Keller: You're always reading the book section and you never buy a book.

Chris *(coming down to settee):* I like to keep abreast of my ignorance. *(He sits on settee.)*

Keller: What is that, every week a new book comes out?

Chris: Lot of new books.

Keller: All different?

Chris: All different.

(Keller shakes his head, puts knife down on bench, takes oilstone up to the cabinet.)

Keller: Psss! Annie up yet?

Chris: Mother's giving her breakfast in the dining room.

Keller *(looking at broken tree):* See what happened to the tree?

Chris *(without looking up):* Yeah.

Keller: What's Mother going to say?

(Bert runs on from driveway. He is about eight. He jumps on stool, then Keller's back.)

Bert: You're finally up.

Keller *(swinging him around and putting him down):* Ha! Bert's here! Where's Tommy? He's got his father's thermometer again.

Bert: He's taking a reading.

Chris: What!

Bert: But it's only oral.

Keller: Oh, well there's no harm in oral. So what's new this morning, Bert?

Bert: Nothin'. *(He walks around broken tree.)*

Keller: Then you couldn't 've made a complete inspection of the block. In the beginning, when I first made you a policeman you used to come in every morning with something new. Now, nothin's ever new.

Bert: Except some kids from Thirtieth Street. They started kicking a can down the block, and I made them go away because you were sleeping.

Keller: Now you're talkin', Bert. Now you're on the ball. First thing you know I'm liable to make you a detective.

Bert *(pulling him down by the lapel and whispering in his ear):* Can I see the jail now?

Keller: Seein' the jail ain't allowed, Bert. You know that.

Bert: Aw, I betcha there isn't even a jail. I don't see any bars on the cellar windows.

Keller: Bert, on my word of honor there's

a jail in the basement. I showed you my gun, didn't I?

Bert: But that's a hunting gun.

Keller: That's an arresting gun!

Bert: Then why don't you ever arrest anybody? Tommy said another dirty word to Doris yesterday, and you didn't even demote him.

(Keller chuckles and winks at Chris, who is enjoying all this.)

Keller: Yeah, that's a dangerous character, that Tommy. *(Beckons him closer.)* What word does he say?

Bert *(backing away quickly in great embarrassment)*: Oh, I can't say that.

Keller *(grabbing him by the shirt and pulling him back)*: Well, gimme an idea.

Bert: I can't. It's not a nice word.

Keller: Just whisper in my ear. I'll close my eyes. Maybe I won't even hear it.

(Bert, on tiptoe, puts his lips to Keller's ear, then in unbearable embarrassment steps back.)

Bert: I can't, Mr. Keller.

Chris *(laughing)*: Don't make him do that.

Keller: Okay, Bert. I take your word. Now go out, and keep both eyes peeled.

Bert *(interested)*: For what?

Keller: For what! Bert, the whole neighborhood is depending on you. A policeman don't ask questions. Now peel them eyes!

Bert *(mystified, but willing)*: Okay. *(He runs offstage back of arbor.)*

Keller *(calling after him)*: And mum's the word, Bert.

(Bert stops and sticks his head through the arbor.)

Bert: About what?

Keller: Just in general. Be v-e-r-y careful.

Bert *(nodding in bewilderment)*: Okay. *(He exits.)*

Keller *(laughing)*: I got all the kids crazy!

Chris: One of these days, they'll come in here and beat your brains out.

Keller: What's she going to say? Maybe we ought to tell her before she sees it.

Chris: She saw it.

Keller: How could she see it? I was the first one up. She was still in bed.

Chris: She was out here when it broke.

Keller: When?

Chris: About four this morning. *(Indicating window above them.)* I heard it cracking and I woke up and looked out. She was standing right here when it cracked.

Keller: What was she doing out here four in the morning?

Chris: I don't know. When it cracked she ran back into the house and cried in the kitchen.

Keller: Did you talk to her?

Chris: No, I — I figured the best thing was to leave her alone. *(Pause.)*

Keller *(deeply touched)*: She cried hard?

Chris: I could hear her right through the floor of my room.

Keller *(after slight pause)*: What was she doing out here at that hour? *(Chris silent, with an undertone of anger showing.)* She's dreaming about him again. She's walking around at night.

Chris: I guess she is.

Keller: She's getting just like after he died. *(Slight pause.)* What's the meaning of that?

Chris: I don't know the meaning of it. *(Slight pause.)* But I know one thing, Dad. We've made a terrible mistake with Mother.

Keller: What?

Chris: Being dishonest with her. That

482

kind of thing always pays off, and now it's paying off.

Keller: What do you mean, dishonest?

Chris: You know Larry's not coming back and I know it. Why do we allow her to go on thinking that we believe with her?

Keller: What do you want to do, argue with her?

Chris: I don't want to argue with her, but it's time she realized that nobody believes Larry is alive anymore. *(Keller simply moves away, thinking, looking at the ground.)* Why shouldn't she dream of him, walk the nights waiting for him? Do we contradict her? Do we say straight out that we have no hope anymore? That we haven't had any hope for years now?

Keller *(frightened at the thought):* You can't say that to her.

Chris: We've got to say it to her.

Keller: How're you going to prove it? Can you prove it?

Chris: For God's sake, three years! Nobody comes back after three years. It's insane.

Keller: To you it is, and to me. But not to her. You can talk yourself blue in the face, but there's no body and there's no grave, so where are you?

Chris: Sit down, Dad. I want to talk to you.

(Keller looks at him searchingly a moment.)

Keller: The trouble is the damn newspapers. Every month some boy turns up from nowhere, so the next one is going to be Larry, so —

Chris: All right, all right, listen to me. *(Slight pause. Keller sits on settee.)* You know why I asked Annie here, don't you?

Keller *(he knows, but —):* Why?

Chris: You know.

Keller: Well, I got an idea, but — What's the story?

Chris: I'm going to ask her to marry me. *(Slight pause. Keller nods.)*

Keller: Well, that's only your business, Chris.

Chris: You know it's not only my business.

Keller: What do you want me to do? You're old enough to know your own mind.

Chris *(asking, annoyed):* Then it's all right, I'll go ahead with it?

Keller: Well, you want to be sure Mother isn't going to —

Chris: Then it isn't just my business.

Keller: I'm just sayin' —

Chris: Sometimes you infuriate me, you know that? Isn't it your business, too, if I tell this to Mother and she throws a fit about it? You have such a talent for ignoring things.

Keller: I ignore what I gotta ignore. The girl is Larry's girl.

Chris: She's not Larry's girl.

Keller: From Mother's point of view he is not dead and you have no right to take his girl. *(Slight pause.)* Now you can go on from there if you know where to go, but I'm tellin' you I don't know where to go. See? I don't know. Now what can I do for you?

Chris: I don't know why it is, but every time I reach out for something I want I have to pull back because other people will suffer. My whole bloody life, time after time after time.

Keller: You're a considerate fella, there's nothing wrong in that.

Chris: To hell with that.

Keller: Did you ask Annie yet?

Chris: I wanted to get this settled first.

Keller: How do you know she'll marry you? Maybe she feels the same way Mother does?

Chris: Well, if she does, then that's the end of it. From her letters I think she's forgotten him. I'll find out. And then we'll thrash it out with Mother? Right? Dad, don't avoid me.

Keller: The trouble is, you don't see enough women. You never did.

Chris: So what? I'm not fast with women.

Keller: I don't see why it has to be Annie.

Chris: Because it is.

Keller: That's a good answer, but it don't answer anything. You haven't seen her since you went to war. It's five years.

Chris: I can't help it. I know her best. I was brought up next door to her. These years when I think of someone for my wife, I think of Annie. What do you want, a diagram?

Keller: I don't want a diagram. . . . I — I'm — she thinks he's coming back, Chris. You marry this girl and you're pronouncing him dead. Now what's going to happen to Mother? Do you know? I don't! *(Pause.)*

Chris: All right, then, Dad.

Keller *(thinking Chris has retreated):* Give it some more thought.

Chris: I've given it three years of thought. I'd hoped that if I waited, Mother would forget Larry and then we'd have a regular wedding and everything happy. But if that can't happen here, then I'll have to get out.

Keller: What the hell is *this?*

Chris: I'll get out. I'll get married and live someplace else. Maybe in New York.

Keller: Are you crazy?

Chris: I've been a good son too long, a good sucker. I'm through with it.

Keller: You've got a business here, what the hell is this?

Chris: The business! The business doesn't inspire me.

Keller: Must you be inspired?

Chris: Yes. I like it an hour a day. If you have to grub for money all day long at least at evening I want it beautiful. I want a family; I want some kids; I want to build something I can give myself to. Annie is in the middle of that. Now . . . where do I find it?

Keller: You mean . . . *(Goes to him.)* Tell me something, you mean you'd leave the business?

Chris: Yes. On this I would.

Keller *(after a pause):* Well . . . you don't want to think like that.

Chris: Then help me stay here.

Keller: All right, but — but don't think like that. Because what the hell did I work for? That's only for you, Chris, the whole shootin' match is for you!

Chris: I know that, Dad. Just you help me stay here.

Keller *(putting a fist up to Chris's jaw):* But don't think that way, you hear me?

Chris: I am thinking that way.

Keller *(lowering his hand):* I don't understand you, do I?

Chris: No, you don't. I'm a pretty tough guy.

Keller: Yeah. I can see that.

(Mother appears on porch. She is in her

early fifties, a woman of uncontrolled inspirations and an overwhelming capacity for love.)

Mother: Joe?
Chris *(going toward porch):* Hello, Mom.
Mother *(indicating house behind her; to Keller):* Did you take a bag from under the sink?
Keller: Yeah, I put it in the pail.
Mother: Well, get it out of the pail. That's my potatoes.

(Chris bursts out laughing — goes up into alley.)

Keller *(laughing):* I thought it was garbage.
Mother: Will you do me a favor, Joe? Don't be helpful.
Keller: I can afford another bag of potatoes.
Mother: Minnie scoured the pail in boiling water last night. It's cleaner than your teeth.
Keller: And I don't understand why, after I worked 40 years and I got a maid, why I have to take out the garbage.
Mother: If you would make up your mind that every bag in the kitchen isn't full of garbage you wouldn't be throwing out my vegetables. Last time it was the onions.

(Chris comes on, hands her bag.)

Keller: I don't like garbage in the house.
Mother: Then don't eat. *(She goes into the kitchen with bag.)*
Chris: That settles you for today.
Keller: Yeah, I'm in last place again. I don't know, once upon a time I used to think that when I got money again I would have a maid and my wife would take it easy. Now I got money, and I got a maid, and my wife is workin' for the maid. *(He sits in one of the chairs.)*

(Mother comes out on last line. She carries a pot of string beans.)

Mother: It's her day off, what are you crabbing about?
Chris *(to Mother):* Isn't Annie finished eating?
Mother *(looking around preoccupiedly at yard):* She'll be right out. *(Moves.)* That wind did some job on this place. *(Of the tree)* So much for that, thank God.
Keller *(indicating chair beside him):* Sit down, take it easy.
Mother *(pressing her hand to top of her head):* I've got such a funny pain on the top of my head.
Chris: Can I get you an aspirin?

(Mother picks a few petals off ground, stands there smelling them in her hand, then sprinkles them over plants.)

Mother: No more roses. It's so funny . . . everything decides to happen at the same time. This month is his birthday; his tree blows down; Annie comes. Everything that happened seems to be coming back. I was just down the cellar, and what do I stumble over? His baseball glove. I haven't seen it in a century.
Chris: Don't you think Annie looks well?
Mother: Fine. There's no question about it. She's a beauty. . . . I still don't know what brought her here. Not that I'm not glad to see her, but —
Chris: I just thought we'd all like to see each other again. *(Mother just looks at*

him, nodding ever so slightly — almost as though admitting something.) And I wanted to see her myself.

Mother *(as her nods halt, to Keller):* The only thing is I think her nose got longer. But I'll always love that girl. She's one that didn't jump into bed with somebody else as soon as it happened with her fella.

Keller *(as though that were impossible for Annie):* Oh, what're you — ?

Mother: Never mind. Most of them didn't wait till the telegrams were opened. I'm just glad she came, so you can see I'm not *completely* out of my mind. *(Sits, and rapidly breaks string beans in the pot.)*

Chris: Just because she isn't married doesn't mean she's been mourning Larry.

Mother *(with an undercurrent of observation):* Why then isn't she?

Chris *(a little flustered):* Well . . . it could've been any number of things.

Mother *(directly at him):* Like what, for instance?

Chris *(embarrassed, but standing his ground):* I don't know. Whatever it is. Can I get you an aspirin? *(Mother puts her hand to her head. She gets up and goes aimlessly toward the trees on rising.)*

Mother: It's not like a headache.

Keller: You don't sleep, that's why. She's wearing out more bedroom slippers than shoes.

Mother: I had a terrible night. *(She stops moving.)* I never had a night like that.

Chris *(looking at Keller):* What was it, Mom? Did you dream?

Mother: More, more than a dream.

Chris *(hesitantly):* About Larry?

Mother: I was fast asleep, and — *(Raising her arm over the audience)* Remember the way he used to fly low past the house when he was in training? When we used to see his face in the cockpit going by? That's the way I saw him. Only high up. Way, way up, where the clouds are. He was so real I could reach out and touch him. And suddenly he started to fall. And crying, crying to me . . . Mom, Mom! I could hear him like he was in the room. Mom! . . . it was his voice! If I could touch him I knew I could stop him, if I could only — *(Breaks off, allowing her outstretched hand to fall.)* I woke up and it was so funny — The wind . . . it was like the roaring of his engine. I came out here . . . I must've still been half asleep. I could hear that roaring like he was going by. The tree snapped right in front of me — and I like — came awake. *(She is looking at tree. She suddenly realizes something, turns with a reprimanding finger shaking slightly at Keller.)* See? We should never have planted that tree. I said so in the first place; it was too soon to plant a tree for him.

Chris *(alarmed):* Too soon!

Mother *(angering):* We rushed into it. Everybody was in such a hurry to bury him. I *said* not to plant it yet. *(To Keller)* I told you to — !

Chris: Mother, Mother! *(She looks into his face.)* The wind blew it down. What significance has that got? What are you talking about? Mother, please . . . don't go through it all again, will you? It's no good, it doesn't accomplish anything. I've been thinking, y'know? — maybe we ought to put our minds to forgetting him?

Mother: That's the third time you've said that this week.

Chris: Because it's not right; we never took up our lives again. We're like a railroad station waiting for a train that never comes in.

Mother *(pressing top of her head):* Get me an aspirin, heh?

Chris: Sure, and let's break out of this, heh, Mom? I thought the four of us might go out to dinner a couple of nights, maybe go dancing out at the shore.

Mother: Fine. *(To Keller)* We can do it tonight.

Keller: Swell with me!

Chris: Sure, let's have some fun. *(To Mother)* You'll start with this aspirin. *(He goes up and into the house with new spirit. Her smile vanishes.)*

Mother *(with an accusing undertone):* Why did he invite her here?

Keller: Why does that bother you?

Mother: She's been in New York for three and a half years, so why all of a sudden — ?

Keller: Well, maybe — maybe he just wanted to see her.

Mother: Nobody comes 700 miles "just to see."

Keller: What do you mean? He lived next door to the girl all his life, why shouldn't he want to see her again? *(Mother looks at him critically.)* Don't look at me like that, he didn't tell me any more than he told you.

Mother *(a warning and a question):* He's not going to marry her.

Keller: How do you know he's even thinking of it?

Mother: It's got that about it.

Keller *(sharply watching her reaction):* Well? So what?

Mother *(alarmed):* What's going on here, Joe?

Keller: Now listen, kid —

Mother *(avoiding contact with him):* She's not his girl, Joe; she knows she's not.

Keller: You can't read her mind.

Mother: Then why is she still single? New York is full of men, why isn't she married? *(Pause.)* Probably a hundred people told her she's foolish, but she waited.

Keller: How do you know why she waited?

Mother: She knows what I know, that's why. She's faithful as a rock. In my worst moments, I think of her waiting, and I know again that I'm right.

Keller: Look, it's a nice day. What are we arguing for?

Mother *(warningly):* Nobody in this house dast take her faith away, Joe. Strangers might. But not his father, not his brother.

Keller *(exasperated):* What do you want me to do? What do you want?

Mother: I want you to act like he's coming back. Both of you. Don't think I haven't noticed since Chris invited her. I won't stand for any nonsense.

Keller: But, Kate —

Mother: Because if he's not coming back, then I'll kill myself! Laugh. Laugh at me. *(She points to tree.)* But why did that happen the very night she came back? Laugh, but there are meanings in such things. She goes to sleep in his room and his memorial breaks in pieces. Look at it; look. *(She sits on bench.)* Joe —

Keller: Calm yourself.

Mother: Believe with me, Joe. I can't stand all alone.

Keller: Calm yourself.

Mother: Only last week a man turned up in Detroit, missing longer than Larry. You read it yourself. You above all have got to believe, you —

Keller *(rising):* Why me above all?

Mother: Just don't stop believing.

Keller: What does that mean, me above all?

(Bert comes rushing on.)

Bert: Mr. Keller! Say, Mr. Keller . . . *(Pointing up driveway)* Tommy just said it again!

Keller: *(not remembering any of it):* Said what? Who?

Bert: The dirty word.

Keller: Oh. Well —

Bert: Gee, aren't you going to arrest him? I warned him.

Mother *(with suddenness):* Stop that, Bert. Go home. *(Bert backs up as she advances.)* There's no jail here.

Keller *(as though to say, "Oh-what-the-hell-let-him-believe-there-is"):* Kate —

Mother *(turning on Keller furiously):* There's no jail here! I want you to stop that jail business! *(He turns, shamed, but peeved.)*

Bert *(past her to Keller):* He's right across the street.

Mother: Go home, Bert. *(Bert turns around and goes up driveway. She is shaken. Her speech is bitten off, extremely urgent.)* I want you to stop that, Joe. That whole jail business!

Keller *(alarmed, therefore angered):* Look at you, look at you shaking.

Mother *(trying to control herself, moving about clasping her hands):* I can't help it.

Keller: What have I got to hide? What the hell is the matter with you, Kate?

Mother: I didn't say you had anything to hide. I'm just telling you to stop it! Now stop it! *(Ann and Chris appear on porch. Ann is 26, gentle but, despite herself, capable of holding fast to what she knows. Chris opens door for her.)*

Ann: Hya, Joe! *(She leads off a general laugh that is not self-conscious because they know one another too well.)*

Chris *(bringing Ann down with an outstretched chivalric arm):* Take a breath of that air, kid. You never get air like that in New York.

Mother *(genuinely overcome with it):* Annie, where did you get that dress!

Ann: I couldn't resist. I'm taking it off before I ruin it. *(Swings around.)* How's that for three weeks salary?

Mother *(to Keller):* Isn't she the most —? *(To Ann)* It's gorgeous, simply gor —

Chris *(to Mother):* No kidding, now, isn't she the prettiest gal you ever saw.

Mother *(caught short by his obvious admiration, she finds herself reaching out for a glass of water and aspirin in his hand, and —):* You gained a little weight, didn't you darling. *(She gulps pill and drinks.)*

Ann: It comes and goes.

Keller: Look how nice her legs turned out!

Ann *(as she runs to fence):* Boy, the poplars got thick, didn't they? *(Keller moves to settee and sits.)*

Keller: Well, it's three years, Annie. We're gettin' old, kid.

Mother: How does Mom like New York? (*Ann keeps looking through trees.*)

Ann (*a little hurt*): Why'd they take our hammock away?

Keller: Oh, no, it broke. Couple of years ago.

Mother: What broke? He had one of his light lunches and flopped into it. (*Ann laughs and turns back toward Jim's yard.*)

Ann: Oh, excuse me! (*Jim has come to fence and is looking over it. He is smoking a cigar. As she cries out, he comes on around on stage.*)

Jim: How do you do. (*To Chris*) She looks very intelligent!

Chris: Ann, this is Jim — Doctor Bayliss.

Ann (*shaking Jim's hand*): Oh, sure, he writes a lot about you.

Jim: Don't you believe it. He likes everybody. In the battalion he was known as Mother McKeller.

Ann: I can believe it. You know — ? (*To Mother*) It's so strange seeing him come out of that yard. (*To Chris*) I guess I never grew up. It almost seems that Mom and Pop are in there now. And you and my brother doing algebra, and Larry trying to copy my homework. Gosh, those dear dead days beyond recall.

Jim: Well, I hope that doesn't mean you want me to move out?

Sue (*calling from offstage*): Jim, come in here! Mr. Hubbard is on the phone!

Jim: I told you I don't want —

Sue (*commandingly sweet*): Please, dear! Please!

Jim (*resigned*): All right, Susie. (*trailing off*) All right, all right . . . (*To Ann*) I've only met you, Ann, but if I may offer you a piece of advice. When you marry, never

— even in your mind — never count your husband's money.

Sue (*from offstage*): Jim?

Jim: At once! (*Turns and goes off.*) At once. (*He exits.*)

Mother (*Ann is looking at her. She speaks meaningfully*): I told her to take up the guitar. It'd be a common interest for them. (*They laugh.*) Well, he loves the guitar! (*Ann, as though to overcome Mother, becomes suddenly lively, crosses to Keller on settee, sits on his lap.*)

Ann: Let's eat at the shore tonight! Raise some hell around here, like we used to before Larry went!

Mother (*emotionally*): You think of him! You see? (*Triumphantly*) She thinks of him!

Ann (*with an uncomprehending smile*): What do you mean, Kate?

Mother: Nothing. Just that you — remember him, he's in your thoughts.

Ann: That's a funny thing to say; how could I help remembering him?

Mother (*It is drawing to a head the wrong way for her; she starts anew. She rises and comes to Ann*): Did you hang up your things?

Ann: Yeah . . . (*To Chris*) Say, you've sure gone in for clothes. I could hardly find room in the closet.

Mother: No, don't you remember? That's Larry's room.

Ann: You mean . . . they're Larry's?

Mother: Didn't you recognize them?

Ann (*slowly rising, a little embarrassed*): Well, it never occurred to me that you'd — I mean the shoes are all shined.

Mother: Yes, dear. (*Slight pause. Ann can't stop staring at her. Mother breaks*

it by speaking with the relish of gossip, putting her arm around Ann, and walking with her.) For so long I've been aching for a nice conversation with you, Annie. Tell me something.

Ann: What?

Mother: I don't know. Something nice.

Chris *(wryly):* She means do you go out much?

Mother: Oh, shut up.

Keller: And are any of them serious?

Mother *(laughing, sits in her chair):* Why don't you both choke?

Keller: Annie, you can't go into a restaurant with that woman anymore. In five minutes 39 strange people are sitting at the table telling her their life story.

Mother: If I can't ask Annie a personal question —

Keller: Askin' is all right, but don't beat her over the head. You're beatin' her, you're beatin' her. *(They are laughing. Ann takes pan of beans off stool, puts them on floor under chair and sits.)*

Ann *(to Mother):* Don't let them bulldoze you. Ask me anything you like. What do you want to know, Kate? Come on, let's gossip.

Mother *(to Chris and Keller):* She's the only one is got any sense. *(To Ann)* Your mother — she's not getting a divorce, heh?

Ann: No, she's calmed down about it now. I think when he gets out they'll probably live together. In New York, of course.

Mother: That's fine. Because your father is still — I mean he's a decent man after all is said and done.

Ann: I don't care. She can take him back if she likes.

Mother: And you? You — *(Shakes her head negatively.)* — go out much? *(Slight pause.)*

Ann *(delicately):* You mean am I still waiting for him?

Mother: Well, no. I don't expect you to wait for him but —

Ann *(kindly):* But that's what you mean, isn't it?

Mother: Well . . . yes.

Ann: Well, I'm not, Kate.

Mother *(faintly):* You're not?

Ann: Isn't it ridiculous? You don't really imagine he's — ?

Mother: I know, dear, but don't say it's ridiculous, because the papers were full of it; I don't know about New York, but there was half a page about a man missing even longer than Larry, and he turned up from Burma.

Chris *(coming to Ann):* He couldn't have wanted to come home very badly, Mom.

Mother: Don't be so smart.

Chris: You can have a helluva time in Burma.

Ann *(rises and swings around in back of Chris):* So I've heard.

Chris: Mother, I'll bet you money that you're the only woman in the country who after three years is still —

Mother: You're sure?

Chris: Yes, I am.

Mother: Well, if you're sure then you're sure. *(She turns her head away an instant.)* They don't say it on the radio but I'm sure that in the dark at night they're still waiting for their sons.

Chris: Mother, you're absolutely —

Mother *(waving him off):* Don't be so damned smart! Now stop it! *(Slight pause.)*

There are just a few things you *don't* know. All of you. And I'll tell you one of them, Annie. Deep, deep in your heart you've always been waiting for him.

Ann *(resolutely):* No, Kate.

Mother *(with increasing demand):* But deep in your heart, Annie!

Chris: She ought to know, shouldn't she?

Mother: Don't let them tell you what to think. Listen to your heart. Only your heart.

Ann: Why does your heart tell you he's alive?

Mother: Because he has to be.

Ann: But why, Kate?

Mother *(going to her):* Because certain things have to be, and certain things can never be. Like the sun has to rise, it has to be. That's why there's God. Otherwise anything could happen. But there's God, so certain things can never happen. I would know, Annie — just like I knew the day he — *(Indicates Chris.)* — went into that terrible battle. Did he write me? Was it in the papers? No, but that morning I couldn't raise my head off the pillow. Ask Joe. Suddenly, I knew! And he was nearly killed that day. Ann, you *know* I'm right!

(Ann stands there in silence, then turns trembling, going upstage.)

Ann: No, Kate.

Mother: I have to have some tea.

(Frank appears, carrying ladder.)

Frank: Annie! *(Coming down)* How are you, gee whiz!

Ann *(taking his hand):* Why, Frank, you're losing your hair.

Keller: He's got responsibility.

Frank: Gee whiz!

Keller: Without Frank the stars wouldn't know when to come out.

Frank *(laughs to Ann):* You look more womanly. You've matured. You —

Keller: Take it easy, Frank, you're a married man.

Ann *(as they laugh):* You still haberdashering?

Frank: Why not? Maybe I too can get to be president. How's your brother? Got his degree, I hear.

Ann: Oh, George has his own office now!

Frank: Don't say! *(Funereally)* And your dad? Is he — ?

Ann *(abruptly):* Fine. I'll be in to see Lydia.

Frank *(sympathetically):* How about it, does Dad expect a parole soon?

Ann *(with growing ill ease):* I really don't know, I —

Frank *(staunchly defending her father for her sake):* I mean because I feel, y'know, that if an intelligent man like your father is put in prison, there ought to be a law that says either you execute him, or let him go after a year.

Chris *(interrupting):* Want a hand with that ladder, Frank?

Frank *(taking cue):* That's all right, I'll — *(Picks up ladder)* — I'll finish the horoscope tonight, Kate. *(Embarrassed)* See you later, Ann; you look wonderful. *(He exits. They look at Ann.)*

Ann *(to Chris, as she sits slowly on stool):* Haven't they stopped talking about Dad?

Chris *(coming down and sitting on arm of chair):* Nobody talks about him any more.

Keller *(rises and comes to her)*: Gone and forgotten, kid.

Ann: Tell me. Because I don't want to meet anybody on the block if they're going to —

Chris: I don't want you to worry about it.

Ann *(to Keller)*: Do they still remember the case, Joe? Do they talk about you?

Keller: The only one still talks about it is my wife.

Mother: That's because you keep on playing policeman with the kids. All their parents hear out of you is jail, jail, jail.

Keller: Actually what happened was that when I got home from the penitentiary the kids got very interested in me. You know kids. I was — *(Laughs.)* — like the expert on the jail situation. And as time passed they got it confused, and . . . I ended up a detective.

Mother: Except that *they* didn't get it confused. *(To Ann)* He hands out police badges from the Post Toasties boxes. *(They laugh. Ann rises and comes to Keller, putting her arm around his shoulder.)*

Ann *(wondrously at them, happy)*: Gosh, it's wonderful to hear you laughing about it.

Chris: Why, what'd you expect?

Ann: The last thing I remember on this block was one word — "Murderers!" Remember that, Kate? — Mrs. Hammond standing in front of our house and yelling that word? She's still around, I suppose?

Mother: They're all still around.

Keller: Don't listen to her. Every Saturday night the whole gang is playin' poker in this arbor. All the ones who yelled murderer takin' my money now.

Mother: Don't, Joe; she's a sensitive girl; don't fool her. *(To Ann)* They still remember about Dad. It's different with him. *(Indicates Joe.)* He was exonerated, your father's still there. That's why I wasn't so enthusiastic about your coming. Honestly, I know how sensitive you are, and I told Chris, I said —

Keller: Listen, you do like I did and you'll be all right. The day I come home, I got out of my car — but not in front of the house . . . on the corner. You should've been here, Annie, and you too, Chris; you'd a seen something. Everybody knew I was getting out that day; the porches were loaded. Picture it now; none of them believed I was innocent. The story was, I pulled a fast one getting myself exonerated. So I get out of my car, and I walk down the street. But very slow. And with a smile. The beast! I was the beast; the guy who sold cracked cylinder heads to the Army Air Force; the guy who made 21 P-40's crash in Australia. Kid, walkin' down the street that day I was guilty as hell. Except I wasn't, and there was a court paper in my pocket to prove I wasn't, and I walked . . . past . . . the porches. Result? Fourteen months later I had one of the best shops in the state again, a respected man again; bigger than ever.

Chris *(with admiration)*: Joe McGuts.

Keller *(now with great force)*: That's the only way you lick 'em is guts! *(To Ann)* The worst thing you did was to move away from here. You made it tough for your father when he gets out. That's why I tell you, I like to see him move back right on this block.

Mother *(pained):* How could they move back?

Keller: It ain't gonna end *till* they move back! *(To Ann)* Till people play cards with him again, and talk with him, and smile with him — you play cards with a man you know he can't be a murderer. And the next time you write him I'd like you to tell him just what I said. *(Ann simply stares at him.)* You hear me?

Ann *(surprised):* Don't you hold anything against him?

Keller: Annie, I never believed in crucifying people.

Ann *(mystified):* But he was your partner; he dragged you through the mud.

Keller: Well, he ain't my sweetheart, but you gotta forgive, don't you?

Ann: You, either, Kate? Don't you feel any — ?

Keller *(to Ann):* The next time you write Dad —

Ann: I don't write him.

Keller: Well, every now and then you —

Ann *(a little shamed, but determined):* No, I've *never* written to him. Neither has my brother. *(To Chris)* Say, do you feel this way, too?

Chris: He murdered 21 pilots.

Keller: What the hell kinda talk is that?

Mother: That's not a thing to say about a man.

Ann: What else can you say? When they took him away I followed him, went to visit him every day. I was crying all the time. Until the news came about Larry. Then I realized. It's wrong to pity a man like that. Father or no father, there's only one way to look at him. He knowingly shipped out parts that would crash an airplane. And how do you know Larry wasn't one of them?

Mother: I was waiting for that. *(Going to her)* As long as you're here, Annie, I want to ask you never to say that again.

Ann: You surprise me. I thought you'd be mad at him.

Mother: What your father did had nothing to do with Larry. Nothing.

Ann: But we can't know that.

Mother *(striving for control):* As long as you're here!

Ann *(perplexed):* But, Kate —

Mother: Put that out of your head!

Keller: Because —

Mother *(quickly to Keller):* That's all, that's enough. *(Places her hand on her head.)* Come inside now, and have some tea with me. *(She goes up steps.)*

Keller *(to Ann):* The one thing you —

Mother *(sharply):* He's not dead, so there's no argument! Now come!

Keller *(angrily):* In a minute! *(Mother turns and goes into house.)* Now look, Annie —

Chris: All right, Dad, forget it.

Keller: No, she doesn't feel that way, Annie —

Chris: I'm sick of the whole subject; now cut it out.

Keller: You want her to go on like this? *(To Ann)* Those cylinder heads went into P-40's only. What's the matter with you? You know Larry never flew a P-40.

Chris: So who flew those P-40's, pigs?

Keller: The man was a fool, but don't make a murderer out of him. You got no sense? Look what it does to her! *(To Ann)* Listen, you gotta appreciate what was doin' in that shop in the war. The both of you! It was a madhouse. Every half hour the Major callin' for cylinder heads, they were whippin' us with the telephone. The trucks were hauling them away hot. I mean just try to see it human, see it human. All of a sudden a batch comes out with a crack. That happens; that's the business. A fine, hairline crack. All right, so — so he's a little man, your father, always scared of loud voices. What'll the Major say? Half a day's production shot. . . . What'll I say? You know what I mean? Human. *(He pauses.)* So he takes out his tools and he — covers over the cracks. All right — that's bad, it's wrong, but that's what a little man does. If I could have gone in that day I'd a told him — junk 'em, Steve, we can afford it. But alone he was afraid. But I know he meant no harm. He believed they'd hold up a hundred per cent. That's a mistake, but it ain't murder. You mustn't feel that way about him. You understand me? It ain't right.

Ann *(she regards him a moment):* Joe, let's forget it.

Keller: Annie, the day the news came about Larry, he was in the next cell to mine — Dad. And he cried. Annie — he cried half the night.

Ann *(touched):* He shoulda cried all night. *(Slight pause.)*

Keller *(almost angered):* Annie, I do not understand why you — !

Chris *(breaking in — with nervous urgency):* Are you going to stop it?

Ann: Don't yell at him. He just wants everybody happy.

Keller *(clasps her around the waist, smil-ing):* That's my sentiments. Can you stand steak?

Chris: And champagne!

Keller: Now you're operatin'! I'll call Swanson's for a table. Big time tonight, Annie!

Ann: Can't scare me.

Keller *(to Chris, pointing at Ann):* I like that girl. Wrap her up. *(They laugh. Goes up porch.)* You got nice legs, Annie! . . . I want to see everybody drunk tonight. *(Pointing to Chris)* Look at him; he's blushin'! *(He exits, laughing, into house.)*

Chris *(calling after him):* Drink your tea, Casanova. *(He turns to Ann.)* Isn't he a great guy?

Ann: You're the only one I know who loves his parents.

Chris: I know. It went out of style, didn't it?

Ann *(with a sudden touch of sadness):* It's all right. It's a good thing. *(She looks about.)* You know? It's lovely here. The air is sweet.

Chris *(hopefully):* You're not sorry you came?

Ann: Not sorry, no. But I'm — not going to stay.

Chris: Why?

Ann: In the first place, your mother as much as told me to go.

Chris: Well —

Ann: You saw that — and then you — you've been kind of —

Chris: What?

Ann: Well . . . kind of embarrassed ever since I got here.

Chris: The trouble is I planned on kind of sneaking up on you over a period of a

494

week or so. But they take it for granted that we're all set.

Ann: I knew they would. Your mother anyway.

Chris: How did you know?

Ann: From *her* point of view, why else would I come?

Chris: Well . . . would you want to? *(Ann still studies him.)* I guess you know this is why I asked you to come.

Ann: I guess this is why I came.

Chris: Ann, I love you. I love you a great deal. *(Finally)* I love you. *(Pause. She waits.)* I have no imagination . . . that's all I know to tell you. *(Ann is waiting, ready.)* I'm embarrassing you. I didn't want to tell it to you here. I wanted someplace we'd be brand-new to each other. . . . You feel it's wrong here, don't you? This yard, this chair? I want you to be ready for me. I don't want to win you away from anything.

Ann *(putting her arms around him):* Oh, Chris, I've been ready a long, long time!

Chris: Then he's gone forever. You're sure.

Ann: I almost got married two years ago.

Chris: Why didn't you?

Ann: You started to write to me — *(Slight pause.)*

Chris: You felt something that far back?

Ann: Every day since!

Chris: Ann, why didn't you let me know?

Ann: I was waiting for you, Chris. Till then you never wrote. And when you did, what did you say? You sure can be ambiguous, you know.

Chris *(looks toward house, then at her, trembling):* Give me a kiss, Ann. Give me

a — *(They kiss.)* God, I kissed you, Annie; I kissed Annie. How long, how long I've been waiting to kiss you!

Ann: I'll never forgive you. Why did you wait all these years? All I've done is sit and wonder if I was crazy for thinking of you.

Chris: Annie, we're going to live now! I'm going to make you so happy. *(He kisses her, but their bodies don't touch.)*

Ann *(a little embarrassed):* Not like that you're not.

Chris: I kissed you. . . .

Ann: Like Larry's brother. Do it like you, Chris. *(He breaks away from her abruptly.)* What is it, Chris?

Chris: Let's drive someplace . . . I want to be alone with you.

Ann: No . . . what is it, Chris, your mother?

Chris: No — nothing like that.

Ann: Then what's wrong? Even in your letters, there was something ashamed.

Chris: Yes. I suppose I have been. But it's going from me.

Ann: You've got to tell me —

Chris: I don't know how to start. *(He takes her hand.)*

Ann: It wouldn't work this way. *(Slight pause.)*

Chris *(speaks quietly, factually at first):* It's all mixed up with so many other things. . . . You remember, overseas, I was in command of a company?

Ann: Yeah, sure.

Chris: Well, I lost them.

Ann: How many?

Chris: Just about all.

Ann: Oh, gee!

Chris: It takes a little time to toss that

off. Because they weren't just men. For instance, one time it'd been raining several days and this kid came to me, and gave me his last pair of dry socks. Put them in my pocket. That's only a little thing — but . . . that's the kind of guys I had. They didn't die; they killed themselves for each other. I mean that exactly; a little more selfish and they'd 've been here today. And I got an idea — watching them go down. Everything was being destroyed, see, but it seemed to me that one new thing was made. A kind of — responsibility. Man for man. You understand me? To show that, to bring that onto the earth again like some kind of a monument and everyone would feel it standing there, behind him, and it would make a difference to him. (Pause.) And then I came home and it was incredible. I — there was no meaning in it here; the whole thing to them was kind of a — bus accident. I went to work with Dad, and that rat-race again. I felt — what you said — ashamed somehow. Because nobody changed at all. It seemed to make suckers out of a lot of guys. I felt wrong to be alive, to open the bankbook, to drive the new car, to see the new refrigerator. I mean you can take those things out of a war, but when you drive that car you've got to know that it came out of the love a man can have for a man, you've got to be a little better because of that. Otherwise what you have is really loot, and there's blood on it. I didn't want to take any of it. And I guess that included you.

Ann: And you still feel that way?

Chris: I want you now, Annie.

Ann: Because you mustn't feel that way anymore. Because you have a right to whatever you have. Everything, Chris, understand that? To me, too. . . . And the money, there's nothing wrong in your money. Your father put hundreds of planes in the air, you should be proud. A man should be paid for that. . . .

Chris: Oh, Annie, Annie . . . I'm going to make a fortune for you!

Keller (offstage): Hello. . . . Yes. Sure.

Ann (laughing softly): What'll I do with a fortune? (They kiss. Keller enters from house.)

Keller (thumbing toward house): Hey, Ann, your brother — (They step apart shyly. Keller comes down, and wryly.) What is this, Labor Day?

Chris (waving him away, knowing the kidding will be endless): All right, all right.

Ann: You shouldn't burst out like that.

Keller: Well, nobody told me it was Labor Day. (Looks around.) Where's the hot dogs?

Chris (loving it): All right. You said it once.

Keller: Well, as long as I know it's Labor Day from now on, I'll wear a bell around my neck.

Ann (affectionately): He's so subtle!

Chris: George Bernard Shaw as an elephant.

Keller: George! — hey, you kissed it out of my head — your brother's on the phone.

Ann (surprised): My brother?

Keller: Yeah. George. Long distance.

Ann: What's the matter, is anything wrong?

496

Keller: I don't know; Kate's talking to him. Hurry up, she'll cost him five dollars.

Ann *(takes a step upstage, then comes down toward Chris):* I wonder if we ought to tell your mother yet? I mean I'm not very good in an argument.

Chris: We'll wait till tonight. After dinner. Now don't get tense, just leave it to me.

Keller: What're you telling her?

Chris: Go ahead, Ann. *(With misgivings, Ann goes up and into house.)* We're getting married, Dad. *(Keller nods indecisively.)* Well, don't you say anything?

Keller *(distracted):* I'm glad, Chris, I'm just — George is calling from Columbus.

Chris: Columbus!

Keller: Did Annie tell you he was going to see his father today?

Chris: No, I don't think she knew anything about it.

Keller *(asking uncomfortably):* Chris! You — you think you know her pretty good?

Chris *(hurt and apprehensive):* What kind of a question?

Keller: I'm just wondering. All these years George don't go to see his father. Suddenly he goes . . . and she comes here.

Chris: Well, what about it?

Keller: It's crazy, but it comes to my mind. She don't hold nothin' against me, does she?

Chris *(angry):* I don't know what you're talking about.

Keller *(a little more combatively):* I'm just talkin'. To his last day in court the man blamed it all on me; and this is his daughter. I mean if she was sent here to find out something?

Chris *(angered):* Why? What is there to find out?

Ann *(on phone, offstage):* Why are you so excited, George? What happened there?

Keller: I mean if they want to open the case again, for the nuisance value, to hurt us?

Chris: Dad . . . how could you think that of her?

Ann *(still on phone):* But what did he say to you, for God's sake?

Keller: It couldn't be, heh. You know.

Chris: Dad, you amaze me. . . .

Keller *(breaking in):* All right, forget it. *(With great force, moving about)* I want a clean start for you, Chris. I want a new sign over the plant — Christopher Keller, Incorporated.

Chris *(a little uneasily):* J. O. Keller is good enough.

Keller: We'll talk about it. I'm going to build you a house, stone, with a driveway from the road. I want you to spread out, Chris, I want you to use what I made for you. *(He is close to him now.)* I mean, with joy, Chris, without shame . . . with joy.

Chris *(touched):* I will, Dad.

Keller *(with deep emotion):* Say it to me.

Chris: Why?

Keller: Because sometimes I think you are . . . ashamed of the money.

Chris: No, don't feel that.

Keller: Because it's good money; there's nothing wrong with that money.

Chris *(a little frightened):* Dad, you don't have to tell me this.

Keller *(with overriding affection and self-confidence now, he grips Chris by the*

back of the neck, and with laughter be-
tween his determined jaws): Look, Chris,
I'll go to work on Mother for you. We'll
get her so drunk tonight we'll all get
married! *(Steps away, with a wide gesture
of his arm.)* There's gonna be a wedding,
kid, like there never was seen! Champagne,
tuxedos — ! *(He breaks off as Ann's voice
comes out loud from the house where she
is still talking on the phone.)*

Ann: Simply because when you get excited you don't control yourself. . . . *(Mother
comes out of house.)* Well, what did he
tell you for God's sake? *(Pause.)* All right,
come then. *(Pause.)* Yes, they'll all be here.
Nobody's running away from you. And
try to get hold of yourself, will you?
(Pause.) All right, all right. Good-bye.

*(There is a brief pause as Ann hangs up
receiver, then comes out of kitchen.)*

Chris: Something happen?
Keller: He's coming here?
Ann: On the seven o'clock. He's in Co-
lumbus. *(To Mother)* I told him it would
be all right.
Keller: Sure, fine! Your father took sick?
Ann *(mystified):* No, George didn't say
he was sick. I — *(Shaking it off)* I don't
know, I suppose it's something stupid;
you know my brother — *(She comes to
Chris.)* Let's go for a drive, or some-
thing. . . .
Chris: Sure. Give me the keys, Dad.
Mother: Drive through the park. It's
beautiful now.
Chris: Come on, Ann. *(To them)* Be back
right away.
Ann *(as she and Chris exit up driveway):*
See you.

*(Mother comes down toward Keller, her
eyes fixed on him.)*

Keller: Take your time. *(To Mother)* What
does George want?
Mother: He's been in Columbus since this
morning with Steve. He's gotta see Annie
right away, he says.
Keller: What for?
Mother: I don't know. *(She speaks with
warning.)* He's a lawyer now, Joe. George
is a lawyer. All these years he never even
sent a postcard to Steve. Since he got back
from the war, not a postcard.
Keller: So what?
Mother *(her tension breaking out):*
Suddenly he takes an airplane from New
York to see him. An airplane!
Keller: Well? So?
Mother *(trembling):* Why?
Keller: I don't read minds. Do you?
Mother: Why, Joe? What has Steve sud-
denly got to tell him that he takes an
airplane to see him?
Keller: What do I care what Steve's got
to tell him?
Mother: You're sure, Joe?
Keller *(frightened, but angry):* Yes, I'm
sure.
Mother *(sits stiffly in a chair):* Be smart
now, Joe. The boy is coming. Be smart.
Keller *(desperately):* Once and for all, did
you hear what I said? I said I'm sure!
Mother *(nods weakly):* All right, Joe. *(He
straightens up.)* Just . . . be smart.

*(Keller, in hopeless fury, looks at her,
turns around, goes up to porch and into
house, slamming screen door violently
behind him. Mother sits in chair downstage, stiffly, staring, seeing. Curtain.)*

READING COMPREHENSION

Select the best choice to complete each sentence below. Then write the complete sentence on your paper.

1. Kate said that Larry _____.
   a. would come back
   b. died nobly for his country
   c. hadn't suffered long

2. Chris had asked Ann to visit because he _____.
   a. knew his mother wanted to see her
   b. wanted to move to New York
   c. wanted to ask her to marry him

3. Joe Keller was afraid that Chris and Ann's marriage would _____.
   a. upset Larry
   b. be like pronouncing Larry dead
   c. be a scandal in the neighborhood

4. Joe Keller and Ann's father went to prison for _____.
   a. selling cracked cylinder heads
   b. price-fixing
   c. stealing military secrets

For Discussion

1. Why was the apple tree planted? What does it become a symbol of?

2. Why do you think Joe and Chris were dishonest with Kate about Larry's death? Do you think they were right?

3. The first act ended with Kate and Joe worried about the arrival of George Deever. Why do you think they were worried? Does this make an effective ending for the act? Why or why not?

UNDERSTANDING LITERATURE

Characters and Conflict in a Play. The first act in a play lays the foundation for everything that comes later. It introduces you to the characters. It presents the background and the rising action of the plot, the problems and conflicts the characters must resolve.

The first act of *All My Sons* reveals the characters' personalities, problems, and relationships with each other.

On your paper, match each character listed below with his or her description.

1. Kate   a. moved to New York to get away from unhappy memories

2. Joe   b. a doctor who is not totally content

3. Chris   c. a loyal but demanding person, who believes Larry will return

4. Ann   d. likes to joke with kids, is proud of his success

5. Jim   e. believes the stars rule our lives

6. Frank   f. wishes to marry the woman he loves

Writing

Choose one character from the play and write a character study. Describe (a) the character's personality, (b) the conflicts he or she faces, and (c) his or her relationship with the other characters in the play.

Act Two

As twilight falls, that evening. On the rise, Chris is discovered sawing the broken-off tree, leaving stump standing alone. He is dressed in good pants, white shoes, but without a shirt. He disappears with tree up the alley when Mother appears on porch. She comes down and stands watching him. She has on a dressing gown, carries a tray of grape juice drink in a pitcher, and glasses with sprigs of mint in them.

Mother *(calling up alley)*: Did you have to put on good pants to do that? *(She comes downstage and puts tray on table in the arbor. Then looks around uneasily, then feels pitcher for coolness. Chris enters from alley brushing off his hands.)* You notice there's more light with that thing gone?

Chris: Why aren't you dressing?

Mother: It's suffocating upstairs. I made a grape drink for Georgie. He always liked grape. Come and have some.

Chris *(impatiently)*: Well, come on, get dressed. And what's Dad sleeping so much for? *(He goes to table and pours a glass of juice.)*

Mother: He's worried. When he's worried he sleeps. *(Pauses. Looks into his eyes.)* We're dumb, Chris. Dad and I are stupid people. We don't know anything. You've got to protect us.

Chris: You're silly; what's there to be afraid of?

Mother: To his last day in court Steve never gave up the idea that Dad made him do it. If they're going to open the case again I won't live through it.

Chris: George is just a damn fool, Mother. How can you take him seriously?

Mother: That family hates us. Maybe even Annie —

Chris: Oh, now, Mother . . .

Mother: You think just because you like everybody, they like you?

Chris: All right, stop working yourself up. Just leave everything to me.

Mother: When George goes home tell her to go with him.

Chris *(noncommittally)*: Don't worry about Annie.

Mother: Steve is her father, too.

Chris: Are you going to cut it out? Now, come.

Mother *(going upstage with him)*: You don't realize how people can hate, Chris; they can hate so much they'll tear the world to pieces.

(Ann, dressed up, appears on porch.)

Chris: Look! She's dressed already. *(As he and Mother mount porch)* I've just got to put on a shirt.

Ann *(in a preoccupied way)*: Are you feeling well, Kate?

Mother: What's the difference, dear. There are certain people, y'know, the sicker they get the longer they live. *(She goes into house.)*

Chris: You look nice.

Ann: We're going to tell her tonight.

Chris: Absolutely, don't worry about it.

Ann: I wish we could tell her now. I can't stand scheming. My stomach gets hard.

Chris: It's not scheming; we'll just get her in a better mood.

Mother (*upstage, in the house*): Joe, are you going to sleep all day?

Ann (*laughing*): The only one who's relaxed is your father. He's fast asleep.

Chris: I'm relaxed.

Ann: Are you?

Chris: Look. (*He holds out his hand and makes it shake.*) Let me know when George gets here.

(*He goes into the house. Ann moves aimlessly, and then is drawn toward tree stump. She goes to it, hesitantly touches broken top in the hush of her thoughts. Offstage Lydia calls, "Johnny!" Sue enters and halts, seeing Ann.*)

Sue: Is my husband — ?

Ann (*turns, startled*): Oh!

Sue: I'm terribly sorry.

Ann: It's all right, I — I'm a little silly about the dark.

Sue (*looks about*): It is getting dark.

Ann: Are you looking for your husband?

Sue: As usual. (*Laughs tiredly.*) He spends so much time here, they'll be charging him rent.

Ann: Nobody was dressed so he drove over to the depot to pick up my brother.

Sue: Oh, your brother's in?

Ann: Yeah, they ought to be here any minute now. Will you have a cold drink?

Sue: I will, thanks. (*Ann goes to table and pours.*) My husband. Too hot to drive me to the beach. Men are like little boys; for the neighbors they'll always cut the grass.

Ann: People like to do things for the Kellers. It's been that way since I can remember.

Sue: It's amazing. I guess your brother's coming to give you away, heh?

Ann (*giving her drink*): I don't know. I suppose.

Sue: You must be all nerved up.

Ann: It's always a problem getting yourself married, isn't it?

Sue: That depends on your shape, of course. I don't see why you should have had a problem.

Ann: I've had chances —

Sue: I'll bet. It's romantic . . . it's very unusual to me, marrying the brother of your sweetheart.

Ann: I don't know. I think it's mostly that whenever I need somebody to tell me the truth I've always thought of Chris. When he tells you something you know it's so. He relaxes me.

Sue: And he's got money. That's important, you know.

Ann: It wouldn't matter to me.

Sue: You'd be surprised. It makes all the difference. I married an intern. On my salary. And that was bad, because as soon as a woman supports a man he owes her something. You can never owe somebody without resenting them. (*Ann laughs.*) That's true, you know.

Ann: Underneath, I think the doctor is very devoted.

Sue: Oh, certainly. But it's bad when a man always sees the bars in front of him. Jim thinks he's in jail all the time.

Ann: Oh . . .

Sue: That's why I've been intending to ask you a small favor, Ann. It's something very important to me.

Ann: Certainly, if I can do it.

Sue: You can. When you take up housekeeping, try to find a place away from here.

Ann: Are you fooling?

Sue: I'm very serious. My husband is unhappy with Chris around.

Ann: How is that?

Sue: Jim's a successful doctor. But he's got an idea he'd like to do medical research. Discover things. You see?

Ann: Well, isn't that good?

Sue: Research pays 25 dollars a week minus laundering the hair shirt. You've got to give up your life to go into it.

Ann: How does Chris —

Sue *(with growing feeling):* Chris makes people want to be better than it's possible to be. He does that to people.

Ann: Is that bad?

Sue: My husband has a family, dear. Every time he has a session with Chris he feels as though he's compromising by not giving up everything for research. As though Chris or anybody else isn't compromising. It happens with Jim every couple of years. He meets a man and makes a statue out of him.

Ann: Maybe he's right. I don't mean that Chris is a statue, but —

Sue: Now darling, you know he's not right.

Ann: I don't agree with you. Chris —

Sue: Let's face it, dear. Chris is working with his father, isn't he? He's taking money out of that business every week in the year.

Ann: What of it?

Sue: You ask me what of it?

Ann: I certainly do. *(She seems about to burst out.)* You oughtn't cast aspersions like that; I'm surprised at you.

Sue: You're surprised at me!

Ann: He'd never take five cents out of that plant if there was anything wrong with it.

Sue: You know that?

Ann: I know it. I resent everything you've said.

Sue: You know what I resent, dear?

Ann: Please, I don't want to argue.

Sue: I resent living next door to the Holy Family. It makes me look like a bum, you understand?

Ann: I can't do anything about that.

Sue: Who is he to ruin a man's life? Everybody knows Joe pulled a fast one to get out of jail.

Ann: That's not true!

Sue: Then why don't you go out and talk to people? Go on, talk to them. There's not a person on the block who doesn't know the truth.

Ann: That's a lie. People come here all the time for cards and —

Sue: So what? They give him credit for being smart. I do, too; I've got nothing against Joe. But if Chris wants people to put on the hair shirt let him take off his broadcloth. He's driving my husband crazy with that phony idealism of his, and I'm at the end of my rope on it! *(Chris enters on porch, wearing a shirt and tie now. She turns quickly, hearing. With a smile.)* Hello, darling. How's Mother?

Chris: I thought George came.

Sue: No, it was just us.

Chris *(coming down to them):* Susie, do me a favor? Go up to Mother and see if you can calm her. She's all worked up.

Sue: She still doesn't know about you two?

Chris (*laughs a little*): Well, she senses it, I guess. You know my mother.

Sue (*going up to porch*): Oh, yeah, she's psychic.

Chris: Maybe there's something in the medicine chest.

Sue: I'll give her one of everything. (*On porch*) Don't worry about Kate; a couple of drinks, dance her around a little. . . . She'll love Ann. (*To Ann*) Because you're the female version of him. (*Chris laughs.*) Don't be alarmed, I said version. (*She goes into house.*)

Chris: Interesting woman, isn't she?

Ann: Yeah, she's very interesting.

Chris: She's a great nurse, you know, she —

Ann (*in tension, but trying to control it*): Are you still doing that?

Chris (*sensing something wrong, but still smiling*): Doing what?

Ann: As soon as you get to know somebody you find a distinction for them. How do you know she's a great nurse?

Chris: What's the matter, Ann?

Ann: The woman hates you. She despises you!

Chris: Hey. . . . What's hit you?

Ann: Gee, Chris —

Chris: What happened here?

Ann: You never — Why didn't you tell me?

Chris: Tell you what?

Ann: She says they think Joe is guilty.

Chris: What difference does it make what they think?

Ann: I don't care what they think; I just don't understand why you took the trouble to deny it. You said it was all forgotten.

Chris: I didn't want you to feel there was anything wrong in your coming here, that's all. I know a lot of people think my father was guilty, and I assumed there might be some question in your mind.

Ann: But I never once said I suspected him.

Chris: Nobody says it.

Ann: Chris, I know how much you love him, but it could never —

Chris: Do you think I could forgive him if he'd done that thing?

Ann: I'm not here out of a blue sky, Chris. I turned my back on my father; if there's anything wrong here now —

Chris: I know that, Ann.

Ann: George is coming from Dad, and I don't think it's with a blessing.

Chris: He's welcome here. You've got nothing to fear from George.

Ann: Tell me that. . . . Just tell me that.

Chris: The man is innocent, Ann. Remember he was falsely accused once and it put him through hell. How would you behave if he were faced with the same thing again? Annie, believe me, there's nothing wrong for you here, believe me, kid.

Ann: All right, Chris, all right. (*They embrace as Keller appears quietly on porch. Ann simply studies him.*)

Keller: Every time I come out here it looks like Playland! (*They break and laugh in embarrassment.*)

Chris: I thought you were going to shave.

Keller (*sitting on bench*): In a minute. I just woke up, I can't see nothin'.

Ann: You look shaved.

Keller: Oh, no. (*Massages his jaw.*) Gotta be extra special tonight. Big night, Annie. So how's it feel to be a married woman?

Ann (*laughs*): I don't know, yet.

Keller (*to Chris*): What's the matter, you slippin'? (*He takes a little box of apples from under the bench as they talk.*)

Chris: The great *roué*!

Keller: What is that, *roué*?

Chris: It's French.

Keller: Don't talk dirty. (*They laugh.*)

Chris (*to Ann*): You ever meet a bigger ignoramus?

Keller: Well, somebody's got to make a living.

Ann (*as they laugh*): That's telling him.

Keller: I don't know, everybody's gettin' so damn educated in this country there'll be nobody to take away the garbage. (*They laugh.*) It's gettin' so the only dumb ones left are the bosses.

Ann: You're not so dumb, Joe.

Keller: I know, but you go into our plant, for instance. I got so many lieutenants, majors, and colonels that I'm ashamed to ask somebody to sweep the floor. I gotta be careful I'll insult somebody. No kiddin'. It's a tragedy: You stand on the street today and spit, you're gonna hit a college man.

Chris: Well, don't spit.

Keller (*breaks apple in half, passing it to Ann and Chris*): I mean to say, it's comin' to a pass. (*He takes a breath.*) I been thinkin', Annie . . . your brother, George. I been thinkin' about your brother George. When he comes I like you to *brooch* something to him.

Chris: Broach.

Keller: What's the matter with brooch?

Chris (*smiling*): It's not English.

Keller: When I went to night school it was brooch.

Ann (*laughing*): Well, in day school it's broach.

Keller: Don't surround me, will you? Seriously, Ann . . . you say he's not well. George, I been thinkin', why should he knock himself out in New York with that cut-throat competition, when I got so many friends here; I'm very friendly with some big lawyers in town. I could set George up here.

Ann: That's awfully nice of you, Joe.

Keller: No, kid, it ain't nice of me. I want you to understand me. I'm thinking of Chris. (*Slight pause.*) See . . . this is what I mean. You get older, you want to feel that you — accomplished something. My only accomplishment is my son. I ain't brainy. That's all I accomplished. Now, a year, 18 months, your father'll be a free man. Who is he going to come to, Annie? His baby. You. He'll come, old, mad, into your house.

Ann: That can't matter anymore, Joe.

Keller: I don't want that to come between us. (*Gestures between Chris and himself.*)

Ann: I can only tell you that that could never happen.

Keller: You're in love now, Annie, but believe me, I'm older than you and I know — a daughter is a daughter, and a father is a father. And it could happen. (*He pauses.*) I'd like you and George to go to him in prison and tell him . . . , "Dad, Joe wants to bring you into the business when you get out."

Ann (*surprised, even shocked*): You'd have him as a partner?

Keller: No, no partner. A good job. (*Pause. He sees she is shocked, a little mystified. He gets up, speaks more nervously.*) I want him to know, Annie . . . while he's sitting there I want him to know that when he gets out he's got a place waitin' for him. It'll take his bitterness away. To know you got a place . . . it sweetens you.

Ann: Joe, you owe him nothing.

Keller: I owe him a good kick in the teeth, but he's your father.

Chris: Then kick him in the teeth! I don't want him in the plant, so that's that! You understand? And besides, don't talk about him like that. People misunderstand you!

Keller: And I don't understand why she has to crucify the man.

Chris: Well, it's her father, if she feels —

Keller: No, no.

Chris (*almost angrily*): What's it to you? Why — ?

Keller (*a commanding outburst in high nervousness*): A father is a father! (*As though the outburst had revealed him, he looks about, wanting to retract it. His hand goes to his cheek.*) I better — I better shave. (*He turns and a smile is on his face; to Ann.*) I didn't mean to yell at you, Annie.

Ann: Let's forget the whole thing, Joe.

Keller: Right. (*To Chris*) She's likeable.

Chris (*a little peeved at the man's stupidity*): Shave, will you?

Keller: Right again.

(*As he turns to porch, Lydia comes hurrying from her house.*)

Lydia: I forgot all about it. (*Seeing Chris and Ann*) Hya. (*To Joe*) I promised to fix Kate's hair for her tonight. Did she comb it yet?

Keller: Always a smile, hey, Lydia?

Lydia: Sure, why not?

Keller (*going up on porch*): Come on up and comb my Katie's hair. (*Lydia goes up on porch.*) She's got a big night; make her beautiful.

Lydia: I will.

Keller (*holds door open and she goes into kitchen; to Chris and Ann*): Hey, that could be a song. (*He sings softly.*) "Come on up and comb my Katie's hair. . . . Oh, come on up, 'cause she's my lady fair — " (*To Ann*) How's that for one year of night school? (*He continues singing as he goes into kitchen.*) "Oh, come on up, come on up, and comb my lady's hair — "

(*Jim Bayliss rounds corner of driveway, walking rapidly. Jim crosses to Chris, motions him, and pulls him down excitedly. Keller stands just inside kitchen door, watching them.*)

Chris: What's the matter? Where is he?

Jim: Where's your mother?

Chris: Upstairs, dressing.

Ann (*crossing to them rapidly*): What happened to George?

Jim: I asked him to wait in the car. Listen to me now. Can you take some advice? (*They wait.*) Don't bring him in here.

Ann: Why?

Jim: Kate is in bad shape, you can't explode this in front of her.

Ann: Explode what?

Jim: You know why he's here; don't try to kid it away. There's blood in his eye; drive him somewhere and talk to him alone.

(*Ann turns to go up drive, takes a couple of steps, sees Keller, and stops. He goes quietly on into house.*)

Chris (*shaken, and therefore angered*): Don't be an old lady.

Jim: He's come to take her home. What does that mean? (*To Ann*) You know what that means. Fight it out with him someplace else. (*Ann comes back down toward Chris.*)

Ann: I'll drive . . . him somewhere.

Chris (*goes to her*): No.

Jim: Will you stop being an idiot?

Chris: Nobody's afraid of him here. Cut that out!

(*He starts for driveway, but is brought up short by George, who enters there. George is Chris's age, but a paler man, now on the edge of his self-restraint. He speaks quietly, as though afraid to find himself screaming. An instant's hesitation and Chris steps up to him, hand extended, smiling.*)

Chris: What're you sitting out there for?

George: Doctor said your mother isn't well. I —

Chris: So what? She'd want to see you, wouldn't she? We've been waiting for you all afternoon.

(*He puts his hand on George's arm, but George pulls away, coming across toward Ann.*)

Ann (*touching his collar*): This is filthy, didn't you bring another shirt?

(*George breaks away from her, and moves down, examining the yard. Door opens, and he turns rapidly, thinking it is Kate, but it's Sue. She looks at him; he turns away and moves to fence. He looks over it at his former home. Sue comes downstage.*)

Sue (*annoyed*): How about the beach, Jim?

Jim: Oh, it's too hot to drive.

Sue: How'd you get to the station — Zeppelin?

Chris: This is Mrs. Bayliss, George. (*Calling, as George pays no attention: staring at house*) George! (*George turns.*) Mrs. Bayliss.

Sue: How do you do.

George (*removing his hat*): You're the people who bought our house, aren't you?

Sue: That's right. Come and see what we did with it before you leave.

George (*walks down and away from her*): I liked it the way it was.

Sue (*after a brief pause*): He is frank, isn't he?

Jim (*pulling her off*): See you later. . . . Take it easy, fella. (*They exit.*)

Chris (*calling after them*): Thanks for driving him! (*Turning to George*) How about some grape juice? Mother made it especially for you.

George (*with forced appreciation*): Good old Kate, remembered my grape juice.

Chris: You drank enough of it in this house. How've you been, George? — Sit down.

George (*keeps moving*): It takes me a minute. (*Looking around*) It seems impossible.

Chris: What?

George: I'm back here.

Chris: Say, you've gotten a little nervous, haven't you?

George: Yeah, toward the end of the day. What're you, big executive now?

Chris: Just kind of medium. How's the law?

George: I don't know. When I was studying in the hospital it seemed sensible, but outside there doesn't seem to be much of a law. The trees got thick, didn't they? *(Points to stump.)* What's that?

Chris: Blew down last night. We had it there for Larry. You know.

George: Why, afraid you'll forget him?

Chris *(starts for George):* Kind of a remark is that?

Ann *(breaking in, putting a restraining hand on Chris):* When did you start wearing a hat?

George *(discovers hat in hand):* Today. From now on I decided to look like a lawyer, anyway. *(He holds it up to her.)* Don't you recognize it?

Ann: Why? Where — ?

George: Your father's — He asked me to wear it.

Ann: How is he?

George: He got smaller.

Ann: Smaller?

George: Yeah, little. *(Holds out his hand to measure.)* He's a little man. That's what happens to suckers, you know. It's good I went to him in time — another year there'd be nothing left but his smell.

Chris: What's the matter, George, what's the trouble?

George: The trouble? The trouble is when you make suckers out of people once, you shouldn't try to do it twice.

Chris: What does that mean?

George *(to Ann):* You're not married yet, are you?

Ann: George, sit down and stop — ?

George: Are you married yet?

Ann: No, I'm not married yet.

George: You're not going to marry him.

Ann: Why am I not going to marry him?

George: Because his father destroyed your family.

Chris: Now look, George . . .

George: Cut it short, Chris. Tell her to come home with me. Let's not argue; you know what I've got to say.

Chris: George, you don't want to be the voice of God, do you?

George: I'm —

Chris: That's been your trouble all your life, George; you dive into things. What kind of a statement is that to make? You're a big boy now.

George: I'm a big boy now.

Chris: Don't come bulling in here. If you've got something to say, you could be civilized about it.

George: Don't civilize me!

Ann: Shhh!

Chris *(ready to hit him):* Are you going to talk like a grown man or aren't you?

Ann *(quickly, to forestall an outburst):* Sit down, dear. Don't be angry, what's the matter? *(He allows her to seat him, looking at her.)* Now what happened? You kissed me when I left, now you —

George *(breathlessly):* My life turned upside down since then. I couldn't go back to work when you left. I wanted to go to Dad and tell him you were going to be married. It seemed impossible not to tell him. He loved you so much. *(He pauses.)* Annie — we did a terrible thing. We can never be forgiven. Not even to send him a card at Christmas. I didn't see him once since I got home from the war! Annie, you don't know what was done to that man. You don't know what happened.

Ann *(afraid):* Of course I know.

George: You can't know, you wouldn't be here. Dad came to work that day. The night foreman came to him and showed him the cylinder heads ... they were coming out of the process with defects. There was something wrong with the process. So Dad went directly to the phone and called here and told Joe to come down right away. But the morning passed. No sign of Joe. So Dad called again. By this time he had over a hundred defectives. The Army was screaming for stuff and Dad didn't have anything to ship. So Joe told him ... on the phone he told him to weld, cover up the cracks in any way he could, and ship them out.

Chris: Are you through now?

George *(surging up at him):* I'm not through now! *(Back to Ann)* Dad was afraid. He wanted Joe there if he was going to do it. But Joe can't come down. ... He's sick. Sick! He suddenly gets the flu! Suddenly! But he promised to take responsibility. Do you understand what I'm saying? On the telephone you can't have responsibility! In a court you can always deny a phone call and that's exactly what he did. They knew he was a liar the first time, but in the appeal they believed that rotten lie and now Joe is a big shot and your father is the patsy. *(He gets up.)* Now what're you going to do? Eat his food, sleep in his bed? Answer me; what're you going to do?

Chris: What're you going to do, George?

George: He's too smart for me. I can't prove a phone call.

Chris: Then how dare you come in here with that rot?

Ann: George, the court —

George: The court didn't know your father! But you know him. You know in your heart Joe did it.

Chris *(whirling him around):* Lower your voice or I'll throw you out of here!

George: She knows. She knows.

Chris *(to Ann):* Get him out of here, Ann. Get him out of here.

Ann: George, I know everything you've said. Dad told that whole thing in court, and they —

George *(almost a scream):* The court did not know him, Annie!

Ann: Shhh! — But he'll say anything, George. You know how quick he can lie.

George *(turning to Chris, with deliberation):* I'll ask you something, and look me in the eye when you answer me.

Chris: I'll look you in the eye.

George: You know your father —

Chris: I know him well.

George: And he's the kind of boss to let 121 cylinder heads be repaired and shipped out of his shop without even knowing about it?

Chris: He's that kind of boss.

George: And that's the same Joe Keller who never left his shop without first going around to see that all the lights were out.

Chris *(with growing anger):* The same Joe Keller.

George: The same man who knows how many minutes a day his workers spend in the toilet.

Chris: The same man.

George: And my father, that frightened

mouse who'd never buy a shirt without somebody along — that man would dare do such a thing on his own?

Chris: On his own. And because he's a frightened mouse this is another thing he'd do — throw the blame on somebody else because he's not man enough to take it himself. He tried it in court but it didn't work, but with a fool like you it works!

George: Oh, Chris, you're a liar to yourself!

Ann *(deeply shaken):* Don't talk like that!

Chris *(sits facing George):* Tell me, George. What happened? The court record was good enough for you all these years, why isn't it good now? Why did you believe it all these years?

George *(after a slight pause):* Because you believed it. . . . That's the truth, Chris. I believed everything, because I thought you did. But today I heard it from his mouth. Your Dad took everything we have. I can't beat that. But she's one item he's not going to grab. *(He turns to Ann.)* Get your things. Everything they have is covered with blood. You're not the kind of girl who can live with that. Get your things.

Chris: Ann . . . you're not going to believe that, are you?

Ann *(goes to him):* You know it's not true, don't you?

George: How can he tell you? It's his father. *(To Chris)* None of these things ever even cross your mind?

Chris: Yes, they crossed my mind. Anything can cross your mind!

George: He knows, Annie. He knows!

Chris: The voice of God!

George: Then why isn't your name on the business? Explain that to her!

Chris: What the hell has that got to do with — ?

George: Annie, why isn't his name on it?

Chris: Even when I don't own it!

George: Who're you kidding? Who gets it when he dies? *(To Ann)* Open your eyes, you know the both of them, isn't that the first thing they'd do, the way they love each other? — J. O. Keller and Son? *(Pause. Ann looks from him to Chris.)* I'll settle it. Do you want to settle it, or are you afraid to?

Chris: What do you mean?

George: Let me go up and talk to your father. In 10 minutes you'll have the answer. Or are you afraid of the answer?

Chris: I'm not afraid of the answer. I know the answer. But my mother isn't well and I don't want a fight here now.

George: Let me go to him.

Chris: You're not going to start a fight here now.

George *(to Ann):* What more do you want! *(There is a sound of footsteps in the house.)*

Ann *(turns her head suddenly toward the house):* Someone's coming.

Chris *(to George, quietly):* You won't say anything now.

Ann: You'll go soon. I'll call a cab.

George: You're coming with me.

Ann: And don't mention marriage, because we haven't told her yet.

George: You're coming with me.

Ann: You understand? Don't — George, you're not going to start anything now! *(She hears footsteps.)* Shhh!

(Mother enters on porch. She is dressed almost formally; her hair is fixed. They are all turned toward her. On seeing

George she raises both hands, comes down toward him.)

Mother: Georgie, Georgie.

George *(he has always liked her)*: Hello, Kate.

Mother *(cups his face in her hands)*: They made an old man out of you. *(Touches his hair.)* Look, you're gray.

George *(her pity, open and unabashed, reaches into him, and he smiles sadly)*: I know, I —

Mother: I told you when you went away, don't try for medals.

George *(laughs, tiredly)*: I didn't try, Kate. They made it very easy for me.

Mother *(actually angry)*: Go on. You're all alike. *(To Ann)* Look at him, why did you say he's fine? He looks like a ghost.

George *(relishing her solicitude)*: I feel all right.

Mother: I'm sick to look at you. What's the matter with your mother; why don't she feed you?

Ann: He just hasn't any appetite.

Mother: If he ate in my house he'd have an appetite. *(To Ann)* I pity your husband! *(To George)* Sit down. I'll make you a sandwich.

George *(sits with an embarrassed laugh)*: I'm really not hungry.

Mother: Honest to God, it breaks my heart to see what happened to all the children. How we worked and planned for you, and you end up no better than we are.

George *(with deep feeling)*: You . . . you haven't changed at all, you know that, Kate?

Mother: None of us changed, Georgie. We all love you. Joe was just talking about the day you were born and the water got shut off. People were carrying basins from a block away — a stranger would have thought the whole neighborhood was on fire! *(They laugh. She sees the juice. To Ann.)* Why didn't you give him some juice!

Ann *(defensively)*: I offered it to him!

Mother: *(Thrusting glass into George's hand)*: Give it to him! *(To George, who is laughing)* And now you're going to sit here and drink some juice . . . and look like something!

George *(sitting)*: Kate, I feel hungry already.

Chris *(proudly)*: She could turn Mahatma Gandhi into a heavyweight!

Mother *(to Chris, with great energy)*: Listen, to hell with the restaurant! I got a ham in the icebox, and frozen strawberries, and avocados, and —

Ann: Swell, I'll help you!

George: The train leaves at 8:30, Ann.

Mother *(to Ann)*: You're leaving?

Chris: No, Mother, she's not —

Ann *(breaking through it, going to George)*: You hardly got here; give yourself a chance to get acquainted again.

Chris: Sure, you don't even know us anymore.

Mother: Well, Chris, if they can't stay, don't —

Chris: No, it's just a question of George, Mother, he planned on —

George *(gets up politely, nicely, for Kate's sake)*: Now wait a minute, Chris . . .

Chris *(smiling and full of command, cutting him off)*: If you want to go, I'll drive you to the station now, but if you're staying, no arguments while you're here.

Mother *(at last confessing the ten-*

sion): Why should he argue? *(She goes to him. With desperation and compassion, stroking his hair.)* Georgie and us have no argument. How could we have an argument, Georgie? We all got hit by the same lightning, how can you — ? Did you see what happened to Larry's tree, Georgie? *(She has taken his arm, and unwillingly he moves across stage with her.)* Imagine? While I was dreaming of him in the middle of the night, the wind came along and —

(Lydia enters on porch. As soon as she sees him . . .)

Lydia: Hey, Georgie! Georgie! Georgie! Georgie! Georgie! *(She comes down to him eagerly. She has a flowered hat in her hand, which Kate takes from her as she goes to George.)*

George *(as they shake hands eagerly, warmly):* Hello, Laughy. What'd you do, grow?

Lydia: I'm a big girl now.

Mother: Look what she can do to a hat!

Ann *(to Lydia, admiring the hat):* Did you make that?

Mother: In 10 minutes! *(She puts it on.)*

Lydia *(fixing it on her head):* I only rearranged it.

George: You still make your own clothes?

Chris *(of Mother):* Ain't she classy! All she needs now is a Russian wolfhound.

Mother *(moving her head):* It feels like somebody is sitting on my head.

Ann: No, it's beautiful, Kate.

Mother *(kisses Lydia; to George):* She's a genius! You should've married her. *(They laugh.)* This one can feed you!

Lydia *(strangely embarrassed):* Oh, stop that, Kate.

George *(to Lydia):* Didn't I hear you had a baby?

Mother: You don't hear so good. She's got three babies.

George *(a little hurt by it — to Lydia):* No kidding, three?

Lydia: Yeah, it was one, two, three — You've been away a long time, Georgie.

George: I'm beginning to realize.

Mother *(to Chris and George):* The trouble with you kids is you *think* too much.

Lydia: Well, we think, too.

Mother: Yes, but not all the time.

George *(with almost obvious envy):* They never took Frank, heh?

Lydia *(a little apologetically):* No, he was always one year ahead of the draft.

Mother: It's amazing. When they were calling boys 27 Frank was just 28, when they made it 28 he was just 29. That's why he took up astrology. It's all in when you were born, it just goes to show.

Chris: What does it go to show?

Mother *(to Chris):* Don't be so intelligent. Some superstitions are very nice! *(To Lydia)* Did he finish Larry's horoscope?

Lydia: I'll ask him now, I'm going in. *(To George, a little sadly, almost embarrassed)* Would you like to see my babies? Come on.

George: I don't think so, Lydia.

Lydia *(understanding):* All right. Good luck to you, George.

George: Thanks. And to you . . . and Frank. *(She smiles at him, turns and goes off to her house. George stands staring after her.)*

Lydia *(as she runs off):* Oh, Frank!

Mother *(reading his thoughts):* She got pretty, heh?

512

George (sadly): Very pretty.

Mother (as a reprimand): She's beautiful, you damned fool!

George (looks around longingly; and softly, with a catch in his throat): She makes it seem so nice around here.

Mother (shaking her finger at him): Look what happened to you because you wouldn't listen to me! I told you to marry that girl and stay out of the war!

George (laughs at himself): She used to laugh too much.

Mother: And you didn't laugh enough. While you were getting mad about Fascism, Frank was getting into her bed.

George (to Chris): He won the war — Frank.

Chris: All the battles.

Mother (in pursuit of this mood): The day they started the draft, Georgie, I told you you loved that girl.

Chris (laughs): And truer love hath no man!

Mother: I'm smarter than any of you.

George (laughing): She's wonderful!

Mother: And now you're going to listen to me, George. You had big principles, Eagle Scouts the three of you; so now I got a tree, and this one — (Indicating Chris) — when the weather gets bad he can't stand on his feet; and that big dope — (Pointing to Lydia's house) — next door who never reads anything but Andy Gump has three children and his house paid off. Stop being a philosopher, and look after yourself. Like Joe was just saying — you move back here, he'll help you get set, and I'll find you a girl and put a smile on your face.

George: Joe? Joe wants me here?

Ann (eagerly): He asked me to tell you, and I think it's a good idea.

Mother: Certainly. Why must you make believe you hate us? Is that another principle — that you have to hate us? You don't hate us, George, I know you, you can't fool me, I diapered you. (Suddenly to Ann) You remember Mr. Marcy's daughter?

Ann (laughing, to George): She's got you hooked already! (George laughs, is excited.)

Mother: You look her over, George; you'll see she's the most beautiful —

Chris: She's got warts, George.

Mother (to Chris): She hasn't got warts! (To George) So the girl has a little beauty mark on her chin —

Chris: And two on her nose.

Mother: You remember. Her father's the retired police inspector.

Chris: Sergeant, George.

Mother: He's a very kind man!

Chris: He looks like a gorilla.

Mother (to George): He never shot anybody.

(They all burst out laughing, as Keller appears in doorway. George rises abruptly and stares at Keller, who comes rapidly down to him.)

Keller (the laughter stops; with strained joviality): Well! Look who's here! (Extending his hand) Georgie, good to see ya.

George (shaking hands — somberly): How're you, Joe?

Keller: So-so. Gettin' old. You comin' out to dinner with us?

George: No, got to be back in New York.

Ann: I'll call a cab for you. (She goes up into the house.)

Keller: Too bad you can't stay, George. Sit down. *(To Mother)* He looks fine.

Mother: He looks terrible.

Keller: That's what I said, you look terrible, George. *(They laugh.)* I wear the pants and she beats me with the belt.

George: I saw your factory on the way from the station. It looks like General Motors.

Keller: I wish it was General Motors, but it ain't. Sit down, George, sit down. *(Takes cigar out of his pocket.)* So you finally went to see your father, I hear?

George: Yes, this morning. What kind of stuff do you make now?

Keller: Oh, little of everything. Pressure cookers, an assembly for washing machines. Got a nice, flexible plant now. So how'd you find Dad? Feel all right?

George *(searching Keller, speaking indecisively):* No, he's not well, Joe.

Keller *(lighting his cigar):* Not his heart again, is it?

George: It's everything, Joe. It's his soul.

Keller *(blowing out smoke):* Uh, huh —

Chris: How about seeing what they did with your house?

Keller: Leave him be.

George *(to Chris, indicating Keller):* I'd like to talk to him.

Keller: Sure, he just got here. That's the way they do, George. A little man makes a mistake and they hang him by the thumbs; the big ones become ambassadors. I wish you'd-a told me you were going to see Dad.

George *(studying him):* I didn't know you were interested.

Keller: In a way, I am. I would like him to know, George, that as far as I'm con-cerned, any time he wants, he's got a place with me. I would like him to know that.

George: He hates your guts, Joe. Don't you know that?

Keller: I imagined it. But that can change, too.

Mother: Steve was never like that.

George: He's like that now. He'd like to take every man who made money in the war and put him up against a wall.

Chris: He'll need a lot of bullets.

George: And he'd better not get any.

Keller: That's a sad thing to hear.

George *(with bitterness dominant):* Why? What'd you expect him to think of you?

Keller *(the force of his nature rising but under control):* I'm sad to see he hasn't changed. As long as I know him, 25 years, the man never learned how to take the blame. You know that, George.

George *(he does):* Well, I —

Keller: But you do know it. Because the way you come in here you don't look like you remember it. I mean like in 1937 when we had the shop on Flood Street. And he damn near blew us all up with that heater left burning for two days without water. He wouldn't admit that was his fault, either. I had to fire a mechanic to save face. You remember that.

George: Yes, but —

Keller: I'm just mentioning it, George. Because this is just another one of a lot of things. Like when he gave Frank that money to invest in oil stock.

George *(distressed):* I know that, I —

Keller *(driving in, but restrained):* But it's good to remember those things, kid. The way he cursed Frank because the stock went down. Was that Frank's fault? To listen to him Frank was a swindler. And all the man did was give him a bad tip.

George (*gets up, moves away*): I know those things. . . .

Keller: Then remember them, remember them. (*Ann comes out of house.*) There are certain men in the world who'd rather see everybody hung before they'll take blame. You understand me, George? (*They stand facing each other, George trying to judge him. Ann, coming downstage.*) The cab's on its way. Would you like to wash?

Mother (*with the thrust of hope*): Why must he go? Make the midnight, George.

Keller: Sure, you'll have dinner with us!

Ann: How about it? Why not? We're eating at the lake, we could have a swell time.

(*A long pause, as George looks at Ann, Chris, Keller, then back to her.*)

George: All right.

Mother: Now you're talking.

Chris: I've got a shirt that'll go right with that suit.

Mother: Size 15 and a half, right, George?

George: Is Lydia — ? I mean — Frank and Lydia coming?

Mother: I'll get you a date that'll make her look like a — (*She starts upstage.*)

George (*laughing*): No, I don't want a date.

Chris: I know somebody just for you! Charlotte Tanner! (*He starts for the house.*)

Ann: You go up and pick out a shirt and tie.

George (*stops, looks around at them and the place*): I never felt at home anywhere but here. I feel so — (*He nearly laughs, and turns away from them.*) Kate, you look so young, you know? You didn't

change at all. It . . . rings an old bell. (*Turns to Keller.*) You, too, Joe, you're amazingly the same. The whole atmosphere is.

Keller: Say, I ain't got time to get sick.

Mother: He hasn't been laid up in 15 years.

Keller: Except my flu during the war.

Mother: Huhh?

Keller: My flu, when I was sick during . . . the war.

Mother: Well, sure. . . . (*To George*) I mean except for that flu. (*George stands perfectly still.*) Well, it slipped my mind, don't look at me that way. He wanted to go to the shop but he couldn't lift himself off the bed. I thought he had pneumonia.

George: Why did you say he's never — ?

Keller: I know how you feel, kid, I'll never forgive myself. If I could've gone in that day I'd never allow Dad to touch those heads.

George: She said you've never been sick.

Mother: I said he was sick, George.

George (*going to Ann*): Ann, didn't you hear her say — ?

Mother: Do you remember every time you were sick?

George: I'd remember pneumonia. Especially if I got it just the day my partner was going to patch up cylinder heads. . . . What happened that day, Joe?

(*Frank enters briskly from driveway, holding Larry's horoscope in his hand. He comes to Kate.*)

Frank: Kate! Kate!

Mother: Frank, did you see George?

Frank (*extending his hand*): Lydia told me, I'm glad to . . . you'll have to pardon me. *(Pulling Mother over)* I've got something amazing for you, Kate, I finished Larry's horoscope.

Mother: You'd be interested in this, George. It's wonderful the way he can understand the —

Chris *(entering from house):* George, the girl's on the phone —

Mother *(desperately):* He finished Larry's horoscope!

Chris: Frank, can't you pick a better time than this?

Frank: The greatest men who ever lived believed in the stars!

Chris: Stop filling her head with that junk!

Frank: Is it junk to feel that there's a greater power than ourselves? I've studied the stars of his life! I won't argue with you, I'm telling you. Somewhere in this world your brother is alive!

Mother *(instantly to Chris):* Why isn't it possible?

Chris: Because it's insane.

Frank: Just a minute now. I'll tell you something and you can do as you please. Just let's say it. He was supposed to have died on November twenty-fifth. But November twenty-fifth was his favorable day.

Chris: Mother!

Mother: Listen to him!

Frank: It was a day when everything good was shining on him, the kind of day he should've married on. You can laugh at a lot of it. I can understand you laughing. But the odds are a million to one that a man won't die on his favorable day. That's known; that's known, Chris!

Mother: Why isn't it possible; why isn't it possible, Chris!

George *(to Ann):* Don't you understand what she's saying? She just told you to go. What are you waiting for now?

Chris: Nobody can tell her to go. *(A car horn is heard.)*

Mother *(to Frank):* Thank you, darling, for your trouble. Will you tell him to wait, Frank?

Frank *(as he goes):* Sure thing.

Mother *(calling out):* They'll be right out, driver!

Chris: She's not leaving, Mother.

George: You heard her say it; he's never been sick!

Mother: He misunderstood me, Chris!

(Chris looks at her, struck.)

George *(to Ann):* He simply told your father to kill pilots, and covered himself in bed!

Chris: You'd better answer him, Annie. Answer him.

Mother: I packed your bag, darling.

Chris: What?

Mother: I packed your bag, darling. All you've got to do is close it.

Ann: I'm not closing anything. He asked me here and I'm staying till he tells me to go. *(To George)* Till Chris tells me!

Chris: That's all! Now get out of here, George!

Mother *(to Chris):* But if that's how he feels —

Chris: That's all, nothing more till Christ comes, about the case or Larry as long as I'm here! *(To George)* Now get out of here, George!

George *(to Ann):* You tell me. I want to hear you tell me.

Ann: Go, George! *(They disappear up the driveway, Ann saying, "Don't take it that*

516

way, Georgie! Please don't take it that way.")

Chris *(turning to his Mother):* What do you mean, you packed her bag? How dare you pack her bag?

Mother: Chris —

Chris: How dare you pack her bag?

Mother: She doesn't belong here.

Chris: Then I don't belong here.

Mother: She's Larry's girl.

Chris: And I'm his brother and he's dead, and I'm marrying his girl.

Mother: Never, never in this world!

Keller: You lost your mind?

Mother: You have nothing to say!

Keller *(cruelly):* I got plenty to say. Three and a half years you been talking like a maniac —

(Mother smashes him across the face.)

Mother: Nothing. You have nothing to say. Now I say. He's coming back and everybody has got to wait.

Chris: Mother, Mother —

Mother: Wait, wait —

Chris: How long? How long?

Mother *(rolling out of her):* Till he comes; forever and ever till he comes!

Chris *(as an ultimatum):* Mother, I'm going ahead with it.

Mother: Chris, I've never said no to you in my life, now I say no!

Chris: You'll never let him go till I do it.

Mother: I'll never let him go and you'll never let him go!

Chris: I've let him go. I've let him go a long —

Mother *(with no less force, but turning from him):* Then let your father go. *(Pause. Chris stands transfixed.)*

Keller: She's out of her mind.

Mother: Altogether! *(To Chris, but not facing him)* Your brother's alive, darling, because if he's dead, your father killed him. Do you understand me now? As long as you live, that boy is alive. God does not let a son be killed by his father. Now you see, don't you? Now you see. *(Beyond control, she hurries up and into house.)*

Keller *(Chris has not moved. He speaks insinuatingly, questioningly):* She's out of her mind.

Chris *(in a broken whisper):* Then . . . you did it?

Keller *(with the beginning of plea in his voice):* He never flew a P-40 —

Chris *(struck; deadly):* But the others.

Keller *(insistently):* She's out of her mind. *(He takes a step toward Chris, pleadingly.)*

Chris *(unyielding)* Dad . . . you did it?

Keller: He never flew a P-40, what's the matter with you?

Chris *(still asking, and saying):* Then you did it. To the others. *(Both hold their voices down.)*

Keller *(afraid of him, his deadly insistence):* What's the matter with you? What the hell is the matter with you?

Chris *(quietly, incredibly):* How could you do that? How?

Keller: What's the matter with you!

Chris: Dad . . . Dad, you killed 21 men!

Keller: What, killed?

Chris: You killed them; you murdered them.

Keller *(as though throwing his whole nature open before Chris):* How could I kill anybody?

Chris: Dad! Dad!

Keller *(trying to hush him):* I didn't kill anybody!

Chris: Then explain it to me. What did you do? Explain it to me or I'll tear you to pieces!

Keller *(horrified at his overwhelming fury):* Don't, Chris, don't —

Chris: I want to know what you did, now what did you do? You had 120 cracked engine-heads, now what did you do?

Keller: If you're going to hang me, I —

Chris: I'm listening. God Almighty, I'm listening!

Keller *(Their movements now are those of subtle pursuit and escape. Keller keeps a step out of Chris's range as he talks):* You're a boy, what could I do! I'm in business, a man is in business; 120 cracked, you're out of business; you got a process, the process don't work you're out of business; you don't know how to operate, your stuff is no good; they close you up, they tear up your contracts, what the hell's it to them? You lay 40 years into a business and they knock you out in five minutes; what could I do, let them take 40 years, let them take my life away? *(His voice cracking.)* I never thought they'd install them. I swear to God. I thought they'd stop 'em before anybody took off.

Chris: Then why'd you ship them out?

Keller: By the time they could spot them I thought I'd have the process going again, and I could show them they needed me and they'd let it go by. But weeks passed and I got no kickback, so I was going to tell them.

Chris: Then why didn't you tell them?

Keller: It was too late. The paper, it was all over the front page, 21 went down, it was too late. They came with handcuffs into the shop, what could I do? *(He sits on bench.)* Chris . . . Chris, I did it for you, it was a chance to make something for you. I'm 61 years old, when would I have another chance to make something for you? Sixty-one years old you don't get another chance, do ya?

Chris: You even knew they wouldn't hold up in the air.

Keller: I didn't say that.

Chris: But you were going to warn them not to use them —

Keller: But that don't mean —

Chris: It means you knew they'd crash.

Keller: It don't mean that.

Chris: Then you *thought* they'd crash.

Keller: I was afraid maybe —

Chris: You were afraid maybe! God in heaven, what kind of a man are you? Kids were hanging in the air by those heads. You know that!

Keller: For you, a business for you!

Chris *(with burning fury):* For me! Where do you live, where have you come from? For me! — I was dying every day and you were killing my boys and you did it for me? What the hell do you think I was thinking of, the damn business? Is that as far as your mind can see, the business? What is that, the world — the business? What the hell do you mean, you did it for me? Don't you have a country? Don't you live in the world? What the hell are you? You're not even an animal, no animal kills his own; what are you? What must I do to you? I ought to tear the tongue out of your mouth, what must I do? *(With his fist he pounds down upon his father's shoulder. He stumbles away, covering his face as he weeps.)* What must I do, Jesus God, what must I do?

READING COMPREHENSION

Select the best choice to complete each sentence below. Then write the sentence on your paper.

1. Sue told Ann that everyone in the neighborhood believed that _____.
   a. Joe was really guilty
   b. Chris and Ann made a lovely couple
   c. Chris should take over the business

2. George came to _____.
   a. claim a share of the business
   b. apply for a job as a lawyer
   c. stop Ann from marrying Chris

3. Joe reminded George that his father _____.
   a. never knew how to take blame
   b. loved him very much
   c. lied at the trial

4. George caught a slip Kate made when she said that _____.
   a. she had never liked Steve
   b. Joe hadn't been sick in 15 years
   c. Joe was the lucky one to get away

For Discussion

1. Why do you think Joe wanted to offer to set up George in law practice?

2. Explain how Kate's entrance caused George to change. How does this affect your feelings about him? How does this affect your feelings about Kate?

3. Both Joe's and Chris's ideals are clearly portrayed at the end of the second act. Compare the way they feel. For whom do you feel more sympathy?

UNDERSTANDING LITERATURE

Climax in a Play. By the end of the second act of *All My Sons,* the action has reached a turning point, or *climax*. The events in this act lead to a crisis, and the truth is revealed. The author has set the stage for Act Three — the end of the play where everything will be resolved. The sequence of events in Act Two is important.

1. Below are some events from Act Two. On your paper, put them in order, ending with the climax.

   a. Kate said Joe had not been sick for 15 years.
   b. Frank said Larry's horoscope proved that he was still alive.
   c. Ann said she was staying until Chris asked her to leave.
   d. Joe told the real story of how and why the cracked parts were shipped.
   e. George visited his father in prison.
   f. Chris told Ann and George that he was sure Joe was innocent.

2. Explain what was revealed at the climax of this act. Were you surprised at the climax? Tell why or why not. How do you think that the climax will affect the relationships that Kate, Joe, Chris, and Ann have with one another?

Writing

Imagine that you are a newspaper reporter who has learned the truth about Joe Keller, the leading citizen in your town. Write a three-paragraph news story about the event.

Act Three

Two o'clock the following morning, Mother is discovered on the rise, rocking ceaselessly in a chair, staring at her thoughts. It is an intense, slight sort of rocking. A light shows from upstairs bedroom, lower floor windows being dark. The moon is strong and casts its bluish light. Presently Jim, dressed in jacket and hat, appears, and seeing her, goes up beside her.

Jim: Any news?

Mother: No news.

Jim *(gently):* You can't sit up all night, dear, why don't you go to bed?

Mother: I'm waiting for Chris. Don't worry about me, Jim, I'm perfectly all right.

Jim: But it's almost 2:00.

Mother: I can't sleep. *(Slight pause.)* You had an emergency?

Jim *(tiredly):* Somebody had a headache and thought he was dying. *(Slight pause.)* Half of my patients are quite mad. Nobody realizes how many people are walking around loose, and they're cracked as coconuts. Money. Money-money-money-money. You say it long enough it doesn't mean anything. *(She smiles, makes a silent laugh.)* Oh, how I'd love to be around when that happens!

Mother *(shaking her head):* You're so childish, Jim! Sometimes you are.

Jim *(looks at her a moment):* Kate. *(Pause.)* What happened?

Mother: I told you. He had an argument with Joe. Then he got in the car and drove away.

Jim: What kind of an argument?

Mother: An argument, Joe . . . He was crying like a child, before.

Jim: They argued about Ann?

Mother *(after slight hesitation):* No, not Ann. Imagine? *(Indicates lighted window above.)* She hasn't come out of that room since he left. All night in that room.

Jim *(looks at window, then at her):* What'd Joe do, tell him?

Mother *(stops rocking):* Tell him what?

Jim: Don't be afraid. Kate. I know. I've always known.

Mother: How?

Jim: It occurred to me a long time ago.

Mother: I always had the feeling that in the back of his head, Chris . . . almost knew. I didn't think it would be such a shock.

Jim *(gets up):* Chris would never know how to live with a thing like that. It takes a certain talent — for lying. You have it, and I do. But not him.

Mother: What do you mean . . . he's not coming back?

Jim: Oh, no, he'll come back. We all come back, Kate. These private little revolutions always die. The compromise is always made. In a peculiar way. Frank is right — every man does have a star. The star of one's honesty. And you spend your life groping for it, but once it's out it never lights again. I don't think he went very far. He probably just wanted to be alone to watch his star go out.

Mother: Just as long as he comes back.

Jim: I wish he wouldn't, Kate. One year

I simply took off, went to New Orleans; for two months I lived on bananas and milk, and studied a certain disease. It was beautiful. And then she came, and she cried. And I went back home with her.

And now I live in the usual darkness; I can't find myself; it's even hard sometimes to remember the kind of man I wanted to be. I'm a good husband; Chris is a good son — he'll come back.

(*Keller comes out on porch in dressing gown and slippers. He goes upstage — to alley. Jim goes to him.*)

Jim: I have a feeling he's in the park. I'll look around for him. Put her to bed, Joe; this is no good for what she's got. (*Jim exits up driveway.*)

Keller (*coming down*): What does he want here?

Mother: His friend is not home.

Keller (*comes down to her. His voice is husky*): I don't like him mixing in so much.

Mother: It's too late, Joe. He knows.

Keller (*apprehensively*): How does he know?

Mother: He guessed a long time ago.

Keller: I don't like that.

Mother (*laughs dangerously, quietly into the line*): What you don't like.

Keller: Yeah, what I don't like.

Mother: You can't bull yourself through this one, Joe; you better be smart now. This thing — this thing is not over yet.

Keller (*indicating lighted window above*): And what is she doing up there? She don't come out of the room.

Mother: I don't know, what is she doing? Sit down, stop being mad. You want to live? You better figure out your life.

Keller: She doesn't know, does she?

Mother: She saw Chris storming out of here. It's one and one — she knows how to add.

Keller: Maybe I ought to talk to her?

Mother: Don't ask me, Joe.

Keller (*almost an outburst*): Then who do I ask? But I don't think she'll do anything about it.

Mother: You're asking me again.

Keller: I'm askin' you. What am I, a stranger? I thought I had a family here. What happened to my family?

Mother: You've got a family. I'm simply telling you that I have no strength to think anymore.

Keller: You have no strength. The minute there's trouble you have no strength.

Mother: Joe, you're doing the same thing again; all your life whenever there's trouble you yell at me and you think that settles it.

Keller: Then what do I do? Tell me; talk to me; what do I do?

Mother: Joe . . . I've been thinking this way. If he comes back —

Keller: What do you mean "if"? He's comin' back.

Mother: I think if you sit him down and you — explain yourself, I mean you ought to make it clear to him that you know you did a terrible thing. (*Not looking into his eyes*) I mean if he saw that you realize what you did. You see?

Keller: What ice does that cut?

Mother (*a little fearfully*): I mean if you told him that you want to pay for what you did.

Keller (*sensing . . . quietly*): How can I pay?

Mother: Tell him — you're willing to go to prison. (*Pause.*)

Keller (*struck, amazed*): I'm willing — ?

Mother (*quickly*): You wouldn't go, he wouldn't ask you to go. But if you told him you wanted to, if he could feel that you want to pay, maybe he would forgive you.

Keller: He would forgive me! For what?

Mother: Joe, you know what I mean.

Keller: I don't know what you mean! You wanted money, so I made money. What must I be forgiven? You wanted money, didn't you?

Mother: I didn't want it that way.

Keller: I didn't want it that way, either! I spoiled the both of you. I should've put him out when he was 10 like I was put out, and make him earn his keep. Then he'd know how a buck is made in this world. Forgiven! I could live on a quarter a day myself, but I got a family so I —

Mother: Joe, Joe . . . it don't excuse it that you did it for the family.

Keller: It's got to excuse it!

Mother: There's something bigger than the family to him.

Keller: Nothin' is bigger!

Mother: There is to him.

Keller: There's nothin' he could do that I wouldn't forgive. Because he's my son. Because I'm his father and he's my son.

Mother: Joe, I tell you —

Keller: Nothin's bigger than that. And you're goin' to tell him, you understand? I'm his father and he's my son, and if there's something bigger than that I'll put a bullet in my head!

Mother: You stop that!

Keller: You heard me. Now you know what to tell him. *(Pause. He moves from her — halts.)* But he wouldn't put me away though. . . . He wouldn't do that. . . . Would he?

Mother: He loved you, Joe; you broke his heart.

Keller: But to put me away . . .

Mother: I don't know. I'm beginning to think we don't really know him. They say in the war he was such a killer. Here he was always afraid of mice. I don't know him. I don't know what he'll do.

Keller: Damn, if Larry was alive he wouldn't act like this. He understood the way the world is made. He listened to me. To him the world had a 40-foot front, it ended at the building line. This one, everything bothers him. You make a deal, overcharge two cents, and his hair falls out. He don't understand money. Too easy, it came too easy. Yes, sir, Larry. That was the boy we lost. Larry. Larry. *(He slumps on chair in front of her.)* What am I gonna do, Kate?

Mother: Joe, Joe, please. . . . You'll be all right; nothing is going to happen.

Keller *(desperately, lost)*: For you, Kate, for both of you, that's all I ever lived for. . . .

Mother: I know, darling. I know.

(Ann enters from house. They say nothing, waiting for her to speak.)

Ann: Why do you stay up? I'll tell you when he comes.

Keller *(rises, goes to her)*: You didn't eat supper, did you? *(To Mother)* Why don't you make her something?

Mother: Sure, I'll —

Ann: Never mind, Kate; I'm all right. *(They are unable to speak to each other.)* There's something I want to tell you. *(She starts, then halts.)* I'm not going to do anything about it.

Mother: She's a good girl! *(To Keller)* You see? She's a —

Ann: I'll do nothing about Joe, but you're going to do something for me. *(Directly to Mother)* You made Chris feel guilty with me. Whether you wanted to or not, you've crippled him in front of me. I'd like you to tell him that Larry is dead and that you know it. You understand me? I'm not going out of here alone. There's no life for me that way. I want you to set him free. And then I promise you, everything will end, and we'll go away, and that's all.

Keller: You'll do that. You'll tell him.

Ann: I know what I'm asking, Kate. You had two sons. But you've only one now.

Keller: You'll tell him.

Ann: And you've got to say it to him so he knows you mean it.

Mother: My dear, if the boy was dead, it wouldn't depend on my words to make Chris know it. . . . The night he gets into your bed, his heart will dry up. Because he knows and you know. To his dying day he'll wait for his brother! No, my dear, no such thing. You're going in the morning, and you're going alone. That's your life, that's your lonely life. (*She goes to porch, and starts in.*)

Ann: Larry is dead, Kate.

Mother (*she stops*): Don't speak to me.

Ann: I said he's dead. I know! He crashed off the coast of China November twenty-fifth! His engine didn't fail him. But he died. I know. . . .

Mother: How did he die? You're lying to me. If you know, how did he die?

Ann: I loved him. You know I loved him. Would I have looked at anyone else if I wasn't sure? That's enough for you.

Mother (*moving on her*): What's enough for me? What're you talking about? (*She grasps Ann's wrists.*)

Ann: You're hurting my wrists.

Mother: What are you talking about!

(*Pause. She stares at Ann a moment, then turns and goes to Keller.*)

Ann: Joe, go in the house.

Keller: Why should I —

Ann: Please go.

Keller: Lemme know when he comes. (*Keller goes into house.*)

Mother (*as she sees Ann taking letter from her pocket*): What's that?

Ann: Sit down. (*Mother moves left to chair, but does not sit.*) First you've got to understand. When I came, I didn't have any idea that Joe — I had nothing against him or you. I came to get married. I hoped. . . . So I didn't bring this to hurt you. I thought I'd show it to you only if there was no other way to settle Larry in your mind.

Mother: Larry? (*Snatches letter from Ann's hand.*)

Ann: He wrote it to me just before he — (*Mother opens and begins to read letter.*) I'm not trying to hurt you, Kate. You're making me do this, now remember you're — Remember. I've been so lonely. Kate . . . I can't leave here alone again. (*A long, low moan comes from Mother's throat as she reads.*) You made me show it to you. You wouldn't believe me. I told you a hundred times; why wouldn't you believe me!

Mother: Oh, my God . . .

Ann (*with pity and fear*): Kate, please, please . . .

Mother: My God, my God . . .

Ann: Kate, dear, I'm so sorry . . . I'm so sorry.

(*Chris enters from driveway. He seems exhausted.*)

Chris: What's the matter —

Ann: Where were you? . . . You're all perspired. (*Mother doesn't move.*) Where were you?

Chris: Just drove around a little. I thought you'd be gone.

Ann: Where do I go? I have nowhere to go.

Chris (*to Mother*): Where's Dad?

Ann: Inside lying down.

Chris: Sit down, both of you. I'll say what there is to say.

Mother: I didn't hear the car . . .

Chris: I left it in the garage.

Mother: Jim is out looking for you.

Chris: Mother . . . I'm going away. There are a couple of firms in Cleveland. I think I can get a place. I mean, I'm going away for good. (*To Ann alone*) I know what you're thinking, Annie. It's true. I'm yellow. I was made yellow in this house because I suspected my father and I did nothing about it, but if I knew that night when I came home what I know now, he'd be in the district attorney's office by this time, and I'd have brought him there. Now if I look at him, all I'm able to do is cry.

Mother: What are you talking about? What else can you do?

Chris: I could jail him! I could jail him, if I were human anymore. But I'm like everybody else now. I'm practical now. You made me practical.

Mother: But you have to be.

Chris: The cats in that alley are practical; the bums who ran away when we were fighting were practical. Only the dead ones weren't practical. But now I'm practical and I spit on myself. I'm going away. I'm going now.

Ann (*going up to him*): I'm coming with you.

Chris: No, Ann.

Ann: Chris, I don't ask you to do anything about Joe.

Chris: You do, you do.

Ann: I swear I never will.

Chris: In your heart you always will.

Ann: Then do what you have to do!

Chris: Do what? What is there to do? I've looked all night for a reason to make him suffer.

Ann: There's reason, there's reason!

Chris: What? Do I raise the dead when I put him behind bars? Then what'll I do it for? We used to shoot a man who acted like a dog, but honor was real there, you were protecting something. But here? This is the land of the great big dogs, you don't love a man here, you eat him! That's the principle; the only one we live by — it just happened to kill a few people this time, that's all. The world's that way, how can I take it out on him? What sense does that make? This is a zoo, a zoo!

Ann (*to Mother*): You know what he's got to do! Tell him!

Mother: Let him go.

Ann: I won't let him go. You'll tell him what he's got to do. . . .

Mother: Annie!

Ann: Then I will!

(*Keller enters from house. Chris sees him, goes down near arbor.*)

Keller: What's the matter with you? I want to talk to you.

Chris: I've got nothing to say to you.

Keller (*taking his arm*): I want to talk to you!

Chris *(pulling violently away from him):* Don't do that, Dad. I'm going to hurt you if you do that. There's nothing to say, so say it quick.

Keller: Exactly what's the matter? What's the matter? You got too much money? Is that what bothers you?

Chris *(with an edge of sarcasm):* It bothers me.

Keller: If you can't get used to it, then throw it away. You hear me? Take every cent and give it to charity, throw it in the sewer. Does that settle it? In the sewer, that's all. You think I'm kidding? I'm tellin' you what to do, if it's dirty then burn it. It's your money, that's not my money. I'm a dead man, I'm an old dead man, nothing's mine. Well, talk to me! What do you want to do!

Chris: It's not what I want to do. It's what you want to do.

Keller: What should I want to do? *(Chris is silent.)* Jail? You want me to go to jail? If you want me to go, say so! Is that where I belong? Then tell me so! *(Slight pause.)* What's the matter, why can't you tell me? *(Furiously)* You say everything else to me, say that! *(Slight pause.)* I'll tell you why you can't say it. Because you know I don't belong there. Because you know! *(With growing emphasis and passion, and a persistent tone of desperation)* Who worked for nothin' in that war? When they work for nothin', I'll work for nothin'. Did they ship a gun or a truck outa Detroit before they got their price? Is that clean? It's dollars and cents, nickels and dimes; war and peace, it's nickels and dimes, what's clean? Half the damn country is gotta go if I go! That's why you can't tell me.

Chris: That's exactly why.

Keller: Then . . . why am I bad?

Chris: I know you're no worse than most men but I thought you were better. I never saw you as a man. I saw you as my father. *(Almost breaking)* I can't look at you this way; I can't look at myself! *(He turns away, unable to face Keller. Ann goes quickly to Mother, takes letter from her and starts for Chris. Mother instantly rushes to intercept her.)*

Mother: Give me that!

Ann: He's going to read it! *(She thrusts letter into Chris's hand.)* Larry. He wrote it to me the day he died.

Keller: Larry!

Mother: Chris, it's not for you. *(He starts to read.)* Joe . . . go away . . .

Keller *(mystified, frightened):* Why'd she say, Larry, what — ?

Mother *(desperately pushes him toward alley, glancing at Chris):* Go to the street, Joe, go to the street! *(She comes down beside Keller.)* Don't, Chris . . . *(Pleading from her whole soul)* Don't tell him.

Chris *(quietly):* Three and one half years . . . talking, talking. Now you tell me what you must do. . . . This is how he died; now tell me where you belong.

Keller *(pleading):* Chris, a man can't be a Jesus in this world!

Chris: I know all about the world. I know the whole crap story. Now listen to this, and tell me what a man's got to be! *(Reads.)* "My dear Ann: . . ." You listening? He wrote this the day he died. Listen, don't cry. . . . Listen! "My dear Ann: It is impossible to put down the things I feel. But I've got to tell you something. Yesterday they flew in a load of papers from the States and I read about Dad and your father being convicted. I can't express myself. I can't tell you how I feel — I can't bear to live anymore. Last night I circled the base for 20 minutes before I could bring myself in. How could he have done that? Every day three or four men never come back and he sits back there doing business. . . . I don't know how to tell you what I feel. . . . I can't face anybody. . . . I'm going out on a mission in a few minutes. They'll probably report me missing. If they do, I want you to know you mustn't wait for me. I tell you, Ann, if I had him here now I could kill him — " (*Keller grabs letter from Chris's hand and reads it. After a long pause.*) Now blame the world. Do you understand that letter?

Keller (*speaking almost inaudibly*): I think I do. Get the car. I'll put on my jacket. (*He turns and starts slowly for the house. Mother rushes to intercept him.*)

Mother: Why are you going? You'll sleep; why are you going?

Keller: I can't sleep here. I'll feel better if I go.

Mother: You're so foolish. Larry was your son, too, wasn't he? You know he'd never tell you to do this.

Keller (*looking at letter in his hand*): Then what is this if it isn't telling me? Sure, he was my son. But I think to him they were all my sons. And I guess they were. I guess they were. I'll be right down. (*Exits into house.*)

Mother (*to Chris, with determination*): You're not going to take him!

Chris: I'm taking him.

Mother: It's up to you, if you tell him to

stay he'll stay. Go and tell him!

Chris: Nobody could stop him now.

Mother: You'll stop him! How long will he live in prison? Are you trying to kill him?

Chris (*holding out letter*): I thought you read this!

Mother (*of Larry, the letter*): The war is over! Didn't you hear? It's over!

Chris: Then what was Larry to you? A stone that fell into the water? It's not enough for him to be sorry. Larry didn't kill himself to make you and Dad sorry.

Mother: What more can we be!

Chris: You can be better! Once and for all you can know there's a universe of people outside and you're responsible to it, and unless you know that, you threw away your son because that's why he died.

(*A shot is heard in the house. They stand frozen for a brief second. Chris starts for porch, pauses at step, turns to Ann.*)

Chris: Find Jim!

(*He goes on into the house and Ann runs up driveway. Mother stands alone, transfixed.*)

Mother (*softly, almost moaning*): Joe . . . Joe . . . Joe . . . Joe . . .

(*Chris comes out of house, down to Mother's arms.*)

Chris (*almost crying*): Mother, I didn't mean to —

Mother: Don't, dear. Don't take it on yourself. Forget now. Live. (*Chris stirs as if to answer.*) Shhh. . . . (*She puts his arms down gently and moves toward porch.*) Shhh. . . . (*As she reaches porch steps she begins sobbing. Curtain.*)

READING COMPREHENSION

Select the best choice to complete each sentence below. Then write the complete sentence on your paper.

1. Jim told Kate that Chris would never know how to live with the truth about his father. He said it takes _____.
   a. a better education than Chris has
   b. a certain talent for lying
   c. the ability to forgive

2. Ann told Kate that Kate must _____.
   a. tell Chris she accepts Larry's death
   b. let Chris reenlist in the Army
   c. make Joe go to jail

3. Ann knew Larry was dead because _____.
   a. his best friend wrote to tell her
   b. she saw it in a dream
   c. of the letter he sent her

4. After Chris read the letter aloud, Joe told Chris to _____.
   a. burn it
   b. get the car so they could go to the authorities
   c. read it again

For Discussion

1. How has Ann changed from Act One? What did she do in Acts Two and Three to show she is a strong person?

2. What effect did Larry's letter have on Kate and Joe? How does Chris's reaction add to the drama?

3. Why did Miller end the play as he did? How else could it have ended?

UNDERSTANDING LITERATURE

Theme and Values. The last act of a play brings the plot to a resolution. Now the characters and their beliefs — as well as the author's ideas and basic theme — can be fully understood. Each character in *All My Sons* has his or her own values, or beliefs, about what is true or right in life. Miller also expressed his own values — by his careful structuring of the plot.

On your paper, match each character below with his or her values.

1. Joe   a. "I'm not going out of here alone. There's no life for me that way."

2. Chris   b. There's nothing bigger than the family.

3. Ann   c. ". . . there's a universe of people outside and you're responsible to it. . . ."

4. Jim   d. "The greatest men who ever lived believed in the stars. . . . there's a power greater than ourselves."

5. Frank   e. "The compromise is always made. . . .

Which of the above value statements do you think is closest to Miller's own? Explain your answer.

Writing

In your own words, explain why or why not one of the above themes is important in everyday life.

Section Review

VOCABULARY

Context Clues in Dialogue. Context clues can help you know the meaning of words you do not know. Use context clues to choose the correct meaning for each italicized word below. Write the letter of the correct meaning on your paper.

1. "Sometimes you *infuriate* me, you know that? . . . You have such a talent for ignoring things."
   a. impress
   b. amuse
   c. anger

2. "The story was, I pulled a fast one getting myself *exonerated.* . . . [But] there was a court paper in my pocket to prove I wasn't [guilty]."
   a. shipped out of the country
   b. cleared of charges of wrong-doing
   c. guilty of stealing

3. "I mean if they want to open the case again, for the *nuisance* value, to hurt us?"
   a. current events
   b. annoyance
   c. money

4. "There was something wrong with the process. . . . By this time he had over a hundred *defectives.*"
   a. not perfect parts
   b. new parts
   c. practical parts

READING

Cloze Exercise. Some reading tests use a technique called *cloze* to measure comprehension. In a cloze reading test, words are omitted from a selection. If you understand what you are reading, you will be able to fill in the blanks correctly. Each word you fill in will make sense in the context of the selection.

Here are some lines from "All My Sons." On your paper, write the word that best completes each sentence.

1. "**Ann** (to Kate): . . . You made Chris feel guilty with me. Whether you wanted to or not you've _____ him in front of me."
   a. crippled
   b. ignored
   c. amused

2. "**Ann** (to Chris): . . . Your father put hundreds of _____ into the air. You should be proud."
   a. chemicals
   b. planes
   c. clouds

Now here's a longer passage. This time you supply the words for the blanks. Write them on your paper.

3. "**George:** . . . So Joe told him . . . to weld, cover up the cracks in any way he could, and _____ them out. . . . Dad was afraid. He wanted Joe there if he was going to do it. But Joe can't _____ down. . . . He's sick. Sick! He suddenly gets the flu! Suddenly! But he promised to take responsibility. Do you

529

understand what I'm saying? On the telephone you can't have _____! In a court you can always _____ a phone call and that's exactly what he did. They knew he was a liar the first time, but in the appeal they _____ that rotten lie and now Joe is a big shot and your father is the _____." (p. 507)

WRITING A SPEECH

Playwrights sometimes have characters present *monologues*. A monologue is a long speech that presents an important idea. It can express a theme; it also helps the audience develop a clear understanding of a character's personality or beliefs.

For example, look at Kate Keller's speech in Act One of *All My Sons* on p. 484. This reveals how this character felt about her missing son. Later in the same act on pp. 493–494, Chris gives a speech about the war and how it changed him. And on p. 516, Joe Keller has a speech that describes his feelings about his mistakes.

Below is a list of themes from the play. Select one of the themes. On your paper prepare a speech for yourself or for one of the characters from the play. On your paper, state your theme, then list examples why you, or the character you've selected, agrees or disagrees with the theme.

Themes

1. The family is more important than anything else.

2. We must see ourselves as part of a worldwide community.

3. Compromises have to be made to get through life.

4. The dead are kept alive if they are not forgotten.

Now rewrite your list in paragraph form. Your speech should contain at least five paragraphs. The first paragraph will explain the theme. The second, third, and fourth paragraphs will explain the reasons the theme is important. The last paragraph will contain the conclusion. It will restate the theme and summarize all that went before.

After you have written your speech, reread it with the following checklist in mind:

☐ State the person speaking and the theme.

☐ Give several reasons to support your main idea or theme.

☐ Remember, a monologue is meant to be read aloud. The language you use must sound natural when spoken.

☐ Use words that suit the character's personality and mood. You may wish to use stage directions to help the reader understand the character's feelings.

QUIZ

The following is a quiz for Section 11. Write your answers on your paper in complete sentences.

Reading Comprehension

1. Why did Ann Deever come to visit the Kellers?

2. Why did George Deever come to the Kellers' house?

3. What did Joe Keller do when he realized his factory was producing cracked airplane parts?

4. How did the Keller family learn how and why Larry died?

5. How did the truth about Larry's death affect Joe Keller?

Understanding Literature

6. Describe the character of Kate Keller. What are her strengths? What are her faults?

7. What is the symbolic significance of the apple tree?

8. How does the character of Joe Keller change from the beginning to the end of the play?

9. State the most important theme of the play. How does the title of the play relate to Miller's basic theme?

10. What attitudes does the character of George Deever express? What purpose does he serve in furthering the plot of the play?

COMPOSITION

1. Write a story about Ann and Chris and their lives after the play ends. Describe the conflicts they face and how they resolve them. Do they marry? Are they happy?

2. Pick one of the following characters: George Deever, Ann Deever, Kate Keller, or Chris Keller. Then imagine you are this character, and write a letter to Steve Deever, describing the events of that Sunday in August.

3. Write a scene, with dialogue and stage directions, for when George met his father in prison. Describe the setting and list the characters. Who else would be in the scene? How would they further the plot or help create the setting?

LEVEL FIVE
Glossary

PRONUNCIATION KEY

ă	pat	j	judge	sh	dish, ship
ā	aid, fey, pay	k	cat, kick, pique	t	tight
â	air, care, wear	l	lid, needle	th	path, thin
ä	father	m	am, man, mum	*th*	bathe, this
b	bib	n	no, sudden	ŭ	cut, rough
ch	church	ng	thing	û	circle, firm, heard, term,
d	deed	ŏ	horrible, pot		turn, urge, word
ĕ	pet, pleasure	ō	go, hoarse, row, toe	v	cave, valve, vine
ē	be, bee, easy, leisure	ô	alter, caught, for, paw	w	with
f	fast, fife, off, phase, rough	oi	boy, noise, oil	y	yes
g	gag	ou	cow, out	yōō	abuse, use
h	hat	ŏŏ	took	z	rose, size, xylophone, zebra
hw	which	ōō	boot, fruit	zh	garage, pleasure, vision
ĭ	pit	p	pop	ə	about, silent, pencil, lemon,
ī	by, guy, pie	r	roar		circus
î	dear, deer, fierce, mere	s	miss, sauce, see	ər	butter

PART OF SPEECH LABELS

n.	(noun)	*conj.*	(conjunction)
adj.	(adjective)	*prep.*	(preposition)
adv.	(adverb)	*v.*	(verb)
pron.	(pronoun)	*interj.*	(interjection)

The additional italicized labels below are used as needed to show inflected forms:

pl. (plural)   *sing.* (singular)

STRESS

Primary stress ′
bi · ol′o · gy | bī ŏl′ə jē |
Secondary stress ′
bi′o · log′i · cal | bī′ə lŏj′ĭ kəl |

In this glossary, definitions were chosen to show the meanings of the words as they are used in the selections. Unless otherwise indicated, entries based on © 1977 by Houghton Mifflin Company. Reprinted by permission from The American Heritage School Dictionary.

a•bash |ə băsh'| v. To make ashamed or uneasy; embarrass; disconcert.

af•flict |ə flĭkt'| v. To cause distress to; cause to suffer; trouble greatly: *Mankind is afflicted with many ills.*

ag•ile |ăj' əl| *or* |ăj' īl| *adj.* **1.** Able to move quickly and easily; nimble.

am•big•u•ous |ăm bĭg' yŏo əs| *adj.* Having two or more possible meanings or interpretations; unclear; vague: *an ambiguous statement by the Governor.*

am•phib•i•ous |ăm fĭb' ē əs| *adj.* **1.** Able to live both on land and in water.

an•gli•cize, also **An•gli•cize** |ăng' glĭ sīz'| v. **An•gli•cized, An•gli•ciz•ing.** To make English or similar to English in form, style, or character: *The name Odysseus, or Ulixes in Latin, was Anglicized as Ulysses.*

an•guish |ăng' gwĭsh| n. A pain of the body or mind that causes one agony; torment; torture.

ap•a•thet•ic |ăp' ə thĕt' ĭk| *adj.* Lacking or not showing strong feeling; uninterested; indifferent: *apathetic about school.* —**ap' a•thet'i•cal•ly** *adv.*

ap•pren•tice |ə prĕn' tĭs| n. **1.** A person who works for another without pay in return for instruction in a craft or trade.

art•ful |ärt' fəl| *adj.* **1.** Showing art or skill; skillful: *an artful cook.* **2.** crafty; cunning: *an artful lawyer.*

as•per•sion |ə spûr' zhən| *or* |-shən| n. A damaging or slanderous report or remark: *His speech cast aspersions on my motives.*

awe |ô| n. A feeling of wonder, fear, and respect inspired by something mighty or majestic: *gazing in awe at the mountains.* —v. **awed, aw•ing.** To fill with awe: *The size of the plane awed everyone.* ¶ *These sound alike* **awe, aw.**

awl |ôl| n. A pointed tool for making holes, as in wood or leather.

ax•is |ăk' sĭs| n., pl. **ax•es** |ăk' sēz'| **1.** A straight line around which an object or geometric figure rotates or can be imagined to rotate: *The axis of the earth passes through both of its poles.*

bay•o•net |bā'ə nit| *or* |-nĕt| *or* |bā'ə nĕt'| n. A knife attached to the muzzle end of a rifle for use in close combat.

be•nign |bĭ nīn'| *adj.* **1.** Kind; gentle: *His face was fatherly and benign.*

berth |bûrth| n. **1.** A built-in bed or bunk in a ship or a railroad sleeping car. **3.** A position of employment; a job.

boo•ty |boo' tē| n., pl. **boo•ties. 1.** Loot taken from an enemy in war. **2.** Any seized or stolen goods: *pirate's booty.*

boul•der |bōl' dər| n. A large, rounded mass of rock lying on the ground or imbedded in the soil, and usually different in composition from other nearby rocks.

bul•ly |bool' ē| *adj.* **Informal.** Excellent; splendid.

bust² |bŭst| **Slang.** v. **2.** To cause to become or become bankrupt: *The strike busted several industries.*

cache |kăsh| n. **2.** A supply of something hidden in such a place. ¶ *These sound alike* **cache, cash.**

ca•dav•er |kə dăv' ər| n. A dead body, especially a human body that is to be dissected and studied.

cal•i•co |kăl' ĭ kō| n., pl. **cal•i•coes** *or* **cal•i•cos. 1.** A cotton cloth with a figured pattern printed on it in color. —*adj.* Covered with spots of a different color: *a calico cat.*

cav•al•ry |kăv' əl rē| n. Troops trained to fight on horseback or, more recently, in armored vehicles.

cav•al•ry•man |kăv' əl rē mən| n., pl. **-men** |-mən|. A soldier in the cavalry.

cha•os |kā' ŏs'| n. **1.** Great disorder or confusion.

chide |chīd| v. **chid•ed** *or* **chid** |chĭd|, **chid•ed** *or* **chid** *or* **chid•den** |chĭd'n|, **chid•ing.** To scold; reprove.

cog•wheel |kŏg' hwēl'| *or* |-wēl'| n. A wheel with cogs or teeth in its rim that mesh with those of another wheel to transmit or receive motion.

co•her•ent |kō hîr' ənt| *adj.* **2.** Logically connected; easy to understand: *coherent speech.*

com•pas•sion |kəm păsh' ən| n. The feeling of sharing the suffering of another, together with a desire to give aid or show mercy.

com•po•si•tion |kŏm' pə zĭsh' ən| n. **1.** The putting together of parts or elements to form a whole; the act, process, or art of composing. **3.** A short essay, story, etc., written as a school exercise. **5.** The arrangement of parts or elements forming a whole, as in an artistic work: *the composition of a painting.*

con•clu•sive |kən kloo' sĭv| *adj.* Putting an end to doubt, question, or uncertainty; decisive: *a conclusive argument.*

con•cus•sion |kən kŭsh' ən| n. **1.** A violent jarring; a shock: *A concussion resulted from the blast.*

con•found |kən found'| *or* |kŏn-| v. **1.** To bewilder, puzzle, or perplex: *The pitcher confounded the batter with his knuckle ball.*

coun·te·nance |koun′ tə nəns| *n.* **2.** The face: *the human countenance.*

cred·i·tor |krĕd′ ĭ tər| *n.* A person or firm to whom money is owed.

cres·cent |krĕs′ ənt| *n.* **1.** The figure of the moon as it appears in its first quarter, with concave and convex edges ending in points.

daft |dăft| *or* |däft| *adj.* **1.** Crazy; mad.

daze |dāz| *v.* **dazed, daz·ing.** To stun or confuse, as with a blow, shock, or surprise: *The noise dazed and deafened them.* —**dazed** *adj.*: *a dazed look.*

del·e·ga·tion |dĕl′ ə gā′shən| *n.* **3.** A person or persons chosen to represent another or others.

de·nun·ci·a·tion |dĭ nŭn′sē ā′shən| *or* |-shē-| *n.* The act of denouncing; open condemnation.

des·o·late |dĕs′ ə lāt′| *adj.* **2.** Having few or no inhabitants; deserted: *a desolate wilderness.*

des·o·la·tion |dĕs′ ə lā′ shən| *n.* **1.** The condition of being desolate: *desolation caused by a forest fire.*

di·min·u·tive |dĭ mĭn′ yə tĭv| *adj.* **2.** Expressing smallness or affection, as the diminutive suffixes *-let* in *booklet, -ette* in *dinette,* and *-kin* in *lamb-kin.* —*n.* A diminutive suffix, word, or name.

dis·pose |dĭs pōz′| *v.* **disposed, dis·pos·ing. 3.** To make willing or receptive for; incline: *feeling half disposed to object.*

dis·tinc·tive |dĭ stĭngk′ tĭv| *adj.* Serving to identify, characterize, or set apart from others: *Red berries are a distinctive feature of this plant.*

dis·tract·ed |dĭ străk′ tĭd| *adj.* **1.** Very confused or bewildered: *distracted between joy and sorrow.* **2.** Violently upset in mind, especially by grief.

di·verge |dĭ vûrj′| *or* |dī-| *v.* **di·verged, di·verg·ing. 1.** To go or extend in different directions from a common point; branch out: *a road that suddenly diverged into paths like branches of the letter "Y."*

di·ver·sion |dĭ vûr′ zhən| *or* |-shən| *or* |dī-| *n.* **2.** Something that relaxes or entertains; recreation: *the diversion of a royal hunt.*

dun·der·head |dŭn′ dər hĕd| *n.* A stupid person.*

ec·cen·tric |ĭk sĕn′ trĭk| *adj.* **1.** Odd or unusual in appearance, behavior, etc.; strange; peculiar: *an eccentric hat; an eccentric person; an eccentric habit.*

ec·cen·tric·i·ty |ĕk′ sĕn trĭs′ ĭ tē| *n., pl.* **ec·cen·tric·i·ties. 1.** The condition or quality of being eccentric.

ec·sta·sy |ĕk′ stə sē| *n., pl.* **ec·sta·sies.** A state of intense emotion, especially of joy or delight.

em·phat·ic |ĕm făt′ ĭk| *adj.* **1.** Expressed or performed with emphasis: *an emphatic shake of the head.* **2.** Bold and definite in expression or action: *an emphatic person.*

en·gulf |ĕn gŭlf′| *v.* To cause to disappear by or as if by overflowing and enclosing; swallow up: *The floodwaters engulfed the surrounding farmlands.*

er·rat·ic |ĭ răt′ ĭk| *adj.* **1.** Irregular or uneven in quality, progress, etc.: *His work has been erratic.*

ex·as·per·ate |ĭg zăs′ pə rāt′| *v.* **ex·as·per·at·ed, ex·as·per·at·ing.** To irritate greatly; try the patience of; irk: *Her shrill voice always exasperated him.*

ex·on·er·ate |ĭg zŏn′ ə rāt′| *v.* **ex·on·er·at·ed, ex·on·er·at·ing.** To free from a charge; declare blameless: *The court exonerated the defendant.* —**ex·on′er·a′tion** *n.*

ex·trem·i·ty |ĭk strĕm′ ĭ tē| *n., pl.* **ex·trem·i·ties. 2.** Extreme danger, distress or need: *The victims of the fire called for help in their extremity.*

fa·mil·i·ar·i·ty |fə mĭl′ ē ăr′ ĭ tē| *n., pl.* **fa·mil·i·ar·i·ties. 1.** Acquaintance with or knowledge of something: *His familiarity with the city's streets helped him get around.*

fil·a·ment |fĭl′ ə mənt| *n.* **2.** Any fine or slender thread, strand, fiber, etc.

flo·til·la |flō tĭl′ ə| *n.* **1.** A fleet of boats or other small vessels.

flur·ried·ly |flûr′ əd lē| *adv.* Full of bustling activity; excitedly.*

flus·ter |flŭs′ tər| *v.* To make nervous, excited, or confused: *The staring faces flustered her.*

for·lorn |fôr lôrn′| *adj.* **1.** Deserted; forsaken; abandoned: *a forlorn house.*

forth·right |fôrth′ rīt′| *or* |fôrth′-| *adj.* Straightforward; frank: *ask a forthright question.*

fren·zy |frĕn′ zē| *n., pl.* **fren·zies.** Wild excitement or a display of emotion suggesting madness, often accompanied by vigorous or violent activity: *sharks gone mad and dashing about in a blind frenzy.*

frol·ic·some |frŏl′ ĭk səm| *adj.* Full of fun; frisky; playful: *a frolicsome puppy.*

fun·gus |fŭng′ gəs| *n., pl.* **fun·gi** |fŭn′ jī′| *or* **fun·gus·es.** Any of a group of plants, such as a mushroom, mold, yeast, or mildew, that have no green coloring and that obtain their nourishment from living or dead plant or animal substances. ¶*These sound alike* **fungus, fungous.**

gait |gāt| *n.* **1.** A way of walking or running: *a slow gait; a clumsy gait.*

gal·lant·ry |gǎl′ ən trē| **2.** Chivalrous attention to women; courtliness.

gal·lows |gǎl′ ōz| *n., pl.* **gal·lows·es** *or* **gal·lows. 1.** A framework with a suspended noose, used for execution by hanging.

gaunt |gônt| *adj.* **gaunt·er, gaunt·est. 1.** Thin and bony; haggard; emaciated: *a gaunt face.*

giz·zard |gǐz′ərd| *n.* **1.** An enlarged, muscular part in the digestive tract of a bird, in which bits of sand or gravel collect and in which food is ground and digested.

glock·en·spiel |glŏk′ ən spēl′| *or* |-shpēl′| *n.* A musical instrument consisting of a series of metal bars tuned to the tones of the chromatic scale. It is played by being struck with two light hammers.

grate[1] |grāt| *v.* **grat·ed, grat·ing. 2.** To make or cause to make a harsh grinding or rasping sound by rubbing: *You grate like a jay and squeak like a mouse. He grated the two rocks together.*

grove |grōv| *n.* A group of trees with open ground between them.

guard·i·an |gär′ dē ən| *n.* **1.** Someone or something that guards, protects, or defends: *guardians of law and order.*

hard·tack |härd′ tăk′| *n.* A hard biscuit made only of flour and water; sea biscuit.

has·ty |hā′ stē| *adj.* **hast·i·er, hast·i·est. 1.** Marked by speed; swift; rapid: *a hasty retreat.* —**hast′i·ly** *adv.* —**hast′i·ness** *n.*

hasty pudding. 1. Cornmeal mush.

hav·oc |hǎv′ ək| *n.* Devastation; destruction.

hearth |härth| *n.* **1.** The floor of a fireplace, usually extending into a room.

her·i·tage |hěr′ ĭ tĭj| *n.* **2.** Something other than property passed down from preceding generations; legacy; tradition: *Every country has its heritage of folk music.*

hi·lar·i·ous |hĭ lâr′ ē əs| *or* |-lär′-| *or* |hī-| *adj.* Boisterously funny; provoking much laughter: *a hilarious story.* —**hi·lar·i·ous·ly** *adv.*

hos·tler |hŏs′ lər| *n.* A person who takes care of horses at an inn.*

hot·house |hŏt′ hous′| *n., pl.* —**hous·es** |hou′ zǐz|. A heated building or enclosure with a glass roof and sides, used for growing plants. —**modifier:** *hothouse tomatoes.*

hys·ter·i·cal |hĭ stěr′ ĭ kəl| *adj.* **3.** Marked by uncontrolled emotion; violent or unrestrained: *laughing in hysterical relief.* —**hys·ter′i·cal·ly** *adv.*

im·plore |ĭm plôr′| *or* |-plōr′| *v.* **im·plored, im·plor·ing. 1.** To appeal to (someone) earnestly, anxiously, and humbly; entreat; beseech: *We implore you to help us.*

im·pos·tor |ĭm pŏs′ tər| *n.* A person who deceives by pretending to be someone else.

im·pres·sion·ism, also **Im·pres·sion·ism** |ĭm prěsh′ ə nĭz′ əm| *n.* **1.** A style of painting of the late 19th century, marked by concentration on the impression produced by a scene or object and the use of many small strokes to simulate reflected light. —**im·pres′sion·ist, Im·pres′sion·ist** *n.* & *adj.*

in·cli·na·tion |ĭn′klə nā′ shən| *n.* **2.** A tendency to act in a certain way: *She has an inclination to observe and criticize the faults of others.* **3.** A natural or usual preference: *an inclination to skate.*

in·de·fin·a·ble |ĭn′ dĭ fī′ nə bəl| *adj.* Not capable of being defined, described, or analyzed: *an indefinable feeling.* —**in·de·fin·a·bly** *adv.*

in·dif·fer·ence |ĭn dĭf′ ər əns| *or* |-dĭf′ rəns| *n.* **1.** Lack of concern or interest.

in·dif·fer·ent |ĭn dĭf′ ər ənt| *or* |dĭf′ rənt| *adj.* **1.** Having or showing no interest; not caring one way or the other.

in·fat·u·ate |ĭn făch′ ōō āt′| *v.* **in·fat·u·at·ed, in·fat·u·at·ing.** To fill with a strong and foolish passion or attraction.

in·fir·mi·ty |ĭn fûr′ mĭ tē| *n., pl.* **in·fir·mi·ties. 1.** The condition of being infirm; bodily weakness; frailty. **2.** A disease or disorder that causes this.

in·sin·u·ate |ĭn sĭn′ yōō āt′| *v.* **in·sin·u·at·ed, in·sin·u·at·ing. 1.** To introduce (ideas, thoughts, points of view, etc.) gradually and slyly: *She insinuated her political beliefs into the conversation.* **2.** To convey indirectly; hint covertly: *What are you insinuating?*

in·ti·ma·cy |ĭn′ tə mə sē| *n.* The condition of being intimate, especially close personal relationship.

jinx |jĭngks| *n.* **Informal. 2.** Someone or something supposed to bring bad luck.

keen[1] |kēn| *adj.* **keen·er, keen·est. 4.** Acute; sensitive: *the keen eyes of the jackals.*

KO, also **K.O., k.o.** |kā′ ō′| *v.* **KO'd, KO'ing, KO's. Slang.** To knock out. —*n., pl.* **KO's.** In boxing, a knockout.

535

lu·mi·nar·y |lōō' mə něr' ē| *n., pl.* **lu·mi·nar·ies. 1.** An object, especially a celestial body, that gives off light.

lurch[1] |lûrch| *n.* **1.** An unsteady or abrupt swaying movement. — *v.* To move unsteadily; stagger: *The big, bullying fellow lurched toward Jed.*

mar·i·tal |măr' ĭ təl| *adj.* Of or relating to marriage: *marital vows; marital problems.*

mar·tyr |mär' tər| **2.** A person who sacrifices something important to him to further a belief, cause, or principle.

mar·tyr·dom |mär' tər dəm| *n.* The condition of being a martyr.

murk |mûrk| *n.* Darkness; gloom: *groped his way through the murk of the moonless night.*

mus·ter |mŭs' tər| *v.* **1.** To bring or come together; assemble: *mustered his platoon for inspection. The men mustered for roll call.*

na·tal |nāt′l| *adj.* Of or accompanying birth: *natal injuries.*

ob·sti·nate |ŏb' stə nĭt| *adj.* Stubborn.

or·der·ly |ôr' dər lē| *n., pl.* **or·der·lies. 2.** A soldier assigned to a superior officer to carry orders or messages.

or·ner·y |ôr' nə rē| *adj.* **or·ner·i·er, or·ner·i·est.** Informal. Mean and stubborn: *an ornery child.*

pag·eant |păj' ənt| *n.* **1.** A play or dramatic spectacle usually based on an event in history.

pal·lor |păl' ər| *n.* Unhealthy paleness.

pan·o·ram·a |păn' ə răm' ə| *or* |-rä' mə| *n.* **1.** A view or picture of everything visible over a wide area: *a vast panorama of mountain scenery.*

par·son·age |pär' sə nĭj| *n.* The official residence of a parson (clergyman), as provided by his church.

peev·ish |pē' vĭsh| *adj.* Annoyed; irritable; fretful. —**peev·ish·ness** *n.*

per·i·scope |pěr' ĭ skōp'| *n.* Any of several instruments in which mirrors allow observations of objects that are not in a direct line of sight.

pet·ri·fy |pět' rə fī'| *n.* **pet·ri·fied, pet·ri·fy·ing, pet·ri·fies. 1.** To turn (wood or other organic material) into a stony mass by causing minerals to fill and finally replace its internal structure.

pip·ing |pī' pĭng| —*adj.* Thin, clear, high-pitched, and shrill: *the high, piping notes of the flute.*

plod·der |plŏd' ər| *n.* One who works or acts slowly and wearily.*

pre·lim·i·nar·y |prĭ lĭm'ə nĕr' ē| *adj.* Leading to or preparing for the main event, action, or business: *preliminary sketches for a building.* —*n., pl.* **pre·lim·i·nar·ies.** Something that leads to or serves as preparation for a main event, action, or business: *Without preliminaries, she walked to the edge of the pool and dived in.*

pre·oc·cu·pied |prē ŏk' yə pīd'| *adj.* **1.** Deep in thought; engrossed: *sat quietly all through dinner, frowning and preoccupied.*

pres·ent·ly |prěz' ənt lē| *adv.* **1.** In a short time; soon: *Presently she heard a dog bark.*

pri·me·val |prī mē' vəl| *adj.* Of the earliest ages of the world; primitive.

prin·ci·ple |prĭn' sə pəl| *n.* **2. a.** A rule or standard of behavior: *a woman of dedicated political principles.* **b.** Moral standards in general: *a man of principle.*

pro·claim |prō klām'| *or* |prə-| *v.* **2.** To indicate unmistakably; make plain: *His behavior proclaims him incapable of holding any position of leadership.*

prod·i·gy |prŏd' ə jē| *n., pl.* **prod·i·gies. 1.** A person with exceptional talents or powers: *a child prodigy.*

pro·gres·sive |prə grěs' ĭv| *adj.* **4.** Working for or favoring reforms, as in government, the social system, or education; liberal.

quail[2] |kwāl| *v.* To lose courage; cower: *Harvey's dog looks ferocious, but he quails at the sight of a stranger.*

ram·shack·le |răm' shăk' əl| *adj.* Close to falling apart; broken-down; shaky: *a ramshackle hut.*

rasp |răsp| *or* |räsp| *n.* **2.** A harsh, grating sound.

rau·cous |rô' kəs| *adj.* **1.** Loud and harsh: *raucous cries.* **2.** Boisterous; disorderly: *a raucous party.*

rav·el |răv' əl| *v.* **rav·eled** *or* **rav·elled, rav·el·ing** *or* **rav·el·ling.** To separate into single, loose, threads; fray: *raveled the edge of cloth. The rug raveled.*

red·coat |rĕd' kōt'| *n.* A British soldier during the American Revolution and the War of 1812.

reign |rān| *n.* **2.** Dominant influence or effect; sway: *the reign of theology in the Middle Ages.*

re·lent·less |rĭ lĕnt' lĭs| *adj.* **1.** Mercilessly harsh; unyielding; pitiless: *a relentless killer.* —**re·lent·less·ly** *adv.*

re·morse |rĭ môrs'| *n.* Bitter regret or guilt for having done something harmful or unjust.

ren•e•gade |rĕn′ ĭ gād′| *n.* **1.** Someone who rejects a cause, allegiance, group, etc., in preference for another; a deserter; a traitor. **2.** An outlaw. — *modifier: a renegade leader.*

re•pen•tance |rĭ pĕn′ tns| *n.* Remorse or contrition for past conduct or sin.

re•pen•tant |rĭ pĕn′ tnt| *adj.* Feeling or showing repentance; penitent: *a repentant heart.*

rep•ri•mand |rĕp′ rĭ mănd′| *or* |-mänd′| *n.* A severe scolding or official rebuke.

res•o•lute |rĕz′ ə lōōt′| *adj.* Having or showing strong will and determination: *a resolute voice.* —**res′•o•lute•ly** *adv.*

ret•i•cent |rĕt′ ĭ sənt| *adj.* Hesitant or disinclined to speak out; quiet; reserved: *a reticent child.*

sap•ling |săp′ lĭng| *n.* A young tree.

saun•ter |sôn′ tər| *v.* To walk at a leisurely pace; stroll.

scrim•mage |skrĭm′ ĭj| *n.* A minor encounter between small bodies of troops; a skirmish.*

scut•tle² |skŭt′ l| *v.* **scut•tled, scut•tling.** To sink (a ship) by boring holes in the bottom.

sen•ti•ment•al |sĕn tə mĕn′ tl| *adj.* **3.** Marked by emotion that is excessive or artificial: *a sentimental story.*

shud•der |shŭd′ ər| *v.* To tremble or shiver suddenly and convulsively, as from fear or horror.

sig•ni•fy |sĭg′ nə fī′| *v.* **sig•ni•fied, sig•ni•fy•ing, sig•ni•fies.** **1.** To serve as a sign of: *What does this monument signify?* **2.** To make known: *Peter signified that he wanted to leave early.*

spec•u•late |spĕk′ yə lāt′| **2.** To buy or sell something that involves a risk on the chance of making a substantial profit.

spec•u•la•tor |spĕk′ yə lā′ tər| *n.* Someone who speculates.

spor•tive |spôr′ tĭv| *or* |spōr′-| *adj.* Playful; frolicsome.

stac•ca•to |stə kä′ tō| *adj.* **1.** Short and detached: *staccato musical notes.*

sto•lid |stŏl′ ĭd| *adj.* Having or showing little movement or emotion; impassive: *a stolid soldier.*

suf•fice |sə fīs′| *v.* **suf•ficed, suf•fic•ing.** **2.** To be sufficient or adequate for: *enough water to suffice them for three days.*

sur•vey |sər vā′| *or* |sûr′ vā′| *v.* **1.** To look over the parts or features of; view broadly: *surveyed the neighborhood from a rooftop.* **2.** To examine so as to make estimates or criticisms; investigate:

surveyed the damage done by the storm.

tem•per•ance |tĕm′ pər əns| *or* |-prəns| *n.* **1.** The condition of being moderate or temperate.

tin•der•box |tĭn′ dər bŏks′| *n.* **1.** A metal box for holding tinder.

tran•quil |trăng′ kwĭl′| *or* |trăn′-| *adj.* Free from agitation, anxiety, etc.; calm; peaceful: *a tranquil lake; leading a tranquil life.*

trans•fix |trăns fĭks′| *v.* **2.** To render motionless, as with terror.

trem•u•lous |trĕm′ yə les| *adj.* **1.** Vibrating or quivering; trembling: *speaking with a tremulous voice.*

trib•u•la•tion |trĭb′ yə lā′ shən| *n.* **1.** Great affliction or distress; suffering: *a time of great tribulation for all of us.*

tu•mult |tōō′ məlt| *or* |tyōō′-| *n.* **1.** The din and commotion of a great crowd.

ty•rant |tī′ rənt| *n.* **1.** A ruler who exercises power in a harsh, cruel manner; an oppressor.

var•i•a•tion |vâr′ ē ā′ shən| *n.* **6.** A musical form that is an altered version of a given theme, diverging from it by melodic ornamentation and changes in harmony, rhythm, or key.

ven•i•son |vĕn′ ĭ sən| *or* |-zən| *n.* The meat of a deer, used as food.

vile |vīl| *adj.* **4.** Morally low or base.

vin•di•cate |vĭn′ dĭ kāt′| *v.* To clear of accusation, blame, etc., with supporting proof: *believing that it was time to vindicate himself from such offensive charges.*

vis•age |vĭz′ ĭj| *n.* The face or facial expression of a person.

vul•ner•a•ble |vŭl′ nər ə bəl| *adj.* **1.** Capable of being harmed or injured: *helpless, vulnerable baby birds.*

watch |wŏch| *n.* **3.** A period of duty spent guarding or keeping a lookout: *a two-hour watch.*

wind•fall |wĭnd′ fôl′| *n.* **2.** A sudden piece of good fortune.

writhe |rĭth| *v.* **writhed, writh•ing.** **2.** To move with a twisting or contorted motion: *Snakes were writhing in the pit.*

yearn |yûrn| *v.* **1.** To have a deep, strong desire; be filled with longing: *She yearned for company in her lonely misery.*

Handbook
OF TERMS IN LITERATURE

adaptation   A retelling of a story or novel that changes the original's form, length, or elements of the original while retaining the basic characters and plot.

allegory   A story, play, or poem that has two meanings at the same time, a literal meaning and a symbolic meaning.

author   A person who writes a short story, play, poem, novel, article, essay, or book.

autobiography   An account of a person's life written by that person. An autobiography is an example of nonfiction.

autobiographical fiction   A story or novel that is based on real experiences from the author's life.

biography   An account of a person's life written by another person. A biography is a form of nonfiction.

characterization   The way the author presents the personality of a character. This may be done directly, by describing the character, or indirectly, by showing the character's actions, speech, and thoughts and how they affect the other characters. *Character traits* are the qualities that a character possesses.

characters   People in a story, play, novel, etc. There are *major* and *minor* characters in a story, major characters being more important than minor ones. The *main character* is the most important character.

climax   The part of the plot of a story, novel, or play in which the struggle between opposing forces reaches a crisis (also called a *turning point),* and the outcome becomes known.

conflict   A struggle between characters; between a character and a force of nature; or between opposing views held by different characters. *Internal conflict* lies in the mind of a character who must resolve something.

connotation   The implied meaning of a word or phrase as opposed to its exact dictionary meaning or *denotation.* The connotations of a word are the ideas and feelings associated with it. For example, the *connotation* of *spring* is rebirth and life.

denotation   The exact dictionary meaning of a word as opposed to its implied meaning, or *connotation.*

dialogue   The conversation in a story or play. The exact words the characters say. In a story, quotation marks point out the dialogue.

drama   Means the same as *play.* A work of literature written to be performed before an audience. A drama may be written in parts called *acts.* Acts may be divided into smaller parts called *scenes. Stage directions* tell the director or actors how the stage is to look and how the characters are to move and speak. The *dialogue,* or *lines,* are the words the characters speak.

essay   A short piece of writing on a subject or theme that expresses a specific point of view.

exaggeration   Overstatement of an idea beyond the limits of truth.

fiction   An invented story. Although fiction may be based on actual personal experience, it involves invented characters, actions, and settings.

figurative language   Words used in a special way to give added meaning. In figurative expressions such as "I'm up to my ears in homework," the words are not intended to be interpreted in a word-for-word, or *literal,* sense. Stories, and especially poems, use figurative language to create images, or mental pictures. See also **metaphor, personification, simile.**

538

flashback   A technique that interrupts the present action in a story, play, or novel to tell about something that happened in the past.

foreshadowing   A storytelling device that the author uses to give the reader advance warning or hint of events to come.

historical fiction   A story or novel whose setting is in some period in the past. Often real people from the past or important historical events are used in works of historical fiction.

humor   The quality of being comical or funny.

imagery   Words that create mental pictures, or images, that appeal to one or more of the reader's five senses. For example, "The moon floated above the clouds like a ship lost on the stormy seas" appeals to the reader's sense of sight.

irony   The contrast, or difference, between what is said and what is meant. For example, if we say in conversation that something feels good when it really feels bad, we are using irony. A situation is *ironic* when it is totally different from what the reader or character expected. *Ironic speech* uses exaggeration or understatement to express an idea. For example, "He was so hungry he could eat an alligator."

legend   A story handed down from earlier times. Legends often indicate the beliefs of the people who tell them. Often legends attempt to explain how and why something came to be. The explanations offered in legends often suggest supernatural or magical causes.

lyric poem   A short poem that expresses personal thoughts or feelings. Originally, lyric poems were sung and accompanied by a musical instrument called a lyre.

metaphor   A figure of speech in which there is an indirect or implied comparison between two things. "Her eyes were stars in the midnight sky" is a metaphor.

monologue   A speech in a work of literature that is recited by one character.

mood   The general atmosphere or feeling in a work of literature. Mood is created largely through description and setting.

motivation   The reason a character in a work of literature acts in a particular way. The character's motivation may be stated directly or hinted at by what he or she does, thinks, or says.

mystery story   A term that refers to a work of fiction in which the element of mystery or suspense plays a controlling part. In a *detective story* a mystery involving a crime is solved by a detective through the careful logical analysis of clues.

narrative poem   A poem that tells a story or relates a sequence of events.

narrator   The teller of a story.

nonfiction   Literature about real people and events. Journal accounts, diaries, essays, interviews, biographies, autobiographies, and letters are examples of nonfiction.

novel   A book-length piece of fiction that usually has a plot and deals with human experience.

personification   A figure of speech that describes an object, idea, or animal as if it had human characteristics. For example: "The light spring rain danced upon our heads."

plot   The sequence of events in a short story, novel, play, or poem. The major element in a plot is the *conflict,* or struggle, between opposing forces. *Rising action* is the part of the plot in which the action builds and a problem, or conflict, develops. The *turning point* is the part of the plot in which the struggle between the forces comes to a head in some incident — the *crisis,* or *climax.* The *resolution* is the part of the plot in which the problem is solved.

plot twist   A turn of events in the structure of a story, novel, or play that is unexpected, yet logical based on the reader's knowledge of plot and character.

poem   A piece of literature that uses language chosen for its sound and ability to express and evoke emotion. Many poems use images, or mental pictures, which appeal to the senses. Most poetry is written in lines that have a particular rhythm, or *stress.* Poetry can either be rhymed or unrhymed.

point of view   The vantage point from which the narrator tells the story. In the *first-person* point of view, the narrator is usually a character in the story. This narrator tells the story by using the pronouns "I" or "we." In the *third-person* point of view — the most common form of telling a story — the narrator may or may not be a character in the story. This narrator uses the pronouns "he," "she," or "they." When the narrator, in the third-person point of view, seems to know what every character is thinking and feeling, this narrator is called *omniscient,* or *all-knowing.*

resolution   The part of the plot of a story, novel, or play in which the *conflict* is solved.

rising action   The part of the plot of a story, novel, or play in which action builds and *conflict* develops.

satire   A work of literature that uses irony, sarcasm (biting remarks), and humor to criticize or make fun of people's foolish actions, laws, or practices. The purpose of satire is to call attention, through laughter, to the idea that society needs to be changed.

science fiction   A fantasy story that is often set in the future, on other planets, or in other dimensions in time. Scientific possibilities, such as star travel, may be used in the plot.

setting   The time, place, and general environment of a story. The setting tells when and where the story takes place. Setting is established through description and can evoke a certain atmosphere or mood.

short story   A brief piece of fiction, usually of 500 to 15,000 words in length.

simile   A figure of speech in which two things are compared directly, using *like, as,* or *than.* "Her eyes sparkled like diamonds" is a simile.

stanza   Successive groups of two or more lines in a poem. Stanzas are printed as a unit and are held together by length, rhyme scheme, and meter.

style   A combination of the idea an author wishes to express and the individual way the author expresses the idea.

subplot   A minor plot in a story, novel, or play that generally supports and complicates the main plot.

surprise   A point in the plot of some stories, novels, or plays when something completely unexpected occurs (sometimes called a *plot twist*).

suspense   The tension readers feel because they are uncertain as to how events are going to turn out in a work of literature.

symbol   Something that has meaning in itself and yet stands for something else. For example, in a story, a heart will be itself, but it may also stand for love.

tall tale   A kind of humorous story that was popular on the American frontier. A tall tale casually describes exaggerated, impossible events as if they were normal happenings.

theme   An important truth about life expressed by the author of a work of literature. It may be the author's thoughts about a certain topic, or the author's view of human nature. The theme is conveyed by the whole story — by the title, the plot, the characters, the setting, and the mood.

tone   The attitude that the writer or narrator takes toward his or her subject or reader. A work of literature may be serious or playful, for example, or argumentative or angry. An author may use an emotional tone to appeal to the reader's feelings or a factual tone to reach the reader's mind. The tone can establish both the mood and the effectiveness of the work.

tragedy   A drama that reveals the events in the life of a person, ending in death or great misfortune. The tragic hero is generally a person who has many good qualities. His or her downfall comes from one important error in judgment or flaw in character. Tragedy suggests what an ideal human being would be like and describes the circumstances and personality that keep the hero from fulfilling the ideal.

AUTHOR AND TITLE

Acquainted With the Night, 446
Adams, Abigail, 80
After Twenty Years, 20
Afterward, 328
Ain't I a Woman?, 162
Alcott, Louisa May, 164
All My Sons: Act One, 476; Act Two, 501;
    Act Three, 520
American Crisis, Number 1, The, 82
AMERICAN SAMPLER, AN (Section 1), 16;
    Introduction, 18
AMERICA'S EARLY VOICES (Section 2), 62;
    Introduction, 64
Anderson, Sherwood, 280
Any Human to Another, 309
April Morning, 116
ARTHUR MILLER: A MODERN PLAYWRIGHT (Section
    11), 472; Introduction, 474

Bambara, Toni Cade, 24
Benét, Stephen Vincent, 106, 115
Bernice Bobs Her Hair, 287
Bierce, Ambrose, 170
Bradbury, Ray, 459
Bradstreet, Ann, 70, 71
Bridger, Jim, 196
Brooks, Gwendolyn, 400
Brown, Dee, 67
Buchwald, Art, 407

Calico Dog, The, 359
Casey at the Bat, 179
Chang, Diana, 399
Chestnutt, Charles W., 206
City of Words, A, 394
Civil War Nurse, 164
Cotton Mather, 1663–1728, 115
Crèvecoeur, Jean de, 85
Crockett, David, 86
Crane, Stephen, 233, 236, 247, 249, 250, 257
Cullen, Countee, 309

Day's Wait, A, 311

Day the Sun Froze, The, 86
Dickinson, Emily, 187, 202–204
Didion, Joan, 413
Discovery of a Father, 280
Dose of Pain-Killer, A, 144
Douglass, Frederick, 40
Dream Variations, 304

EARLY AMERICA IMAGINED (Section 3), 102;
    Introduction, 104
Eberhardt, Mignon G., 359
Edwards, Jonathan, 72
Emerson, Ralph Waldo, 141
EPICAC, 428

Fast, Howard, 116
Fleischman, Sid, 196
Field, Rachel, 103
Fire and Ice, 444
Fitzgerald, F. Scott, 287
Fog Horn, The, 462
Franklin, Benjamin, 75, 76
Freeman, Mary Wilkins, 50
Frost, Robert, 425, 444, 446, 449, 450

Georgia O'Keeffe, 453
Giovanni, Nikki, 383, 410
Godasiyo, the Woman Chief, 66

Hemingway, Ernest, 311
Henry, O., 20
Home, 400
Hope Is the Thing With Feathers, 202
Horseman in the Sky, A, 170
Hughes, Langston, 267, 304, 306
Hurricane, The, 44

In Reference to Her Children, 23 June, 1656, 71
I Will Fight No More Forever, 178
I Stand Here Ironing, 412
Irving, Washington, 89

James, Henry, 215
Jim Bridger and the Fiddler Who Wouldn't Fiddle,
    196

Joseph, Chief, 178

Keller, Helen, 34
Kingston, Maxine Hong, 404

Lanier, Sidney, 176
Learning to Read, 40
Legend of Sleepy Hollow, The, 89
Letter to Her Husband, John, 80
Life on the Mississippi, 148
London, Jack, 270
Longfellow, Henry Wadsworth, 46
Love of Life, 270
Lucinda Matlock, 279

Man Said to the Universe, A, 249
Matos, Luis Palés, 44
Masters, Edgar Lee, 279
McCullers, Carson, 386
Midnight Sun, The, 438
Millay, Edna St. Vincent, 48
Miller, Arthur, 473
Mind Over Matter, 343
MODERN EXPERIENCE: 1939–PRESENT, THE
    (Section 9), 382; Introduction, 384
MODERN IMAGINATION: 1939–PRESENT, THE
    (Section 10), 424; Introduction, 426
Mothers, 410

Negro Speaks of Rivers, The, 306

Olsen, Tillie, 412
Open Boat, The, 257
Our Hold on the Planet, 449

Paine, Thomas, 82
Parker, Dorothy, 316
Pit and the Pendulum, The, 190
Poe, Edgar Allan, 190
Poor Sandy, 206

Queen, Ellery, 324, 343

Raven Days, The, 176
Raymond's Run, 24
Red Badge of Courage, The (dramatization), 236
Resolutions, 72
Road Not Taken, The, 450
Rodriguez, Richard, 394

Salem Village, Massachusetts, 106
Sandburg, Carl, 286

Sayings from *Poor Richard's Almanack,* 74
Saying Yes, 399
Serling, Rod, 438
She Sailed for Love, 127
Shock of Recognition, The, 407
Silko, Leslie Marmon, 459
Silver, Joan Micklin, 287
Southbound on the Freeway, 436
Standard of Living, The, 316
Story From Bear Country, 459
Sucker, 386
Swenson, May, 436

Telephone Call, 404
Thayer, Ernest Lawrence, 179
There Was a Child Went Forth, 159
Three Days to See, 34
Tide Rises, the Tide Falls, The, 46
To My Dear and Loving Husband, 70
Travel, 48
Truth, Sojourner, 162
Turn of the Screw, The, 215
Twain, Mark, 144, 148

Under a Telephone Pole, 286

Vegetable Diet, A, 76
VOICE OF COURAGE: Stephen Crane (1871–1900), A
    (Section 6), 232; Introduction, 234
VOICES OF EXPERIENCE: 1840–1898 (Section 4),
    140; Introduction, 142
VOICES OF EXPERIENCE: 1898–1939 (Section 7),
    266; Introduction, 268
VOICES OF IMAGINATION: 1840–1898 (Section 5),
    186; Introduction, 188
VOICES OF MYSTERY: 1898–1939 (Section 8), 324;
    Introduction, 326
Vonnegut, Kurt, Jr., 428

Wayfarer, The, 247
Wharton, Edith, 328
What Is an American?, 85
Whitman, Walt, 17, 159
Wind in the Rosebush, The, 50
Wind Tapped Like a Tired Man, The, 204
Word Is Dead, A, 203
Wreck of the Commodore: Stephen Crane's
    Own Story, The, 250

Yolen, Jane, 127

ACKNOWLEDGMENTS

(continued from page 4)

Brandt & Brandt Literary Agents, Inc. for "Salem Massachusetts," from *We Aren't Superstitious* by Stephen Vincent Benét. Copyright 1937 by Esquire, Inc. Copyright © renewed 1965 by Thomas C. Benét, Rachel Benét Lewis and Stephanie Benét Mahin; "Cotton Mather" from *A Book of Americans* by Rosemary and Stephen Vincent Benét. Copyright 1933 by Rosemary and Stephen Vincent Benét. Copyright © renewed by Rosemary Carr Benét.

Curtis Brown, Ltd. for "She Sailed to Rescue a Lover" from *Pirates in Petticoats* by Jane Yolen. Copyright © 1963 by David McKay Co.

Diana Chang for "Saying Yes," by Diana Chang from *Asian-American Heritage: An Anthology of Prose and Poetry*, edited by David Hsin-Fu Wand, Washington Square Press, published by Pocket Books, 1974.

Crown Publishers, Inc. for adaptation of "April Morning" by Howard Fast. Copyright © 1961 by Howard Fast.

Delacorte Press/Seymour Lawrence for "I Stand Here Ironing," from *Tell Me a Riddle* by Tillie Olsen. Copyright © 1956 by Tillie Olsen; excerpts from the book *Welcome to the Monkey House* by Kurt Vonnegut, Jr. Copyright 1950 by Kurt Vonnegut, Jr. Originally published in *Collier's*.

Doubleday & Company, Inc. for "The Calico Dog," from *The Cases of Susan Dare* by Mignon G. Eberhardt. Copyright 1934 by Mignon G. Eberhardt.

E.P. Dutton, Inc. for excerpts from *Jim Bridger's Alarm Clock and Other Tall Tales* by Sid Fleischman. Copyright © 1978 by Sid Fleischman; excerpts from *Conjure Tales* by Charles W. Chestnutt, retold by Ray Anthony Shepard. Copyright © 1973 by Ray Shepard.

Norma Millay Ellis for "Travel," by Edna St. Vincent Millay from *Collected Poems*. Copyright 1917, 1920, 1921, renewed 1948, 1949 by Edna St. Vincent Millay. Published by Harper & Row, Publishers, Inc.

John Gay's screenplay of *The Red Badge of Courage*. Adapted from the screenplay. A Norman Rosemont Production in association with 20th Century-Fox Television and the NBC Television Network. All rights reserved.

David R. Godine, Publisher, Inc. for excerpts from *Hunger of Memory: The Education of Richard Rodriguez* by Richard Rodriguez. Copyright © 1981 by Richard Rodriguez.

Harcourt Brace Jovanovich, Inc. for "Under a Telephone Pole," from *Chicago Poems* by Carl Sandburg. Copyright 1916 by Holt, Rinehart and Winston, Inc.; copyright 1944 by Carl Sandburg.

Harold Matson Company, Inc. for "The Fog Horn," from *The Golden Apples of the Sun* by Ray Bradbury. Copyright 1953 by Ray Bradbury. Copyright © renewed 1981 by Ray Bradbury.

Harold Ober Associates Inc. for "Discovery of a Father," by Sherwood Anderson from *Reader's Digest Magazine* (November 1939). Copyright 1939 by the Reader's Digest Association. Renewed 1966 by Eleanor Copenhaver Anderson; "Bernice Bobs Her Hair" by F. Scott Fitzgerald. Copyright 1920 by the Curtis Publishing Co., renewed 1948 by Zelda Fitzgerald; excerpt from the poem "Youth" from *Don't You Turn Back* by Langston Hughes. Copyright © 1967, 1969 by Arna Bontemps and George Houston Bass, Executors of the Estate of Langston Hughes. Published by Alfred A. Knopf, Inc.

Harper & Row, Publishers, Inc. for "Home" in "Maud Martha" from *The World of Gwendolyn Brooks*. Copyright 1951 by The Curtis Publishing Company; copyright 1953 by Gwendolyn Brooks Blakely; "Any Human to Another" in *On These I Stand* by Countee Cullen. Copyright 1935 by Harper & Row, Publishers, Inc.; renewed 1963 by Ida M. Cullen; adaptation of "Mind Over Matter" from *The New Adventures of Ellery Queen*. Copyright 1940 by J. B. Lippincott Co., renewed 1968 by Frederic Danney and Manfred B. Lee.

Holt, Rinehart and Winston, Publishers for "Godasiyo, the Woman Chief," from *Tepee Tales of the American Indian Retold for Our Times* by Dee Brown. Copyright © 1979 by Dee Brown; "Acquainted With the Night," "The Road Not Taken," "Fire and Ice," and "Our Hold on the Planet," from *The Poetry of Robert Frost* edited by Edward Connery Lathem. Copyright 1916, 1923, © 1969 by Holt, Rinehart and Winston. Copyright 1940, 1942, 1944, 1951 by Robert Frost. Copyright © 1968, 1970 by Lesley Frost Ballantine.

International Creative Management for adapted version of "Midnight Sun" by Rod Serling. Copyright © 1962 by Rod Serling.

Alfred A. Knopf, Inc. for "Dream Variations" and "The Negro Speaks of Rivers" from *Selected Poems of Langston Hughes* by Langston Hughes. Copyright 1926 by Alfred A. Knopf, Inc. and renewed 1954 by Langston Hughes; excerpts from *China Men* by Maxine Hong Kingston. Copyright © 1977, 1978, 1979, 1980 by Maxine Hong Kingston.

Little, Brown and Company for "Southbound on the Freeway," from *New & Selected Things Taking Place* by May Swenson. Copyright © 1963 by May Swenson. First appeared in *The New Yorker*.

Estate of Carson McCullers for "Sucker" by Carson McCullers. Copyright © 1963 by Carson McCullers.

Macmillan Publishing Co., Inc. for "Some People," from *Poems* by Rachel Field. Copyright © 1957 by Macmillan.

Alida Malkus for her translation of "The Hurricane" by Luis Palés Matos.

Ellen C. Masters for "Lucinda Matlock," from *The Spoon River Anthology* by Edgar Lee Masters. Copyright 1914, 1942 by Macmillan Publishing Co.

G. P. Putnam's Sons for excerpts from *Have I Ever Lied to You?* by Art Buchwald. Copyright © 1966, 1967, 1968 by Art Buchwald.

Charles Scribner's Sons for "A Day's Wait," by Ernest Hemingway from *Winner Take Nothing*. Copyright 1933 by Charles Scribner's Sons; copyright renewed © 1961 by Mary Hemingway.

(Acknowledgments continue on page 544)

ACKNOWLEDGMENTS
(continued from page 543)

Seaver Books for "Story From Bear Country" from *Storyteller* by Leslie Marmon Silko. Copyright © 1981 by Leslie Marmon Silko.

Simon & Schuster, Inc. for "Georgia O'Keeffe" from *The White Album* by Joan Didion. Copyright © 1979 by Joan Didion.

Viking Penguin Inc. for adaptation of "The Standard of Living," from *The Portable Dorothy Parker,* Revised Edition. Copyright 1941 by Dorothy Parker, copyright renewed © 1969 by Lillian Hellman. Originally published in *The New Yorker; All My Sons* by Arthur Miller. Copyright 1947 by Arthur Miller, copyright renewed 1975 by Arthur Miller. *CAUTION:* Professionals and amateurs are hereby warned that *All My Sons,* being fully protected under the Copyright Laws of the United States of America, the British Empire, including the Dominion of Canada, and all other countries of the Berne and Universal Copyright Conventions, is subject to royalty. All rights, including professional, amateur, motion picture, recitation, lecturing, public reading, radio and television broadcasting, and the rights of translation into foreign languages, are strictly reserved. Particular emphasis is laid on the question of readings, permission for which must be secured from the author's agent in writing. All inquiries should be addressed to the author's agent, International Creative Management, 40 West 57th Street, New York, New York 10019.

A. Watkins, Inc. for "Afterward" from *Tales of Men and Ghosts* by Edith Wharton. Copyright 1910 by Charles Scribner's Sons.

William Morrow & Company, Inc. for "Mothers" (10 March 1972) from *My House* by Nikki Giovanni. Copyright © 1972 by Nikki Giovanni; first stanza of "The World Is Not a Pleasant Place to Be" in *My House* by Nikki Giovanni. Copyright © 1972 by Nikki Giovanni.

ILLUSTRATION AND PHOTOGRAPHY CREDITS

Illustrations: pp. 21, 477, 500, 521, Robert Steele; pp. 26–27, 30, Ivan Powell; pp. 53, 56, Tom Stöerrle; pp. 66, 67, 272–273, 275, 415, 418, Sue Rother; p. 73, 77, 235, Walter Brooks; pp. 90, 94–95, 96–97, Arvis Stewart; pp. 106–107, 108, 110–111, 288, 293, 296, 300, Gerry Hoover; pp. 128–129, 132, 135, Rick Porter; p. 146, Rosekrans Hoffman; pp. 171, 172–173, 312–313, Lyle Miller; p. 181, Bill Purdum; pp. 192–193, Jas Szygiel; pp. 198–199, Sylvia Almeida; pp. 209, 210–211, 213, Phil Huling; pp. 216, 220–221, 224–225, Pam Higgins; pp. 258–259, Paul Geiger; pp. 280–281, 282, 405, Steve Tanis; p. 307, Floyd Cooper; pp. 329, 332–333, 335, 338, 400–401, Greg Voth; pp. 345, 348, 353, 356, 399, 440–441, Tom Leonard; pp. 360, 364, 369, 370, 375, Bradley Clark; p. 397, Kathryn Yingling; p. 408, Tim Raglin; pp. 430–431, Brian Cody; p. 445, Jon Friedman; p. 467, Ron Hall.

Photography: p. 19, Association for the Preservation of Virginia Antiquities, John Marshall House, Richmond, Virginia; p. 35, Jack Daly; p. 36, Russ Kinne/Photo Researchers, Inc.; pp. 41, 163, 235, 238, 317, The Bettmann Archive, Inc.; pp. 45, 278, 453, 455, The Metropolitan Museum of Art, New York; pp. 46–47, 166, Museum of Fine Arts, Boston, Massachusetts; p. 48, Smith College Museum of Art, Northampton, Massachusetts; p. 65, Utah Museum of Fine Arts, Salt Lake City, Utah; pp. 70–71, National Gallery of Art, Washington, D.C.; p. 79, Yale University Art Gallery, New Haven, Connecticut; p. 81, Massachusetts Historical Society, Boston, Massachusetts; p. 84, Philadelphia Museum of Art; p. 87, Tom McHugh/Photo Researchers, Inc.; p. 105, The Metropolitan Museum of Art/Associated American Artists; pp. 117, 118, 120–121, 123, 124, 387, 388, 390, 411, Barbara Kirk; p. 143, The Century Association, New York; pp. 150–151, Nathan Benn/Woodfin Camp & Associates; p. 154, Dan McCoy/Black Star Photos; pp. 160–161, North Carolina Museum of Art, Raleigh, North Carolina; pp. 176–177, Photo Researchers, Inc.; p. 189, National Museum of American Art/Smithsonian Institution; p. 202, Jonathan Blair/Woodfin Camp & Associates; pp. 203, 251, The Addison Gallery of American Art, Andover, Massachusetts; p. 204, Mathias T. Oppersdorff/Photo Researchers, Inc.; pp. 240–241, 244, 327, Culver Pictures, Inc.; p. 247, Judith Greene; pp. 248–249, Detroit Institute of Arts; p. 269, New York Historical Society; pp. 254–255, The Cleveland Museum of Art; p. 286, P. W. Grace/Photo Researchers, Inc.; p. 303, Brooklyn Museum of Art; pp. 304–305, Martha Swope; p. 308, F. Grehan/Photo Researchers, Inc.; pp. 385, 450–451, 454, Whitney Museum of American Art, New York; p. 427, Museum of Modern Art, New York; pp. 436–437, Nancy Hoffman Gallery, New York; pp. 446–447, The Art Institute of Chicago; p. 448, NASA; pp. 456–457, Fort Worth Art Center; p. 460, Margaret Durrance/Photo Researchers, Inc.; p. 475, Bruce Davidson/Magnum.

Section Openers: 16–17, 62–63, 102–103, 140–141, 186–187, 232–233, 266–267, 324–325, 382–383, 424–425, 472–473. Photography: Jack George Tauss. Photo Coloration: Marc Tauss.